PRE-COLUMBIAN ART

PRE-COLUMBIAN ART

*Investigations
and Insights*

by Hildegard
Delgado Pang

With a Foreword by
Michael D. Coe

University of Oklahoma Press
Norman and London

This book is published with the generous assistance of Edith Gaylord Harper.

Library of Congress Cataloging-in-Publication Data

Pang, Hildegard Delgado.
    Pre-Columbian art : investigations and insights / by Hildegard Delgado Pang.
        p.   cm.
    Includes bibliographical references and index.
    ISBN 0-8061-2379-6
    1. Indians of Mexico—Art.   2. Indians of Central America—Art.   3. Indians of South America—Art.   4. Indians of Mexico—Antiquities.   5. Indians of Central America—Antiquities.   6. Indians of South America—Antiquities.   7. Mexico—Antiquities.   8. Central America—Antiquities.   9. South America—Antiquities.   I. Title.
F1219.3.A7P26   1992
709'.8—dc20   91-23661
                                                    CIP

The paper in this book meets the guidelines for permanence and durability of the Committee on Production Guidelines for Book Longevity of the Council on Library Resources, Inc. ∞

Dedication

To my parents, Hans and Lisi Schmidt,
for their unwavering support

To Alice Landini, for her sustaining friendship

To Dr. Jack Weinbaum, lost at sea off Cancún
and remembered by his friends

CONTENTS

ILLUSTRATIONS

FIGURES

MAPS

TABLES

THE title of Hildegard Delgado Pang's stimulating book, *Pre-columbian Art*, is something of a misnomer, but misnomers are unavoidable when speaking about the indigenous inhabitants of the Western Hemisphere: consider just the terms "New World," "Indian," and "America," and it becomes clear that we are all prisoners of five centuries of misconceptions and distortions about the cultures that were encountered and destroyed by the European invaders. Dr. Pang has wisely chosen not to cover every single art style of the hemisphere before the "Age of Discovery," from Alaska to Tierra del Fuego, but has focused on the art produced by the very complex societies of Mesoamerica and the Central Andes, where most recent research has been concentrated. But even here there is a problem of what to call this, for Aztec art, for example, was being produced for almost three decades following Columbus's initial landfall in the Antilles; and in the forests of northern Guatemala, the Maya were continuing their old artistic traditions right up to the fall of their capital, Tayasal, in 1697.

Dr. Pang makes it clear that her book is not about "pre-columbian" art per se, but about *research* on it. There is no other book quite like it. Although it is now academically fashionable to adopt an all-encompassing theoretical position which purports to "explain" all past experience (deconstruction, neo-Marxism, feminism, and so forth). Pang does not do this, although she allows the student to find out what, if anything, such theories have contributed to the subject. Instead, she has shown how the art of many cultures, from early civilizations like the Olmec and the Chavín through the Conquest, has been interpreted by scholars grounded in a wide range of disciplines (from archaeoastronomy and art history through zoology!). The interested student can learn about different approaches that have been taken to these early art traditions—not so much grandiose theories, but lesser and more productive ones—and the kinds of insights that have illuminated the changing role that art played in these cultures through time.

Often scholars contradict each other in this endeavor (one has only to turn to the different interpretations which have been put on Olmec stone monuments), but, as Dr. Pang stresses, it is the debates which arise from such conflicts that produce heat and light. As she so rightly puts it, such controversies make the study of pre-columbian art "anything but a musty, arcane endeavor."

Lay it to prejudice in favor of my own profession, but for me some of the most exciting insights into specific bodies of pre-columbian art have been reached by archaeologists without training in art history. I will here cite the work of the late Donald Lathrap on the Tello Obelisk, a masterpiece of the Chavín civilization of the Andes; using a kind of structuralist analysis, Lathrap hypothesized that two crocodilean monsters on the stone could be viewed as a parable on the division of food plants into seed bearers and tubers, at the moment of creation. Another tour de force of art analysis is the work of Christopher Donnan in which he reduces all of the bewildering variety of Moche ceramic art from coastal Peru into a small number of discrete themes or "scenes" that must have been basic to Moche mythology and cosmology. But Hildegard Pang does not play favorites, and the reader will even find in these pages interpretations by such scholarly pariahs as Von Daniken (and his astronauts).

One would be hard put to find much in common between the arts of the Andes and those of Mesoamerica, or even among many of the art styles within those areas beyond long-lasting iconographic traditions. Moche is as different from Nazca as Celtic is from Chinese. What holds these disparate art traditions together intellectually is the interdisciplinary nature of the scholars who study them—a phenomenon hardly to be found at all in the "Old" world, where the study of art is almost wholly the domain of historians of art and of critics. The reader will find that Hildegard Pang is both anthropologist and art historian.

If I had to think of one word to characterize pre-columbian art it would be "vitality," in contrast to what came after it. Art probably had many functions within each of these pre-Conquest societies, but it always played as major a role as it did among the Renaissance Italian cities or Periclean Athens. During the 1920s and 1930s, in response to profound social movements in the Western world, a notion had taken hold that somehow or other these art traditions were communal, egalitarian, and anonymous (see the Mexican muralists, for instance; similar ideas were, and still are, held about African art). The fact is that they are "anonymous" only because in most cases, unlike the West, the names of individual artists and the positions that they held in these societies have been lost, mainly because they worked in a milieu that was nonliterate.

But consider the case of the Classic Maya, who *were* literate, and whose writings we can now read. Recent evidence shows that their scribes, painters, and carvers enjoyed the highest possible status, and in some cases were even royal princes. These gifted individuals probably worked for noble patrons every bit as discriminating as the Medici or the Renaissance popes. Even further, Maya artists went so far as to sign their names to their own works, a form of pride and self-identification that is rare even among those cultures who have complete scripts.

The relation between patronage and art must surely have contributed to the vitality of the works of art shown here. Like it or not, most of this tremendous output was turned out for the elites who controlled these societies; and the artists themselves were sometimes, it seems, members of the same "ruling class." All this came to an end with that most terrible of all human and demographic disasters, the European incursion into the hemisphere. The native social pyramids were all truncated at the top, while enforced conversion to Catholic Christianity and the enslavement or enserfment of once-burgeoning native populations reduced them to a shadow of their former selves. Once-proud indigenous artists and architects were reduced (at best) to low-caste servants of churches and great estates. All of the high art traditions died out at once, to be replaced by a derivative Spanish baroque of numbing sameness and general (but not universal) mediocrity, compared with the glories of pre-columbian art.

All the more reason to welcome this new book, bringing to the reader so much that is new and exciting and controversial in a very lively and important field of study.

PREFACE

THIS is a book about the art of the indigenous peoples of Middle and South America before the European presence. Dozens of critical studies, descriptive overviews, exhibit catalogs, and coffee-table books have been written about pre-columbian art. This book offers a survey of current research and examines how different approaches provide insights into specific pre-columbian cultures and the changing roles of art through time.

Some cultural universals (obtaining food and shelter, assuring security) are life-sustaining. Others (language, kinship networks, political and economic interchanges) minimize conflict and facilitate human relations. Still others combine practical functions with the ability to profoundly enhance the quality of life. One of these is art.

Art in contemporary industrialized societies is often peripheral to other aspects of culture—it may be used for selling products and ideas or for entertainment and aesthetic satisfaction, but it is not truly central to fast-moving, complex lifestyles. Modern technology allows us to interpret, process, and instantly share information and images on a scale hitherto impossible. Sometimes we tune out the overload. Through this enhanced information exchange, governments forge policies with far-reaching consequences. Art contributes minimally to these important decisions.

And yet art is vital to ongoing human development, much as a healthy organism needs sound mental, emotional, and physical properties in balanced interplay. A society that emphasizes materialism over its history or arts can lose cumulative perspective and make short-term, expedient decisions with irreversible long-term consequences. Ethical, moral, and humanitarian elements are critical to these decisions, and they remain vital and alive when preserved and perpetuated through art.

Art both reflects and is critically affected by specific sociohistorical contexts and values. In early, preliterate societies, art interfaced with almost every other aspect of culture. Today, despite changes in its roles, it continues to be a thermometer of cultural well-being. Future scholars may well assess us by the degree of freedom and support given our artists.

The societies that produced pre-columbian

art differ markedly from ours. Because the archaeological record is incomplete and the time and culture gap so enormous, we can only approximate how art functioned within those societies. Perhaps 90 percent of our efforts consist of intuitive but unverifiable speculation. But within that precious remaining 10 percent, careful research allows us to project into and humanize the past with a high degree of accuracy. From past societies we can learn of other world views and other options that enhance our perspective on our own position. If you are unfamiliar with pre-columbian art, be prepared for a feast for the eye and a widening of the mind.

The Middle and South American examples presented chronologically in this book represent an admittedly uneven survey of diverse research orientations and results. Many more were excluded for lack of space. I hope that the extensive bibliography will encourage readers to pursue other areas. Teachers using the book as a text may wish to add supplementary material to enhance particular geographical or theoretical dimensions. The Glossary in the back of the book defines technical terms that are italicized in the text. The Pronunciation Guide and Notes on Languages at the end of the front matter will make it easier to read foreign words.

The examples of pre-columbian art presented here remind us of art as a force in our own culture and as one of the most variable yet constant elements of our common humanity. The act of your sharing in this brief sampling is one more testimony to the effectiveness of art in kindling the human imagination across both time and space.

HILDEGARD DELGADO PANG
Terre Haute, Indiana

ACKNOWLEDGMENTS

THIS book began with the aim of providing students with a one-volume introduction to research into pre-columbian art, keyed to a useful, comprehensive bibliography. I thought that its completion would take 2 or 3 years: instead, it has stretched to over a decade.

One of the pleasures of documenting this exciting and fast-moving discipline has been the chance to meet and correspond with leading scholars in the field. It is with gratitude that I acknowledge my debt to the following individuals who freely provided information on their research, reprints of articles, tips on new developments, permissions to use drawings or photos, and/or words of advice and encouragement: Patricia Rieff Anawalt, Virginia B. de Barrios, Elizabeth Boone, Frank Cancian, Manuel Chambí, Robert Cobean, Michael D. Coe, William Coe, Marvin Cohodas, William Conklin, Alana Cordy-Collins, Christopher Donnan, André Emmerich, Ian Graham, David Grove, Richard Hansen, David Joralemon, Chiaki Kano, Justin and Barbara Kerr, Emily Klein, Ruth Krochok, George Kubler, Charles Lincoln, Gareth Lowe, Patricia Lyon, Joyce Marcus, Guadalupe Mastache, Donna McClelland, Barbara MacLeod, Mary Ellen Miller, Michael E. Moseley, Esther Pasztory, Donald Proulx, Edward Ranney, Dorie Reents-Budet, Merle Greene Robertson, Peter Roe, Anne Rowe, John Rowe, Alan Sawyer, Linda Schele, Rebecca Stone, Karl Taube, Hasso Von Winning, James Vreeland, Charles Wicke, and several anonymous reviewers whose suggestions strengthened the text. I would like to single out Doris Heyden for her never-failing hospitality and decades of encouraging Mesoamerican scholars on both sides of the border.

Institutions and their staffs that were especially helpful in facilitating the acquisition of information, photos, and other material from their collections include the Cleveland Museum of Art, Dumbarton Oaks, the Institute of Andean Studies and editors of *Ñawpa Pacha*, the Instituto Nacional de Antropología e Historia of Mexico, the Krannert Art Museum of the University of Illinois, the Museo Nacional de la Cultura Peruana, the New World Archaeological Foundation, the St. Louis Museum of Art, the Textile Museum, and the Tikal Project.

For technical aspects in producing the book, I am indebted to the staff at University of Oklahoma Press including John Drayton, Patricia Dornbusch, and Sarah Morrison. Photographic reproductions are by Tony Richardson, maps by Norman Cooprider, and tables by Lucinda Roberts, all of Indiana State University. Special thanks go to Robert Chadwick whose eagle eye, innate sense of form, and guiding hand brought the vessel through the shoals of final editing into safe harbor.

In addition I would like to recognize the contributions of numerous Mexican, Guatemalan, Peruvian, European, and Japanese archaeologists and researchers. They are not cited in the Bibliography because it focuses on sources in English that are most accessible to beginning students, but the debt owed them by their North American colleagues and the discipline is enormous.

Finally, although I have scrupulously attempted to credit the many sources and ideas cited, any errors, omissions or misinterpretations are my own.

H. D. P.

GIVEN below are guides to pronunciation of Spanish, Nahuatl, Mayan, and Quechua and notes on other characteristics of the languages.

SPANISH

Pronunciation Equivalents

Vowels

a	as in *father*
e	midway between *e* and *ai* as in *met* and *maid*
i/y	like *i* in *machine*
o	as in *note*
u	as in *rule*

Consonants generally as in English, but

c	hard (as in *can*) before *a, e, o,* and *u* or at the end of a word; otherwise soft (like *s* in *so*)
ch	as in *chat*
g	hard (as in *go*) before *a, o,* and consonants; soft (as in German *ich*) before *e* and *i*
h	unpronounced
j	like *ch* in German *ich*
ll	like *y* in *you*
ñ	like *ny* in *canyon*
ts	as in *hats*
x	like *ks* in *kicks* between vowels; like *s* in *so* preceding consonants

Stress

Stress is on the penultimate syllable of words ending either in a vowel or in the consonants *n* or *s* and on the last syllable of all others, unless indicated otherwise by an acute (′) accent.

NAHUATL

Distribution

Nahuatl place-names occurred throughout Mesoamerican areas under Aztec influence; the language is still spoken in Central Mexico.

Pronunciation Equivalents

Pronunciation is as in Spanish, except for the following:

PRONUNCIATION GUIDE AND NOTES ON LANGUAGES

ll	long *l* as in *ill* (Ex.: *chimalli*, shield)
e	final *e* is always pronounced
qu	*k* before *e* and *i* (Ex.: Quetzal-cóatl)
x	like *sh* in *she* (Ex. *xicolli*, a sleeveless jacket
z	like *s* in *sit* (Ex.: *zacatl*, blade of grass)

The letters *tl* are common at the beginning (*Tl*aloc), middle (tla*tl*i), and end (quexquemi*tl*; atla*tl*) of words and are pronounced by releasing air at sides of the tongue (as in a*tl*as).

The vowels a, e, i, and o have an alternate elongate form, shown in some orthographies by a macron (e.g., ō) that can change the meaning of the word.

Glottal stops separate some vowels and are indicated by *h* (Ex.: E*h*écatl). These are enunciated when the vocal chords contract, then open, producing a mild explosive sound (as in re*e*nter, *Is* it?, co-ordinated).

Consonants also have aspirated (like *p* in *pot*) and glottalized forms (*p'* as in *spa*, *t'* as in *stick*, *k'* as in *skim*, and *kw'* as in *squash*).

Stress

Stress is on the penultimate syllable (Ex.: poch-*te*ca) unless indicated otherwise by an acute accent mark.

Other Characteristics

Nahuatl is a *polysynthetic* language, meaning that phrases and entire sentences are contained in long, composite words formed by compounding or agglutinating prefixes, infixes, and suffixes onto root morphemes (ex.: *tlihuizcihuatl*, "She is a worthless woman"; *timimacáxtoca*, "You think you are feared but you are not").

Reduplication of an initial consonant and vowel indicate repetitive action or intensification of a characteristic: For example, *teonaná-catl* (*teo*, "god," *nacatl*, "flesh"), "flesh of the gods" (sacred, hallucinogenic mushrooms); Tla-mimilolpa, a residential area within Teotihua-cán; Huehuetenango (*hue*, "old"; *tenango*, "place"), "old, old town."

Among frequent Nahuatl suffixes are *loca-tives* indicating place. For example:

-co, -go	(as in Mexi*co*, "place of the Mexica [Aztecs]")
-can, -yan, -chan	(as in Tlalo*can*, "Tlaloc's place"; Teotihua*cán*, "Place where the gods were born"; Mi*can*, "Realm of the dead")
-tlan, -tla	(as in Tenochti*tlán*, "Near the nopal cactus buds")
-tenango, -tenanco	(as in Quezal*tenango*, "Town of the quetzal")
-apan	(as in Papalo*apan*, [*papalotl*, "butterfly"; *apan*, "near the water"], "Butterfly River")
-tepec	(meaning "hill," as in Chapul-*tepec*, "Grasshopper Hill")

MAYAN

Distribution

Mayan was and still is spoken in the Maya lowlands and highlands, including parts of Belize, El Salvador, and Honduras. Related Huaxtec dialects are still found in Veracruz and San Luis Potosí, Mexico.

Pronunciation

Pronunciation is as in Nahuatl, except for the following:

c	always hard, as in *can*
x	as *sh* in *she* (Ex.: Xelhá)
qu	as *k* in *kit* before *e* and *i* (Ex.: Palenque)
u	like *w* in *wash* before a vowel (Ex.: *U*axactún, *u*ayeb)

There are five vowels (a, e, i, o, u), each with long (written doubled: aa) and short forms.

Several consonants (*c'*, *ch'*, *tz'*, *dż*, *p'*, *t'*) have frequently used glottal forms (Ex.: *Dz*ibil-chaltun).

Glottal stops may occur before or between vowels

Stress

Stress is usually on the final syllable (Ex.: Xi-balb*a*, Hunah*pu*)

Other Characteristics

Like Nahuatl, Mayan dialects are polysynthetic.

Classifier infixes describe qualities of goods being counted (two *large* blades); *proclitic* words denote the sex of a given title or name (Ex.: *Zak* in Zak Kuk indicates that the person called Kuk is a female, in this case, Lady White Quetzal, Pacal's mother, at Palenque).

In the Yucatec Mayan dialect, changes in pitch, including rising/falling and flat tones, can change the meaning of words.

Common Maya site name suffixes include -tun ("stone," as in Uaxactun, "Eight Stones") and -ha ("by the water," as in Altún Ha, "[Site of] Stone by the Water").

QUECHUA

Distribution

In pre-columbian times, Quechua was spoken in southern Ecuador, highland Peru, and northern Bolivia. Its use is still widespread in highland Peru.

Pronunciation

Pronunciation is as in Nahuatl, but the consonants b, d, f, g, and j are not used. Strong glottalization of the consonants v, p, t, ch, and k (written doubled—vv, pp, tt, etc.—in some orthographies) produces a harsh, gutteral effect. Ll, pronounced like y in you, is a frequent phoneme.

Stress

Stress is normally on the penultimate syllable.

Other Characteristics

Quechua is also a polysynthetic language in which utterances are composite words, rich in complex meanings.

A classical dialect, topa simi ("royal speech"), spoken in Cuzco, was of higher status than ordinary Quechua (runa simi, "speech of the people").

Onomatopoeia, the use of words that sound like what they describe, and repetition of syllables, are common in Quechua (Ex.: Lekeleke and Kotchitchi, names of birds using repeated syllables that imitate the sound of the birds' calls, and huahua, "baby").

In status-conscious Inca society, honorifics, such as yupanqui ("esteemed") and topa ("royal") were important parts of rulers' titles.

Frequently used suffices and their meanings are:

-callanka	multiple-doored hall
-camac	creator (Ex.: the deity Pachacamac)
-cancha	walled enclosure (Ex.: Coricancha, "Golden Enclosure" [of the Sun])
-cocha	water (Ex.: the deity Viracocha)
-llacta	town
-kuna	plural
-mama	woman (Ex.: Pachamama, "Earth Mother")
-marca	fortress (Ex.: Pañamarca)
-pata	terrace
-puncu	gate
-runa	man
-tampu, -tambo	rest stop or house (Ex.: Paucartambo)
-wasi, -hausi	house of (Ex.: Intihuasi, "House of the Sun")

PRE-COLUMBIAN ART

ABBREVIATIONS

CUP	Cambridge University Press
DO	Dumbarton Oaks
EMM	Editorial Minutiae Mexicana
FCE	Fondo de Cultura Económica, Mexico
IAS	Illinois Archaeological Survey
INAH	Instituto Nacional de Antropología e Historia, Mexico
KAM	Krannert Art Museum, University of Illinois
MNCP	Museo Nacional de la Cultura Peruana
MNA	Museo Nacional de Antropología, Mexico
NP/IAS	Ñawpa Pacha, Institute of Andean Studies, Berkeley
NWAF	New World Archaeological Foundation
PM/HU	Peabody Museum, Harvard University
RLSS	Robert Louis Stevenson School, Pebble Beach, California
TM	The Textile Museum, Washington, D.C.
TP/UPM	Tikal Project, University Museum, University of Pennsylvania
UCLA/CLAS	University of California at Los Angeles, Center for Latin American Studies
UCP	University of California Press
UNMSM	Universidad Nacional Mayor de San Marcos, Peru
UWP	University of Washington Press

Pre-columbian art is the art of native peoples of the Americas prior to the arrival of Christopher Columbus and other Old World explorers. The geographic area encompassed extends from the Arctic Circle to the southern tip of South America. Art was a vital part of pre-columbian cultures, which included bands of nomadic hunter–gatherers and semisedentary tribes, local chiefdoms, and complex states. Its forms and functions varied accordingly, and we are only beginning to appreciate its scope and complexity.

This book surveys recent research on art from pre-columbian Middle and South America. The focus is on Mesoamerican and Central Andean art, representing the two areas within Middle and South America that produced ancient high civilizations. These areas also provide the most complete combinations of extensive archaeologically retrievable art remains (often with glyphic texts), complementary ethnohistorical sources, and oral traditions. They have therefore generated active, intensive, and exciting research based on cross-disciplinary cooperation and interpretation. Unfortunately, space limitations preclude inclusion of pre-columbian Circum-Caribbean groups, the northern Andean area, and the Amazon Basin, and it is with genuine regret that I omit other major Mesoamerican regions (western Mexico, Oaxaca, and Veracruz, for example) and topics (pre-columbian codices, to name just one).

The subjects covered were selected because their well-defined styles have attracted concentrated scholarship and research strategies that have yielded especially fruitful results accessible in English sources to both students and general readers. I have deliberately and even-handedly presented multiple, sometimes conflicting, interpretations to convey the stimulating intellectual exchanges that accompany ongoing research. For text use, instructors will want to add individual assessments and supplementary material. The large bibliography that accompanies this text will lead readers to important recent citations as well as to many older, classic studies.

DEFINITIONS OF ART

Art is a product of individual cultures, not all of which view it as a discrete category. What Western critics consider an art form might have been a decorated utilitarian object or a power-charged icon in its original context. Finding such objects in an art gallery or analyzed by an art critic would baffle their original makers and users.

Most English dictionaries define art as the result of creative human efforts that elicit emotional, aesthetic, and/or conceptual responses by means of images or sounds. Richard Anderson (1989, 11–12) notes that *art* derives from the Latin *ars*, referring to the creative use of learned skill. Art may express beauty and originality, fear or veneration, *apotropaic* power, or human interaction with ancestral and supernatural forces. Through *iconography*, art combines direct imagery with intellectually recognized symbols and meanings. Despite outward similarities among cultures, iconography is actually highly culture-specific: A cross may suggest the cardinal directions to one culture, the concepts of Christian crucifixion and resurrection to another.

Art form and content change over time in response to shifting perceptions and values. Even someone with little "art background" can see differences of perspective, body proportion, and costume in Renaissance depictions of saints and those found in churches today or among images of Christ from the Americas, Africa, and Asia, despite their shared religious symbolism. Sometimes visual clues are less overt, like the unconscious, culturally ingrained gestures that reveal the identity of an otherwise perfectly trained counterspy. When a culture reacts to stimuli such as religious revival, foreign occupation, or strong outside influences, art forms can be sensitive barometers of, and causal elements in, cultural change.

To sum up, all art (1) is a creative product of human imagination, (2) requires human skill in its execution, (3) evokes culturally conditioned responses, (4) embodies or symbolically represents aspects of the physical or spiritual world, (5) changes through time through contributions of individual artists, and (6) both reflects and affects the cultural context within which it is produced.

SCOPE OF ART FORMS

Under the preceding definition, art forms may be tangible or intangible, durable or evanescent, static or in constant flux. Traditionally, the *visual arts* include plastic (architecture, sculpture, metalwork, textiles, and ceramics) and graphic (painting, engraving, and etching) forms as well as costume and body ornamentation. The nontangible, *aural arts*, based on sound, embrace instrumental and vocal forms (song, incantations, proverbs, recitation of poetry, and mythology). The *kinetic arts*, based on movement (dance, theater, storytelling performance, and mime) overlap with the other categories. Pre-columbian scholars broaden these traditional categories to include interactive or interacting phenomena such as rituals that combine face and body painting, masks, costumes, stylized movement, recitation, and music in an appropriate architectonic setting into a total experience that itself is art. They also look beyond form to interpret the purposes, uses, and messages of art as perceived by its creators and targeted recipients.

ARCHITECTURE AS ART

Architecture, the designing and building of structures, makes use of both technology and art and combines practical and aesthetic aspects. Like painting or sculpture, it can convey specific iconographic messages. The first built structures probably were imitations of earlier natural shelters. In time, they were geared to human activities: barter, group meetings, and worship, for example. The dead, too, had their own elaborate tombs and citylike necropolises.

As buildings were clustered into growing towns and cities, their interrelationships and spacing became important. The placement of specialized structures added to the visual statement they made. Construction materials reflected durability or aesthetics, displayed wealth, or made visual metaphors for spiritual qualities. Associated paintings, mosaics, and sculptures added decoration and clarified structural function. Proportions and relative siting of individual buildings became architectural statements about successions of earthly rulers or diagrams of the cosmos.

Regional styles in architecture help archaeologists to identify interaction between sites and their relative chronologies. Renovation and enlargements at fixed calendric intervals have also been invaluable in refining construction phases when base dates from inscriptions or associated artifacts are known.

ATTITUDES TOWARD PRE-COLUMBIAN ART

Much as we single out our own culture's fine arts for display, we fill entire museums with pre-columbian masks and sculpture because, despite their unfamiliar canons, we respond to them emotionally. We are touched and affected, fascinated or repelled, depending on individual aesthetic perspectives.

Sixteenth-century Europeans saw pre-columbian art as exotic and esoteric. Although impressed by its technical excellence, none tried to assess it by the standards of the societies that created it. Ethnocentric evaluations continued into the 1800s, when published descriptions of stelae, architecture, and codices laid the foundation for twentieth-century attempts to understand this ancient art within its wider context.[1]

CHARACTERISTICS OF PRE-COLUMBIAN ART

Although the formal aspects of pre-columbian art can be determined directly from art forms, its intended meaning, function, and effect on users are inextricably linked to its sociocultural context, which we interpret through ethnohistoric sources, archaeological reconstruction, and analogy with modern tribal peoples. As with contemporary small-scale, preliterate societies, pre-columbian art was closely tied to a cohesive world view that tended toward conservatism and traditional presentation rather than individual innovation. Form was structured to present symbolism correctly rather than for its own sake (excepting strictly decorative pieces: jewelry, for example), and although we may never know artists' personal motives, blatant individualism and commercialism were lacking. However, recent tentative identification of some Maya and Inca artists' names and signatures suggests that some pre-columbian societies recognized and appreciated individual artistic skills. Although most artists appear to have worked comfortably within traditional parameters, there was enough variation in design and technique (see sections on Maya funerary pottery: Chapter 6, and Paracas and Huari textiles: Chapters 9 and 11) to isolate individual craftsworkers and possible workshop groups.

Research since 1960 has shown increasingly how pre-columbian art fulfilled functions of documentation, education, and, sometimes, manipulation of information. Study of pre-columbian art has also helped us understand the timing, mechanisms, and nature of major cultural events in those societies. Researchers have discovered that distinctive religious and political symbols, ceramics, textiles, and/or architectural canons accompanied and sometimes helped create ecomomic expansion or political demise.

Part of the energy and intellectual challenge of pre-columbian studies lies in the development of new, often alternative, and fiercely protected and defended explanations of data from ongoing excavations. Most difficult to reconstruct, and perhaps irretrievable, are the lives of the common classes, who lacked commemorative stelae and high-status grave goods but were the mainstay of the cultures that produced the art.

Evidence for myth, poetry, dance, music, and specifics of ritual is relatively incomplete. Graphic and plastic forms have survived best, but here, too, remains are selective and skewed toward elite class values and concerns, leaving us ignorant about other groups and areas of pre-columbian art. The Spaniards were diligent tomb looters, and contemporary pot hunters are making inroads into what is left. What we recover is only a tiny fraction of what was— a skeleton that we audaciously (and often, no doubt, incorrectly) attempt to reflesh through careful induction and artful surmise.

INTERDISCIPLINARY METHODS OF APPROACH

How can we effectively study art so different from ours in form and intent? The careful use of evidence from archaeology, ethnohistoric sources, cultural anthropology, art criticism, art

---

[1] Janet Berlo (1985, 1–27) gives an excellent summary of the trajectory of pre-columbian Mesoamerican art studies; it is keyed to a comprehensive bibliography of 1,533 citations. Kendall (1977) with 2,100 entries, lists additional sources for the reader who wishes to pursue topics beyond those covered here.

history, epigraphy, biology, history, medicine, architecture, astronomy, and other disciplines enables scholars both to interpret art forms and develop historical, materialistic, and ideological profiles of their creators.

Archaeology: Aims and Methods

Archaeologists, like good detectives, reconstruct past scenarios by inference from partial and selective remains. Their interpretations are restricted by the time span separating materials of the past from the present, poor preservation of artifacts, the absence of living informants, lack of provenience data for some finds, and occasional problems in dating objects or complications involving reuse of objects by later groups.

Archaeological excavation proceeds by horizontal layers (strata: hence the term stratigraphic excavation), which act as controls for recording the positions of artifacts and provide a relative chronology: In undisturbed stratigraphy, the oldest material lies at the bottom, the most recent on top. Carbon-14 dating and other radioactive methods give more specific dates. Similar objects from other, dated sites permit cross-dating and inferences about trade, migrations, and exchange of ideas.

Seriation, the plotting of artifact forms and types according to their initial appearance, increase, decline, and demise, can also indicate chronological change where good stratigraphy is absent. Thus ceramic distinctions (characteristics of clay and temper inclusions, vessel shapes, and decoration techniques such as those highlighted for Paracas wares in Chapter 9) can provide relative dates, whereas thermoluminescence dating, which measures energy stored as electrons within fired clay and released as light by reheating, can provide more specific dates.

Dating is important because it allows archaeologists to place their findings within specific time divisions such as phases (chronological periods with particular artifact assemblages) and horizons (relatively short periods during which cultural traits and assemblages achieved a wider distribution). Horizon styles, characterized by the pervasive and rapid spread of specific art forms and motifs, have been especially noteworthy in pre-columbian Peru.

Location is another important consideration.

The spatial context in which artifacts are found, including associated artifacts and cultural features such as hearths or workshop debris, reveals important aspects about their production and is essential to their restoration: A cluster of flint spalls may indicate a workshop area; jade and turquoise fragments may be rejoined as a funerary mask or a complex mosaic. Temples, residences, tombs, trash pits (middens), and offering caches associated with construction phases have all yielded artifacts and valuable information.

Interdisciplinary cooperation maximizes the usefulness of archaeological data. Physicists, geologists, petrographers, and metallurgists identify colorants, fibers, alloys, tempers in clay, and locations from which raw materials may have been quarried or traded, allowing archaeologists to reconstruct techniques of manufacture with surprising accuracy.[2] Paleographers contribute by deciphering hieroglyphs. Comparison with recent objects described by ethnographers can help explain "problematic" finds.

Contemporary excavations transcend mere recovery and description of artifacts. Interpretations of subsistence bases, production of goods, demography, settlement patterns and urbanization, exchange patterns and social interaction, and processual aspects of cultural origin, development, and decline represent the cutting edge of Mesoamerican archaeology in providing cultural contexts critical to understanding pre-columbian art.

Ethnohistory

A frequent link between archaeological data and ethnographic observation of living people is ethnohistorical description, that is, accounts written by traders, soldiers, explorers, missionaries, and settlers, of Indian culture before its acculturation to European ideas. Such sources, however, must be used with care. Writers unconsciously incorporated sixteenth- and seventeenth-century European ideas and often embellished their accounts: Conquistadors inflated the number of battle casualties and captives, missionaries the number of converts. The art of the indigenous populations was of minor

---

[2] For example, the excellent summaries of pre-columbian metallurgy in Emmerich (1965) and of metallurgy, jade working, and lapidary techniques in Lothrop (ed.) (1961, 35–80, 242–247).

concern to monarchs interested in New World tribute, and most chroniclers viewed American Indians as cultural inferiors. Some accounts were written years after European contact, when cultural disintegration had set in. Nonetheless, these sources provide continuity between archaeological evidence and the earliest reliable ethnographic descriptions of the late nineteenth and early twentieth centuries.

There has been considerable criticism of the use of ethnohistorical sources describing late groups such as the Aztecs or Postclassic Maya to extrapolate backward over thousands of years in interpreting far earlier Olmec or Teotihuacán culture. George Kubler (1962, 1967a,b) warns of the dangers of conceptual disjunction as beliefs alter over time and symbols acquire different meanings. Other scholars insist on the basic unity of the pre-columbian Mesoamerican world view and combine insights from direct analysis of pre-columbian art, ethnohistoric references, analogies with other pre-columbian cultures, and survivals among ethnographic Mesoamerican groups.

Cultural Anthropology

Cultural anthropologists describe contemporary cultures. *Ethnographers* (ethno: culture, -graphy: recording of) work with modern subcultures, including tribal and peasant peoples. *Ethnologists* (ethno: culture; -ology: science, or study of), make cross-cultural comparisons to isolate broader patterns and significant parallels. Their focus is *emic*—attempting to record how a culture functions as perceived by its members.

Seeing art in particular cultural contexts facilitates understanding of its interaction with other cultural institutions. Some ethnographic studies explore the interplay between art forms, their contexts, their creation, and their effects on members of a society. Ethnographic insights may be particularly useful where elements of pre-columbian art survive today in altered but recognizable form. Ethnographically recorded myth, for example, may help identify figures represented in pre-columbian art, and surviving ceremonies may hold clues to antecedent forms.

Other interpretive approaches are also productive. *Ethnoarchaeology*, whereby archaeologists gain insights into particular problems

through focused ethnological studies, has helped resolve questions about settlement patterns, factors affecting the preservation and distribution of artifacts, and relationships of craftsworker groups to artistic styles and patterns of use.

Art Criticism

Art critics study the qualities facilitating the appreciation and interpretation of art. They enhance perception, opening our eyes, ears, and minds beyond initial impressions to new, deeper insights. By increasing our understanding, they encourage a more knowledgeable appreciation, a "second look" with wiser eyes.

Art evokes aesthetic responses through our sensory mechanisms—direct, pure reactions not based on step-by-step reasoning. Critics of art, by stressing its universality, neutralize its particular cultural contexts. They concentrate on *formal*, or *structuralist*, analysis to explore both the qualities (texture, configuration, and composition) that catalyze response and the interaction of those qualities that produces the complete form. They consider elements of realism and of *hieratic perspective* and the ordering of visual form through repetition, opposition, and symmetry of pattern and color.

In *qualitative analysis*, art critics assess standards of skill and subjectively ascribe particular aesthetic qualities: For example, a work may be arresting, sensuous, voluptuous, monumental, or beautiful; it may embody energy, tension, or passivity and evoke responses of unrest, excitement, wonder, or torpor. Such evaluations vary from critic to critic and culture to culture and indeed have changed drastically throughout the history of art criticism.[3] In using Western aesthetic standards to evaluate pre-columbian art, critics may in fact impute characteristics that exist only in modern Western eyes.

Not all critics limit their comments to relativistic perceptions. Some feel that all art has a universal ability to evoke aesthetic response and create emotional impact. Its ability to con-

[3] For samples of divergent critical reviews under a single cover, Sylvan Barnet's delightful little guide (1981) is excellent. Theoretical concepts of art criticism such as style, creativity, aesthetic appreciation, philosophy of art, and criteria of judgment are explored in various issues of *The Journal of Aesthetics and Art Criticism. The British Journal of Aesthetics* provides a continental perspective.

vey precise meaning nonverbally is more culture specific, however. Indeed, the question whether universally accepted criteria of aesthetic excellence truly exist is only beginning to be explored.

In the meantime, art critics sensitize us to aesthetic attributes and nuances of form, enabling us to think and feel beyond our first impressions and to experience artworks with a heightened, more articulate awareness.

Art History

Art historians document the development of art, including its changes in form and meaning, throughout space and time. They can answer questions about style and iconography relatively easily for Western art, which has written documentation, clearly identified artists, schools, and sponsors, and well-established provenience and chronologies. For pre-columbian art, however, these specifics are lacking. To compensate, art historians have combined formal analysis with supportive data from excavations and ethnohistorical sources and made significant contributions to the field.

A concept derived from the Western tradition and frequently employed for evaluating and ordering art is *style*, the distinctive organization of formal properties that characterizes the art of a place, group, individual, or period. Artists working within a style share similar conceptualization and execution; art historians identify style by recognizing shared details of perspective, composition, color, proportion, and emphasis or omission of features. *Attribute analysis* involves studying the range of stylistic features and how they may be combined. Its structuralist approach is akin to identifying the basic sounds of a language and their combination into longer utterances. *Iconics*, the study of how "building-block" design motifs may be combined to create new forms, is similar to the concept of "deep structure" in transformational grammar, which is thought to underlie the creation of all human speech. Computer-generated databases of images have given new thrust to such iconic studies.

By combining attribute analysis, iconics, and knowledge of the raw materials and techniques of manufacture available at a given time and place, art historians develop the parameters of style. Using such parameters, a "pre-columbian" mural fragment may be revealed as a forgery because of incorrect proportions or the presence of iconic elements not known until decades later. Having several pieces of a known provenience makes tests of inferences about distribution patterns and zones of artistic influence possible.

The concept of style has been criticized and even rejected. Kubler (1962), comparing it to outdated nineteenth-century perceptions of biological evolution that identify relationships based on form, considers it insufficient to explain multiple changes of art through time. He suggests, instead, using systems description, emphasizing process as well as form to detail variables of cultural interaction spurring or hindering the development of local art. To Kubler, the concept of style, originally intended to help bring order to the diversity of art forms, may actually impose interpretation and selectively shape the history of art. Nevertheless, style is still important in most art-historical descriptions of archaeological and ethnographic art.

Another area of art-historical interest is the transmission of meaning through visual imagery. Technically, *iconography* deals with representation of ideas through images, whereas *iconology* examines how visual symbols convey temporal and cultural values.

Finding the intended meaning behind imagery is particularly difficult in art lacking emic documentation. Scholars must determine what, if anything, was meant, and sometimes even what is represented. One way to start is by arranging all known images from a particular group or period into categories of similar forms and their variants. Meaning may then sometimes be inferred by noting which basic motifs occur together. Knowing these associations, an investigator can recognize changes in form, substitutions, or the introduction of new elements that may signal evolving shifts in meaning or even deliberate manipulation of images, for example, by intrusive ethnic elements intent on introducing new values.

Studies correlating changes in visual images with their inferred meanings are becoming increasingly sophisticated as investigators draw upon the results of cross-disciplinary research for new data on pre-columbian dynastic successions, population movements, trade and tribute networks, and ethnographic survivals of customs and artifacts to give their interpretations context and validity.

NEW RESEARCH APPROACHES

One of the welcome new trends in pre-columbian art scholarship is the perception of art as a discrete artifact system that can influence and affect other cultural institutions and not act merely as a passive "mirror" that reflects ongoing events. Several studies (for example, Klein 1986, 1988b) explore pre-columbian art in its wider sociocultural contexts as a medium deliberately conceived to support the religious or political ideas and interests of governmental and priestly elites and to further specific aims of public policy. This function is perhaps clearer to twentieth-century scholars viewing the art in retrospective than it was to the pre-columbian public participating in the interplay.

Another area of current interest is the relationship between images and glyphic texts (Berlo 1983; Hanks and Rice 1989). Scholars are increasingly aware that the primacy of written, linear texts that explain ancillary illustrations is a Western concept inappropriate to pre-columbian representations, where glyphic texts merely convey historic specifics (names of persons, places, titles, dates, and events), whereas images provide far richer and subtler qualifying details at multiple, less explicit levels of deeper meaning (M. Graham 1986, 96–97; Klein 1988b, 44).

Several scholars now incorporate principles of *semiotics* in their work. This practice seeks to extrapolate underlying cultural values from pre-columbian imagery by exploring the relationships between signs as a communication system (syntactics) that also includes their creators and users (pragmatics), in addition to the traditional iconographic focus on semantic meanings. Semioticians work directly from the structure of artworks, eschewing ethnographic and ethnohistoric comparisons. Art systems, viewed as "volumes" of encoded, unwritten information, are being examined especially closely at Teotihuacán, a complex Early Classic site with a comprehensive lexicon of visual symbols and no known system of formal writing.

New approaches and the more traditional iconographic studies are both benefitting increasingly from computerized information retrieval and analysis. By transferring cumbersome photographic archives of pottery, stelae, textiles, site plans, and design inventories onto computer or laser disks and cross-indexing iconographic motifs and details of manufacture, form, and design, researchers are uncovering significant, formerly obscure, correlations and adding a substantive statistical base to previously more speculative, subjective interpretations.

Still, let it be noted, the results continue to be just that—interpretations, not fact, and they have their opponents. New data from excavations and breakthroughs in glyph interpretation lead to the excitement and challenge of additional tentative, often alternative and conflicting interpretations that in turn may be abandoned as future finds are made. The ensuing debates between scholars generate both light and heat and make the study of pre-columbian art anything but a musty, arcane endeavor. Several of these valuable, sometimes contradictory contributions are summarized in this volume, and more are sure to come.

PART ONE

MESOAMERICA

M ESOAMERICA is an archaeological culture area of enormous ecological and cultural
diversity (see Map 1).[1] Geographically, it includes the southern two-thirds of Mexico, all of
Belize, Guatemala, and El Salvador, and western Honduras, Nicaragua, and Costa Rica. Pre-
columbian Mesoamerican cultures shared certain traits, including the use of hieroglyphic
writing, stelae, codices, and complex calendars;
the importance of corn as a central item in the
diet; the *temazcal*; the ball game (a ritual game
played in special courts); the *volador*; and the
use of speech scrolls in art to indicate human
utterances.

Our knowledge of Mesoamerican cultures is
most accurate and complete with regard to their
material culture, geographic distribution, and
chronological spread. Questions of beliefs, behavior, symbolism, and values are far more hypothetical, especially for earlier cultures where
internal texts and ethnohistorical descriptions
are lacking. We do know that high civilizations
such as those of the Aztecs and the Maya developed monumental architecture (temples with
elaborate pyramid bases), glyphic notation,
densely populated urban centers, hereditary
rulership, well-defined social and professional
classes, and far-reaching cultural influence
through trade and/or militarism.

Modern scholars divide the Mesoamerican
archaeological sequence into major time periods—the Preclassic, Protoclassic, Classic, and
Postclassic—several of which are further subdivided (see Table 1). The dates for these periods
are tied to a Maya ceramic sequence associated
with Long Count hieroglyphic dates that are interpreted using the GMT (Goodman-Martinez-
Thompson) correlation (see Chapter 5). GMT
dates, preferred by most archaeologists, run
about 260 years later than Long Count readings
using the alternative Spinden correlation that is
preferred by some Mexican and North American archaeologists because its earlier readings
mesh well with certain Central Mexican radiocarbon dates. The developments that characterize these major pan-Mesoamerican periods
and the predominant groups within them are
described next.

[1] The term *Mesoamerica* was first created and defined by Mexican anthropologist Paul Kirchhoff. A fuller description of its implications may be found in Kirchhoff (1952).

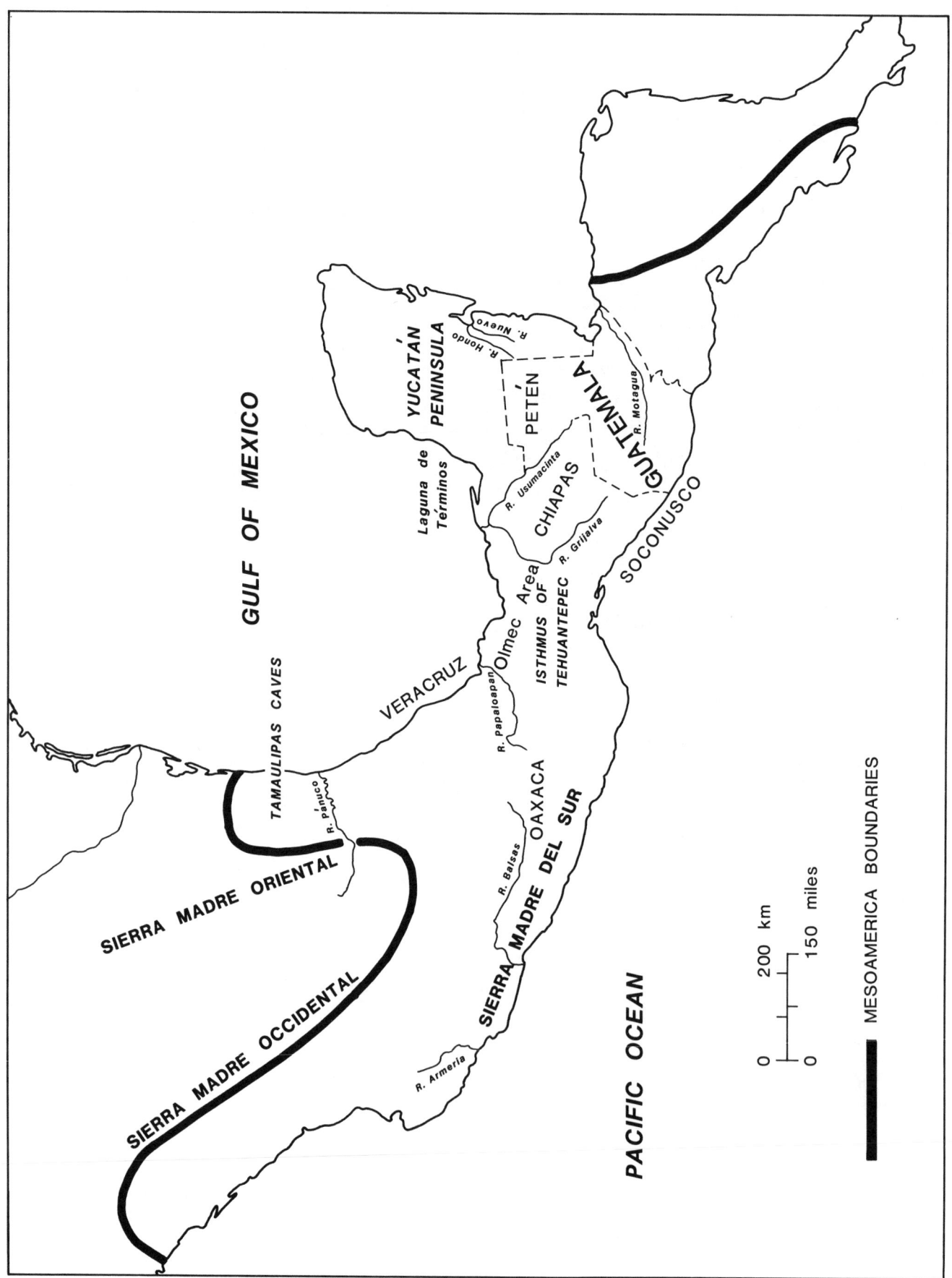

Map 1. Mesoamerica: boundaries, important sub-areas, and geographical features

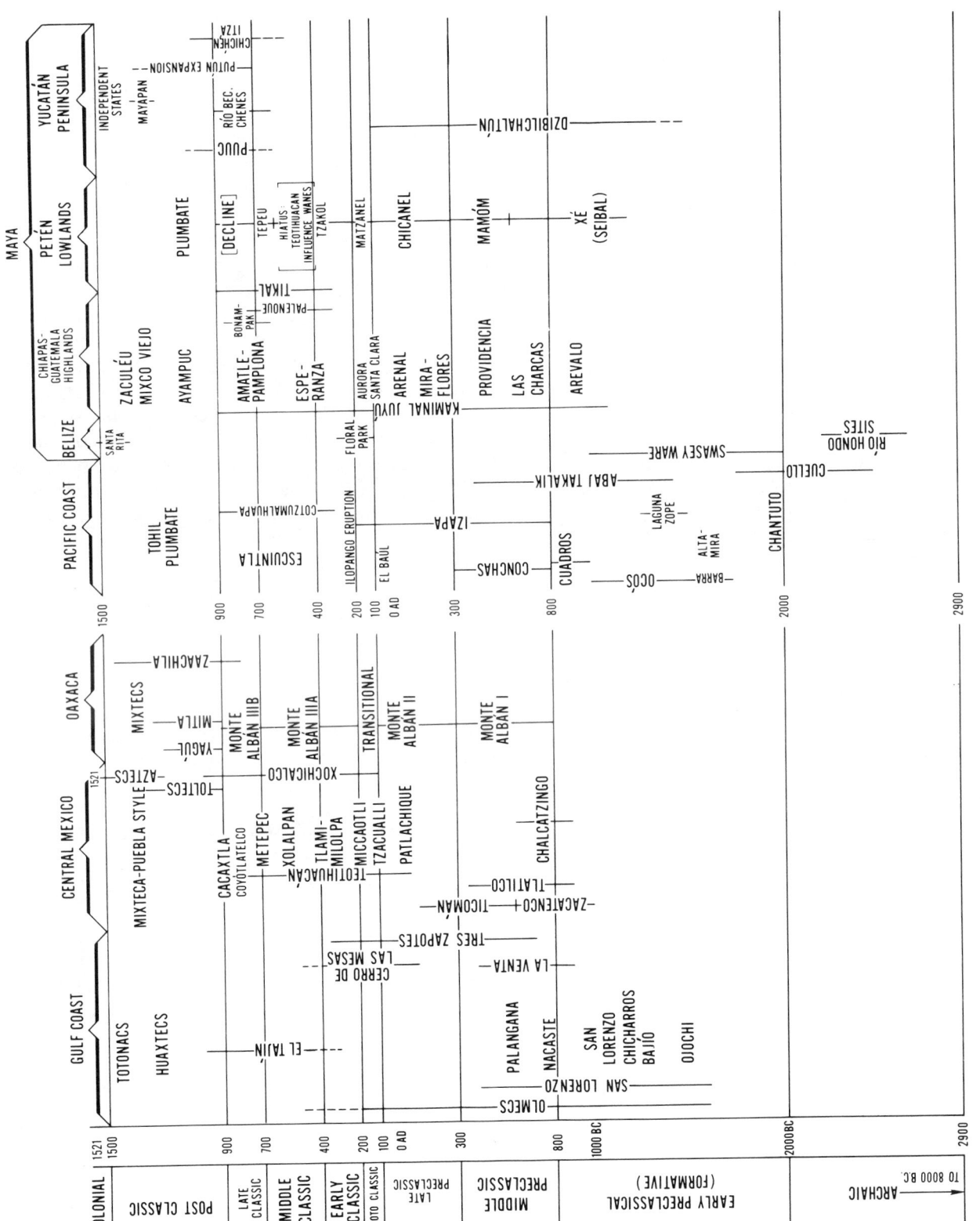

Table 1. Mesoamerica: archaeological periods and regional sequences

PRECLASSIC PERIOD (2000 B.C.–100 A.D.)

This period, called Preclassic by Mexican archaeologists and Formative by many North Americans, is characterized by settled village life and *milpa* agriculture involving crops (corn, beans, squash, chili) that were domesticated during the preceding Archaic period (8000–2000 B.C.). The long Archaic transition from hunting and foraging to deliberate food production and sedentary life was particularly well documented at sites in the Tehuacán Valley of southeastern Puebla, Mexico, in the 1960s and 1970s by Richard S. MacNeish's *The Prehistory of the Tehuacán Valley* (Volumes 1–6 published in Austin by the University of Texas press; his latest volume, a summary of the development of agriculture throughout the world, will be published in 1991 by the University of Oklahoma Press). Although peripheral to pre-columbian art, this transition nonetheless laid the baseline of settled life and the matrix of cultural complexity out of which later artists would so successfully operate.

Preclassic cultures can be identified by the presence of pottery vessels (typically *tecomates*), handmade clay figurines, weaving, increased populations living in villages and towns, and concomitant sophistication in institutions and beliefs. Among them, the Olmecs are noteworthy because of their early ceremonial centers, use of hieroglyphic notation, and development of a distinctive art style.

The Olmecs

The Olmecs are one of Mesoamerica's oldest and most intriguing cultures. Their origins and ethnic affiliations are as yet unclear, and they represent one of the major foci of current archaeological investigation. Their "hearth area" consisted of the Gulf Coast lowlands of southern Veracruz and western Tabasco. The most impressive and extensive evidence of Olmec culture is found at the Early through Middle Preclassic sites of San Lorenzo and La Venta and at the Late Preclassic Tres Zapotes and Laguna de los Cerros sites (see Map 2).

Olmec culture reached its apogee by 900 to 700 B.C. as the Olmecs traded with and expanded their cultural influence to Central and West Mexico, Oaxaca, the Pacific Coast of Chiapas and Guatemala, the Maya lowlands, and even western El Salvador and Copán in Honduras where they went in search of obsidian, kaolin clay, cacao, hematite, jade, and other exotic resources. The most famous Central Mexican Olmec "frontier" town is Tlatilco, where burials discovered by bricklayers contained Olmecoid figurines, clay seals, and pottery bowls together with local Preclassic wares. In West Mexico, cave paintings near Juxtlahuaca and Oxtotitlán (see Map 2) depict Olmec themes. At Chalcatzingo, in the state of Morelos (see Map 2), a relief with three figures carrying paddles and a bound, seated, ithyphallic figure (Fig. I.1) suggests that violence may have accompanied the spread of Olmec influence. (Others interpret the scene as a fertility rite.) At Teopantecuanitlán near Copalillo, Guerrero (Map 2), four flame-browed, torch-carrying frontal Olmecoid stone figures, set into patio walls and tentatively dated at 1200 B.C., predate examples of Gulf Coast Olmec monumental art and thereby raise exciting questions about early West Coast contributions to the development of Olmec style.

Following the violent collapse of San Lorenzo and the subsequent demise of La Venta by 400 B.C., the Olmec heritage continued at the Late Preclassic sites of Tres Zapotes and Laguna de los Cerros. Pacific Coast sites show a mixture of Olmec and local iconography that contributed strongly to the Classic Maya style. Elsewhere, Preclassic villages continued to evolve, unaffected by Olmec influence.

PROTOCLASSIC PERIOD (A.D. 100–250)

From A.D. 100 to 250 at rapidly developing sites in present-day Oaxaca, coastal Guatemala, and Belize, regional art and ceramic styles, ceremonial architecture, evidence of polytheism, and advances in hieroglyphic writing and calendric computation laid the groundwork for the development of Classic period high cultures. The stimuli and mechanisms that explain these critical, transitional Protoclassic developments are still being defined.

CLASSIC PERIOD (A.D. 250–900)

The Classic period is characterized by florescent high cultures with sophisticated urban centers, calendric and writing systems, fully developed art styles, religious pantheons, monu-

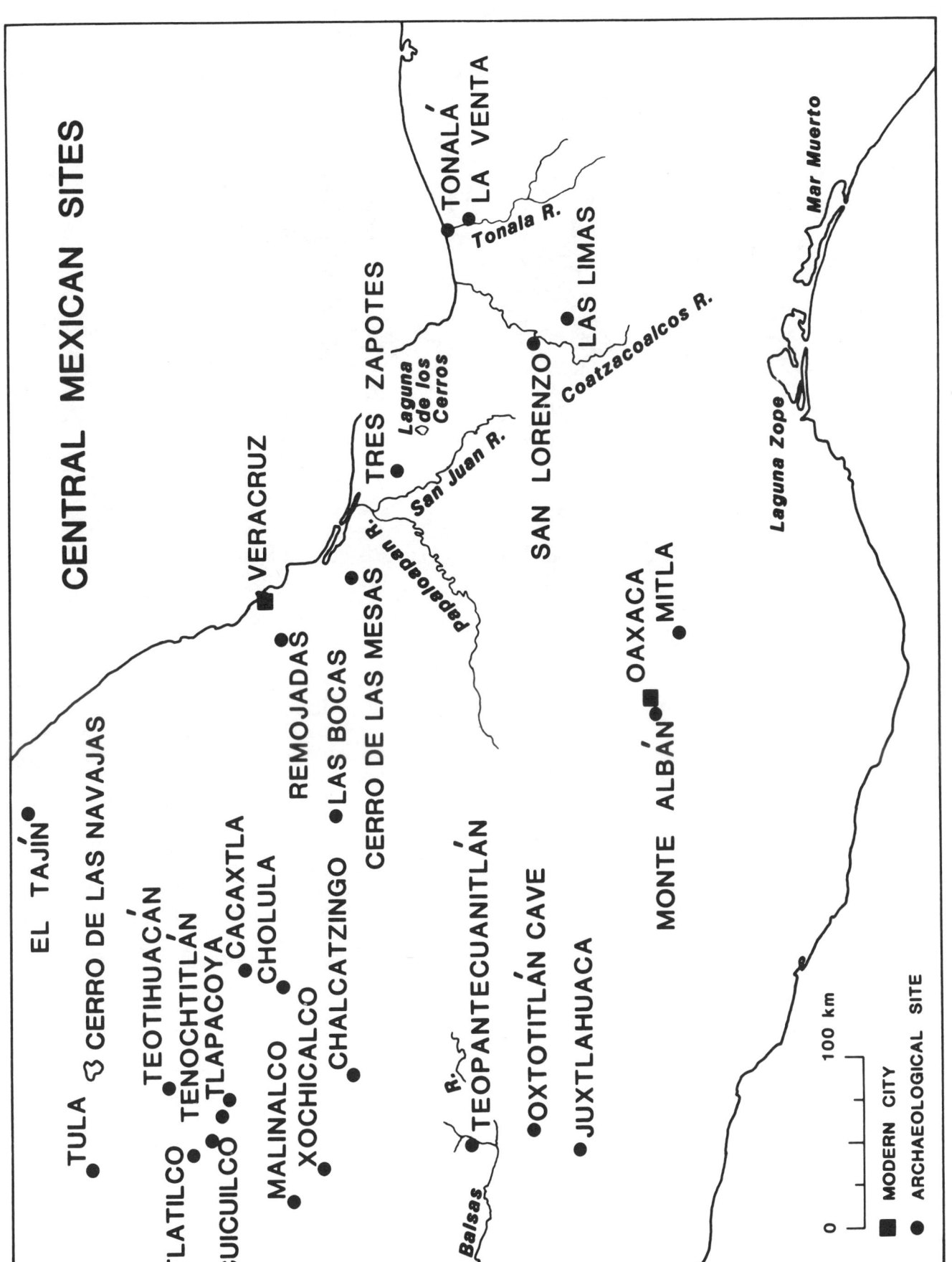

Map 2. Central Mexico and Gulf Coast sites

I.1. War (?) scene with ithyphallic bound figure from Chalcatzingo, Morelos. (Courtesy MNA)

mental architecture, institutionalized militarism, and extensive interregional trade. Here we must bypass important developments in West Mexico, Oaxaca, and the Gulf Coast in order to concentrate on the most important Central Mexican site, Teotihuacán, and the Classic period Maya.

Teotihuacán

The impact of Teotihuacán (see Map 2) was felt throughout Mesoamerica during the Classic period, and long after its demise in the eighth century, its cultural legacy remained. The fifteenth-century Aztecs called the ruins *Teotihuacán*, which means "Place of the Gods," and this is how tourists visiting the site, just 42 kilometers (25 miles) northeast of Mexico City, know it today.

Teotihuacán was unique in its rapid, brilliant rise. No secondary Early Classic centers in Central Mexico could compare in either size or complexity. Local springs and rivers, fertile soils, and outcrops of *obsidian* helped underwrite Teotihuacán's growth. Its trade network extended to present-day Guatemala and the Maya lowlands and saw the introduction of Teotihuacán pottery forms and architectural canons. In exchange for Gulf and Pacific shells, jade, hematite, onyx, and turquoise, Teotihuacán produced obsidian blanks for transport to foreign markets (obsidian blades are so sharp that they are manufactured today for use as surgical blades).

Between A.D. 650 and 750 Teotihuacán was destroyed by fire and partially abandoned. According to René Millon (1967), the fall was preceded by population reductions and slackening political power, perhaps the result of intrusions by less-cultured northern peoples. Around A.D. 650, or a little later, the city's northern temples and public structures were burned ritually either by outsiders or internal dissidents in the standard Mesoamerican manner denoting conquest.[2] Survivors maintained Teotihuacán's legacy at nearby Cholula, in the present-day state of Puebla, and Xochicalco, in the present-day state of Morelos, cities with long-standing ties with Teotihuacán (see Map 2). A group using red-on-buff Coyotlatelco pottery that is common in the Late Classic central highlands continued to live at the abandoned site of Teotihuacán.

The Maya

On the Yucatán Peninsula in the present-day Guatemalan state of Petén and the jungles of

[2]Millon (1981, 237). The Spaniards also razed native temples, building Christian churches on the rubble, to show the superiority of the new Catholic gods over the idols they replaced.

East Mexico and in the Central Guatemalan and West Honduran highlands (Maps 1 and 5), the Maya developed large Preclassic centers around a base of intensive cultivation. Incorporating Olmec and Pacific Coast elements with indigenous features, they created a brilliant culture that dominated Eastern Mesoamerica. Their distinctive limestone architecture and polychrome narrative pottery, their sophisticated mathematical reckonings and calendrical observations, and their rich cosmology were unique in the New World.

The Maya were able to sustain large populations for centuries in spite of the heavily leached soils of the swampy jungle lowlands. Aerial surveys have revealed networks of raised fields and human-made canals that permitted intensive cultivation of swampland and indicate highly organized and efficient corporate labor.

Classic Maya rulership was hereditary, validated through both earthly and divine ancestry. Major centers controlling districts of political influence were bound by political, kinship, and exchange marriage alliances, and territories were expanded through frequent raids. Trade brought on goods from Central America, the Pacific Coast, and the Central Mexican plateau.

Maya intellectual achievements include accurate astronomical observations and 260-day and 365-day interdigitating calendars. One observation marked the celestial positions of the planet Venus over millennia. Agricultural cycles and rites were keyed to both the 365-day solar calendar and the 260-day sacred calendar, a system shared by many Mesoamerican groups. The solar year had 18 months of 20 days each (a total of 360 days) and an added period of 5 unlucky Uayab days; the sacred calendar had 13 months of 20 days each. The two coincided every 18,980 days (52 years) at the end of a major time cycle. The synchronized interface of the two calendars is called the Calendar Round. Time units and numbers had patron gods who controlled them and affected their good or bad fortune; thus auguries of good or difficult times could be made for recurring time cycles.

Between A.D. 750 and 800 the great Middle Classic lowland Maya centers began to decline, reacting to the disruption of trade routes following Teotihuacán's demise, strained resources, increased population, the demands of an expanding elite, cultural intrusions from Central Mexico, and competition among regional capitals. The result was skirmishes, instability, malnutrition, and, probably, political anarchy and internal rebellion. By A.D. 900, commemorative stelae were no longer erected, and most central lowland sites had been abandoned.

On the Yucatán Peninsula, Maya culture continued unabated, nourished by seagoing Gulf Coast trade under Putún (Mexicanized, Chontal-speaking) Maya merchants. In the Guatemalan highlands, Maya sites were moved to higher, more defensible locations. In Central Mexico a new group of "northern barbarians," the Toltecs, invaded the areas of the settled Mesoamerican peoples.

POSTCLASSIC PERIOD
(A.D. 900–EUROPEAN CONTACT)

The Postclassic period was a time of reintegration in response to the disruption that followed the demise of the great Classic centers. Refugees from sacked cities populated nearby sites or moved into new areas to resettle. *Chichimec* incursions increased along the northern Mesoamerican frontier, first as the Toltecs (ca. A.D. 900) and later as the Aztecs who, in the thirteenth century, intruded upon the settled Mesoamerican peoples.

The Early Postclassic was also a period of unprecedented cultural exchange and eclecticism. Maya influence occurs at Central Mexican sites, whereas on the Yucatán Peninsula, Maya culture was nourished by Gulf Coast trade under the seagoing Putún. Architectural parallels between the Yucatec site of Chichén Itzá and the Central Mexican Toltec capital of Tula are particularly strong. In the Guatemalan highlands, the Maya moved to higher, more defensible locations as militarism increased.

The Toltecs

Impinging on Central Mexico's post-Teotihuacán reintegration was the Early Postclassic arrival of the Toltecs, a northwestern Chichimec people who synthesized Veracruz, Maya, and Central Mexican elements into a brilliant new culture. The Postclassic Toltec stronghold was at Tula (Map 2), where the Toltecs amplified their nomadic and raiding heritage into full-scale cults of militarism and human sacrifice.

These innovations are symbolized in the famous legend of Quetzalcóatl, the "Feathered

Serpent." According to the most commonly accepted version, Quetzalcóatl was the son of a local Nahua woman and Mixcóatl, leader of the Toltec migration. Assuming the ancient title Feathered Serpent, he founded Tula (where both his image and the Venus symbol occur frequently) and initiated a golden age of prosperity. Eventually, he was overthrown by followers of Tezcatlipoca (Smoking Mirror), the god of war and darkness, and in A.D. 987 he fled with a small band of followers to the Gulf Coast.[3] There he either immolated himself and rose into the sky as Venus, the Morning Star, or headed eastward across the gulf on a raft. Western Maya coastal ports indeed mention the arrival of Kukulkán ("Feathered Serpent" in Mayan) and his (possibly Putún Maya) escorts in that year. An alternative account has Quetzalcóatl abandoning Tula shortly before its fall in 1168 A.D. after a dispute with a rival leader, Huémac. Quetzalcóatl promised to return in his natal year, 1 Reed, which repeated itself every 52 years in the Mesoamerican Calendar Round. In the meantime, new nomadic peoples from the north swamped the Mesoamerican frontier, and Tula fell under their sway.

Late Postclassic Groups

During the thirteenth century, the final waves of Chichimec peoples reached the Valley of Mexico, and local powers filled the vacuum left by the demise of Tula. Among them were the Aztecs, or Mexica. According to their legends, the Aztecs settled in the Valley of Mexico around A.D. 1200, after lengthy migrations in

[3]Davies (1974) notes multiple mythical overlays to the legend and connects this exodus with possible new Chichimec incursions.

search of the sign that their patron god, Huitzilopochtli, had promised them: an eagle eating the red buds (the symbol of human hearts) of a large prickly-pear cactus. (The eagle, with the ribbonlike sign for war in its beak reinterpreted as a snake, appears on Mexico's red-, white-, and green-banded flag and on most Mexican coins.)

At first, the Aztecs served as mercenaries for the people of the city of Culhuacán and other groups along the shores of the Valley of Mexico's five interconnected lakes. Despised as barbarians, they were eventually shunted to a swampy islet already occupied at its northern end by the settlement of Tlatelolco. From this simple beginning in 1325, they expanded through warfare and military alliances and eventually conquered Tlatelolco and the other valley powers. When the Spaniards reached them, in 1521, they had established a major commercial and military empire.

In the Maya area, Postclassic Yucatán centers continued to flourish. One of the best known is Chichén Itzá, famed for its sacred *cenote,* into which gold, jewelry, and young children were thrown as sacrifices.

By 1250, Chichén had been supplanted by nearby Mayapán when the Cocom family overcame the Itzas of Chichén and controlled trade for the entire peninsula. Putún Maya traders worked the coastal ports in large canoes, and eventually another Mexica-oriented group, the Xiu, overcame Mayapán in 1441. Subsequently, Yucatán was divided by struggles between sites contending for leadership. When the Spaniards, fresh from their conquest of Central Mexico, turned to the Yucatán a decade later, they found a scattered and divided people ripe for easy conquest, a pale shadow of the grandeur of their Classic-period ancestors.

THE Olmecs are one of Mesoamerica's oldest and most intriguing cultures. Their ceremonial centers, early use of hieroglyphic notation, and sophisticated cult images distinguish them from other Preclassic cultures. Because these traits were developed more fully in subsequent Classic cultures, some archaeologists consider the Olmecs a "Mother Culture"; to others they were merely the most prominent of several emerging regional civilizations with a shared ideological system.

ARCHAEOLOGICAL BACKGROUND

The major Olmec sites of San Lorenzo, La Venta, Tres Zapotes, and Cerro de las Mesas lie in the humid tropical lowlands of the Gulf Coast of Mexico, often refered to as the Olmec hearth area (see Map 1). Archaeological exploration of the area began in the early 1920s with the discovery of giant carved basalt human heads at several sites. In 1925, La Venta was discovered and cleared by Franz Blom and Oliver La Farge, who noted similarities to Maya forms in its stelae and who uncovered a giant stone head like one found earlier at the nearby site of Tres Zapotes. In the late 1930s, Matthew Stirling found three more giant stone heads plus enough other monuments to persuade the National Geographic Society to fund additional digging. Four field seasons produced a basalt-columned sunken courtyard with a tiger-masked stone sarcophagus, important monoliths, and jade figurines as well as additional Olmec monuments at Tres Zapotes and Cerro de las Mesas.

Inconclusive stratigraphy and a tentative ceramic sequence prompted new excavations at La Venta in 1955 by Philip Drucker, Robert Squier, and Robert Heizer. Carbon-14 dates of 800–400 B.C. confirmed the site as Middle Preclassic and the Olmec as forerunners of the Early Classic Maya.

In the mid-1960s, Michael D. Coe, of Yale University, turned to the tantalizing question of Olmec origins. Near the modern, southern Veracruz village of San Lorenzo Tenochtitlán, three closely clustered Olmec sites had been known since 1945: San Lorenzo (see Map 2), Río Chiquito (also known as Tenochtitlán), and Potrero Nuevo. Coe's 1966–1968 excavations with Richard Diehl at San Lorenzo (Coe and Diehl

CHAPTER 1

THE OLMECS

1980) produced firm archaeological contexts for five giant stone heads found previously at San Lorenzo and a sequence tied to carbon-14 dates and stratigraphy, detailing early phases of Olmec development.

The first settlers at San Lorenzo arrived around 1600 B.C. Their pottery was similar enough to contemporary Pacific Coast wares at Ocós, also excavated by Coe, that he calls the two groups "country cousins." Traits identified specifically as Olmec appear abruptly in pottery and sculpture around 1150 B.C. and continue until about 900 B.C., when San Lorenzo's huge stone heads, torsos, and bas reliefs, mutilated by pitting and decapitation, were buried in north–south and east–west lines on a red gravel floor. The fill with which they were covered eventually eroded out, toppling them into adjoining ravines.

The major destruction at San Lorenzo may have been triggered by external forces, internal dissatisfaction, and revolt, or ritual actions. At any rate, Olmec power subsequently shifted to La Venta, and people with a different ceramic tradition occupied San Lorenzo for another two centuries and then deserted it. La Venta continued until about 400 B.C., after which Olmec culture declined in the face of rising central Mexican principalities such as Teotihuacán that were probably based on irrigation agriculture.

Reconstruction of Olmec culture is hindered by these early dates, which preclude direct references to the Olmecs in ethnohistoric and ethnographic sources. Epigraphic sources are also scarce: Only a few preliminary calendric or name glyphs occur at Olmec sites.

Olmec sculpture, pottery, jades, paintings, and settlement patterns, however, all attest to a well-formulated religious system maintained by a priesthood at ceremonial centers and supported by outlying settlements through riverbank cultivation. Macrobotanic and faunal remains confirm the presence of maize and manioc, hunted animals, and lacrustine resources. Maize was probably steamed into tamales rather than roasted as tortillas because clay *comales* or griddles are absent.

ARCHITECTURE

Time, climate, and human intervention have combined to create a notoriously incomplete record of Olmec architecture. Because of the tropical Gulf Coast climate, preservation of organic material is rare. Wood-and-thatch structures have long since decayed, and only earthen mounds show where they once stood. Much of the stone architecture, having survived for millennia, has been lost in this century to pot hunters and the construction of air strips and oil refineries.

Nonetheless, it is evident that Olmec sites were shaped at least partly by their ecological setting. The swampy Gulf coastal plain is dotted with lagoons and therefore lacks the carrying capacity to sustain dense human occupation. The settlement pattern is one of hut clusters representing multiple, dispersed populations that presumably were the labor base for construction of the stone monuments and altars at ceremonial sites such as San Lorenzo and La Venta.

San Lorenzo

The site of San Lorenzo, in southern Veracruz near the Río Chiquito branch of the Coatzacoalcos River (Map 2), consists of mounds and courts set on an artificially modified hill 50 meters (164 feet) high from which human-made ridges project to form a pattern interpreted by Michael Coe as a huge eastward-flying bird effigy (Map 3). Gullies between the ridges formed the "wings" and "tail"; the head and part of the northeast wing, Coe feels, were never completed. Not all of Coe's peers see the bird outline: One reviewer noted that a few more rainy seasons might easily erode additional feathers into shape.

The ceremonial center of San Lorenzo consists of North, Central, and South courts (collectively labeled "Group A") along the bird's back (Map 3). The South and Central courts are flanked by paired rectangular north–south–oriented mounds with the largest mound (Mound 3-1 on Map 3) at their juncture. The smaller North Court is bounded to the west by an extension of the Central Court's lateral west mound (which angles to enclose a ball-court-like depression called the Palangana Complex) and to the east by an artificial water-collection depression, or laguna.

More than 200 smaller house mounds (not shown on the map) with an estimated five

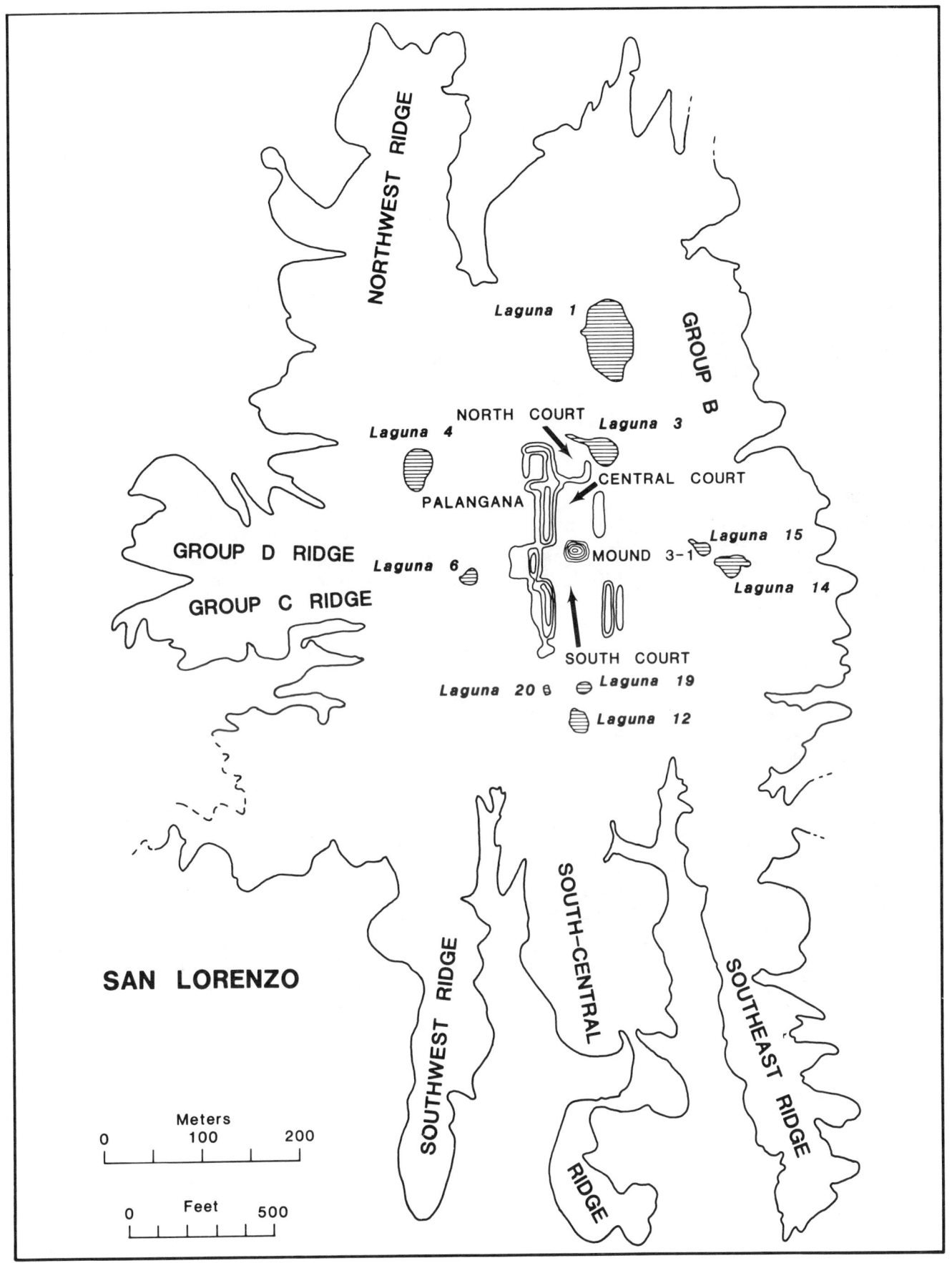

Map 3. Site map of San Lorenzo, showing architectural groupings and ridges suggestive of bird wings. (For a detailed map, see Coe and Diehl 1980, vol. 1, map 2)

people per residence, suggest a population of approximately 1,000 people during San Lorenzo's height, 1150–900 B.C. Some mounds occur in linear, "Main Street" formations; others cluster in U-shaped groups around courts. Interspersed lagunas (Map 3) perhaps represent borrow pits from which soil was taken to build the ridges. Some have geometric shapes and may have been sacred baths.[1] U-shaped basalt-lined troughs with slab covers extended in feeder lines from lagunas to a main aqueduct where Stirling earlier uncovered a duck-shaped stone monument with waterlike glyphs. This monument could have fit the main trough and ritually released accumulated water through a rounded hole in its bottom.

Developmental Phases

San Lorenzo's developmental phases, based on ceramic and architectural changes, chronicle a history of over 800 years (Coe and Diehl 1980; Coe 1981). During the Ojochi phase (1500–1350 B.C.), ceramic forms show close connections with Pacific coast sites. The Bajio phase (1350–1250 B.C.) saw conceptualization and initial construction of the site's effigy form. White clay Olmec-type figurines and "proto-Olmec" pottery appear in the Chicharras phase (1250–1150 B.C.), with full-scale Olmec stone sculpture and pottery appearing in the subsequent San Lorenzo phase (1150–900 B.C.), the site's apogee, during which artificial lagunas connected by basalt-lined conduits and the site's North, Central, and South courts and adjoining platform mounds were built. During the subsequent Nacaste phase (900–700 B.C.), outside influences are reflected by new figurines and pottery types, and a deliberate destruction and burial of monuments around 900 B.C. By 600 B.C., during the Palanguna phase, increasing ties with Tres Zapotes, La Venta, and the Maya lowlands were reflected in ceramic forms and in architectural constructions such as a four-sided, earth-walled ball court and the three courts of Group A, which may represent an imitation of Complex A at La Venta (see later discussion). San Lorenzo was finally abandoned

around 400 B.C. and was reoccupied again around A.D. 900 by Postclassic groups who renovated some of the structures and placed offerings under the plaza floors.

Laguna de los Cerros

The huge, 93-acre (37.6-hectare), largely unexcavated site of Laguna de los Cerros (Map 2), located 55 kilometers (34.18 miles) northwest of San Lorenzo, probably is contemporary with San Lorenzo and is equally important. Its ceremonial center consists of a series of earthen platforms around plazas and a large northern mound with the same alignment, 8° west of true north, as at San Lorenzo. Eventual excavations here will surely provide additional details of early Olmec architecture and culture.

La Venta

The occupation of La Venta in the Middle Preclassic period (900–300 B.C.) overlaps occupation of San Lorenzo, and archaeologists theorize that La Venta's rise may have contributed to San Lorenzo's violent disruption. Located on an island 3 miles (4.8 kilometers) long 40 feet (12 meters) above the swampy backwaters of Tabasco's Tonalá River some 10 miles (16 kilometers) inland from the Gulf Coast, it was long believed to have served as an important unoccupied ceremonial center for outlying villages. However, excavations by William Rust (The University Museum, University of Pennsylvania) "have revealed Middle Preclassic villages along an ancient river course just north of La Venta, as well as substantial construction remains (house floors, storage pits, urn burials), and a serpentine workshop near the ceremonial center itself" (Henderson 1988, 866), indicating a resident population at the site. La Venta is the source of some of the most famous pieces of Olmec sculpture.

The stone architecture at La Venta, like the shaped ridges and monuments buried under tons of fill at San Lorenzo, was the result of a sizable, well-organized work force. The extent of the effort is staggering. Enormous quantities of serpentine for portable sculpture and mosaic offerings associated with construction phases came from Pacific Coast sources 100 miles (160 kilometers) away. David Grove (1984) estimates

---

[1] Coe (1968, 64) proposes this explanation because themes on both San Lorenzo and La Venta monuments show water as a highly revered substance.

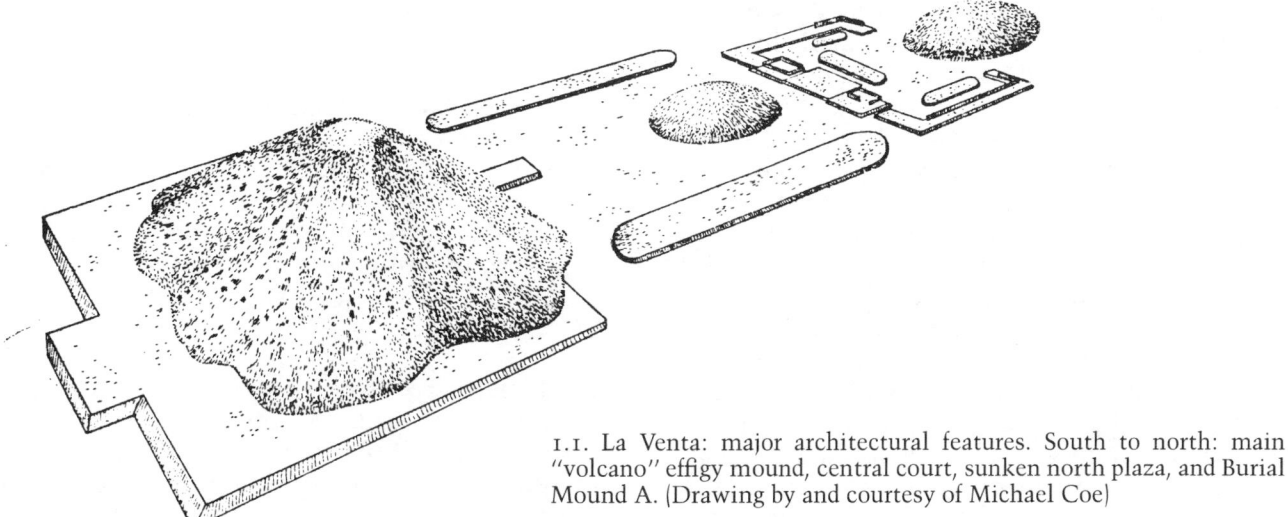

1.1. La Venta: major architectural features. South to north: main "volcano" effigy mound, central court, sunken north plaza, and Burial Mound A. (Drawing by and courtesy of Michael Coe)

that, at 100 pounds (45.3 kilograms) per person, 20,000 loads of serpentine were carried in to create the southwest platform offering, only one of several at the site. Basalt blocks quarried at Cerro Cintepec, in the Tuxtla Hills, 60 miles (96.5 kilometers) to the west, may have been ferried along the coast and up the Tonalá River by raft and then hauled on rollers to the site. Thousands of hours of additional labor created the monuments, altars, aqueduct system, and structures with red, yellow, orange, and white imported clay floors.

Three major complexes lie from south to north along an axis 8° west of true north (Fig 1.1): a large, fluted mound, a central court, and a north court associated with ritual and burial activities. The 110-foot-high (33.5 meter) mound, with its ten lobes, may have been a volcano effigy. Resting on a low, apronlike platform with a southern projection, it is the largest artificial structure at any Olmec site. Its north face overlooks the central court, which contains a smaller mound enclosed by long, low, rectangular north–south-oriented platform mounds.

North of the Central Court, the sunken North Court, paved with colorful clay, is surrounded by an adobe wall that originally supported a row of vertically set basalt columns, some over 9 feet (2.7 meters) high and weighing up to 2,000 pounds (one ton). Ritual caches and burials indicate concentrated ceremonial activity. At the court's north end, a four-tiered

truncated mound (Mound A-2 on Figure 1.1) faces the court; its sloping walls are reminiscent of the later Teotihuacán *talud*, with an unworked center section that presumably once supported a central stair. Low, square platforms set off the North Court's south-facing entrance.

Over fifty caches of jade and serpentine ranging in size from a handful of figurines to massive mosaics were placed under platforms, corners of structures, and stair bases during phases of architectural renovation. The most famous caches are identical 14.8 × 19.8 foot (4.5 × 5.9 meter) jaguar-mask mosaics filled with colored clay laid down and immediately covered by the platforms flanking the entrance to the North Court. In a smaller cache, fifteen serpentine and jade human figurines set in sand attentively face a lone granite figure against a backdrop of six upright celts. These caches must have embodied powerful forces, for their locations were carefully noted and later uncovered for reverent reviewing and, perhaps, power renewal activities.

Burials were also coordinated with the orientation of the site and mounds. La Venta's five tombs all follow the center line of the site. Tomb A, found under the mound at the north end of the North Plaza, is a rectangular cairn, walled and roofed with basalt slabs like those that fence in the plaza. It contained two adolescent male burials with jade figurines and beads. Tomb B, south of the mound, contained a single burial in a lidded sandstone sarcophagus with a snarling flame-browed jaguar head at one end, which has unfortunately disintegrated since excavation. Altars and stelae were also coordinated with architectural features, among them three giant stone heads north of and one south of the North Plaza mound facing outward as if to protect the site from harm. Unfortunately, they were not powerful enough to avert twentieth-century bulldozing and construction of a refinery for Pemex, Mexico's nationalized gas industry, an air strip, and the related oil town of La Venta, which leveled most of the site, precluding accurate future reconstructions.

Following La Venta's decline, Tres Zapotes rose to prominence (Table 1). Over fifty mounds at that site await future excavation. Its monuments blend Olmec and Izapan (see Chapter 3) features, and slope-and-panel *talud–tablero* mound facings foreshadow Teotihuacán's distinctive style. Another Early Classic site, Cerro de las Mesas (Map 2) has yielded a cache of Olmec jades and stelae with figures in a style that has Izapan, Olmecoid, and Mayan affinities.

Influence of Olmec Architecture

Although all major Olmec sites shared common traits—basalt aqueducts, diagnostic pottery and figurines, giant stone heads, and a similar art style, for example—they exhibit individual variation. San Lorenzo lacked La Venta's figurine and jaguar-mask caches, elite burials, and volcano-effigy mound; La Venta, with its unique natural island setting, escaped San Lorenzo's cataclysmic monument defacement. Collectively, Olmec architecture pioneered features that became Mesoamerican standards for the next 2,000 years. These include:

1. Architecture aligned along a site axis 8° west of true north, indicating considerable skill in astronomical reckoning.
2. Long, flat platform mounds grouped around a central plaza as bases for houses and temples.
3. Mounds over burials beneath house or temple floors.
4. Mounds with sloping stone-faced walls and, at late sites, prototypes of Teotihuacán's talud and tablero construction.
5. Deliberate bilateral symmetry of burials, architectural structures, paired buried monuments and/or caches, and (at San Lorenzo) contours of the site itself.
6. Offerings associated with periodic construction phases, probably keyed to an early version of the Calendar Round.
7. Stela/altar pairing and specialized structures such as ball courts.
8. Ceremonial precincts that either independently, or as sacred areas within later urban centers, became foci of religious architecture for centuries to come.

ART

Basalt and serpentine sculpture, pottery figurines, and clay seals are our primary material for the study of Olmec iconography. Most pieces are found associated with burials or ceremonial architecture; others, such as San Lorenzo's monument lines, have been redeposited to form what Coe calls an "antimuseum," removed from public display. Still others are found in household refuse or construction fill. Unfortunately, some of the most important engraved or incised objects, now in museum or private collections, were looted and lack any archaeological provenience whatsoever.

Style

Basalt and jade objects from the Olmec area have been known for over a century. In 1929, on the basis of their general similarity, Marshall Saville assigned examples in the American Museum of Natural History collections to an ancient style that he named "Olmec." Its more specific parameters were defined in 1942 at a Sociedad Mexicana de Antropología archaeological round table at which Miguel Covarrubias, a respected Mexican artist, described Olmec style as centering around a "were-jaguar" infant with cleft head, a wide flat nose, a snarling down-turned mouth with fangs or toothless infantile gums, slanted eyes, flame-shaped brows, and a body that combined jaguar claws and spots with the torso and limbs of a pudgy human infant (Figure 1.2).

As more monuments were discovered, additional diagnostics were added. Serpent–jaguar combinations were noted. Pouting-mouthed priests held little were-jaguars who carried serpent-headed ceremonial bars, "knuckle dusters" (objects shaped like brass knuckles), or perforators (awl-shaped objects used for autosacrificial bloodletting). The style description

1.2. Front and profile views of God IV, rain deity, from San Lorenzo showing diagnostic Olmec features. (From Coe and Diehl 1980, fig. 494; courtesy of the authors and the University of Texas Press; copyright © 1980)

covered both large pieces (comprehensively described in de la Fuente 1977) and smaller ones with proportions suggesting monumentality. De la Fuente (1973; 1977, 345–356 and Figures 1–17a) finds the 1.618 Classic Greek and Renaissance "Golden Mean" ratio in Olmec giant stone heads (Figure 1.3) and seated figures, where its harmonic proportions reflect "the perfect order in nature and the cosmos" (author's translation, de la Fuente 1977, 347).

Style Subdivisions

Once Olmec style had been defined and described, scholarly interest turned to its regional subdivisions, origins, chronological development, and diffusion into other areas. Formal studies have led to several attempts at style subdivisions. C. William Clewlow, Jr., and his coauthors (1967) propose three sequential site styles at Laguna de los Cerros, San Lorenzo, and La Venta. The art historian Susan Milbrath (1979), comparing modeling (roundness or flatness), detail, postures, proportions, and relation

of figures to background composition and to each other, reaches slightly different conclusions as to monument dates.[2] Charles Wicke (1971), using statistical Guttman scaling, seriates sequentially stylistic traits of the giant stone heads (Fig. 1.4a) and votive stone axes (Fig. 1.4b).

David Grove and Susan Gillespie (n.d.) have outlined broader chronological patterns of change in the Olmec symbol system, along with their possible political implications. During the Early Preclassic, colossal heads probably represented individual rulers whose abilities to control forces of fertility and rain were closely tied to altars, paw-wing, reptilian, were-jaguar, fire serpent, and other motifs on pottery, and clay figurines of bald-headed babies. After 900 B.C., green stone and serpentine were used for new figurine types, and incised motifs sym-

[2] A caveat: stylistic analysis is not an infallible technique. Kubler's (1962, 67) Tres Zapotes–La Venta–San Lorenzo succession of giant heads on stylistic grounds was subsequently contradicted by carbon-14 dates.

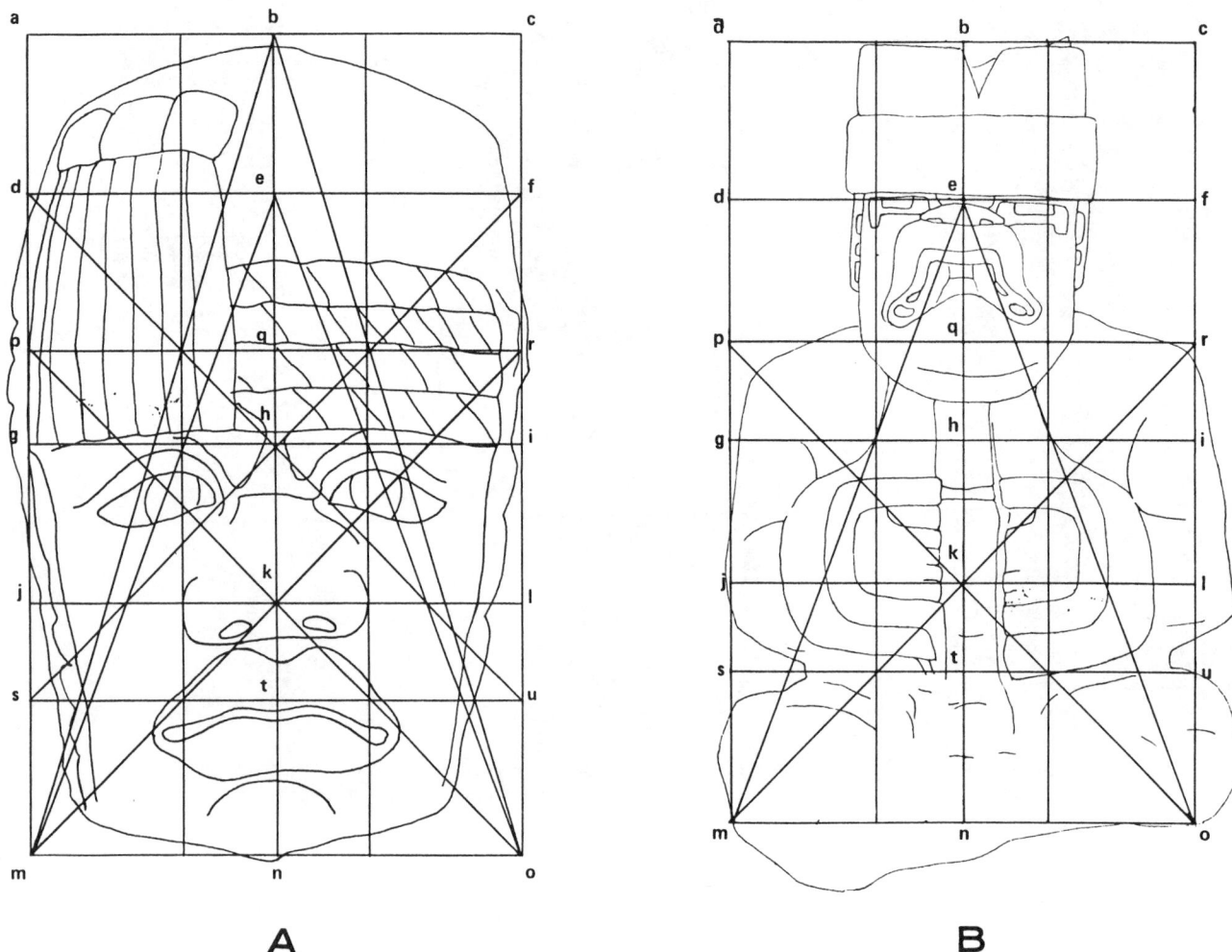

A B

1.3. Golden-mean proportions applied to (A) giant stone head from San Lorenzo and (B) San Lorenzo Monument 10. (From de la Fuente 1973; figs. 3 and 4; courtesy Instituto de Investigaciones Estéticas, Mexico)

bolizing hereditary rulership and its validation through bloodletting, formerly unimportant in Olmec ritual, became popular (Grove and Gillespie n.d.; Joyce, Edging, Lorenz, and Gillespie 1990).

Origin and Diffusion

Issues related to the origin and diffusion of Olmec style have been debated for decades, particularly since Olmecoid objects and representations have also been found in West Mexico and at select sites in Central Mexico, Oaxaca, Chiapas, and even Costa Rica. Recently, Olmecoid stone sculptures from Teopantecuanitlán near Copalillo, Guerrero, carbon-14 dated sev-

eral centuries before monumental art developed at Gulf Coast Olmec sites, have reopened the issue of origins outside the Gulf Coast Olmec hearth area. To Grove (n.d.), the early pieces suggest an older, widely shared ideology that predated "Olmec" style and accompanied Early Preclassic public architecture, multilevel settlement hierarchies, and increasingly complex rituals in Oaxaca, the Gulf, West, and Pacific coasts, and Central Mexico where developing "Olmecoid" motifs were used concurrently in distinctive, local manners. In San José Mogote, in the state of Oaxaca, and Tlatilco, in Central Mexico, for example, the distribution of pottery with "Olmec" fire-serpent and were–jaguar motifs in different residential wards suggests their

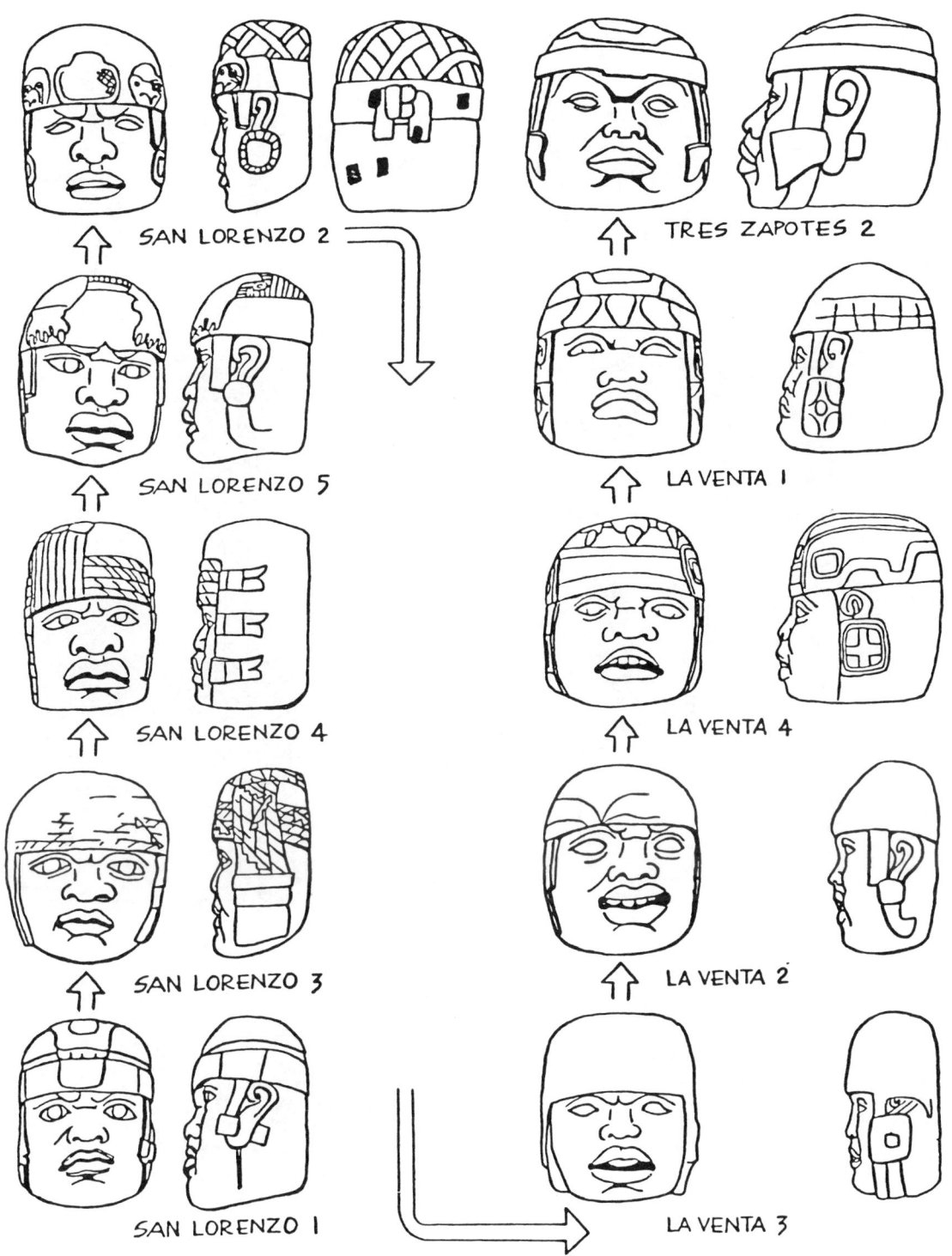

SAN LORENZO 2

TRES ZAPOTES 2

SAN LORENZO 5

LA VENTA 1

SAN LORENZO 4

LA VENTA 4

SAN LORENZO 3

LA VENTA 2

SAN LORENZO 1

LA VENTA 3

1.4a. Seriation by Charles Wicke of Olmec colossal heads. (From Wicke, 1971, 70; courtesy Charles Wicke)

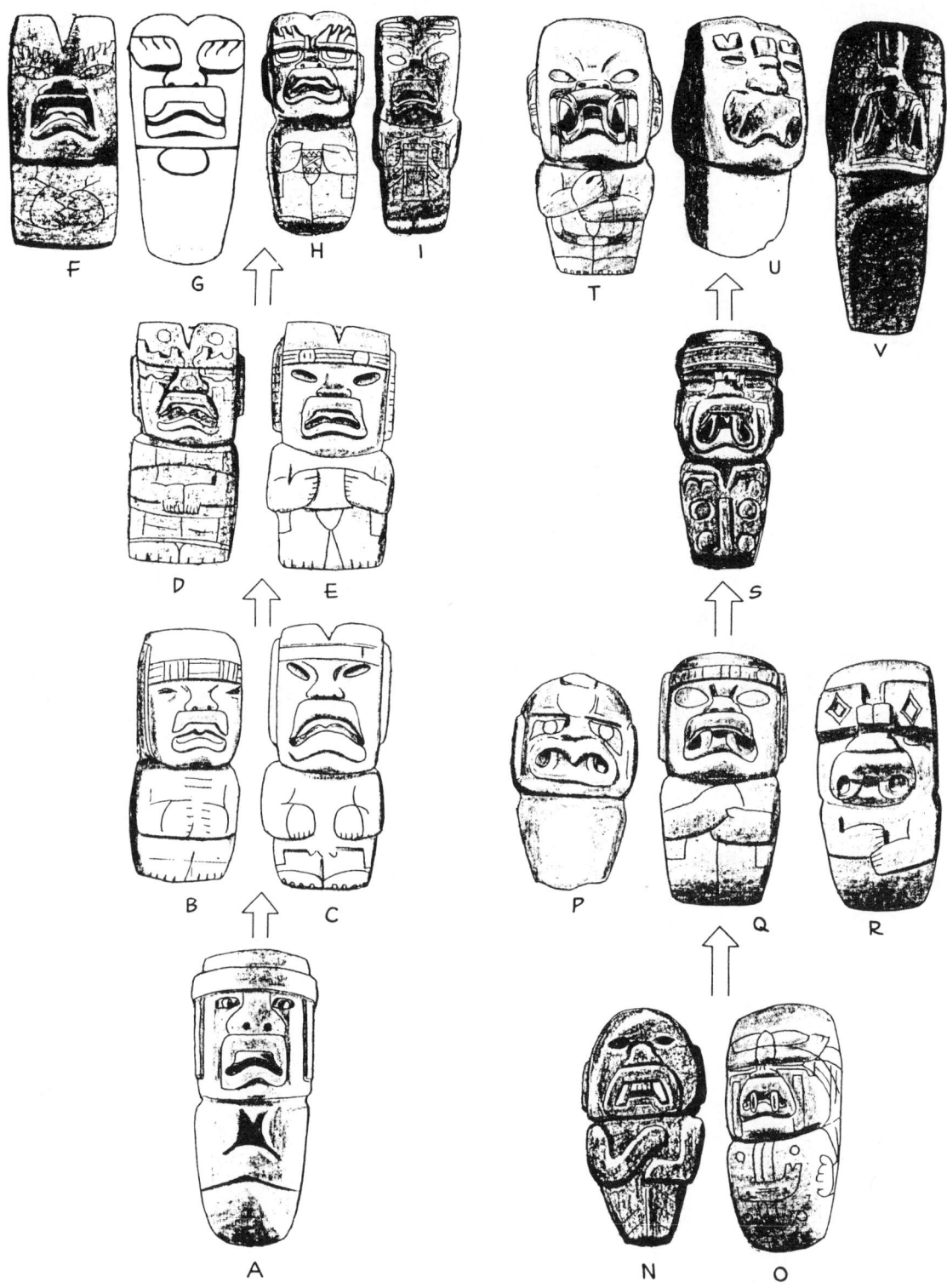

1.4b. Olmec votive axes. The arrows indicate chronological development (From Wicke 1971, 133; courtesy Charles Wicke)

use as emblems of corporate descent groups and their apical ancestors (Marcus 1989, 171–173; Tolstoy 1989, 101–102). Grove also questions the model that Olmec iconography always accompanied resource exchanges to Middle Preclassic "trade nodes," pointing out that "Olmec" motifs are absent in highland Guatemala, a major source for Olmec obsidian but *do* occur at Tlatilco and Tlapacoya where Gulf Coast–Central Mexican exchanges of obsidian and iron ore mirrors were minimal. He further suggests that Gulf Coast Olmec iconography was often more abstract than "frontier art" at distant sites, where explicit representations more effectively introduced unfamiliar concepts.

Post-Olmec Substyles

Other scholars have focused on post-Olmec regional substyles. In an early developmental scheme, Covarrubias (1946) detailed the Olmec were–jaguar's presumed transformation into Zapotec, Mixtec, Aztec, Totonac, and Mayan rain deities (Figure 1.5). At Monte Albán, in Oaxaca, cylindrical Young Fire God braziers and *danzante* stones (Figure 1.6) with outlines of mutilated, inert figures may represent a revival of Olmec style imperfectly remembered, perhaps by rulers emulating the prestige the Olmec once enjoyed.[3] Olmecoid jaguar altar/thrones, ceremonial bars, feline-saurian-serpents, jaguar–infants, crossed bands, and U-shaped elements appear between 200 B.C. and A.D. 200 at Pacific Coast sites and subsequently in Early Classic Maya art.

Iconography of the Olmec "Were–Jaguar" and Associated Motifs

Several meanings have been proposed for the pervasive "were–jaguar" motif. Portions of jaguarlike beings astride recumbent women on incomplete basalt monuments from Potrero Nuevo and Río Chiquito (Figure 1.7) led Matthew Stirling in 1955 to speculate that were–jaguars were the offspring of jaguar–human mating and therefore totemic ancestral beings from whom the Olmec claimed descent.[4] Car-

ried by adult priests, they were interpreted as potential infant sacrifices for rain. Still others saw in their slanting, almond-shaped eyes and mongoloid appearance deformed children whose abnormality indicated supernatural powers. The cleft forehead was interpreted as either *spina bifida*, the split skull characteristic of stillborn babies, the furrowed brow of a male jaguar, or the flexible upper skull fontanelle of a recently born infant.

Another interpretation, by Peter Furst (1981), involves *Bufo marinus*, a frog found in San Lorenzo excavations whose skin secretes a hallucinogenic substance perhaps used by Olmec shamans, or witch doctors. Interpreting the cleft foreheads as earth openings (figuratively, the vagina of Mother Earth) through which humans and others reached the earth's surface, Furst proposed the were–jaguar–toad. As the earth receives the dead and generates new life, adult toads shed and eat their skins, appearing to devour themselves and be endlessly reborn. Bands of protruding half-swallowed skin, Furst feels, resemble the bifurcated fangs of many were–jaguar representations.

Another explanation elaborates on the jaguar component. Jaguars, along with serpents, are ancient Mesoamerican zoomorphs affiliated with night, the underworld, agility, and power. These qualities, appropriate symbols of Olmec rulers, and the Olmec image of a jaguar issuing from a standing human's genitals in a cave at Oxtotitlán, Guerrero (Figure 1.8) led Coe (1972) to characterize the jaguar as an expression of royal descent.

Other investigators emphasize the were–jaguar's polymorphic nature (Muse and Stocker 1974; Stocker, Meltzoff, and Armsey 1980). Building on initial identifications by Donald Lathrap, they identify saurian, particularly crocodilian, elements. Rosemary Joyce and colleagues (Joyce, Edging, Lorenz, and Gillespie 1990) agree and also identify a fish (*xoc*) zoomorph with a crescent eye, sharklike teeth, fins, and crossed bands as body markings. They feel that this sharklike figure and its abstractions (as a serrated, cross-hatched oval, crossband motifs, and the scallop-edged "knuckle

---

[3] Scott (1978, 17). For a good review of other regional adaptations of the Olmec style after the collapse of La Venta, see Parsons (1981).

[4] Davis (1981) doubts that the monuments in question (Monument 1 from Río Chiquito, 3 from Potrero Nuevo, and 20 from

Laguna de los Cerros) show human–jaguar copulation; positions, he argues, are indefinite, and the humans have loincloths in place with no genitalia shown. He proposes alternative interpretations of battle action or vanquishing of a foe.

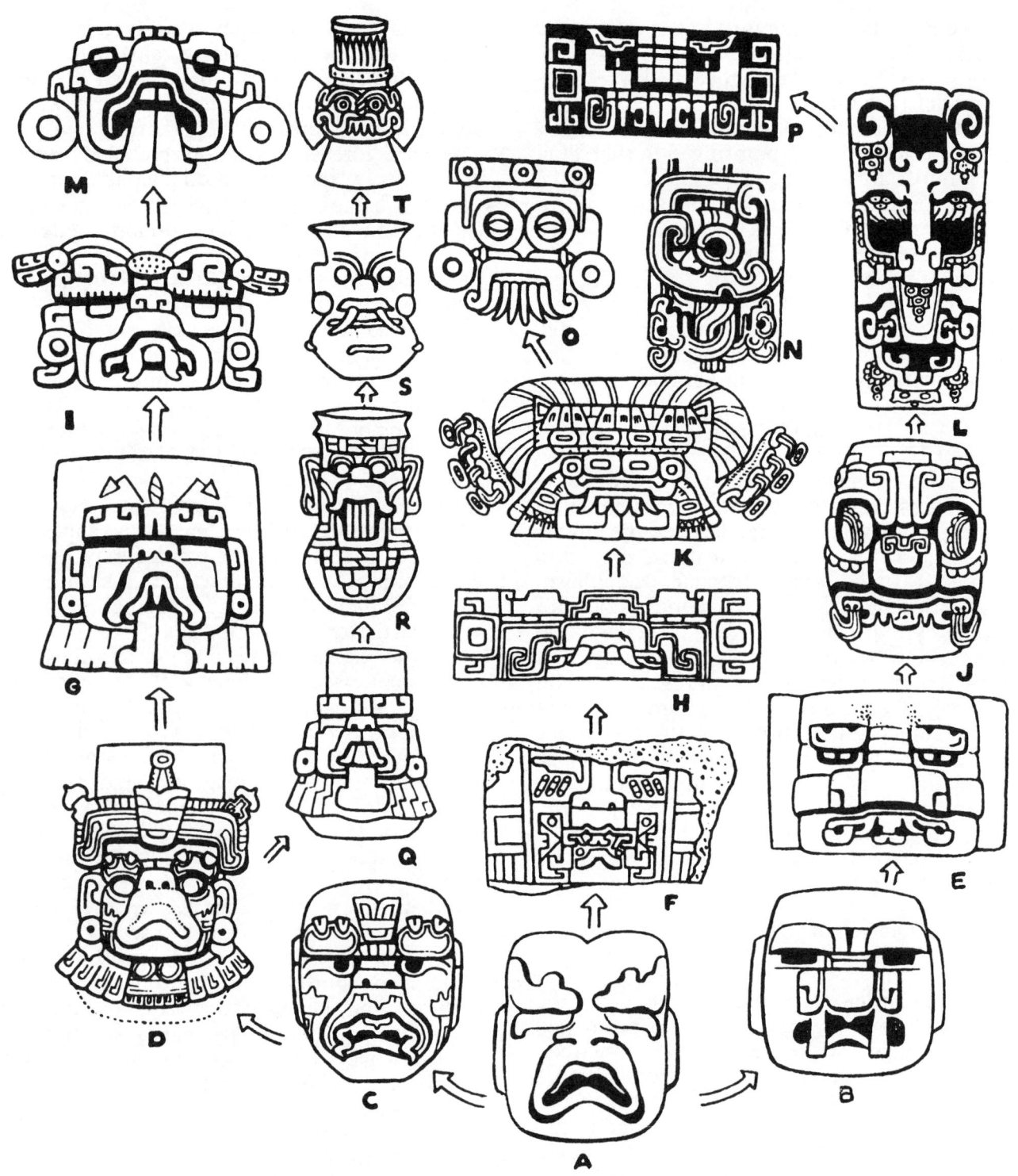

1.5. Chart by Miguel Covarrubias suggesting evolution from Olmec masks (*A–C*) of Oaxacan (*left*), Central Mexican (*center*), and Mayan (*right*) rain deities. (From Covarrubias 1946; courtesy Cuadernos Americanos)

1.6. *Danzante* ("dancing") figures from Monte Albán, Oaxaca, considered portraits of captives in an Olmec-derived style. (Caso 1946, figs. 23, 25, 27; drawings by Agustín Villagra, courtesy INAH)

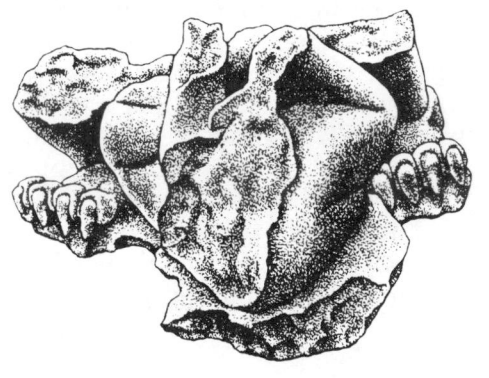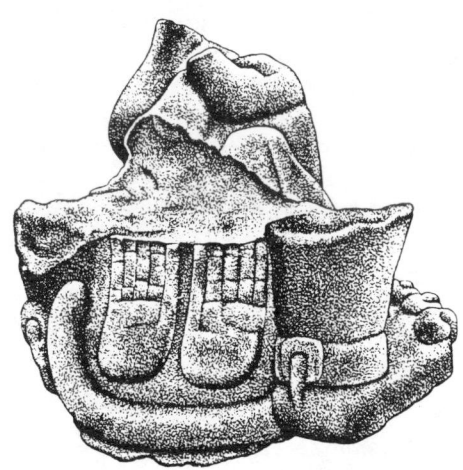

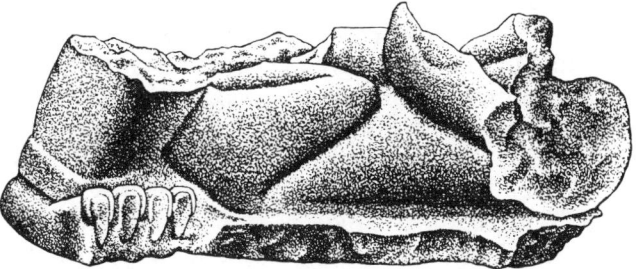

1.7. Possible jaguar–human mating, Monument 3, Potrero Nuevo. (From Diehl 1980, fig. 497; courtesy of the authors and the University of Texas Press; copyright © 1980)

1.8. Polichrome mural from Oxtotitlán. Guerrero: jaguar as royal-descent indicator. (Courtesy David Grove)

duster" held by Olmec priests) denote bloodletting along with stilleto-like "ice pick" jadeite perforators, stingray spines, and sharks' teeth recovered from excavations. Grove (1987, 61–65) feels that hand-held torch motifs were also bloodletting accoutrements, noting that their name (*tah, chah*) in several Maya dialects is a homophone for "bloodletter" (*ta, cha*). Clearly we are just beginning to understand the "were–jaguar" and other enigmatic composite images, their interrelationships, and their parallels with elements in Classic Maya art.

Iconography of Monumental Art

Giant Stone Heads

The 2 to 3 meter (6 to 9 foot) tall, 12- to 24-ton *cabezas colosales* (giant basalt heads) found at major Olmec sites have been subjects of ongoing speculation. Some see Negroid aspects in their round, broad faces, their flat, wide noses, and their thick lips, and suggest migrations from Black Africa into the Olmec heartland. A technological explanation is far more likely: The Olmec, working with stone implements and sand as an abrasive, economized by remov-

ing as little of the stone surface as possible. Headdresses, tubular ear plugs, and facial features are carved in bas relief, thereby saving laborious removal of tons of material.

The heads have been described as captured enemy chiefs, Olmec lords, or players of the ritual ball game, because of their helmetlike headgear and the discovery of Mesoamerica's earliest ball court at San Lorenzo. With seventeen complete heads now available,[5] differences in iconographic elements are more apparent and can suggest important intersite dynastic and political relationships. Studies by Clewlow and colleagues (1967) confirm that the heads portray discrete individuals. Their helmetlike headdresses bear specific emblems that identify their wearers (Figure 1.9). Particularly exciting is the discovery that the jaguar-claw (or eagle-claw) emblem on the headgear of La Venta Head 4 is also worn by a figure with the same puffy face and overbite on San Lorenzo Monument 14 (Figure 1.10c), a table-top altar strikingly like La Venta Altar 4. The San Lorenzo figure was also probably connected by a rope (indicating kinship) to the main altar figure. The inference is that the La Venta Head 4 ruler was related to the San Lorenzo lord. Use of similar emblems may link ancestors with later rulers, just as giant heads with similar physiognomy but different emblems indicate genetically related rulership. (A recently found cache of about twenty-five life-size jade masks from Arroyo Pesquero, south of La Venta, with physiological and age differences and distinctive facial incising, may likewise be individual ruler portraits (Coe 1989, 78).

Altars

Olmec monolithic art also includes carved, rectangular stone altars, so called because of their ledged, tablelike tops that often bear a frontal jaguar image (Figure 1.10 and 1.11a). Their deep frontal niches contain a seated adult male, sculpted in the round, grasping a thick cord that leads around the base to the side panels, where low-relief figures hold the ends of the cord and face the front of the monument. The seated front figure often holds a little were–

[5] Three from the Tres Zapotes area, four from La Venta, and eight from San Lorenzo.

a

b

c

d

1.9. Giant stone head with headgear bearing a 3-macaw emblem, San Lorenzo, Monument 2. (From Coe and Diehl 1980, fig. 425; courtesy of the authors and the University of Texas Press; copyright © 1980)

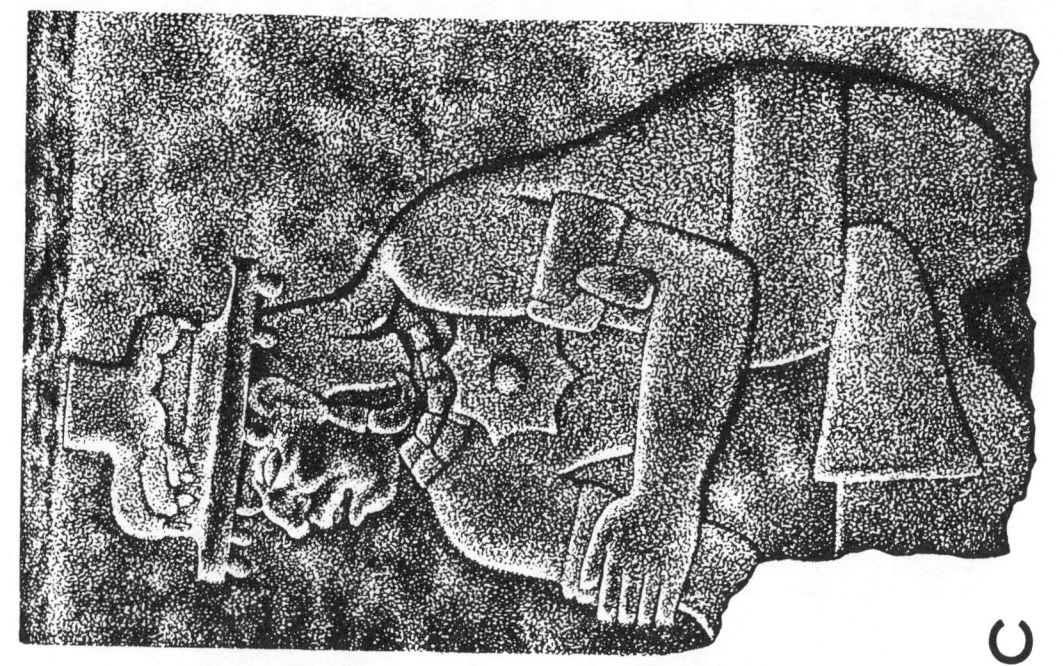

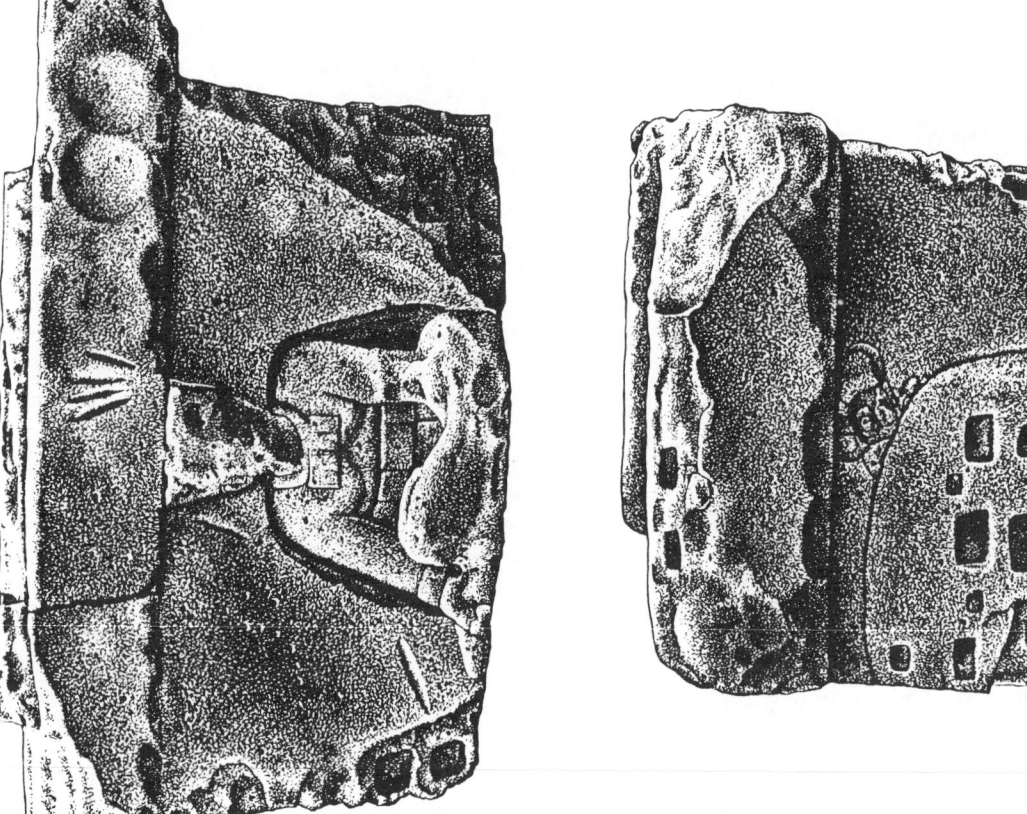

1.10. (*A, B*) altar/throne, Monument 14, San Lorenzo; (*C*) enlargement of left-end figure with same facial type and claw headgear emblem as on La Venta giant Head 4. (From Coe and Diehl 1980, figs. 438, 439; courtesy of the authors and the University of Texas Press; copyright © 1980)

1.11a. Altar 4 from La Venta, with frontal jaguar image. (From Bernal 1969, pl. 14; photo courtesy of University of California Press)

1.11b. Polychrome mural of a bird–man on a jaguar throne resembling Olmec altars: Oxtotitlán, Guerrero. (Courtesy David Grove)

jaguar across his lap, whereas side figures carry animated were–jaguars in their arms. Seven altars have been found at La Venta, two at San Lorenzo, one at Laguna de los Cerros, and none at Tres Zapotes.

A cave painting from Oxtotitlán, in the state of Guerrero, provides a new slant on these altars. A masked bird–man figure, with left arm raised and left knee bent, sits regally on a wide jaguar mask strongly resembling the frontal mask of many so-called altars (Figure 1.11b). Grove (1973) therefore feels that "altars" are actually thrones whose iconography, by detailing the depicted ruler's divine origins, validates his right to rule. The frontal niche of the altars is sometimes edged with a wide band and bifurcated fangs or vegetation symbols; by analogy with Petroglyph 1 from the site of Chalcatzingo (Figure 1.12) and other monuments, the niche represents a jaguar's mouth, symbolizing a cave. The seated figure holding the were–jaguar can thus be interpreted as emerging from the underworld, a clear indication of his divine origin (Grove 1981, 61). He is bound to the side figures by a "rope of kinship" linking genealogical relatives and visually confirming hereditary rights to rulership.

Identification of niche figures as specific Olmec lords, emblem glyphs, and *cabeza colosal* portraits may eventually facilitate establishing the genealogical ties that link historical individuals. If Olmec altars are thrones, they may be prototypes of the Classic Mayan jaguar throne. The altar/ throne and the early versions of a "ceremonial bar" held by important lords (Figure 1.12) appear to be major Olmec contributions to the accoutrements of later Maya ceremonialism.

Comparative Ethnohistorical Contributions

Ethnohistoric data play only a minor part in most Olmec research. However, information about Central Mexican (Aztec) deities has been used recently to interpret Olmec were–jaguar image variants as prototypes of major Postclassic gods.

New motivation for a comprehensive, systematic inventory of Olmec motifs came through a fortuitous, accidental discovery. In 1965, two children at play unearthed a major Olmec serpentine figure from a house mound at Las Limas, a small village just south of Coe's San Lorenzo excavations in Veracruz. The figure,

1.12. Petroglyph 1, Chalcatzingo, Morelos, with ceremonial bar–holding seated figure in jaguar-mouth cave facing jaguar "flame-brow" clouds releasing phallic, earth-fertilizing raindrops. (Courtesy INAH)

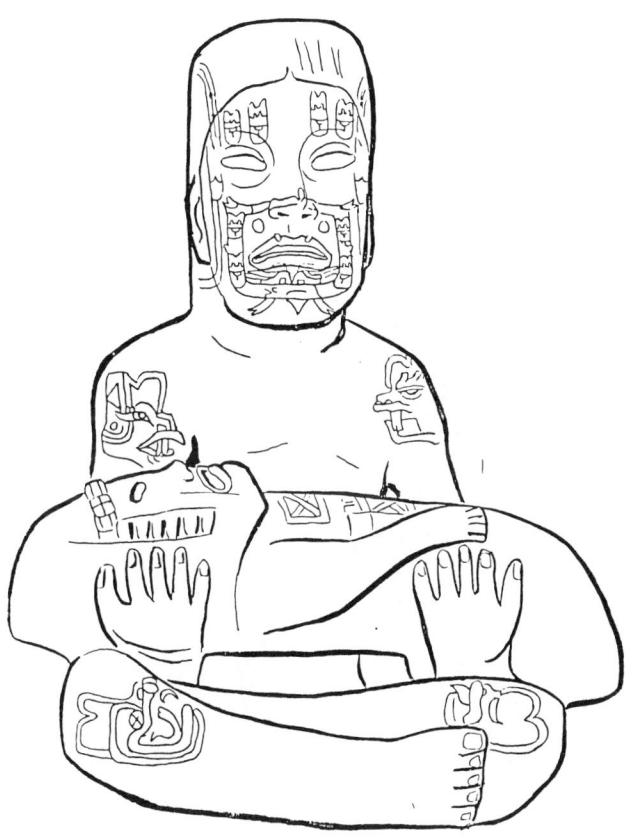

1.13. Stone seated figurine from Las Limas, Veracruz. (From Wicke 1971, 31; courtesy Charles Wicke)

like those in altar niches, sits cross-legged holding a bundlelike were–jaguar infant across its lap (Figure 1.13). When archaeological authorities came to investigate, they found the figure in a household altar, surrounded by burning candles and revered by villagers as a slightly aberrant Madonna and Child.

Of immediate interest to art historians was the elaborate incising of a slightly different jaguarlike head on each shoulder and knee and the complex mouth mask incised from the figure's nose to its chin. Additional incised bands appear at the side of the face with celt-shaped free forms above the brows (Figure 1.13 and 1.14). Multiple-element fine-line incising had been seen previously on Olmec serpentine pieces (Figure 1.15), but this new find was the first instance of jaguar mask variants so clearly and carefully shown on a single piece.

Michael Coe, who saw the figure shortly after its discovery, immediately surmised that these mask variants and the lap-held infant repre-

sented prototypes of several central Mexican Postclassic gods. His student David Joralemon identified them as a dragonlike god (Quetzalcóatl, on the right knee); a death god (left knee); a fire serpent (left shoulder); a god of regeneration (on the right shoulder); and a rain deity (the carried infant). Joralemon subsequently collected all available representations of Olmec motifs and reduced them to 182 component parts (Figure 1.16) grouped into significant combinations (Joralemon 1971, 6–18).

Joralemon's deity identifications were complicated by the Olmec (indeed, Mesoamerican) predilection for combining animal, human, and vegetal features on a single figure and assigning given deities shifting associations and alternate forms. Nonetheless, he bravely proposed ten specific Olmec gods, some with as many as five variant forms, including prototypes of Aztec gods of corn (Centéotl [God II]), rain (Tlaloc and dwarf Tlaloques [God VI; Figure 1.14b and Fig. 1.17 a–c]), wisdom (Quetzalcóatl, the "Feathered Serpent" [God I: Fig. 1.14e]), fire (Xiutecuhtli [God III: Fig. 1.14c]), and death (Mictlantecuhtli [God VIII: Figure 1.14c]). Joralemon subsequently isolated three deity pairs that he feels illustrate a philosophical Olmec dualism (1976, 53) and continues to restructure his categories (described and given ideological context in Coe 1989a).

Alternative viewpoints hold that the Olmec motifs depicted natural forces and not gods; that Olmec deities could not have maintained recognizable continuity to Aztec forms; or that Joralemon's dictionary forces the data into artificial groupings. Joralemon counters that Olmec–Aztec comparisons are entirely valid, because the basic Mesoamerican religious system has remained relatively stable (Joralemon 1976, 59).

Ethnographic Insights

Ethnographic descriptions of recent cultures, like ethnohistorical data, have been used to interpret Olmec art even though Hispanization and modernization have wiped out indigenous culture in the Olmec hearth area. Ethnographic descriptions of other parts of Mesoamerica, Colombia, Ecuador, and Peru detail deeply rooted belief systems that may have parallels in earlier Olmec cosmology.

A widespread, deeply seated belief in both

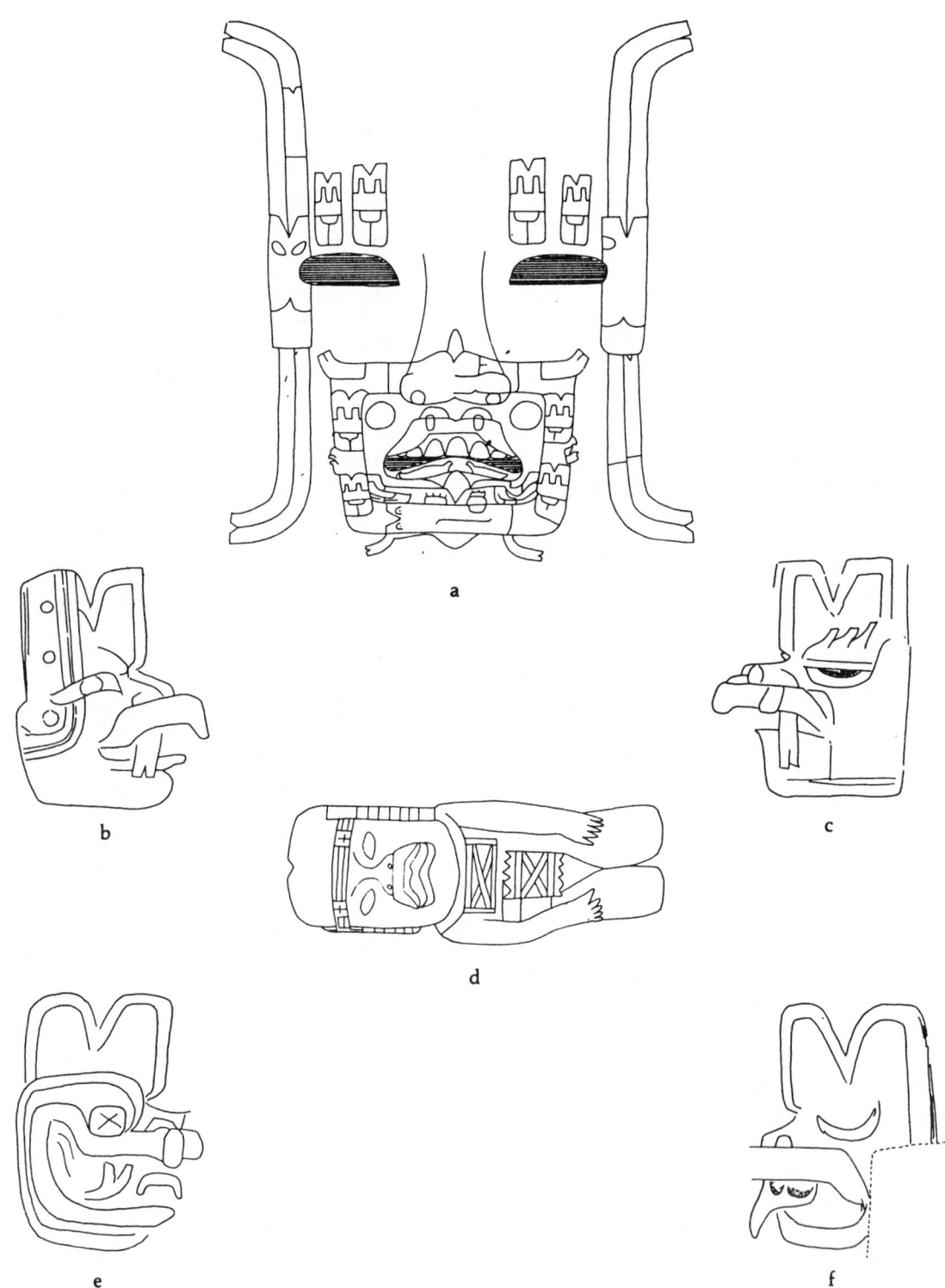

1.14. Incised designs from the Las Limas figurine: (*a*) facial incising; (*b*) right shoulder: God VI, war; (*c*) left shoulder: God III, fire; (*d*) infant figure carried on lap: God IV, rain; (*e*) right knee: God I, wisdom; (*f*) left knee: God VIII, death. (From Nicholson 1976a, p. 32, fig. 3; drawings by P. David Joralemon, copyright © 1976 by UCLA/CLAS)

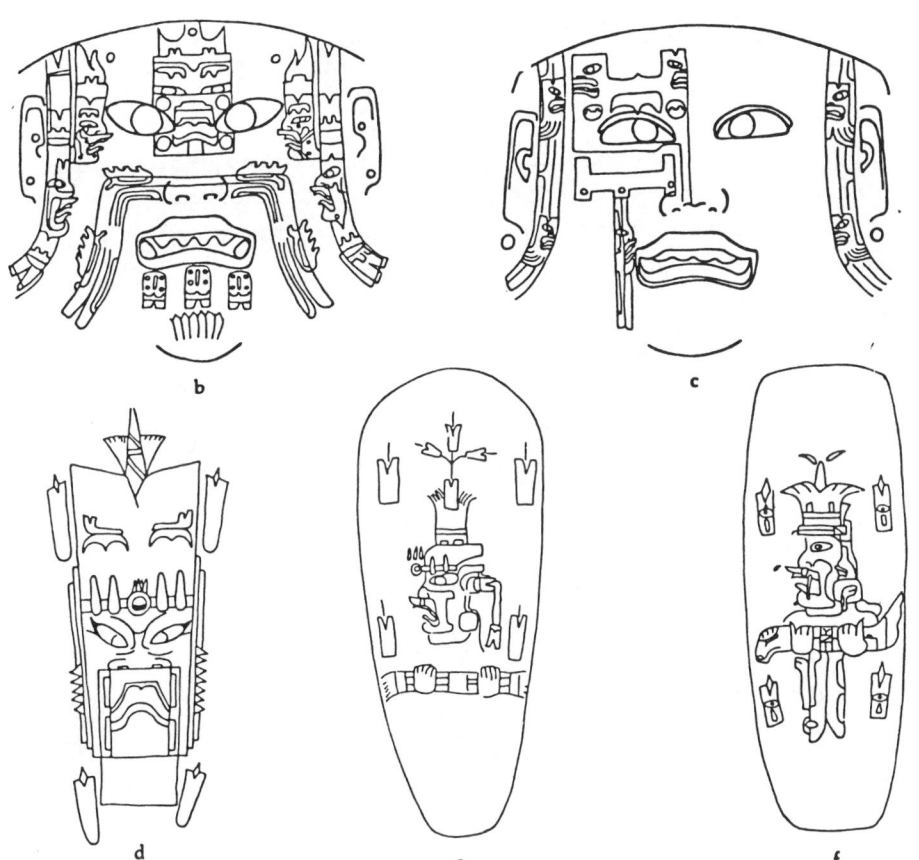

1.15. Multiple-pattern engravings on jade and basalt: (*top*) jade masks from Arroyo Pesquero, Veracruz; (*bottom*) jade celts from Arroyo Pesquero, Veracruz. (From Nicholson [ed.] 1976, p. 41, fig. 8; drawings by P. David Joralemon, copyright © 1976 by UCLA/CLAS)

tropical South America and Mesoamerica is the affiliation between jaguars and shamans (Furst 1968). Shamans can transform themselves into jaguars; in death, they revert to feline form. Thus Olmec were–jaguars may be shamanic or even royal alter egos. To the modern Maya, the jaguar is an animal counterpart of shamans in Chamula Indian myth. Jaguars are also a *nagual* of village elders able to communicate with ancestors among the Tzotzil Indians of Chiapas, Mexico.[6] In addition, ethnographic analogy hints at an intriguing explanation for the mutilation and destruction of monuments at La Venta and San Lorenzo (Grove 1981). At San Lorenzo, sculptures were deliberately battered and pitted (Figure 1.9), defaced and decapitated, and drilled with slots and niches (Figure 1.10, lower left) prior to careful linear burial. Coe feels that this destruction coincided with the

collapse of the site, perhaps through internal revolution or a countercult (there being no evidence of violent outside invasion). Grove thinks that purposeful symbolic mutilation of monuments accompanied the death of rulers, ends of dynasties, or the completion of calendric cycles.

An ethnographic parallel for mutilation occurs among the Canelos Quichua of Ecuador, whose ruling chiefs derive their power from the underworld and concentrate it in stools or ceremonial seats (Grove 1981, 63). When they die, their power becomes uncontrolled and dangerous, and the stools containing it are buried or destroyed. Olmec thrones, too, may have been "power charged": They not only depicted the source of a ruler's power by showing him emerging from the underworld but embodied his political and religious power while in office. Consequently, they might have required neutralization upon his death. Grove notes that stela and sculpture mutilation centered on a figure's head and face and occurred over a long pe-

[6] Gossen (1974, 273); Holland (1964, 304).

A Dictionary of Olmec Motifs and Symbols

The 182 motifs included in this section, each designated by an arabic numeral, are given verbal and graphic descriptions wherever possible. Important variations are labeled with small letters. Every occurrence of a particular motif may be found by referring to the illustrations listed at the end of the description.

1 *General Body Form.*

   A *Human.* 1, 2, 3, 4, 6, 7, 9, 10, 11, 13, 14, 15, 17, 18, 19, 20, 22, 33, 36, 90, 132, 142, 150, 178, 188, 196, 206, 208, 209, 244, 245, 259, 263.

   B *Jaguar.* 17, 38, 39, 93, 94, 95, 96, 97, 143, 145, 262, 263.

   C *Bird.* 4, 11, 42, 191, 192, 193, 194, 197, 198, 202, 204.

   D *Snake.* 55?, 56?, 243, 244, 245, 246, 247, 248, 250, 251, 252.

   E *Fish.* 3, 11.

2 *Typical Olmec Face.* Almond-shaped eyes, wide flattened nose, and mouth with flaring upper lip and drooping corners. 2, 3, 4, 9, 10, 11, 13, 15, 16, 17, 18, 19, 20, 21, 23, 26, 27, 36, 61, 132, 142, 148, 150, 154, 159, 187, 199, 208, 209, 245, 246, 259.

3 *Cleft or Cloven Head.* Extremely common characteristic of Olmec deities. Cannot be considered definitive for any one god. 5, 8, 10, 29, 36?, 43, 44, 61, 120, 122, 123, 126, 135, 146, 148, 153, 155, 157, 161, 162, 163, 164, 165, 166, 172, 173, 175, 181, 182, 183, 184, 185, 186, 189, 206, 207, 208, 209, 211, 214, 215, 219, 220, 222, 225, 228, 230, 232, 233, 235, 236, 237, 238, 239, 241, 242, 249, 253, 256, 257.

4 *Eye Plaque.* Squared panel, often with frontal view of an Olmec god, appearing on the forehead above the eye. 10?, 26, 27, 72, 128, 137, 138, 139, 146.

5 *Flame Eyebrows.* Branched or scroll-like elements representing eyebrows. Definitive for God I and common for Gods II and III. 38?, 248?

   A *Three or four repetitions of squared-off element.* 90, 91, 93, 95, 96, 99, 101, 120, 121, 126, 137, 138, 140, 143, 144, 145, 147, 152, 154, 160, 161, 162, 163, 164, 171, 176, 191, 199.

   B *Curvilinear, shorthand version of Type A brow.* 10, 90, 97, 101, 102, 103, 117, 118, 129, 136, 137, 138, 142, 146, 149, 172, 192, 195, 199, 201, 202, 257.

   C *Brow with only one rise.* 30, 33, 100, 131, 144, 145, 148, 151.

   D *Brow with two rises.* 101, 130, 155, 180, 184, 198, 199.

   E *Brow with three rises.* 94, 141, 148, 157, 159, 165, 177, 179, 180.

   F *Brow with two hoop elements.* 135, 175.

1.16. First page from Joralemon's Olmec dictionary (Joralemon 1971, p. 7; courtesy P. David Joralemon and DO)

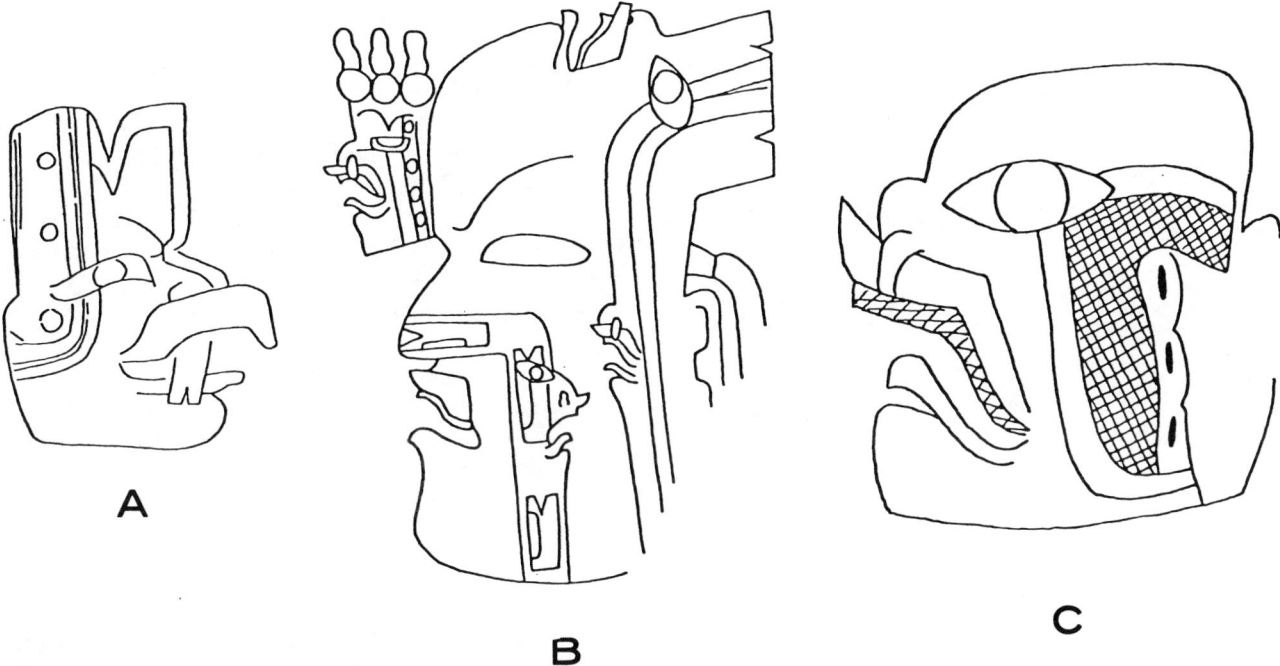

1.17. God VI variants (possibly a Xipe antecedent) with cleft head, open mouth, and a curved band passing through Type-D eyes: (A) Las Limas figure, (B) jade of unknown provenience, with four subsidiary God VI profiles, (C) pottery bowl, Tlapacoya. (From Joralemon 1971, p. 79; courtesy P. David Joralemon and DO)

riod. The decapitated stone head, where the ruler's power-in-image was concentrated, was buried with his body in at least one instance at Chalcatzingo. To Grove, the extra time and labor spent in burying mutilated monuments suggests that reverent Southwestern U.S. Indian custom of "killing" mortuary pottery (de-liberately breaking a central hole to release the pot's spirit) rather than violent iconoclasm at San Lorenzo (Grove 1984, 159–161).

The Olmecs will always be one of the great pre-columbian enigmas, but interdisciplinary cooperation is quietly adding to our understanding of their art and culture.

CHAPTER 2

TEOTIHUACÁN

TEOTIHUACÁN, a famous tourist Mecca 50 kilometers (31 miles) northeast of Mexico City, began as one of several Late Preclassic sites. By A.D. 150, it had eclipsed its formerly larger neighbor, Cuicuilco, in both size and importance. Its subsequent growth was phenomenal. Between A.D. 450–650, it was the largest city of its time in the world, with an urban area of over 20 square kilometers (12½ square miles) and a stable population estimated at 125,000 to 200,000 people (Millon 1981, 208). Its decline between A.D. 650–750 was accompanied by burning of temples and gradual, subsequent abandonment.

ARCHAEOLOGICAL BACKGROUND

In 1905, the Mexican archaeologist Leopoldo Batres began excavations at Teotihuacán. He mistook stone rubble surrounding the site's largest structure, the Pyramid of the Sun, for remains of its last construction phase and continued to bore inward, seeking better preserved earlier architecture. By the time he realized that there were no substructures, rain had eroded away the original outer dimensions of the pyramid. As a consequence of Batres's mistake, the Pyramid of the Sun that we see today has five stages instead of the original four, flecked by exposed tenon stones that held the original plaster facing.

In 1917, another Mexican archaeologist, Manuel Gamio, excavated the Temple of the Feathered Serpent and the Ciudadela (Citadel). He also surveyed nearby villages and established a pottery workshop for his peasant workers: Today their descendants make figurine replicas that are sold to tourists. Laurette Séjourné, Pedro Armillas, Eduardo Noguera, Sigvald Linné, and others later explored several of Teotihuacán's residential compounds. Mexico's Instituto Nacional de Antropología e Historia reconstructed important buildings along the Avenue of the Dead between 1960 and 1964. An ambitious survey by René Millon, Bruce Drewitt, and George Cowgill (1973) has produced a comprehensive site map. Other researchers (Sanders, Parsons, and Santley 1979; Wolf 1976) have plotted rural sites and described the ecological basis underlying Teotihuacán's precipitous rise to prominence.

Until the 1940s, Teotihuacán was believed to be the ancient Toltec capital of Tula because the Toltecs had been the most powerful pre-Aztec presence in Central Mexico, and Teotihuacán was the only large ruin around. In 1941, Wigberto Jiménez Moreno found ethnohistoric sources locating Tula further north and west, and ceramic and architectural studies confirmed Teotihuacán's construction in the first century A.D. by an unknown people.

Teotihuacán supported a large population through *milpa* horticulture (and perhaps irrigation agriculture) of corn, squash, *amaranth*, and *maguey*, in addition to lacrustine fish and birds. Channels diverted water from the Río San Juan to adjacent croplands, and there are tenuous indications of prototypal *chinampas*, or floating gardens.

From earliest times, the population was urban: Only 10 to 15 percent lived in adjacent, dispersed settlements. There is clear evidence of a priestly administrative class, although it is uncertain whether political and religious authority was held by a single individual or by a group. Artisans and merchants occupied residential districts, and poorer individuals inhabited crowded, slumlike compounds such as Tlamimilolpa.

Six ceramic phases keyed to stratigraphic excavations define Teotihuacán's growth and decline.[1] During the Patlachique phase (100 B.C.–A.D. 0), Teotihuacán was one of several small Late Preclassic settlements. Some time during Early Classic Tzacualli (A.D. 0–150), people using *talud–tablero* construction came from near present-day Tlaxcala and joined the local population, perhaps lured by the nearby obsidian outcroppings and natural springs. The Pyramid of the Sun and the Pyramid of the Moon were built, and Teotihuacán began processing obsidian and building extensive trade contacts. The Miccaotli phase (A.D. 150–250) saw further expansion, and by the Tlamimilolpa phase (A.D. 250–450), Teotihuacán covered over 20 square kilometers (12½ square miles). Housing compounds were interspersed with workshops that produced trade items for much of Central and South Mexico. The Xololpan phase (A.D. 450–650) represented boom times, but around A.D.

500 images of warriors and weapons appear. The subsequent Metepec phase (A.D. 650–750) opened with evidence of burning in several of the city's temples: Charcoal from a hearth or burned area in a small structure in the Temple of the Sun plaza is carbon-14 dated to about A.D. 650 (Robert Chadwick, personal communication). Emigration followed, and by 750 only a much smaller population remained.

ARCHITECTURE

Teotihuacán's distinctive architecture had antecedents at other Central Mexican sites (Map 2). Cuicuilco, a major ceremonial center until its destruction by the volcano Xitle between A.D. 0 and A.D. 100, had several truncated, stepped platforms and a 150-meter in diameter (492-foot) circular, stepped pyramid with east and west access ramps. The main platform at nearby Tlapacoya had multiple tiers with stuccoed, dressed-stone talud faces and stairs connecting the several levels. These antecedent forms provided an architectural basis dramatically amplified at Teotihuacán.

Site Plan

Teotihuacán's layout and public architecture were conceived and executed during the Tzacualli phase (A.D. 0–150) in a century and a half of extraordinary physical and intellectual activity. At this time, the enormous Pyramid of the Sun was completed and the Pyramid of the Moon, the Temple of Quetzalcóatl, the East Avenue, and many of the temples and palaces along the Avenue of the Dead were under construction by a work force that already numbered between 70,000 and 100,000 people during the first century A.D. in an early version of urban accretion. Between A.D. 150 and 500, the size of the site continued to increase dramatically as the population expanded and buildings with uniform rubble fill were built over earlier structures.

The city's layout was carefully planned. Major architectural complexes lie to either side of a north–south oriented 4-kilometer (2.5-mile), stepped *via sacra*, the Calle de los Muertos, or Avenue of the Dead (Figure 2.1; Map 4). East and West avenues intersect this axis at the Ciudadela complex and Great Compound, dividing Teotihuacán into quarters laid out in a gridiron

---

[1] See Millon (1981, Fig. 7-7, p. 207) for a concordance of the Teotihuacán Mapping Project's phase names and the Mexican Instituto Nacional de Antropología e Historia's Proyecto Teotihuacán phase numbers

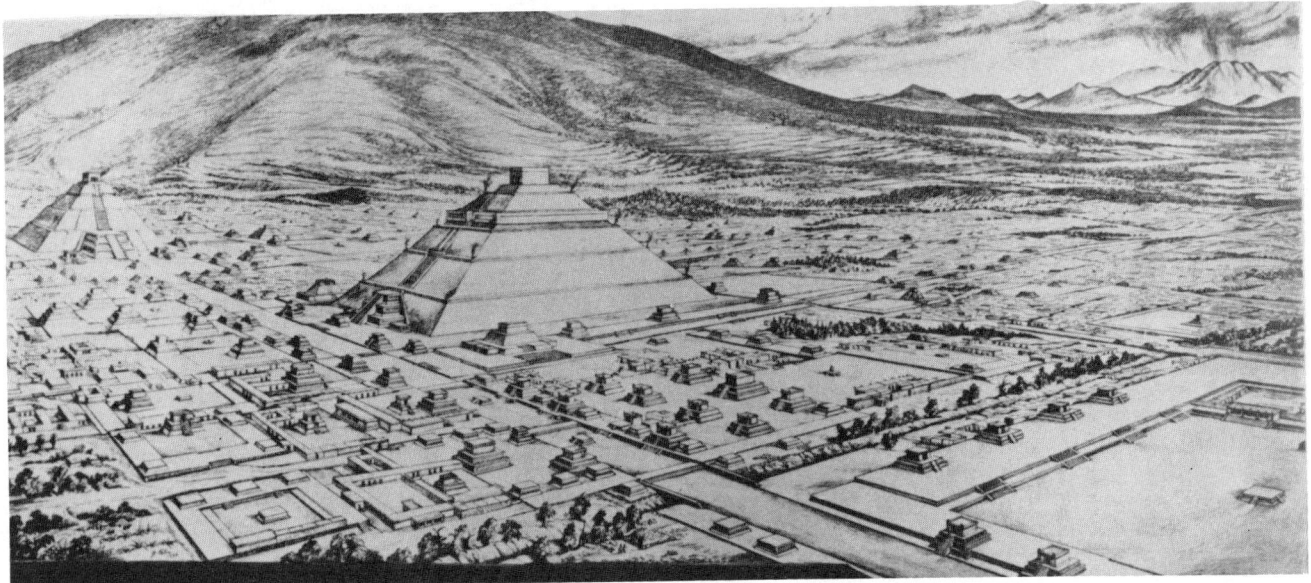

2.1. View of the Citadel (*lower right*), the Pyramid of the Sun (*left of center*), and the Pyramid of the Moon, at the end of the Street of the Dead. (From Marquina 1951, pl. 10; reconstruction and drawing by Feliciano Peña; courtesy INAH)

pattern and separated by narrow streets (Map 4). As the city grew, this basic layout was essentially maintained.

Talud and Tablero Construction

Temples were built on stepped pyramids or platforms whose exteriors display Teotihuacán's distinctive talud and tablero construction. Each temple level consisting of a sloping, dressed stone wall, or talus (*talud*), surmounted by a vertical, rectangular framed panel (*tablero*), and

2.2. Talud–tablero construction in Teotihuacán architecture: sloping wall (talud) topped by horizontal panel (tablero). (From Heyden and Villaseñor 1984, p. 18; drawing by Alberto Beltran, courtesy EMM)

was divided by a central stair with low, flat balustrades (*alfardas*) (Figure 2.2). Fill behind the talud was interspersed with upright slabs to support the weight of the overlying tablero, whereas tablero frames were stabilized by ledgelike slabs driven deep into the rubble or adobe brick fill. The stone exteriors of porous *tezontle* were held in place with what René Millon calls "Teotihuacán concrete," a mixture of crushed volcanic scoria and mud mortar. Firewood for burning tons of limestone to produce lime plaster for hundreds of structures may have hastened deforestation and dessication in the valley.

The framelike tableros were usually two to three times the height of their supporting talud, giving structures a strongly horizontal visual pull. George Kubler poetically describes the effect: "The sloping talud is always shadowed by the tablero. From a distance, the tablero appears to float upon a cushion of shadow" (1984, 57). Exteriors were painted red and white, and recessed tableros contained painted murals or carved stucco or stone heads held in place by tenons. Teotihuacán at its height was far more colorful than the stone reconstruction we see today.

The Core Area

The backbone of ceremonial architecture is the Avenue of the Dead (from the Aztec *miccaotli*, "way of the dead"), a 40-meter-wide (131 foot)

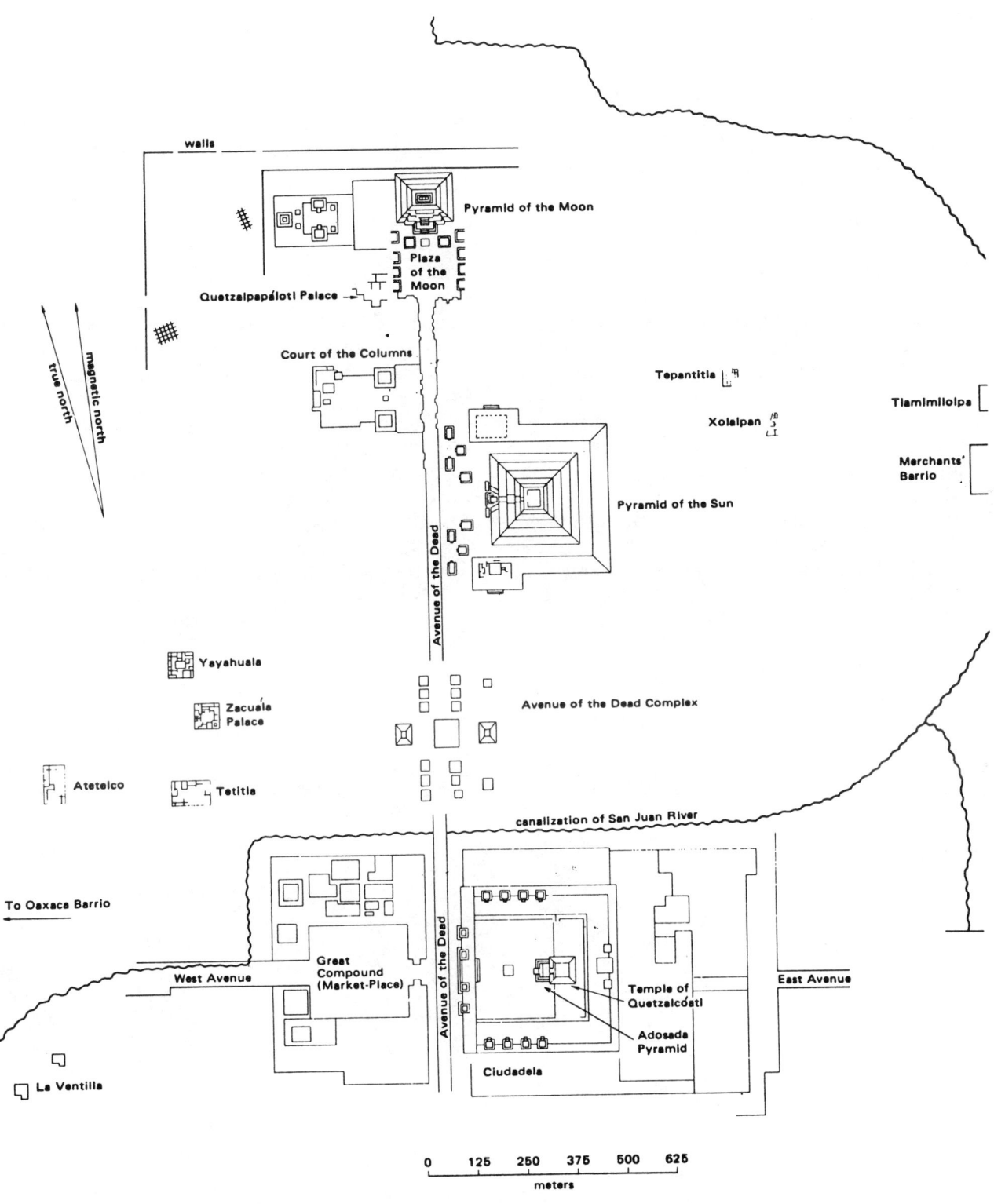

walls

true north
magnetic north

Pyramid of the Moon

Plaza
of the
Moon

Quetzalpapáloti Palace →

Court of the Columns

Tepantitla

Xolalpan

Tlamimilolpa

Merchants'
Barrio

Avenue of the Dead

Pyramid of the Sun

Yayahuala

Zacuala
Palace

Avenue of the Dead Complex

Atetelco

Tetitla

canalization of San Juan River

To Oaxaca Barrio

West Avenue

Great
Compound
(Market-Place)

Avenue of the Dead

Ciudadela

Temple of
Quetzalcóatl

Adosada
Pyramid

East Avenue

La Ventilla

0   125   250   375   500   625

meters

Map 4. Simplified map of the civic-ceremonial center of Teotihuacán. (From Weaver 1981, fig. 20, p. 19; courtesy of Muriel Porter Weaver and Academic Press)

paved north–south esplanade extending 4 kms (2.5 miles) in a series of terraces connected by low stairs (Map 4). These landings regulated the flow of priestly processions and provided changing vistas for tourists and visiting pilgrims, as they still do today. Over a hundred painted buildings lined the avenue, including the Temple of the Jaguar, the Temple of the Mythical Animals, the Temple of Agriculture, and the Viking Group (named after the foundation that financed its excavation). Many were decorated with murals whose original colors remain intact.

The dominant structure, facing the avenue on its east side, is the enormous Pyramid of the Sun, which is 61 meters (200 feet) high and 213 meters (698 feet) across its base as reconstructed (Fig. 2.1). The pyramid may have supported a temple to the sun, or perhaps twin temples like those found in later Maya and Aztec architecture.

Second in size is the 36-meter-high, (116 foot) four-tiered Pyramid of the Moon at the avenue's north end (Figure 2.1 and Map 4). Its complex south face has three projecting, sloping-walled tiers with a five-tiered "half pyramid," a talud–tablero exterior landing attached to the lower two tiers. A balustraded center stair connects these interlocking faces with the unrestored top tier of the main pyramid. South of this ex-

tension, a large, square, ground-level courtyard framed by talud–tablero platforms encloses a low, flat ceremonial platform and the remains of a "holy of holies" structure with multiple altars.

Teotihuacán's priests and rulers probably lived in "palace" complexes like the Palace of the Quetzal–Butterfly (Quetzalpapálotl) discovered in 1962 west of the Plaza of the Moon. Its mural-adorned rooms face a patio with square carved columns showing the mythical bird–butterfly. Originally polychrome, they support a tablero-edged flat roof bordered by upright stone merlons that, inverted, are almost identical to the slab tripod feet found on Teotihuacán cylinder vessels.

Further south, the huge, square Ciudadela enclosure on the east side of the Avenue of the Dead contains residential complexes flanking an ornately decorated pyramid, the Temple of Quetzalcóatl (the Feathered Serpent). On its partially excavated six-tiered east face, massive heads of Quetzalcóatl alternate with flat-snouted, tusked, scroll-browed agnathous heads bearing "double-donut" goggle eyes suggesting the Aztec rain god Tlaloc (Figure 2.3). Undulating, rattle-tailed serpent bodies striated like flowing water and Gulf Coast bivalve and conical shells fill the background; additional Quet-

2.3. Quetzalcóatl (Feathered Serpent) and Tlaloc (rain deity) on Temple of Quetzalcóatl tablero. (Courtesy INAH)

zalcóatl heads adorn the stair balustrades. We can only speculate about the splendid temple that once crowned these ornate painted and obsidian-inlaid façades.

After A.D. 300, a new four-tiered pyramid (the Adosada Pyramid) was built over the Temple of Quetzalcóatl's sculptured walls, and a 400-meter-long (438 yard) ceremonial precinct was created by enclosing the pyramids and a small central altar within a wide, 3-meter (9.8-foot) high wall topped by low talud–tablero temple or palace bases. Across the Avenue of the Dead to the west is the Great Compound, which probably served as an open-air market space.

Residential Areas

In the city's residential neighborhoods (barrios, in Spanish), over 2,000 one-story walled apartment compounds consisting of rooms facing open patios and serviced by temples housed 60 to 100 people each (Millon 1981; 203–210). Nearly 400 such compounds, including a walled precinct attached to the west face of the Pyramid of the Moon, were workshops for processing black or banded-gray obsidian from Otumba, a town in the basin of Mexico east of Teotihuacán, and the highly prized green variety from Cerro de las Navajas (Hill of the Blades) in Pachuca, in the state Hidalgo. Over 140 other compounds housed workshops for shellwork, figurines, utilitarian pottery, or Teotihuacán's distinctive Thin Orange ceramic ware. Compounds from which Gulf Coast and lowland Maya pottery have been recovered were probably merchants' barrios, used for warehousing trade goods. One example, the Oaxaca barrio, contains Monte Albán-type tombs and pottery spanning several centuries.

Other apartment compounds were for local residents. Standardized compounds that centered kin-based groups around a shrine preserved group identity and created barriolike units facilitating political administration of the population (Millon 1981, 210–212). Complex murals found in apartment compounds at the outlying settlements of Teopancaxco, Atetelco, Tetitla, Tepantitla, Xolalpan, and Zacuala (Map 4) housed moderately wealthy inhabitants. In contrast, crowded, tenementlike units and generally poorer burials at other residential compounds such as Tlamimilolpa and La Ventilla B suggest that they were occupied by low-status rural or foreign immigrants. Windowless, gar-

retlike rooms at Tlamimilolpa may also represent temporary quarters for pilgrims and other rural transients requiring short-term lodging.

Implications of the Architecture

Teotihuacán qualifies as an urban center in terms of both size and internal complexity. Demographic projections from house-mound counts propose a densely packed population of 150,000 to 200,000 at the city's height, whereas the architecture bears witness to diverse social, economic, and political activities. Residential structures and burial distinctions imply as many as six social classes; the market area and obsidian and pottery-making workshops show how goods were made and circulated. The relatively rapid construction of the Pyramid of the Sun, the Pyramid of the Moon, and the Ciudadela, and the city's preconceived layout suggest efficiently directed labor by a centralized political administration. These combined data confirm Teotihuacán as the New World's first true city, stimulating new theories and models for the rise of Mesoamerican urbanism and formation of states (Sanders and Price 1968; Sanders 1974).

Geomantic Considerations

Architecture coordinated with astronomical events and geomantic concepts may explain why Teotihuacán was an important pilgrimage center (Aveni 1980, 222–234). The Pyramid of the Sun, for example, aligns with the rising point of the Pleiades, signaling the zenith of the sun's passage over the site (Dow 1967, 326–334). During his mapping project, Millon found identical "sighting" crosses centered within concentric circles on building floors and on stones atop Cerro Colorado, a hill due west of the Pyramid of the Sun, and on Cerro Gordo ("Mother of Stone" in Nahuatl), a mountain source of water and stone 7 kilometers (4.3 miles) north of the city that rises like a guardian behind the Pyramid of the Moon.

Geomancy links site locations to lucky or unlucky topographic features. According to geomancy, subterranean energies affect human fortunes, and site selection and architecture can encourage good or repel harmful influences. Thus building over a sacred spot can ensure a city's future success. Such considerations may explain the siting of the Pyramid of the Sun.

The Pyramid of the Sun Cave

In 1971, a 100-meter-long tunnel under the Pyramid of the Sun exposed a stairway cut into bedrock and leading to a natural four-chambered cave containing ancient remnants of drainage conduits, perhaps used for rituals to evoke rain. Two basalt-disk fragments (mirror backs?) with bird–man and jaguar–man images indicate that Gulf Coast influences may have been important in Teotihuacán's brilliant rise.

Doris Heyden (1975, 1981) and John Carlson (1981) find illuminating references in ethnohistoric and ethnographic sources linking caves to animistic topography. To the later Aztecs, caves represented both life, as the place whence the first humans emerged to the earth's surface, and death, as the entry to the underworld. Mesoamerican Indians today still make cave offerings. Springs, according to Aztec myth, were the cave eyes (*ojos de agua*) of the dismembered earth goddess Tlaltecuhtli, while her mouth released earth's rivers. In Teotihuacán's famous Tlalocan mural (Figure 2.4), life-sustaining water flows from a mountain cave; in another mural, a figure with a huge quetzal headdress

2.4. Figures from Tlaloc's paradise, (Tlalocan) mural, Tepantitla. (From Séjourné 1956, fig. 13, p. 100; drawing by Abel Mendoza, courtesy INAH)

2.5. Fertility figure with Tlaloc aspects, from Tepantitla, above the Tlalocan mural. (Courtesy INAH)

and water dripping from her hands, whom art historians call the Great Goddess, rises over a cave from which a spring gushes (Figure 2.5).

Heyden feels that Teotihuacán's Pyramid of the Sun cave may have represented a sacred *axis mundi* connecting earth to the thirteen heavens and nine underworlds traversed daily by the sun, revered as a focus for pilgrimage and later as an oracle by the Aztecs. The original cave–shrine, sanctified by enclosing it within a sacred mountain in the form of a huge pyramid, may have been the cosmic axis of this sacred city where the gods were born.

ART

Teotihuacán's art encompasses a wide range of media and techniques, while exhibiting consistent proportions and a cohesive, unified style characterized by Esther Pasztory as "conventionalized, flat, ornamental, and heraldic" (1978, 112).

Stonework

In stonework, small serpentine and jade masks are easily recognizable by their flat, triangular faces and broad forehead clefts at the top, as if in remembrance of the Olmecs, wide, horizontal brows over narrow, deep-set eyes, broad mouths with slightly parted lips, and a strong sense of horizontality (Figure 2.6). Large figures are static and cubistic: The 24-ton Goddess of Water parallels architectural horizontality with her tablerolike headdress and taludlike skirt (Figure 2.7).

Pottery Figurines

Pottery figurines are lively and animated; many have articulated arms and legs. Their faces, at first hand-modeled (Miccaotli and Tlamimilolpa phases) and later mass produced with molds (Xolalpan phase), show the diagnostic Teotihuacán facial proportions (Figure 2.8).

2.6. Incised stone mask with wide, flat forehead and diagnostic facial proportions. (From Séjourné 1956, fig. 15, p. 66; courtesy INAH.)

2.7. Monolithic stone image of Goddess of Water with strong horizontal planes at headpiece and skirt. (Courtesy MNA)

2.8. Small clay figurine with wide headband. (Courtesy INAH)

(Head molds found in cornfields are used by peasants to produce authentic-looking copies for tourists today.) Some large, mold-made figurines are hollow and contain smaller, more ornate figures in the torso, the front section of which may be lifted away. A few seem to represent gods analogous to the later Aztec Xipe Totec and a paunchy, fat god.

Pottery

Teotihuacán pottery has a limited number of distinctive forms and designs. Small rectangular or ovoid clay pieces with two or three upright holes, perhaps for holding blood or incense offerings, are appropriately dubbed *candeleros*, whereas a vaselike vessel with a narrow neck, flared lip, and a globular body is called a *florero*. Neither of these forms achieved the distribution of the Teotihuacán slab-footed tripod cylinder (Figure 2.9). These vessels had domed, nubbin-handled lids and carved or painted stucco decoration depicting striding masked priests and water symbols and were in vogue between A.D. 300 and 650. Elaborately headdressed faces in low relief adorn the fronts of complex

2.9. Cylinder tripod with talud–tablero slab legs, showing in profile a priest carrying a knife with a human heart and a tri-lobed liquid symbol. (Séjourné 1966, fig. 19; courtesy FCE)

Xololpan-phase *incensarios* (Figure 2.10), which were widely imitated as Teotihuacán's influence spread.

Murals

Painted murals are unusually prominent as interior decoration of temple and palace walls. They were painted on wet stucco following pressed guidelines with colors and dark outlines added. Their characteristic flatness centers attention on the basic forms depicted; overlapping of images is rare. Subjects blend with backgrounds, appearing two-dimensional because of minimal contrast in color values (A. Miller 1973, 25–32, and Appendix 2).

Most murals show religious or military figures, symbolic animals, rituals and cult objects, or mythical scenes; formal writing, historical personages, and visual narratives are notably absent. Water symbolism (pendant drops, shells, "eyes" in water bands, and jade ovals flowing from cuffed hands) (Figure 2.11) and priests wearing goggle-shaped eye masks reminiscent of the Mesoamerican rain deity Tlaloc and marching warriors occur so frequently that Kubler (1967, 12) speaks of "liturgical" repetition. Gridlike, angular figures with stiff postures and standardized forms reflect what Pasz-

2.10. Teotihuacán incensario with complex modeling. (Courtesy The St. Louis Art Museum, gift of Morton D. May)

tory (1978, 119) considers the "rational planned approach to making images," an approach also evident in Teotihuacán architecture.

In composition, repetition and symmetry predominate. Marching priests, jaguars (Figure 2.12), or human figures in front view are repeated across wall sections and borders of murals. In the Atetelco compound's White Patio, zoomorphized priests in a reticulated grid form wallpaperlike patterning. Occasionally, small, informal, individualistic figures (as in the Tlalocan patio mural, Figure 2.4) appear as counterparts of Teotihuacán's lively clay figurines.

Attempts have been made to relate murals to architectural and ceramic phases and to political orientations. Clara Millon (1972), using motif seriation, has divided the murals into six periods. Early mythical scenes are succeeded by

2.11. Mural of the Cuffed Hands, Tetitla. (Redrawn by the author from a copy by Agustín Villagra; courtesy INAH)

2.12. Coyote mural, Atetelco. (Redrawn by the author from a copy by Agustín Villagra; courtesy INAH)

monumental themes such as giant striding jaguars during Teotihuacán's expansion, whereas late murals of eagle warriors carrying atlatls and impaling human hearts with darts and knives (Figure 2.13) suggest increasing militarism and secularization. Archaeological corroboration of this trend comes from Saburo Sugiyama's (1989) excavations of over forty burials of bound soldiers with obsidian projectile points and pyrite-black mirrors apparently sacrificed to commemorate the dedication of the Temple of Quetzalcóatl in the Ciudadela around A.D. 200 (Sugiyama 1989). Pasztory (1988a; 1988b, 57, 71–75; n.d.) also sees increasing self-expression

in late Teotihuacán murals and believes it indicates weakening of the centralization and communal orientation that had developed out of earlier village traditions.

Iconography

Description, identification, and interpretation of Teotihuacán symbols and motifs has intrigued many scholars. Laurette Séjourné (1956) and Robert Rands (1955) described Teotihuacán water symbols and their parallels in other Mesoamerican cultures. Alfonso Caso (1966) summarized many interpretations of symbols and

2.13. Warriors holding dart bundles and knives impaling human hearts. (Redrawn by the author after Séjourné 1956, figs. 42 and 30)

deities. Various writers agree that the cuffed "sacred hands" (Figure 2.11) showering streams of shells, water creatures, butterflies, flowers, and jade denote fertility. George Kubler (1973) points out similarities between the profiles of talud-tablero architecture, the slab feet of cylinder tripod vessels, and the butterfly nose ornament worn by priests and considers all three as indicators of sacredness. Peter Furst (1974) identifies morning glories on Tepantitla murals as possible sources of vision-producing seeds used in fertility cults.

Important Motifs

The most complete and systematic study of Teotihuacán motifs is Hasso von Winning's *La Iconografía de Teotihuacán: Los Dioses y Los Signos* (1987). Among the major motifs he identifies are:

1. *Water–blood symbols.* These appear as water "eyes" (upper right, Figure 2.5), trilobed (Figure 2.9) and multilobed water drops (Figure 2.5), and lobed blood drops from impaled human hearts (upper right, Figure 2.13). Terrance Stocker and Michael Spence (1973) identify similar lobed elements on Olmec headdresses (Figures I.1 and 1.2), on the famous San Lorenzo duck-basin water font, on Teotihuacán-influenced Mayan and Guatemalan Pacific Coast (Escuintla) ceramics, on Oaxacan stelae and murals, and at the site of Xochicalco as hearts dripping trilobed drops of blood. M-shaped pieces of flaked obsidian and flint at Teotihuacán and Tula may also representa this symbol. Heyden (1987, 124–126) notes the continuity of this symbol in the Postclassic, when it appears as a water-vegetation indicator on Aztec pottery. A modern Mayan occurrence may be the foil-covered M-element seen on rain deity masks at the Zinacantan, Chiapas, Carnival (Figure 2.14; Bricker 1981, 139).

2. *The Reptile's Eye glyph (Figure 2.15).* It consists of a frontal eye with a curl-dot, rayed, or feathered brow and lashes (Figure 2.15). With a flame brow, it becomes the "radiant eye." Von Winning (1961) reads it as a symbol of fertility and abundance; Kubler (1967) as an earth sign.

3. *A four-symbol pattern bound by a cord* (Figure 2.16a,1). According to Von Winning, it consists of (a) vertical lines (falling rain), (b) eyes in rivers or springs (groundwater), (c) dia-

2.14. Masked dancers with trilobal motifs associated with Mayan rain deities, during Carnival, Chiapas, Mexico. (Photo courtesy Frank Cancian)

mond bands (fire or burning incense), and (d) horizontal bars between comblike elements (bound sticks representing year cycles in the Central Mexican calendar: Figure 2.16a,2). He (1977, 20) reads the combination as a "mnemonic prayer formula" in an "incipient stage of a partial writing system" seeking rain in coming year cycles through prayer offerings of incense. Its fire/water opposition may also relate to the later Aztec *atl-tlachinolli* symbol, which Séjourné (1956, 108–109) interprets as "burning water" (Figure 2.16c).

4. *An owl/hand-on-shield/crossed darts motif* (Figure 2.17). To Von Winning (1948), this motif indicates death and the underworld because the owl (and its Mayan equivalent, the moan bird) are nocturnal birds, and militarism, because of the darts and shield.

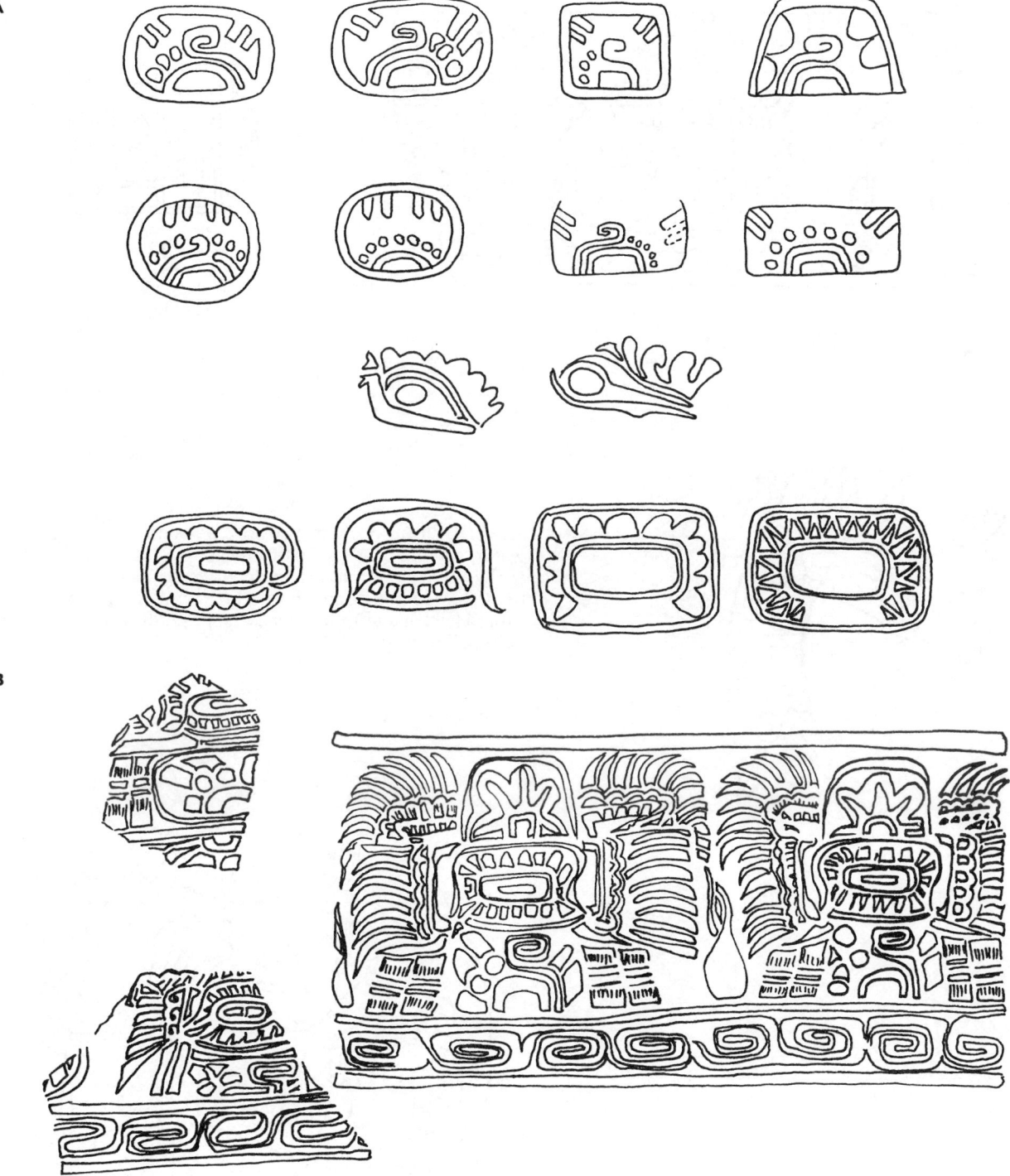

2.15. (A) *Upper two rows,* stylized Reptile's Eye glyph; *third row,* Serpent Eye; *bottom row,* Feathered Eyes. (B) Radiant or Feathered Eye over Reptile Eye glyphs on cylinder tripod vessels. (Adapted by the author from drawings by Hasso von Winning, courtesy Hasso von Winning)

A

1

2

B

2.16. (A) "Four Symbol pattern" of bound rain, lightning, water, and fire bands: (1) pattern band; (2) figurine headdress, with ordering of bands altered (courtesy Hasso Von Winning); (B) *Atl-tlachinolli* Aztec fire–water symbol for Flowery War (from Heyden and Villaseñor 1984, p. 57; drawing by Alberto Beltran, courtesy EMM)

2.17. Detail of Owl–Hand on Shield-Crossed Darts motif on a ceramic warrior figure. (Collection of the MNA; drawing by the author)

Motifs as Communication Systems

George Kubler (1967a), James Langley (1986), Janet Berlo (1983), and others have explored how Teotihuacán motif combinations may have functioned as communication systems conjoining the functions of text and image. Kubler's structuralist interpretation is that motif clusters are analogous to "grammatical positions," with secondary motifs enriching and expanding primary ones, as adjectives do for nouns. Large, compound figures shown frontally, like Teotihuacán's complex clay incensarios (Figure 2.10), are the most visually effective way to display multiple iconographic elements (Berlo 1982, 86–90); they are often flanked by smaller figures. Combined with a complex oral tradition, such densely encoded images could have been "read" as effectively as any linear, written text and probably conveyed multiple levels of meaning.

Langley, like Kubler, worked directly from Teotihuacán signs and used ethnohistorical analogy sparingly. He used computer analysis to facilitate comparisons of chronology, range of variants and alternate forms, and the kinds of artifacts involved. After identifying sign clusters, he ranked their components in a hierarchy of importance and compared their known occurrences, thereby correlating cognate signs with parallel functions, mutual substitutions, and statistically significant combinations. The result (Langley 1986) was an illustrated, annotated compendium of 229 confirmed, probable, and "problematical" signs, which included the comb and bar (a firewood bundle), butterfly (warrior, soul), Reptile's Eye, trapeze-ray (sun, year sign), and trilobe drops (blood). Their systematic, repetitive use, he feels, encodes early militaristic and sacrificial aspects of Teotihuacán culture and characterizes an "emergent writing system."

Some Teotihuacán symbols may indeed have had more widespread recognition. Clara Millon (1973) identified a three-tasseled headdress that is both worn and depicted separately as a cult object. This diagnostic headgear consists of a tablerolike three-tasseled panel, a midsection bearing jade symbols, and a lower band of spearpoints (Figure 2.18) and appears on Teotihuacán murals and on pottery. Millon also found this headdress on the Bazán Stone, a stela from Oaxaca (Figure 2.19), as a glyph in a Zapotec Indian text that accompanies depiction of a Teotihuacán outsider near a footprint indicating travel. The combination suggests Teotihuacán political and trade inroads into South Mexico. The three tasseled headdress also appears in Guatemala at Kaminaljuyú and on Tikal Stela 31 (see Figure 5.4, right side) atop a goggle-eyed figure on the shield of a figure garbed in Teotihuacán-style clothing. Millon proposes that the peripatetic headpiece symbolized the patron deity of Teotihuacán's ruling lineage and identified

2.18. Figure (right) wearing a Three Tasseled Headdress, preceded by a Three Tassel Headdress cult object; one of four such figures with affiliated sacred animals on a bowl from Calpulalpan, Tlaxcala, in a Teotihuacán-type grave. (From Séjourné 1966, fig. 117; courtesy FCE)

2.19. The Three Tasseled Headdress among Zapotec glyphs near the foot of a Teotihuacanoid figure (*left*). Footprints may indicate a traveling merchant. On the "Bazan Stone," Monte Albán, Oaxaca. (Marquina 1951, fig. 16, p. 349; courtesy INAH)

Teotihuacán trade, political, and military ambassadors in foreign lands.

The Techinantitla and Tlacuilapaxco Murals

The 1988 publication of an additional corpus of Teotihuacán mural fragments (Berrin 1988) pro-

vided scholars with important new images. The pieces, a bequest by architect Harald Wagner to San Francisco's de Young Memorial Museum in 1976, had been looted in the early 1960s from the Techinantitla and Tlacuilapaxco compounds of Teotihuacán's Amanalco barrio, a mere 500 yards east of the Pyramid of the Moon plaza. They were carefully restored through joint

Mexican–North American collaboration, and in 1986 over half were returned to Mexico, a milestone in cooperative international museography. Fitting together and interpreting the incomplete pieces and matching them with counterparts sold in the mid-1960s to museums and dealers in Houston, Saint Louis, and Milwaukee and with fragments found at the site took over 10 years of intensive inderdisciplinary cooperation (Berrin 1988, 24–44, 78–113, Klein 1990).

Both male and female deities (or deity impersonators?) appear in the Amanalco fragments. Researchers have bestowed several red-and-green Tlaloc-like male figures with the title of "Storm Gods," including benign water–fertility and malevolent fire–militarism variants (the former carry jars or crop plants; the latter wear tasseled headdresses or carry lightning bolts). Pasztory (1988b) contrasts them to a complex of female, skirt-wearing, Tlaloc-like figures portrayed in other Teotihuacán barrios (Figure 2.5, 2.6) whom she calls the "Great Goddess." These female figures also exhibit life-nourishing and life-taking aspects when they take on celestial fire and crocodilian earth forms, and their benign, cuffed hands generate icon-laden, life-sustaining water (Figure 2.11).

Murals from the Wagner bequest also portray nonreligious themes. An important segment of the Techinantitla murals is a procession of figures in tassel headdresses that are interpreted as legendary founders, rulers, or generals in ritual procession (R. Millon, in Berrin 1988, 91). Several have accompanying name glyphs consisting of a tassel headdress crowning a lower element (trilobe drop with feathered eye, raptor claw, feathered serpent on a mat, goggle-eyed mask, Tlaloc-like storm god head, etc.). Upper wall fragments show the tassel headdress and a separate element as a two-part notation suggesting incipient columnar writing (C. Millon 1973, 119–121). Millon interprets the headdress as a referent to military position, noting its similar use in so designating the tassel-headdressed procession leader on the Calpulalpan bowl (Figure 2.18, right) and on the atlatl- and shield-carrying figures on Tikal Stela 31 (Figure 5.4). The tasseled generals procession may thus represent "revered military ancestors" who expanded Teotihuacán's frontiers and validated blood sacrifice rituals (C. Millon 1973, 121–132).

Militarism and sacrifice are themes in other mural fragments. Paintings from Tlacuilapaxco show walking, profile figures (warrior–priests?) in feathered coyote headdresses "sowing" streams of dots (blood?) and flowers in front of terraced plots of land into which five bloodied maguey spines (implements of autosacrifice) are imbedded: Also present are heavily adorned scrolls emanating from the mouths of figures that may represent chants specifying offerings or benefits sought (Pasztory 1988b, 195–200). Coyotes, a martial symbol, march with long sacrificial knives, and in one scene they tear out the heart of a sacrificial deer spurting a huge trilobe of blood (Pasztory 1988b, 206–221). These images correspond well with the increasing emphasis on sacrifice and military groups indicated by the aforementioned ritual burial of guardianlike warrior groups with obsidian points and slate disks on the south side and at the four corners of the Temple of Quetzalcóatl shortly before its completion (Sugiyama 1989).

Equally intriguing is a reconstructed row of flowering plants with nine compound glyphs in their stems composed of up to four separate signs. These glyphs may be toponyms or may identify lineages or plant names. They are keyed in both color and sequence to each plant's distinctive bud or fruit, another exciting indication of precise symbolic notation used to convey complex, multivalent meaning.

ETHNOHISTORIC PARALLELS VERSUS INTERNAL EVIDENCE

The use of Aztec images and ethnohistoric references to Postclassic beliefs in interpreting Teotihuacán iconography is part of a broader debate: whether to work directly from pre-columbian materials, avoiding outside coeval, ethnohistoric, and ethnographic comparisons because of the likelihood of intervening shifts in meaning or to combine such material cautiously with contextual analysis in a synthetic approach, allowing for reinterpretation, revivals, social and ethnic biases, and other twists and bends in evolving iconography. The contextual, purist position elaborates internal evidence; the synthesists (nicknamed "upstreamers") seek connections between late forms and their antecedents within a long-term, conservative Mesoamerican tradition. In the former group, George Kubler (1967a, 12) resists parallels of his Teotihuacán water complex deity with Tlaloc, the Aztec rain god, and other Nahuatl labels, arguing that major disjunctions of meaning may have occurred in the interim. Conversely, H. B. Nicholson (1976), Cecelia Klein (1975, 1986), Esther Pasztory (1978, 1988a), and others have emphasized the strong internal unity of Mesoamerican tradition and used ethnohistoric data to strengthen analytic interpretations.

Tlaloc Variants and the Four-Symbol Pattern

A case in point is Teotihuacán's most easily recognizable deity—a figure with donut-ring eyes, a "moustache" upper lip, a forked serpent tongue, and associated water symbolism. This figure has long been identified as a prototypal Tlaloc with multiple (red, corn, lightning, jade) aspects and interchangeable jaguar, feathered serpent, butterfly, owl, and quetzal attributes (Séjourné 1956; Pasztory 1973). Comparing versions of these Teotihuacán figures with images of the Aztec Tlaloc (Figure 2.20), Pasztory (1974) identified two main types at Teotihuacán: (a) a peaceful, donut-eyed Rain–Tlaloc A (Figures 2.21a and b) with smiling crocodilelike lips, wearing a five-knot headdress with a trapeze-ray symbol and carrying lightning-serpent staffs or jars bearing Tlaloc faces and (b) a goggle-eyed Jaguar–Tlaloc B (Figure 2.22) with a forked tongue, "handlebar moustache," and minus serpent

staffs, Tlaloc jars, and the trapeze-ray symbol in his three-tassel headdress (see C. Millon 1973). Pasztory related Jaguar–Tlaloc B to jaguars with netted bodies believed to symbolize the underworld midnight sun. Jaguar–Tlaloc B appears abroad with warrior or military cult aspects and the tasseled headdress, in political contexts associated with Teotihuacán expansion, perhaps symbolizing Teotihuacán's patron deity or ruling dynasty. The figure may have carried through via Tula to the Late Postclassic Aztec pantheon along with Teotihuacán antecedents of the Aztec gods Xochipilli and Huehuetéotl and Great Goddess antecedents of the earth–moon deity Xochiquétzal (Pasztory 1988a; Von Winning 1987).

Hasso von Winning also finds parallels at Teotihuacán with ethnohistoric descriptions of Aztec ritual. He identifies the comb and bar element of Teotihuacán's four-symbol pattern (Figure 2.16a) as an early version of the sacred Aztec xiuhualpilli (firewood bundle) illustrated in Spanish accounts, codices, and Aztec stone sculpture, which symbolized 52 completed years, and the New Fire ceremony, which opened the next time cycle (von Winning 1979). In spite of the absence of calendrical glyphs, he feels that Xolalpan-phase representations of priests holding flaming bundles support the hypothesis that the New Fire ceremony originated at Teotihuacán.

Autochthonous Images

On the other hand, as scholars explore the range of primary art sources more fully, they may reassess earlier interpretations. Esther Pasztory (n.d., 2–4) now feels that the Aztec–Teotihuacán connection was less strong than she suggested in her earlier publications because most Aztec gods have no prototypes at Teotihuacán and major Teotihuacán images such as the Net Jaguar fail to continue into the Aztec pantheon. She and others now refer to Teotihuacán's goggle-eyed figures by the more neutral term "Storm Gods" rather than as Tlalocs, and identify Teotihuacán's most important and powerful deity as a female Great Goddess rather than as a Xochiquétzal prototype. The front-facing Great Goddess, with her female costume, bird headdress, masklike "butterfly" nose ornament, and associated yellow and red zigzag bands, rains down water and jade symbols from her cuffed

2.20. Postclassic Aztec version of Tlaloc, from the *Codex Laud*. (Drawing by the author)

A

B

2.21. (*A*) Tlaloc A carrying rain serpent and Tlaloc jar, Tetitla (after Séjourné 1966; drawing by the author); (*B*) Tlaloc A with rain jars, Tepantitla (from Pasztory 1974, fig. 4; courtesy Esther Pasztory and DO)

2.22. Pasztory's Tlaloc B type alternating with flayed-skin faces, on a Zacuala cylinder tripod. (Redrawn by the author after Séjourné 1966, courtesy FCE)

hands that are sometimes shown alone, but she may also reveal claws and bared teeth in association with weapon-bearing birds denoting military associations (Pasztory 1988b, n.d.). In contrast to these major cult images, Teotihuacán's Storm God effigy jars and "Old Man" braziers seem to be practical household continuations of older Preclassic forms.

Implied Cultural Values

Pasztory (n.d.) has carried semiotic interpretation further, setting aside Aztec parallels in an effort to isolate broader underlying meanings and internalized cultural patterns inherent in art form, independent of written texts and specific identifications of deities and cults. She notes that Teotihuacán's art style is deliberately abstract, nonnarrative, and nonnaturalistic and that it is based on flat geometric forms and depicts a high percentage of animals, whereas profile human figures are standardized and depersonalized in contrast to individual dynastic rulers shown in other Classic-period and later Aztec art. This focus on purity of concept with no overt references to earlier groups such as the Olmecs suggests to her that Teotihuacán may have been attempting to embody cosmic, utopian perspectives through its orderly, planned, grid layout of ceremonial areas and multifamily apartment complexes and that it was perhaps ruled by ranked lineages rather than by prominent individuals in dynastic succession. Teotihuacán's standardized serpentine masks, mold-made faces on clay figurines, and the Adosada Pyramid masking the front of the Pyramid of the Moon likewise suggest hidden elements, depersonalization, social uniformity, and a non-individualistic, collective, ongoing Preclassic outlook that may have helped Teotihuacán successfully integrate diverse ethnic elements into an expanded urban setting. Thus, even in the absence of ancillary glyphic texts and supportive Aztec analogies, Teotihuacán's symbol system internally encodes the presence and evolution of major cultural values that can be partially corroborated by archaeological data and further tested as new materials appear.

TEOTIHUACÁN INFLUENCE AND THE LATE CLASSIC AFTERMATH

Another important research issue is the spread of Teotihuacán influence into other areas. Ta-

2.23. Incensario in Teotihuacán style, probably from Escuintla in coastal Guatemala. (Courtesy The St. Louis Art Museum, gift of Morton D. May)

lud–tablero architecture, cylinder tripods, and iconographic elements ("Tlaloc" images, the trapeze-ray year sign) have a spotty distribution in Veracruz, Oaxaca, Guatemala, and the Maya area between A.D. 400 and 700 as indicators of Teotihuacán cultural penetration. Looted Teotihuacán-style incensarios (Figure 2.23) and cylinder tripods from Escuintla, in coastal Guatemala, probably accompanied Teotihuacán's extended commercial outreach into the highlands, including Kaminaljuyú (Hellmuth 1978; Berlo 1982).

Teotihuacán iconography appears in the Maya lowlands as early as A.D. 435. At Tikal on Stela 31, two Teotihuacanoid figures flank the Maya ruler Stormy Sky (Figure 5.4), and Teotihuacanoid pottery is found in royal tombs. At Kaminaljuyú, copies of Teotihuacán cylinder tripods and Thin Orange ware accompany burials in Classic tombs, and Platform Mounds A and B are multi-story talud–tablero constructions.[2]

To William Sanders (1974; Sanders and Michels 1977), Kaminaljuyú represents an important Teotihuacán redistribution center established by traveling merchants who spread Teotihuacán architecture and religion, with the tripartite headdress-wearing shield god shown on Tikal Stela 31 as their patron. In an alternative interpretation, Charles Cheek (1977, 158 *et passim*), considering architectural and ceramic changes, sees gradual assimilation of Teotihuacán traits by the Kaminaljuyú elite who managed Teotihuacán's economic interests, followed by intensification of assimilation during a Teotihuacán political takeover and subsequent rapid abandonment as Teotihuacán influence ceased. Kenneth Brown (1977) concurs that Kaminaljuyú meets the requisites as a Teotihuacán "port of trade."

During the seventh and eighth centuries, Cholula, Cacaxtla, and Xochicalco, in Central Mexico, and El Tajín, in Veracruz (see Map 2), began competing commercially and militarily with Teotihuacán, perhaps hastening its decline, while incorporating Teotihuacán, Maya, and Oaxacan influences into their art (Cohodas 1989b). In the Maya area, stelae at Piedras Negras, Seibal, Yaxchilán, Aguacateca, and Dos Pilas show rulers as warriors wearing Teotihuacán-derived insignia (the Central Mexican trapeze-ray year sign and Tlalocs) with traditional Maya costume.

By A.D. 750 Teotihuacán influence in South Mexico and the Maya area had come to an end, and the ascending Central Mexican military states rushed in to fill the vacuum. In Tabasco and Campeche, Gulf Coast Chontal Putún and Itzá groups, "Mexicanized" by participation in the Teotihuacán network, opened new coastal ports and expanded to Chichén Itzá and the Usumacinta- and Puuc-area sites. Revived commercial connections with Central Mexico resulted in strong architectural and iconographic parallels between the rising Toltec city of Tula and Chichén Itzá as "Epiclassic restructuring" (Cohodas 1989b) phased out many lowland sites, stimulated Puuc sites, and led to Early Postclassic dominance by Tula and Chichén. Teotihuacán as a monopolistic obsidian producer, cosmopolitan trading center, innovator of religious concepts and ceremonial goods, and hallowed shrine "where the gods were born" was gone, but its memory lingered on in goggle-eyed earth monsters carved on the bottom of large Late Postclassic stone sculpture, a possible Aztec reference to Teotihuacán–Tula descent (Pasztory 1988a), and in other deities possibly derived from prototypes at Teotihuacán.

---

[2] Pasztory (1978). Structure B-4 at Kaminaljuyú is in fact an Early Classic replica of the Pyramid of the Moon (Miller 1986, 81).

CHAPTER 3

THE MAYA

ANTECEDENTS

POSSIBLE NON-MAYA ANTECEDENTS

Paleoindian

THE earliest records of human occupation in the Maya area are 11,000-year-old Paleoindian campsites in highland Guatemala and Belize. This preceramic, preagricultural way of life based on hunting and foraging persisted into the Archaic period, between 8000 and 2000 B.C., as people adapted to a variety of environments and took the first halting steps toward incipient plant domestication and a semisedentary way of life.

Altamira and La Victoria

By 3000 B.C., early village life based on shellfish foraging and marine resources appeared along the Pacific Coast Soconusco area of Chiapas, Mexico, and southwestern Guatemala (Map 1; for sites, see Map 5). By 2000 B.C., splinter groups moved inland to the coastal plain, and by 1700 B.C. their descendants at Altamira on the Chiapas coast produced Barra-Complex *tecomates* and incised, punctate-zoned bowls resembling wares from El Salvador and Nicaragua, from the sites of Valdivia and Machalilla in Ecuador, and from Puerto Hormiga in north Colombia, where pottery was being made as early as 3000 B.C. They may also have received South American crops. At Altamira and nearby Laguna Zope, archaeologists have found small obsidian flakes that were perhaps used for grating manioc, a South American tuber.

By 1500 B.C., Ocós (1500–1000 B.C.) and Cuadros (1000–850 B.C.) phase wares appear at La Victoria in coastal Guatemala. Ocós pottery again hints at sporadic connections with Ecuador. By the end of the Early Preclassic, multiple Pacific Coast villages were in touch with early Olmec San Lorenzo, Central Mexico, and Central and South America.

Olmec Expansion

Olmec commercial expansion also acted as a major catalyst for Pacific Coast sites. With the rise of La Venta, Olmec influence extended south to Costa Rica, presumably linked to cacao cultivation and distribution. Possible trading centers (colonies?) occur at several sites in

MAYA SITES

0   200 km

0   150 mi

GULF OF MEXICO

Dzibilchaltún

Chichén Itzá

Mayapán

Cobá

Uxmal   Kabah   Yaxuná   Xelhá

Jaina   Sayil   Tulum

Labná

Edzná

Hochob

Laguna de Términos

Xicalango

Xpuhil

Beçan

Santa Rita

Río Bec   Cerros

San Estevan   Cuello

Usumacinta R.   *Candelaria R.*   Calakmul   El Pozito

Comalcalco   *Hondo R.*   Lamanai

El Mirador   *New R.*

Palenque   Uaxactún

Tikal

Piedras Negras   Naranjo

Chiapa de Corzo   Yaxchilán

Bonampak   Seibal

Xoc   Altar de Sacrificios

CARIBBEAN SEA

G U A T E M A L A

Pijijiapan   Quiriguá

Chantuto   San Martin   *Motagua R.*

Izapa   Jilotepeque   Copán

Ocos   El Chayal

Abaj Takalik   Kaminaljuyú

El Baul

Cozumalhuapa

PACIFIC OCEAN

Map 5. Maya sites

Chiapas; Abaj Takalik and El Baúl in Guatemala (Map 5); and Chalchuapa and Quelapa in El Salvador where Olmecoid monuments may portray traders or enclave founders. Olmec entrepreneurs tapped into Guatemalan highland obsidian (from San Martín Jilotepeque and El Chayal) and penetrated into Chiapas and the Petén lowlands, where pottery at Chiapa de Corzo, a were–jaguar boulder carving at Xoc, Chiapas, and a jadeite bloodletter and Olmecoid celts at Seibal (Map 5) indicate Olmec Middle Preclassic influence or presence.

Later on, Olmec influence ended abruptly. By 400 B.C., La Venta had collapsed; nearby Tres Zapotes continued for a few hundred years, but the Olmec trade network was broken. This particularly affected the Soconusco area, where commercial colonies, now controlling cacao distribution independently, flourished as competing chiefdoms and integrated the Olmec legacy into their own cultural base in a synthesis sometimes called Izapan culture after the site of Izapa in Chiapas. Because many researchers view Izapan art as an important catalyst of Classic Maya art, we will highlight key studies here.

The Izapan Sphere

The full picture of Pacific Coast contributions is still being written. Today the rich volcanic Soconusco soils sustain cane and coffee plantations that limit large-scale excavations, although stelae are known through surface finds.

An exception is Early Preclassic–Late Classic Izapa (Map 5), 35 kilometers (22 miles) from the Pacific Coast near Tapachula, Chiapas. Excavations by the New World Archaeological Foundation between 1961–1965 identified eighty-nine stelae, eighty clay-faced platform mounds in addition to numerous plazas, altars, and boulder sculptures, and produced an accurate site map showing stela–altar pairs in situ with respect to architecture (G. Lowe et al. 1982, 159). Most stelae occur at the base of platforms facing a central plaza in mound groups A–E and date between 300 B.C. and 50 B.C.

Izapan stelae share iconographic elements with Pacific Coast and Guatemalan highland monuments, yet in other respects are strikingly different, suggesting overlapping Olmec, early Mayan, and local art styles representing distinct ethnic groups and uneven Olmec penetration. Linguistic research has not clarified the picture.

Most likely, several dialects prevailed as natives and newcomers intermingled, and their art reflects this diversity and creative synthesis.

Outside Influences

Several researchers identify potential outside stylistic influences. Mino Badner (1972) finds elements in Izapan jaguars, serpents, raptorial birds, and crocodiles resembling Chavinoid motifs from Early Horizon highland Peru. Olmec-derived elements noted by Michael Coe (1965b) and Jacinto Quirarte (1973, 1976) include U or inverted-U signs, crossed and diagonal bands, the Saint Andrew's cross motif, downward-looking deities (as on Stela D from Tres Zapotes), stela and altar pairing, long-lipped figures reminiscent of were–jaguars, and—on Izapan Miscellaneous Monument 2—a human figure in a niche resembling Olmec Stela 2 from Tres Zapotes (Norman 1973, 1976, 282–283).

At Izapa, artists combined these elements into a distinctive local style in what appear to be mythical, narrative scenes within framing bands. Jacinto Quirarte (1973, 1974, 1976, 1977) divides these scene frames into top-line sky bands with shorthand jaguar features and baseline earth bands with parallel diagonals and multiple scrolls, triangles, and frets. Both frame complex scenes of mythical polymorphic beings interacting in pairs, groups, and in sky-to-earth contexts.

Izapan Stelae

To illustrate the variety of Izapan representations, I reproduce overlay tracings of select stelae from V. Garth Norman's monumental *Izapa Sculpture* (1973, 1979) and note some of his interpretations.

Stela 1 (Figure 3.1). This stela shows a fishing or rain deity with ankle and wrist fishfins carrying a jar on his back from which emanate cloud scrolls. The deity sieves fish through a hand-held net. The scene takes place between a basal water band spewed out by two deity masks and a stylized jaguar mask sky panel above which a seated figure stretches a scrolled (umbilical?) cord over what may be the number 5 (in dots) and a day glyph. Norman (1973, 89–91) interprets the scene as a water cycle. Water evaporates up into the net and onto the figure's arms and is blown by his breath into cloud scrolls

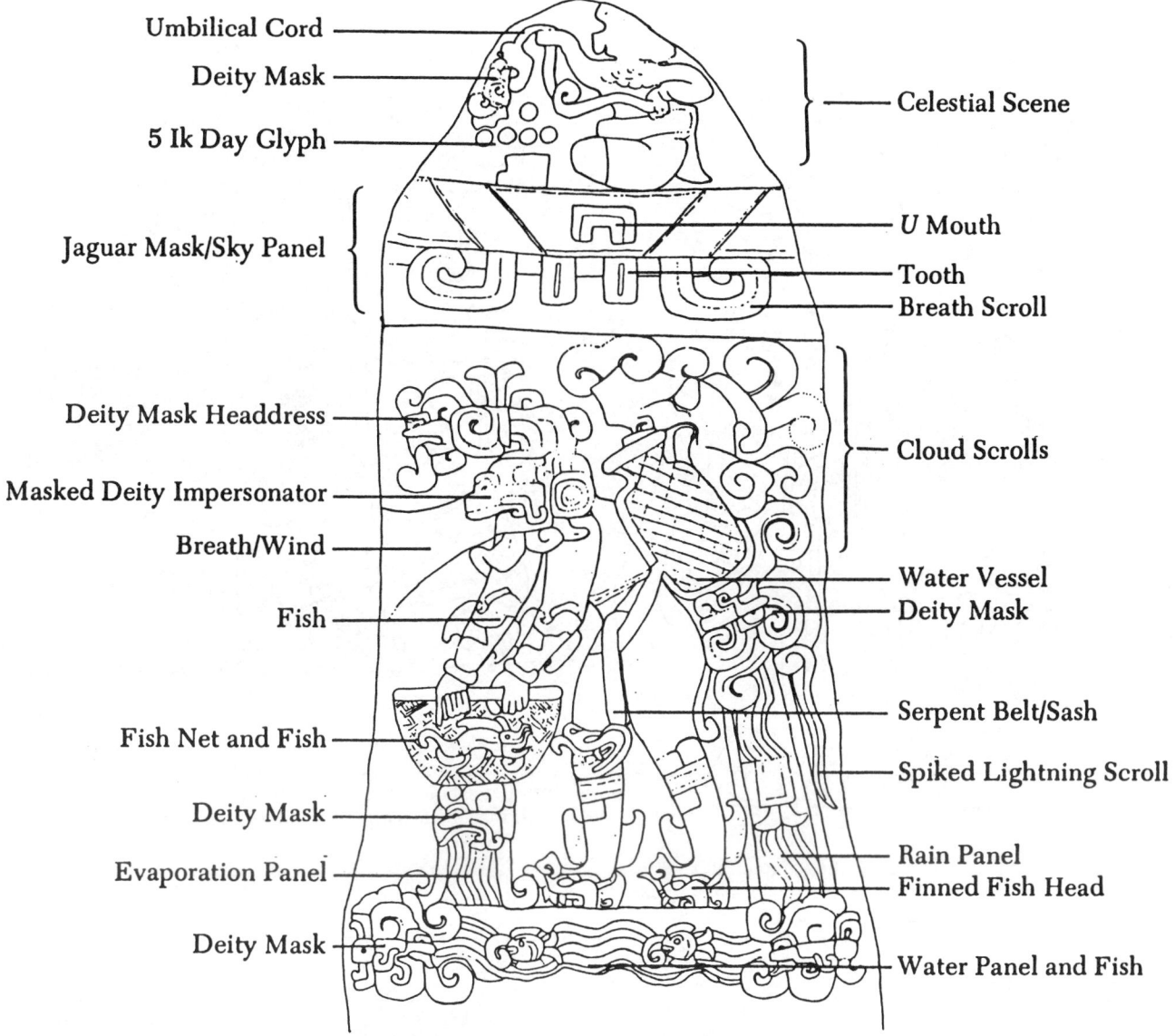

Umbilical Cord

Deity Mask

5 Ik Day Glyph

Celestial Scene

Jaguar Mask/Sky Panel

U Mouth

Tooth

Breath Scroll

Deity Mask Headdress

Cloud Scrolls

Masked Deity Impersonator

Breath/Wind

Water Vessel

Deity Mask

Fish

Fish Net and Fish

Serpent Belt/Sash

Spiked Lightning Scroll

Deity Mask

Evaporation Panel

Rain Panel

Finned Fish Head

Deity Mask

Water Panel and Fish

3.1. Stela 1, Izapa: masked deity impersonator with dorsal water vessel, holding fish in a net over a basal water panel. (Norman 1973, 1976, fig. 3.1; courtesy NWAF)

that condense, clockwise, into the storage jar, are released by its deity mask as rain, and fill the water panel for a new cycle.

Stela 12 (Figure 3.2). On this stela, a stylized U-serpent, profile mask, and complex sky and base panels frame a scene in which an inert jaguar, possibly bleeding from the mouth, is suspended by ropes over a fire tended by two squatting humans.

Stela 21 (figure 3.3). Stela 21 is a ritual or perhaps historical decapitation scene witnessed by an individual in a jaguar-topped litter borne by

two costumed carriers. The executioner holds a knife and the still-bleeding severed head above the victim's prone body. Rain scrolls hang from the sky band, and a glyph may identify one of the protagonists.

Stela 23 (Figure 3.4). Between sky and wave-scrolled water bands, a scroll-masked-profile diving god holds a long double volute in his right hand and an unknown object in his left, guiding bands of falling rain to the water below. Norman (1976, 129–130) thinks this antecedent of the rain god Chac, who Maya Indians be-

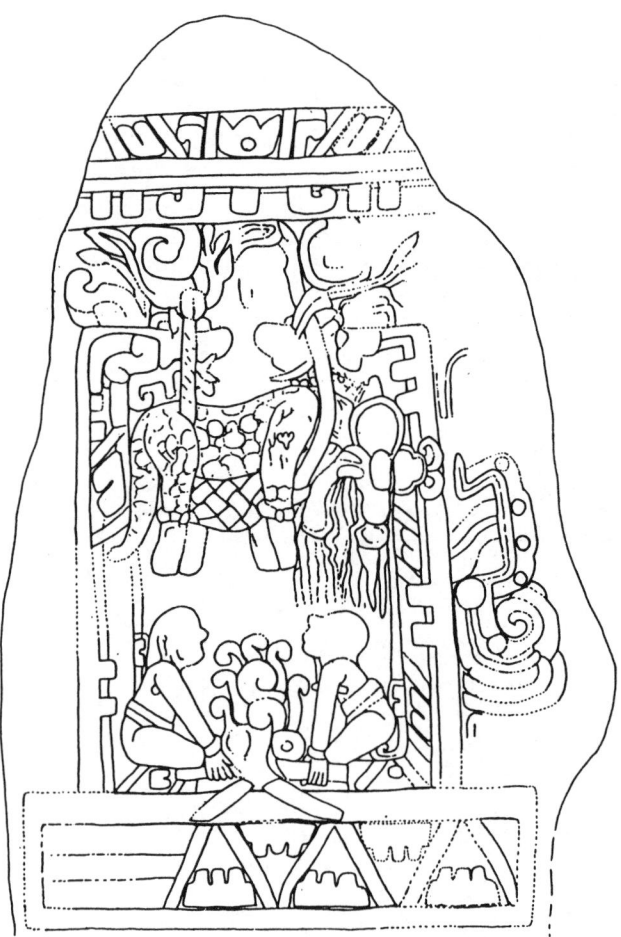

3.2. Stela 12, Izapa: scene including a complex sky, a three-prong-element base, and side serpent–jaguar mask panels, with a jaguar suspended by ropes over crouching humans beside smoke scrolls. (Norman 1973, fig. 3.12; courtesy NWAF)

3.3. Stela 21, Izapa: a knife-wielding executioner holds a bleeding head over a decapitated body, observed by a faceless litter-borne person surmounted by a scrolled jaguar with insect-head tail glyph. (Norman 1973, fig. 3.20; courtesy NWAF)

lieve pours rain from heavenly water jars, is creating a storm: The slightly more ferocious toothed sky serpent and basal mask on the left signify stormy, flood-producing rain, whereas the more benign right-hand masks represent gentle crop-nourishing rains.

Stela 50. The stela's design, following the boulder's natural shape, shows a masked skeleton seated in profile on a wide base panel (Figure 3.5). From its abdomen, a long coil loops beyond the knees through a scrolled deity half-mask into the hands of a right-facing human with veined insectlike wings. The skeleton may be a death god or, with its *kan* cross and doglike headdress ornament, five-dotted (quincunx), kin ("day" or "sun" glyph)-shaped pelvis, and projecting eyetooth, a solar/Venus god.

Death is linked to rebirth via the umbilical cord leading to the winged sky figure.

Stela 5. Norman calls Stela 5 (Figure 3.6) "supernarrative," with its complex interplay between twelve to fifteen humans, twelve zoomorphs and over twenty-five plants and objects in over sixty separate motifs (Norman 1976, 166). A huge two-headed U-serpent's body and heads (51 and 9) frame the action over a triangled earth panel resting on a scrolled line of waves. A thick eight-branched tree divides the scene into halves. Multiple humans sit at ground level while two bird-headed figures (A and B) and many smaller animated humans occupy the midground. At the bottom, Norman sees two priests—tutors of the bird gods (2 and 6) recording sacred lore, with an attendant (1) holding a fringed umbrella at right. Object 3, between figures 2 and 4, may be an infant, an idol, a child sacrifice, a mummy, or bone bundle, with an effigy head symbolizing the ancestors of fig-

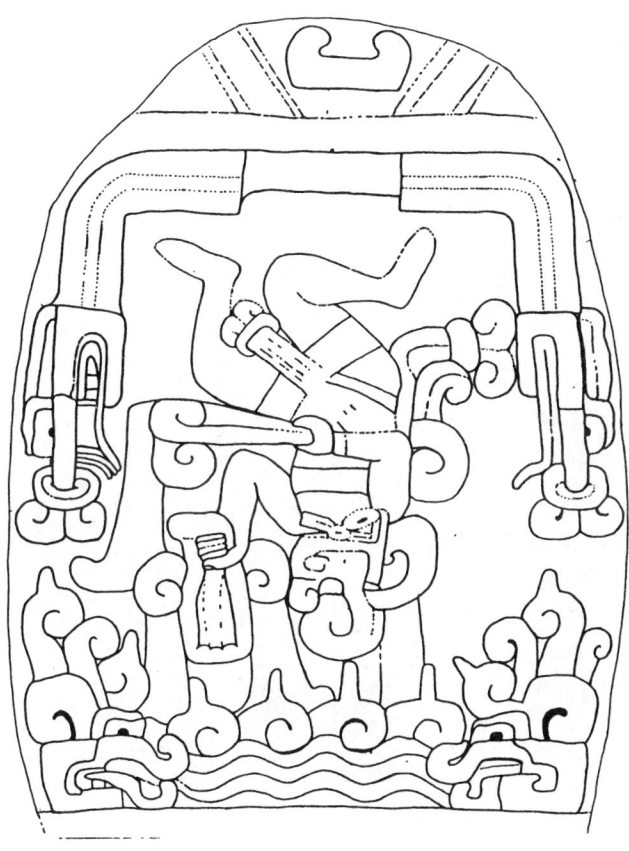

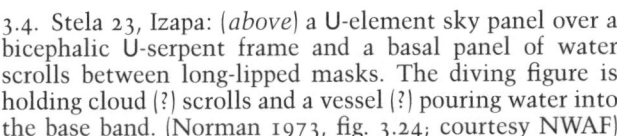

3.4. Stela 23, Izapa: (*above*) a U-element sky panel over a bicephalic U-serpent frame and a basal panel of water scrolls between long-lipped masks. The diving figure is holding cloud (?) scrolls and a vessel (?) pouring water into the base band. (Norman 1973, fig. 3.24; courtesy NWAF)

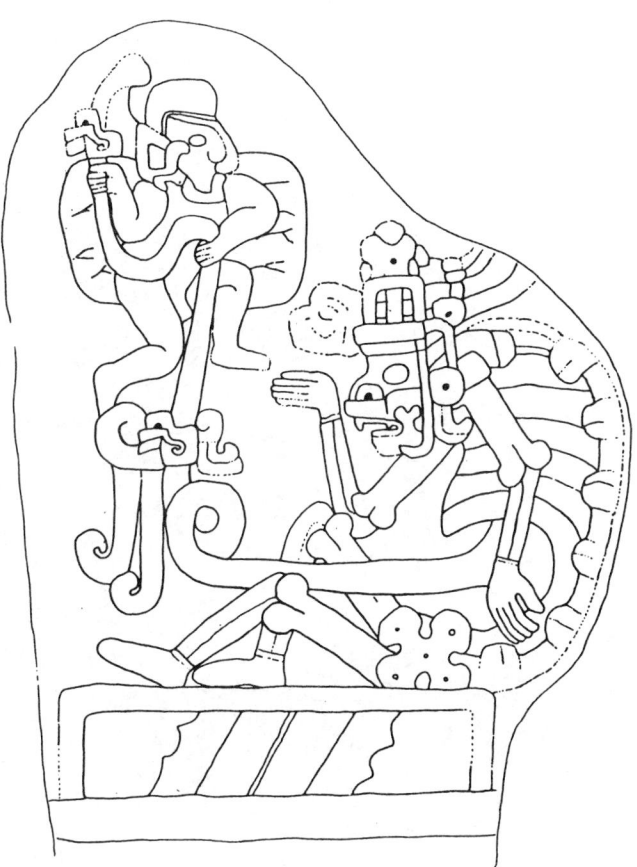

3.5. Stela 50, Izapa: skeletal figure with kin-glyph pelvis, *kan* cross headdress, alveolar mask, and a scrolled cord from the rib cage leading to a deity mouth mask and a mask held by a human with veined butterfly wings. (Norman 1973, fig. 3.35; courtesy NWAF)

ures 2 and 4; there are other possibilities. Norman's left-side analysis is equally complex, and the reader is referred to the original publication for details. Other stelae depict diving gods, trees with a crocodilian body as roots, and masked figures with outstretched arms as if dominating natural forces. Clearly, many potential scenarios are possible, especially because a sequential chronology is lacking and the enormous range of iconographic elements is still not completely known (Norman 1976, 41).

Stelae at Other Sites

Stelae from nearby El Baul, Abaj Takalik, El Jobo, Bilbao, Chalchuapa in El Salvador, and Kaminaljuyú (Map 5), in contrast, combine Olmec, Izapan, and early Maya traits. At Abaj Takalik, Monument 1 and reworked Olmec Monument

23 show Olmec features; Stela 2's profile figures and descending, scroll-enveloped gods (Izapan features) enclose a glyph later used by the Maya in calculating *Long Count* dates (for an explanation of Long Count dates, see Appendix One in Chapter 5), and Stela 5 depicts two Maya figures facing Long Count dates, with Izapan figures on the sides. Reflecting this mix, Kaminaljuyú's beautiful, deliberately mutilated Late Preclassic Stela 10 has an undeciphered proto-Maya text accompanying a birdwing-caped figure with a trident "weeping eye" wielding an "eccentric" obsidian object and a bearded, fanged god carved in Maya style (Figure 3.7). The striding figure on Kaminaljuyú's Stela 11 carries an identical eccentric obsidian: The pose, long-lipped god masks, biphed tongue breechcloth, stiff cape, downward-peering sky god, spiked incensarios, and scrolled baseline are direct ties with the Izapan style.

3.6. Stela 5, Izapa: a complex mythical scene between sky and water panels, with a central tree dividing multiple human, animal-masked, bird, fish, and falling-rain images. (Norman 1976, fig. 4.1; courtesy NWAF)

Ties to the Classic Maya

Still unresolved is what and how these Pacific Coast chiefdoms contributed to Classic Maya art and culture. Michael Coe feels that the Izapan style funneled modified Olmec ideas (prototype ceremonial bars, long-lipped masks transitional between Olmec were–jaguars and Mayan Chacs, and diagonal/U-elements that appear later in Maya sky bands and glyphs) to the Maya, whereas other Olmec elements (rulers carrying royal infants, ballgame iconography, deities and glyphs, bloodletting perforators, hematite mirrors, calendric notation, and ceremonial bars) may have reached them from Veracruz via Oaxaca and Chiapas (Coe 1977, 186–190).

Other researchers emphasize that Izapan ste-

3.7. Stela 10, Kaminaljuyú, with a bearded, fanged diety (*upper right*), a trident-eyed figure hold-ing a eccentric flint (*upper left*), a profile figure with a fanged back-mask (*below*), and calendric, undeciphered proto-Mayan glyphs. (Coe 1987, fig. 28; courtesy Michael D. Coe)

lae lack Maya texts, calendrics, and static poses of historical figures. Virginia Smith, based on a thorough trait analysis, regards Izapan art as "a unique local phenomenon," definitely not in-termediary between Olmec and Maya art styles (1984, 48–49). Lee Parsons (1986), after chrono-logically ordering 125 Kaminaljuyú stone sculp-tures dating between 700 B.C.–A.D. 700, finds Kaminaljuyú's Miraflores and Arenal substyles much more Mayan than anything at Izapa. Com-pounding the question of origins is Stela 1 from La Mojarra, Veracruz, found submerged in the Acula River in 1986 in the heart of Olmec territory. Its Long Count dates of A.D. 143 and 158 and long text in archaic glyphs accompany an ornately dressed profile figure in, of all things, full-blown Izapan style (Winfield Capi-taine 1988).

"PROTO-MAYA" AND MAYA CHRONOLOGY UP TO THE EARLY CLASSIC

Archaic and Early Preclassic

A long, detailed sequence documenting the transition from nomadic to sedentary life, like that of Tehuacán for Central Mexico, is lacking for the Maya area. Tantalizing evidence of early settled life appears in the coastal Belize lowlands, with part-time sea- and lagoon-based settlements dating to 4000 B.C. and year-round occupation with horticulture by 3000 B.C. toward the end of the Early Preclassic, inland villages such as Cuello along the New and Hondo rivers (Map 5). Grave goods indicate distant trade connections at this early date and include jadeite from the Motagua River, shell for bracelets from the Gulf of Honduras, and quartzite for *metates* and *manos* from the Maya Mountains to the south. By 900 B.C., Cuello, Santa Rita, El Pozito, and San Estevan (Map 5) were producing a sophisticated, red-slipped pottery called Swasey ware.

Middle Preclassic

During the Middle Preclassic (800–300 B.C.), people moved from the Pacific Coast and Belize into the Guatemala highlands and Petén lowlands to establish the village precursors of Late Preclassic and Classic regional centers: Kaminaljuyú, Chiapa de Corzo, Altar de Sacrificios, and Seibal; El Mirador, Tikal, and Uaxactún in the Petén lowlands, and Cerros in Belize (Map 5). Early, local pottery traditions such as the Xé Complex from Seibal and Altar de Sacrificios on the Pasión River suggest loose informal contacts until around 600 B.C. when a waxy, textured ware called Mamóm spread throughout the lowlands as a result of increasing interaction between major centers. Long-distance exchange in obsidian, jade, and magnetite stimulated established sites such as Cerros, El Mirador, and Kaminaljuyú, which sorted obsidian from local sources to adjacent Pacific Coast lowland and Petén Maya sites.

Late Preclassic

Late Preclassic (300 B.C.–A.D. 100) lowland and highland Maya sites continued to grow. The most important was El Mirador (Map 5), with architectural complexes that include El Tigre and the 70-meter-high (230-foot) Danta, the largest known human-made structure in Mesoamerica. Cerros in Belize flourished as part of a coastal trade network. Inland, construction began on the North Acropolis at Tikal and the beautiful jaguar-serpent-masked E-VII-sub pyramid at Uaxactún. In Guatemala, Kaminaljuyú prospered by exporting obsidian for blades and basalt for sculpture and metates. The uniformity of Late Preclassic red-slipped Chicanel ceramics throughout the Petén confirms continuing intersite ties as a powerful Maya elite regulated importation of high-status Gulf and Pacific coast shells, stingray spines for bloodletting, and resist-decorated orange and brown Usulután pottery from El Salvador.

Protoclassic

During the Protoclassic (*a.d.* 100–250), Cerros and El Mirador collapsed, and monument building faltered at other sites. Uaxactún and Tikal survived to lead the second wave of new regional centers. Pacific coast sites were abandoned around A.D. 200–250 when ash fall from the eruption of Ilopango, a major volcano near San Salvador, may have disrupted food-resource procurement and cacao production for almost 200 years (Sheets 1980), and people fled to resettle in the Guatemalan highlands and Belize. The rising Central Mexican power of Teotihuacán exerted influence on the weakened Pacific Coast trade network and established a particularly strong presence at Kaminaljuyú that, as a Teotihuacán co-partner or colony, linked with Tikal as a lowland distribution center. The influx of new goods and ideas transformed Tikal into the dominant Early Classic lowland center with powerful new dynastic rulers. By A.D. 250, the foundations of Classic Maya culture were in place, and the earlier Preclassic groundwork was about to produce an even more splendid second florescence.

IN its long development, Maya architecture exhibits great temporal and regional variety. Structurally, however, it remained limited: With only a few exceptions, the Maya never learned about broad supported roof construction and used only small, thick-walled interiors.

TECHNIQUES AND MATERIALS

The favored lowland building material was readily available limestone, which is easily worked when wet but hardens with weathering. Blocks were positioned over a rubble or cement core, held in place by mortar, and coated with plaster. Powdered lime made from burned, crushed limestone was mixed with water and *sascab*[1] to make cement, with sand or volcanic ash for finer mortar, and with organic gums for stucco plaster used on floors, exteriors, modeled decorations, and as a polished base for interior murals.

TYPES OF STRUCTURES

Ordinary Dwellings

Peasant houses, like contemporary Maya huts, were built on low adobe-plastered or stone-faced earthen platforms around courts. Their vertical posts interwoven with branches (wattle) were daubed with white adobe, and the houses had steep thatched grass roofs covering a floor of tamped earth.

Temples and Pyramid Bases

The earliest temples were "god houses," slightly fancier elaborations of peasant huts. In time, limestone temples were built on stone-faced bases resembling the underlying earthen platforms. Eventually these bases became pyramidal to better raise the gods' dwellings well above those of mere mortals.

Pyramids of fitted limestone over a rubble core took many forms. Most were square or rectangular, with multiple bodies and one, two, or four medial stairways leading to the truncated top. In the Petén, extremely tall pyramids had steep stairs with narrow risers; Yucatán

CHAPTER 4

MAYA ARCHITECTURE

---

[1] Terms descriptive of Mayan architecture are defined in a handy lexicon by Loten and Pendergast, 1984. See also Glossary, this volume.

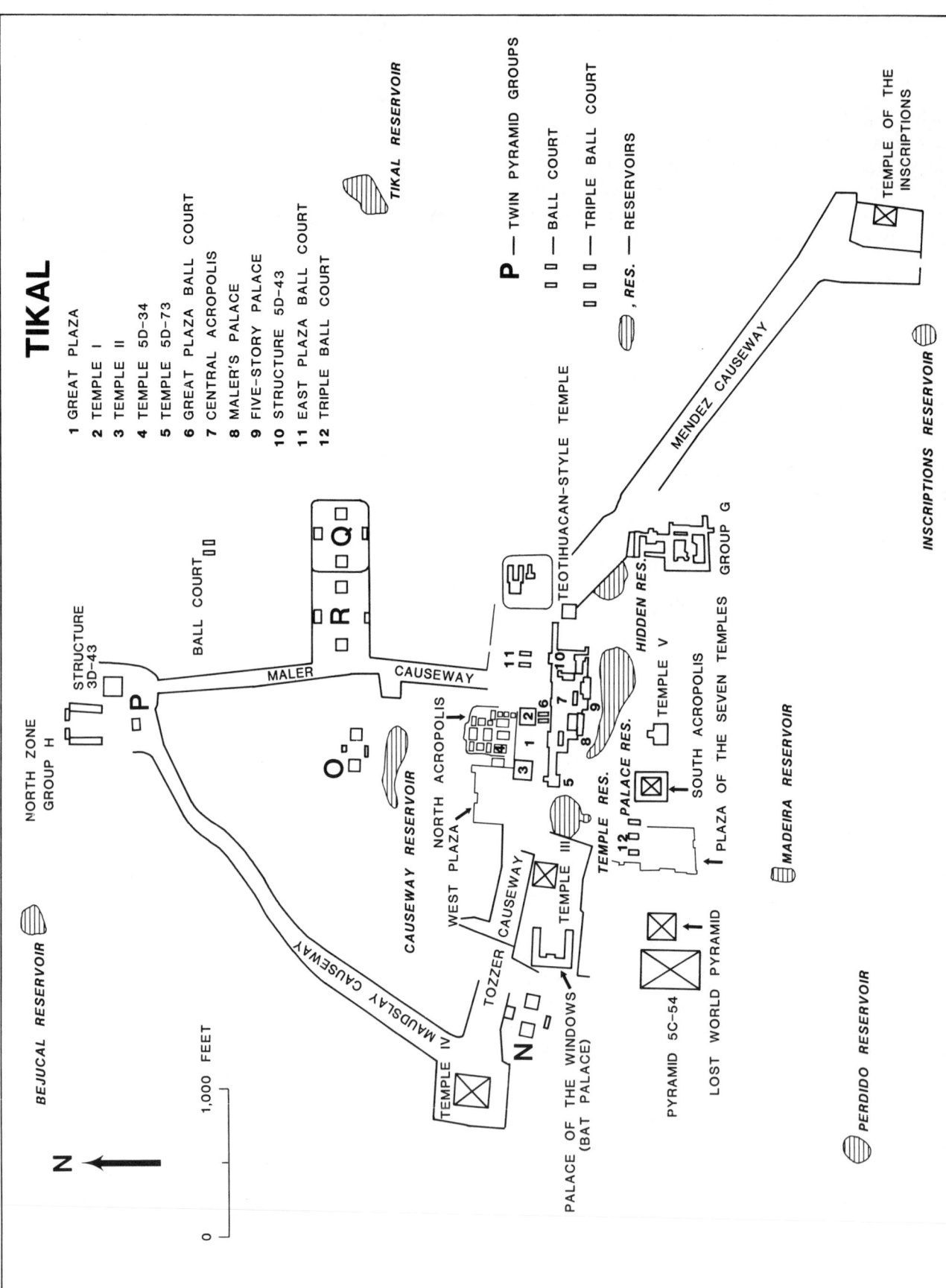

TIKAL

1 GREAT PLAZA
2 TEMPLE I
3 TEMPLE II
4 TEMPLE 5D-34
5 TEMPLE 5D-73
6 GREAT PLAZA BALL COURT
7 CENTRAL ACROPOLIS
8 MALER'S PALACE
9 FIVE-STORY PALACE
10 STRUCTURE 5D-43
11 EAST PLAZA BALL COURT
12 TRIPLE BALL COURT

P — TWIN PYRAMID GROUPS

▯▯ — BALL COURT

▯▯▯ — TRIPLE BALL COURT

◓ , RES. — RESERVOIRS

TIKAL RESERVOIR

BEJUCAL RESERVOIR

NORTH ZONE
GROUP H

STRUCTURE
3D-43

BALL COURT

MALER   CAUSEWAY

N

1,000 FEET

0

PALACE OF THE WINDOWS
(BAT PALACE)

TEMPLE IV

TOZZER CAUSEWAY

MAUDSLAY CAUSEWAY

CAUSEWAY RESERVOIR

NORTH ACROPOLIS

WEST PLAZA

TEMPLE III

TEMPLE RES.

PYRAMID 5C-54

LOST WORLD PYRAMID

TEMPLE V

PALACE RES.

SOUTH ACROPOLIS

PLAZA OF THE SEVEN TEMPLES

TEOTIHUACAN-STYLE TEMPLE

HIDDEN RES.

GROUP G

MADEIRA RESERVOIR

MENDEZ CAUSEWAY

PERDIDO RESERVOIR

INSCRIPTIONS RESERVOIR

TEMPLE OF THE
INSCRIPTIONS

Map 6. Tikal: a simplified map of major architectonic features. (For a detailed map, see Carr and Hazard 1961)

architects favored squatter, broad horizontal stairs. Ornamentation included huge stucco masks, projecting apron moldings, flat vertical or sloping faces, and carved-stone relief work.

Undecorated lower walls were usually separated from upper decorated entablatures by a molding, with a cornice or upper molding at the roof. Small, narrow, windowless rooms were clearly for ritual rather than public use, with a smaller back sanctuary for religious images and ritual. Structurally weak walls made of a rubble core covered with dressed stone instead of stacked stone blocks were built 1 to 1.5 meters (3 to 5 feet) thick for stability and set no more than 4 meters (12 feet) apart to effectively support the steep sloping sides of corbeled-vault ceilings, whose angle was in imitation of the interior of peasant hut roofs.

The Maya corbeled arch lacked both the potential for wide, ample Central Mexican rooms with beam ceilings and the structural stability of the Old World's true arch in which close-fitting trapezoidal blocks in a tight curve are secured by a central capstone. The Maya arch was built by overlapping horizontal slabs inward from each wall until they were close enough to be spanned by a heavy flat capstone. Each slab, projecting slightly beyond the one below it, was tenoned into a mortar and rubble core and secured by the weight of the stones above it. The steep angle of incline was plastered smooth or created with beveled stones, forming a high triangular vault often as tall as the narrow room beneath it. Wooden crossbeams provided extra thrust and may have been used to hang objects or woven screens. The resulting buildings, in Stierlin's (1964, 136) succinct phrase, "resembled hollow monoliths."

A prominent lowland feature is the roof comb or *cresteria*, supported by the front or back wall of single-room temples or on the center wall of double-roomed temples. Crests of solid masonry or latticelike openwork often bore large stucco-modeled designs or multiple figures of rulers as important billboard-like surfaces for iconographic display. Some were actually taller than their temples: Temple V at Tikal (Map 6) is 30 feet (9.1 meters) tall and supports a 52-foot (15.8 meter) cresteria. Lintels, tablets, murals, and panels were also important display adjuncts, with glyphic texts identifying accession transfer, subjugation of enemies, and defunct rulers as divine ancestors.

Palaces

Temples and other structures were grouped around paved open plazas used for victory celebrations, accessions, royal funerals, and, if contemporary Maya villages are a guide, huge outdoor markets. In contrast, low rectangular platforms with wide stairways underlay multiroom "palaces" up to 300 feet (91.4 meters) long, which may have been quarters for priests, lounges for incoming traders and storage of goods, or places of council and decision making. At Copán and Quiriguá (Map 5), their widestaired landings were probably used as reviewing stands (Proskouriakoff 1963, 47–49).

Specialized Structures

Specialized structures include high "observatories" at Palenque and Chichén Itzá, with multidirectional upper-level windows for possible astronomical and calendric sightings. *Chultunes* held food or rainwater fed by stone-paved aprons during storms (Matheny 1986, 8), refuse, and occasional burials. Ordinary citizens were buried in slab-lined crypts below house floors; rulers in Tikal, Comalcalco, Kaminaljuyú, and Palenque, at plaza level in front of or within commemorative mounds or pyramid temples with glyphs on crypt walls for identification. Sweatbaths (*temascales*), still found in Mesoamerican Indian villages today, were used for curing and ritual purification. Piedras Negras had eight, with sherd-lined hearths for heating stones, drains for water to create steam, and benches for the participants.

An easily recognizable specialized structure is the I- or double-T-shaped ball court, consisting of two wide end zones joined by a long, narrow playing alley. Classic period courts such as that at Copán had sloping sides against which the ball was deflected and above which the audience sat on viewing platforms. The Great Ball Court at Chichén Itzá, of Late Classic or Early Postclassic date, had vertical walls with an inset stone ring for instant scoring, as described later.

The Ball Game

The lowland Maya ball game, *tlachtli*, was played with a solid rubber ball that each team tried to move into the opponents' end zone by deflecting it with knees, hips, elbows, or shoulders. Because the heavy, soccer-sized ball ricocheted off court walls with tremendous speed and force, players wore protective knee, elbow, and shoulder pads, a helmet, and a thick (presumably leather), padded yoke at the waist. Quick scoring and an instant victory occurred when a player "trick-shot" the ball cleanly through a stone ring set at high center of each court wall. At this rare feat, pandemonium reigned, and the winning team could storm the audience and snatch the jades worn by wealthy patrons. Court walls at Chichén Itzá in Yucatán and El Tajín in Veracruz also show losing team captains undergoing heart sacrifice or decapitation, with serpents representing blood spurting from their severed necks (Schele and Miller 1986, 241–264).

By integrating pottery representations and limited sixteenth-century ethnohistoric Spanish chronicle descriptions with architectonic data, Mary Ellen Miller, Stephen Houston, and Linda Schele have further interpreted the ball game as a rite of kingship in which notable prisoners of war played and were subsequently sacrificed to honor their captor's victory. The carved blocks that form a tier of thirteen steps known as Hieroglyphic Stairway 2 at Yaxchilán show the Late Classic ruler Bird Jaguar about to deflect a ball containing his bound captive Jeweled Skull against the risers of a hieroglyphic staircase, a setting possibly also used for public captive torture and display as shown in the Bonamak murals (see Figure 6:2). Miller, Houston, and Schele (Schele and Miller 1986, 249–251; Miller and Houston 1987, 49–52, 55, 63) feel that this and other ball-playing scenes with skulls or bound captives depicted as the ball against a staircase backdrop are "conflations" of related sequential events, the "resonant images" of a warlike game and its postgame staircase sacrifice.

Two known glyphs refer to ball-game playing; others suggest that ball-playing rulers may have identified themselves with the legendary Hero Twins of the *Popol Vuh* post-Contact epic or with Gods I (Chac Xib Chac) and III (Jaguar God variants) of the Palenque Triad in defeating underworld opponents and reenacting battle victories (Schele and Miller 1986, 252–253; Miller and Houston 1987, 60–63), later memorializing these commemorative events in architecturally associated murals, stone altars,

ballcourt markers, and friezes. Additional interpretations and descriptions of courts have appeared (see Scarborough and Wilcox 1989).

STRUCTURE GROUPINGS

Combinations of basic structural types were influenced by topography, aesthetics, and the functions of structure clusters. In ceremonial areas, temple pyramids enclosed an open plaza on three or all four sides, frequently with stela/atlar pairs at their base. Palace groups around plazas presumably had residential, educational, or administrative functions. Pairs of facing pyramids, U-placed groups of three, or a pyramid facing a platform with several structures may be what Kubler (1984, 210) refers to as "geomantic groups," oriented for viewing significant astronomical phenomena, representing microcosms of the perceived universe, or keyed to topographic features with mythical associations.

Cohesive multilevel clusters of buildings together form irregular and assymetrical acropolis groups with small stairways connecting their different levels. Some acropolis groups are contiguous; at Tikal (Map 6), separate units, perhaps identifying special functions, rites, or discreet lineage groups, are linked by long paved walkways (*sacbés*) through the intervening rainforest, that center both eye and mind and offer ideological links as well as physical access. Low-walled sacbés were up to 246 feet (75 meters) wide. Some link adjacent cities. The longest, between Cobá and Yaxuná (Map 5), is 30 feet (9 meters) wide and 60 miles (96.5 kilometers) long; shorter causeways connect Uci and Cansahcab, Ake and Izamal, and Uxmal and Kabah.

Rebuilding and enlargement altered architectural configurations as populations grew and physical needs and spiritual perceptions changed. Outer temples encase earlier ones; wings were added, and separate buildings fused together.

Complex reconstruction phases are hard to conceptualize from verbal description, site plans, and photos. Funds permitting, a few buildings have been restored so that we may understand their original forms. For most, reconstruction is less costly at the drawing board or through computer graphics. One of the most skilled artists was Tatiana Proskouriakoff, who started out drawing artifacts for the Carnegie Institution of Washington digs, moved on to architectural interpretation, and became a devoted Mayanist, creating major decipherments of dynastic glyphs and interpretations of Maya art styles. Her *Album of Maya Architecture* (1963) is a good place to look for the basic elements of Maya architectural design.

SITE PLANS

Knowledge of Maya site plans is still limited. In many sites only the large central structures and ceremonial complexes have been surveyed, and only a select few, including Tikal, Dzibilchaltún, Mayapán, Comalcalco, Edzná and Seibal (see Map 5), have been mapped in their entirety. At this stage we can compare intersite construction and styles; understanding the interaction between structures has only begun.[2]

Broad generalizations can nevertheless be made. First, Maya sites lack the controlled gridlike axiality of Teotihuacán and Aztec Tenochtitlán. Individual complexes were influenced by uneven topography and are generally oriented to the cardinal points and linked by sight lines between the major structures. To avoid flooding, Petén structures were built on artificially terraced rises around low-lying *bajos*, forming "island cities" or "archipelago cities," well integrated with their natural surroundings (Kubler 1984, 207). Through awareness of the aesthetics of topography, verdant rises at Palenque and Yaxchilán became deliberate visual display settings for both architecture and sculpture.

Second, random and unplanned long-term growth resulted in assymetrical site plans. Outlying areas expanded irregularly as topography permitted. Internal sectors became more compact or encroached into other areas to gain space, as commercial specialization required more workshop area; also there was a growing priesthood, requiring new palace and temple complexes; and rising elites, requiring architecture and stelae to validate their divine origins. Even in flatter Yucatán, unhindered by vagaries of topography, site expansion responded to changes in social needs and perceived cosmographic relationships rather than following a rigidly preconceived plan.

A third characteristic of growth involves urbanization. For years archaeologists, concentrating on temple and palace excavation, described the great Petén sites as vacant ceremonial centers with caretaker priests. We know now that most large sites have ceremonial areas with extensive residential sectors in close proximity. These semiurban "central places" or "organizational centers" are recognized as cities on the basis of their size, populations, monumental architecture, and the complex interaction between their specialized social, political, military, religious, commercial, and craftsworking classes.

Finally the relative site sizes suggest a hierarchy of primary centers and dependencies based on site complexity, node positions along trade routes, and epigraphic evidence. Primary site glyphs and dynastic names at minor sites probably indicate military alliances and political intermarriages as mechanisms of linkage (Marcus 1976).

ARCHITECTURAL DEVELOPMENT AND REGIONAL STYLES

Preclassic to Protoclassic (2000 B.C.–A.D. 250)

From small Early Preclassic Belize and Pacific Coast hut/plaza clusters, Maya architecture developed rapidly. By the Middle Preclassic, villages of wattle-and-daub huts dotted the Chiapas and Guatemalan highlands as well as the central lowlands, and small temple pyramids occur at several sites.

The Late Preclassic saw a marked increase in lowland ceremonial construction, probably reflecting increased cultural and commercial contacts with the Pacific Coast and southern highlands. Quadrilaterally symmetrical stuccofaced, stepped, radial pyramids with sets of large, chevron-toothed, biphed-tongued jaguar–serpent masks flanking each stair appear at El Mirador's Pava and El Tigre complexes (Matheny 1986, 15–21), at Piedras Negras, Palenque, Tikal (deliberately mutilated, in the North Acropolis), Kohunlich, and Lamanai and Cerros in Belize (Map 5). One of the first examples uncovered is Uaxactún's radial pyramid E-VII-sub, fortuitously preserved by overlying constructions; in 1988, nine additional sets of intentionally buried, beautifully preserved Late Preclassic long snouted masks were found by Juan

---

[2] Descriptions of architecture at individual Maya sites, beyond the scope of this book, may be found in Stierlin 1964 and Heyden and Gendrop 1975. For settlement patterns, see details in Vogt and Leventhal, eds. (1983).

Antonio Valdes of the Proyecto Nacional Tikal on Uaxactún Group H complex structures (Richard D. Hansen, personal communication, 1988).

Interpretations of Radial Pyramids

To Kubler (1962) and Coggins (1980), these unique structures are architectonic representations of the four-lobed Maya symbol for cyclical completion, an interpretation strengthened by Uaxactún E-VII-sub's orientation keyed to solstice and equinox sunrises demarcating celestial cycles. Freidel and Schele (1988a, 561) relate radial pyramids to the Classic period quincunx glyph (four corner dots around a center point) and concepts of paired and quadripartite opposition, with the two sets of masks as the quadrilateral circles and a priest standing on the stair as the cosmic center. (For interpretations of the iconography of Late Preclassic radial pyramid masks, see page 90). Arthur Miller interprets radial pyramids as architectonic images of natural forces (water, the sun), reinforcing the cyclical nature of time in calendar round inscriptions, and of rulership, through which ancestor kings continued in contact with their living descendants (A. Miller 1986, 17–40). Marvin Cohodas (1980), noting their quadripartite directional associations, astronomical functions, and usual absence of temple superstructures, feels that they were used for public ceremonies of sympathetic magic celebrating the solar agricultural calendar, a matter of ongoing concern because radial pyramids, minus masks, continued as important components of later Classic period sites.

Protoclassic Period (A.D. 100–250)

This brief transitional period saw the collapse of El Mirador, Cerros, and several other flourishing Late Preclassic sites and a marked decline in construction at Lamanai and Tikal as incipient contacts by some sites combined with the rising polity of Teotihuacán added new elements to the trade equation. By A.D. 100, the basic architectural layout of temple pyramids and complementary platforms containing tombs bounding open plazas was well established and ready for elaboration by prospering Early Classic sites.

Early Classic (A.D. 250–400)

During the Early Classic period, Central Mexican concepts influenced several expanding Maya centers. Kaminaljuyú's Esperanza-phase pyramids incorporated taluds and tableros, and tombs contain imported Teotihuacán Thin Orange ware and slab-footed cylinder tripods with Teotihuacán and Maya motifs. In the central lowlands, Tikal reflects Teotihuacán influence in architecture, tomb pottery, and stela portrayal of Teotihuacán figures. Architecture at lesser sites remained essentially Mayan. Astronomical orientation became important: For example, Uaxactún's Structure E-VII (built over E-VII-sub) was an observatory for sighting solar equinox and solstice positions along the corners and centerline of three temples at the west end of its plaza. Palaces and specialized structures proliferated to meet the needs of a growing, increasingly stratified society.

Middle Classic (A.D. 400–700)

Between A.D. 400–500, contacts continued to be strong with the Gulf Coast, Oaxaca, Teotihuacán-influenced Kaminaljuyú, and Pacific Coast sites. Then Teotihuacán's long-distance trade connections began to falter. By 600, its wider influence had waned even at Kaminaljuyú, and by 750 Teotihuacán no longer influenced any Maya-region site.

As Teotihuacán influence weakened, Cholula and Xochicalco, in Central Mexico, El Tajín, in Veracruz, and Monte Albán, in Oaxaca, rose to fill the vacuum in a burst of eclecticism that highlights the Middle Classic period (Pasztory 1978). Sites in Central Mexico, Veracruz, and Oaxaca modified Teotihuacán's talud–tablero architecture by adding an upper flaring cornice, like an inverted talud above the tablero. In early Puuc-style Yucatán platforms, a smaller version appears as *binder moldings* on columns. Round temple bases and radial pyramids returned to popularity, possibly as symbols of completed time cycles. Sites in Oaxaca, Veracruz, and the Yucatán turned to stone mosaic and modeled stucco for decorating building facades (Pasztory 1978, 108–112).

In the Maya area, Teotihuacán's withdrawal and intersite raiding triggered a minihiatus decline at several sites—a mild dress rehearsal for the great tenth-century Petén collapse still ahead. Construction and stela erection decreased, and burial offerings declined in quantity and quality. By A.D. 600, Maya sites had adjusted, but Tikal's Kaminaljuyú–Teotihuacán enhanced hegemony was over, and its political authority shared with new regional centers (Copán, Palenque, Yaxchilán, and Calakmul; see Map 5) whose emblem glyphs now appear as indicators of these sites' growing importance. Construction resumed as the new power redistribution returned stability to the lowlands and architects developed distinctive regional styles.

At Tikal, tall, stepped, "skyscraper" pyramids topped by corbel-vaulted, narrow-roomed masonry temples with heavy roof combs break the forest canopy. The Usumacinta-River-area architects compensated for hillier topography through skillful assymetrical placement of lower buildings at different levels. Some temples (at Piedras Negras, for example) have massive walls and heavy crests; others have ample double rooms. At Palenque, architects gained inner space in several ways. They sloped upper walls inward to reduce the weight borne by walls. Deep interior wall niches, piers (wall sections) alternating with very wide, multiple doorways, and hollow lightweight "honeycomb" roof crests also helped to reduce upper weight. Walls could thus be made thinner, and interior rooms were larger. These innovations give Palenque an allover impression of delicacy and lightness (Figure 4.1).

A third regional "style" occurs in the Motagua Drainage at Copán, Honduras, and Quiriguá, Guatemala. Here roof crests are absent, and architectural sculpture reached unique ornateness. Stelae and altars are rich in baroque detail; freestanding grotesques, feline figures, and deity masks adorn walls and corners, and Copán's Hieroglyphic Stairway has over 2,000 glyphs in high relief.

Regional styles accompanied the rise of ruling dynasties. Arthur Miller (1986) relates this to an intellectual shift from cyclical, nature-based reasoning to linear concepts, shown on stelae presenting Long Count dates of linear time measured from a fixed base date. In architecture, masks of natural forces were replaced by images of individual rulers and glyphic texts recording their life events. Chapters 5 and 6 detail how architecture, visual images, and writ-

4.1. Characteristics of Palenque architecture: (top) perspective view of the Temple of the Sun; (bottom) cross section of the Temple of the Cross, showing the roofed interior sanctuary at back, the center wall dividing corbel-vaulted rooms, the hollow roof crest, and piers above stairs. (Marquina 1951, pl. 199, after M. A. Fernández; and pl. 201, a drawing by J. G. Gómez R.; courtesy INAH)

ing at Tikal and Palenque were conjoined to reaffirm a ruler's divine descent, royal ancestry, and earthly right to rule.

Late Classic (A.D. 700–900)

The Late Classic saw lowland sites peak and enter a final decline. Between A.D. 700–800, new regional centers prospered, and Tikal regained momentum under dynamic new rulers. However, their promising economic base was being eroded by enterprising Putún or Chontal Maya

4.2. Temple pyramid of the Río Bec style, Xpuhil, Quintana Roo. (Sodi Morales 1976, p. 54; drawing by Alberto Beltran, courtesy EMM).

who moved among Gulf Coast and Yucatán ports in enormous paddle and sail-powered canoes and stimulated far more rapid, less costly oceangoing trade with Central Mexico. This diverted goods from the old land and river routes managed by the great lowland Maya sites, undercutting prosperity and generating internal discontent, class conflicts, leadership crises, and warfare between centers in reciprocal negative feedback, a classic *systems analysis* example of the self-defeating situation. Rulers may have associated the upheaval with unfavorable prognostications accompanying recurrent katun periods (see Chapter 5 Appendix), for pollen samples show a switch from diversified planting to corn monoculture, perhaps done to free labor for intensified temple and monument construction in an effort to ritually turn things around. Agricultural productivity and resources were strained; disease and malnutrition are attested to in bones from the period. By A.D. 889, Long Count stelae glorifying the ruling dynasties disappeared as populations dwindled and gradually moved away.[3]

Late Classic Yucatán sites (Cobá, Edzná, Dzibilchaltún) flourished through the peninsula's increasingly active contacts with Central Mexico while maintaining their centuries-old export of salt and cotton to the lowlands. Petén architectural concepts filtered back in the exchange. Three overlapping, distinctive Late Classic architectural styles resulted—Puuc, Río Bec, and Chenes.

Río Bec

The Río Bec sites of Río Bec, Becan, and Xpuhil (Map 5) in Campeche predictably show similarities with Tikal. Most striking is Xpuhil's replication of Tikal's tall pyramids. Xpuhil's three, nearly vertical, round-cornered towers with steep unclimbable mock stairways sport huge stucco masks, topped by dummy solid-stone temples with high, masked roof combs (Figure 4.2). The temple "doorways" are huge open-mouthed monster heads, set in walls encrusted with complex geometric stucco and stone sculpture. Upper facades of low palaces have three-dimensional sculpted masks above undecorated or bas-relief piers separating the doorways. On pyramids, projecting apron moldings, like solid tableros, resemble Tikal's, whereas rounded corners of bunched stone columns recall the uprights of thatched huts. At other sites, building corners have stacked Chac masks projecting long noses like elephant trunks and doorways framed by open-mouthed serpentlike masks.

[3] For an excellent summary and evaluation of these multiple factors and arguments of their proponents, consult Lowe 1985, 88–111. Using epigraphic, demographic, and ceramic data in systems analysis and computer simulation, Lowe illustrates how their interaction could have created a stress threshold for major centers that affected dependent sites until the lowland collapse was complete.

Chenes

Further north, the adjacent Chenes style is named after the area's numerous *cenotes* (*chenes*, as in the name Chichén Itzá, "Mouth of the Well of the Itzá Lineage"). Buildings at Hochob have such active baroque-mosaic lower friezes that the eye can scarcely rest. The long noses of stylized rain-bringing Chac masks project from building corners like curled tapir snouts probing the air. Temple entrances are the maws of monster masks with moustache-like upper lips extruding serrated teeth (Gendrop 1980). Structures are lower, but otherwise Chenes is a cognate of Río Bec. Here, too, built-on columns recall the shape of simple huts, topped by elegant openwork crests.

Puuc

The Puuc style, named after the low northwestern Yucatán Puuc Hills, peaked in the eighth and ninth centuries at Uxmal, Labná, Kabah, Edzná (Map 5), Oxkintok, Xkalumkin, and Sayil (Pollock 1980). Thin slabs of veneer masonry tenoned into a cement core provided background for intricately fitted stone mosaics (Figure 4.3). Designs included crisp textile-like patterns recalling those at the sites of Yagul and Mitla in Oaxaca, stylized long-nosed Maya Chacs, rattle-tailed feathered serpents, and the ubiquitous stepped fret. Where decoration was dense, the effect was electric. Kabah's Structure 1, the Codz Poop, has a facade of 250 Chac masks with shared eyes and tentacle noses that is an energized tapestry of movement (Figure 4.4a). Such ornate decoration usually occurs on wide, slightly outward-sloping panels over undecorated, multiple-doored lower sections of long, low buildings set on wide-staired platforms facing plazas, quite in harmony with the flat, open Yucatán topography. Some upper panels have

parallel collonades or binder moldings imitating cord-lashed house posts. Thatch huts are even directly portrayed in stone on building walls at Labná and Uxmal.

Inside, long, narrow rooms with corbel vaults connect to windowless back rooms. Hollow Petén-style roof crests rest on the center or back wall or project over the front of the roof as flying facades, lavishly decorated with spools or colonettes. Sets of short colonettes also separate buildings from their platform stairs.

Archaeologists variously date Puuc style between A.D. 600–900 and note its early ninth-century spread northward to Dzibilchaltún and southwestward into Campeche (Kowalski 1987, 25–48). The style ends suddenly, with structures at midcompletion at several sites.

The Late Classic–Postclassic Continuum (A.D. 800–Contact)

During the Late Classic and Early Postclassic, Putún Maya merchants expanded westward into Central Mexico, southward up the Usumacinta River to the lowland site of Seibal, and eastward into the Yucatán to open new markets and sources of goods. Architectural innovation accompanied the intensified interchange.

Xochicalco

The fortified hilltop site of Xochicalco, in the Mexican state of Morelos (Map 2) confirms strong Late Classic–Early Postclassic Maya influence in Central Mexico. The Teotihuacanoid talud–tablero platform base under its Temple of the Feathered Serpent bears high-relief feathered serpents with seated, crosslegged figures with Maya profiles and costumes in their coils and the Central Mexican day glyph "9 Wind," calendar name of the legendary Feathered Serpent ruler, Quetzalcóatl. Xochicalco's ball court

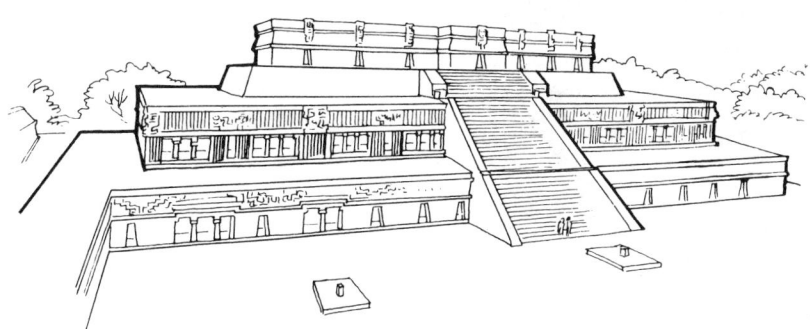

4.3. The Palace at Sayil, Yucatan (Puuc-Chenes style). (Sodi Morales 1976, p. 55; drawing by Alberto Beltran, courtesy EMM)

is identical in dimensions and form to those at Tula (see Map 2), the Toltec capital, a site with strong architectural ties to Maya Chichén Itzá.

Cacaxtla

Further evidence of Maya penetration into Central Mexico comes from Cacaxtla, another "eclectic" hilltop site 20 miles (21.8 kms) west of Tlaxcala (Map 2). Here palaces of eighth-century Mexican architecture contain murals that appear to show Central Mexicans defeating Maya warriors. In Building B, atlatl and shield-carrying (Central Mexican?) jaguar warriors gore dark-skinned bird-helmeted (Putún Maya?) opponents, perhaps documenting initial Gulf Coast intrusions. Later murals in Building A appear to show them reconciled. On the North Mural, the black-faced Jaguar leader holds a dripping spear near the glyph 9 Wind, as stated, a Quetzalcóatl referent. Its jamb has a jaguar-garbed figure in a long-nosed Maya mask. On the truly eclectic South Mural, the bird-helmeted warrior stands on a bearded feathered serpent holding a Maya-like bicephalic ceremonial bar, framed by turtles and shells, with a background quetzal, Teotihuacán "facing hands" and feathered eye glyphs. On its jamb, a dancing black figure holds Maya God N issuing from his shell.

Cacaxtla's murals combine Gulf Coast scrollwork and ballplayer yokes; Maya costume (heel-cup sandals, garters, sky-band belts), cranial deformation, ceremonial bars, deities (bearded dragons, God N); bar and dot numbers; and Teotihuacán flat scene borders, glyphs (feathered reptile eyes, half-stars, hearts dripping blood, dot plus day glyph dates), atlatls, Tlaloc jars, and the trapeze-ray year sign (Foncerrada de Molina 1980, 196; Quirarte 1983; Kubler 1984, 169). Mary Ellen Miller (1986b) observes that Cacaxtla's jaguar–bird opposition appears also in the Maya Bonampak murals and finds the quality of both paintings to be similar and decidedly Maya in sensibility.

International Style. This intriguing "international style" is a product of intensified Late Classic Yucatec–Gulf Coast–Central Mexican contacts stimulated by ongoing trade outreach and population dispersal following the collapse of Teotihuacán. Its timing and dynamics are the focus of intense ongoing research. Sixteenth-century Spanish chronicles identify Cacaxtla's

4.4a. Kabah: Codz Pop facade, with Puuc-style Chac masks (photo courtesy Doris Heyden).

4.4b. Chichén Itzá: stone mosaic Chac masks at the corner of the Temple of the Warriors (photo by the author).

builders as people called Olmeca-Xicalanca. Donald McVicker proposes that they may represent a combination of "Mexicanized Maya" Putún traders and Teotihuacán survivers (perhaps priestly elite) who had fled to the Gulf Coast and subsequently returned inland as "Mayanized Mexicans" (McVicker 1985). Later waves of this influx may have introduced Maya-derived traits to Tula.

Chichén Itzá and Tula

This Late Classic/Postclassic international style also occurs at Chichén Itzá (see Map 5), a northern Yucatec site named "Well of the Itzá"

because of its large cenotes and settlement by the Maya Itzá lineage. Chichén clearly shows both Puuc and Central Mexican influences. Structures with Late Classic Mayan Puuc features are the Temple of the Three Lintels, the Iglesia ("Church") and Monjas ("Nuns") palaces in the Nunnary Group, the Akab Dzib palace, and the Red House, with Puuc-style stone mosaic reliefs, heavy walls, corbel vaults, veneer masonry, and Mayan Chac masks (Figure 4.4b). The circular Caracol ("shell") observatory may reflect the Central Mexican association of round pyramids with Quetzalcóatl.

The Central Mexican site with the closest parallels to Chichén is Tula, the Toltec capital located 60 kilometers (37.3 miles) north of Mexico City, in the state of Hidalgo. In its earliest stages in the mid-seventh century, Tula shows ceramic connections with adjacent post-Teotihuacán groups. There are plentiful visual and glyphic references to Quetzalcóatl, who supposedly founded the site. At its height in the tenth century, Tula was a major political center with an estimated population of over 100,000. Its main architectural features included six ball courts, a large pyramid with a temple dedicated to Quetzalcóatl in his Venus aspect, residential areas, major plazas, and a stone wall of serpent bodies (*coatepantli*). Warriors wearing butterfly pectorals and carrying Central Mexican atlatls, or spear throwers, are depicted on three-dimensional and bas-relief stone Atlantean pillars that supported flat temple roofs. They, along with eagles and prowling jaguar referents to human sacrifice, suggest that militarism was important in the site's development and expansion. Tula eventually was sacked around A.D. 1168, probably as a result of Chichimec incursions triggered by a prolonged period of drought.

The parallels in site layout, building construction, and iconography between Tula and Chichén Itzá have intrigued scholars for years. Chichén's Castillo ("castle") or Temple of Kukulkán (Mayan for "feathered serpent"), Court of the Thousand Columns, Temple of the Warriors, and Great Ball Court have strikingly similar counterparts in Tula.[4] Reclining Chacmools (Figure 4.5a), colonnaded halls with wide flat roofs, friezes of jaguars and eagles eating sacri-

[4] One must bear in mind however that Mexican archaeologists in the 1940s were guided by Chichén architecture in reconstructing Tula's Pyramid B with features of Chichén's Temple of the Warriors.

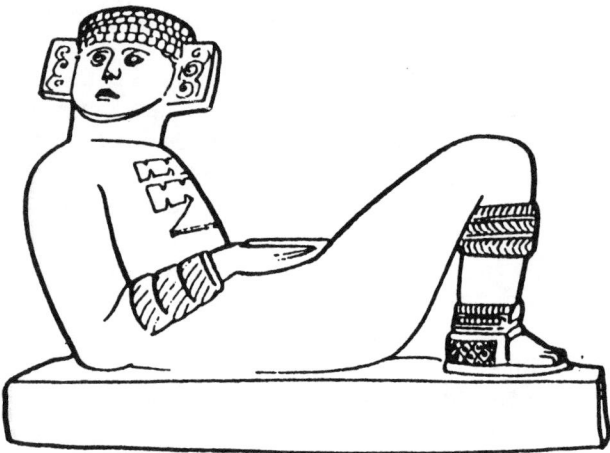

4.5a. Chichén Itzá: Chacmool similar to those at Tula, Hidalgo. (Sodi Morales 1976, p. 59; drawing by Alberto Beltran, courtesy EMM)

4.5b. Chichén Itzá: eagle eating a human heart, Platform of the Eagles and Jaguars. (Photo by the author)

4.5c. Chichén Itzá: feathered serpent columns at the entrance of the Temple of the Warriors. (Photo by the author)

Mexican referents. Toltec-looking warriors in canoes with shields and atlatls observe Maya villages (Figure 4.6), conquer them, and make alliances with seated Maya lords. Others may commemorate Maya Gulf Coast or Central Mexican conquests. Gold disks from Chichén's sacrifical cenote have eagle-headdressed Central Mexican physical types spearing and performing heart sacrifice on Maya captives.

Interpretations of Chichén–Tula Similarities

Architectural and sculptural parallels between the two sites were traditionally seen as indicators of an early Postclassic military, or at least cultural, Toltec "invasion," associated in legend with the flight of Quetzalcóatl eastward by sea as bearer of Central Mexican culture to the Yucatán. Recent research, however, indicates

ficial hearts (Figure 4.5b), serpent balustrades and columns (Figure 4.5c), and caryatid or Atlantean warrior columns (Figure 4.5d) also occur at both sites.

Chichén's murals likewise contain Central

4.5d. Chichén Itzá: caryatid columns of warriors. (Photo by the author)

4.6. Mural, Chichén Itzá, probably showing reconnoitering Putún. (Sodi-Morales 1976, p. 89; drawing by Alberto Beltran, courtesy EMM)

far earlier Maya contacts during the Early and Middle Classic periods with Teotihuacán and the sites that rose after its collapse.

Many scholars feel that Nonoalca and Olmeca-Xicalanca groups, mentioned in sixteenth-century Spanish chronicles, were the catalysts for Yucatec–Central Mexican interaction well before Tula's rise and Quetzalcóatl's postulated Postclassic arrival and see Tula as a Putún Maya trade partner or even a colony of Chichén rather than as instigator of a Postclassic Toltec invasion.

Evidence supporting these earlier, Classic period exchanges includes proposed dates of A.D. 600–900 for Chichén's Castillo and Great Ball Court, presumably built by early Mexicanized (Putún) Maya or pre-Toltec Mexican immigrants (Cohodas 1978; Wren, pp. 20–21, in Cog-

gins and Shane 1984). Cohodas (1989b) notes iconographic shifts at Chichén from Middle Classic fertility and ball game themes to Late Classic–Postclassic Maya/Mexican ethnic opposition of warriors, prisoner display, and sacrifice as violence marked these cultural exchanges. Toltec–Maya architectural elements and Chichén's (Toltec-influenced) Sotuta and Puuc Cehpech wares also occur at other Late Classic Yucatec sites (Lincoln 1986, 164–183; Kowalski 1987, 48–51) as further evidence of ongoing acculturation.

Thus the emerging picture for the Yucatán is one of complexity, unevenness, and overlap, with "entradas" of Central Mexican ideas and/or people intensifying between A.D. 800–1200. Ties between Chichén and Tula were two-way and strong. Chontal-speaking Putún groups, linked with the Postclassic Maya Itzá lineage in historic Yucatec chronicles, may have cultivated Chichén as a trading colony and acted as a conduit for Central Mexican influences. Conversely, several scholars[5] feel that

[5] George Kubler (1984, 288), noting Tula's lack of Toltec art corresponding to that at Chichén, calls Tula a possible "stylistic out-

Maya ideas, carried inland by "Mayanized" Mexicans from Veracruz, were directly imitated at Tula in the ongoing exchange (McVicker 1985, 95–98). The stimulus was clearly beneficial to both.

Epigraphic Studies

Epigraphic studies by Ruth Krochok (1988) show that Chichén texts document group participation by matrilineally related individuals (some apparently brothers) in public events, in contrast to the usual Mayan record of a ruler's life events. Krochok suggests that they may reflect a new political system to accompany the more fluid, sea-based trade, with wealth acruing to merchants and symbiotic trade networks rather than sustaining a single divine lineage. Charles Lincoln (1988) concurs and proposes that Chichén developed a "new social order" of complementary dual offices of kingship, Kakupacal ("Fire in His Shield") and Kukulkán ("Feathered Serpent"), reflecting bilineal descent, represented graphically by solar disks and the feathered serpent, in legend by the Hero Twins Xbalanque (Palenque GIII) and Hunahpu (GI)

---

post" of "Mexican ideas, clothed in Maya forms." Mary Ellen Miller (1985) sees Tula's chacmool sculptures as Classic Maya in origin, representing captive figures and the Maya perception of Tlaloc as a war/sacrifice symbol.

and the Central Mexican gods Tezcatlipoca (Mayan God K) and Quetzalcóatl (Kukulkán), and historically by the Cocom and Xiu lineages.

The Decline of Chichén Itzá

Whatever its government, Chichén Itzá prospered under the Putún Itzá from trade and pilgrimages to its sacred cenote. By the early thirteenth century, however, challenges appeared from the rival Cocom lineage whose power base lay on the northeastern coast of Yucatán, and in A.D. 1221 Chichén collapsed, perhaps to Mexicanized Putún warriors organized by the Cocom. The dispossessed Itzá fled southward, and the city of Mayapan (Map 5), under Cocom domination, took control of Yucatán commerce. Smaller than Chichén, Mayapán's defensive walls, palaces, and Feathered Serpent temple were crudely built.

In A.D., 1441 Mayapán fell to a third dynasty, the Xiu, a Mexican group based at Uxmal who vanquished the Cocom and established additional smaller settlements at Mani and Tibolón. By the late fifteenth century, the Yucatán had fragmented into small competing states. Following Spanish incursions in the 1530s and 1540s, Itzá survivors retreated into the Petén and built an island settlement called Tayasal near modern Flores, where their descendants finally surrendered to the Spaniards in 1690.

WE have already noted possible Preclassic Olmec and Pacific Coast contributions and the role of architecture and iconography in assessing Late Classic/Postclassic developments. Important research continues in both areas, along with a ferment of new interpretations. In Chapter 5 and 6, we will highlight three of several major areas in which interdisciplinary studies of Classic period art have enhanced our understanding of lowland Maya culture: (1) the identification of dynastic lineages and their interaction, as exemplified at Tikal, Copán, and Caracol (Chapter 5); (2) rituals of dynastic accession and validation and their iconography, as exemplified at Bonampak and Palenque (Chapter 6); and (3) linkages between religious iconography and Maya myths and identification of ceramic artists and workshops through the study of Maya funerary pottery (Chapter 6). The reader should be aware that equally important and comprehensive results may be expected from ongoing research at other major Maya sites.

One of the most important achievements in Maya studies over the past two decades has been our ability to recognize the images and names of historic rulers at most of the important Classic lowland sites and in some instances to confirm sequences of succession covering several hundred years. Part of this success is due to the decipherment of glyphs denoting major life events and royal kinship relationships. More recently, we have begun to understand individual rulers' ritual responsibilities and economic, political, and military interaction with other sites.

A key factor in appreciating how lowland Maya dynastic lineages functioned during the Classic period is an understanding of how they developed out of earlier forms of political rule. One way of "backtracking" to these origins is by tracing prior forms of the symbols of authority publicly displayed by the great Classic rulers.

PROPOSED ORIGINS OF THE ICONOGRAPHY OF RULERSHIP

Some researchers feel that they have found antecedents for the iconographic symbols of Classic period Maya rulership at several Late Preclassic sites in the Maya lowlands. They propose that Preclassic Maya beliefs by an egalitarian popula-

CHAPTER 5

MAYA ART

IDENTIFICATION OF DYNASTIC LINEAGES AND THEIR INTERACTION

tion first centered around the worship of natural forces and that a rising elite class during the Late Preclassic deliberately attempted to link the power of rulership with the ability to contact and control some of these cosmic forces through the medium of royal ancestors (Freidel and Schele 1988a, b). By the Early Classic, individual rulers representing royal dynasties appear in art. Wearing costumes and carrying paraphernalia that reinforce their divine sun–Venus descent, they are shown beneath floating embodiments of ancestors and with glyphic texts documenting their divine descent and thereby their right to rule. Architecture, sculpture, and epigraphy conjoin to document this shift in the social and political order and seem to have been deliberately used by emerging elite rulers to effect and consolidate the change (Schele and Freidel 1990:96–129).

Masks On Radial Pyramids

As noted in Chapter 4, several important Late Preclassic Maya centers in Guatemala, Belize, and Mexico have distinctive radial pyramids with a staircase on each of their four sides flanked by panels of large stucco masks with jaguar and human features. The most distinctive examples occur at Cerros, Uaxactún, Lamanai, Tikal, El Mirador (see Map 5), and at Kohunlich, in Mexico, near the Guatemalan border.

Researchers have interpreted these large frontal masks as personifications of a variety of widely worshiped natural forces ancestral to Classic period supernaturals such as the Cauac Monster (a mythical being symbolizing earth and stone), the Jaguar God of the Underworld, representing the sun during its night passage below the earth (M. E. Miller 1986a, 60; Tate 1982; Matheny 1986), the Palenque Triad, and/or the Hero Twins (to be described shortly: see Freidel and Schele 1988a, b). David Freidel, Mary Ellen Miller, and Linda Schele further identify Cerros Structure 5C-2's masks as a directionally oriented cosmogram, with blunt-snouted, kin-solar, cheek-infixed masks as Sun Jaguars interacting celestially with the upper, longer-nosed Venus masks: On the east side, Venus as Morning Star precedes the rising sun, whereas west of the stair, as in the sky, Venus as Evening Star follows the setting sun (Schele and Miller, 1986, 106–108; Freidel and Schele 1988b, 80–83; Schele and Freidel 1990: 111– 117, 120). The

double-headed sky serpents that arch over the Cerros masks may be derivatives of similar sky-serpent bands that frame the upper part of mythical scenes on Izapa stelae.

The great masks of these sculptured pyramids at Cerros and other Late Preclassic centers were later replaced by Classic-period architecture with sculptured images of actual rulers wearing the same kinds of headdresses and ear flares, who now represented the human embodiment of the Sun, Venus, and other cosmic forces (Freidel and Schele 1988b, 78–80).

The Palenque Triad and the Hero Twins

David Freidel and Linda Schele (1988b, 81–85) also find Preclassic antecedents for two of three Classic period gods who represent the deification of the Sun and Venus and the patron of royal lineages. These three gods collectively form the Palenque Triad, so called because they were identified through inscriptions at Palenque as divine ancestors of Palencano rulers. The Triad are referred to individually as Gods I, II, and III (GI, GII, and GIII for short). Born as brothers 18 days apart, their Classic-period characteristics are as follows:

1. GI (born first: alias God B, the barbed god). GI represented Venus and was sometimes anthropomorphized as Chac Xib Chac, an axe-brandishing executioner in sacrifice scenes.
2. GII (born last: alias God K or Bolon Tzacab). GII was the patron of royal lineages and sacrifice, with an easily recognizable forehead flare and serpent foot.
3. GIII (born second: alias Ek Ahau). GIII was the Jaguar nighttime sun, one of the Lords of Xibalbá (the Underworld), and represented darkness, death, and war (Schele and Miller 1986, 48–51).

Two of the Palenque Triad gods have also been identified by Floyd Lounsbury (1985, 51–58) with another set of important Classic period divinities, the Hero Twins who are described as mythical ball players and monster slayers in the epic *Popol Vuh* myth. Using linguistic, iconographic, and glyphic evidence, Lounsbury and others equate GI/Venus with Hero Twin Hunahpu and GIII with his younger brother Xbalanque, the Jaguar Sun. Others, particularly Michael Coe (1989b, 165–168), point out inconsistencies that they feel make the connection invalid. GII, of royal lineages, seems to have no known Preclassic prototype.

We shall return to the Hero Twins in greater detail in Chapter 6 as represented on Classic period pottery. The point to be made here is that several scholars find Twin and Triad prototypes in what they interpret as radial-pyramid Sun and Venus masks at Cerros and Uaxactún, representing natural forces in the process of becoming deified. Michael Coe (1989b, 62–64) points out possible additional prototypes from several Late Preclassic stelae at Izapa that may already show one or both Hero Twins and Vucub Caquix (7 Macaw), the bird–monster patron of the preceding world era, who was hunted and killed by the Twins and is the mythical Serpent-Wing Bird so frequent in Classic Maya sculpture.

Antecedents of Royal Regalia

Freidel and Schele further trace the consolidation of cosmic forces into the personae of divinely descended human rulers through elements of costume and accessory paraphernalia used by Classic-period rulers. By the Early Classic, royal accoutrements reinforcing divine descent included:

1. A "stocking-capped" Jester God diadem with possible antecedents in a Late Preclassic "crown" with a three-pointed center element.
2. A royal headdress possibly derived from radial pyramid masks, which appears to "disgorge" the ruler's face in divine descent.
3. The Preclassic Sky Serpent as a portable bicephalic, serpent-headed ceremonial bar.
4. Small hand-held effigies of the Jester God and God K (GII, symbol of dynastic lineages).
5. Portrayal under a saurian Celestial Monster whose long-snouted front head (with crossed-band *lamat*–Venus infixes) and rear head (with solar–kin infixes) disgorge, respectively, the faces of GI as Venus and GIII as the Underworld Sun (Freidel and Schele 1988b, 58–80).

To Freidel and Schele, this shift from cosmic symbols to accoutrements validating rulership reflects a deliberate reformulation of Preclassic beliefs to ease the potentially stressful transformation from egalitarianism to elitism. The decoding of symbolic elements carried by changing architecture and sculpture is an excellent example of structuralist analysis relating cultural, iconographically expressed belief systems to the realities of social behavior (Freidel and Schele 1988b; Schele and Freidel 1990).

We turn now to the ritual and political expression of these symbols by the lowland Classic elite.

CLASSIC-PERIOD DYNASTIES AND HISTORICAL FIGURES

One of the breakthroughs in documenting the shift from egalitarianism to dynastic rulership has been the identification of individual rulers along with their dates of reign, political activities, and ritual responsibilities. Such data are particularly complete for Tikal and Palenque and are rapidly being recovered from Copán, Caracol, Yaxchilan, Naranjo, and other interacting lowland sites.

TIKAL

Tikal, largest (75 square miles, 194.2 k²) and best investigated Classic lowland Maya site (Map 5), lasted for over 500 years. It was strategically positioned in the Petén jungles of Guatemala between two important Caribbean and Gulf Coast trade arteries, the San Pedro Martír and Belize rivers. Ample forest resources combined with irrigated raised fields ensured a stable food base for its estimated peak population to 75,000 to 100,000 people.

Intensive excavations by the University of Pennsylvania (1956–1970, under Edwin Shook and William Coe) and subsequently by Guatemalan archaeologists corroborate Tikal's urban dimensions and functions. The city's core (Map 6) was the now-restored Great Plaza, with its towering east and west pyramids (Temple I, Temple of the Giant Jaguar, and Temple II, Temple of the Masks), built around A.D. 700. There are three major building clusters: the Late Preclassic–Early Classic North Acropolis and the Late Classic Central and South acropolises. Broad sacbés form a triangle connecting the Great Plaza and Temple IV, with the five-precinct North Group at its apex.

Tikal's pyramids were funerary monuments build over royal tombs. Fourteen densely clus-

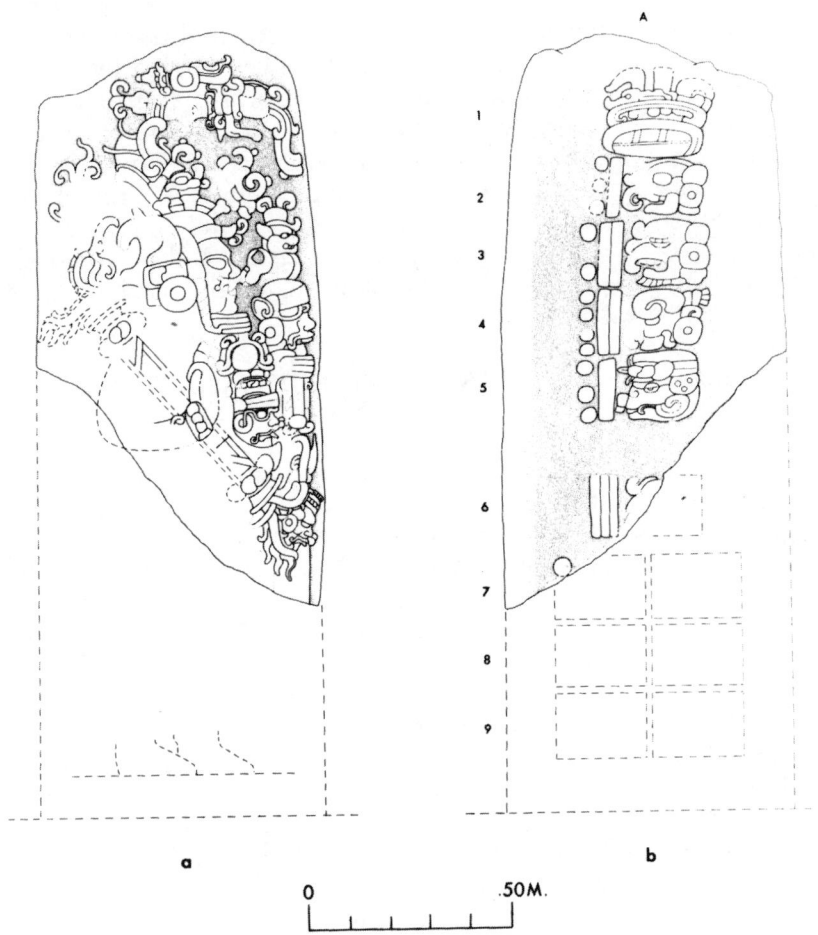

5.1. Stela 29, Tikal, (a) front and (b) back: an Early Classic ruler holds a ceremonial bar. The other numbers and letters indicate glyph positions. (Jones and Satterthwaite 1982, fig. 49; drawing by William Coe, courtesy TP/UPM)

tered North Acropolis structures formed a necropolis for Late Preclassic and Early Classic rulers in a tentative dynastic sequence from A.D. 376–768 as proposed by Clemency Coggins and Christopher Jones (Coggins 1975, 1979, 1980, 1983; Jones 1969, 1977; Jones and Satterthwaite 1982) on the basis of architectural and art styles, funerary offerings, stela portraits, and glyphic texts.

The sequence begins with Stela 29's earliest lowland Mayan Long Count date (A.D. 292), first use of Tikal's "knotted bundle" emblem glyph (as a knotted headband on the head below the ruler's chin: Figure 5.1) and portrayal of an unidentified Early Classic ruler holding a diagonal ceremonial bar with bearded serpent ends and a "football-helmeted," scroll-lipped sun–jaguar head (Figure 5.1). A downward-looking "ancestor" wearing a long-nosed headdress may link Stela 29 to Preclassic Pacific Coast Izapan sculpture.

Jaguar Paw: Early Classic Beginnings

Jaguar Paw, the first named Early Classic ruler, reigned from an as yet undetermined date until A.D. 377. He may be shown on Stela 29 and also stands over a bound captive on Guatemala's famous Leiden Plate, a miniature stelalike jadeite belt pendant dated in Long Count at A.D. 320 and probably made in Tikal, on which he carries a U-shaped double-headed serpent ceremonial bar; he wears hip masks, a wide Mayan "sky-band" belt, and an elaborate animal headdress topped with a tassel-capped "jester" head. Linda Schele's careful drawing isolates the regalia of royalty in this densely coded image (Figure 5.2). His looted tomb (Burial 22) is in North Acropolis Structure 5D-26.

Curl Nose and Central Mexican Influences at Tikal

Curl Nose, possibly an immigrant from Teotihuacán or Kaminaljuyú, ruled at Tikal from

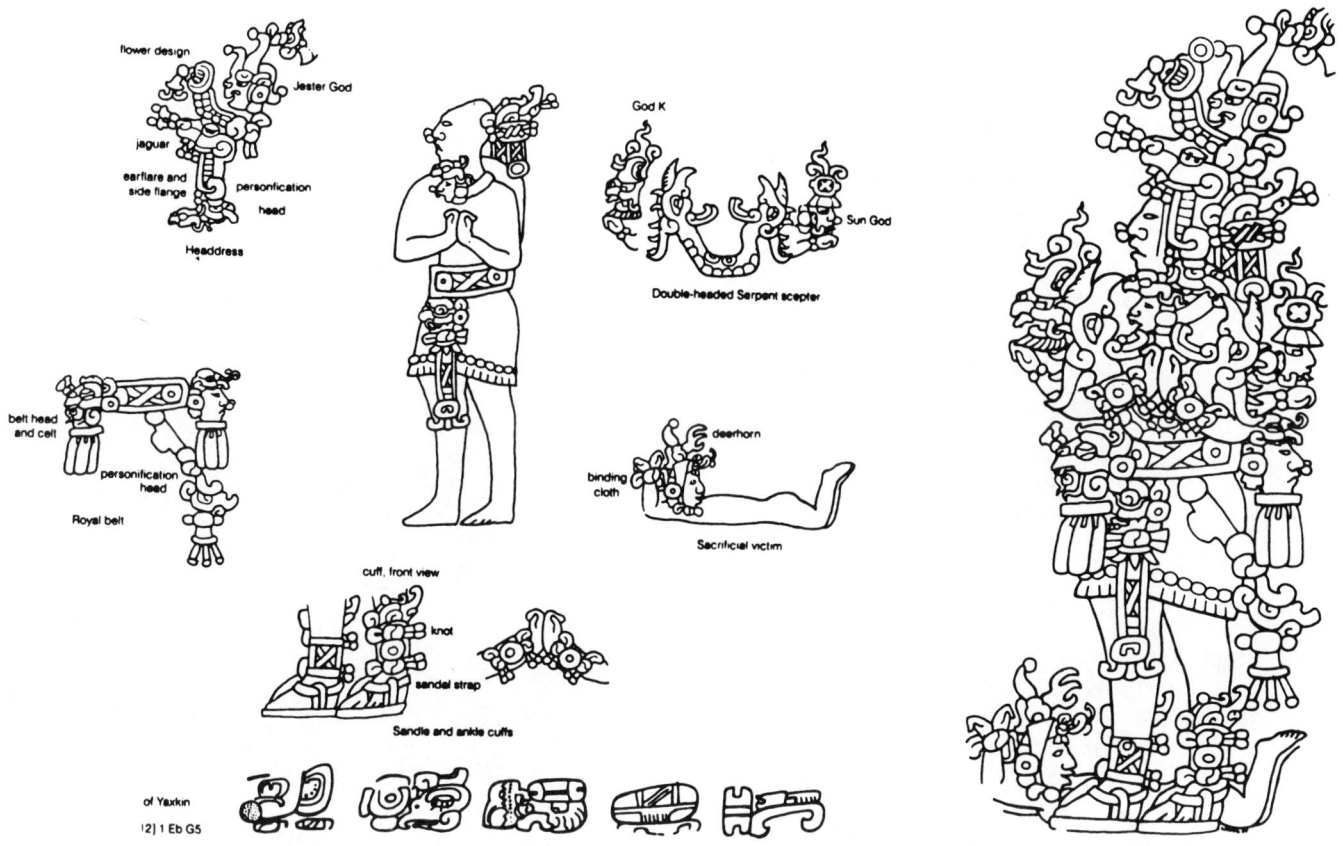

5.2. Breakdown of costume elements and glyphic text (*left*) on the front of the Leiden Plaque (*right*), depicting an Early Classic ruler, Balam Ahau Chaan. (From Schele and Miller 1986, pl. d; drawing courtesy Linda Schele)

A.D. 379 to A.D. 426. He may have married one of Jaguar Paw's daughters and founded a new Sky Dynasty (Coggins 1979), as recorded on Stela 4 (Figure 5.3) where he sits, puffy-faced, on an animal-head throne in a frontal Central Mexican position, wearing a quetzal–feathered–jaguar headdress and shell necklace and crooking a ceremonial bar (?) in his elbows. A long-nosed Chac (rain god) legitimizing his rule as a surrogate ancestor looks down from above.

Coggins feels that Curl Nose introduced important Central Mexican ideas during his 47-year rule, solidifying Teotihuacán trade connections and adding the Teotihuacán rain god Tlaloc to the Maya pantheon. Other researchers (Klein 1990:96) are not so sure, noting that representations of the tasseled headdress and certain Central Mexican costume and military accoutrements appear earlier in the Maya area than at Teotihuacán. That Curl Nose's accession predates the Teotihuacán enclave at Kami-naljuyú calls his putative Kaminaljuyú origins into question and suggests that he may have had a less direct role in sponsoring Central Mexican innovations at this time of reciprocal influences when Maya ideas, conversely, were also reaching Teotihuacán. Whatever the mechanisms of adoption, Tlaloc in Mayanized form gained war and sacrifice connotations and identification with the Mayan water deity Chac (God B) and long-lipped lineage deity God K (Coggins 1983).[1]

Curl Nose and the Introduction of Katun-Completion Stelae (see Appendix). Curl Nose also may have introduced katun-completion stelae at Tikal. During his rule, stelae were erected with abbreviated dates commemorating the ending of 7,200-day katun periods every 19-

[1]See Schele and Freidel 1990 for an important summary of known dynastic sequences and very readable vignettes that imaginatively reconstruct key events in important rulers' lives.

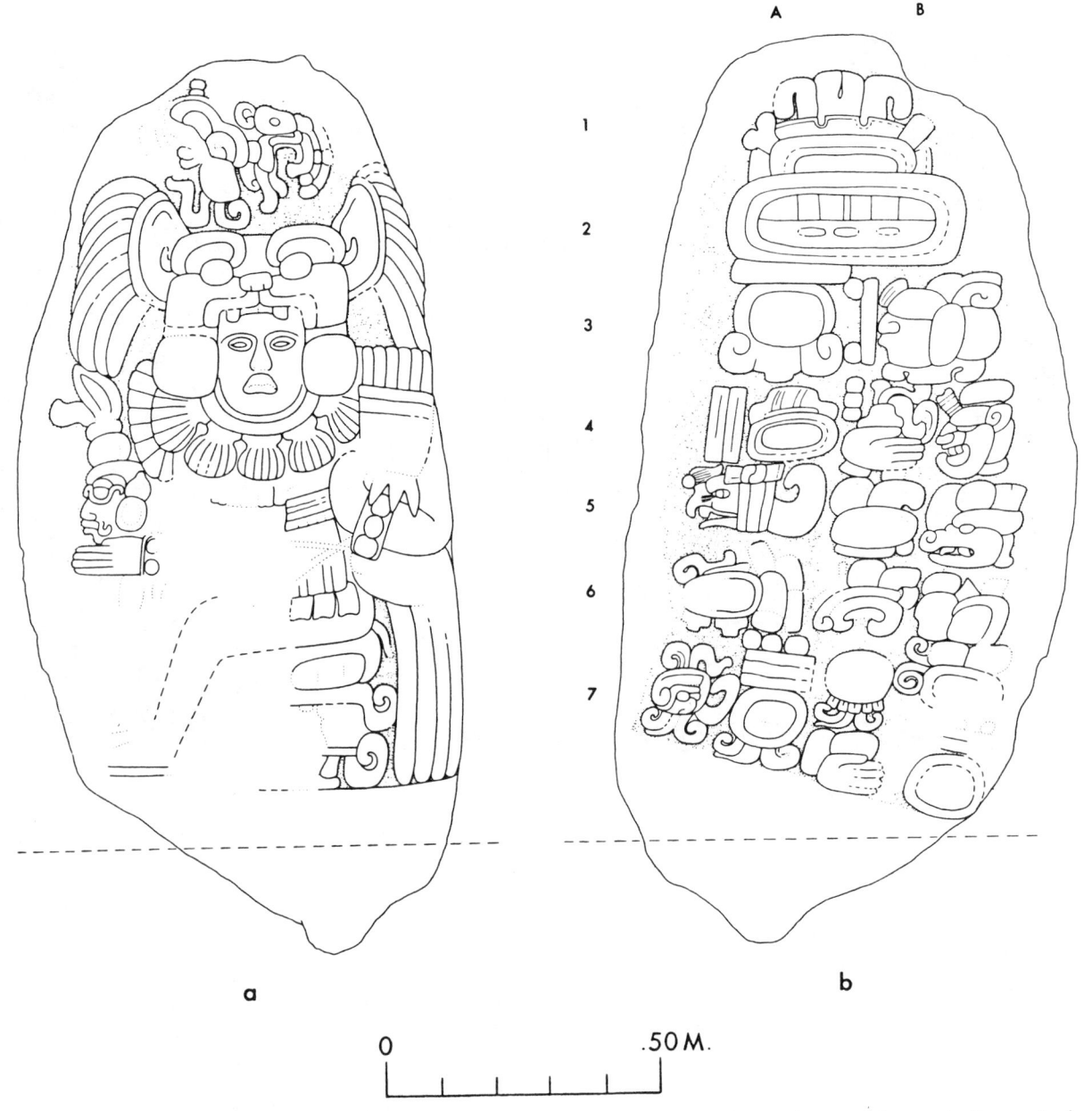

5.3. Stela 4, Tikal, front (*a*) and back (*b*). Accession of Curl Nose in A.D. 379. Numbers and letters indicate glyph positions. (Jones and Satterthwaite 1982, fig. 5; drawing by William Coe, courtesy TP/UPM)

plus years and the ends of even more significant 13-katun cycles totaling 256.25 years (Coggins 1983, 59). Similar recording of katun endings appears even earlier at nearby Uaxactún where katun-completion Stelae 18 and 19 date to A.D. 357, twenty-two years before Curl Nose's accession. Uaxactún's Stela 5 (A.D. 337) shows clear highland influence, suggesting that here, too, katun recording may represent a Central Mexican intrusion.

The presumed outsider's (Curl Nose) reign began just before the end of Baktun 8 and continued into Baktun 9, an omen-ridden transition that also fell on a critical Katun 8 Ahau (see Appendix at the end of this chapter). Coggins thinks that Curl Nose's appearance may represent deliberate Mexican moves into the anxiety-ridden lowlands to establish their presence at Tikal by this important target date. Tikal Stela 18 (A.D. 396) marks the end of the first katun of Curl Nose's long and innovative rule.

When he died in 426, Curl Nose was buried under North Acropolis Structure 5D-34 (Burial 10), accompanied by nine sacrificed individuals, Central Mexican Thin Orange wares, and Teotihuacanoid stucco-painted vessels with Tlaloc and an open-mouthed, facially painted Xipe Totec, the Central Mexican god of rebirth.

Stormy Sky: Prosperity for Tikal

Stormy Sky, succeeding his father Curl Nose in 426, further cemented Teotihuacán–Maya rela-tions. He also established local dynasties in Yaxchilán, Quiriguá, and Copán where Tikal's sculptural style and emblem glyph were adopted until these sites became sixth-century regional centers with their own emblem glyphs (Marcus 1976; Sharer 1985). At Río Azul, glyphs and murals identify Stormy Sky's son's burial in looted Tomb 1. Two associated unlooted tombs "may be those of actual Teotihuacanos" (Henderson 1988, 867).

Stormy Sky's most striking appearance is on Stela 31, perhaps making the first katun comple-tion within his reign (Figure 5.4). With a "cleft-

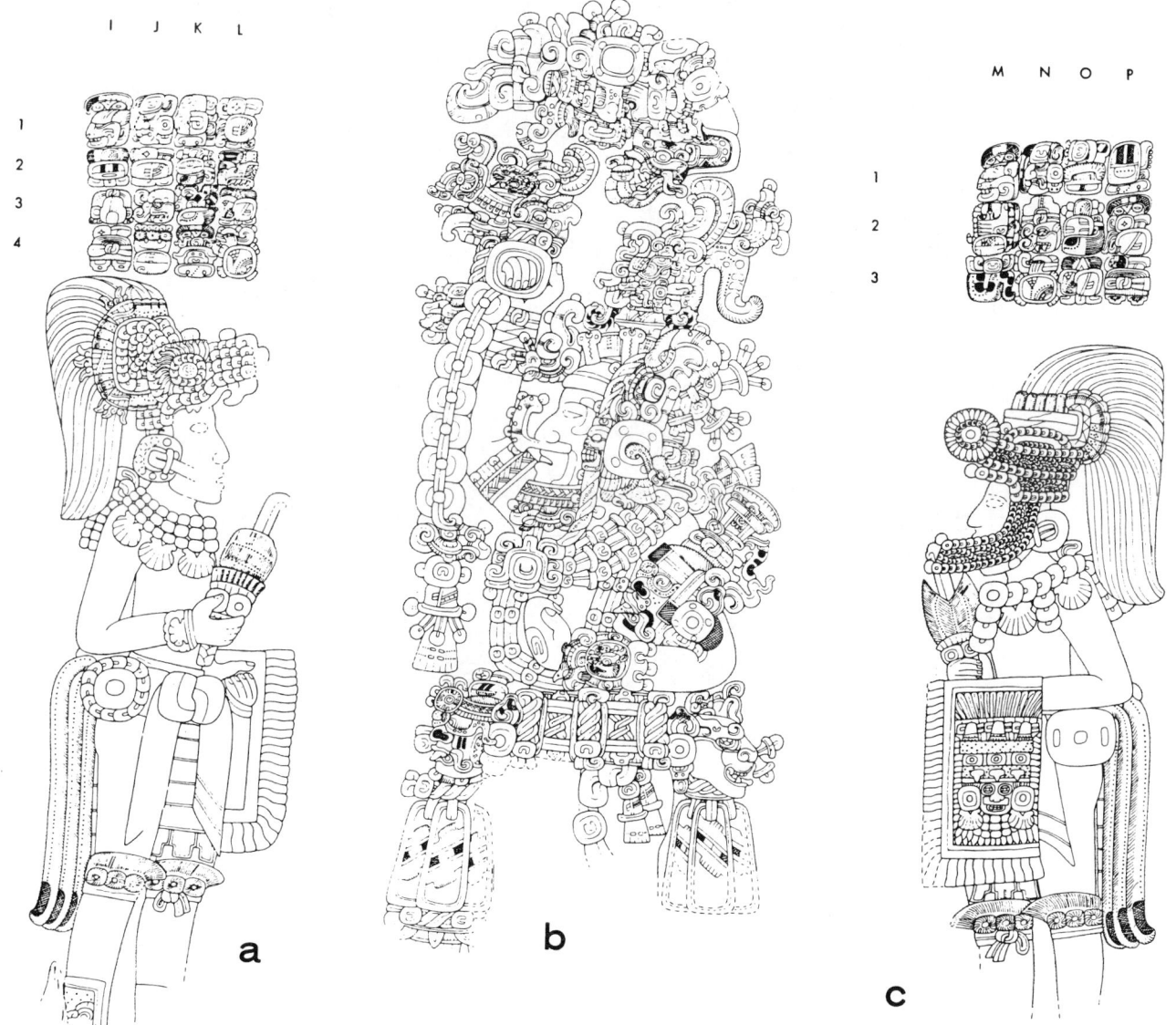

5.4. Stela 31, Tikal, (a, c) sides, (b) front: Stormy Sky between Teotihuacanoid figures, with ancestor face above. Numbers and letters indicate glyph positions. (Jones and Satterthwaite 1982, fig. 51; drawing by William Coe, courtesy TP/UPM)

5.5. Stela 1, Tikal: probably Stormy Sky with a bicephalic serpent-headed ceremonial bar. Feathered panels show a multiple-deity image. (Jones and Satterthwaite 1982, fig. 1; drawing by William Coe, courtesy TP/UPM)

sky" lineage glyph on his headdress, he raises a long-nosed agnathous Chac head and chainlike pendant while cradling a snag-toothed, scroll-eyed, and scroll-lipped Sun–Jaguar with a Tikal-glyph topknot at his left elbow. His costume has both Mayan and Teotihuacán elements. A profile face (of his father, Curl Nose?) with a hand for its jaw (indicating death) attached to a serpent body looks down from above.

On the stela's sides are two figures identified either as Teotihuacán "ambassadors" or as Curl Nose in Teotihuacán-derived garb, with feathered-eye owl headdresses and feathered shields displaying Tlaloc faces. According to Coggins, a water (Cauac) shield glyph above them may signify Teotihuacán, whereas their feathered atlatls denote Tlaloc's lightning-hurling aspect as ancestor of Mayan gods whose forehead smoking was (visual metaphors for lightning bolts) at first symbolized the new Mexicanized dynasty and later became God K on *manikin* rulership scepters (Coggins 1979, 1980).

Stelae 1, 2 (Figure 5.6), and 26 may depict Stormy Sky, ornately clad, between elaborate, feathered, winglike panels carrying a ceremonial bar ending in huge bearded serpents disgorging seated figures.

Stormy Sky presumably died in A.D. 456. His headless, handless body was buried between two sacrificed retainers in a tomb (Burial 48) cut into bedrock under Structure 5D-33-3 in the North Acropolis. This is called the "Painted Tomb" because of its many wall glyphs. A few years later, another shrine (5D-33-2) was erected, and 13 katuns later (in A.D. 713), Lord Ah Cacau, a ruler reviving Tikal's golden past, took Stela 31 into the shrine's rear room for memorial rituals and then carefully buried it in the fill of a new memorial structure—5D-33-1st.

The Middle Classic Hiatus at Tikal. In the years that followed, stelae honor Sky Dynasty rulers including Kan Boar (A.D. 457–488), Jaguar Paw Sky (A.D. 488–537), and Double Bird (A.D. 537–562). Then, between A.D. 538–682, Tikal underwent a temporary decline along with several other lowland sites. During this Middle Classic hiatus, architectural construction and monument erection lagged, and broken stelae appear in building fill. Archaeologists attribute this to the military defeat in 562 of Tikal by the site of Caracol (Chase and Chase 1989, 6–9). Coggins (1975) feels that during the disruption, Tikal's old Jaguar Paw lineage challenged and perhaps shared power with an intrusive Sky Dynasty.[2]

Ah Cacau (Double Comb or Ruler A): Return to Greatness

Ah Cacau's accession in 682 occurred exactly 13 katuns (256 1/4 years) after Stormy Sky's, a particularly auspicious period for a cyclical repetition of past greatness. Lord Ah Cacau ritually welcomed the new Katun 8 Ahau on 9.13.0.0.0 (A.D. 692) and inaugurated a neo-Mexican phase that restored prosperity to Tikal (Schele and Freidel 1990: 195–214). Moving rapidly and decisively, he encouraged marriage alliances with nearby sites, such as the wedding of a Tikal noblewoman, "Woman of Tikal," to a lord from Naranjo, which resulted in the birth of the great Naranjo ruler, Scroll Squirrel (Marcus 1976, 57–60). One translation of Ah Cacau's name as "Producer of Chocolate" may denote resurgent involvement in the Soconusco cacao trade. He also recalled Tikal's past greatness by erecting stelae honoring Stormy Sky and deliberately amplified the latter's Central Mexican commemoration of katun cycle endings.

Katun-Completion Rituals and Twin Pyramid Groups. One of Ah Cacau's innovations was the construction of Twin Pyramid Groups (TPGs: Map 6) to display katun-completion stelae. TPGs consist of two four-staired, radially symmetrical pyramids facing each other across the east and west ends of a plaza, a tall, nine-doored structure (perhaps symbolic of the nine-layered Underworld) at the south end, and a stela–altar pair with caches of incised obsidian pieces and/or human skull and bones within a walled enclosure to the north.

To celebrate the important 9.13.0.0.0 katun transition in A.D. 692, Ah Cacau erected Stela 30 showing himself as katun keeper holding a diagonal two-segment expanded ceremonial bar and "sowing" with his right hand. He also had accompanying Altar 14 built, bearing a huge 8 Ahau ringed by glyphs of the 9.13.0.0.0 date, his name, and the Tikal emblem glyph, inside the north walled enclosure of TPG 3D-1 (Figure 5.6). He was still in office when Katun 14 ended, and he had constructed TPG 5C-1 to display Stela 16, a magnificent frontal portrait of him-

---

[2] The novel *Tikal* (Peters 1983) describes how conflict between the native Jaguar Paw and usurping Sky clan could have weakened Tikal and contributed to the Classic Maya demise.

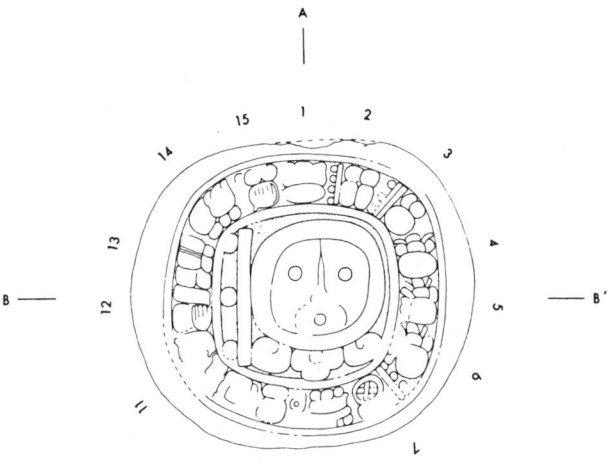

5.6. Altar 14, Tikal, with 8 Ahau glyph: (a) line drawing and (b) photo. Numbers and letters indicate glyph positions. (Jones and Satterthwaite 1982, figs. 50b and 103d; drawing by William Coe; drawing and photo courtesy TP/UPM)

self in a resplendant quetzal-feather back ornament. He daintily holds a slender two-segment expanded ceremonial bar (with jade inlay?), wears a round mosaic bird (?) head pectoral with lateral trident prongs above a bar gorget ornament, and carries a Tlaloc pouch (Figure 5.7). Altar 5 shows caped individuals wearing bloodspotted streamers (?) tending a skull-and-bone pile, possibly Ah Cacau's wife's or mother's.

Mortuary Architecture. Two of Tikal's most imposing structures, Temples I and II, document both Ah Cacau's familial ties and Maya concepts of filial obligation and remembrance of honored ancestors. These two regal structures face each other across the Great Plaza (Map 6). They are symbolically linked by a stela row on the plaza's north side, much as husband–wife pairs sit facing each other in painted pre-columbian genealogical manuscripts from South Mexico. Appropriately, archaeologists identify Temple I as a posthumous memorial to Ah Cacau probably built by his son and Temple II as a memorial to Lady 12 Macaw, Ah Cacau's wife.

Temple I (the Temple of the Giant Jaguar, named after its Lintel 3) contains Ah Cacau's valuted tomb (Burial 116). Its grandiose construction, magnificently carved wooden lintels, and sumptuous grave goods confirm Tikal's returning prosperity. Included with Ah Cacau's poorly preserved bones are exquisite objects of pottery and jade and thirty-seven intricately incised bone tubes. Several (Figure 5.8) depict Ah Cacau and a lizard, monkey, parrot, and furry mammal in a long canoe paddled by a Stingray Spine god (with fish attributes and a stingray spine through his nose) and an Old Jaguar god (together called the Paddlers or Floaters, perhaps representing ancestors), moving through wave scrolls, bubbles, and wave stacks or descending into the watery Underworld with its wide-eyed passengers.

Exterior architectural detail further memorializes the royal couple. Temple I's roof comb was adorned with a sculpture of Ah Cacau on his throne. Temple II (the Temple of the Masks) portrays Lady 12 Macaw on its Lintel 2 in an elaborately figured cape (Figure 5.9. Temple I's zapote-wood door Lintels 2 and 3 record Ah Cacau's inauguration date and show him seated under a towering jade-scaled feathered serpent and a magnificent jaguar (Figures 5.10, 5.11). In spite of these magnificent posthumous memorials in art, Ah Cacau's exact death date is unknown.

Yax Kin Caan Chac (Ruler B)

Yax Kin succeeded Ah Cacau in A.D. 734, three years after the close of Katun 15 (9.15.0.0.0). Ah Cacau may have been too frail to perform the appropriate katun ceremonies: TPG 4D-1 has only plain Stela 55 and uncarved Altar 47 in its enclosure. Yax Kin's inaugural Stela 21, dated

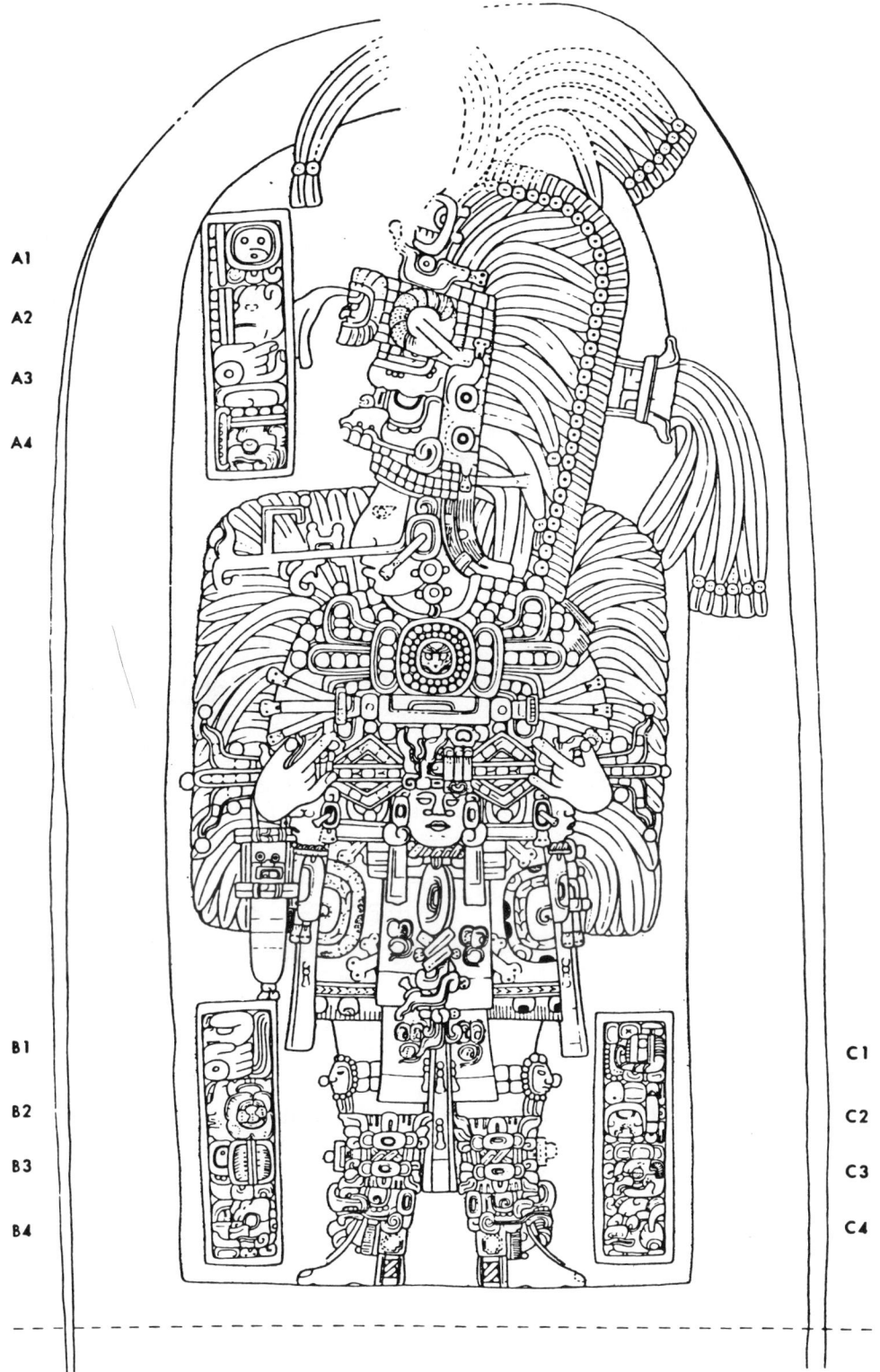

A1
A2
A3
A4

B1
B2
B3
B4

C1
C2
C3
C4

5.7. Stela 16, Tikal: Ah Cacau with ceremonial bar and Tlaloc pouch. Numbers and letters indicate glyph positions. (Jones and Satterthwaite 1982, fig. 22; drawing by William Coe, courtesy TP/UPM)

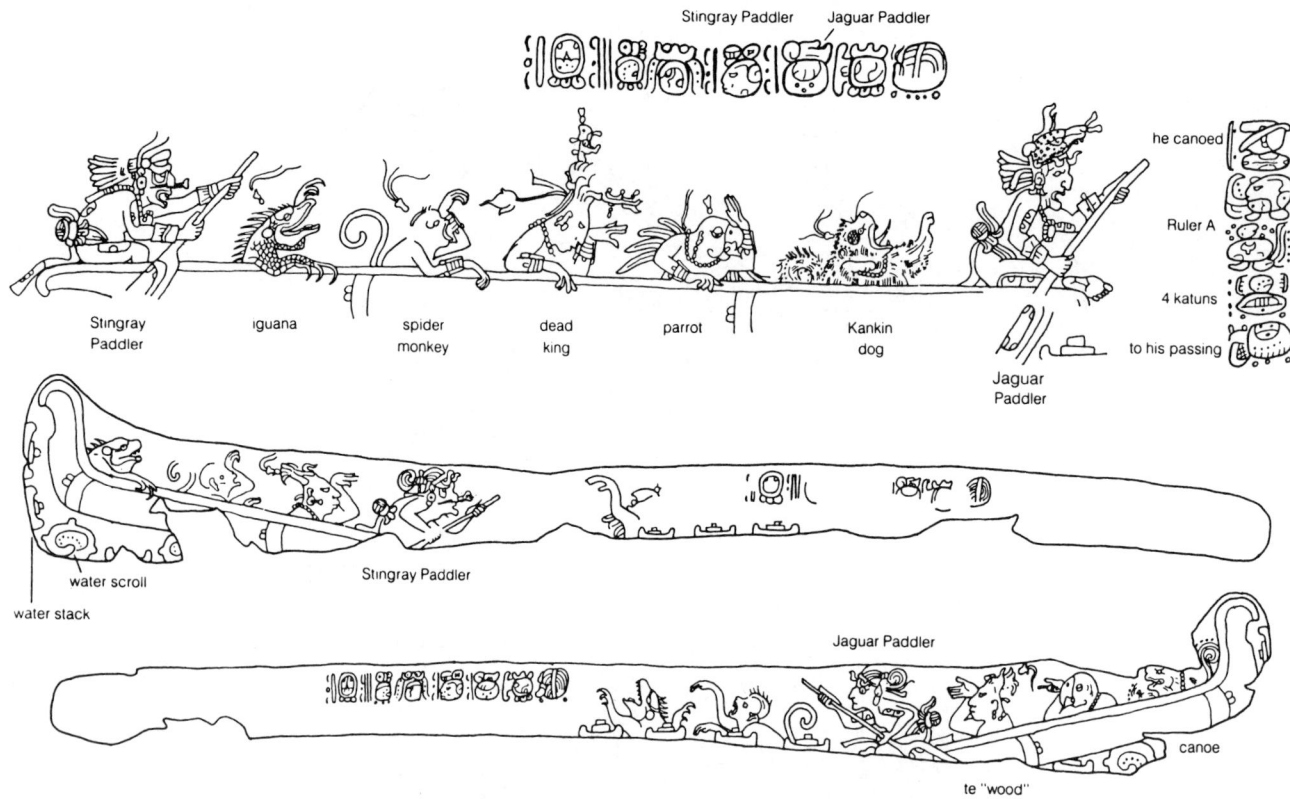

Stingray Paddler   Jaguar Paddler

Stingray
Paddler   iguana   spider
monkey   dead
king   parrot   Kankin
dog

Jaguar
Paddler

he canoed

Ruler A

4 katuns

to his passing

water scroll   Stingray Paddler

water stack

Jaguar Paddler

canoe

te "wood"

5.8. Incised bones, from Tikal Burial 116, showing a sinking canoe bearing a dead ruler, animals, and the Paddler Twins, entering Xibalbá, the Maya underworld. (Schele and Miller 1986, p. 270, fig. VII.1; drawing courtesy of Linda Schele)

9.15.5.0.0, stands before Tikal's largest pyramid, Temple VI (Temple of the Inscriptions) built toward the end of his reign. Its long glyphic roofcomb facade records a Baktun 5.0.0.0.0 (1139 B.C.!) Olmec-period date (a remembered ancestry?) and other dates referring to Tikal's early settlement, dynastic beginnings, unknown Early Classic events, and possibly Yax Kin's death. On Inaugural Stela 12, he performs the katun-end ceremony of sowing seed, incense, or drops of blood (Love 1987; Stuart 1988) corroborated by a "hand-scattering" glyph (first identified by Stuart 1988) in the text. Accompanying Altar 9 shows a prone prisoner who is bound. On subsequent Stela 5, Ruler B again holds a fringed pouch and (reconstructed) manikin scepter beside a prone, bound prisoner. In 751, Yax Kin commemorated the end of Katun 9.16.0.0.0, 2 Ahau 13 Tzec, by building TPG 3D-2 for Stela 20 (Figure 5.12) and Altar 8. He faces left, wearing an arm shield and holding a three-celt war staff and fringed purse; behind him is an ornately spotted and clawed, scarfed jaguar throne.

Altar 8 again exhibits a prone, bound captive, perhaps for tun-completion sacrifice (Coggins 1983, 47).

Details of Yax Kin's life are unknown to us, but carved Lintels 2 and 3 from his tall memorial Temple IV (Map 6) portray him in regal splendor. He may also have adorned Temple IV's roof comb where remains of large ear spools were once part of the great mask. On Lintel 2, he sits, childlike, with heels not reaching the ground, on a mat-hassock throne with an arm shield and (reconstructed) manikin scepter, protected by a huge human figure with outstretched arms (Figure 5.13); on Lintel 3 he appears frontally with arm shield and spear on a high-backed throne draped by an enormous bearded serpent disgorging a deity, surmounted by a moan bird with outstretched wings (Figure 5.14). His tomb should be under Temple IV (still unexcavated) but may in fact be Burial 196 from low platform 5D-73 near the Great Plaza. An incised bone dates it to 9.16.3.0.0 (A.D. 766), 2 years before the next ruler's inauguration, and a jade-mosaic

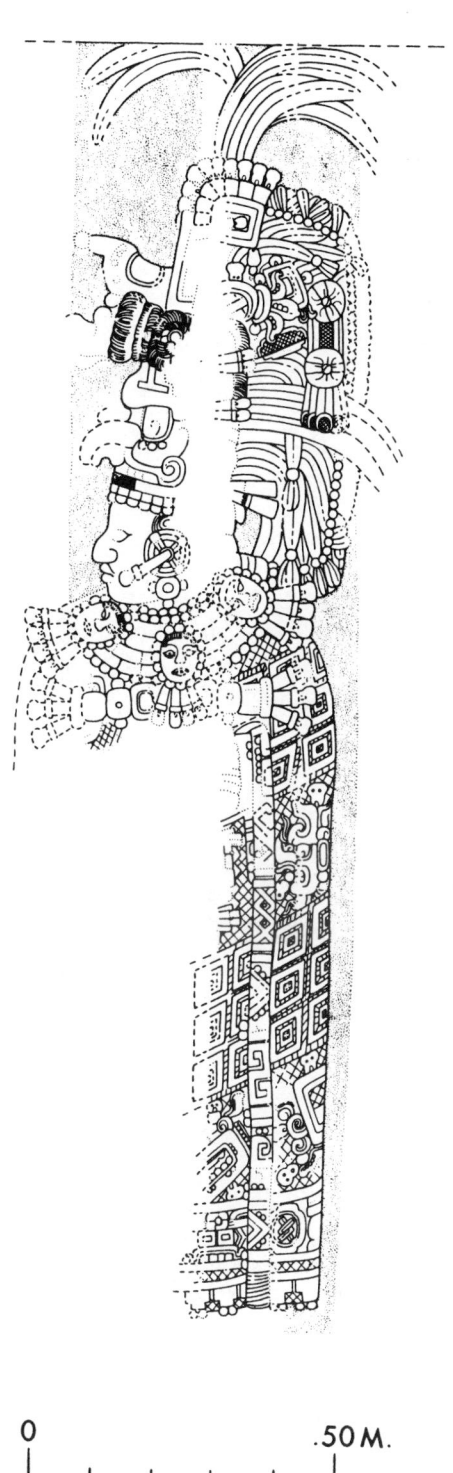

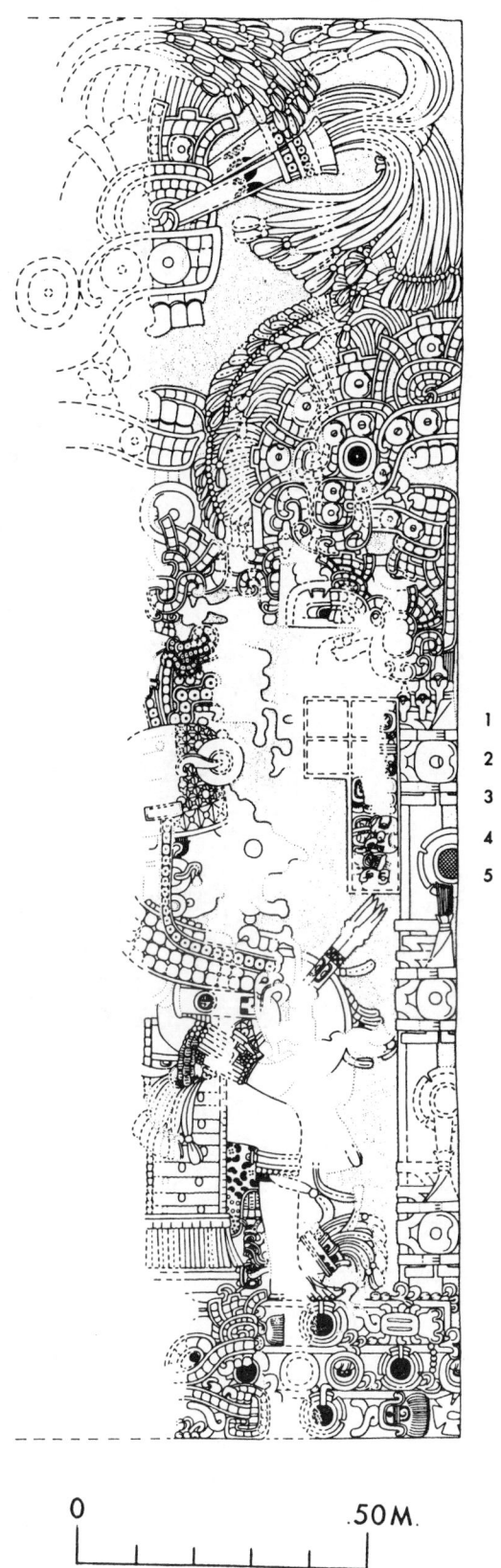

A   B

1
2
3
4
5

0   .50 M.

0   .50 M.

5.9. Temple II, Lintel 2, Tikal: probably 12 Macaw, wife of
Ah Cacau. (Jones and Satterthwaite 1982, fig. 71; drawing
by William Coe, courtesy TP/UPM)

5.10. Temple I, Lintel 2: Ah Cacau beneath a serpent pro-
tector. Numbers and letters indicate glyph positions.
(Jones and Satterthwaite 1982, fig. 69; drawing by William
Coe, courtesy TP/UPM)

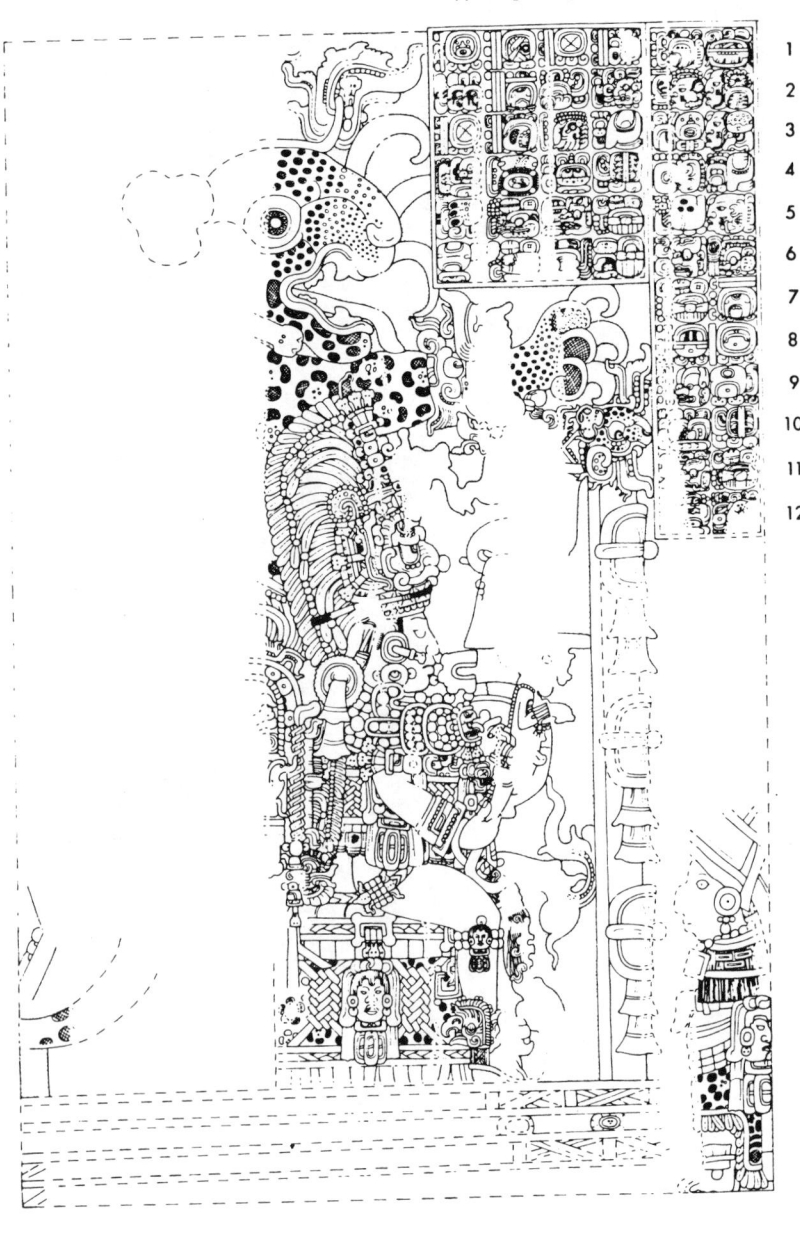

A B C D E F

1 2 3 4 5 6 7 8 9 10 11 12

0 .50 M.

5.11. Temple I, Lintel 3: Ah Cacau beneath a jaguar protector. Numbers and letters indicate glyph positions. (Jones and Satterthwaite 1982, fig. 70; drawing by William Coe, courtesy TP/UPM)

vessel with portrait lid parallels one found in Yax Kin's father's (Ah Cacau) tomb.

Chitam (Ruler C)

Chitam, Yax Kin's son, succeeded him in 768 after an interval during which Katun 16 ended and an unidentified twenty-eighth ruler reigned. Three years later, he raised the katun-end cele-

bration to new heights by building Tikal's largest TPG, 4E-4. Its enclosure displays the beautifully preserved Stela 22 on which he holds an expanded ceremonial bar while scattering, for 9.17.0.0.0 katun-end rites recorded along with his accession date (Figure 5.15).

Lord Chitam ruled through Katun 18 (A.D. 790) when he again conducted katun-end rites as shown on Stela 19 in TPG 4E-3, Tikal's sec-

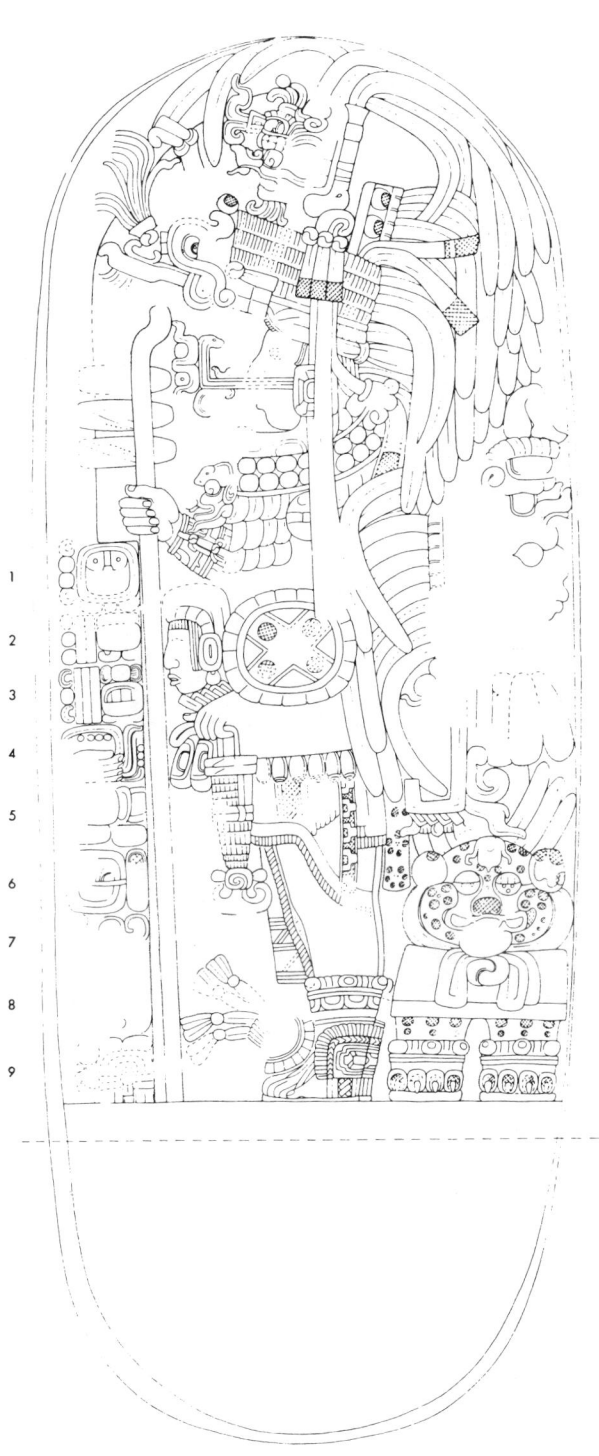

5.12. Stela 20, Tikal: Yax Kin (Ruler B) on jaguar throne. Numbers indicate glyph positions. (Jones and Satterthwaite 1982, fig. 29; drawing by William Coe, courtesy TP/UPM)

ond largest TPG (Map 6), built for what must have been spectacular ceremonies. On both stelae, he is watched by celestial ancestors in tentacular jeweled coils (Stuart 1984, 10). His fringed pouch may have contained seeds, copal for incense (Love 1987), or grain for divining prophesies of the incoming katun. The "hand-scattering" glyph, also found at Copán, Quiriguá, and Naranjo, ends the accompanying texts.

Lord Chitam's tomb may lie under Temple III (Map 6) where Lintel 2 (Figure 5.16) portrays a turkey-thighed potbellied ruler in jaguar costume and headpiece in front of a mat-hassock throne with an "eccentric" obsidian trident matching that of two sparsely clad attendants with eroded name glyphs on either side.

With Chitam's death, successions become obscure as Tikal's fortunes dwindled. TPG construction and stela erection ceased as Tikal suffered increasing competition from Putún coastal traders. Dennis Puleston (1979, 64–70) thinks the Maya anticipated collapse ordained by the katuns and created a self-fulfilling prophecy. An unknown Tikal ruler with skull-mask back ornament and expanded ceremonial bar valiantly celebrated Katun 10.2.0.0.0 (A.D. 869) on Stela 11, but Tikal was now a dying city. Nearby Jimbal's Stela 2, dated A.D. 889, is the last katun-marking stela in the Tikal area.

Copán

Copán is an important site whose pivotal influence is documented by its stelae and monuments. Located in Honduras at the southeastern periphery of the Maya lowlands (Map 5), it was well established by A.D. 564 with its own emblem glyph and ruling dynasty. Excavations in the 1930s and 1940s by the Carnegie Institution of Washington and the Peabody Museum at Harvard explored its central acropolis in the Principal or Main Group area, including an East and West plaza, associated ball court, and a tall platform-mound (Structure 26) with a Hieroglyphic Stairway of sixty-two steps bearing over 1,800 sculpted glyphs that comprise the longest known pre-columbian text. Reconstruction of the Main Group continued between 1975–1980 under the direction of Gordon Willey and Claude Baudez. Subsequent excavations have explored Copán's residential areas of Las Sepulturas, northeast of the Main Group, and El Bosque, west of the Main Group, in an effort to es-

5.13. Temple IV, Lintel 2: Yax Kin backed by a giant human protector. Numbers and letters indicate glyph positions. (Jones and Satterthwaite 1982, fig. 73; drawing by William Coe, courtesy TP/UPM)

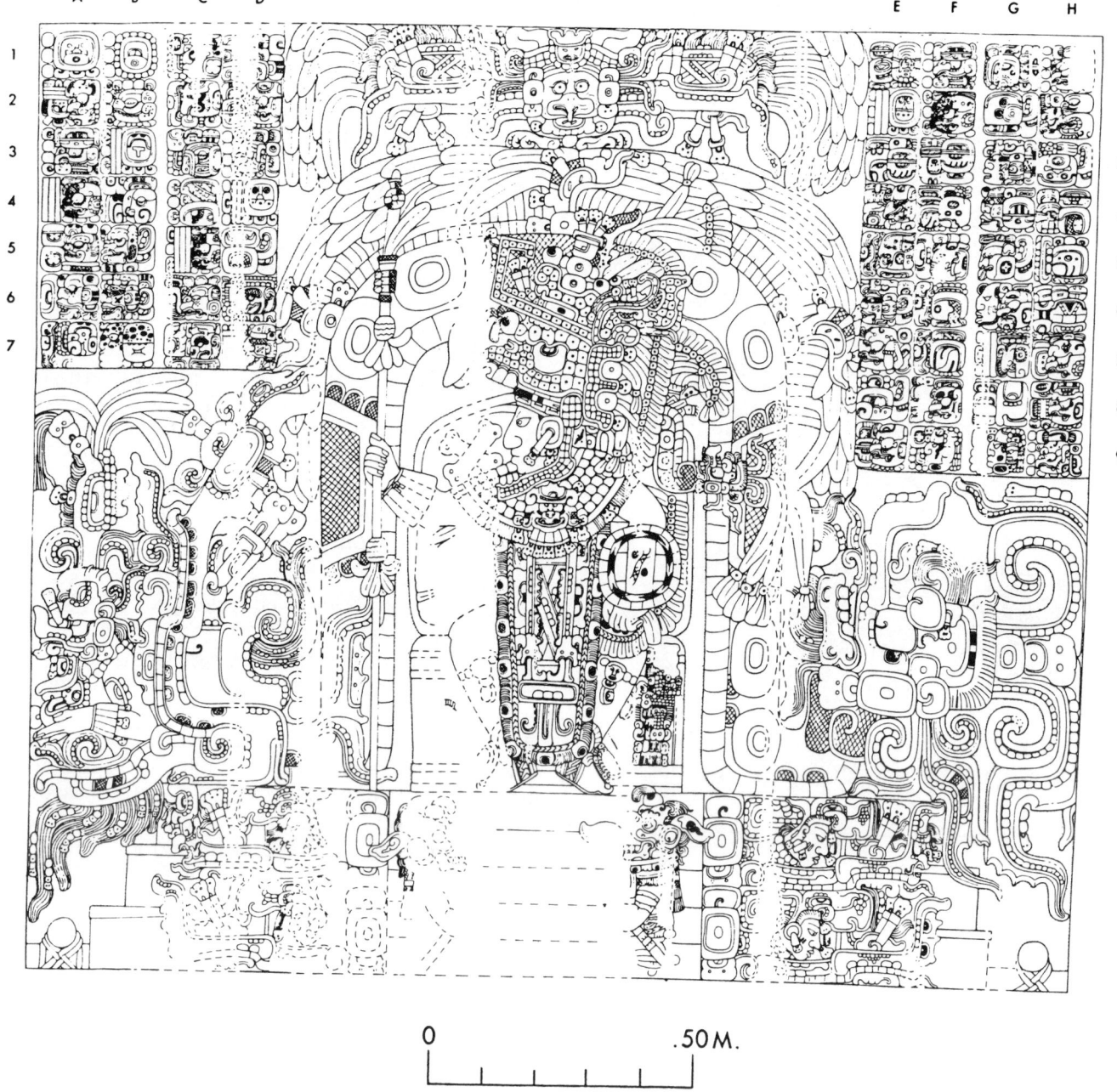

5.14. Temple IV, Lintel 3: enthroned Yax Kin atop a tiered pyramid under an arching feathered serpent. Numbers and letters indicate glyph positions. (Jones and Satterthwaite 1982, fig. 74; drawing by William Coe, courtesy TP/UPM)

tablish the range and nature of nonceremonial architecture.

The Copán Succession

Through the translation of glyphic texts from stelae, altars, and the Hieroglyphic Stairway, we can now trace the succession of Copán's sixteen known rulers (Fash and Fash 1990; Schele and Freidel 1990:306–345). Dynastic rule was established in the early fifth century by Yax K'uk Mo', revered in later texts as the founding royal ancestor. The accession of the twelfth ruler, Smoke Imix (Smoke Jaguar), in A.D. 628, saw major architectural expansion and competition with the nearby site of Quiriguá. Unfortunately,

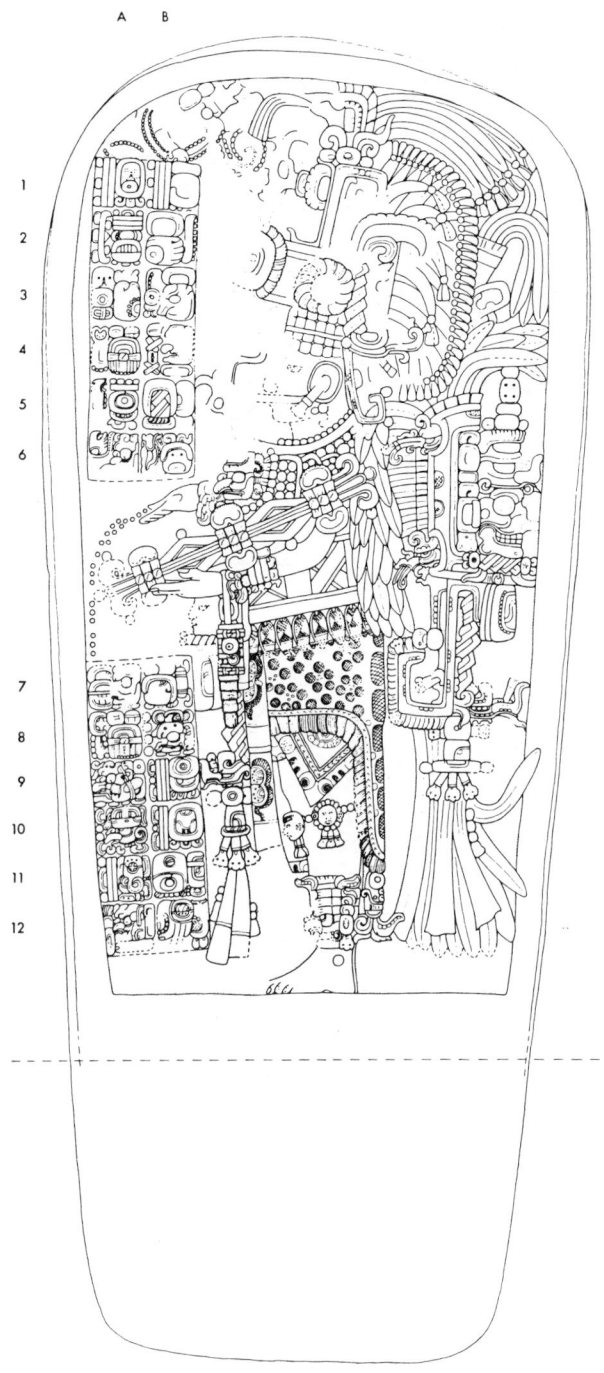

5.15. Stela 22, Tikal: in profile, Chitam (Ruler C) in the "scattering" pose. Numbers and letters indicate glyph positions. (Jones and Satterthwaite 1982, fig. 33; drawing by William Coe, courtesy TP/UPM)

his successor, 18 Rabbit, was captured and decapitated after a successful raid by Quiriguá's fourteenth ruler, the renowned Cauac Sky, sending Copán into temporary political decline, with a 20-year gap in inscriptions.

Copan's next ruler, Smoke Monkey, sought consensus and recovery by governing in conjunction with a council of *holpops*, nobles of local wards who are depicted on the only building erected during his brief rule (Fash and Fash 1990, 32). Smoke Monkey was followed by Smoke Shell, who constructed the Hieroglyphic Stairway touting the exploits of past rulers in order to reestablish dynastic legitimacy after 18 Rabbit's humiliating defeat. The sixteenth ruler, Yax Pac (Rising Sun), who ruled from A.D. 762 to A.D. 800, continued to extol past rulers as mighty warriors on stelae and altars, even though the accompanying architecture was of such poor quality that Copán's power during his reign was likely far less than artistic imagery would suggest (Schele and Freidel 1990:320–343). The dynasty ended shortly thereafter, but occupation by elite groups continued into the Early Postclassic until at least A.D. 1100, with evidence of ongoing construction.

Scribes and Rulers

The role of scribes in creating the images and texts so important in reconstructing Copán's past has been clarified by the excavation of the main building in the elite residential Sepulturas area, called the House of the Bacabs (four world bearers) or Pauahtuns (monkey scribes associated with God N; see glossary) and described by Webster (1989). The structure, which dates to the long eighth-century reign of Yax Pac (Rising Sun), has sculptures of seated *pauahtun* scribes with a stylus in one hand and a paint pot in the other on its facades and was probably a residence for scribes or a monument to the head of a scribal lineage, his ancestors, and his patron god. A scribal bench in its central room seems to commemorate *bacabs*, ancestral scribes from the lineage, and a bicephalic monster representing earth.

The high prestige and probable noble status of scribes is reflected in the manner of their interment at Copán. A scribal burial dating to about A.D. 450 at the House of the Bacabs, perhaps that of the lineage founder, contained a codex, whereas the lavish grave goods accompanying a scribe burial discovered in 1989 under the Hieroglyphic Stairway included codex sections and paint pots containing red coloring (Fash and Fash 1990, 30). The latter individual may have been a son of the ruler, Smoke Imix.

A B   E   F   C D

0   .50 M.

5.16. Temple III, Lintel 2: a pot-bellied Chitam (?) between trident-bearing attendants. Numbers and letters indicate glyph positions. (Jones and Satterthwaite 1982, fig. 72; drawing by William Coe, courtesy TP/UPM)

Thus we are identifying not only dynastic rulers but historical artists through their signatures and actual physical remains and are beginning to understand more fully their elite kinship ties and their roles in reinforcing a rigidly hierarchical society.

Caracol

Caracol, 76 kms (47.2 miles) southeast of Tikal in Belize, is another large lowland site, with a core population density that exceeds Tikal's and has multiple causeways radiating outward to peripheral settlement areas. At its height during the Middle Classic period, it, too, was involved in warfare with adjacent sites (Chase and Chase 1987, 1989). Although its dynastic sequence is still incompletely known, inscriptions on a ball-court altar found in 1985 tell that, after prior skirmishes, Caracol's Lord Water vanquished Tikal's ruler Double Bird in A.D. 562. This defeat, coupled with the malaise created by Teotihuacán's earlier withdrawal from her Kaminaljuyú–Tikal trade connections, finally explains the severe Middle Classic hiatus disruption and desecration of monuments at Tikal.

In A.D. 631, Lord Water's son, Kan II, waged another successful war against the site of Naranjo. As a result of these campaigns, Caracol's fortunes ascended between A.D. 562–652. After a brief eighth-century decline, perhaps reflecting counterraids, Caracol rebounded with additional conquests using the effective Central Mexican atlatl, or spear thrower. Representations document increasing warfare, sacrificial rites, and *tzompantlis*, racks to display trophy skulls, reinforcing the broader archaeological evidence for Late Classic site-specific and inter-site expansion and decline.

W̲E are uncertain where the pan-Mesoamerican interdigitating 260-day religious and 365-day solar/agricultural calendars began. Middle Preclassic Oaxaca and Late Preclassic Veracruz with their early calendric glyphs are possibilities. By 36 B.C., the first Maya Long Count stela (see below) appears at Chiapa de Corzo in Chiapas. Pacific coast stelae at El Baul (Stela 1) and Abaj Takalik (Stela 2) are only slightly later. By the Early Classic period, the combination of Calendar Round and Long Count dates was rapidly adopted in the Maya lowlands for commemorating major historical events.

THE CALENDAR ROUND

The Maya used two concurrent, cyclical calendar systems to mark the passage of time. The first, a 260-day sacred calendar (the *tzolkin*), consisted of 13 months formed by combining numbers from 1 to 13 with a repeating sequence of 20 different day names and was used for divination and the scheduling of religious ceremonies. The second was a 360-day solar calendar (the *haab*), used for determining agricultural cycles and crop planting. The haab consisted of 18 named months, each containing 20 days preceeded by a number from 0 to 19, plus a year's end period of 5 unlucky days bridging the beginning of the next haab reckoning.

The two calendars coincided every 18,980 days, marking the end of a major 52-year time cycle called the Calendar Round. Calendar Round dates record a day's position in both the tzolkin and the haab, that is, 13 Ahau, 18 Cumku. Days, months, and numbers were associated with patron gods who controlled them and affected their good and bad fortunes, thus auguries of good or difficult times could be made for recurring time cycles.

THE LONG COUNT

The Long Count represented a supplementary, linear method of fixing a date by recording the elapsed time between it and a mythical baseline date of 3114 B.C. This elapsed time segment was broken down into its total number of kins (days), uinals (20-day "months"), tuns (18 uinals, or a "short" haab year of 360 days), katuns (20 tuns, equaling 7,200 days or 19.71 of our

APPENDIX TO CHAPTER 5

THE MAYAN CALENDAR

365-day years), and baktuns (20 katuns, equaling 144,000 days or 394.25 years).

Long Count dates were recorded on stelae with an oversized introductory glyph followed by the glyphs for baktuns, katuns, tuns, uinals, and kins. Each time unit glyph was preceded by a number from 0 to 19 in bar-and-dot notation, with a bar representing 5, dots representing units of 1, and a shelllike symbol representing 0. A Long Count date, for example, might read 9 baktuns, 17 katuns, 0 tuns, 0 uinals, and 0 kins (shortened in texts to 9.17.0.0.0). The Long Count date was clarified by designating the day's position in the ritual and solar calendars, that is, 9.17.0.0.0 13 Ahau 18 Cumku.

KATUN-COMPLETION DATES AND THE SHORT COUNT

By the Late Classic, katun-completion stelae at Tikal and other sites replaced Long Count dates with an abbreviated three-glyph version consisting of the katun number (the second number in a Long Count date such as 9.17.0.0.0) followed by the designation of the day ending the katun in the religious and solar calendars, that is, Katun 17 13 Ahau 18 Cumku. An even shorter method was the Short Count designation used in the Postclassic "count of the katuns" (u kahlay katunob), whereby a katun was designated only by its completion day (in the preceding example, Katun 13 Ahau). Katuns always ended on an Ahau day numbered from 1 to 13 because 13 katuns or 256.25 years later the same-numbered katun again recurred.

ASSOCIATED PROGNOSTICATIONS, RITUALS, AND ARCHITECTURE

Clemency Coggins (1983, 52–53) sees additional implications behind Maya katun recording. She notes that the lowland Maya associated completed katuns with prophecies concerning those to come. Rulers are shown on stelae ritually commemorating katun endings by "sowing" small pelletlike objects that have been interpreted as seeds, copal incense, or drops of autosacrificial blood. During the Late Classic, these stelae were erected within special architectural complexes called Twin Pyramid Groups (see the section, Katun-Completion Rituals and Twin Pyramid Groups).

Note: An invaluable computer alternative to manually converting Maya Calendar Round and Long Count dates into Gregorian or Julian dates and vice versa is the program BARSDOTS, prepared by former math teacher Sid Hollander. Among other helpful data, it calculates astronomical positions, associated Maya patron deities, and equivalent Aztec dates and also counts forward or backward from a given date. To obtain a diskette, or for further information, contact Sid Hollander, 30 N. E. 186 Terrace, Miami, FL 33179.

IN Chapter 5, we have seen how dynastic rule developed during the Early Classic period at major lowland sites. We now also know much more about the accession rites by which identifiable, named rulers assumed power and the meaning behind the iconographic symbols that they deliberately and publicly displayed to assert their divine right to rule. Some of these symbols are derived from Maya mythology, key elements of which appear as striking scenes on polychrome painted pottery. We turn now to studies that examine this rich corpus of visual referents and their connection with important rituals and beliefs.

DYNASTIC RITUALS AND ICONOGRAPHY

Our understanding of the rituals of accession and paraphernalia of rulership has been particularly enhanced through study of art at the sites of Bonampak and Palenque.

Bonampak

Bonampak is a small jewel of a site set in the Chiapas jungles of Mexico a scant 26 kms (14 miles) south of the larger site of Yaxchilán, with which it had close relations (Map 5). It consists of a series of block masonry temples set on a terraced hillside south of its main plaza, plus additional unexplored structures. Its last Late Classic ruler was Chaan-Muan, who appears alone or with his mother and his wife (in garments bordered with Central Mexican Tlaloc masks and year signs) on three stelae dated between A.D. 700 and 800, performing autosacrifice or dominating a kneeling, bound captive (Mathews 1980).

The Bonampak Murals

Bonampak is world famous for its narrative murals on the walls and ceiling vaults of three contiguous temples set on the verdant hillside. The murals were first reported to the outside world in 1946 by Giles Healy, a photographer filming Lacandón Indians of the area, and created an immediate sensation. Painted in over a dozen colors on a wet lime ground, the murals showed complex group scenes and documented hitherto unknown details of Maya warfare, sacrifice,

CHAPTER 6

MAYA ART

RITUALS OF ACCESSION AND VALIDATION, AND ICONOGRAPHY OF "CODEX-STYLE" CERAMICS

6.1. A copy of a Bonampak mural, by Agustín Villagra, showing musicians. (Courtesy INAH)

costume, and ceremony covering a 2-year sequence and involving over 200 individuals.

The murals were left uncompleted when Bonampak was abandoned, perhaps after an unsuccessful battle following the one depicted.

The succession of events in the murals, interpreted by Karl Ruppert, J. Eric S. Thompson, and Tatiana Proskouriakoff (1955) and most recently and thoroughly by Mary Ellen Miller (1986b), is as follows:

Room 1. In Room 1, a child is presented to the ruler Chaan-Muan, two of his wives, and fourteen lords as the heir-apparent. Elsewhere, lesser nobles (*cahals*) dress and confer, possibly as war leaders (*batabs*) discussing battle plans or preparations for performance in a later celebration announced by a parade of parasol-carrying attendants and musicians with upright drums, rattles, and deer-antler–tortoise-shell clappers who accompany dancers dressed as fantastic clawed, tentacled water creatures (Figure 6.1).

Room 2. In a panoramic, three-wall battle scene, jaguar-skin-clad Bonampak warriors led by Chaan-Muan and aided by the planet Venus in ascent triumph over enemy Maya armed with lances and shields. A second, "judgment" scene takes place on a platform stairway, where a jaguar-skin-garbed Chaan-Muan, his white-robed wife with outspread fan, and assorted cahals survey disheveled naked captives who, as

potential sacrifice victims, raise their hands, fingernails dripping blood, in supplication. A decapitated trophy head rests nearby on a bed of leaves (Figure 6.2).

Room 3. Room 3 shows lords in enormous hoodlike headdresses and stiff waist panels

6.2. Bonampak murals: "judgment scene." (After Agustín Villagra; courtesy INAH)

posed on pyramid steps with an axe-wielding executioner as war trumpets celebrate the victory. In another scene, royal family members engage in ritual bloodletting, piercing their tongues with thorns or stingray spines proffered by a portly slave.

Interpretations

These vivid scenes collectively provide key information about the ceremonies preceding the accession to lowland Classic rulership. The young child carried by women in two different scenes is interpreted as the prince–regent, presented to the court as ruler–designate. The accompanying text confirms that his public presentation, the ritual celebrating his designation almost a year later, and the battle to secure captives for sacrifice were all timed to coincide with key movements of the planet Venus as an ally (Miller 1986b, 150). Ceremonies in his honor included ritual bloodletting by both captives and relatives and war prisoner sacrifice.

Linda Schele (Schele 1984, 12–14, 29, 42–43) and Mary Ellen Miller (Schele and Miller 1986) cite evidence for similar activities honoring young prince–regents of about 5 years of age at other major sites. What Schele calls the "na event" (named after its initial glyph in inscriptions) is also documented at Piedras Negras, Palenque, and Naranjo. Na-event bloodletting by the wife of an incumbent ruler when his predecessor died also induced visions summoning ancestors to impart their wisdom during his coming reign. Late Classic pre-accession rites also included ritual circuits to a series of sacred caves in order to contact gods and ancestors. Karen Bassie-Sweet (1991) has identified texts and iconography on stelae and relief sculpture that commemorate pre-accession and period-ending rituals held at sacred caves to reconfirm links with the supernatural world. It is likely that these ceremonies survive in the contemporary highland Maya ritual circuits made by cargo holders to sacred caves and mountain shrines.

Besides visually documenting pre-accession rituals in progress, the Bonampak murals also provide striking witness to Late Classic lowland political disruption. Miller (1986b, 151) believes that Bonampak succumbed to Late Classic competition between sites and that the infant in the murals never lived to become ruler. The murals are an invaluable historical documentary of these unsettled times.

At the Classic lowland site of Palenque, coordinated interdisciplinary research has identified another royal lineage and increased our understanding of additional rites and paraphernalia of royal accession and death.

Palenque

Palenque began as a small sixth-century site in the tropical Chiapas highlands of East Mexico (Map 5). Its largest structure (Map 7) is the Palace Complex, an aggregate of rooms around patios containing a four-story tower and interior stucco reliefs of Maya lords. Southwest of the palace, the Temple of the Inscriptions, named for its interior hieroglyphic panels, tops a 65-foot (19.8 meter) truncated pyramid. A southeastern complex contains the Temple of the Sun, the Temple of the Cross, and the Temple of the Foliated Cross. There are other minor structures at the site.

In 1952, Mexican archaeologist Alberto Ruz Lhuillier, working in the Temple of the Inscriptions, uncovered an 80-foot rubble-filled stairway with thirteen corbel vaults leading to a 30-foot-long (9.1 meter) crypt with a solid-stone sarcophagus containing the remains of a male burial (Figure 6.1).

The discovery confirmed that some Mesoamerican pyramids contained royal tombs and provided a huge corpus of exciting new iconographic material. The tomb walls were lined with stucco-relief figures. The sarcophagus

6.3. Palenque, Temple of the Inscriptions: cross-section view showing Pacal's crypt. (Sodi Morales 1976, p. 35; courtesy EMM)

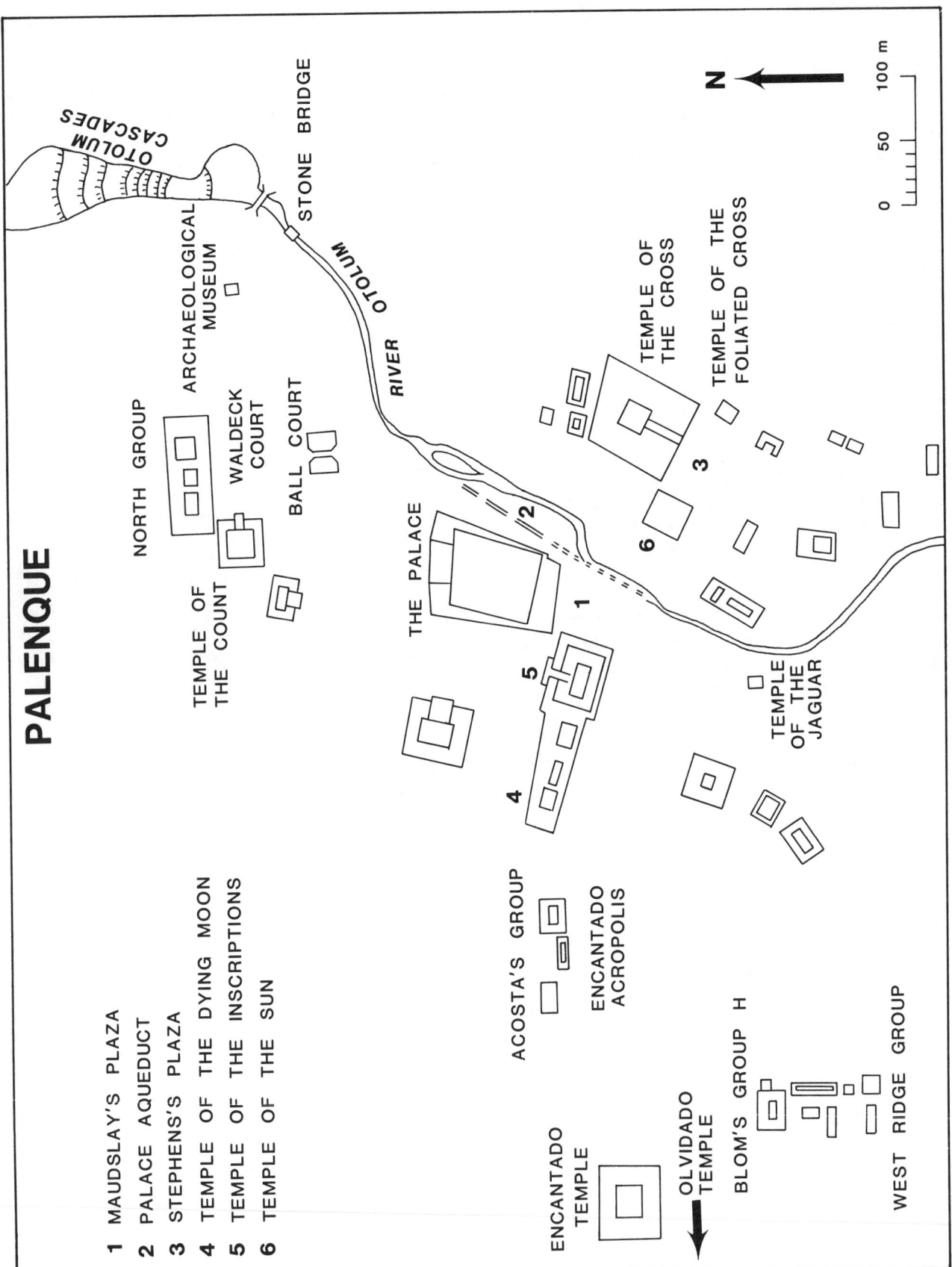

PALENQUE

1 MAUDSLAY'S PLAZA
2 PALACE AQUEDUCT
3 STEPHENS'S PLAZA
4 TEMPLE OF THE DYING MOON
5 TEMPLE OF THE INSCRIPTIONS
6 TEMPLE OF THE SUN

N

0   50   100 m

OTOLUM CASCADES

STONE BRIDGE

RIVER OTOLUM

NORTH GROUP

ARCHAEOLOGICAL MUSEUM

TEMPLE OF THE COUNT

WALDECK COURT

BALL COURT

THE PALACE

TEMPLE OF THE CROSS

TEMPLE OF THE FOLIATED CROSS

TEMPLE OF THE JAGUAR

ACOSTA'S GROUP

ENCANTADO ACROPOLIS

ENCANTADO TEMPLE

OLVIDADO TEMPLE

BLOM'S GROUP H

WEST RIDGE GROUP

Map 7. Palenque: important structures and architectural features

6.4. Pacal's sarcophagus lid, Temple of the Inscriptions, Palenque. (Drawing courtesy Merle Greene Robertson)

bears multiple carved figures, and the lid shows the complex image of an individual lying at the base of a cruciform plant (Figure 6.4).

Within the sarcophagus lay a male with jade objects in his hands and mouth, jade ear spools, necklaces, and rings, jade sun-god figures at his sides, and a jade-mosaic facial mask that had crumbled from its wooden backing. (This mask was one of the priceless pieces stolen from Mexico's National Museum of Anthropology during Christmas 1985 and recovered in 1989.) A hollow psychoduct passageway connects the sarcophagus with one of the overlying temple's pier sculptures of his mother and provides a

"breath-of-life" channel by which the dead ruler could communicate with his descendants.

Art: Techniques and Style

An ongoing series of Palenque Round Table volumes (M. G. Robertson 1974a, b, 1979, 1980, 1990; Robertson and Benson 1985) by scholars who convene periodically at the site has helped interpret Palencano art. The following pages present some of their important contributions.

In her own series on Palencano art (M. G. Robertson 1983, 1985a, b), one of its most devoted scholars, Merle Greene Robertson, describes the close collaboration between sculptors and architects. Wall and roof-comb figures were modeled in stucco on a flat stone armature ("bones"). Stucco detail was then added, first underclothing, then outer clothing, ornaments, and headgear, as if dressing a gigantic doll. The results were painted in symbolic colors: red for people and objects of the human world, blue for divine beings and objects, and yellow for jaguars and possible Underworld beings and objects, with death indicated by cross-hatching.

Iconography

Iconographic studies have been immeasurably assisted by glyphic decipherments in the decades following the previously mentioned sarcophagus discovery.

Heinrich Berlin (1958) for years insisted that Maya glyphs recorded specific historical events. In 1960, Tatiana Proskouriakoff, observing that inscriptions at Piedras Negras stela clusters covered a normal human life span, proposed glyph readings for birth (an "up-ended frog" glyph), accession (a "toothache" glyph) and death (Figure 6.5). Texts at other sites were re-examined; today the name glyphs of important rulers from Piedras Negras, Yaxchilán (Figure 6.6), Copán, Tikal, Palenque, and other sites have been identified. In 1958, Berlin deciphered "Emblem Glyphs" referring to Copán, Tikal, and Palenque, and other researchers rapidly supplemented the list (Figure 6.7). Additional elements of Maya grammar, phonetic values, and glyph translations (the Quadripartite Badge for rulership, bloodletting, ball playing, cacao, and many social and kinship positions) have since been proposed by Linda Schele, Victoria Bricker, Floyd Lounsbury, David Stuart, Peter

6.6. Jaguar names from Yaxchilán and their glyphs. (Marcus 1976, fig. 4.16; drawing courtesy Joyce Marcus and DO)

Shield-Jaguar

Shield-Jaguar

Bird-Jaguar

Bird-Jaguar

Lord Jaguar

Knotted-Eye Jaguar

Bird-Jaguar

Bat-Jaguar

6.5. Mayan event glyphs: (a) "up-ended frog," indicating birth; (b) "toothache" variants, indicating accession; (c) two versions of the "seating" glyph; (d) marriage; (e) capture; (f) death; (g) "hand grasping fish," indicating death of a noble, and the blood-letting glyph. (Marcus 1976, fig. 1.2; drawing courtesy Joyce Marcus and DO)

Mathews, Yuri Knorosov, Nicolai Grube, Barbara MacLeod, and other dedicated scholars.

Glyphic texts identify the ruler in Palenque's sarcophagus as Lord Shield (phonetically, in Maya, Pacal), who died in A.D. 683 after a long, prosperous reign. He was succeeded by his first son, Chan Bahlum (Snake Jaguar), who ruled until A.D. 701, after which his second son, Kan Xul, ruled for another 18 years. Women were also monarchs: among them Pacal's mother, Lady Zac Kuk (White Quetzal) and before her, Lady Kan Ik. At this writing, the birth, accession, death dates, titles, and personal names of Palenque's rulers from A.D. 387 to 799 are known, with the exception of a 30-year gap (Schele 1986, 111–112). Inscriptions also identify their bilateral descent, spouses, and divine mythical ancestors.

The identity of a facing tall-and-short, Mutt-and-Jeff pair on carved stone tablets in the Temple of the Cross (henceforth abbreviated

Calakmul (?)   Motul de San José (?)   Toniná

Copán   Quiriguá   Seibal

Tikal   Tikal   Naranjo

Palenque   Palenque   Palenque

Yaxchilán   Yaxchilán   Piedras Negras

6.7. Emblem glyphs of important Maya sites. (Marcus 1976, fig. 1.7; drawing courtesy Joyce Marcus and DO)

TC) (Figure 6.8, 6.9a, 6.9b) the Temple of the Foliated Cross (TFC) (Figure 6.10), and the Temple of the Sun (TS) (Figure 6.11) had long eluded researchers. Linda Schele (1974, 1976) proposes that the small figure is Lord Pacal shown posthumously as a deified ancestor transferring rulership regalia to the large figure, his son Chan Bahlum who succeeded him 132 days after his death.

Merle Greene Robertson and Linda Schele identify consistent physical abnormalities within the Palencano ruling dynasty. Pacal's ancestor, Pacal I, has the same right clubfoot shown by Pacal on the sarcophagus lid (Figure

6.4) and on Palace House D (Robertson, Scandizzo, and Scandizzo 1976). Chan Bahlum had six fingers on one hand and six toes on one foot; Pacal's second son may also have had a left clubfoot, possibly resulting from royal inbreeding (Robertson 1979b).

Robertson further notes that shortly before Pacal died, small hand-held manikin scepters of serpent-footed God K (Figure 6.12), perhaps denoting the user's spirit co-essence or *way* (Houston and Stuart 1989) began to replace the serpent-ended ceremonial bar carried by rulers; simultaneously, the infant Chan Bahlum is represented on four TI piers above Pacal's tomb as a human baby with God K's serpent leg, a six-toed human foot, and a God K forehead flare on the now missing head (Figure 6.13). Pacal, on his sarcophagus lid, also sports a forehead flare (Figure 6.4), clearly a God K attribute.

What can we in the twentieth century learn from this information? To Robertson, Pacal comes across as an astute politician and image builder. With death approaching, he built the Temple of the Inscriptions crypt for his burial and deified his lineage in TI texts as descendants of the Palenque Triad gods. Through the deliberate use of images identifying Pacal's and Chan Bahlum's foot deformities with God K's serpent foot and manikin scepter to transfer royal accession, Palenque's rulers consolidated their political hold by dramatically reproclaiming themselves as living gods directly descended from the serpent deities of Mesoamerica's distant past.

The Sarcophagus Lid from the Temple of the Inscriptions (see Figure 6.4). The white-limestone sarcophagus lid is probably Palenque's most reproduced image. It has even been interpreted as a "space traveler" strapped behind a "central oxygen machine" adjusting "control knobs" (Figure 6.14).

According to the generally accepted interpretation proposed by Linda Schele (1976; Schele and Miller, 1986, 282–285), the lid depicts a highly transcendental scene. A supine Lord Pacal rests on an image of the Underworld Sun, formed by two facing skeletal heads with scrolled eyes wearing large, square, jade earplugs with inverted Ahau (sun) face pendants. Both sink into a gaping skeletalized Earth Monster jaw with large canines and four slatlike center teeth extending to the corners and up the sides of the lid. On its bowl-like headdress, en-

6.8. Palenque, Temple of the Cross, center tablet. (Schele 1976; courtesy Linda Schele and RLSS)

closing an X-shaped kin/sun sign, are the four elements of the Quadripartite Badge of Rulership: (1) a shell (at Pacal's feet), (2) a stingray spine for autosacrificial bloodletting, at his rump, (3) a half-cartouche enclosing a glyph: usually a crossed band but in this case a per-centage-shaped *cimi*/death sign, and (4) (far right) a triple-leafed plant symbolizing fertility and growth.

Schele believes that this critical instant of transformation finds Pacal suspended between earth and heaven, with the upper portions of the crosslike ceiba tree/world axis that links the two rising behind him. In the bright, pre-cious upper world, the tree's arms and top end in jeweled serpent heads, their upcurled lips lined with tubular and round jade beads. A feathered-serpent-wing bird, perhaps the divine

6.9a. Palenque, Temple of the Cross, west jamb: Chan Bahlum as invested ruler with royal scepter. (Schele 1976, fig. 6; courtesy Linda Schele and RLSS)

6.9b. Palenque, Temple of the Cross, east jamb: God L (Jaguar Lord of the Underworld). (Schele 1976, fig. 6; courtesy Linda Schele and RLSS)

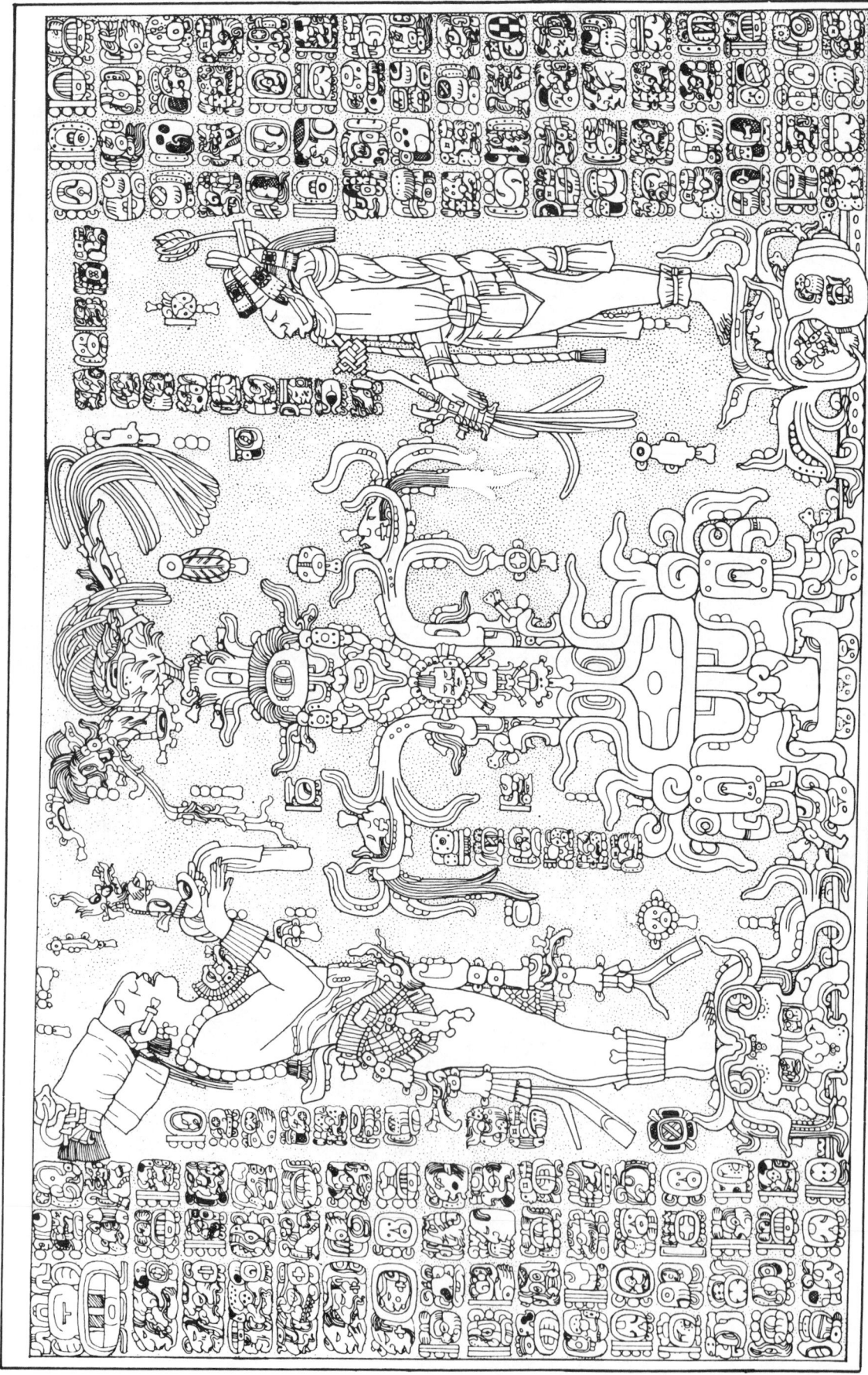

6.10. Palenque, Temple of the Foliated Cross, central tablet. (Schele 1976, fig. 10; courtesy Linda Schele and RLSS)

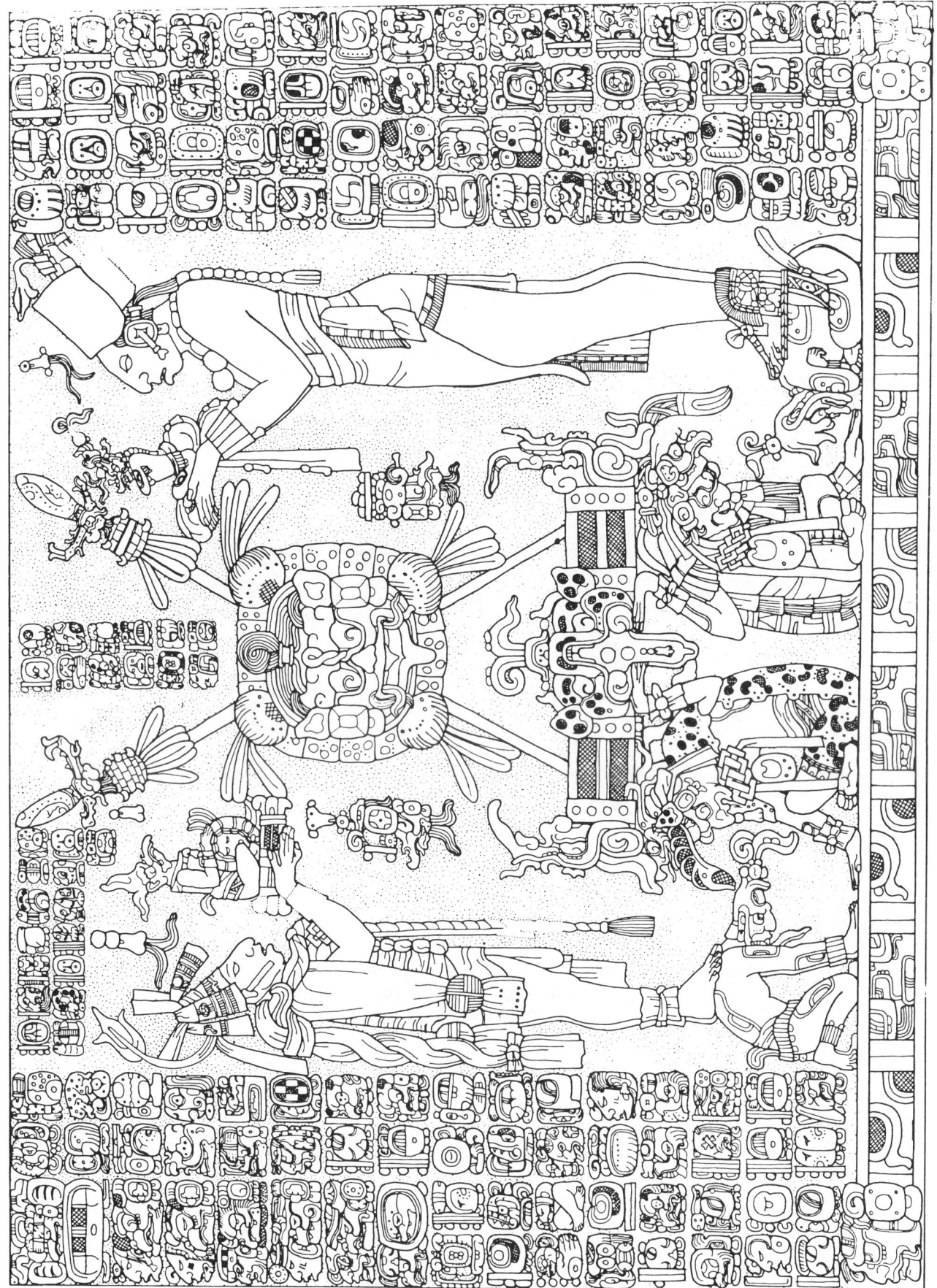

6.11. Palenque, Temple of the Sun, center tablet (Schele 1976, fig. 12; courtesy Linda Schele and RLSS)

6.12. Palenque: God K, the Flare God, from (a) Temple of the Inscriptions; (b) sarcophagus lid; (c) Temple 14; (d) Temple of the Sun; (e) a tablet at Dumbarton Oaks; (f) Palace, House A, pier b; and (g) Palace, north substructure, tier 3. (Schele 1974, 51, fig. 11; courtesy Linda Schele and RLSS)

Vucub Caquix who was slain by the legendary Hero Twins, perches on top with a twisted-mat mouth pendant, surveying the scene.

Draped around the tree's branches is a jade-ringed, flexible ceremonial bar ending in open-mouthed bearded serpent heads disgorging two important Palencano deities. The left serpent head displays the image of God K, the "Flare god" of royal lineages with his smoking forehead torch. God K is also carried as a manikin scepter with one of his legs, shown as an elongated snake, as its handle (Figure 6.12e). The right serpent head disgorges the long-nosed Jester god, wearing his diagnostic curved, peaked "stocking cap" tipped with a tassel-like bone tip. The Jester God is also carried in manikin

form as a rulership symbol (Figure 6.15). The background area of the sarcophagus lid is filled by numerous freeform shells, jeweled Ahau masquettes, jade–bone elements, and joined triple jade beads (the number 3?). A sky band of sun and night glyphs frames the sides, with profile head blocks at the top and bottom.

According to Schele's interpretation, the lid, with its solar, death and Under Upperworld symbolism, shows Pacal's transformation into God K, whose forehead flare bursts from his own forehead (Schele and Freidel 1990:225–234). Like the setting sun, he enters the Underworld to be reborn and renewed. With its complex multivalent iconography, this scene represents one of the strongest visual statements of

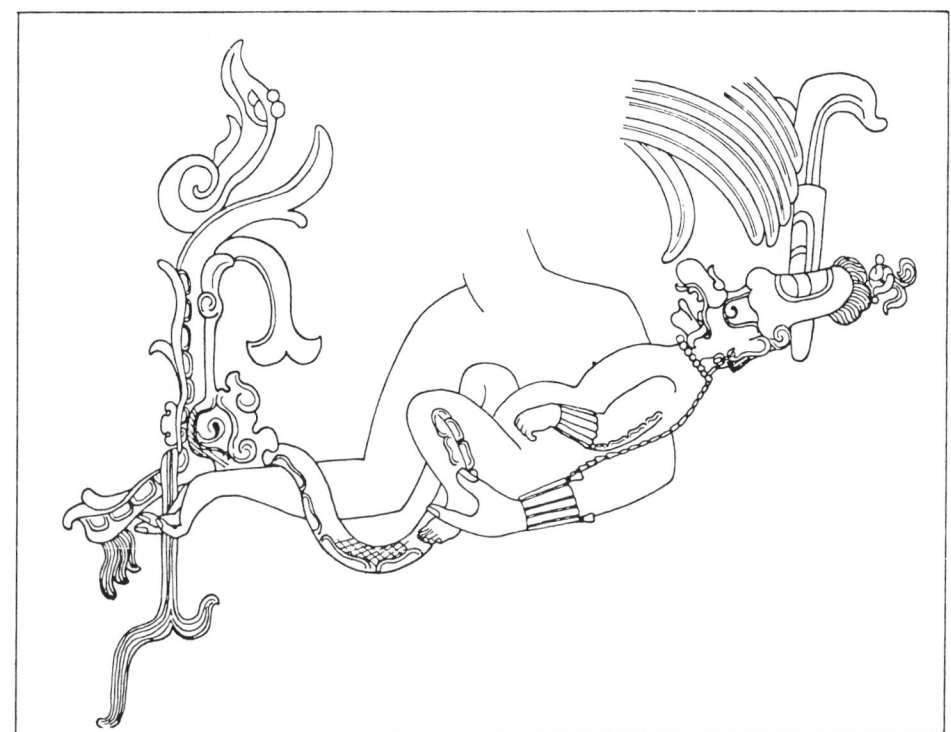

6.13. Palenque: Chan Bahlum as an infant in arms with six toes and the serpent foot and flare headpiece of God K. (Composite drawing from piers b, c, d, and e, from Robertson 1979, 131, fig. 8; courtesy Merle Greene Robertson and RLSS)

a   b

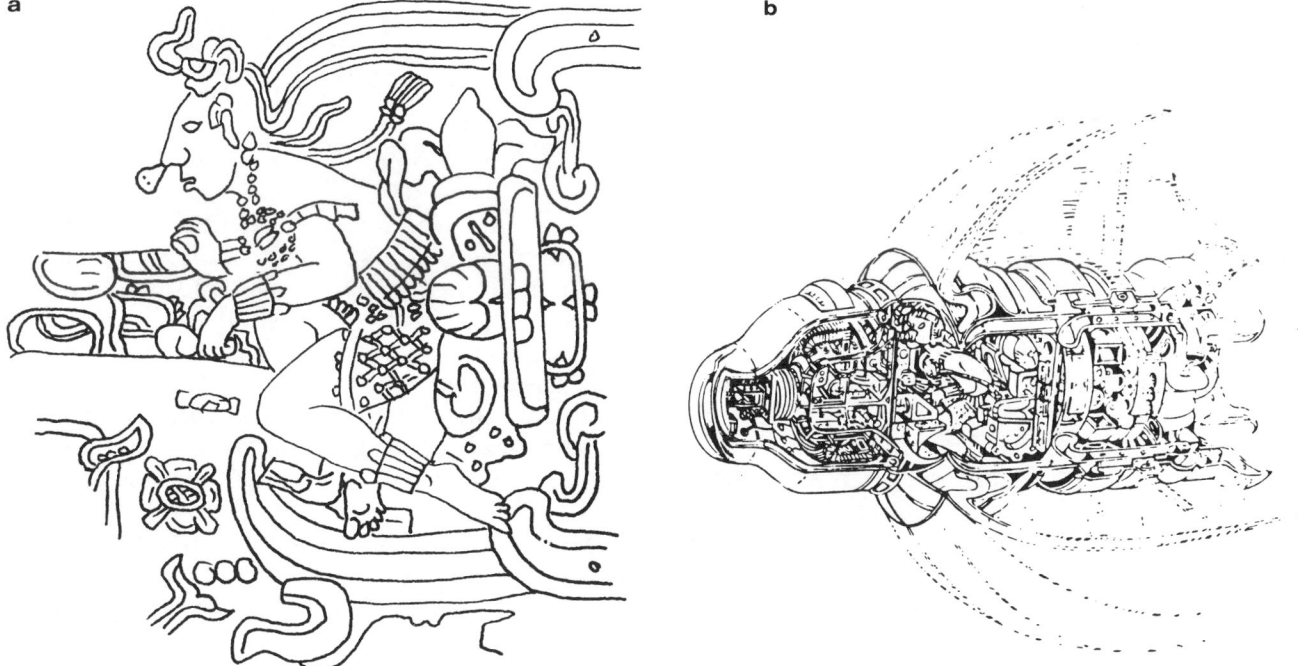

6.14. (a) Pacal's sarcophagus image rotated 90 degrees (cf. Fig. 6.4) to match (b) a spaceship astronaut's position in a nose cone. Von Daniken writes: "The observer of the Palenque relief will be struck by the fact that the 'Indian on the Sacrificial Altar' is dressed in a very modern way. Just below his chin is a kind of roll-neck pullover. The tightly fitting upper part of his suit ends at the wrists in turned back cuffs. He wears a broad belt with a safety fastening round his waist, trousers with a wide mesh pattern and tight socklike garments down to the ankles—the perfect outfit for an astronaut! In my view, the apparatus in which the space traveller crouches so tensely, presents the following technical characteristics. The central oxygen machine lies in front of the strapped-in astronaut, as do the energy supply and communications system, not to mention the manual controls and equipment for observations outside the spacecraft. In the bow of the ship, i.e. ahead of the central unit, large magnets are recognisable. Presumably their purpose was to create a magnetic field around the ship's hull that would prevent it from being struck by particles when travelling at high speeds in outer space. Behind the astronaut we can see a nuclear fusion unit. Two atomic nuclei, probably hydrogen and helium, which finally merge, are schematically depicted. I find it important the rocket exhaust is shown in stylised form at the end of the spaceship *outside* the frame." (von Daniken 1974, figs. 99, 99a; courtesy Econ-Verlag GMBH, Duesseldorf)

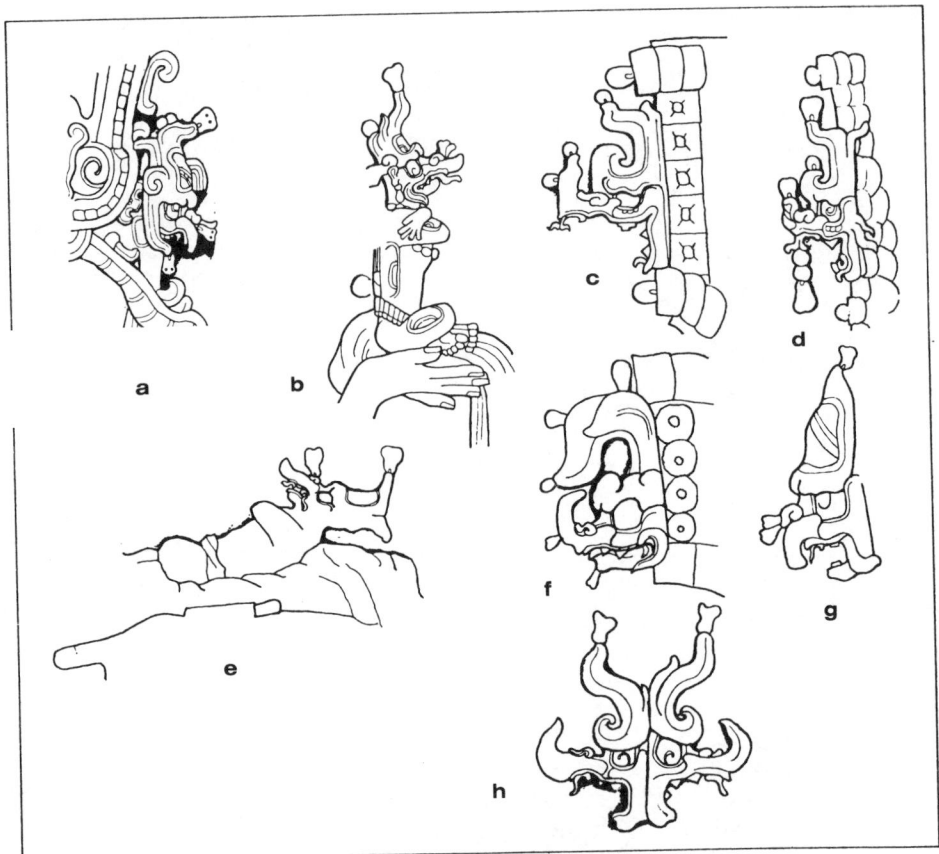

6.15. Palenque: the Jester God, from (a) sarcophagus lid, Temple of the Inscriptions; (b) Temple of the Foliated Cross; (c) Palace tablet; (d) Tablet of the Slaves; (e) Temple of the Cross; (f) Oval Palace Tablet; (g) east side, sarcophagus, Temple of Inscriptions; (h) Palace, House A, pier c. (Schele 1974, 50, fig. 10; courtesy Linda Schele and RLSS)

death and apotheosis known from pre-columbian times.

The Temple of the Cross Tablet and Jambs (see Figures 6.8, 6.9a,b). Glyphs at the Temple of the Cross record the birth and parentage of Palenque Triad God I. The temple is also dedicated to the Feathered Serpent god of the north, Venus, and the ancestral dead. Its central tablet (Figure 6.8) appropriately represents oppositions of life and death and validation of rulership through divine descent (Schele 1974; Cohodas 1976; Schele and Freidel 1990:242).

Here, too, the setting is a trilevel cosmos, with the Underworld represented by a front-view/double-profile subterranean sun. From its Quadripartite Badge headdress, a cruciform axis-mundi tree rises, its arms ending in jeweled serpent heads analogous to the Central-Mexican bearded Fire Serpent (*xiucóatl*) symbolizing *devouring* or *death*. At its top, a right-profile serpent–bird displays the same necklace and pectoral, matted jade mound element, serpent-head wing, and beaded Ahau tail masquette as on the sarcophagus lid. The familiar flexible serpent "bar" of alternating *yax* (green, new) and *mol* (water, jade) water/rebirth symbols, ending in upturned, agnathous serpent heads trailing matted jade elements, hangs over the world tree's arms against jade-bone, shell-triple-dot, and jeweled Ahau masquette background motifs. The basal border blocks are earth, sun, moon, and Venus signs. Lateral hieroglyphic texts refer to pre-Pacal rulers and the birth of the Palenque Triad deities (Schele and Freidel 1990: 246–248).

The smaller human figure (left) is probably Pacal, deified in death. He stands on an Underworld Sun mask, wears tasseled and braided death robes and cuffed-cloth divinity wristlets, and holds a staff topped by a long-nosed deity wearing a Quadripartite Badge headpiece. On the right, Chan Bahlum presents a recumbent Jester God manikin with crossed arms and legs on a twisted napkin. The interchange records Chan Bahlum's succession and Pacal's victory over death. The remarkably complete jambs show Chan Bahlum as an invested ruler passing the royal scepter (Figure 6.9a) to the old jaguar god of the Underworld and the west (Figure 6.9b).

Cohodas (1974, 160–161) feels that TC iconography emphasizes the Underworld where, in Aztec myth, the sun mates with the moon during the summer solstice, dies, and is reborn as new corn. The moon ushers in the rainy season that nurses the young corn with celestial mother's milk. These death–rebirth metaphors reenforce Pacal's rebirth as a deity, in which form he passes the accoutrements of rulership to his son. Chan Bahlum, Palenque's new lord and the temple's builder, may in fact be buried in the pyramid below.

The Temple of the Sun Tablet and Jambs (see Figures 6.11, 6.16, 6.17). The Temple of the Sun is located on the west, setting-sun side of the Cross Group. Its patron deity is Palenque God III, the Lord of Xibalbá, with iconography of war, death, and sacrifice (Schele and Freidel 1990:243).

On the center tablet (Figure 6.11) Pacal faces his son and heir–designate, separated by a huge shield and crossed, feather-ornamented, obsidian-tipped spears marked with *cauac* curls and dots (like those on decapitation axes) emerging from open serpent jaws (Figure 6.16). The shield, with the cruller-nosed, scroll-eyed ace of the

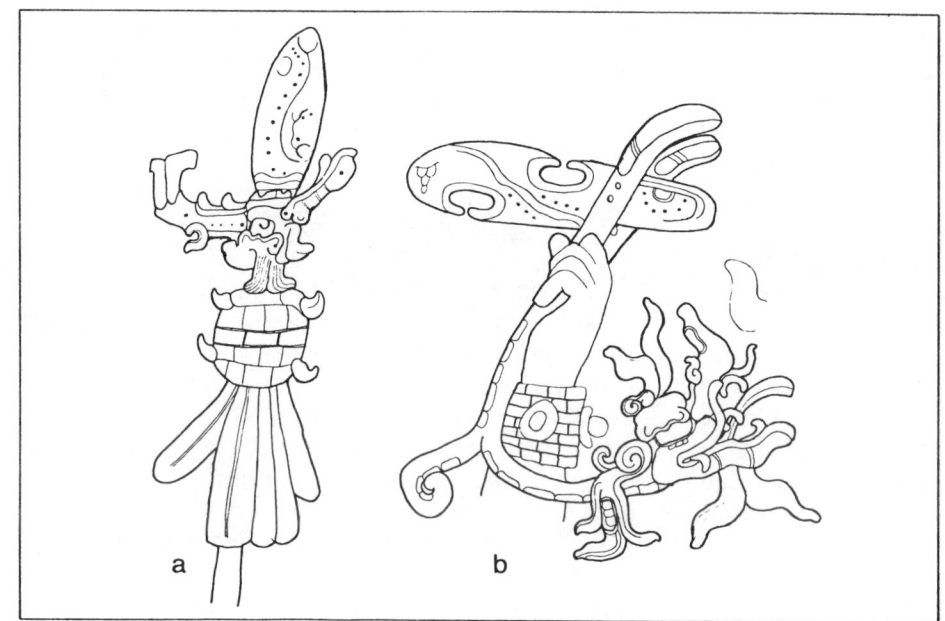

6.16. Palenque: (*a*) Temple of the Sun serpent spear compared with (*b*) serpent axe from Dumbarton Oaks tablet. (Schele 1974, 52, fig. 13; courtesy Linda Schele and RLSS)

6.17. Palenque: shield-bearing gods from (*a*) Temple of the Sun, (*b*) Tablet of the Slaves, (*c*) Palace Tablet. (Schele 1974, p. 52, fig. 12; courtesy Linda Schele and RLSS)

Jaguar god of the Underworld (the setting sun), is propped up on a wide, rigid ceremonial bar with agnathous skeleton–serpent ends and an open-mouthed jawless jaguar (the nightly devourer of the sun) at its center (Cohodas 1976, 160–161), supported by two crouching Underworld lords wearing matted gorgets: on the left, a jaguar-pelted God L with fire aspects and deity wristlets and on the right a bacab with a solar eye.

Pacal (left), in Underworld garb, stands on a kneeling Ahau-faced god proffering a cross-legged manikin on a traylike "earth bar" (Figure 6.17). The manikin wears an "eccentric"-flint-shaped headdress with cauac symbols and holds a miniature faced shield with crescent eye flaps and an open mouth resembling the Aztec god Xipe Totec's flayed-skin masks. Chan Bahlum (right) stands on a cross-armed, cross-legged God M and offers a God K effigy on a twisted napkin. The transfer of power takes place on a long earth-bar basal border of alternating *caban* earth signs and stylized, face-up sun-god heads ending in large Ahau profiles at the lower corners of the tablet.

The fragmentary jambs restate the descending-sun-devoured-by-earth symbolism. On the south jamb, Pacal offers an agnathous jaguar (the Underworld Sun) on an earth bar. The north-jamb figure, probably Chan Bahlum (with head missing and a six-toed left foot) holds a staff or spear. The lateral jamb borders have *ceh* month glyphs that Cohodas glosses as the descending sun in deer form, sinking toward a cauac earth-monster head with a blade as tongue.

The Temple of the Foliated Cross Tablet and Jambs (Figure 6.10). To Cohodas (1974), the symbolism of the TFC, on the east, rising-sun side of the Cross Group, implies rebirth and agricultural fruition and documents the birth of GII (God K) of the Triad and the accession of Chan Bahlum.

Again, the center of the tablet is a cruciform world tree. It rises from a large mask of the front head of the bicephalic earth monster Itzamna (in contrast to the back, Underworld-signifying head on the TC), with small, inverted Ahau heads at its base and a headdress with a large kan cross signifying "water" or "precious." On the tree trunk sides are sun-god heads in profile from whose tops grow crosslike arms stylized as corn plants with Young Corn god heads in

place of ears. The tree is topped by a large, square-eyed, Tau-toothed sun-god mask wearing a beaded sun-faced pectoral. A serpent-wing bird perches above.

Pacal and Chan Bahlum are in their usual presentation positions. Chan Bahlum (left) wears a long-nosed-god pectoral, long-lipped back and front waist pendants, and a shell thigh ornament and offers a seated cross-legged and armed Jester-god manikin on a folded cloth while standing on an agnathous Cauac monster head. Pacal, in his knotted "curtain-pull" funereal garments, neck muffler, and mat pectoral, stands on a conch shell with an emerging god whose hand nurtures corn-plant scrolls sprouting a Young Corn god head. His offering is a ceremonial perforator, or bloodletter. Its identification by Joralemon (1974) as a symbol of accession transfer is an iconographic breakthrough that deserves a minidescription of its own.

Maya Autosacrificial Bloodletting

Devotional autosacrifice is widely represented in Maya codices, stelae, and pottery. Individuals run ropes with entwined thorns through their tongues or perforate ears and penis with maguey tips or stingray spines. The cord, spines, and blood-spattered bark paper were presented as offerings or perhaps direct nourishment (Stuart 1984) to the appropriate god.

Joralemon identified a deified God-K-effigy-handled bloodletter in a bloodletting scene on a long-known Maya painted vase and closeups of the implement in the lower section (Figure 6.18). He then realized that Pacal's TFC tablet offering was also a bloodletter. Subsequent investigation uncovered representations of bloodletters at Yaxchilán, Copán, Bonampak, Tikal, Altar de Sacrificios, and the Chamá region of Guatemala (Figure 6.19).

Scholars now connect perforators and the associated bloodletting glyph to important Maya rituals (Schele and Miller 1986; Stuart 1988). The birth of an heir was commemorated by his father's offering blood to the ancestors. His family and captives shed blood at his first public presentation. A ruler's mother, wife, and/or war prisoners he captured joined him in bloodletting accession rites (shown on Yaxchilán Lintel 24 where Lord Shield Jaguar watches as his kneeling wife, Lady Xoc, with bloodstained

6.18. Rollout of vase from Huehuetenango, Guatemala, showing six figures holding and/or using deified bloodletters (*upper register*) and bloodletters with long-lipped deity masks wearing banded, plumed headdresses. (From Gordon and Mason 1925–1928, pl. 27; courtesy The University Museum, University of Pennsylvania)

cheeks, runs a cord through her tongue [Figure 6.20]).

Autosacrificial bloodletting also may have commemorated time-period endings (as in Tikal's "sowing stelae") and established communication with ancestors who appear in the mouths of what Schele calls "Vision Serpents" summoned by the devotee (Schele and Freidel 1990:68–70). On Yaxchilán Lintel 25, Lady Xoc, holding a bowl containing perforators and bloodied paper, raptly regards a coiled serpent disgorging an armed warrior that is rising from another bowl with paper and rope (Figure 6.21b) whereas on Lintel 15, another of Bird Jaguar's wives seems to converse with an ancestor in her vision serpent's maw (Figure 6.21a). Stephen Houston and David Stuart (1989) feel that Lintel 15's accompanying text identifies the serpent as the *way* or spiritual co-essence of God K, the Maya god of royal lineages, who acted as intermediary when members of Maya royalty summoned their ancestors through ritual autosacrifice.

Maya bloodletting continued into Colonial times. Bishop Landa describes participants strung together with cotton cord through their perforated penises before their idol. Ear bloodletting while intoxicated is still practiced by the contemporary Lacandón Maya of Chiapas.

Palenque's Classic Period Rise

The emphasis of Palencano iconography on accession to politico–religious office raises the question of Palenque's relationship to other Maya cities. Some consider Palenque a special burial necropolis because of its pyramid crypt and supposed location as gateway to Xibalbá where lowlands and highlands merge.[1] Ruler Pacal's affinities with God K, of royal lineages, would have added to the site's luster (Robertson, Scandizzo, and Scandizzo 1976, 85). There is no doubt that Palenque's prominence increased dramatically under Pacal's rule.

In 672, Pacal began construction of his TI tomb, oriented to receive the setting wintersolstice sun when viewed from the Palace Tower (Schele 1977, 42–56). His son, Chan Bahlum, subsequently built the TC, TFC, and TS to celebrate his own accession. The manipulation of art by rulers to reinforce their own purported divinity may well have accelerated Palenque's rise. Politically, the site became one of four regional capitals by A.D. 731 (Marcus 1976, 131),

[1] A. Miller (1974, 45). Schele thinks that Chan Bahlum may lie under the Temple of the Cross, Lord Hok under Temple XI, and one of Pacal's parents under the Temple of the Count (Ferguson and Royce 1977, 28).

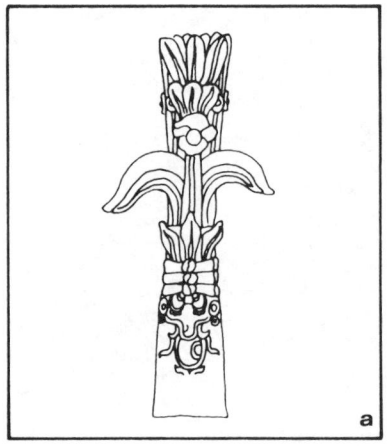

Stela D, Copan.

Limestone Panel from the Bonampak area.

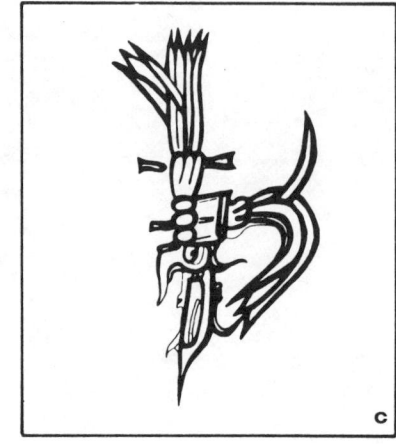

Huehuetenango Vase.

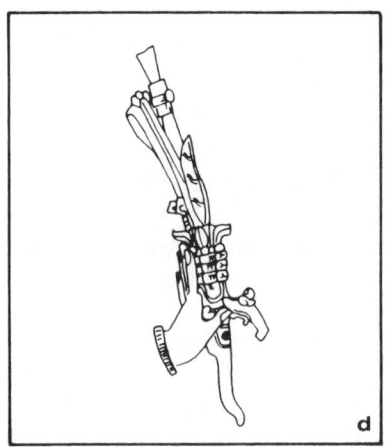

Panels from the door jambs, Temple of the Foliated Cross, Palenque.

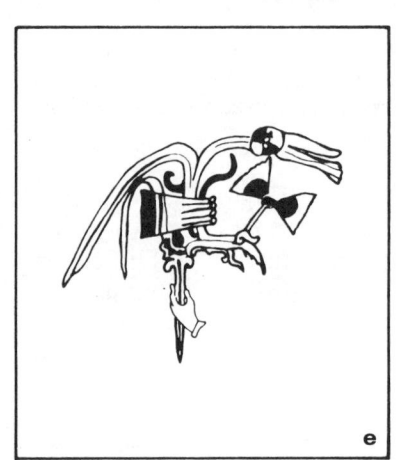

Polychrome plate from the Chama region.

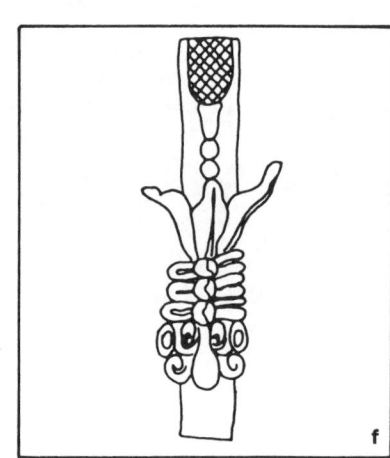

Stela A, Copan.

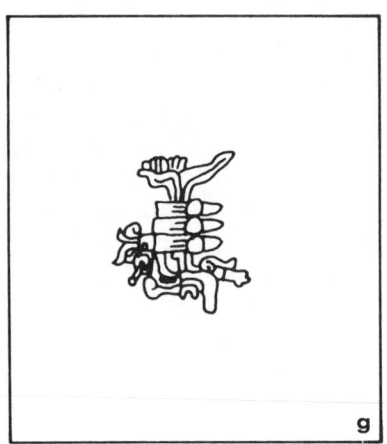

Limestone Panel from the Bonampak area.

Huehuetenango Vase.

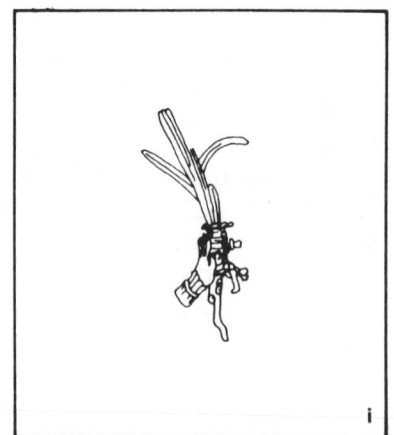

Tablet of the Foliated Cross, Palenque.

6.19. Mayan ceremonial bloodletters, identified by Joralemon. (Joralemon 1974, p. 20, fig. 24; drawing courtesy P. David Joralemon and RLSS)

6.20. Yaxchilán: Lintel 24, with Lord Skull Jaguar and Lady Xoc in bloodletting scene. (Drawing by Ian Graham, courtesy Ian Graham and PM/HU)

remaining a major center until A.D. 800. It was apparently a very special city that still may hold a surprise or two in reserve.

RELIGIOUS ICONOGRAPHY, MYTH, AND OTHER INSIGHTS FROM LOWLAND "CODEX-STYLE" POTTERY

Another major area of research is the interpretation of both painted scenes and glyphs on Classic lowland "Codex-Style" painted pottery, renowned for its delicate black-line images, sophisticated proportions, and elegant portraits of Maya elite, divinities, and assorted mythical creatures.

Linking Iconography to Myth: Xibalbá and the Hero Twins

In 1973, Michael Coe proposed that funerary pots found by him and Nicholas Hellmuth in museum and private collections showed denizens of the mythical Maya Underworld, Xibalbá, interacting with the recently dead. Coe based this supposition on iconographic clues that included Underworld jaguar masks, cimi-like death markings, death-eye necklaces, and sacrificial scarfs worn by human participants and Underworld deities already identified in Maya codices and ethnohistoric description.

To the Maya, Xibalbá, "the Nine Beyonds," represented the sun's Underworld path through four descending levels, a nadir, and four ascending levels beneath the mortal world, as opposed to its heavenly daytime movement through six ascending levels, zenith, and six descending levels to the evening horizon. Heaven, Earth, and Underworld were laid out in the four cardinal directions, connected by the ceiba-tree world axis so frequently represented at Palenque. Like the sun, the gods moved on all three planes and had matching counterparts in the worlds above and below.

Coe's major source of reference was the *Popol Vuh* or *Book of Counsel*, a long oral tradition recorded by an anonymous, newly literate Indian in the Maya Quiché dialect shortly after the Conquest and found by Father Francisco Ximénez in the Guatemalan village of Santo Tomás Chichicastenango. Here Coe found exploits of two sets of legendary twins that to him, matched many pottery themes.

The Saga of the Hero Twins

The first twins were 1 Hunahpu (1 Hunter) and 7 Hunahpu (7 Hunter). On pottery, they are represented as a pair of bejeweled "Young Lords" (Coe 1989b, 166) with body god-markings and tonsured hair. Karl Taube (1985) identifies twin 1 Hunahpu with Classic-period references to God E, the Maya maize god and eventual father of the Hero Twins.

1 Hunahpu and 7 Hunahpu were both exceptional ball players. The Underworld Lords, displeased by their noisy playing and envious of their skills, summoned them to a ball contest in Xibalbá. After being humiliated by the gods and failing in a series of ordeals, they lost the ceremonial match and were beheaded. Coe's Vase 42 (the "Princeton Vase," Figure 6.22) may show 7 Hunahpu's execution witnessed by Underworld God L, the aged cigar-smoking god, and his comely female attendants (Coe 1973, 92). Figure 4, with her dainty finger on kneeling

A

B

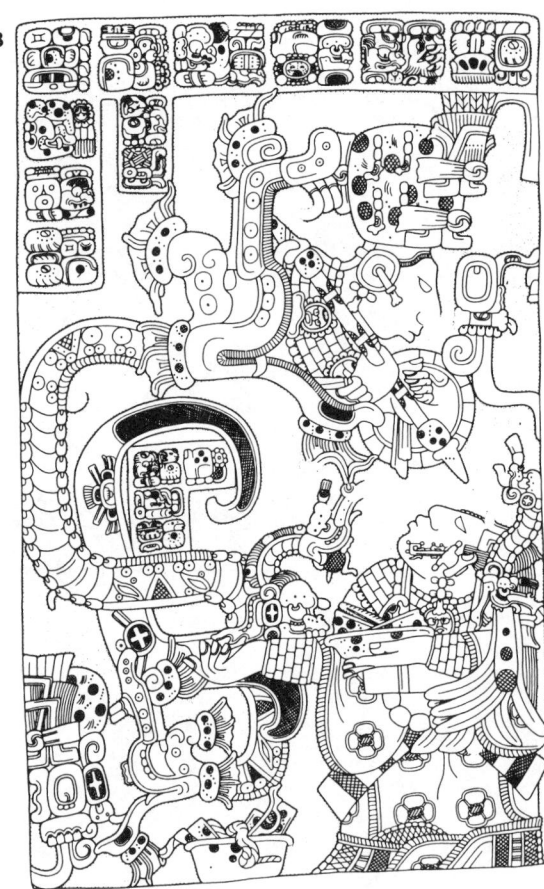

6.21. Yaxchilán, (*A*) Lintel 15, (*B*) Lintel 25: vision scenes in which the devotee holds a bowl containing bloodletters and bloodstained paper, facing a vision serpent disgorging an ancestor or armed warrior. (Drawings by Ian Graham, courtesy Ian Graham and PM/HU)

6.22. Underworld God L with female court attendants and a decapitation, possibly of 7 Hunahpu. (Vase 42, collection of Mr. and Mrs. William Kaplan, New York; drawing by Diane Griffiths Peck, in Coe, 1973, p. 92; courtesy Michael D. Coe)

Figure 5's ankle, points to the execution where a masked Figure 3 attached to the victim by a death-eye cord watches as Figure 2, with god-marked upper arm and back, beheads bound Figure 1, with god-marked ribs and thigh. A rabbit scribe beneath the dias seems to record the scene on a jaguar-skin-covered codex.

Following the execution, 1 Hunahpu's head, hung in a tree like a beautiful fruit, with its spittle impregnated Xquic, "Little Blood," or "Blood Girl" (the Young Moon), daughter of one of the Underworld Lords. After a Snow White-like escape from her father's wrath when friendly executioners simulated her blood with cochineal sap, Xquic fled to earth surface to bear the new Hero Twins, Hunahpu (the Blowgun Hunter), and Xbalanqué (Jaguar Deer, or, perhaps, Jaguar Sun, according to Lounsbury 1985), the ancestral sun.

The twins are identified by Coe on pottery as "Headband Gods" because of their turbanlike headgear. Hunahpu has a spotted cheek like that in the glyph for the twentieth calendrical day, Ahau, which is called Hu-nahpu in the Maya Quiché dialect (Coe 1989b, 167). Xbalanque has jaguar-skin cheek markings befitting the (X)balam part of his name, which means "jaguar."

As they grew, both twins became skilled blowgun hunters. One of their feats was to cleanse the world of monsters and to shoot Vucub Caquix (7 Macaw), a superhuman bird monster who presided over the previous (Fourth Sun) world epoch and its protohuman wooden manikins, thereby precipitating the creation of the Fifth Sun and of full-scale human beings. Vucub Caquix, in his *nance* fruit tree, appears as the target of the Hero Twins' blowguns on several ceramic vases (Coe 1989b, 169–173) and as the so-called principal bird deity or serpent-wing bird atop the "foliated cross" world-tree representations on the Temple of the Cross and Temple of the Foliated Cross tablets (Figures 6.8 and 6.10) and Pacal's sarcophagus lid (Figure 6.4) at Palenque.

Like their father, 1 Hunahpu, and their uncle, 7 Hunahpu, the twins also became exceptional ball players, and again the Underworld Lords sent a challenge. Aided by mosquitos' biting the lords so they called each others' names in annoyance and anger (an event perhaps shown on a bas-relief vase cited by Coe 1973, 24), the

twins weakened their adversaries by magically using the revealed names during their reception in Xibalbá.

The lords had humiliated the first twins by duping them into greeting wooden images and sitting on hot stones, but the new twins saw through the "dummy" and "hot-seat" ruses. Impressed, the lords further tested them by boarding them in difficult residences. In the House of Gloom, they were given pine torches and cigars for light and commanded to return them unused in the morning. By adding fireflies (perhaps the flare-toting insect on the Metropolitan Vase: Figure 6.23), they easily complied. In the House of the Deadly Cama Zotz Vampire Bats, they slept protected inside their blowguns: Several vases show bats with death-eye collars malevolently spreading their wings or hovering over the twins.

In the challenge ball match, the twins soundly trounced their hosts. Sore losers, the Underworld Lords sacrificed the twins and threw their bones to a water jaguar (shown on a Late Classic vase, according to Robicsek and Hales 1988). The twins bounced back as magicians and performed on "armadillo" dance for the lords, possibly illustrated on another vase located by Coe. After sacrificing and reviving the Lords' dog (perhaps the dog on the Metropolitan Vase (Figure 6.23), they cut each other into slivers and miraculously rematerialized. Lounsbury (1985, 53–55) interprets this vase as showing Hunahpu, with axe, sacrificing Xbalanque as infant jaguar sun to entertain the Underworld Lords, with skeletal Death God A as witness. The drunken lords insisted on performing the trick, and the twins obliged (Vase 16 [Figure 6.24] shows a twin about to kill God N emerging from his snail shell) but neglected to revive them again. Their victory over death complete, the twins were transformed into the sun and moon and the first twins, 1 Hunahpu and 7 Hunahpu, became the Morning and Evening stars.

Additional Iconographic Identifications

Both Coe (1989b) and Floyd Lounsbury (1985) give broader identity to the Hero Twins by linking them with gods in the Palenque Triad, with conflicting results. Lounsbury, using linguistic, iconographic, and glyphic evidence, equates Hero Twin Hunahpu with Triad GI and Xbalan-

1   2   3   4   5

6.23. Underworld ritual: sacrifice by god G I (*1*) of Jaguar God of the Underworld (*2*) with attendant skeletal figure (*3*), dog (*4*), and insect (*5*). (Vase 45, Museum of Primitive Art, New York; drawing by Diane Griffiths Peck, in Coe, 1973, p. 99; courtesy Michael D. Coe)

6.24. Twin pulling God N from shell while brandishing knife. (Vase 16 from Chama, Guatemala; collection of Gillett G. Griffin, Princeton, N.J.; drawing by Diane Griffiths Peck, in Coe, 1973, p. 47; courtesy Michael D. Coe)

que with G III, the Underworld Sun. Coe disagrees (1989b, 166), pointing out that the *Popol Vuh* names Xbalanque as the sacrificer of Hunahpu (not Hunahpu's sacrificing Xbalanque, depicted as the infant-jaguar victim on the Metropolitan Vase [Figure 6.23], according to Lounsbury). Coe adds that the *Popol Vuh* identifies Hunahpu, not Xbalanque, as the twin transformed into the sun (Lounsbury considers these discrepencies as textual corruptions). Coe concludes that G I is not a Hero Twin but is Chac

(God B, creator of rain and lightning), and that G III is twin Hunahpu because G III's glyph contains a head-form infix of the day glyph Ahau, which is translated as Hunahpu in Maya Quiché.

Coe's studies and Nicholas Hellmuth's splendid photos and drawings have stimulated additional identifications of Maya Underworld supernaturals. Among them are God L with his balding, wrinkled head, moan-bird headdress, and solicitous young female attendants; the

6.25. Preparations for scaffold sacrifice. (Vase 33, collection of Edward H. Merrin Gallery, New York; drawing by Diane Holsenbeck, in Coe, 1973, p. 76; courtesy Michael D. Coe)

netted-bag-headdressed, snail-shell resident God N (Pauah Tun); the Water Lily (Underworld) Jaguar with Ahau curl eye, tau-shaped incisors, and a lily blossom, often with an attendant nibbling fish in his hair, and serpent-legged God K with his distinctive forehead flare. Decapitation and sacrifice scenes are frequent. Dumbarton Oaks Vessel 16 (Fig. 6.25) shows a scaffold sacrifice that Karl Taube (1988) interprets as a rain fertility ritual, hunting sacrifice, and accession ceremony.

Codex Scenes and Themes

Going one step further, thorassic surgeon/Maya specialist Francis Robicsek (Robicsek and Hales 1981) purposes that themes from 308 "Codex-Style" vessels are "sequential time frames" from a lost Late Classic funerary codex. The accompanying glyphs, translated by epigrapher and coauthor Donald Hales, identify additional Xibalbá dwellers including death gods Hun Cimi ("1 Death," a black-skulled skeleton, and Vucub Cimi "7 Death," with a white skull); the god-disgorging Bearded Dragon; the long-lipped Cauac Monster bearing grape-cluster water symbols; Ancestral Bundle gods, and a sacrificed infant were–jaguar.

Robicsek also notes scenes with particular themes:

1. *Old Gods Interacting with Young Lords.* Here the victorious Hero Twins, aided by dwarfs,

humiliate the Old Gods by disrobing them (Figure 6.26)

2. *Old God Emerging from Bearded Dragon Maw.* Here the god faces a Young Lord or fondles a full-breasted, nubile female wrapped in draconic coils (the "Dragon Lady") while God K (whose serpent foot is the Bearded Dragon's tail) and Ancestral Bundles observe (Figure 6.27)

3. *Death of a Deer-Eared Old Man.* The old man exudes stench scrolls and foliated farts on a bier attended by women who soothe or ride loin-clothed deer.

4. *Sacrifice of an Infant or Adolescent Were–Jaguar.* According to Lounsbury (1985), Vase 4 (Figure 6.23) shows Xbalanque (2) as a were–jaguar being executed on a Cauac Monster platform by a death-eye necklaced, celt-brandishing Hunahpu/GI (1), with skeletal Xibalbá Lord 1 or 7 Death (3) reaching to receive the infant. An Underworld canine (4) and an insect with deity-wing markings and a "glow-chamber" tail ([5], possibly one of the firefly helpers of the Hero Twins?) monitor the scene. Robicsek and Hales (1988) further pursue the implications of this theme.

5. *Scenes with Death Symbols.* The same trio (GIII as Water Lily Jaguar, the death god, and Executioner GI) often appear with a decapitated head and/or "Macabre Triadic Bowl" containing a long bone, death eye, and skull or severed head (below GI's upraised foot in Figure 6.28).

6.26. Hero Twins removing Old God's moan-bird hat, costume, and stamping on a recumbent Old God. (Vessel 2, in Robicsek and Hales 1981, p. 15; rollout photograph copyright © 1981 by Justin Kerr)

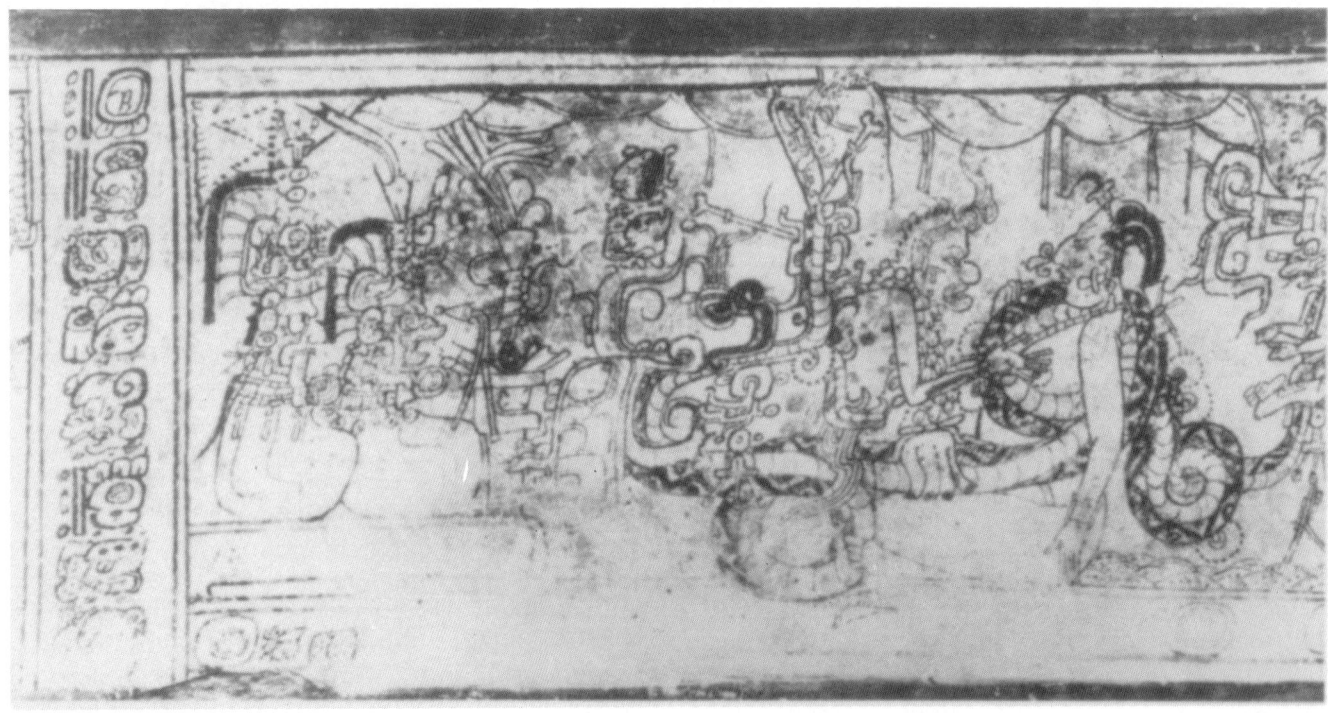

6.27. Old God with enema bib emerging from Bearded Dragon, caressing Dragon Lady; observed by Bundle Gods and Flare God. (Vessel 12a, in Robicsek and Hales 1981, p. 19; rollout photograph copyright © 1981 by Justin Kerr)

Other frequent scenes noted by Robicsek and Hales involve *hunters* (the Hero Twins?) with blow guns, deer-eared *trumpeters* blowing conch shells as they emerge from Bearded Dragon jaws, *scribes* carving ink pots or producing codices, *confrontations* between (Putún Maya?) warriors and unarmed (local?) lords carrying bundles and layered packages (perhaps codices), and figures emerging from cracks in turtle shells that may denote the resurrection of either 1 or 7 Hunahpu out of a cleft turtle shell symbolizing the Underworld after their sacrificial death. Taube

6.28. Water Lily Jaguar, 1 Death, and axe-wielding GI Executioner with a severed head at his ankle and one leg raised over a bowl containing a severed hand, bone, and eye. (Vessel 30, in Robicsek and Hales 1981, p. 25; rollout photograph copyright © 1981 by Justin Kerr)

(1985) and Coe (1989b) see the latter as a visual metaphor for 1 Hunahpu as maize god representing the germination of young corn.

Alternate Interpretations

The Coe–Robicsek identification of funerary scenes and *Popol Vuh* themes has been challenged by other scholars because of the nine-century gap between the *Popol Vuh* and Classic-period vases and the sometimes questionable authenticity and undocumented provenience of their pottery sample. Cohodas (1989a) notes that many vessels combine elements from unrelated *Popol Vuh* episodes and eschews such analogies, concentrating instead on their iconographic themes to identify artists, schools, and workshops. He and others (Taylor 1982, 114–119) note that "creative restoration" by art dealers enhancing vessels for resale can also skew scholarly interpretations.

Stephen Houston and David Stuart (1989) feel that the purported Underworld Gods and denizens are in fact "co-essences" or spirit companions of the lords depicted on vases, named as such by a distinctive glyph that is half Ahau–Sun God face and half-spotted jaguar skin, accompanied by the phonetic complements *wa* and *ya*, giving a reading of *way*, a contemporary Maya term for spirit companion. They strengthen their argument by citing the ongoing indigenous belief that every person has a spiritual co-essence and offer examples of stela texts where the "way" glyph identifies the way of lords and even gods depicted on stelae and lintels.

Codex-Style Subdivisions and Individual or Workshop Styles

Besides producing major iconographic studies, scholars of Maya "Codex-Style" vessels have identified regional and workshop substyles and even specific individual artists.

Codex-Style vessels differ from other Classic Maya painting and drawing styles (reconstructed from Tikal by Coggins 1975) in their fine linear, iconographically rich portrayals of historical or mythical figures. Based on brush-stroke differences, Robicsek and Hales (1981) recognize five Codex substyles: (1) plain-line (with uniform lines); (2) codex baroque ("curlicues and filigrees"); (3) whiplash (rapid, sure lines of varying thickness); (4) calligraphic (slow, deliberate, sometimes retouched strokes); and (5) fine-line (work of spidery thinness).

Identifying personal styles or shared traditions in which an artist, teacher, or institution exerted influence is more difficult. Photographers Barbara and Justin Kerr, whose stunning rollout photos have contributed so much to Codex-Style studies, recognize a surrealistic fineline "Fantastic Painter," a second style in sequential war-sacrifice processions, and additional vases by the painters of the Princeton (Figure 6.22) and Metropolitan (6.23) vases (Kerr and Kerr 1988, Figures 7.18; 7.17–7.19; 7.1–7.9 and 6.10–6.15).

Marvin Cohodas (1989a), working with nearly 200 vases from Codex Site "A," an as-yet-unidentified source, further describes the Metropolitan Master, Fantastic, Calligraphic, and Backwards Glyph artists and the Painters of the Frontal Rabbit and Ringed Eye. He details shifts in the Metropolitan Painter's glyph elaboration, iconographic content, and use of themes that may indicate influences and exchanges of ideas between workshops as well as individual artistic development. Reents (1985) links quality differences in Naranjo–Holmul pottery to increased production for middle- and lower-class use, possibly by extended-family workshops.

Petén area Codex-Style sites have been tentatively identified on stylistic and epigraphic grounds (Robiscek 1981; Cohodas 1989a) near El Perú, San José Motul, Xultún and Naj Tunich Cave, and Naranjo. The Maya Polychrome Ceramics Project, a joint effort by art-historian Dorrie Reents-Budet and Ronald Bishop of the Smithsonian Institution's Conservation Analytical Lab, has combined stylistic investigations with trace-element chemical analyses using a database of over 1,200 vases and 14,500 sherds to identify individual and workshop styles and their site locations (Reents-Budet, personal communication). Criteria of vessel form, iconography, colors and painting techniques, and supplementary glyphs help isolate stylistically related pieces, whereas trace-element profiles of clay types identify pieces from the same area, distinguish Codex Style from other fine-line

wares, and suggest stylistic subdivisions that can be tested by future archaeological excavation.

Epigraphic Interpretations of Pottery Texts

In his original descriptions, Michael Coe (1973, 1978) interpreted a series of glyphs on "Codex-Style" vessel rims, which he called the Primary Standard Sequence, as rebirth formulas to facilitate the deceased's passage through Xibalbá. More recent phonetic readings by David Stuart, Stephen Houston, Karl Taube, Nicolai Grube, and Barbara MacLeod (cited in Cohodas 1989a) have amplified their decipherment. Stuart (1989) suggests instead that these glyphs act as name tags to introduce the name and title of the vessel's donor or recipient (and, elsewhere on the pot, the name of the artist–creator: Stuart 1989, 156), and describe the vessel's manufacture (carved or painted), form (plate, bowl), and function (for atole or ritual cacao drinking).

Felicitous corroboration of the latter interpretation has come through collaboration between archaeologists, epigraphers, and chemists. Several early Classic-period vessels from Tomb 19 at the northeastern Guatemalan site of Río Azul, discovered in 1984 after looters had ransacked the site, contained well-preserved organic material identified from theobromine and caffeine traces as residues of cacao (Hall et al. 1990). The Primary Standard text on Tomb 19's Vessel 15, a unique pot with a bayonet-type screw on its ("child-proof") lid, listed its owner, the vessel form, and its intended use (i.e. "for ca-ca-wa," or cacao drinking). Barbara MacLeod's eagerly awaited Ph.D. dissertation (MacLeod 1990) details the phonetic readings and sociocultural implications for a by now sizable corpus of Primary Standard variants from ceramic sources.

CONCLUSION

Maya research today is crackling with the excitement of new archaeological discoveries, epigraphic breakthroughs, and cutting-edge research that details new interpretations of Maya art. Epigraphy and iconographic interpretations have clarified new aspects of political organization and government and the role of public art in documenting autosacrifice, accession, royal intermarriage, military celebrations with participating *cahales*, and ancestral validation of rulership rights. Tomb inscriptions and funerary pottery affirm continuing postmortuary status of the elite as memoralized revered ancestors. Perhaps future studies will enable us to better understand the role of art in the lives of the ordinary, nonelite Maya as well.

It is hard to imagine what key insights the next decades will bring. Surely cooperating North American, Mesoamerican, and European Maya scholars will continue to derive new and tantalizing insights from excavated art objects, if Mesoamerican political unrest, funding cutbacks, and relentless pot hunters do not beat archaeologists to the draw.

CHAPTER 7

THE AZTECS

ARCHAEOLOGY AND ETHNOHISTORY

BY a quirk of fate, we know more about some aspects of Aztec culture through ethnohistoric sources than from archaeological excavation. The Spaniards razed much of the Aztec island capital in 1521, destroying the major temples and replacing them with Colonial churches and buildings. Today modern Mexico City covers ancient Tenochtitlán, its sister settlement of Tlatelolco, and adjacent lakeshore kingdoms, limiting their archaeological retrieval. Suburbs bear their proud names, and bus marquees reading Culhuacán, Tlacopan, Azcapotzalco, Coyoacán, Chalco, Tlalpan, and Texcoco are a lingering legacy of the past.

Major Ethnohistoric Sources

Important sixteenth-century ethnohistoric sources include Durán's (Durán, 1971) survey of Aztec gods and rites and Sahagún's encyclopedic accounts in Nahuatl (translated into English by Anderson and Dibble: 1950–1976) based on data from Indian informants (both profusely illustrated). Other primary sources are Fernando Alvarado Tezozomoc, Diego Muñoz Camargo, Juan Bautista Pomar, and other Indian or part-Indian chroniclers, and pictorial codices prepared for the Crown by native artisans shortly after Spanish contact.

Aztec Background and Development

According to these sources, the Aztecs (Mexica) were semibarbarian nomads from northwestern Mexico. Led by their leaders Tenoch and Mexitli, they arrived in Central Mexico around A.D. 1200 after centuries of migration from the mythical Aztlán ("White Place" or "Place of the Herons") and Chicomostoc ("Place of the Seven Caves"). The valley was already occupied by small lakeshore kingdoms, descendants of survivors from Teotihuacán, Toltec Tula, and acculturated Chichimecs from earlier intrusions. These settled people denigrated the Aztecs but hired them as mercenaries because of their raiding skills. Shunted among the least desirable lands, the Aztecs finally settled on an unoccupied island in the southwestern section of the valley's five interconnected lakes. They named it Tenochtitlán after their leader and/or the large *tenoch* (prickly pear) cactus with a perching eagle eating its fruits that divinely sanctioned their arrival and built a thatch-roofed shrine to their tribal war god, Huitzilopochtli ("Southern Hummingbird," or "Hummingbird on the Left [of the Sun's Pathway]"), who had led them and promised them greatness as the People of the Sun. This small hut after many reconstructions became the great Templo Mayor.

The Aztecs soon upgraded themselves in the local hierarchy by allying with winning groups and eliminating rivals. In 1428, they defeated the hated Tecpanecs of Azcapotzalco, their former overlords, and, with Tlacopan and Texcoco, formed the powerful Triple Alliance. Their joint ventures generated tribute, and the Aztecs enlarged their island settlement with *chinampas* (so-called floating gardens), converting swampy areas into farming plots. Under strong rulers, they expanded into the Gulf Coast, West Mexico, and Oaxaca. Tenochtitlán absorbed its neighbor Tlatelolco in 1473 and became a city of 200,000. When the Spaniards arrived in 1519, the Aztecs were an expanding conquest state sustained by tribute, with only the Tarascans in West Mexico and the Tlaxcalans in the state of Puebla as holdouts. The state extended from the Gulf to the Pacific and south to the edge of the Maya world.

Aztec Social, Political, and Economic Organizations

The Aztecs were a stratified society with *macehualli* (commoners), craftsworkers, serfs (*mayeque*), merchant–spies (*pochteca*), priests, warriors, and nobles (*pilli*), including lords (*tecuhtli*) of the ruling lineages from among whom the Aztec ruler, titled Huey Tlatoani ("Great or Revered Speaker"), was elected by a council of distinguished elders. His chief male advisor was the powerful Cihuacóatl (Snake Woman), a sort of combination secretary of state and military strategist who helped formulate state policy and tried important cases. The state regulated agricultural and craft production and redistributed tribute from conquered territories.

Long-distance trade brought both raw and finished goods to the markets of Tenochtitlán and Tlatelolco, where government officials taxed them, monitored transactions, and settled disputes. *Mantas* of woven white cotton, quills of gold dust, and sacks of cacao beans as pseudo-currency supplemented barter exchanges: Archaeologists have found cacao beans drilled, filled with sand, and skillfully plugged as evidence of pre-columbian counterfeiters at work! The huge markets had sectors for particular goods (meats, vegetables, live animals, pottery, jewelry, firewood, curative herbs) as Mexican and Guatemalan Indian markets still do today. The Templo Mayor's caches confirm the scope of Aztec tribute and trade for exotic luxury items: They include Pacific and Gulf Coast shells, Mezcala-style carvings from the state of Guerrero in West Mexico, stone figures from Oaxaca, and even an Olmec mask that may represent a cherished heirloom from an ancient, sacred past (Berdan 1987).

The state sponsored its citizens' education. Commoners studied in the *telpochcáltin* or lower schools; those of high birth graduated into the *calmecac* and learned about hieroglyphic writing, history, myths, the workings of the 365-day solar and 260-day religious calendars, and public rites and ceremonies. Warriors trained at the Telpochcalli ("House of War") in martial arts and use of the powerful *macana*, a club edged with two rows of razor-sharp obsidian blades. Future priests were drilled in the sacred 260-day *tonalpohualli* of 20 day names numbered from 1 to 13 and the auguries, rituals, and patron deities associated with each 13-day week. They also learned astronomical observation, calculation, and the sacrifices appropriate for each goddess or god.

ARCHITECTURE

Mexico City today is a sprawling mixture of enormous government structures adjacent to neighborhood *vecindades* and slums; Colonial churches tilt into the ancient lake beds beside ultramodern high rises of glass. Aztec Tenochtitlán lies beneath busy paved streets and yields its secrets only during pipeline or subway construction or planned excavations such as that of Tlatelolco's Plaza de las Tres Culturas[1] and the Templo Mayor.

[1] Here Aztec ruins lie within a few yards of a Colonial church and a modern high-rise apartment complex, the latter heavily damaged by the 1985 earthquake.

Tenayuca, Santa Cecilia Acatitlán, and Malinalco

Fortunately, we can learn about the Aztecs from Postclassic sites outside Mexico City. Tenayuca's pyramid is a cognate of the Templo Mayor, with a snake wall (*coatepantli*) in situ on three sides and fire-serpent heads at the base of its stair balustrades. A smaller temple at Santa Cecilia Acatitlán has been completely reconstructed. The Aztec shrine of Malinalco (Map 2) near Toluca, with its serpent entrance carved out of bedrock, contains banquettes lined with serpent, jaguar, and eagle sculptures. Associated stonework depicts gods, human attendants, and animals down to the lowly grasshopper with great realism. Burnished orange pottery painted in fine black lines, onyx vessels, obsidian (black, gray, or greenish volcanic glass) ear spools, quartz-crystal skulls, vertical and horizontal wooden drums, and canoes miraculously preserved in the old lake beds also help reconstruct the Aztec millieu.

Ethnohistorical Descriptions of Tenochtitlán

Sixteenth-century descriptions of Tenochtitlán are neither lengthy nor very precise. The Nuremberg Map of 1524 illustrating Cortés's

Map 8. Plan of Tenochtitlán and causeways. (Reproduced from Heyden and Villaseñor 1984, p. 15; courtesy of Editorial Minutiae Mexicana)

letters to the Spanish king Carlos V shows Tenochtitlán's causeways, major canals, and sacred precinct in a schematic sixteenth-century European style and lacks specific detail. Codices illustrate the Templo Mayor (*Atlas de Durán*, Sahagún's *Primeros Memoriales, Códices Matritenses, Códice Ixtlixóchitl, Códice Aubin*), Moctezuma II's palace (*Códice Mendoza*), and portions of outer Tenochtitlán or a nearby island town (*Plano en Papel de Maguey*). Thus our picture of Tenochtitlán still remains incomplete.

Tenochtitlán was an island in the southwest portion of five shallow, intergrading lakes, connected to the mainland by wide, bridged causeways running south to Coyoacán and Iztapalapa, west to Tacuba and Chapultepec, and north to Tepeyac (Map 8). Mexico City's streets still follow the causeway routes. A dike separated Lake Texcoco's eastern, salty water from the sweetwater southern lakes, Chalco and Xochimilco, and a double-conduit aqueduct brought fresh water from Chapultepec Hill on the western mainland to supplement the city's springs.

Archaeological Excavation of Tenochtitlán

Specific building locations were eventually forgotten as Colonial structures covered their ruins. In 1900, a sewer-construction project cut into a corner of the Templo Mayor, and further excavations in 1914, 1934, and the 1960s revealed substructures and important pieces of sculpture. In 1978, the discovery of a beautifully carved stone disk of the dismembered goddess Coyolxauhqui launched a full-scale excavation of the Templo Mayor area by Mexico's Instituto Nacional de Antropología e Historia between 1978 and 1982. Apartments and a major bookstore were torn down, but the rest of the sacred precinct still lies unaccessible beneath the modern city. Parts of the Metro subway system have hit interesting features such as an exquisite local barrio temple at the Pino Suarez station, now sandwiched between modern underground shops, but these few meandering corings leave most of ancient Tenochtitlán untouched.

Layout of Tenochtitlán

What was Tenochtitlán like at its height in 1519, on the eve of the Spanish Conquest? Educated guesses place its population at between 150,000 and 300,000 in a 35-square-mile (90 square kilometer) area that included adjoining Tlatelolco, making it "the largest and most highly urbanized city in the New World" for its time (Calnek 1976, 287–288). At the center of its four quarters of gridded districts, a sacred precinct enclosed a large twin-staired pyramid and several smaller temples.

Pasztory (1983, 117) thinks that Tenochtitlán's grid plan may be modeled after Teotihuacán, which was revered by the Mexica as the oracular birthplace of the sun in the fifth great age of creation, because Tenochtitlán's reticulated avenues, orientation, cruciform axis, and standard measure of length are almost identical with Teotihuacán's. The island setting, on the other hand, may recall their original Aztlán homeland. Its four quarters may represent the four cosmic world quarters divided by the east–west sun's path and a perpendicular north–south axis, whereas its ceremonial precinct marked a fifth direction, the sacred center of the universe (in Nahuatl, *Cem Anahuac Yolóco*, or "Heart of the One World").

Each city quarter had its own temples, replaced by Spanish churches that still stand today, and contained 80 to 100 residential districts (*tlaxilacalli*) for clans or lineages (*calpulli*), often representing a craftmaking, merchant, or other profession. These districts of up to 2,000 people had local temples, meeting plazas, markets, and schools and were further subdivided into neighborhoods.

Causeways

Dividing the quarters were broad avenues leading in the south and west to the great causeways—in the north through Tlatelolco to the Tepeyac causeway and in the east to probable embarcation points to Texcoco beyond the Great Dike (Map 8). Five main canals crisscrossed the city with numerous feeders facilitating canoe access and irrigation for *chinampa* gardens associated with house plats that Edward Calnek, working with Colonial deeds and house plans, has correlated to existing city streets (Calnek 1972, 1976). Large chinampas lay at Tenochtitlán's southern and eastern edges where fishermen and farmers produced much of the city's food.

The Templo Mayor

At Tenochtitlán's center, under the busy modern Zocalo, lay the administrative palaces (Tec-

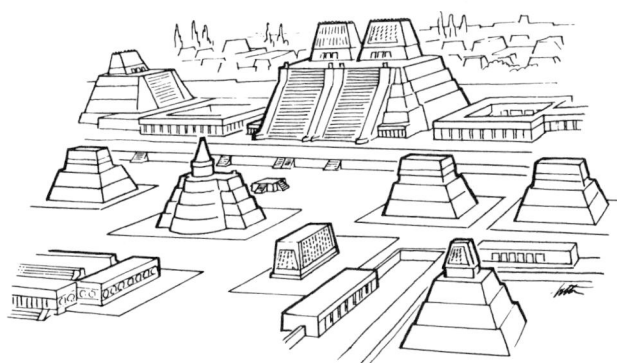

7.1. Tenochtitlán's ceremonial center: schematic drawing by Alberto Beltran. (Heyden and Villaseñor 1984, p. 12; courtesy EMM)

pan), the main market, and the temple precinct or Teocalli (Figure 7.1). Within the Teocalli, the dominant structure was the Templo Mayor, the culmination of successive enlargements of the original Huitzilopochtli shrine beginning in 1325. In 1521, ethnohistorical sources describe the temple as a west-facing, multistage, double-staired pyramid topped by twin temples to the tribal war god Huitzilopochtli on the right (south) painted red with a skull-decorated roof facade, and Tlaloc the water god on the left, adorned with vertical blue and white bands.

Construction Phases. Archaeological data from the 1978–1982 excavations suggest seven enlargement phases (Matos Moctezuma 1988, 64–83) that do not always dovetail with descriptions in ethnohistoric sources (see Umberger, León-Portilla, and Nicholson, in Boone, ed., 1987, for other interpretations). Mexican excavation of the Temple II phase (ca. A.D. 1400) exposed twin temples on a two-staired 35-foot-high (10.6 meter) pyramid base with a beautifully painted *chacmool* in front of the Tlaloc temple and a trapezoidal sacrificial stone in situ before Huitzilopochtli's shrine (Map 9, Area 3). Temple III (1427–1440), built after the defeat of Atzcapotzalco, was larger, in keeping with expanding Aztec influence. Eight upright, life-sized stone standard bearers were found ceremonially repositioned at the base of the Huitzilopochtli stair, covered by subsequent Temple IV construction (Map 9, above the Coyolxauhqui area).

Temple IV had two subphases. IVa construction (1440–1469) covered Temple III; during IVb, between 1469–1481, the front was ex-

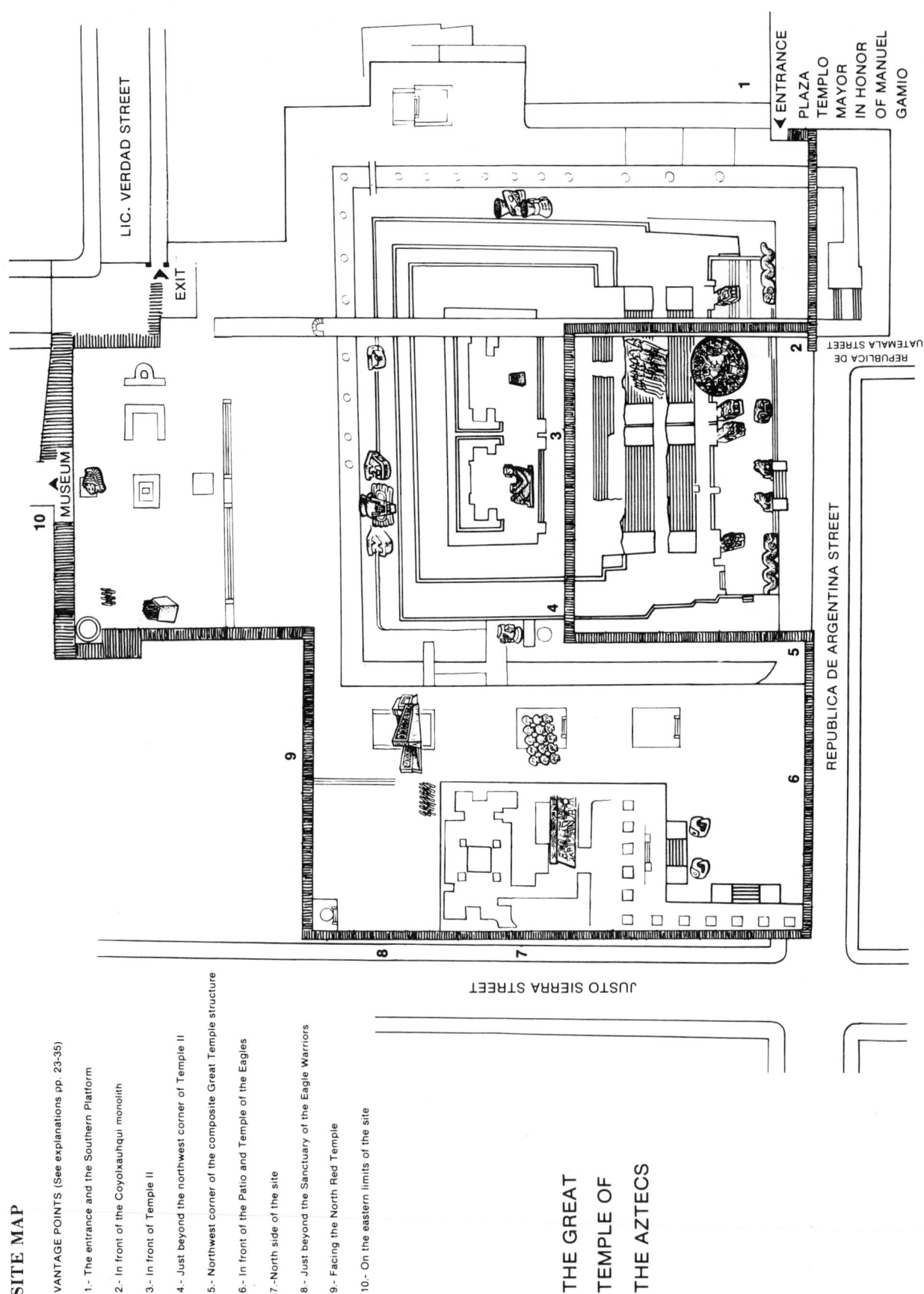

SITE MAP

VANTAGE POINTS (See explanations pp. 23-35)

1.- The entrance and the Southern Platform

2.- In front of the Coyolxauhqui monolith

3.- In front of Temple II

4.- Just beyond the northwest corner of Temple II

5.- Northwest corner of the composite Great Temple structure

6.- In front of the Patio and Temple of the Eagles

7.- North side of the site

8.- Just beyond the Sanctuary of the Eagle Warriors

9.- Facing the North Red Temple

10.- On the eastern limits of the site

THE GREAT
TEMPLE OF
THE AZTECS

LIC. VERDAD STREET

ENTRANCE
PLAZA
TEMPLO
MAYOR
IN HONOR
OF MANUEL
GAMIO

REPUBLICA DE GUATEMALA STREET

REPUBLICA DE ARGENTINA STREET

JUSTO SIERRA STREET

EXIT

MUSEUM

Map 9. Map of the Templo Mayor, Tenochtitlán. (From Heyden and Villaseñor 1984, pp. 36–37; courtesy Editorial Minutiae Mexicana)

panded by twin, low-balustraded stairs ending in huge flame-feathered fire-serpent heads below Huitzilopochtli's temple and scroll-nosed/lipped water serpents on Tlaloc's side (Map 9, Area 2). Under the Huitzilopochtli temple, a huge stone disk of the dismembered goddess Coyolxauhqui lay between the fire serpents to receive the bodies sacrificed to her brother. A low platform with 20-foot-long (6 meter) writhing corner serpents extending from the pyramid base contained pits with a cremation and two carved Fine Orange urns that Umberger (1987, 428–437) interprets as possibly the remains of Moctezuma I. A stair on the Tlaloc side with twin frogs representing water-sustained animals atop its balustrades is nicknamed the "Altar of the Frogs" (Map 9, Area 2). Remains of Temples V–VII (1481–1520) consist mainly of foundation segments because these outer structures were leveled to clear the La Traza area for Colonial construction.

Other Tecpan Structures

The Templo Mayor excavations have exposed additional sacred precinct structures. As part of a Stage VI (1486–1502) three-room temple complex north of the Templo Mayor, the "Temple of the Eagles" (Map 9, Areas 6, 7, 8) has eagle-headed stair balustrades and an interior "Sanctuary of the Eagle Warriors" containing murals and banquettes with marching priests and warriors in Toltec style. To the south, the small stone Altar of the Skulls with 240 carved human skulls suggests *tzompantlis* described in Spanish sources. East-facing twin Red Temples with red-painted Teotihuacán talud–tablero sides at the Templo Mayor's back corners face a walled patio decorated with Teotihuacán circles containing a sunken circular pit and a columnar upright altar (Map 9, Area 8).

Unlocated to date are ethnohistorically described circular Quetzalcóatl temples, ball courts, gladiator sacrifice stones, palaces, and temples to the gods Xipe Totec, Tezcatlipoca, and captive gods. Sahagún mentions seventy-two major and minor structures. One can only speculate what remains beneath the city streets.

ART

Attitudes toward Aztec Art

Ever since the seventeenth century, Aztec art has been interpreted with changing perceptions by nonnative critics (Keen 1971). Considered horrendous and barbaric by the Spaniards, it was, by the late nineteenth century, influencing Gaugin and thereafter Henry Moore and Giacometti. Early twentieth-century art critics began describing it in more positive terms as major museum exhibits increased public acceptance. In Mexico, it became associated with *indigenismo*, the nationalistic appreciation of Mexico's Indian population and pre-columbian heritage. Past studies (for example Klein 1986) have increasingly explored its wider cultural context and its material as well as ideational effects.

Style

Professional art historians have defined the parameters of Aztec style. In a seminal article, H. B. Nicholson (1960) reexamined the Central Mexican Mixteca-Puebla style of codex and polichrome pottery decoration and concluded that it encompassed a Toltec substyle integrating Teotihuacán elements, a Mixtec substyle incorporating the Toltec substyle with local Oaxaca canons, and an Aztec substyle of Central Mexican features influenced by Mixtec artisans imported as tribute.

Diverse ethnic elements are dramatically confirmed by the wide range of art objects unearthed in the Templo Mayor (Pasztory 1983; Berdan 1987). Aztec synthesis of Toltec, Gulf Coast, and Mixteca-Puebla features is also evident in Azec monolithic sculpture (Nicholson 1971a; Townsend 1979; Solís Olguín 1982).

Reconstruction of Aztec painting style is problematic because few Aztec murals have survived.[2] Elizabeth H. Boone (1982a) has described Aztec painting based on remains at Malinalco and post-Conquest codices that retain elements of pre-Conquest style. Flat figures drawn in straight or angular lines and direct, unshaded colors are evenly distributed. They have smaller head-to-body proportions and are less stiff than in late Postclassic Mixtec codices. Place, personal name, conquered town, and day glyphs in the post-Conquest *Borbonicus* and *Tonalamatl Aubin* differ considerably from those in Borgia-group Mixteca-Puebla codices and Mixtec co-

---

[2] These include a Tlaloc mural associated with a decorated altar on Argentina Street, Mexico City (Matos Moctezuma 1988, 29); the Templo Mayor Stage II Tlaloc shrine pillars and interior murals of striding, staff-bearing figures (*ibid.* 66); Teotihuacanoid water motifs on Stage VI's Temple C and Red Temple; and fragments from nearby Malinalco.

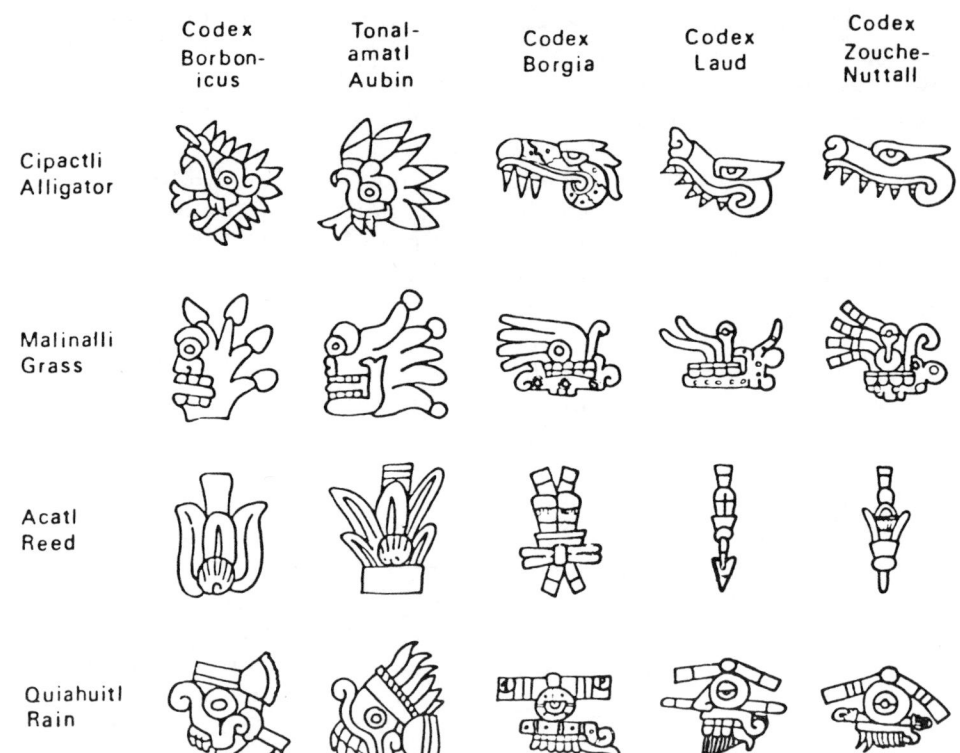

7.2. Style differences in four day signs from Aztec (*Borbonicus, Aubín*), Borgia-group (*Borgia, Laud*), and Mixtec (*Zouche-Nuttall*) codices. (Boone 1982a, fig. 151; drawing courtesy Elizabeth Boone)

dices from western Oaxaca (Figure 7.2). Nancy Troike cautions that major misinterpretations can result from using Central Mexican concepts to analyze Mixtec materials because the two styles indeed differ in both content and execution (Troike 1981).

Iconography

Aztec iconography is rich and distinctive. Deities of fertility, celestial creativity, and war/sacrifice (Nicholson 1971b; Brundage 1985) have mutually interchangeable attributes and insignia not found in the Mixteca-Puebla area, and many Aztec symbols for natural forces or sacred objects are unique. Major themes include cyclical transformation, sacrifice by gods or humans, life/death or death/rebirth alternation, and images of rulers and secular events (Pasztory 1983). Nicholson (1973) feels that differentiation from other substyles occurred during the last few decades before Spanish Conquest.

Symbols

Basic iconographic units, stylized *symbols* (water, flower, fire, star, heart, etc.), are combined into *emblems* (sky bands, feathered or fire serpents, solar disks). Lineage insignia, costumes and masks, body and facial painting, and carried accoutrements identify particular deities, *texiptla* (deity impersonators), priests, or rulers and nobles who merit the right to wear their regalia (Klein 1986). Number and time-period glyphs and human, deity, and place names add further specificity.

Symbol size, placement, and interrelationships also assist in conveying the simultaneous, multivalent meanings characteristic of both Aztec graphic art and poetry. Deities, for example, have dual Underworld and Upperworld forms, variants for the cardinal directions, multiple names and aspects, and insignia and accoutrements shared with other members of their cluster. The Christian concept of the Trinity pales in comparison with the iconography shared by congeries of related Aztec deities.

Art, Ritual, and World View

Aztec behavior and belief were strongly influenced by a corpus of myths only partially recoverable from ethnohistoric accounts. From them we know that a large array of gods either embodied or personified and/or influenced powerful natural forces. Some were considered ancestors of rulers. Others offered examples for human emulation. Aztec supernaturals had multiple, shared iconographic attributes, and rich, metaphoric titles, like African praise names, leading Spanish chroniclers to describe a huge, complex pantheon.

Architecture, too, visually represented multivalent Mexican beliefs. Matos Moctezuma (1987) feels that the Templo Mayor represented the navel of the universe to the Aztecs and acted as an *axis mundi*, vertically marking the terrestrial midpoint between the nine Underworld levels and the thirteen layered heavens, and horizontally the center of the four world quarters of east, west, north, and south. The Tlaloc temple at the top symbolizes Tonacatepetl, the Mountain of Sustenence, Water, and Plenty, and the Huitzilopochtli temple represents Coatepec ("Serpent Mountain"), where the divine solar ancestor Huitzilopochtli slew his sister, the goddess Coyolxauhqui. Thus the Templo Mayor visually reinforces concepts of identity as Huitzilopochtli's chosen "People of the Sun," solar sacrifice, agricultural fertility, and war. Broda (1987) adds that the Templo Mayor may have been further conceived as a single sacred mountain signifying Earth as dual giver of life-sustaining crops and receiver of the human sacrifices performed at its summit. Architectural iconography was invisibly reinforced by offerings of shells, Tlaloc effigies, jaguar skulls, and skeletons with egg-shaped jade balls in their mouths (symbols of Tepeyolotl, "Heart of the Mountain"), and human skulls with sacrificial, Tlaloc-face, mosaic-inlaid knives through their noses or impaled in balls of resin, cached within the substructures.

The Nature of Aztec Rituals

In the Aztec world view, humans could reenact mythical events as a tie to the sacred past and honor, strengthen, nourish, and maintain their pantheon and the cosmic forces it governed through offerings of corn, amaranth dough images, and quail sacrifice, and appropriate rituals, with a human texiptla first representing them and then sacrificed as the honored deity. Rituals were conducted as important public, state functions and by priests at local temples and individual homes. Autosacrificial bloodletting of the ears, tongue, and penis (Figure 7.3) was utilized as a substitute for offering human life, whereas ritual cannibalism permitted absorption of a vanquished enemy's bravery or a sacrificed texiptla's divinity. The annual public ritu-

7.3. Priests practicing auto-sacrifice. Note the maguey thorn bloodletters (*puas*) in the grass bundle (*upper right*). (Fray Diego Durán, *Libro de los Dioses y Ritos*; original in the Biblioteca Nacional de Madrid; reproduced in Horcasitas and Heyden 1971, pl. 11, p. 333, courtesy University of Oklahoma Press)

als, fasts, and feasts during the eighteen 20-day months created social cohesion as collective petitions for crop fertility, harvest celebrations, or memorials for the dead, and intimidation of conquered and potential enemies through prisoner sacrifice. Ceremonies of ruler accession, military or ball-game victories, and temple dedications accompanied by large-scale human sacrifice to national gods further underscored political power publicly and helped maintain the state. Festivals were manipulated to facilitate tribute redistribution, reinforce class distinctions, and encourage militaristic expansion (Klein 1986).

Cultural Implications of Aztec Art

Aztec artists furthered these ends by producing deity images and cult objects from stone, wood, precious jade, and gold, and depicting ritual situations and their iconography on monuments, murals, and in codices. These representations often employed exotic materials (shell, turquoise) requiring long-distance trade or tribute and skills by imported craftsworkers and sometimes became visual statements of political dominion. Thus state-directed art was involved in the most basic aspects of Aztec culture. Its production required the acquisition of exotic raw materials through both trade and tribute. By reinforcing mythologies validating Aztec political domination, it was used to manipulate both local and subjugated populations. Its images visually represented and helped to ritually control an extensive array of deities representing natural forces, human and agricultural fertility, and the institution of sacred warfare (Klein 1986). A look at major congeries comprising Aztec religion will show these forces in more detailed interplay. We next turn to these.

The Aztec Pantheon: Characteristics and Representation

Fertility. Maize fertility was embodied by Centéotl ("Corn deity"), the young maize god, whose impersonator with corncobs on his headdress and back was sacrificed in the eleventh festival month, and Xilonen ("Young Corn Ear or Doll"), his female counterpart, whose young virgin texiptla was feted at the Cintéopan, the Corn Temple, blessed seeds during the fourth month and was then beheaded, becoming the goddess in her death. Chicometóatl ("Seven

Serpents"), she of the seven ears of corn (for which serpents are a verbal/visual metaphor) and goddess of ripening corn, was likewise impersonated by a texiptla with a huge square headdress accompanied by young girls bringing ears of corn to her temple during the eleventh month. The texiptla's sacrifice commemorated the death of the moon goddess in giving birth to vegetation and corn: Her body was flayed and worn by devotees or displayed, stuffed with straw and wearing sacrificial garments, on a litter of corn and harvest crops (Anawalt 1982, 54–56; 1984, 167–169). These fertility–vegetation goddesses often had lunar aspects and were impersonated by texiptlas wearing towering headdresses with rosettes representing buds or flayed human skins symbolizing their potential for new growth.

7.4. Tlazoltéotl, in flayed victim's skin, giving birth. (From *Codex Borbonicus*, folio 13, in Bibliothèque de l'Assemblée Nationale Française, Paris; redrawn by the author)

téotl's yarn ball and spindle headdress, U-shaped nose ornament, and broom were attributes used by her texiptla who was later sacrificially decapitated. In the *Codex Borbonicus* (Figure 7.4), she wears a crumpled-looking human skin while giving birth in hocker position to Centéotl, the young corn god. A little Dumbarton Oaks collection image of this event (sadly, perhaps a fake) is one of the most brutally direct representations of parturition known. It is not recommended for viewing by pregnant friends.

Individual devotion was shown to these and other deities by autosacrificial bloodletting, using maguey thorns or stingray spines to lacerate legs, ears, genitals, or tongue (Figure 7.3). Blood fell on hand-made paper that was then offered in the temples. Rulers celebrating military victories or electoral bloodletting (Klein 1987) and priests during religious ceremonies used more elaborate wood or stone perforators, possibly hummingbird-shaped ones resembling exacavated jade Olmec stilettoes (Figure 7.5) because hummingbirds represented Huitzilopochtli ("Hummingbird on the Left") and the Cihuateteo, women who died in childbirth. As Aztec death symbols, hummingbirds are shown sipping human blood through their beaks.

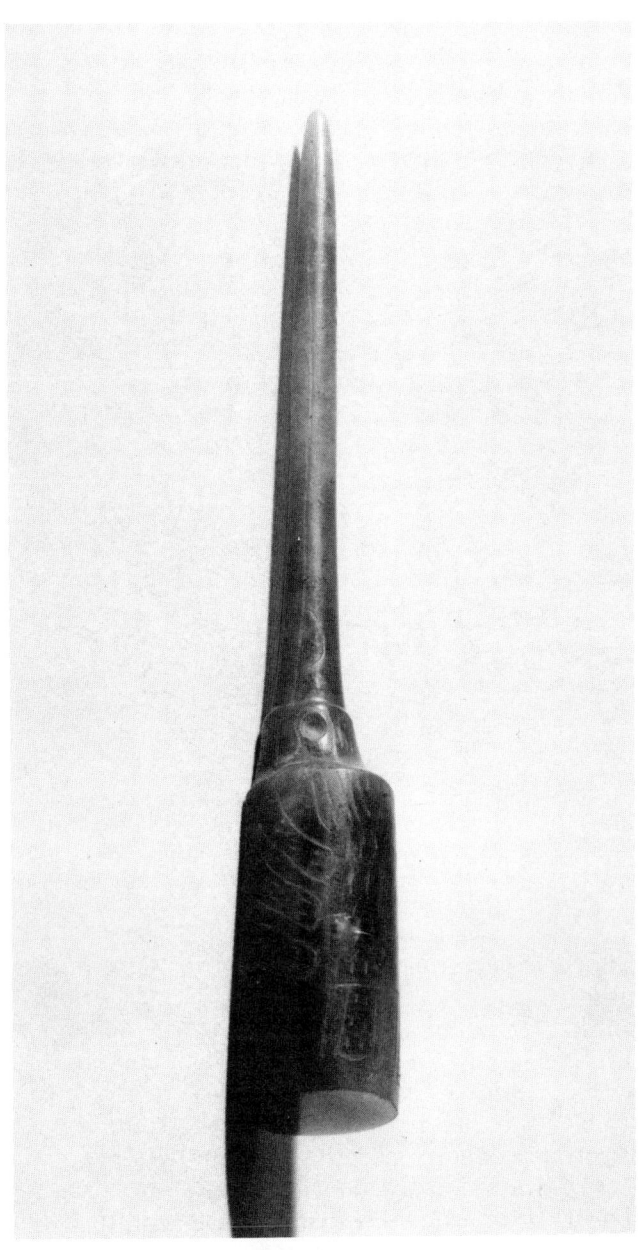

7.5. Jadeite Olmec stiletto representing the head and beak of a bird, perhaps a hummingbird. Possibly used as a bloodletter. (Courtesy DO)

Other fertility deities were Xochipilli ("Prince of Flowers"), a young god of dance and music with flower designs on his skin, and Tlazoltéotl ("Eater of Filth"), a Huaxtec Indian female deity who "ate" the sins confessed to her and also symbolized sexual intercourse, desire, and lust as adjuncts to human fertility.[3] Tlazol-

[3] For a particularly full description of Tlazoltéotl–Ixcuina, see Sullivan (1982).

7.6. Xipe Totec with diagnostic pointed cap, quail pendant, and flayed victim's skin (*Codex Borgia*, folio 25, in the Biblioteca Apostalica Vaticana, Rome; redrawn by the author from Seler 1904–1909)

Xipe Totec ("Our Lord the Flayed One") has traditionally been considered a fertility god representing life potential within death (Caso 1958; Nicholson 1972) but may in fact be a god of war and sacrifice (Broda 1970). In codices (Figure 7.6) he (or his texiptla) wears swallow-tailed streamers on his conical cap and belt, a sacrificial quail pendant, and a dry, seed-cover-like skin costume and mask cut from flayed victims stitched at the back and shoulders, so that only his lips and eyes showed through (Figure 7.7). Traditional interpretations parallel this life within death with seasonal crop renewal and the sun's daily death and resurrection.

With slightly different facial painting and a smoking mirror at his nape, Xipe becomes a Red Tezcatlipoca ("Smoking Mirror"; Figure 7.8). Xipe was honored with an earth-fertilizing sacrifice of war captives shot with arrows on a wooden frame (*Tlacacaliliztli*: Figure 7.9), and a final consecration of the skin costumes in a cave in the Xipe temple during the second ritual

7.8. Xipe Totec wearing a smoking mirror, as Red Tezcatlipoca. (*Codex Borbonicus*, folio 14; original in the Bibliothèque de l'Assemblée Nationale Française, Paris; redrawn by the author)

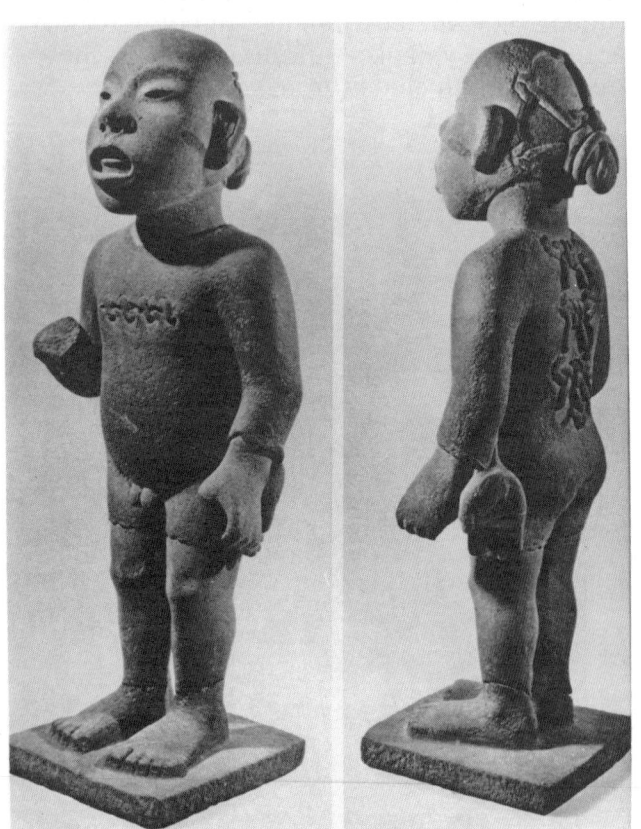

7.7. Clay sculpture of Xipe Totec. Note tie cords at the head and back, and the dangling hand of the skin costume. (Photo courtesy MNA)

month, Tlacaxipehualiztli. Another ceremony honoring Xipe was *tlahuahuanaliztli* (mock combat) in which enemy captives tied to a large ringlike stone, the *temalacatl* ("sacred spindle whorl") confronted Aztec warriors armed with real obsidian-set *macanas* with their own dummy weapons edged with feathers (Figure 7.10). Valiant survivors occasionally chose prestigious heart sacrifice death over freedom: The fact of death became secondary to the manner of death. Broda (1970) interprets these ceremonies, which both celebrate martial skills and underscore Aztec supremacy through tribute collection and redistribution, as a deliberate calendrical restatement of political power to discourage external rebellion and promote internal unity.

Earth. Several female deities represent Earth in her generative or death-receiving aspects. Victims offered to the ancient Toci ("Our Grandmother," and mother of Cihuacóatl, the birth goddess) were dashed on stones, offered through heart sacrifice or arrow sacrifice or roasted on her Divine Hearth during the eleventh month

7.9. An arrow sacrifice (*top*) and gladiatorial sacrifice (*bottom*). (*Historia Tolteca-Chichimeca*, p. 53; original in the Bibliothèque de l'Assemblée Nationale Française, Paris; reproduced from Preuss and Mengin 1937, pl. 15 [Berlin, Baesler Archiv])

under the direction of a female priestess. The shrine in Tepeyac of Tonantzin ("Our Holy Mother," perhaps an alter-image of Toci or Coatlicue) became the site for the Basílica of Mexico's Catholic Virgen de Guadalupe in a relatively easy Our-Mother to Our-Lady mental transition. A younger earth goddess and patroness of weavers was Xochiquétzal, ("Flower-Feather"), recognizable by the quetzal feather tufts on her headdress. Children of royal lineage were sacrificed to her in the thirteenth month

with a special flint knife after craftsworkers brought floral offerings to her image and entertained her doomed impersonator.

Earth was both bringer of plant life and receiver of human and solar death. The most impressive death representations are monolithic statues of Coatlícue ("Serpent Skirt"), a huge, flaccid-breasted figure with a skirt of interwoven serpents, immensely clawed upraised hands and feet for feeding on buried bodies, a skull back-ornament with pendant, shell-tipped

7.10. Gladiatorial conflict honoring Xipe Totec (on hill): a prisoner of war tied to a round stone (*left*), and a jaguar warrior with real *maçana* (*right*). (Fray Diego Durán, *Libro de los Dioses y Ritos*; original in the Biblioteca Nacional de Madrid; reproduced from Horcasitas and Heyden 1971, pl. 15, p. 337, courtesy University of Oklahoma Press)

leather braids, fanged faces at her bone joints, and a necklace of human hands, hearts, and skulls. Her decapitated head is replaced either by a skull or by gushing blood represented as two facing, profile serpent heads forming a single visage (Figure 7.11). As mother of Huitzi-

lopochtli and Coyolxauhqui (of whom more later) Coatlícue combines massive creative and destructive aspects.

Cihuacóatl ("Snake Woman") shows similar duality as patroness of birth, midwives, sorceresses, and the Cihuateteo, women who had

7.11. A stone sculpture of Coatlicue, unearthed in Mexico City's main plaza in 1790. (Heyden and Villaseñor 1984, p. 21; drawing by Alberto Beltran, courtesy EMM)

7.12. Cihuacóatl, "She of the Skirt of Serpents," with sacrificial face-knife headband, raising a weaving batten as a sword. (*Codex Magliabecchiano*, folio 45r.; original in the Biblioteca Nazionale Centrale, Florence; after Seler 1904–1909, p. 88, fig. 367b)

died in parturition. Her sword or sharp, eagle-feather-decorated weaving batten, skeletal white body, blade tongue, face joints, and headband of knives or hearts (Figure 7.12) signify her appetite for sacrificial hearts and blood. Her texiptla was ritually killed in festivals in the eighth month.

Cecelia Klein has shown that Aztec gods were often venerated as ancestors of rulers (1976, 234–238) and, by extension, patron deities of specific cities. Thus the cult of Cihuacóatl in Culhuacán, Xochimilco, and Cuitlahuac (cities in the southern Chinampaneca "floating-garden" lake area conquered by Tenochtitlán) was taken up by the Aztecs as a tool of state publicizing military conquest, and the title and costume of Cihuacóatl were awarded to the victorious general Tlacaélel, who organized Aztec military forays for prisoners to nourish the goddess (Klein 1986, 151–152; 1988b, 237–240 and 245–247). Klein suggests that many Aztec de-

ities operated at multiple social levels in multivalent roles, petitioned and/or feared by commoners while simultaneously reformulated as a state cult underscoring successful conquests and intimidating potential enemies (1986b, 248–251).

Earth, welcomer of the dead and receiver of sacrificial bodies, was the Earth Monster Tlaltecuhtli ("Earth Lord"), who shares Coatlícue's immense clawed, upraised hands and feet, curved fang faces at body joints, necklace of sacrificed hands and hearts, and skull back-ornament with braided pendants (Klein 1975, 71). In her female aspect, she lies bellydown in birth-hocker position with bent clawed arms and legs spread open, her head raised to the west to devour the setting stars and human dead. These pass below to her navel (Mictlán, realm of the dead) and are then reborn from her womb on the eastern horizon.

Tlaltecuhtli often appears on stone discs or *cuauhxicalli* sacrificial eagle bowl bottoms, with taloned, cuffed gloves ending in long paper strips, *chalchihuite* (precious jade stone) round-els on her face, long curled, feather-tufted hair, and a face-knife tongue. In other reliefs, her stylized, upturned mouth contains multiple tongue knives, and she sports a round, jade-rimmed navel and skull-and-crossbones skirt (Townsend 1979, 23–27; Figure 7.13). Even when shown three-dimensionally, her hands are raised to the shoulders, and her head is thrown back (Figure 7.14).

In shorthand form, Tlaltecuhtli splays herself on the above-the-stairs landing of an Aztec stone sculpture (Figure 7.15) known as the Teocalli de la Guerra Sagrada or "Holy House of Sacred War" (Townsend 1979, 49–63; Klein 1986,

7.14. Seated, three-dimensional Tlaltecuhtli from the Mexico City subway excavations. Note fanged serpent heads at feet, knees, and elbows; severed hand–heart necklace with trophy head pendant. The upturned hands and face are not visible in this photo. (Photo courtesy MNA)

7.13. Upward facing Tlaltecuhtli with (*top*) terraced mouth containing rounded teeth and four blades at center; round eyes above scrolled brows; "diadem" above falling hair; (*center*) round navel disc; clawed "serpent head" hands and feet; and (*bottom*) skull-bones skirt. (Original in a private collection; reproduced from Nicholson 1971a, fig. 43, p. 428; photo by G. Echaniz, courtesy MNA)

338–349). This miniature model of an Aztec temple is associated with *itzimiquiztli* ("death by the knife"), in which priests held the victim by the hands and feet over a sacrificial stone while a high priest opened the victim's chest with an obsidian knife, removed the heart (Figure 7.16), and rolled the body down the pyramid steps (Figure 7.17). Related motifs adorn the structure's sides, including masked, costumed priests and a skull and sacrificial knife exhaling the fire-and-water symbol of war fought to procure sacrificial victims. Two *cuauhxicalli* bowls for heart offerings top the teocalli's balustrades, and its backrest shows a hummingbird-head-dressed Huitzilopochtli (or the emperor Ahuí-

zotl?), left, with a fire-serpent foot and Huitzilopochtli, Tezcatlipoca, and Xiuhtecuhtli costume aspects (Klein 1987, 342–343), and Tezcatlipoca (Moctezuma II?), right, facing a giant 4 Movement-dated solar disc, focus of offerings to the sun (Figure 7.18b). After climbing the stairs, victims walked symbolically into Tlaltecuhtli's gaping jaws and sacrificial knife tongues on the landing (Figure 7.19) and were sacrificed by priests directly over her skull back-ornament.

Tlaltecuhtli as an earth cleft appears on the Dedication Stone honoring the Templo Mayor's completion in 1487 (Figure 7.20). As the ruler Ahuízotl ("Water Dog," right) and previous emperor Tizoc ("Bloody Leg," his brother, left) autosacrificially pierce their ears, their blood spurts past a woven grass ball with two inserted bloodletters and a pair of smoking "frying-

7.15. Temple of Sacred War (*Teocalli de la Guerra Sagrada*): model of a solar-cult temple. Tlaltecuhtli's image is carved on the landing above the steps. (Photo courtesy INAH)

7.16. Aztec heart sacrifice with five priests securing the victim to the sacrificial stone (Fray Diego Durán, *Libro de los Dioses y Ritos*; original in the Biblioteca Nacional de Madrid; reproduced from Horcasitas and Heyden 1971, pl. 7, p. 329, courtesy University of Oklahoma Press)

7.17. Heart sacrifice (*top*) with victim's body hurled to pyramid base. (*Codex Magliabecchiano*, folio 70r.; original in the Biblioteca Nazionale Centrale, Florence; reproduced from *Codex Magliabecchiano, Codices Selecti*, vol. 23 [Graz: Akademische Druck-u. Verlagsanstalt, 1970])

pan" incense ladles into Tlaltecuhtli's waiting mouth. Finally Mictlantecuhtli ("Lord of Mictlán," earth as land of the dead) received sacrificial victims plus the normal human dead.

Water and Moisture. Chief among water deities was Tlaloc ("Makes Grow," derived from the root *tlalli*, "Earth"), lord of heavenly precipitation, shown anthropomorphically with round donut eyes and a tusked, "moustache" upper lip, carrying lightning serpents and a thunder celt (Figure 2.20). Similar Tlaloques, little mountain gods, assisted Tlaloc by dumping jars of rain. Both received sacrifices of drowned noble children whose weeping encouraged rains via imitative magic, exemplified by Templo Mayor Offering 48, a stone cist containing eleven Tlaloc effigy jars, turquoise pectorals, shells, and the skulls and bones of forty-two children ranging in age from 3 months to 7 years (Matos Moctezuma 1988).

Johanna Broda (1987) widens Tlaloc's water associations to include mountains as sources of springs, based on small, stone "mountain-idol" caches in the Templo Mayor, itself a huge, offering-laden sacred mountain in the Aztec cosmovision. She theorizes that Tlaloc's Aztec earth aspect is a continuation of Esther Pasztory's Teotihuacán Jaguar (Type B) Tlalocs. Pasztory, for her part, traces martial Tlalocs with year-sign headdresses to Late Classic Xochicalco,

Cacaxtla, and select lowland Maya sites, perhaps as a title or indicator of Teotihuacán dynastic connections and notes Tlaloc and the year-sign headdress on stelae at Tula as well. She feels that the Aztecs adopted Tlaloc as a patron deity of past high cultures and recast him as the rain–earth deity father of their own Huitzilopochtli. His appearance on archaic, Toltec-style chacmools (Figure 7.21) reasserts Aztec claims to dynastic Toltec ancestry.

Tlaloc's female consort Chalchiuhtlicue ("Jade Skirt"), the patroness of oceans, rivers, and fishermen, is accompanied by a wavy water background, water or "preciousness" symbols, and a white-dotted, blue back-ornament in the codices. Her texiptla, like Tlaloc's, was sacrificed in the sixth month of the ritual cycle. Because her domain of earthly waters complements Tlaloc's heavenly rains, it is appropriate that the "presence of the sea" is strong in other Templo Mayor caches of Gulf- and Pacific-Coast shells, coral, stingray autosacrifice spines, shark's teeth, and crocodile skulls (Broda, 1987).

Fire. Xiutecuhtli ("Lord of Fire," also called "Lord of the Year" or "Lord of Turquoise") is one of the oldest gods, with affinities to Huehuetéotl, the wrinkled Preclassic "Old, Old God" of Fire. His attributes include a headdress with paired fire drills, a butterfly pectoral, and a *xiucóatl*, or fire serpent. Priests maintained a

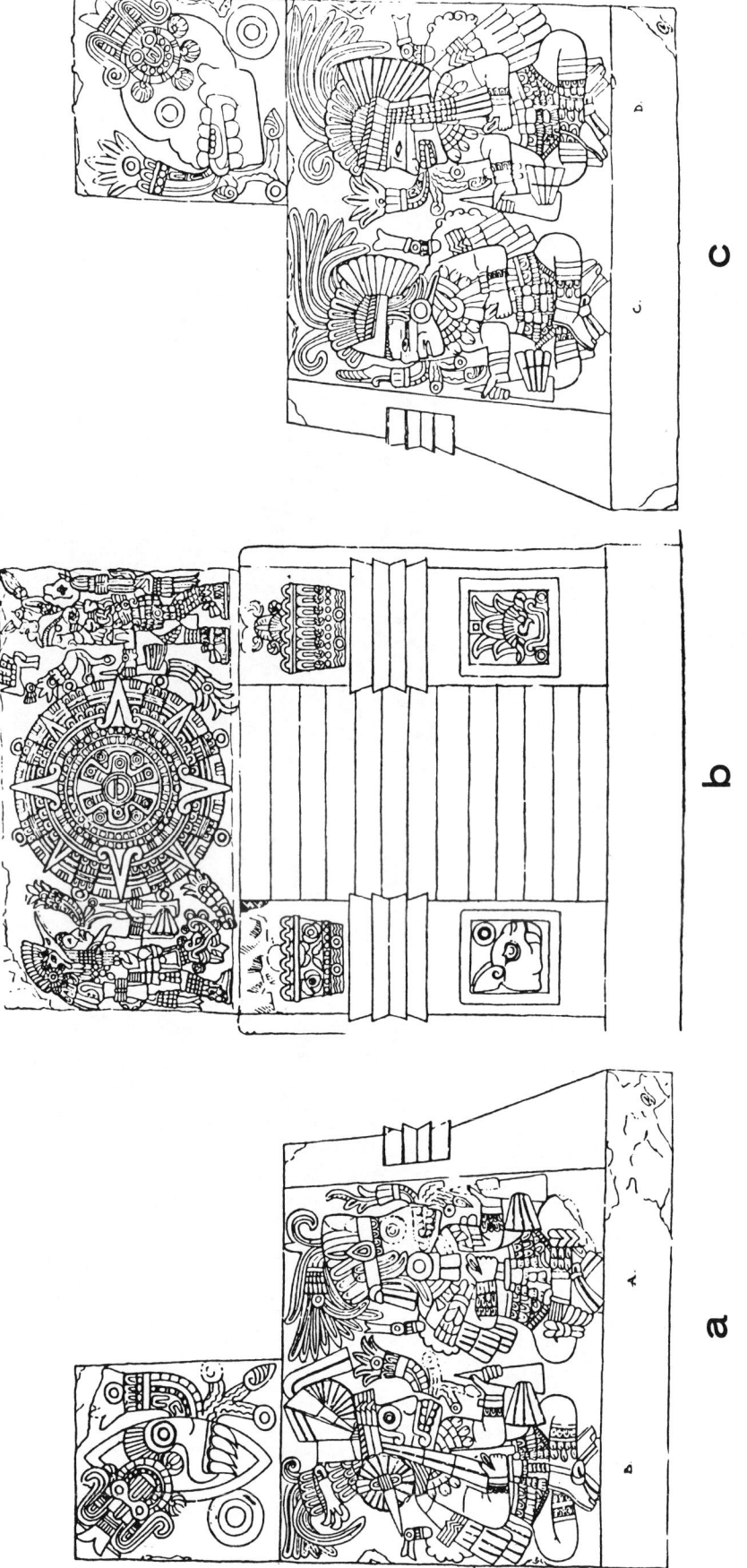

7.18. Carvings on the Temple of Sacred War (after Palacios): (*a*) the left side, showing the date "1 Knife" (face-knife with smoking mirror at ear and *atl-tlachinolli* war symbol at mouth, over two seated priests holding copal bags and perforators; (*b*) front balustrades with dates "4 Rabbit" (*left*) and "2 Reed" (*right*) at base, *cuauhxicalli* at top, Huitzilopochtli (?) (*left*, with bird headpiece) and Tezcatlipoca (or Moctezuma II?, *right*) facing "4 Ollin" solar disc; (*c*) the right side showing the date "1 Death" (smoking mirror and *atl-tlachinolli* over two-seated, cross-legged figures). (Townsend 1979, fig. 22b, e, f; drawings by Emily Umberger, courtesy DO)

7.19. Top of *Teocalli:* open, fanged Tlaltecuhtli mouth (*top*) with four-knifed tongue facing the stairs, scroll-browed eyes, clawed arms and legs, tasseled skull back ornament; date "2 House," stylized yarn ball and perforators between paper torches atop temple roof. (Marquina 1951, fig. 12; courtesy INAH)

7.20. Dedication Stone commemorating completion of the Templo Mayor: (*left*) Tizoc and Ahuizotl (*top right*) holding bloodletters, facing a grass ball with inserted perforators dripping blood into an upturned Tlaltecuhali mouth; (*below*) year sign "8 Reed." (Courtesy MNA)

7.21. Archaic-style Chacmool, a survival from Toltec antecedents, now with a Tlaloc eye mask. (Courtesy MNA)

perpetual flame at his Tenochtitlán shrine. During the tenth month, his texiptlas were roasted in a huge bonfire and then retrieved for heart removal.

Far more critical was the New Fire Ceremony at 52-year cycle conclusions when negative cosmic forces threatened the world's end. All hearths were extinguished, and Tenochtitlán waited anxiously as a procession of priest–texiptlas representing the most important gods crossed the southern causeway to initiate world-renewal ceremonies atop Cerro de la Estrella, "Hill of the Star." Just before midnight, a distinguished war captive's heart was offered to Xiutecuhtli, and a fire priest twirled a fire drill with tinder in his chest cavity. Its sparks were nurtured into a roaring bonfire immolating his body and announcing to watchers across the valley that another 52-year cycle would begin with the dawn. Runners carried the flame, Olympic fashion, to Huitzilopochtli's temple; from there it went to other major temples, local temples, and hearths of individual homes. The honored victim, like Christ, had offered himself on behalf of others, and Xiutecuhtli, Lord of the Year, had accepted his sacrifice, ensuring 52 more years of life.

Sun and War. A trinity of major gods share solar and war aspects as foci of heart sacrifice rituals. Tonatiuh ("Sun That Lights") carried a rayed solar disk like a miniature calendar stone on his back and was strengthened by heart sacrifice for his nightly battle through the Underworld. Huitzilopochtli ("Hummingbird on the Left"), the Aztec tribal deity, gained martial–solar attributes with time: By 1520 the gladiatorial and heart sacrifices of his festival, Panquetzaliztli, rivaled those to Tonatiuh. In codices, he wears a hummingbird mask and round, gold solar pendant and carries a shield ornamented with down balls. Spanish conquistadores saw his Templo Mayor idol, covered with gold, gems, and seed pearls encrusted with sacrificial blood.

Tezcatlipoca ("Smoking Mirror"), god of royal lineages, magicians, night, war, and death, had Toltec antecedents and red, blue, black, and white forms linked to the cardinal directions and other gods. A smoking mirror reflecting future events adorns his head and replaces one foot bitten off in a fight with the Earth Monster. He carries martial regalia: an atlatl, a bundle of darts, and a war shield covered with down balls and horizontal divisors similar to those of his "brother" Huitzilopochtli.[4] The oracular mirror and his capacity for jaguar transformation suggest aspects of shamanism (Brundage 1979, 81–83). Texcatlipoca's texiptla was royally feted for a year, heart-sacrificed in the fifth month, then ritually eaten by select nobles and the texiptla-elect.

Manipulation of Natural Forces and Crisis Management

Aztec ritual was directed toward maintaining powerful natural forces in smoothly operating harmony and ameliorating natural disasters that were the result of disharmony. The interplay between these forces and humans is documented both in visual arts and myths.

The Legend of the Five Suns. One of the most compelling Aztec myths concerns the five Suns, major cycles of creation and destruction. During the first four Suns, the world was destroyed by voracious jaguars, cataclysmic winds, rains of fire, and floods. The Fifth Sun, ushering in the Toltecs, is designated by 4 Ollin (four dots plus the X-shaped "Movement" or "Earthquake" day sign), the date of its creation and impending destruction by earthquake.

The Fifth Sun was created at Teotihuacán by gods who sacrificed themselves in a bonfire to form the sun, moon, and energy for their celestial movements. Quetzalcóatl then molded humans from corn and ancestor bones from previous Suns, animating them with his blood ("divine semen") from penis autosacrifice. Humans, therefore, could maintain the Fifth Sun by reenacting its mythical creation through autosacrifice and resacrifice, renewing its smaller 52-year increments through the New Fire Ceremony. The fact that the Fifth Sun was also the last gave urgency to the contract.

The Five Suns myth appears iconically on the famous Aztec Calendar Stone (Figure 7.22). Its large, central Ollin sign has symbols of the four preceding Suns in its arms, surrounded by an inner ring of the 20 day signs. The center face, with its taloned claws and sacrificial-knife tongue, is either Tonatiuh, the daytime Sun, or the nighttime Underworld Sun (Klein 1976, 103–113, and 1977).

---

[4]Klein (1976, 163–164) considers Huitzilopochtli as his most frequent alter-aspect because of names, directions, dwelling places and other iconic features they share.

7.22. Aztec Calendar Stone: (*center*) "4 Movement" sign and solar face; (*outside*) band of twenty day signs and solar rays, encircling fire serpents with heads at base. (Heyden and Villaseñor 1984, p. 4; drawing by Alberto Beltran, courtesy EMM)

The Coyolxauhqui–Huitzilopochtli Myth. Huitzilopochtli is associated with sacrifice and war through a second Aztec myth of divine conflict. A large stone disk (Figure 7.23) unearthed in 1978 at the bottom of the Templo Mayor stairway (Map 8 Area 2) graphically depicts his sister Coyolxauhqui ("Painted Bells"), a moon goddess according to Seler and Mexican interpretations but symbol of a defeated enemy to Klein (1988b, 241–243) as the first sacrificial victim. Coyolxauhqui and her 400 Huitznahua ("Star"?) warrior brothers, offspring of earth goddess Coatlicue ("Skirt of Snakes"), plotted to kill their mother for her unseemly "immacu-late conception" by a ball of fluff. At the moment of attack, Huitzilopochtli burst from her womb in full splendor, killed his siblings, carved out their hearts, and hurled their dismembered bodies to the bottom of Coatepec ("Serpent Hill").

Relationship of Sacrifice to Cosmic Myths

Each year the Aztecs reenacted this myth during the feast of Panquetzaliztli from Huitzilopochtli's temple atop the Templo Mayor, a replica, according to Matos Moctezuma (1984, 138, 149; 1987, 198–203) of Coatepec, as victims'

7.23. The Coyolxauhqui Stone depicting the dismembered moon goddess, discovered under Mexico City's streets in 1978. (Heyden and Villaseñor 1984, p. 4; drawing by Alberto Beltran, courtesy EMM)

hearts were offered to Huitzilopochtli and their bodies tossed down the great staircase onto the Coyolxauhqui disk below. Their heart/blood energy enabled the sun to vanquish the night-time underworld of Coyolxauhqui and the Huitznahua and return victorious on the morning horizon to outshine them and nurture all earthly life. Ongoing sacrifice reaffirmed the symbiotic contract between Huitzilopochtli and his People of the Sun, for without it the sun would die and their world would end.

Nature constantly reinforced the concept of sacrificial death engendering new life. The sun alternated with the nighttime moon and stars; its light weakened in fall and winter and revived in spring and summer. The monthly moon waxed and waned. New vegetation grew from seeds of crops that had been consumed and died. Life-bringing rains alternated with parching droughts. With such examples, it was clear that human life, too, must end to recharge the ongoing symbiosis of waxing and waning natural forces.

Conversely, imbalances could be corrected through appropriate ritual and increased sacrifice. When Ahuítzotl's canal overflowed, flooding Tenochtitlán to the first level of the Templo Mayor, oracles said increased child sacrifices petitioning Tlaloc to "turn off the water" were necessary. Bernal Díaz del Castillo reports that the coming of the Spaniards triggered massive human sacrifice to divine its significance and stave off disaster.

Art, Ritual, and State Policy

Cosmic rationales for offering human life meshed so well with Aztec political and military interests that they became official state policy. Festivals involving sacrifice of war prisoners intimidated allies, glorified war that brought in the tribute that supported the expanding, nonproductive upper classes (Klein 1986), and further motivated soldiers toward future combat. Thus an interesting question arises: Were myths validating solar sacrifice deliberately embellished to further Aztec conquests? If so, a likely candidate is Tlacaélel, Cihuacóatl-advisor to the fifteenth-century emperor Itzcóatl and a key figure in defeating the rival principality of Azcapotzalco. R. C. Padden (1967) describes him as a "brilliant psycopath" with a military power base of Azcapotzalco war heroes who rewrote Aztec history, naming the hitherto insignificant Mexica direct heirs of Toltec royalty and elevating Huitzilopochtli, formerly a minor tribal patron deity, to major status with Toltec major gods Quetzalcóatl and Tezcatlipoca. This charter provided a rationale for simultaneously nourishing the god and extending the domains of Huitzilopochtli's chosen people through war. His revamped image received its final polish in 1487 through completion of the Templo Mayor, sanctified by massive human sacrifice that left no doubts about his power and that of the Aztecs.

War for Procurement of Sacrificial Victims

Divinely mandated sacrificial war produced simultaneous economic, political, and religious benefits (Conrad and Demarest 1984, 44–52). With the defeat of Azcapotzalco in 1428, the Aztecs gained both independence and several tribute-paying dependencies. Emperors Itzcóatl and Moctezuma I moved into Oaxaca and Veracruz; prisoners graced the sacrificial altars, and tribute filled the coffers. Jaguar and Eagle warriors in the increasingly prestigious military machine entered battle willingly: Death on the field or as a captive guaranteed transmutation into a companion of the sun, and valor brought recognition, upward social mobility, and the right to wear godly insignia (Klein 1986, 151–153). As an expanding conquest state, the fortunes of the Mexica were on the rise.

Xochiyaóyotl: The Flowery War. In 1450 disaster came. The gods, dissatisfied with the quality of sacrifices, sent droughts causing widespread famine. Foreign wars were suspended, resulting in a dearth of captives at the same time that oracles showed the gods hungry for human hearts. The need shaped the institution: Tlacaélel, now advisor to Moctezuma Ilhuicamina, devised a ritualized conflict, the Flowery War (Xochiyaóyotl), in which warriors (whose colorful costumes resembled bright flowers) from six nearby cities under Aztec domination battled at a prearranged place and time. Killing was avoided because the aim was to take live prisoners; when each side had enough, the battle was stopped, again by "gentleman's agreement." Xochiyaóyotl supplied large numbers of sacrificial victims quickly without protracted logistics and had the added advantage of soothing Huitzilopochtli's finicky palate with an all-Nahuatl diet.

The Xochiyaóyotl solution worked. It kept the troops fit for foreign ventures and was self-reinforcing through the motivation of hero death and solar resurrection. As an institution that sustained ritualized sacrifice, militarism, solar worship, and the Aztec identity as people of the sun, Xochiyaóyotl is an excellent example of how cultural needs generate innovative behavioral solutions.[5]

As the empire grew, increased population and a rising, nonproductive nobility strained Tenochtitlán's chinampa system and resource base, leading to further military expansion for tribute. Deities from conquered populations, held hostage in the special Temple for Foreign Gods in an intimidating show of Aztec power, required additional sacrifices (Townsend 1979, 34–35; Klein 1986, 51–54; 1988b, 246–247, 250). The burgeoning pantheon, ceremonies for ruler accession and temple consecration (such as that for the Templo Mayor in 1487), and re-

quirements for managing occasional natural disasters motivated additional prisoner-generating foreign ventures and Coronation wars waged by the incumbent to validate his right to rule and prove his military abilities (Townsend 1987, 394–398).

Art in Support of Ritual and State Policy

Even as they participated in this milieu, Aztec artists helped sustain it by producing the images and cult objects underlying the ideology that perpetuated political and economic conquests and the luxury items used by the elite social class that planned and directed them.

Aztec "idols" are described ethnohistorically; the best surviving depictions of them are in codices and as stone sculpture. Archaeologically retrieved flint knives for sun-sustaining heart sacrifice had mosaic-inlay handles of crouching warriors (Figure 7.24) or eagles, symbol of the celestial sun; deified "face knives" with shell- and turquoise-mosaic eyes and mouths appear in codices and were bound with skulls imbedded in *copal* balls in the Templo Mayor. Sculptors produced elaborately carved *cuauhxicalli* ("eagle bowls") for heart/blood offerings to the sun. Small ones display death heads. Larger examples such as the Tizoc Stone, a sacrificial platform (Figure 7.25), show military exploits of the emperor who commissioned them. Cuauhxicalli are also held over the bellies of reclining, frontally facing chacmools, Toltec/Maya-derived figures with earth–Tlaloc imagery found in situ near major temples (see Figure 7.21).

Artists rendered the role of Xochiyaóyotl, the Flowery War, iconographically by combining its glyph, *atl tlachinolli* (consisting of conjoined water and fire bands) with symbolism connoting solar sacrifice and the founding of Tenochtitlán. Figure 7.26 shows a prickly-pear cactus rising from the open mouth of the splay-legged goddess Tlaltecuhtli, representing earth. On it, an eagle (the sun) perches and feeds on red cactus buds (*quauhnochtli*: eagle cactus fruit, "sweet food of the gods" according to Sahagún) that represent the hearts of sacrificial victims. The atl tlachinolli symbol, a reminder of how victims were obtained, dangles from its beak. Sacrificial blood, the sun's drink, was *teo-atl* ("sacred water") or *chalchiuh-atl* ("precious water"), glossed by combining the *atl* flowing-water symbol with shells and eyelike chalchi-

[5] Frederick Hicks (1979) and others, in an alternate interpretation, regard Xochiyaóyotl as a government attempt to draw attention away from failure to subjugate recalcitrant enemies such as the Tlaxcaltecans.

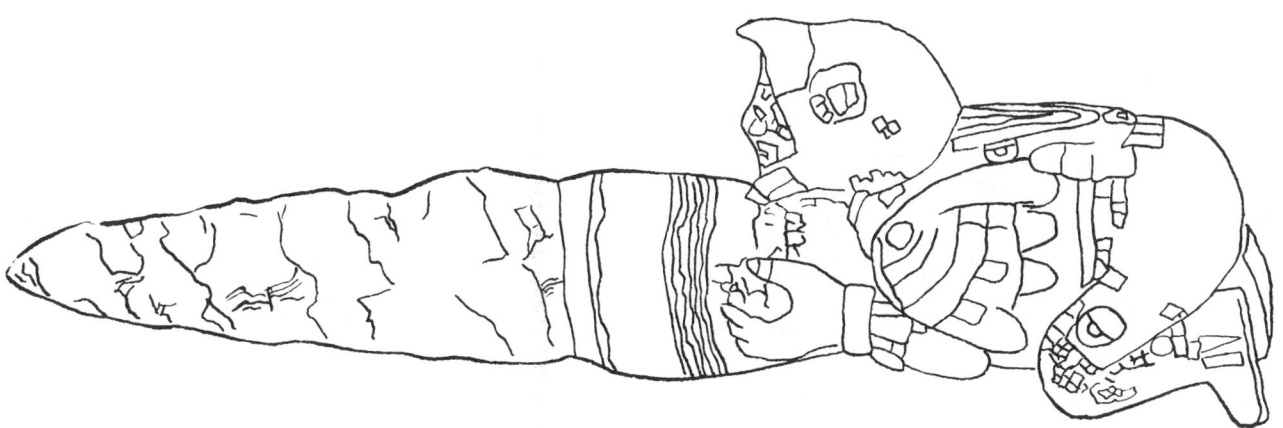

7.24. Aztec sacrificial knife with mosaic-inlay handle. (Drawing by the author of original in British Museum)

7.25. The Cuauhxicalli of Tizoc, with repeated scenes of the emperor Tizoc holding a captive by the hair. (Courtesy INAH)

huites of precious jade. The *tzompantli*, the display rack for the skulls of sacrificial victims, is shown in codices (Figure 7.27) and in sculpture by the 240 stone skulls on the walls of the Templo Mayor's Phase-VI Temple B (Matos Moctezuma 1988, 78).

Mexica craftsworkers further reinforced the system by accoutering the priests and rulers who guided it. Weavers, dyers, and feather workers produced the elaborate costumes worn by some of the texiptlas and collaborated with goldsmiths to garb and bejewel rulers and the lesser elite, using exotic trade materials and designs restricted to the privileged classes. Patricia Anawalt (1990) proposes that the distinc-

tive reticulated design with central dots on the blue-and-white, batik- and plangi-decorated cape worn by Aztec emperors matches the design in tribute textiles shown in codices paid in tribute by thirteenth- and fourteenth-century Toltec-influenced areas, validating their right to rule by visually restating their claim to ancestral Toltec connections.

Detailed study of minor arts such as costume and masks by a thorough investigator can produce impressively far-ranging cultural data. Cecelia Klein (1986) artfully describes how Aztec masks functioned as tribute, insignia recognizing military exploits, symbols of conquest, political titles, and hereditary indicators

of social status. Similar contextual analysis of other pre-columbian artforms may expose equally complex, interrelated socioeconomic connections beyond their explicit iconography. The legacy of Aztec artists documents a complex culture and a coherent cosmovision, the interpretation of which represents an exciting challenge to ongoing scholarship.

Ethnographic Vestiges

During the sixteenth century, the Aztec pantheon was subsumed under the guise of Catholic saints. Artists once more synthesized an alien style and religion, producing feather-work portraits of Christ and adding Tezcatlipoca's obsidian mirror to sculptures of Christian saints for extra power even as Spanish priests, eager for converts, linked Church ceremonies and saint days with Aztec festivals. Aztec ideas about sacrificial death to maintain life were channeled into safer Catholic alternatives.

7.26. Eagle with *atl-tlachinolli* ("Flowery War" sign) in beak, atop a nopal cactus with tunas symbolizing human hearts, rising from a Tlaltecuhtli (Earth) mask mouth. An incomplete Chalchiuhtlicue (earth, water) goddess is on the *lower right*. (Townsend 1979, p. 51; courtesy DO)

7.27. Tenochtitlan's Templo Mayor and *tzompantli*, as portrayed in the *Atlas de Durán*. (Heyden and Villaseñor 1984, p. 16; courtesy EMM)

The transition had its rocky moments. In the Maya area, sixteenth-century heart sacrifice was still performed on children crucified in the newly learned Christian manner. Robicsek and Hales (1984, 54) suggest a syncretistic appreciation of methods: "We can easily imagine how, when a converted Maya . . . heard of Abraham's planned sacrifice of Isaac, the story of Jesus's crucifixion, or the legends of the martyrs, his own heart must have filled with satisfaction at the thought, 'These Spanish barbarians are not so uncivilized after all'." The great Aztec festivals survive today as vestigial animal sacrifices for rain or good crops in remote Guatemalan and Mexican Indian villages. The Fifth Sun and heart sacrifice are no longer of concern.

Indians did identify readily with the European Day of the Dead (November first) because of their own ninth-month "Small Feast Day of the Dead" and tenth-month "Great Feast Day of the Dead". (Its preceding hallowed evening or Hallow'e'en', October 31, has taken a different, lighter turn in North America with costumed children trick or treating). Throughout Central Mexico, all-night vigils with food and candle offerings are held in Indian cemeteries: The most famous is on the island of Janitzio in Lake Pátzcuaro, in the state of Michoacán. Mestizos celebrate with *pan de muerto* breads and sweet rolls decorated with skulls and crossed bones and exchange gifts of candy skulls with the recipient's name iced on the brow.

Mexicans today know of the great Aztec sacrificial cults from museums, schools, and books, not from memory or ongoing tradition. The concept of Xochiyaóyotl, the Flowery War, survives as a transmogrified symbol on Mexican coins and the flag that show an eagle perched on a cactus biting a snake, the Spanish misrepresentation of the original atl-tlachinolli glyph. An era has passed, with death today reduced to grinning candy skulls and humorous wire and papier-maché folk figures, but it revives through Aztec sacrifice-related art to remind us, if we read between the lines, of our own tenuous "Fifth Sun" existence in a nuclear age.

EPILOGUE

In 1519, after skirting the Yucatán Peninsula, a small group of Spaniards under Hernan Cortés landed at Veracruz near the spot where Quetzalcóatl, the Feathered Serpent priest, had bade farewell to his faithful followers almost six centuries before. The year was a repeat of 1 Reed, his promised date of return.

Word quickly reached Moctezuma, who was already obsessed by portents of comets and a bird with a cephalic mirror showing men on strange beasts. Now, confronted by pale, blond, and red-haired beings who arrived in mountains that moved on water, rode swiftly across the land on huge snorting animals the Indians thought were immortal,[6] accompanied by snarling mastifs unlike the small, fat *escuintles* the Mexica raised for food, carrying flame-spurting muskets, Moctezuma vacillated between eliminating them as mortal intruders or welcoming them as returning gods. The overwhelmingly pervasive hold of gods and their cults on the Aztec mind tipped the decision. As Nicholson[7] movingly puts it:

> Late pre-Hispanic central Mexico was ruled more effectively by these shadow beings conjured out of the endless flow and surge of human hopes and fears than by any ostensibly mighty *huey tlatoani* [politico–religious ruler] reclining arrogantly on his jaguar-skin-draped throne. Only a full appreciation of this basic fact will allow any genuine understanding—however imperfect in many respects—of the extraordinary culture which produced the man who, in possession of more power than any other mortal in native North America could, in effect, deliver—without a blow in its defense—his populous, thriving empire to a tiny band of audacious strangers.

In the end, Moctezuma received Cortés in Tenochtitlán as a living god. With a welcome like that of the Rastafarians for Emperor Haile Selassie as a god-incarnate when he visited Jamaica or the tumultuous reception that would be given to a second coming of Christ in our own time, the Aztecs received in their midst the instruments of their destruction. In a few short years the Spaniards overcame all opposition, and the mighty Aztec empire was gone.

---

[6] One source mentions the Indian belief that horse and rider were one, so that seeing Spaniards dismount was a major shock. Another records a Spanish priest's discovery of a remote Maya group who had deified a runaway horse and fed it offerings of flowers. When it died, they thought they had killed a god and were remorseful for decades thereafter.

[7] Nicholson 1971b, 444–445. For readers wanting more insight into Aztec culture, I recommend *Aztec* (Jennings 1980). This vivid novel accurately incorporates the major personae of the Aztec rise as its hero, Miztli, suffers more adventures and misadventures than are any normal mortal's due.

PART TWO

PRE-COLUMBIAN SOUTH AMERICA

LEAVING Mesoamerica, we turn now to South America, where a second great florescence of high civilization developed in the Central Andean area of Peru, southern Ecuador, and northern Bolivia.

GEOGRAPHIC DIVISIONS

The Central Andean area is traditionally divided into North Coast, Central Coast, and South Coast and North, Central, and South Highland areas (Map 10). Over forty small, permanent or semipermanent rivers drain southwestward from the Andean foothills through narrow valleys to the Pacific. The coastal desert, dry because the cool off-shore Humboldt Current limits ocean evaporation and rainfall, is an archaeologist's dream for preservation of otherwise perishable materials.

In the highlands, people have lived for millennia in narrow northwest–southeast-oriented intermontane *callejones* that parallel the Andean cordilleras and permit farming of potatoes and highland grains. To the east, the Andean escarpment drops sharply from its *ceja de la montaña* ("brow of the mountains") to the tropical Amazon Basin below. Several major rivers (the Marañón and Huallaga in the north; the Apurimac and the Urubamba in the south) originate a scant 100 miles (160.9 kilometers) from the Pacific Coast to merge with the Amazon and eventually empty into the Atlantic 4,000 miles (6,436 kilometers) away. The eastern Andean slopes (the Montaña) with their major river systems and valuable tropical products form the third great subdivision of the Peruvian culture area.

THE ARCHAEOLOGICAL SEQUENCE

Central Andean archaeological cultures parallel those of Mesoamerica in terms of their broad development (Willey 1971; Lumbreras 1974). Early hunter–foragers may have arrived as early as 21,000 years ago and left stone and bone artifacts in highland caves. Eventually highland and lowland domesticates supplemented wild animals, plants, and abundant marine food resources. Sedentary villages, towns, and urban centers rose throughout Peru, to be interrupted in their development by the coming of the

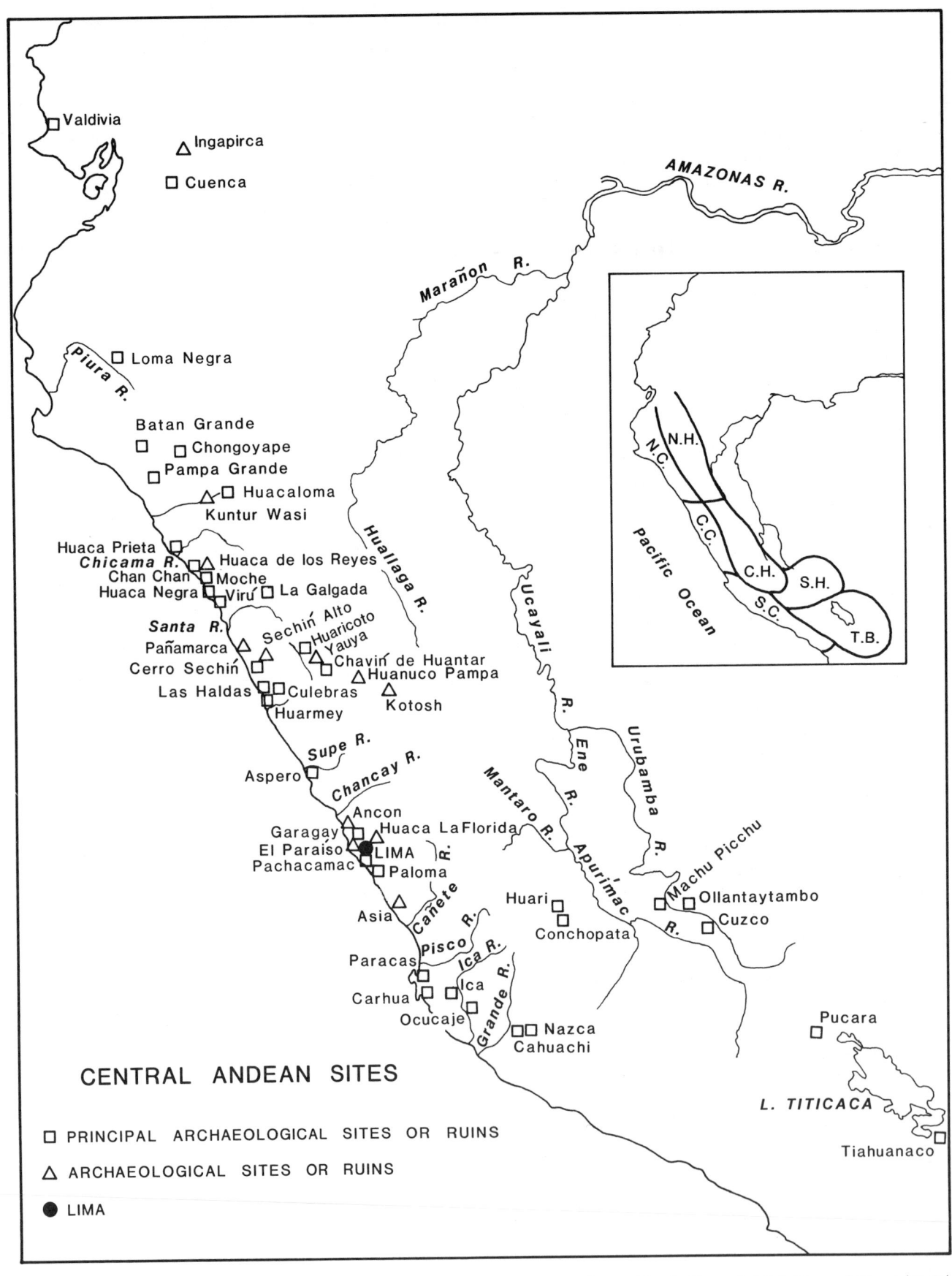

Valdivia

△ Ingapirca

□ Cuenca

AMAZONAS R.

Marañón R.

Piura R.

□ Loma Negra

Batan Grande
□   □ Chongoyape
□ Pampa Grande
△ □ Huacaloma
Kuntur Wasi

Huallaga R.

Huaca Prieta □
Chicama R. □ △ Huaca de los Reyes
Chan Chan □ Moche
Huaca Negra □ △ Viru □ La Galgada

Santa R.

Sechin Alto
△ Huaricoto
Pañamarca △ △ □ Yauya
Cerro Sechin □ □ □ Chavin de Huantar
Las Haldas □ □ Culebras △ Huanuco Pampa
□ Huarmey △ Kotosh

Ucayali R.

Supe R.

Chancay R.

Mantaro R.

Ene R.

Apurimac R.

Urubamba R.

Aspero □

Ancon
Garagay △ △ Huaca LaFlorida
El Paraiso ● LIMA
Pachacamac □ □ Paloma

Asia △

Cañete R.

Pisco R.

Ica R.

Grande R.

Huari □
□ Conchopata

Machu Picchu □ □ Ollantaytambo
□ Cuzco

Paracas □
Carhua □ □ Ica
Ocucaje □ □ □ Nazca
Cahuachi

Pucara □

L. TITICACA

CENTRAL ANDEAN SITES

□ PRINCIPAL ARCHAEOLOGICAL SITES OR RUINS

△ ARCHAEOLOGICAL SITES OR RUINS

● LIMA

Tiahuanaco □

Insert map: Pacific Ocean, N.C., N.H., C.C., C.H., S.H., S.C., T.B.

Map 10. Peru: Central Andean sites and geographical features. Insert map shows North Coast (N.C.), Central Coast (C.C.), South Coast (S.C.), North Highland (N.H.), Central Highland (C.H.), South Highland (S.H.), and Titicaca Basin (T.B.) subdivisions.

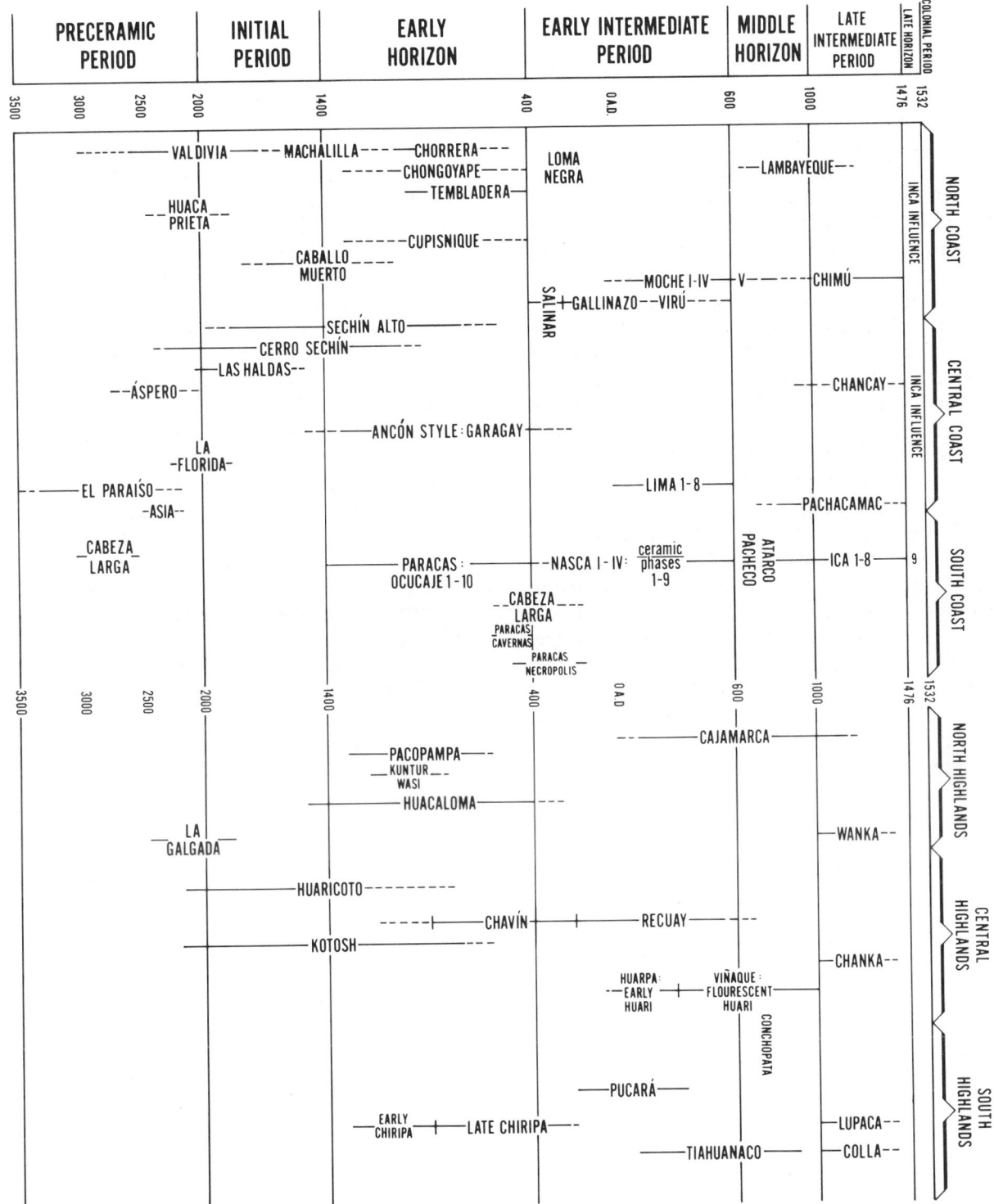

Table 2. Central Andean Peru: archaeological periods and regional sequences

Spaniards in 1532. An excellent overview of this progression, including descriptions of major projects, shifts in research emphases, and key bibliographic citations for the major archaeological periods, may be found in Burger (1989).

The archaeological sequence (Table 2) includes Preceramic, Initial period, Early Horizon, Early Intermediate, Middle Horizon, Late Intermediate, and Late Horizon divisions. The three horizon divisions are still widely used, though their utility is increasingly being questioned because the art styles they represent lasted longer and had a more spotty geographical distribution than had been originally thought.

During the long Preceramic period, which ended at about 2000 B.C., small communities inhabited Peru's intermontane valleys and coastal riverbanks where oases of vegetation (lomas) were nurtured by ocean fog. Around 3500 B.C., Pacific currents changed, and the Humboldt Current developed a cold upper-level flow that cut off the fogs so vital to lomas growth. It also brought up algae from the ocean depths that attracted numerous fish reserves and guano-producing ocean birds. These marine resources became "sea harvests" for coastal peoples so that domesticated food plants were only an incidental supplement.

A domesticate of far greater impact was cotton, a cross between wild Asiatic and indigenous American types. It appeared at around 3000 B.C. and extended the bast-fiber textile production already underway. Finely netted, warp-float, twined, and eventually loom-woven cloths mark the beginnings of Peru's long textile heritage and, with pyro-engraved domesticated bottle gourds, were used centuries before the appearance of pottery, in contrast to the cluster appearance of textiles, pottery, corn, and settled life in Mesoamerica. Corn appears on the coast between 2500 and 2000 B.C., perhaps coming from Mesoamerica, and potatoes were domesticated internally in the highlands.

The Initial period (2000–1400 B.C.) marks the appearance of pottery and settled life, with large-scale ceremonial structures in some areas. In the North–Central Coast, Las Haldas, beginning in the late Preceramic around 2000 B.C., peaked at about 1800 as a preagricultural town based on fishing resources that may have supported a population of 10,000 people. Kotosh is a major highland ceremonial site, located in the Montaña and known through Japanese excava-

tion. Its earliest phase contains three temple structures and bones of llama offerings. Llama sacrifice was also found at the North Coast Virú Valley Temple of the Llamas by 1800 B.C. These and other sites maintained themselves on the basis of sea resources, manioc, peanuts, maize, and, in the highlands, potatoes, grains and coca.

The Early Horizon (1400–400 B.C., though dates vary with different sources) marks the appearance of complex, cult-related art motifs best represented at the Central Highland site of Chavín de Huantar in several highland and coastal areas. However, recent data indicate that Chavinoid motifs already occur at coastal centers during the preceding Initial period and that the development of Chavín's diagnostic art style may be a late Early Horizon development.

The Early Intermediate period (400 B.C.–600 A.D.) covers the reemergence of local cultures after Chavín influence had waned. These include Moche on the North Coast, Nasca on the South Coast, and Pachacamac on the Central Coast.

The Middle Horizon (A.D. 600–1000) once again saw a limited horizon style as religious motifs from the South Highland site of Tiahuanaco spread through the Central Highland site of Huari to select coastal and highland cultures. In other areas, non-Huari states remained in control.

The Late Intermediate period (1000–1476) was again marked by regionalism as large cities such as Chan Chan in the North Coast (Chimú culture), Chancay in the Central Coast, and the Ica culture in the South Coast emerged from Middle Horizon influences and broke out into independent patterns.

During the Late Horizon (1476–1532), a truly pan-Andean horizon style accompanied the spread of Inca political influence into both highlands and coast, only to be interrupted and demolished by the Spaniards under Pizarro.

CHAPTER 8

CHAVÍN

THE Early Horizon is best known for the highland ceremonial center of Chavín and the widespread distribution of art in the Chavín style throughout both highland and coastal sites as a horizon style.

In order to understand the rise of Chavín, scholars have attempted for decades to amplify the Preceramic, late Initial period, and Early Horizon context of Chavín's beginnings.

Origins

Part of the difficulty in separating out sites with pre-Chavín similarities from sites affected by the spread of developed Chavín iconography had been the lack of a firm chronology for early sites and, indeed, for Chavín itself. Excavations by Luís Lumbreras and Richard D. Burger have produced a sequence based on ceramics and architecture that finally makes comparison and cross-dating possible (Lumbreras 1974; Burger 1984). According to Burger (1981, 1984), Chavín was occupied between 850–200 B.C., and its fully developed iconography spread after 600 B.C. Recently, sites have been found with Chavinoid architecture and iconography that predate Chavín's occupation by several centuries, confirming that the site's major ceremonial architecture and its full-blown art style developed more recently than had been thought.

Preceramic and Initial Period Settlements

Archaeologists have known for years that South America's northwest coast sustained early, successful settlement several millennia before the birth of Christ. One of the most intriguing examples is the site of Valdivia on the Guaylas Coast of Ecuador, where coastal fishers used a gray, rocker-stamped pottery by 3000 B.C. A slightly later, fishing–collecting culture, Machalilla, produced more sophisticated ceramics in the same area and slightly to the north. Valdivia and Machalilla are among the earliest South American pottery producers and users.

Contemporary shoreline settlements on the Peruvian coast lacked pottery but developed early textile traditions. Junius Bird found horticulturalists who wove complex twined textiles living in multiple-room houses by 2500 B.C. at Huaca Prieta near the North Coast Chicama Valley (Map 10). Subsequent excavation in the Jequetepeque Valley to the north revealed Initial-period pottery-using sites with terraced platforms and U-shaped mound complexes containing sunken, circular courts, repeatedly rebuilt after floods and landslides.[1]

Preceramic Huaca Negra, Culebras, Las Haldas, and Huarmey on the North Coast, Aspero, Huaca La Florida, Ancon, Chilca, and Asia on the Central Coast, and Cabeza Larga on the South Coast (Map 10) confirm that sedentary maritime–horticultural adaptation was widespread. Large masonry platforms at the 13-hectare site of Aspero in the Supe Valley contain caches of twined textiles and burials with beads and feather work, indicating Preceramic status differentiation, corporate labor, and ceremonial activity (Feldman 1983). El Paraíso, inland from the Chillón River, is even bigger (50 hectares), with six huge mounds, courts, and rooms with corridors.

Late Initial Period/Early Horizon Sites with Chavinoid Features

Coastal Sites. By 1200 B.C., a number of coastal sites with populations of several hundred people had adobe brick structures far larger and more numerous than anything in Mesoamerica. North Coast Jequetepeque Valley sites have U-complexes and both circular and rectangular sunken courts (Ravines 1985). Caballo Muerto's Huaca de los Reyes temple niches contain friezes depicting a frontal human standing on or flanked by profile feline heads with Chavinoid crossed canines and a serpent-head sash. Downcoast in the Casma Valley, Cerro Sechín's pre-1300 B.C. stone walls show long-haired profile and frontal trophy heads with closed eyes, profile staff-bearing warriors, and dismembered arms and legs. Nearby Sechín Alto has a granite-faced pyramid fifteen times larger than Chavín's Castillo with multiple platforms, rectangular patios, and plazas with two sunken courts. South of the Casma Valley, Las Haldas's large stepped pyramid and two circular sunken courts date to 1200 B.C., well before Chavín's Castillo. Other Central Coast sites also have complex truncated mounds and platforms with U-shaped

arms: Garagay, in addition, has polychrome friezes with Chavinoid elements that date to 1000 B.C. Researchers relate the rise of these Central Coast ceremonial sites to the introduction of new root crops, irrigation, and *mita*-like corporate labor and theorize that the land enclosed by U-platforms produced sacred gardens connected with water-management rituals in the temples (Williams 1985; Moseley 1985, 48–49) well before Chavín's Old and New Temple construction.

Highland Sites and the Kotosh Religious Tradition. The highlands tell a similar story of established occupations followed by elements of "Chavín-style" architecture and/or sculpture well before the construction of Chavín's great temple. In the North Highlands, La Galgada on the Upper Santa River has early Initial-period courts within U-platforms and pottery, goldwork, and textiles with Chavinoid features; however, temples here and at Shillacoto (Map 10) have superimposed hearths containing burned pepper seeds suggesting distinctive rituals, perhaps fumes for sweatbath purification (Burger and Burger 1980; Grieder and Bueno 1981, 45–51; Grieder and Bueno 1985). In the Cajamarca Basin, Japanese excavations date Late Huacaloma fragments of a seven-color mural and Chavinoid stone carvings to 1000–500 B.C. Kuntur Wasi (La Copa), long considered to be contemporary with Chavín because of its carved stone feline–human sculptures, produced Initial period rectangular buildings with central hearths; Huaricoto, 55 kilometers (34 miles) from Chavín in the Callejón de Huaylas, also has early hearths with animal bone and coastal shell offerings within stone-lined sunken courts, followed by Early Horizon Chavinoid material and dressed stone shrines.

These highland late Preceramic and Initial period sites participated in what Lucy and Richard Burger call the "Kotosh Religious Tradition" of sunken-court firepits for cyclical offerings within walled sacred precincts. Kotosh, on the Huallaga River of the east Andean Montaña, dates back to ca. 2000 B.C., with late Preceramic temple wall-niches, one with two sets of crossed clay arms on its walls. Its earliest, Wairajirca and Kotosh phases, pottery has strong tropical affiliations. During the late Early Horizon, Kotosh, Huaricoto, and other North–Central Highland sites peacefully integrated Chavín influences with ongoing firepit rituals,

---

[1] Ironically, several have succumbed to one great final flooding from the Gallito Ciego dam project (Ravines 1985, 224–226).

suggesting a source other than the North Highlands for Chavín's distinctive art.

Early Horizon Chavín

The site of Chavín de Huántar lies at an altitude of 10,285 feet (2,135 meters) on the eastern slopes of the Cordillera Blanca in the North–Central Highlands near the Río Mosna, one of the tributaries of the mighty Marañon (Map 10). The area has good soils in which potatoes, *quinoa*, beans, and *oca* are grown and is within an easy 2- to 3-hour walk to higher pastures so that a "vertical archipelago" of different cropping is possible (Burger 1984, 8). It is also an area of frequent landslides that have buried parts of the site in both archaeological and recent times, redepositing material and making excavation difficult.

Chavín's archaeological features cover an area of at least 40 hectares (almost 99 acres), making it one of the New World's largest settlements for its time (Burger 1984, 235). Its temple complex lies between the juncture of the Mosna River and its smaller tributary, the Huacheseca (Wacheksa); surveys by Burger extend the habitation zone to the far side of the Huacheseca that was canalized within stone walls and crossed via a polished stone-slab bridge (rather like Cuzco's central plan centuries later!).

Chavín's organic, internal growth occurred in several increments. John Rowe (1962, 1967) attempted to assess this development within a tentative sequence of phases, from A through F, based on stylistic seriation of architecture and sculpture. These phases are discussed in greater detail in the subsequent section on Chavín art. Several seasons of excavation by Peruvian archaeologist Luís G. Lumbreras (1974, 71–72) produced conflicting results but added important information on Chavín's architecture, ceremonial offerings, and ceramic types. More recently, Richard Burger has linked ceramics from stratigraphic contexts to firm carbon-14 dates and defined three ceramic phases (Burger 1981; 1984, 17, 277). These are the Urabarriu phase of earliest settlement (850–460 B.C.), the Chakinani phase characterized by classic Chavín-style incised pottery (460–390 B.C.), and the Janabarriu phase of maximum site expansion, cult activity, and ceremonial construction (390–200 B.C.).

Chavín was not an empty religious center but a major settlement of over 2,000 people located on an important highland–Montaña route with walls to regulate access (Burger 1984, 221–224). Chert, obsidian-, bone- and shell-working areas indicate occupational specialization, whereas terracing and complex architecture with galleries and drainage systems imply the organization of a large work force, perhaps drawn from the Upper Santa River Basin. Fragments of carved white granite with complex Chavín imagery and cult shrines found at two nearby sites, Pójoc and Waman Wain, suggest that Chavín was a synchoritic settlement linked to populations in support hamlets through shared rituals and symbiotic exchange of goods and services (Burger 1982, 21–23).

Architecture

At Chavín, Late Preceramic and Initial period North and Central Coast architectural traits (U-shaped platforms and circular, sunken courts) and motifs were brilliantly synthesized with new motifs, probably of tropical inspiration, and the site flourished as a ceremonial center with sophisticated architecture during the Janabarriu phase (390–200 B.C.) as coastal centers fell into decline (Burger 1981, 600).

El Castillo, Chavín's main structure, is a composite of stone-faced platforms that underwent several reconstructions and probably served as temple foundations. They were lower and far more complex than Mesoamerican pyramids, with a multilevel honeycomb of rooms, ramps, passageways, galleries measuring up to 6 by 15 feet (1.8 by 4.5 meters), and air ventilator shafts and ducts connecting to the outside. Rooms originally contained sacred images; many have wall niches containing offerings of llama, fish, and guinea-pig bones. South Coast marine shells in the Gallery of the Offerings indicate active trade or perhaps pilgrimages (Lumbreras 1974). After Chavín's collapse, most of the cult images were removed, and interior galleries were reused by later people as tombs.

Platform exteriors were dressed with granite slabs, and three-dimensional human, serpent, and feline heads, some still in place, were sunk into the walls with pegs or tenons (Figure 8.1a, b) giving the effect of a sculptured frieze (Figure 8.2). Low-relief carving decorates lintels, cornices, columns, altars, and exterior walls.

El Castillo's construction began during the

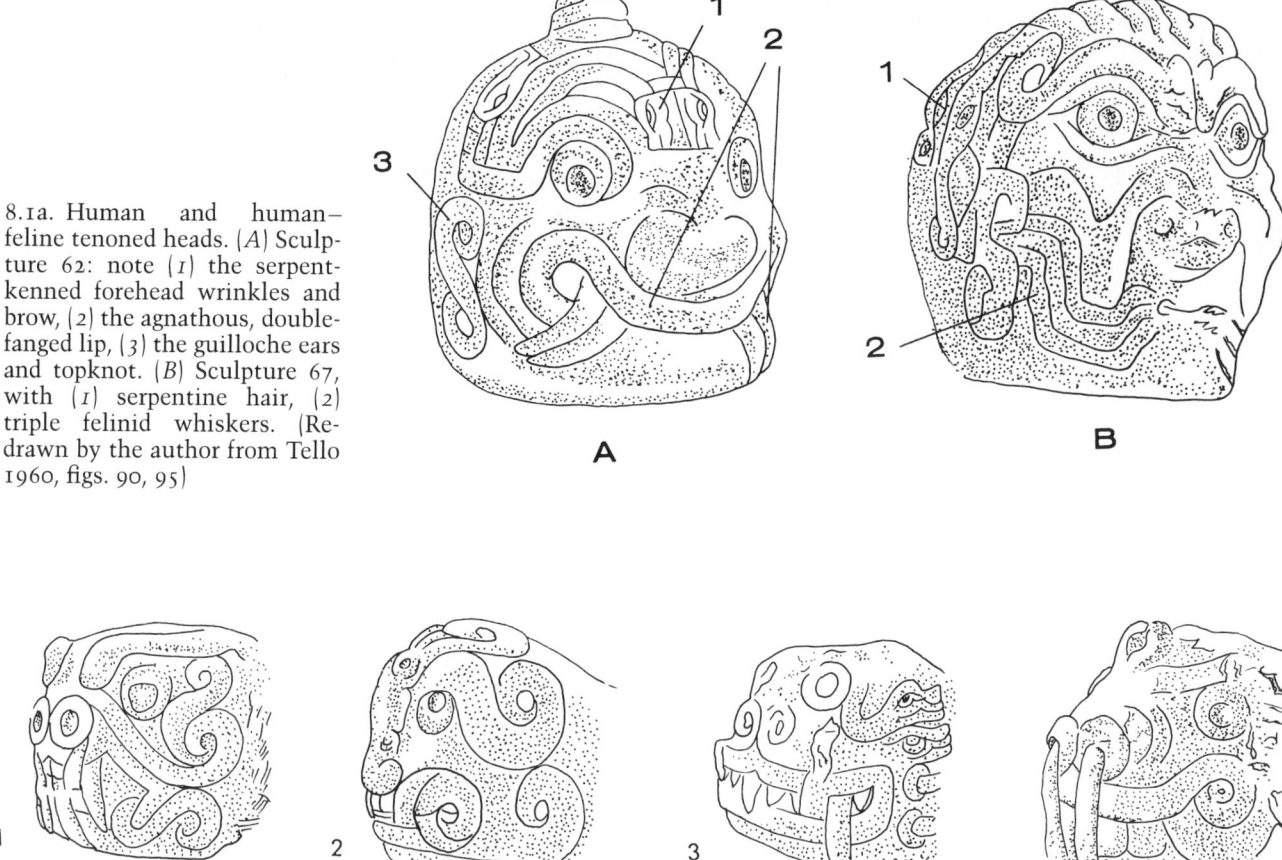

8.1a. Human and human–feline tenoned heads. (*A*) Sculpture 62: note (*1*) the serpent-kenned forehead wrinkles and brow, (*2*) the agnathous, double-fanged lip, (*3*) the guilloche ears and topknot. (*B*) Sculpture 67, with (*1*) serpentine hair, (*2*) triple felinid whiskers. (Redrawn by the author from Tello 1960, figs. 90, 95)

8.1b. Feline and reptilian tenoned heads: (*1*) Sculpture 70, with six-fanged mouth; (*2*) Sculpture 71, with scrolled mouth and brow; (*3*) Sculpture 91, a "serpentine monster" with serpent-kenned whiskers and brow; (*4*) Sculpture 95, a "monster" with nasal streamers, "slat" teeth, and "smiling" moustache-lip. (Redrawn by the author from Tello 1960, figs. 98, 99, 119, 123)

8.2. Placement of heads on the western facade, Structure A, Chavín. (Tello 1960, fig. 7; courtesy UNMSM)

8.3. East facade of Chavín Temple, showing Black and White Portal. (Photo by Luis Lumbreras, courtesy MNCP)

Urabarriu phase (850 B.C.) with a 15-meter-high (49.2 foot) east-facing U-shaped structure—the Old Temple. Its arms enclose a sunken, circular plaza lined with large 70 by 80 cm (28 by 31 inch) carved blocks depicting fanged, clawed humans carrying Strombus-shell horns and the barrel-like San Pedro cactus, above a lower row of profile felines (Lumbreras 1977, 11−14). Inside, a cross-shaped gallery still houses a 4.5-meter-high (15 foot) cult object, the Lanzón, or Great Image.

During the Chakinani phase (460–390 B.C.), additions expanded the Old Temple's north and south wings. By 400 B.C., religious beliefs apparently shifted, and during the subsequent Janabarriu phase (390–200 B.C.), cult imagery proliferated, and the south wing became the main focus of worship as the New Temple, with an entrance portal and stairs leading up to two smaller entrances at midlevel of the platform face (Figure 8.3). New, long, low platforms recreated the Old Temple's U-form, this time enclosing a sunken rectangular court with 90-meter (295 foot) sides and four low entry stairs.

The New Temple entry, the Black and White Portal, was particularly elaborate, with its south face of white granite slabs and north face of black limestone (Figure 8.4). Its lateral cylindric

8.4. The Black and White Portal of Chavín's Castillo. (Photo by Luis Lumbreras, courtesy MNCP)

columns show an upward-looking feline/hawk-beaked figure on the right and a masked eagle figure on the left like matched winged angels guarding the image within (Figure 8.5). Fragments of cornices, now fallen, were also carved with feline–avian motifs (Figure 8.6), and the doorway lintel also shows hawks and eagles (Figure 8.7).

With its elaborately ornamented ceremonial architecture, Chavín became an important late

A

B

8.5. (A) Hawk-masked guardian, North Column, Black and White Portal: note the tear band, continuous mouth band as wing axis, agnathous jaguar head on staff, anklets, and kilt border; jaguar heads with shared mouth and eye on diagonal panels. (B) Eagle-masked guardian, South Column, Black and White Portal. (Rowe 1967, figs. 8 and 9; drawings courtesy John Rowe)

A

B

8.6. Jaguar-masked birds: from (A) cornice facing Black and White Portal, with jaguar heads on wing and tail feathers, kilt edging, and knees; mouth-band backbone; and (B) from New (South Wing) Temple cornice. Note "mouth-band" anklets over foot disgorged as "tongue," profile jaguar heads disgorging the leg as a "tongue," mouth band disgorging wing feathers. (Rowe 1967, figs. 11 and 12; drawings courtesy John Rowe)

A

B

8.7. (A) Jaguar-masked hawk from above the doorway lintel, Black and White Portal, with tear band, mouth band as wing axis, inverted jaguar mask at chest, serpent-keened lip; (B) jaguar-masked eagle from above the door-way lintel, Black and White Portal—a simplified version with jaguar eye and brow at ends of continuous mouth band denoting wing axis. (Rowe 1967, figs. 15 and 16; drawings courtesy John Rowe)

Early Horizon center outshining contemporary Garagay, Las Haldas, and Caballo Muerto that declined as Chavín's New Temple was being built.

ART

Chavín's complex art style, well preserved on stone, in contrast to more perishable coastal remains, attracted early excavators, among them Peruvian archaeologists Julio Tello and Rafael Larco Hoyle. Tello's reports focused on the elaborately carved monuments and ceremonial architecture; accordingly, he viewed Chavín as a center of origin ("cultura matríz"), the inspira-

tion for all later Andean high cultures. In the absence of sound chronologies based on architectural and ceramic sequences, art resembling Chavín's at subsequently excavated coastal and highland sites was interpreted as Chavín-derived during a pervasive Chavín horizon style.

Possible Sources

We now know that Initial period coastal sites, already described, are one highly likely source of origin. Tello proposed influences from the eastern montaña because Chavín's jaguars, condors (an early identification), and serpents are important in the beliefs of contemporary montaña tribes (Tello 1960). Larco Hoyle, a North Coast landowner, concluded that North Coast Nepeña Valley pilgrims inspired Chavín. Others see Chavín as an indigenous Central Highland development or see similarities to early double-spout and bridged pottery from Ecuador (Lathrap 1971, 89–90).

Diffusionists look farther afield. Michael Coe has pointed to specific shared designs and a general similarity of jaguar themes between Olmec and Chavín, perhaps spread through oceanic contacts by Olmec-influenced people from the Mesoamerican West Coast; Heine-Geldern looks to the terminal phases of Chou Dynasty China for similarities (Coe 1962, 1963; Heine-Geldern 1959). The question is still unresolved.

Spread of Chavín Motifs

Once full-blown cult iconography was enshrined in the New Temple at Chavín, Chavinoid themes proliferated to both highlands and coast, accompanied by an increase in temple building, agricultural settlements, and population expansion. Highland Kuntur Wasi (La Copa) in the north and Yauya in the Middle Marañón drainage (Map 10) share Chavín motifs on stone sculpture, whereas North Coast Cupisnique and Vicus produced thick, massive black pots resembling Chavinoid carved stone, with stirrup spouts larger than their globular bodies. A cache of gold crowns and pendants from North Coast Chongoyape faithfully mirrors Chavín iconography, whereas South Coast pottery and textiles show direct continuing connections. Both coasts transferred motifs from Chavín stone carving to cloth and clay because of the local absence of stone. Only the

South Highlands participated less actively in the shared cult imagery.

Chavín imitations or trade pieces accompany indigenous wares in habitation, ritual, and burial areas, indicating use by local residents rather than administrators or foreign garrisons. The accepting cultures had no fortifications, and Chavín's population was too small to sustain extensive conquest. Ideas probably spread through cult missionaries, pilgrim–converts returning home from visits to highland shrines, and/or imported Chavín artisans, perhaps accompanied by desirable new strains of corn as has been suggested by excavations in the Virú Valley (Katz 1969, 94). Cult acceptance may also have accelerated due to coastal disequilibrium and lowered food production from a fifth-century climatic disaster triggered by El Niño, the sporadic, torrential rains that sometimes inundate the South American coast during the Christmas season, according to another recent suggestion.

Chavín Style

The classic descriptions of Chavín style are by John Rowe (1962, 1967). Subjects include raptorial birds (eagles with markedly curved beaks and hawks with tear bands at the base of the eye); jaguars identifiable by their pelage markings; profile serpents; and human figures, with various other birds, animals, plants, and marine life in secondary roles. Their interplay on the same figure is one of the most complex known in any art form.

Rowe sees Chavín style as basically representational but expressed in a figurative, metaphorical manner. Its diagnostics include frequent *bilateral symmetry*; *rhythmic, sequential repetition* of elements; use of *modular bands* to set out a design; *mutual use of a design element* by several figures; use of *basic units of curved lines, straights, and scrolls*; and the extensive use of *kennings*.[2]

Consistent visual kennings signal qualities

<hr/>

[2] Kennings in Old Norse tenth-century court poetry are indirect references to a subject through something with similar characteristics. Rowe gives the examples "The seal's field roared in wrath under the banners," alluding to the sea's sweeping waves that suggest the movement of troops in battle. This is a kenning twice removed:

  the seal's field = the sea = moving army

Kennings thus go beyond simile ("the waves of men"). They tease the senses through subtle associations in a highly sophisticated form of punning.

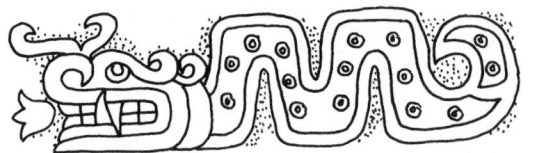

8.8. Figures with feline–serpent attributes from the cornice at the southwest corner, New Temple. Note the jaguar's tail and kenned as (*1*) the "tongue" of the profile rump mask and (*2*) the "neck" of the frontal head at its tip; (*3*) the foot kenned as the profile ankle mask's "tongue." (Redrawn by the author from Rowe, J. 1967, fig. 17)

that we can recognize but only partially appreciate. Favorites at Chavín are:

1. Jaguar tongues for flexible body appendages such as arms, legs (Figure 8.5), or tails (Figure 8.8 bottom, 1). To identify the kenning as a tongue, it is set in a fanged jaguar mouth with flared nostrils and upturned eyes (see foot in Figure 8.8 bottom, 3).

2. Jaguar necks used in the same way. A kenned leg (or arm) forms the "neck" of a jaguar face set at midpoint, and its foot issues from the agnathous mouth as a "tongue" (Figures 8.5, 8.8). The neck metaphor is also suggested when small jaguar heads appear at the end of the kenned feline tails (Figure 8.8 bottom, 2).

3. Serpents as kennings for human or animal hair (Figures 8.8, 8.9), eyebrows (Figures 8.1b, 3; 8.9), feathers (Figure 8.7), feline whiskers (Figure 8.8 bottom), and even facial wrinkles (Figure 8.1a, 1)! The serpent body carries the implication of undulation and ends with an easily identifiable serpent head.

4. Jaguar-mouth bands as metaphors for backbones (Figure 8.5b), wing bones (Fig-

ure 8.5a, b; 8.7a, b), or tails (Figure 8.7b). Their two lips contain single or paired canines separating undifferentiated triangular teeth.

5. Jaguar mouth bands in the genital area of winged figures holding staffs (Figure 8.5, right) suggesting a toothed or denticulate vagina and female gender (Lyon 1978, 99–102).
6. Jaguar mouths to ken "divinity" on anthropomorphic and anthropomorphized bird and animal figures.

Kennings may be used in layers, as when an anthropomorphic divinity's profile jaguar face has a masklike eagle or hawk beak kenned out beyond it (Figures 8.5, 8.6, 8.7). The number of kennings on a figure corresponds to its importance.

Chavín figures usually appear against undifferentiated backgrounds devoid of perspective, although teeth do overlap jaws and claws curl over palms of grasping hands. In staff-bearing figures, the staff actually lies behind the figure's elbows and clenched hands (Figure 8.5). Some anthropomorphic figures combine frontality and profile, including splayed feet and wings (Figure 8.6), or profile "walking legs" and head (Figure 8.5a) on frontal torsos. Profile figures emphasize body outlines of head, wing, leg, and foot (Figure 8.7) or single front and rear legs (Figure 8.8). Upturned eyes (Figure 8.6b, 8.7a) and guilloches double as fillers (Figure 8.1a, 3, 8.1b, upper left and right) and as jaguar pelage markings (Figure 8.8, bottom).

Rowe's Phases

In the absence of carbon-14 dates, Rowe used the associations of motifs with architectural features to define stylistic phases. His divisions are:

Phase AB: The Great Image/Lanzón/Smiling God (Figure 8.9). Burger (1984) tentatively links Phase AB with his Urabarriu archaeological stage (850–460 B.C.). Its principal stone image, the javelinlike Lanzón, is set into the floor and ceiling of a cross-shaped gallery in the Old Temple. It is a 14-foot-10-inch (4.53 meter) keeled, rectangular, eastward-facing white granite monolith that Rowe feels represents the oldest deity worshiped at Chavín, the anthropomorphized feline Great Image.

The figure rests on a tapering base with vertical, twined guilloche striping. Its feet are carved

8.9. The Lanzón in its temple setting. (Drawn by the author from a photo)

as if viewed from above, with upcurved claws touching at center front beneath a tabbed kilt of upward-facing jaguar heads sharing a continuous mouth band. The right, heavily clawed arm is raised; the left one hangs empty at the figure's side. The head is kenned with serpent eyebrows over great globular fishlike eyes with upturned pupils; serpents also ken the hair and kilt fringes. The scrolled upturned mouth corners made Rowe (1962, 19) nickname the image the "Smiling God." A single, great curved fang curls down from each corner across a lower lip that does not join the upper lip properly and may, with its double row of teeth, have been carved on later. Pendant ear discs drop over what looks like a second skeletal jaw with vertebral-looking teeth. From the back of the head, a narrower section of lip band sharing jaguar heads like those on the kilt rises to the ceiling like some heavily kenned essence—a spiraling New World counterpart of the Buddhist *ushnisha*. Patterson (1971, 46) suggests that the Great Image may have functioned as an oracle because, near its top, a hole connects to the chamber above where a person could have crouched to project his/her voice to worshippers in the room below.

Phase AB also includes the cornice blocks from the New (South Wing) Temple (El Castillo: Figure 8.6) that depict jaguar-faced, bird-beaked figures with splayed wings and legs ending in long curved talons. The wings are joined to the body by agnathic jaguar profiles, and the tail feathers extrude like multiple tongues from an agnathic, frontal jaguar mask, the eyes of which are appendages on a continuous mouth-band backbone. Feathers are kenned with one or (in Figure 8.6) paired jaguar masquettes.

Phase C: The Tello Obelisk (Figure 8.10a, b). During this phase, which probably corresponds to Burger's Chakinani phase (460–390 B.C.), new extensions were added on the Old Temple's north and south wings. Rowe's type indicator is the elaborately kenned Tello Obelisk, found out of context in the plaza facing the new South Wing Temple. It is one of the most complex of all Chavín sculptures and was surely a cult object of great importance. It represents two caymans (a small tropical alligator), each covering two sides of the obelisk. The head is in profile with four tusks protruding from the upper lips across the lower lip, and body parts are kenned with a plethora of floral, jaguar, shell, and other details blocked out and numbered by Rowe to facilitate their iconographic identification (Figure 8.10). The caymans end with profile jaguar heads disgorging a fishlike spread tail. The upper end of the stone depicting what seem to be emanations from the forehead and nostrils is a narrow, notched section like that of the Lazón.

Phase D: Black and White Portal Sculptures: Column Hawk/Eagle Figures; Cornice Hawk/Eagle Profiles; Proto-Staff God (Figures 8.5; 8.7; 8.11). Rowe regards Phase D as "the anchor point in this sequence" because its diagnostic

pieces, the facing hawk and eagle "guardian angels" on the round portal columns and the rows of profile hawks and eagles on the cornice above were all carved and set into place within a very short period of time.

The column figures (Figure 8.5) are bird–humans with splayed, heavily kenned wings and upturned jaguar faces ending in bird beaks. They wear decorated costume panels, have vertebral mouth-band kennings, and hold what may be horizontal "ceremonial bars" or knives. The hawk guardian on the north column (Figure 8.5, left) is recognizable by the tear band intersecting the eye and carries a rigid jaguar-headed implement. The eagle-masked guardian (Figure 8.5, right) is more complex, with elaborate costume panels and a "toothed vagina" area that suggests to investigator Pat Lyon (1978, 99) that it may be female. It holds a fish-tabbed staff or knives (?), their rigidity kenned by the continuous mouth/backbone motif. Both probably stood as "guardian angels" at the entrance of the Staff God's shrine.

Above the doorway lintel, a frieze of profile hawks (with eye bands, Figure 8.7a) and eagles with serpent–jaguar kennings (Figure 8.7b) repeats the avian theme. Also dated by Rowe as Phase D is a small simple Staff God image found in the New Temple patio (Figure 8.11).

Phase EF: The Raimondi Stela (Figure 8.12) with Staff God. This phase, and the preceding Phase D, correspond to maximum population growth and ceremonial activity and probably correspond to the Janabarriu occupation (390–200 B.C.) at Chavín (Burger 1984, 244–246).

The 6-foot-high carved slab called the Raimondi Stela, found in a house in Chavín in 1873, was probably the major cult object associated with the South Temple. It depicts what Rowe calls the Staff God and probably replaced the Smiling God/Lanzón when the South Wing (Castillo) became the new cult center. Its frontal human figure holds two staves kenned with inverted jaguar heads emitting modular-band volute tongues resembling organ pipes. The figure's face is a composite: An inverted face at the chin shares its mouth with the center face, and a second inverted face at the forehead shares its eyes.

Above the main face a great towering protuberance of four inverted caymanlike heads with curved corner canines, short, rounded poker-chip teeth, and a large, prominent central eye-

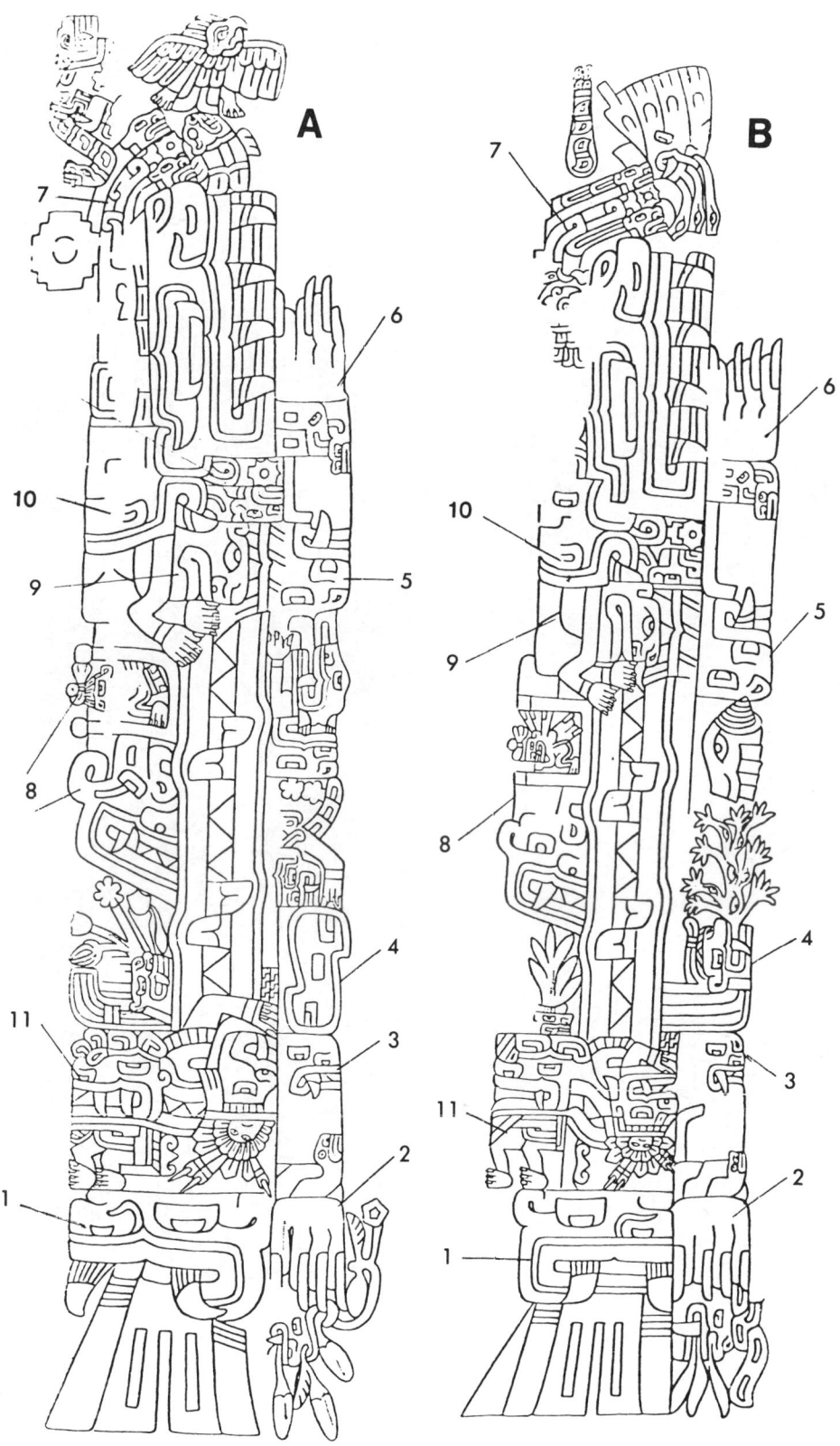

8.10a. Caymans (*A*) female and (*B*) male, Tello Obelisk: (*1*) jaguar-kenned tail, (*2*) hind food holding vegetation, (*3*) knee, (*4A*) seedlike genitalia, (*4B*) penis, (*5*) elbow, (*6*) front paw, (*7*) forehead ornament, (*8*) dorsal jaguar head and glyph, (*9*) inverted shoulder feline, (*10*) neck mouth-mask, (*11*) jaguar-headed rump figure. (Tello 1960, fig. 8)

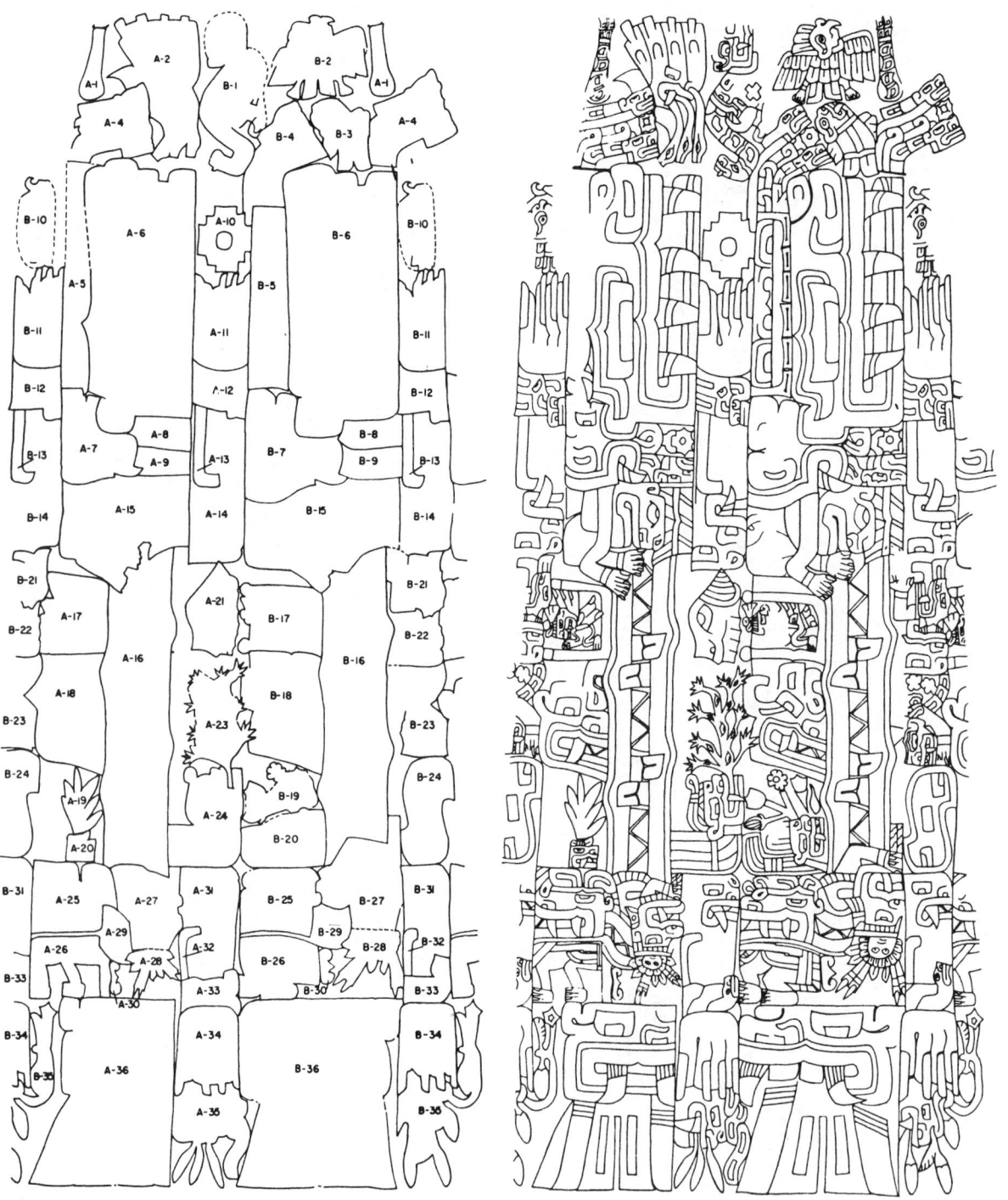

8.10b. Key to individual Tello Obelisk design motifs by Rowe. (Lyon 1978, pl. 28; drawing courtesy John Rowe)

8.11. Smiling Staff God, New Temple patio. (Rowe 1967, fig. 21; drawing courtesy John Rowe)

tooth, edged by long-stemmed volutes and serpent heads, issues forth and shows the Chavín delight in difference of detail within a format of repetition. With this complex piece, the style completed its "progression from three dimensional imagery to flat relief and from early powerful, daemonic representations to docile patterning" (Conklin 1971, 18).

Rowe's scheme was a preliminary one in which he conjoined letters (Phases AB, EF) to be expanded through new data. Chronological associations are difficult because most Chavín sculptures have been moved from their original locations. Archaeologists and art historians have responded to this problem in two ways: (1) by undertaking tighter formal analyses of known Chavín art and (2) by correlating datable architectural and ceramic sequences from Chavín and other sites to style changes at Chavín.

Refinement of Rowe's Phases

The most comprehensive attempt to enlarge upon and refine Rowe's chronology is that proposed by Peter Roe (1974). He finds that Rowe's original sequence has essentially held firm.

8.12. The Raimundi Stela. (Drawn by the author from a photo)

56

57

Feature 56 is a primary-figure extremity. It can function as either a foot or a hand depending on orientation. The fingers are elongated, as are the fingernails. The latter, however, project straight forward and do not curve. The formerly plain bracelet becomes a simple twined snake. Feature 57, a foot, differs only in being shorter.

58

Feature 58 is a secondary-figure hand form. Note the realistic rendering with all five digits present. Note also how the hand increases in width as the tips of the fingers are approached.

59

Feature 59 is a secondary-figure foot form. Here again the shape is a "U" spreading apart toward the tips. The number of toes may be variously reduced.

60

Feature 60 indicates the first iconographic evidence of the existence of the trophy-head cult. Small severed heads are carried in the hand of mythical or non-mythical human figures.

61

Feature 61 depicts the first appearance of weapons, more specifically, atlatl and darts. As above, this feature appears in the hand of a human figure.

62

Feature 62 is an elaborate version of the collared cat-snake. The bulbous quality of the mouth and nose is characteristic.

63

Feature 63 is a subsidiary-figure simple snake-head variant. Note that all the anatomical features are separate.

64

Feature 64 marks the first appearance of the exceedingly simplified snake head in the Chavín sequence. The mouth becomes the extension of the eyebrow line, disappearing as a separate element, and the nose is omitted.

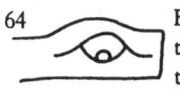

65

Feature 65 is an elaborate hair arrangement. The hair is indicated by vertical lines and is piled up.

66

Feature 66 is an abstract, geometric, decorative motif, developed out of the pelage markings of AB Feature 22 by the addition of a central hole. Apparently, they are no longer exclusively pelt markings since they can appear independently.

67

Feature 67 is an angular fret motif that has developed out of Feature 21 by the loss of the interstitial spaces.

68

Feature 68 is a stylized spinal column that appears to be bifurcated by a straight line.

69

Feature 69 is a decorative motif/filler figure which consists of a series of rays with recurved tips. The shank is not exceedingly long in relation to the curl. There is a space where the tip recurves.

70

Feature 70 is a peculiar finger-ray that appears as part of a secondary figure.

PERIOD C-D

71

Feature 71 is a primary-figure eye form. While the eyebrow element is derived from earlier prototypes, differing in that it has two projections, the earlier simple lower line has become a projection extending above the eye proper.

72

Feature 72 is a main-figure continuing mouth band. It differs from the earlier Feature 14 in having another canine interrupt the smaller rounded teeth.

73

Feature 73 is a primary-figure mouth form. Note the lips projecting at right angles to the mouth and the conservative points in the lip above the bases of the canines.

74

Feature 74 is a human-like hand where, however, talons have replaced fingernails to give a zoomorphic effect.

75

Feature 75 evolves out of Feature 20. Here the scales, instead of continuing in a straight line, form a right angle, indicating an increase in complexity and plasticity.

8.13. Page from Roe's Glossary of Chavín features. (Roe 1974, p. 14; courtesy Peter Roe and DO)

Roe seriated the major stone carvings at Chavín and nearby sites, using component design units. In 89 pieces, he recognized and plotted 148 "building blocks" or features into clusters of shared features. He then arranged the order of pieces into a sequence where some features died out as others appeared in a piece, just as one might seriate U.S. homes from 1900 according to the presence or absence of washing machines, radios, TVs, microwave ovens, home videogames, and the like without ever knowing dates to arrive at a correct relative sequence.

With his pieces arranged to show waxing or waning of each design feature, Roe plotted them against Rowe's style phases. They matched well, and he now had not only Rowe's phase-diagnostic elements but those from his wider universe of 148 grouped into the Rowe style system. The only change needed was insertion of the CD phase because of a strongly transitional piece.

The next step was a Glossary of Features (Figure 8.13) to facilitate recognition of their variants and recombinations. These recombinations sometimes involved deliberate repetition of elements combined with bilateral symmetry to produce highly complex images, as in the face-to-face figures of the Yauya Stela (Figure 8.14) from the Middle Marañon area, and the Lintel of the Jaguars from the Monumental Stairway at Chavín (Figure 8.15). The Yauya Stela's scaly tailed cayman–feline, strongly resembling the Tello Obelisk caymans (Figure 8.10) but with small fish rather than plant details, appears to meet its clone head on. The Lintel of the Jaguars presents facing, mirror-image jaguars. The rhythmic, sequential repetition of their upper face (Figure 8.15, bottom, a), dorsal, fanged frontal face infixes (b–c), neck profile face (d), backbone mouth band (e), brow curl (f), kenned "beard" serpents (g), legs (h), kenned neck hairs (i), and underbelly front face infixes (j) is so exact that Roe (1974) thinks a template may have been used.

Once he had identified the range of features used in Chavín art, Roe plotted their presence within Rowe's phases to trace their chronological development. Seriation clearly showed the evolution of specific features such as mouths, mouth bands, and eyes (Figure 8.16).

Roe then applied these criteria to eighty-three pieces from more distant areas and proposed that Chavín influence spread into nearby Central and North Coast valleys in Phase C, peaked in Phase D, and faded in EF as local traditions resurged (Figure 8.17). These conclusions have subsequently been challenged as "Chavín-derived" sites have yielded pre-Chavín carbon-14 dates. For example, Caballo Muerto and Cerro Sechín's stone carvings appear to be earlier than Roe's D and EF phases (Samaniego, Vergara, and Bischoff 1985). Thomas and Shelia Pozorski (1987) note that C-14 dates have compacted the South Coast Ica ceramic sequence (discussed in the next chapter) that was the basis of Rowe's original seriation into his Phases D-E. They further suggest that Chavín's Old and New temples were built simultaneously and that the stylistically different sculptures in Rowe's Phases A-E were actually contemporaneous. Clearly, stylistic seriation may require refining once ceramic and architectural sequences with firm dates are in.

Ethnographic and Botanical Clues

Additional interpretations of Chavín iconography are suggested by Douglas Sharon's (1972, 1974) work with a contemporary North Coast shaman. Sharon's informant frequently uses the hallucinogenic San Pedro cactus (*Trichocereus pachanoi*), a tall ribbed relative of the southwestern saguaro held on Chavín sculpture by a human with claws like a jaguar (Figure 8.18), one of the alter-ego forms of shamans in tropical forest areas that are a possible source of Chavín concepts. Alana Cordy-Collins (1977a) notes that the San Pedro cactus also appears on Chavinoid coastal pottery with jaguars and with deer, an animal used by modern shamans to detect malevolent spirits, and on an Ica Valley painted textile accompanying jaguars, winged deer, shamans, hummingbirds, a deity, acacia seed pods, and an unidentified third hallucinogen. She sees these representations as a remnant of an earlier shamanic past surviving into the period of sedentary agriculture.

Another ethnographic contribution links contemporary Indian mountain cults to fertility spirits with Chavín iconography. Johan Reinhard finds Chavín's proximity to Mount Huantsan on the east side of the Cordillera Blanca significant and speculates that Chavín's Staff God may be an early antecedent of Illapu, the Inca mountain-dwelling storm god. Chavín's hawks

A

B

8.14. The Yauya Stela: (A) actual condition (redrawn by the author from Tello 1960, fig. 34); (B) the Yauya Stela: hypothetical reconstruction showing a "spread-eagled" cayman with a mouth band and other features of the Tello Obelisk cayman. See fig. 8.10a for key. (Roe 1974, fig. 11; courtesy Peter Roe and DO)

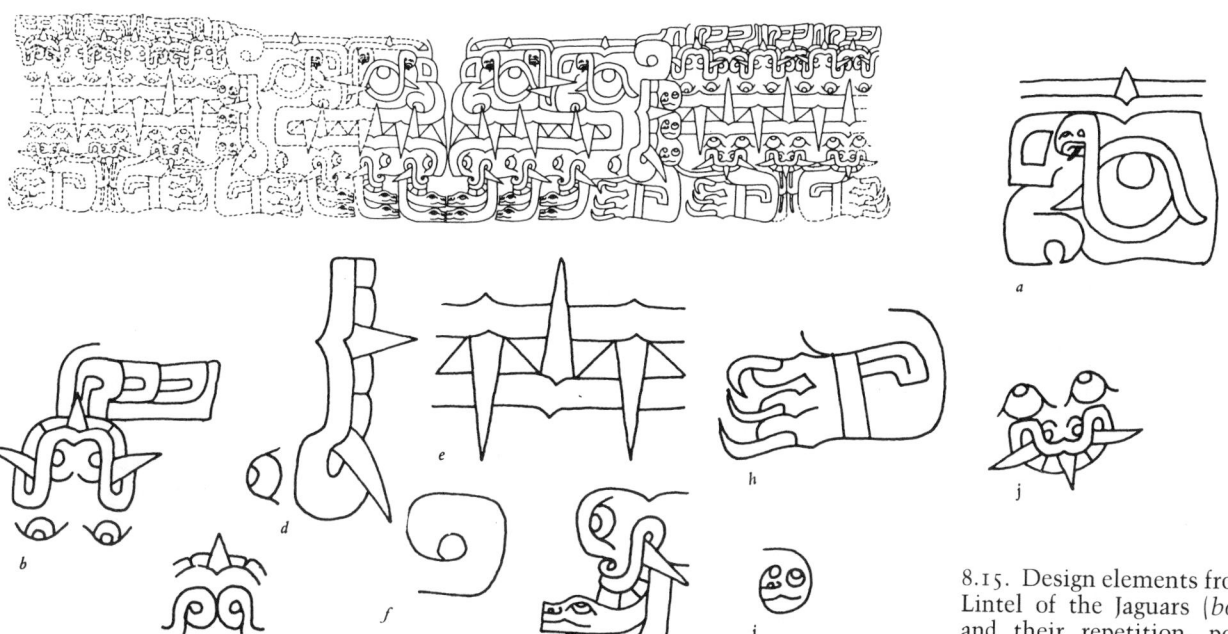

8.15. Design elements from the Lintel of the Jaguars (*bottom*) and their repetition, possibly using templates (*above*). (Roe 1974, figs. 9, 10; courtesy Peter Roe and DO)

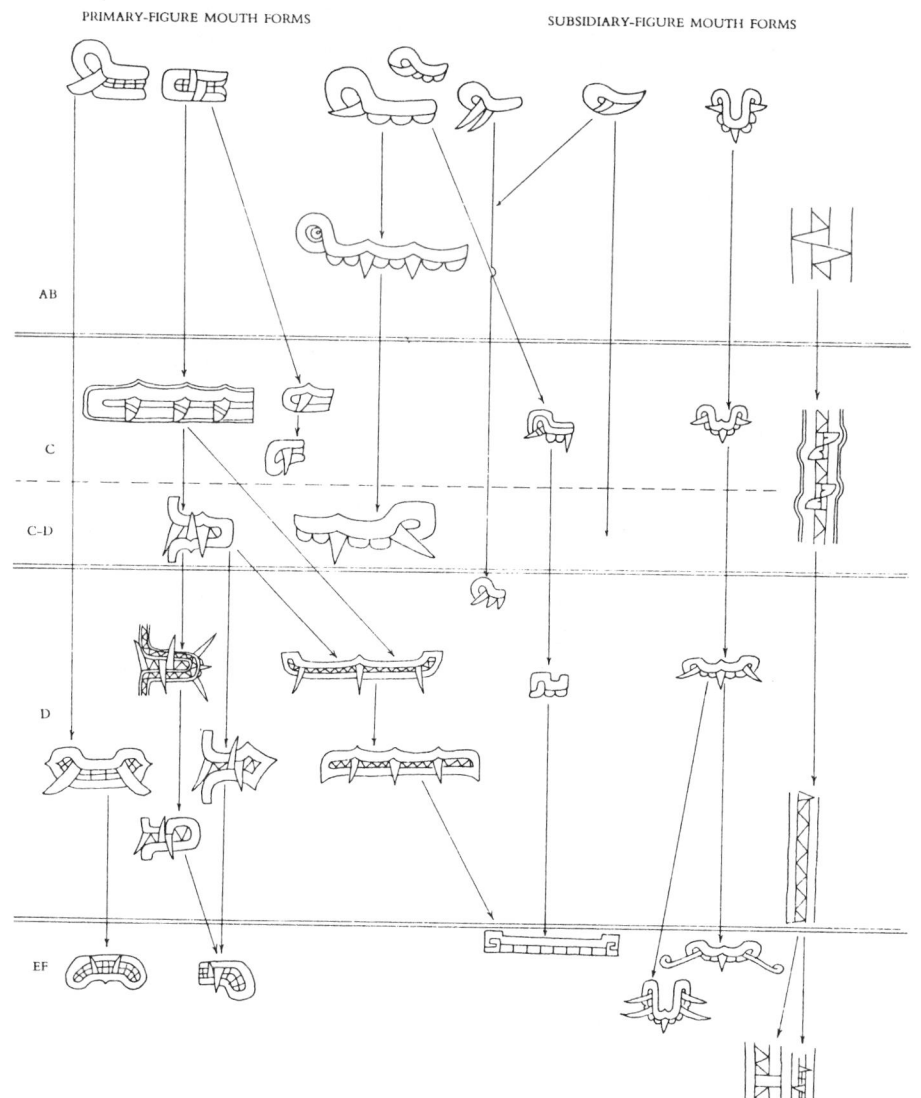

PRIMARY-FIGURE MOUTH FORMS

SUBSIDIARY-FIGURE MOUTH FORMS

AB

C

C-D

D

EF

8.16. Seriation of Chavín mouth types. (Roe 1974, chart 5, p. 74; courtesy Peter Roe and DO)

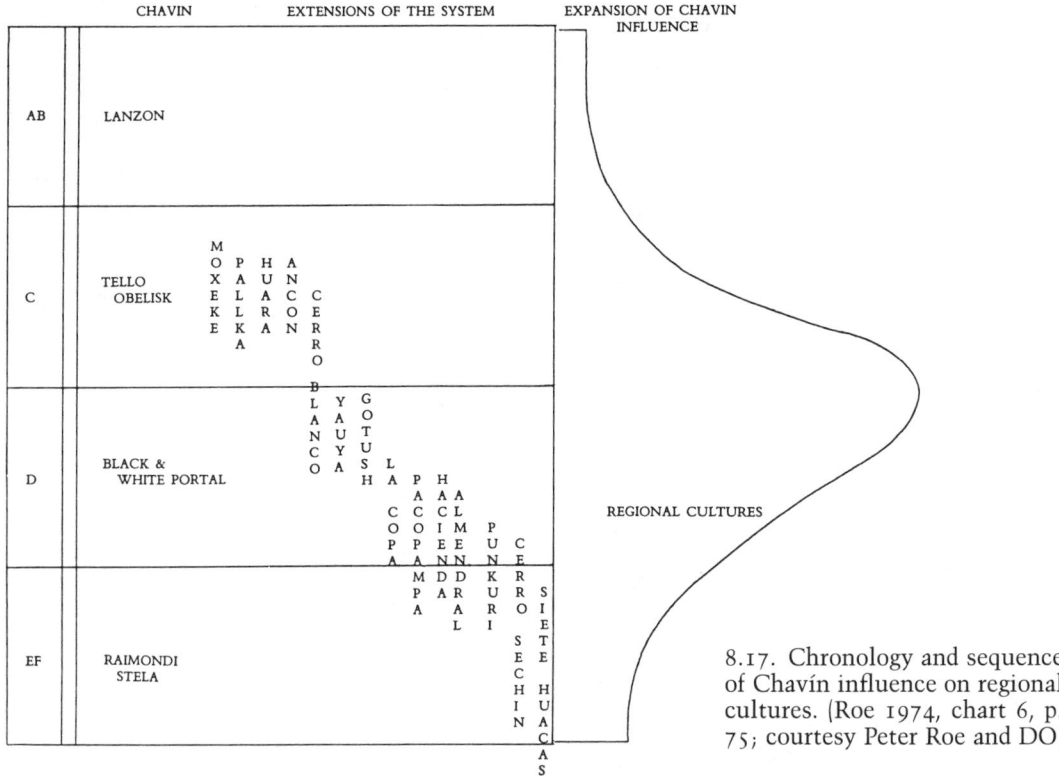

8.17. Chronology and sequence of Chavín influence on regional cultures. (Roe 1974, chart 6, p. 75; courtesy Peter Roe and DO)

8.18. Supernatural figure holding San Pedro cactus: Chavín. (Cordy-Collins 1977a, fig. 2; drawing courtesy Alana Cordy-Collins)

and eagles could have served as mountain-god messengers, with the ubiquitous snakes and felines associated with mountain lightning (Reinhard 1985a, 403–404).

Donald Lathrap (1971, 75–77) has strengthened the case for tropical Chavín origins by identifying tropical anacondas, jaguars, and harpy eagles on the site's major carvings. He concludes from ceramic evidence that the Eastern Andean Highlands and the montaña were part of an "interaction sphere," the collapse of which "during the early half of the first millennium b.c. . . . would appear to relate to the emergence of the Chavín horizon" (Lathrap 1971, 96). University of Tokyo excavations at Kotosh in the South Highlands confirm highland–montaña contacts. At Kotosh, Initial period (pre-Chavín) incised Waira-Jirca and Kotosh-phase Amazon-like pottery occurs full-blown between 2000–1200 B.C.; subsequent Chavinoid elements (such as feline mouths: see Figure 8.19) appear during the Early Horizon Chavín Phase (1200– 870 B.C.).

One of the most complex Chavín sculptures, the Tello Obelisk (Figure 8.10) is part of Lathrap's evidence. On it, two caymans are shown in profile. Their closed mouths lack a lower tooth

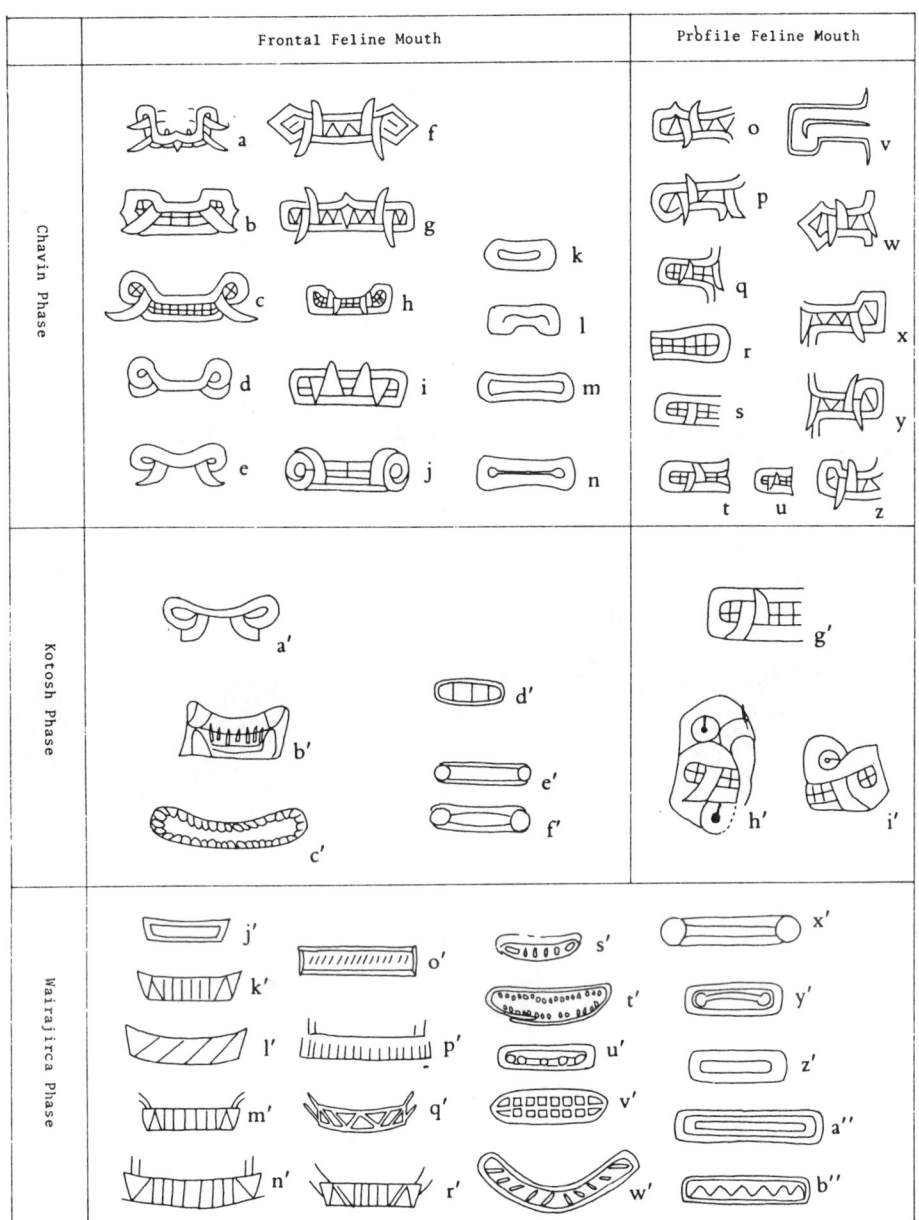

8.19. Comparison of Wairajirca, Kotosh, and Chavín-phase feline mouths from Kotosh, in the Upper Huallaga area. (Kano 1979, fig. 13; courtesy Chiaki Kano and DO)

row, like many agnathic or jawless Chavín heads that are perhaps cayman derived and that in later phases gained a lower lip and canines as jaguar images came into vogue (Lathrap 1973, 339). Peruvian archaeologist Julio Tello segregated out the components of each cayman as alter-images: Cayman A with its jaguar penis extruding a branched plant, as a water–rain–germination deity, and Cayman B with its seed-like genitalia representing the heat and dryness of summer and fall. Lathrap sees Cayman A as a masculine rain bringer with Underworld associations because of his six-leafed achira plant, a possible peanut, and his emerging manioc-plant penis (Figure 8.20, b) (all underground tubers) and Cayman B as a female symbolizing dry-season harvests, celestial because she bears the above-ground-growing bottle gourd and aji fruit (Figure 8.20, a). The obelisk's plants represent tropical forest cultigens that were a major catalyst in Chavín's rise.

Not all scholars agree. However, these inter-

8.20. (*a*) Above ground bottle gourd (*left*) and aji plants (*right*) associated with "Sky" cayman; shown as elements B19-20 and B34-35 in Rowe's key to Tello Obelisk motifs; see fig. 8.10b above. (*b*) Underground achira tuber (*left*) and manioc plants (*right*) of "Underworld" cayman; A19-20 and A23-24 in Rowe's key and fig. 8.10b above. (From Lathrap 1973, pp. 98–99, figs. 1–4, reproduced with permission of IAS)

pretations show how ethnographic legends and studies of plant uses can help interpret ancient iconographic elements.

To conclude, little is known about Chavín's abrupt collapse shortly after 200 B.C. Rapid intrusion of alien influences is reflected by the appearance of Huarás "white-on-red" pottery, named after a nearby highland site (Burger 1981, 595; 1984, 250). Further excavation is needed to clarify the nature of late Early Horizon highland interaction. For now, Chavín stands as the brilliant, culminating synthesis of developing coastal iconography catalyzed by tropical elements. The resulting art style influenced all of the major Central Andean cultures that followed.

AREA AND BACKGROUND

CHAPTER 9

PARACAS

An early recipient of Chavinoid influence was the narrow Paracas Peninsula on Peru's South Coast (Map 10), a sand-swept spit of land that juts out between the Chincha and Pisco rivers. Here an Early Horizon culture of fishers and farmers lived in small settlements on the peninsula and at the edges of the adjacent Ica, Nasca, and Chinca valleys.

Peninsula Sites

Paracas culture first came to public attention in 1925, when Julio Tello, director of Peru's National Museum of Anthropology and Archaeology, visited the peninsula with North American archaeologist William Duncan Strong and his wife and discovered a series of well-preserved burials on the flanks and adjoining beach of a low ridge called Cerro Colorado.

For years, the Lima, Peru, black market had sold beautifully embroidered textiles to leading U.S. and European museums. Their source was discovered in 1905 when the mule of an itinerant fruit vendor crossing the Paracas Peninsula stepped into a hollow cavity, exposing a mummy bundle and its offerings. The vendor looted the area during his trips, assisted by a local merchant whose Lima contacts funneled the pieces into willing hands abroad. For 20 years, they kept the location secret. In 1925 Tello was shown the area by the muleteer. In the beach sands, facing the Bahía de Paracas, he found skulls with pronounced cranial deformation and named the site Cabeza Larga, "Elongated Head." On the cerro's crest, bottle-shaped tombs cut into the hard subsoil contained additional mummy bundles: These he called Paracas Cavernas (Figure 9.1a).

Two years later, Tello's assistant and successor, Toribio Mejía Xesspe, located an even more spectacular cemetary under refuse on the cerro's northern slope, with bundles containing old men with extreme fronto-occipital cranial deformation wrapped in fine embroidered mantles. Forty percent had trephined skulls, with discs of bone cut away by using obsidian knives to relieve pressure on the brain. Many had survived the operation with metal plates inserted to close the aperture. Their bodies lay

191

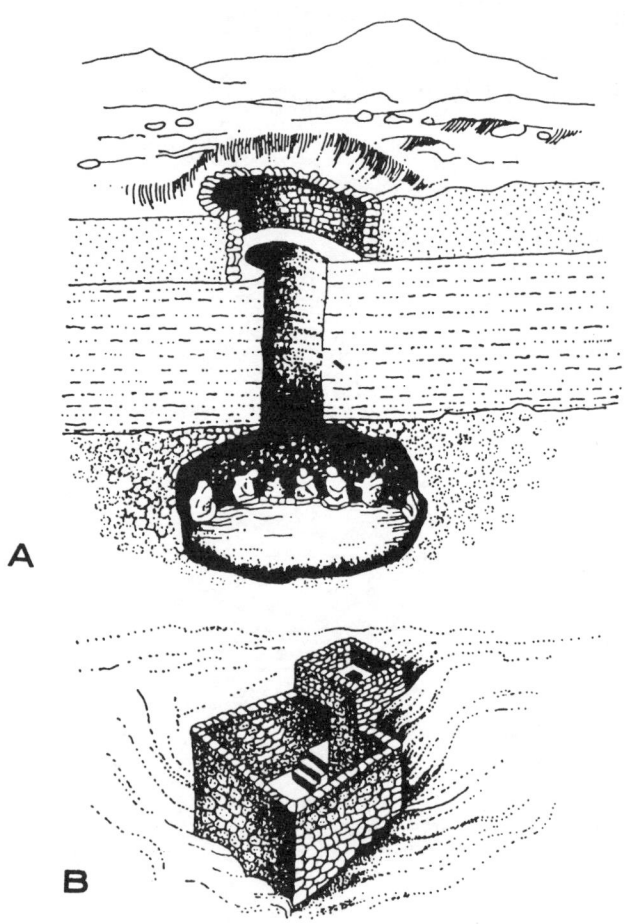

A

B

9.1. (A) Paracas Cavernas-type tomb and (B) Paracas Necropolis-type tomb. (Bankes 1977, p. 91; courtesy Phaidon Press)

beneath house floors in rectangular stone chambers roofed with huarango wood branches and whale ribs covered with reed, part of a village with an estimated population of 3,700 (Paul 1989, 4). Tello interpreted the crypts as the anterooms, patios, and chambers of a "City of the Dead" that he named Paracas Necropolis (Figure 9.1b). During the next 3 years, Tello and Mejía Xesspe (Tello 1959; and, posthumously published by Mejía Xesspe, Tello 1980) recovered an incredible 429 Necropolis mummy bundles that were brought to Lima for storage and study.

Adjacent Valley Sites

Archaeological excavation has documented the presence of villages with semisubterranean houses at Huaca Soto and Huaca Alvarado in the Chincha Valley and Tajajuana, Cerillos, and Ocucaje in the Ica Valley. As at most coastal sites, construction of adobe brick produced less imposing architecture than the stone pyramids at highland sites. Toward the end of the Early Horizon, large towns began to coalesce, some with multiple-walled fortifications reflecting unsettled times as Chavín's influence began to wane.

Chavín Characteristics at Paracas

In contrast to the North and Central coasts, where Chavín influences were more diluted, people of the Paracas cultures were in direct and continuing contact with highland Chavín. Their pottery and textiles sensitively mirror changes in Chavín style. Many, from grave lots with known associations, can be anchored to chronologies from other dated sites and tied to John Rowe's stylistic sequence for Chavín. The Paracas (Ocucaje) ceramic sequence seriated by Dorothy Menzel, John Rowe, and Lawrence Dawson (1964, summarized in the next section) is especially important because its ten phases are so accurate that they have been used as Early Horizon subdivision markers for the entire South Coast area.

ART

Paracas art is best known for its distinctive pottery and textiles, placed as grave goods with high-status males, that graphically document the transition from strong Chavín influences into the Early Intermediate South Coast Nasca style.

Pottery

Paracas potters incised designs into burnished, leather-hard gray or brown clay and, after firing, filled them with thick, crusty mineral colors of matte reds, oranges, yellows, browns, and rusts, using nopal-cactus or algarrobo-tree resins as binder. The most popular forms are double-spouted jars, with a spout and false-spout effigy figure joined by a flat straplike handle above a globular body. Also frequent are shallow round-bottomed bowls with outcurving or everted walls, occasional effigies, and single- or double-chambered "whistling jars" with a small hole in the effigy spout through which air is forced when the filled vessel is tipped.

The Ocucaje Sequence

Menzel, Rowe, and Dawson named this Paracas-style pottery "Ocucaje" after a narrow fertile area of the Ica Valley that provided their main sample. They carefully seriated vessel forms, designs, and techniques of manufacture, guided by changes in representations, feature clusters, and the appearance of supernaturals such as the Oculate Being. The resulting tight sequence is a model of what careful seriation can accomplish. The final tabulation plots 461 design features and was aided immensely by the known association of pottery groups in specific grave lots.

From the overview, broad trends became clear. Phases 1 through 8 had the strongest Chavín connections, whereas 9 and 10 became increasingly independent, with proto-Nasca decoration and form. Chavín influence affected design but had little influence on vessel shape: Except for a few early stirrup-spout jars, the traditional double-bridged and bridged-effigy-spout jar, low bowl, and polichrome decoration prevailed. Curvilinear design gradually became rectilinear, and horizontality was emphasized as bowls became lower and globular bodies compressed. Feline mouths widened into parallel lip bands with round or square corners, later with points. Guilloches became frets; volutes, long-stemmed "recurved rays." Modular-band-dominated late designs look as if they had been laid out on lined paper. Ultimately, Phase 9 and 10 designs returned to more representational naturalistic forms.

The following brief illustrated summary shows Menzel, Rowe, and Dawson's use of one Chavín theme (the frontal jaguar head) on one form (bird-spouted jars) to trace some of the major changes from Chavín-influenced wares to wares of the succeding culture in the area—Nasca.

Phases 1 through 2 mark the first appearance of Chavín influence, corresponding to Rowe's AB Chavín phase and the curvilinear Great Image. The Phase 1 vessel (Figure 9.2) is a typical North Coast stirrup-spout alien to Paracas. Its feline spots and face are curvilinear, with sub-triangular opposable fangs and a double tooth row beneath rounded eyes and brow bands.

By Phase 2, the vessel has a double bridged spout with the blind spot as a bird (Figure 9.3). Its jaguar has an agnathous, fanged mouth with

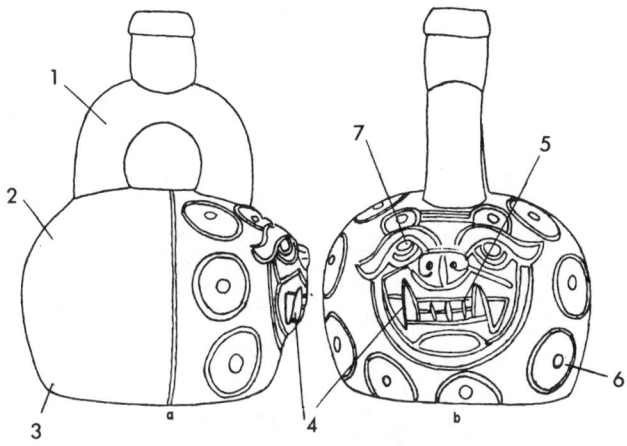

9.2. Ocucaje Phase 1 vessel with (1) stirrup spout, (2) globular body, (3) flat base showing jaguar with (4) subtriangular opposable fangs, (5) double-row incisors, (6) feline spots, (7) rounded brow and pupils. (Menzel, Rowe, and Dawson 1964, figs. 1a, b; courtesy UCP)

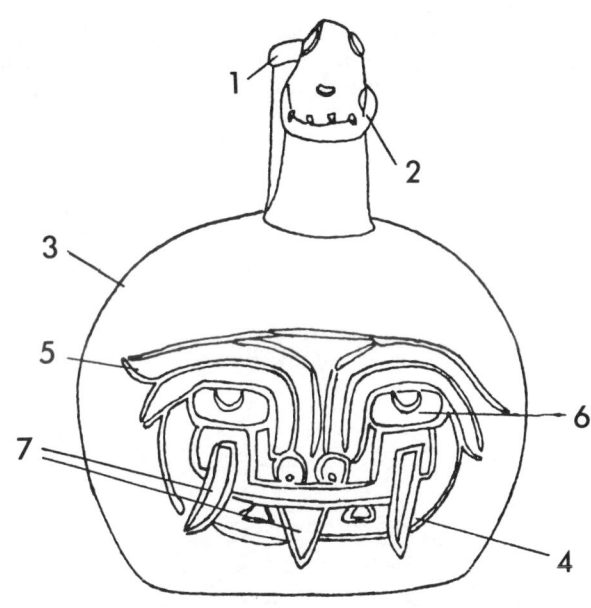

9.3. Ocucaje Phase 2 vessel with (1) pouring spout, (2) blind bird-effigy spout, (3) globular body, (4) agnathic jaguar face with (5) curved, point-ended brow, (6) rectangular, humanoid eye, (7) single fangs and "eyetooth." (Menzel, Rowe, and Dawson 1964, fig. 1c; courtesy UCP)

a central eyetooth and lacks ears and spots. Flattening and horizontal stretching create a sub-rectangular face and eye sockets.

During Phase 3 (Rowe's Phase C), the Staff God replaced the Great Image at Chavín in the new South Wing. As the cult shifted focus, new Chavín influences reached regional sites. On

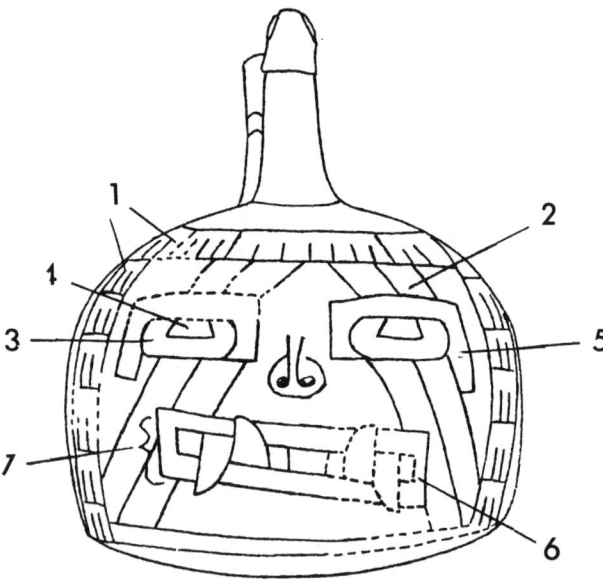

9.4. Phase 3 vessel with (1) facial frame, (2) double "hawk" tear bands, (3) subrectangular iris, (4) parabolic pupil, (5) feline brow, (6) lips with squared corners, (7) lips and tear markings formed by modular bands. (Menzel, Rowe, and Dawson 1964, fig. 2a; courtesy UCP)

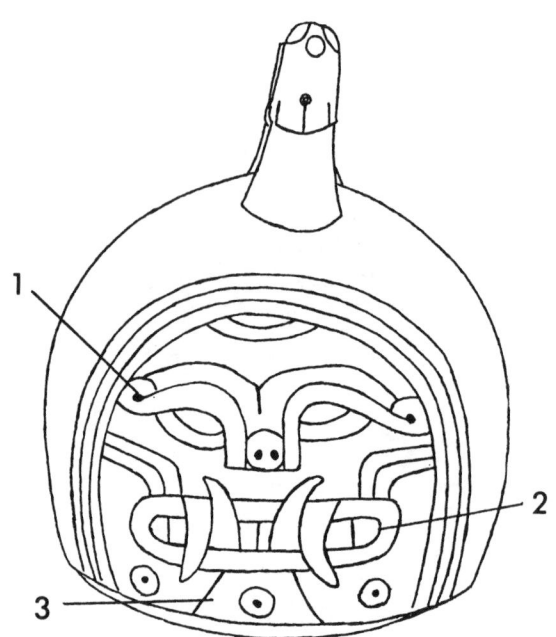

9.5. Phase 4 vessel with (1) dotted finial brow tip ornament, (2) curved lip corners and fangs, (3) defined chin-wisker area, within triple modular-band facial frame. (Menzel, Rowe, and Dawson 1964, fig. 2b; courtesy UCP)

the Ocucaje Phase 3 vessel (Figure 9.4), an enlarged, framed jaguar head covers half its surface. Brows, lips, and enclosed teeth resemble horizontal strips, foreshadowing modular bands.

Influences corresponding to Chavín D reached Paracas in Phases 4 and 5. Other sites missed the "second wave" and continued developing variants based on earlier stimuli through Phases 7 or 8. On Phase-4 pottery (Figure 9.5), the facial frame, brows, and whiskers on a prominent chin area become double or triple modular bands. Chavín Phase D influences include curved fangs, corner-pointed lips, and serpent appendages. In Phase 5 (Figure 9.6), the head becomes even more rectangular within its modular band frame curved at the top to indicate ears, and the face is further compressed into horizontal bands.

Ocucaje 6 and 7 amplified and consolidated features of Phases 4 and 5, adding a geometric bowl design of possible Chavín influence. Phase-6 vessels are broader and squatter (Figure 9.6). Chin and side whiskers, eyes, and mouth are all triple, modular bands; overlapping canines are diagonal slashes. The interbrow furrow becomes an ornamental subunit of recurved rays, like the EF Raimondi Stela's long, stemmed volutes at Chavín. Lines unconnected with other lines end in dot finials (Figure 9.7).

Phase 7 sees the design area spread behind the bird spout (Figure 9.8a). Negative-painted spots signal jaguar identity. Open-ended lips extend to the facial frame. Recurved ray nose ornaments persist (Figure 9.8b). With more horizontal space available, chin whiskers add on rectangular "eye panels" and side panels with ball-band fillers. Dots or ball bands also fill the expanded space above the eyes. Up to twelve modular bands complete the facial design.

Phase 8, keyed with 7 to Chavín phase EF, moved toward artistic independence. Vessels became taller, allowing designs to spread out and in some cases appear against open ground instead of narrow modular bands. The Oculate Being, a large-eyed human head (Figure 9.9) appears, later gaining a feline body, whiskers, and tail, and carrying knives, darts, and trophy heads. Potters and weavers followed their own bent, and local traditions developed in several southern valleys. Phase-8 jaguar designs wrap three-quarters of the way around the vessel, adding side panels of radiating recurved rays,

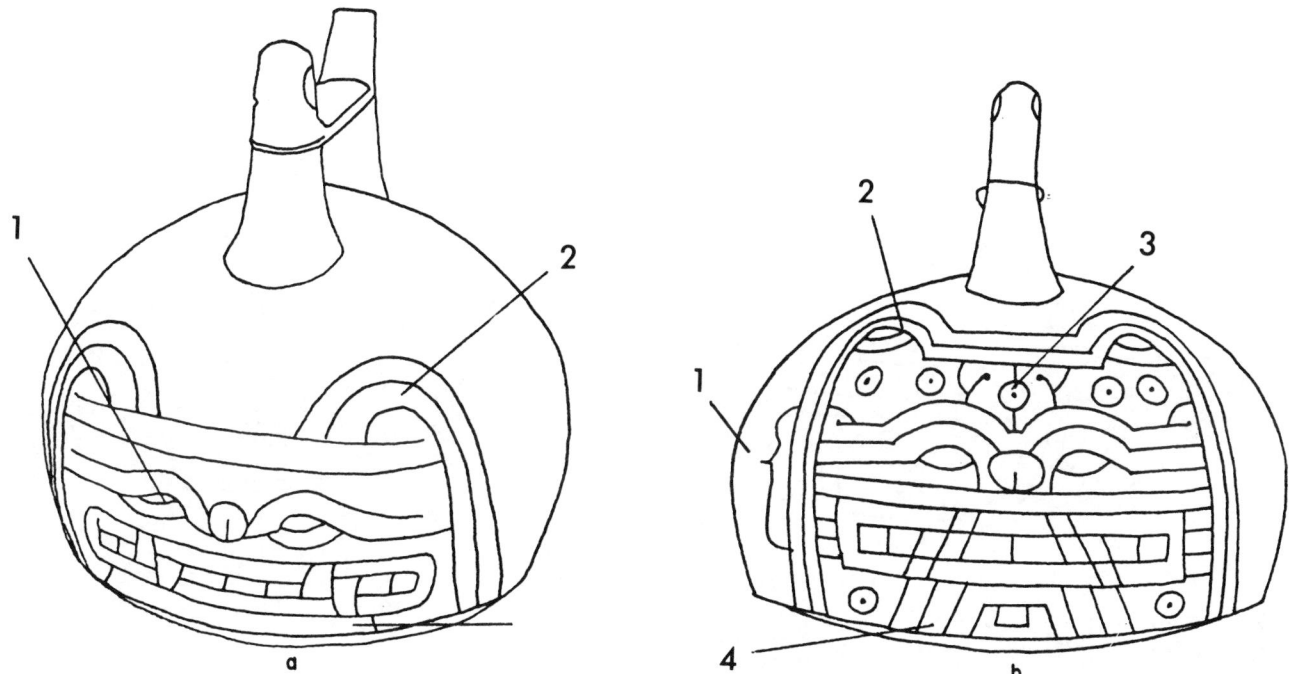

9.6. (a) Phase 5 vessel with (1) lenticular eye, (2) modular band frame including ears, (3) compressed mouth and teeth (Menzel, Rowe, and Dawson, 1964, fig. 3a; courtesy UCP). (b) Phase 6 vessel with (1) eyes, mouth, side whiskers, and (2) ears, all subsumed as modular bands; (3) dot finials at forehead; diagonal slash canines, and (4) modular band chin whiskers. (Menzel, Rowe, and Dawson 1964, fig. 3b; courtesy UCP)

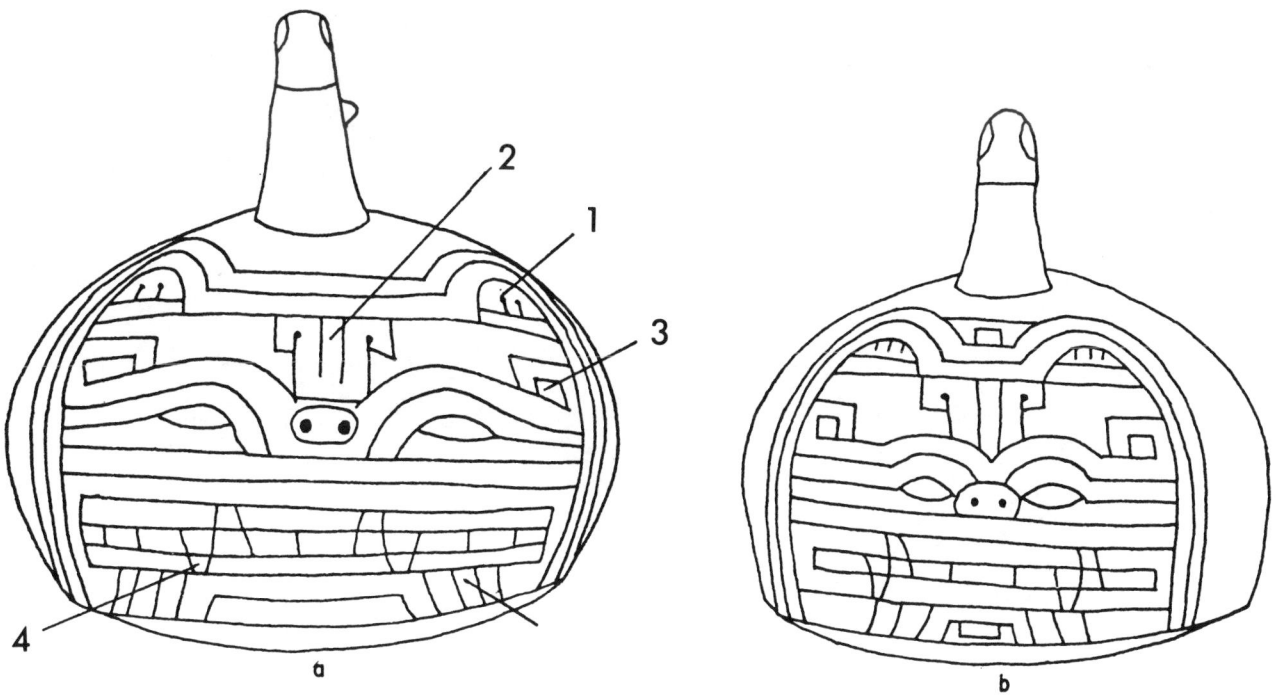

9.7. Phase 6 vessels with dot finials at end of (1) ear, (2) forehead ornament lines, (3) fret brow ends, (4) canines overlapping lip band, (5) triple-band chin and whiskers. (Menzel, Rowe, and Dawson 1964, fig. 4; courtesy UCP)

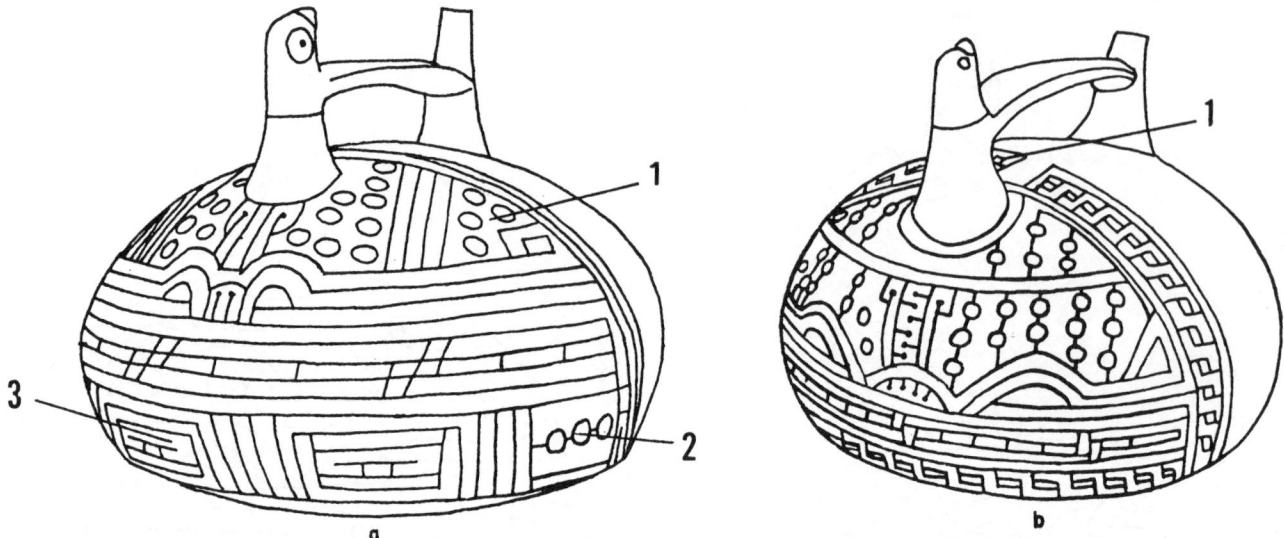

9.8. (a) Phase 7 vessel with (1) forehead and (2) jowl-area circle fillers; recurved-ray forehead ornament; open-ended lip; (3) "eye" panels in chin-whisker area; (b) phase 7, 8 vessel with ladder-design nose ornament, dot finials at nose, (1) face frame extending behind bird-effigy spout. (Menzel, Rowe, and Dawson 1964, figs. 6a, b; courtesy UCP)

9.9. The Oculate Being on Ocucaje Phase 8 pottery: (a) spouted bottle, (b) bowl, (c) spouted bottle. Note trophy-head whisker tips, hair (with ball-band divisors), modular-band canines and chin whiskers. (Menzel, Rowe, and Dawson 1964, fig. 43; courtesy UCP)

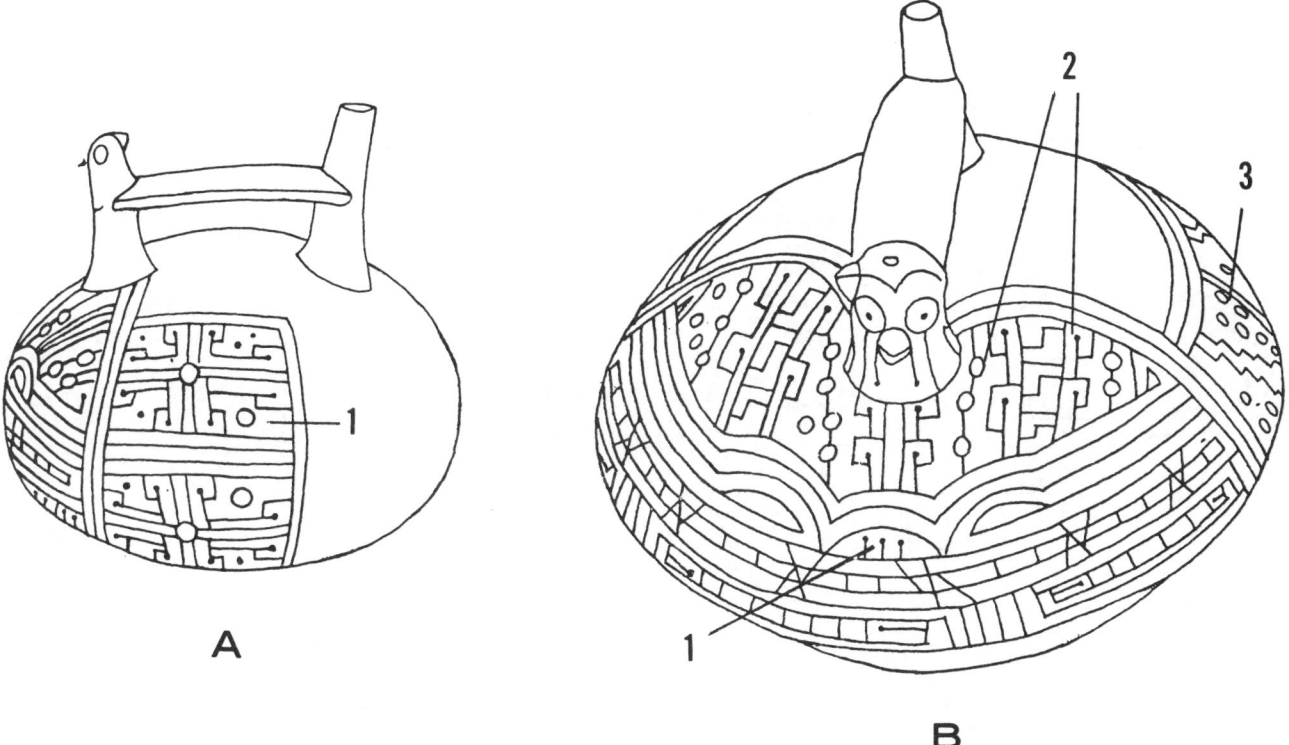

9.10. (A) Phase 8 double-bridged-spout vessel with (1) expanded side panels with radial ray bands; (B) Phase 8 double-bridged-spout vessel with (1) dot-finial nose, (2) ball-band and recurved-ray fillers, and (3) expanded side panels. (Menzel, Rowe, and Dawson 1964, fig. 7a, b; courtesy UCP)

circles, or other designs as appendages to the facial outline bands (Figure 9.10). Faces gain add-ons of repeat fang sets or chin-whisker "eye rectangles" on spaghetti-thin modular bands.

Fortifications from Phases 8 through 10 indicate local warfare that could have interfered with dwindling Chavín contacts. By Phase 9, Chavín influences had ended, and potters amplified the repertoire of Phase 8 with proto-Nasca elements (Figure 9.11a, b).

Ocucaje Phase 10 introduced naturalistic plant, animal, and human forms and proliferated older themes such as the Oculate Being, now with serpent appendages; also X-ray-view cat, bird, snake, or human figures. White-slipped ware shows Topará influence from the adjacent northern Cañete, Chincha, and Pisco valleys. Phase 10 formalized proto-Nasca subjects and style and set the stage for Early Intermediate Phases 1 and 2, during which early Nasca elements continued to affect the Ica Valley.

What have we learned about Chavín influ-

ences from Ocucaje pottery? First, that Chavín ideas were adopted in pulses probably keyed to the internal development of Chavín's Great Image and Staff God cults. Second, that whereas some sites absorbed little from Chavín or assimilated early influences and then went their own way, Paracas maintained close contacts, sensitively reflected Chavín's style changes, and passed them into the Nasca tradition and to select southern highland groups.

Textiles

Textiles offer another record of Chavín influence. The South Coast offers ideal preservation of perishable materials. As a result, textiles from both controlled excavation and *huaquero* pillaging are available for study (King 1965a, b).

The Carhua Textiles

The best known Paracas painted textiles come from Carhua (Karwa) and Chuchio along the

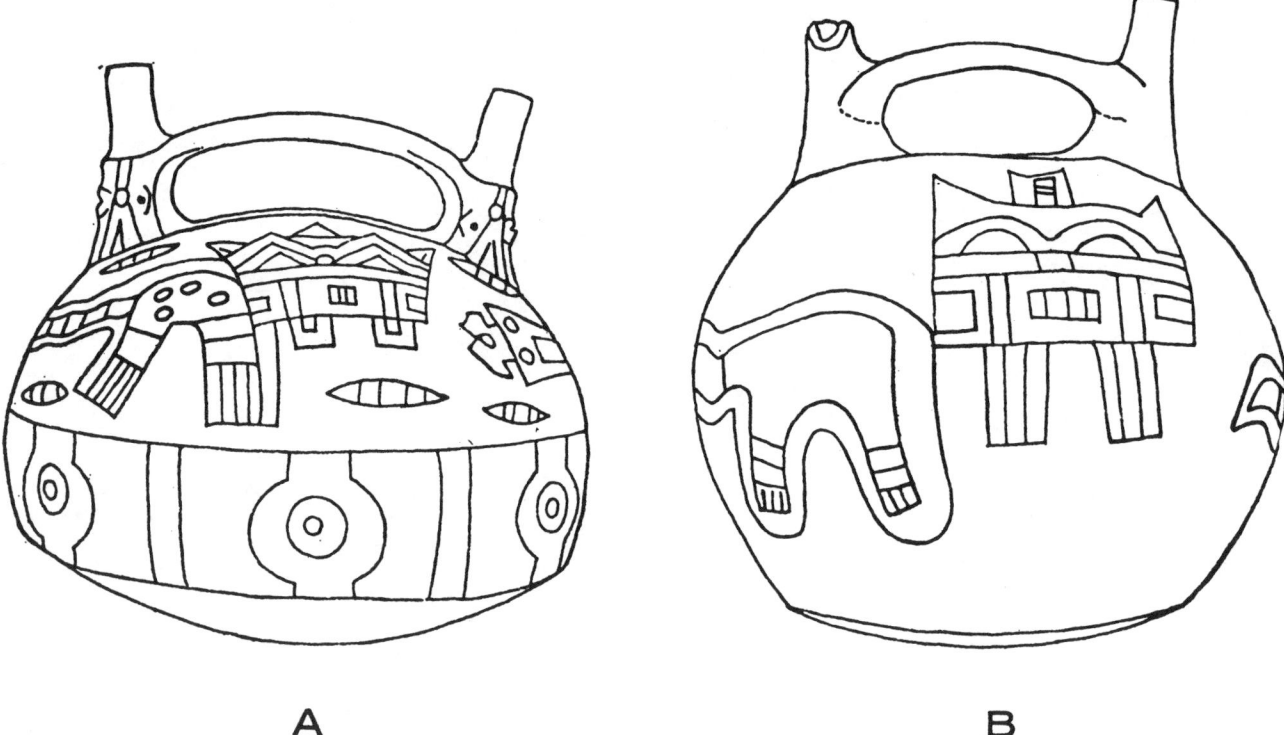

A   **B**

9.11. (A) Phase 8 and (B) Phase 9 vessels with double spouts connected by a round, upcurved bridge, with proto-Nasca felines retaining modular-band paws, brows, chin whiskers. (Menzel, Rowe, and Dawson 1964, figs. 8a, b; courtesy UCP)

Bahía de Independencia south of the peninsula and from Callango on the Lower Ica River (Map 10). Michael Coe donated two purchased Callango pieces to Dumbarton Oaks in 1960. A decade later, 120 Early Horizon fragments were on the market as a result of renewed huaquero activity.

The most thorough and comprehensive study of these textiles is by Alana Cordy-Collins (1976). She assigns them to the middle of the Chavín sequence (Rowe's Phases D and EF) because of their agnathous frontal masks (Figure 9.12) with fanged, upcurled lip and central eye-tooth (Roe's Feature 101) like the Yauya Stela's (Figure 8.14), and split-faced, double-profile feline heads (Figure 9.13). She also has matched many of the over 200 fragments to reconstruct larger pieces (Cordy-Collins 1979). Her identification of cotton plants and a tiny portion of a Staff God foot on one fragment permitted extrapolation to larger images with the same plant in the god's headdress.

Larger painted textiles, perhaps temple wall hangings, are as heavily kenned and iconographically complex as Chavín stone sculpture with its multiple visual axes for faces within figures and "contour rivalry" as motifs share outlines suggestive of the "multiplicity-within-unity" of "a supernatural environment in which earthly rules do not apply" (Stone 1983, 67–70). One fragment (Figure 9.14) shows portions of two large back-to-back figures wearing a continuous mouth-band-edged kilt with a back ornament and tassels kenned with serpent and bird-masked jaguar heads. Profile jaguar faces demarcate the knees and taloned feet. Frontal figures holding staffs (Figure 9.15) are surely close cousins to Chavín's Staff God. Rebecca Stone, using Patricia Lyon's (1978) criteria, subdivides those with eyes as breasts and toothed, "denticulate vaginas" holding vegetal staffs as female; triangle-loinclothed figures holding animal staffs as male; and those holding snakes as neuters (Stone 1983, 63–67). Figure 9.16 is a highly elaborated version of the Chavín South Wing cornice splayed-bird guardian (Figure 9.16a), identical in layout but with greater emphasis on detail.

The purity of Chavín style in early Paracas textiles (Figure 9.17) makes it likely that they

9.12. Early Horizon painted textile with two agnathous, five-fanged, frontal deity faces. South Coast provenience, probably highland woven. (Conklin 1971, fig. 1, TM 1977.35.3; courtesy TM)

were imports. Many Carhua textiles in fact show North and Central Coast characteristics of spin and weave (Stone 1983, 53–54). Textiles would have been an ideal medium for transmitting Chavín iconography because of their portability and the ease with which designs could be painted or traced from low-relief sculpture

(Cordy-Collins 1976). Conklin (1971, 19) feels that painted textiles replaced earlier structurally decorated ones as more "missionary" textiles were exported or taken home by returning coastal pilgrims, much as Chinese Buddhist priests brought back copies of holy sutras from India. Carhua may have copied imported textiles locally under Chavín emissaries and/or weavers, judging from the "pure" style of both fabrics and pottery found there.

Paracas Cavernas and Necropolis

Although Cabeza Larga, Paracas Cavernas, and Paracas Necropolis are separate burial areas, their proximity and overlapping chronology suggest that the peninsula is a multiple-component area with cemeteries for different social classes. Cavernas burials (800?–150 B.C.; probably contemporary with Ocucaje phases 7–10 and Early Horizon 7–10) are more lavishly appointed than those at Cabeza Larga (800–150 B.C.?); the latter may represent village fishers and corn-and-bean farmers. The opulent needle-knit, deity-imaged Necropolis burials (150–5 B.C.; Early Horizon 10–Early Intermediate 1 and 2) with their surrounding satellite bundles may be revered shamans or lineage elders and their kin, facing eternity in a separate, elite cemetary.

Burial Characteristics. The Paracas dead have survived to the twentieth century in an excellent state of preservation, some with their red hair still intact. Bodies may have been eviscerated and were probably smoked prior to becoming the core of a mummy bundle.

To form a mummy bundle, the dead were seated upright in baskets or on coils of cotton padding, flexed, bound tightly, and wrapped in cotton shrouds, alternating layers of plain and patterned mantles with inserted items (slings, feather fans, gold jewelry, and shell necklaces and bracelets) to a 4-foot (1.2 meter) diameter. Some bundles had sixty different cloths and weighed up to 200 pounds. Anne Paul estimates that weaving the plain cloth background for a large bundle may have required up to 29,493 hours and embroidering the designs another 40,000 hours (Paul 1989, 32–33).

As a final step, the bundle was lashed to a mat bottom and topped with a padded-cotton false head, wearing a painted mask with feline features or a trophy-head-holding deity (Figure 9.18) or a wooden head with inlaid shell eyes, a

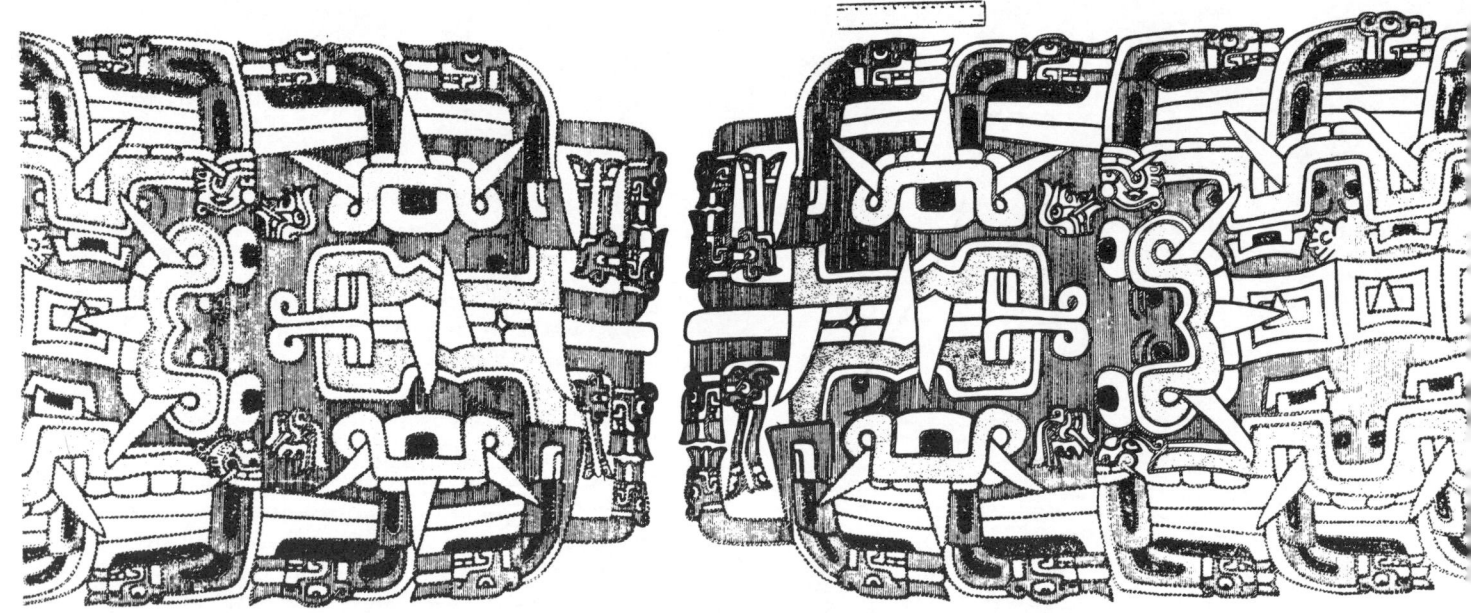

9.13. Ica Valley painted textile, Early Horizon 1. Note the agnathous mouth with a central eyetooth at the neck and as an eyebrow, single-toothed mouths as vertebrae, and the continuous lip bands and serpent kennings at the sides of the figures. (Adapted from a tracing in Roe 1974, fig. 17, p. 50; courtesy Peter Roe and DO)

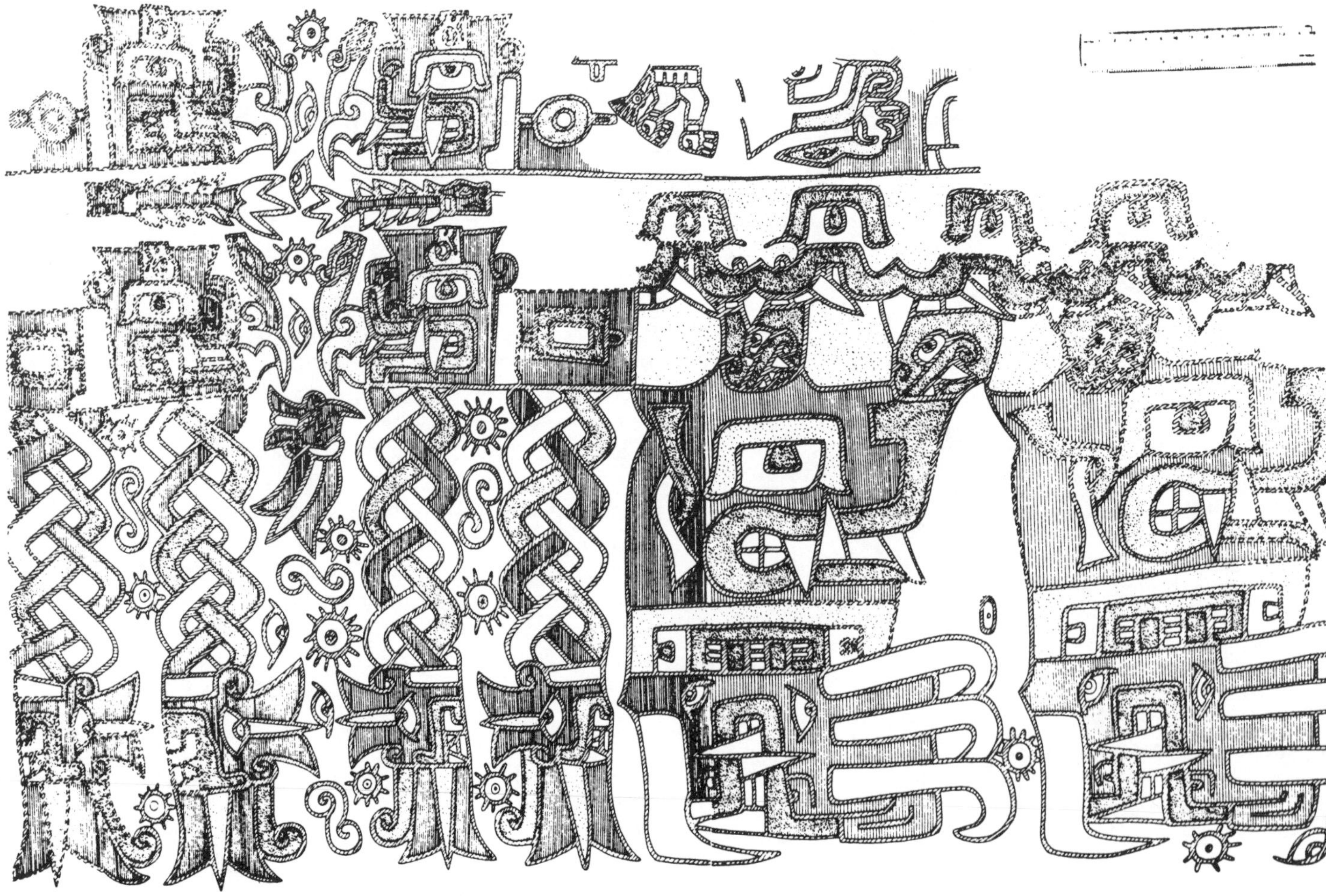

9.14. Ica Valley Early Horizon painted textile fragment: back-to-back figures in tasseled kilts. Note feline heads at feet and knees; continuous mouth-band kilt edge; four feline masks above tassels, with serpent-kenned kilt edge; four feline masks above taseels, with serpent-kenned bird masks separated by serpent-headed fish. (Roe 1974, fig. 17, adapted from a tracing; courtesy Peter Roe and DO)

9.15. Early Horizon painted textiles with frontal human figures. (Roe 1974, fig. 13, adapted from Rowe 1962, and fig. 14, adapted from a tracing; courtesy Peter Roe and DO)

9.16a. Cornice, southwest corner of the Temple at Chavín. (Roe 1974, fig. 1, adapted from Rowe 1967, fig. 12; courtesy Peter Roe and DO)

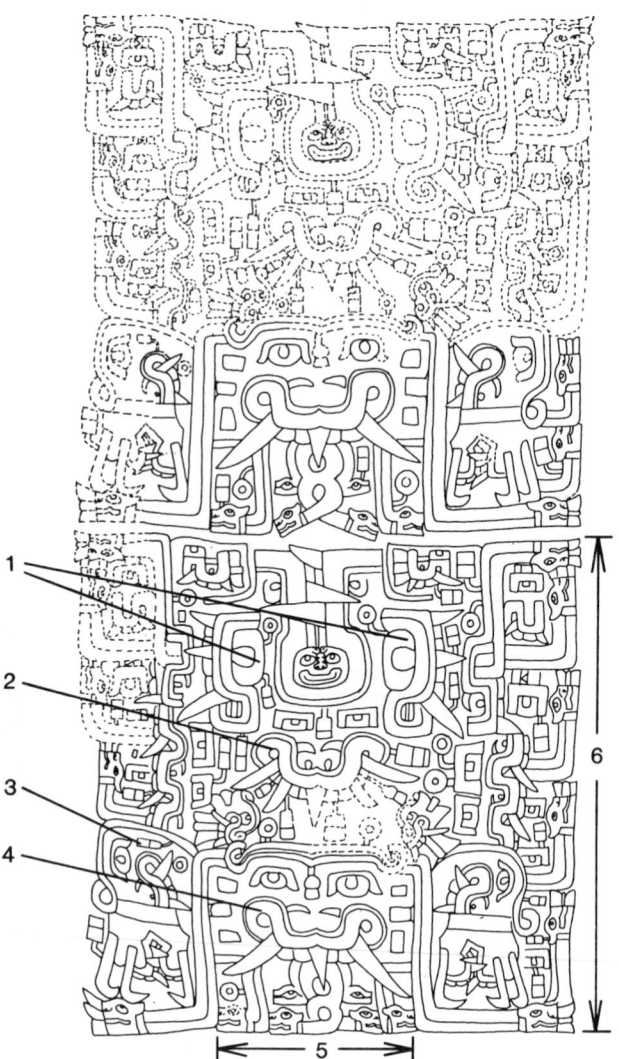

turban, and false hair (Vreeland and Cockburn 1980, 139 ff.). Smaller satellite bundles surrounding the large bundles suggest a burial hierarchy, with status indicated by a bundle's bulk and the quality of its textiles. Food was wrapped in cloth or placed in bowls nearby. Accompanying double-bridged-spout jars presumably held *chicha*. Cane staffs wrapped with animal tendon bands and obsidian-tipped darts marked the graves. Some bundles contained feet or amputated limbs, mummified alpacas, or birds; in one unique case, the central object was a bag of black beans!

Textile Analyses

Paracas textiles have been the subject of numerous technical studies (Means 1932; O'Neale 1942; Bird and Bellinger 1954; d'Harcourt 1962; Tello 1959, 1980). Cavernas and Cabeza Larga weavers produced gauze, double and triple cloth, and patterned weaves. Necropolis wool mantles were executed in loop and stem-stitch embroidery (Figure 9.19) that can run horizontally, vertically, or diagonally and is called "needle knitting" because of its chainlike appearance. Embroiderers used this simple stitch to cover huge surfaces in glowing colors and produce three-dimensional tab edging for robes and funerary mantles (Figures 9.20, 9.21a, b) in a unique example of stitching as sculpture. Dye analyses identify over 100 shades of color.

Seriating the textiles has been a slow, ongoing process. Tello died before adequately publishing his field notes, and mummy bundles at the museum deteriorated, lost labels, and even disappeared. Since 1973, some museum bundles have been matched to his notes. Other Necropolis textiles, looted by huaqueros when a political crisis suspended Tello's excavations in 1930, were cut into pieces and sold to museums and collectors all over the world. Researchers are only now reconstructing the components of original bundles (Paul 1980–1981). Jane Dwyer, another outstanding Paracas textile researcher,

9.16b. Early Horizon painted textile with stylized elaboration of 9.16a: key body parts in both include (1) split jaguar heads sharing mouth; (2) full-face, agnathous jaguar at neck; jaguar heads as (3) knees, (4) rump mask, (5) tail and (6) wing feathers. (Roe 1974, fig. 19, adapted from Rowe 1962; courtesy Peter Roe and DO)

9.17. (*a, left*) Fragment of a Chavinoid Paracas painted hanging from Corowa, *ca.* 1000 B.C.; property of Alan C. Lapiner and André Emmerich (Sawyer 1972, fig. 3; photo courtesy André Emmerich); (*b, below left*) Sculpture 11, from the Castillo or Temple at Chavín (redrawn by the author from Tello 1960, fig. 39; courtesy UNMSM)

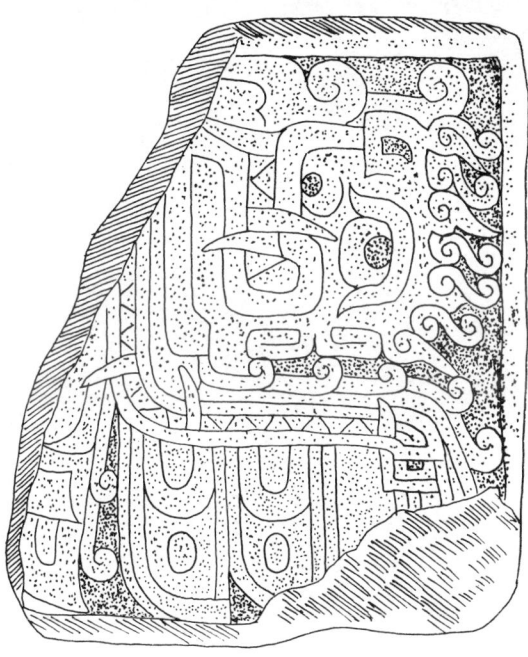

Paul's (1980) important work on Necropolis styles.

Paracas Substyles. During Early Horizon 9, when Chavín influence was replaced by influences from adjacent valleys, Cavernas textiles changed from Early Horizon 7–8 painted decoration to structural patterning with supplemen-

9.18. Painted cloth mummy mask, Early Horizon 10; TM 91.968. (Dawson 1979, fig. 12; courtesy TM)

has compiled a data bank of over 1,100 known fragments as a basis for further study.

One of the most complete chronological descriptions of Paracas textiles is J. P. Dwyer's 1971 Ph.D. dissertation, parts of which are summarized in later articles (E. Dwyer and J. P. Dwyer 1975; Dwyer 1979). Her substyles and serialization of stylistic and iconographic change in pieces with archaological or stratigraphic associations are summarized next. Incorporated as well are comments from Anne

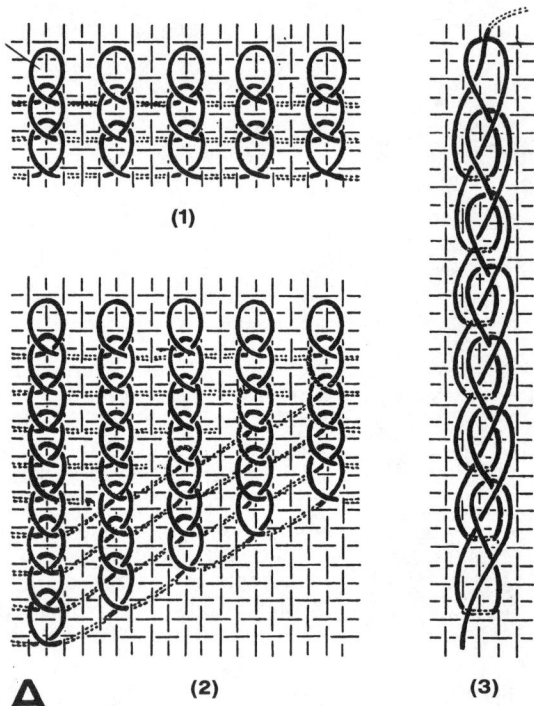

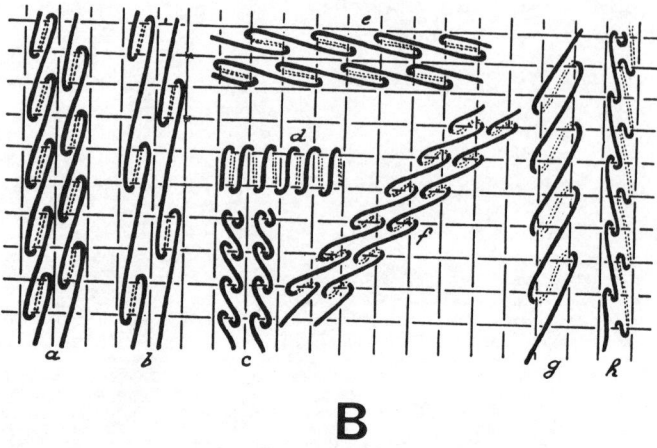

9.19. (*A, left*) Loop-stitch embroidery: (*1*) horizontal lines, (*2*) oblique lines, (*3*) vertical lines (D'Harcourt 1962, fig. 90a–d; courtesy UWP); (*B, above*) stem-stitch embroidery: vertical, horizontal, and diagonal covering stitches. (D'Harcourt 1962, fig. 92a–c; courtesy UWP)

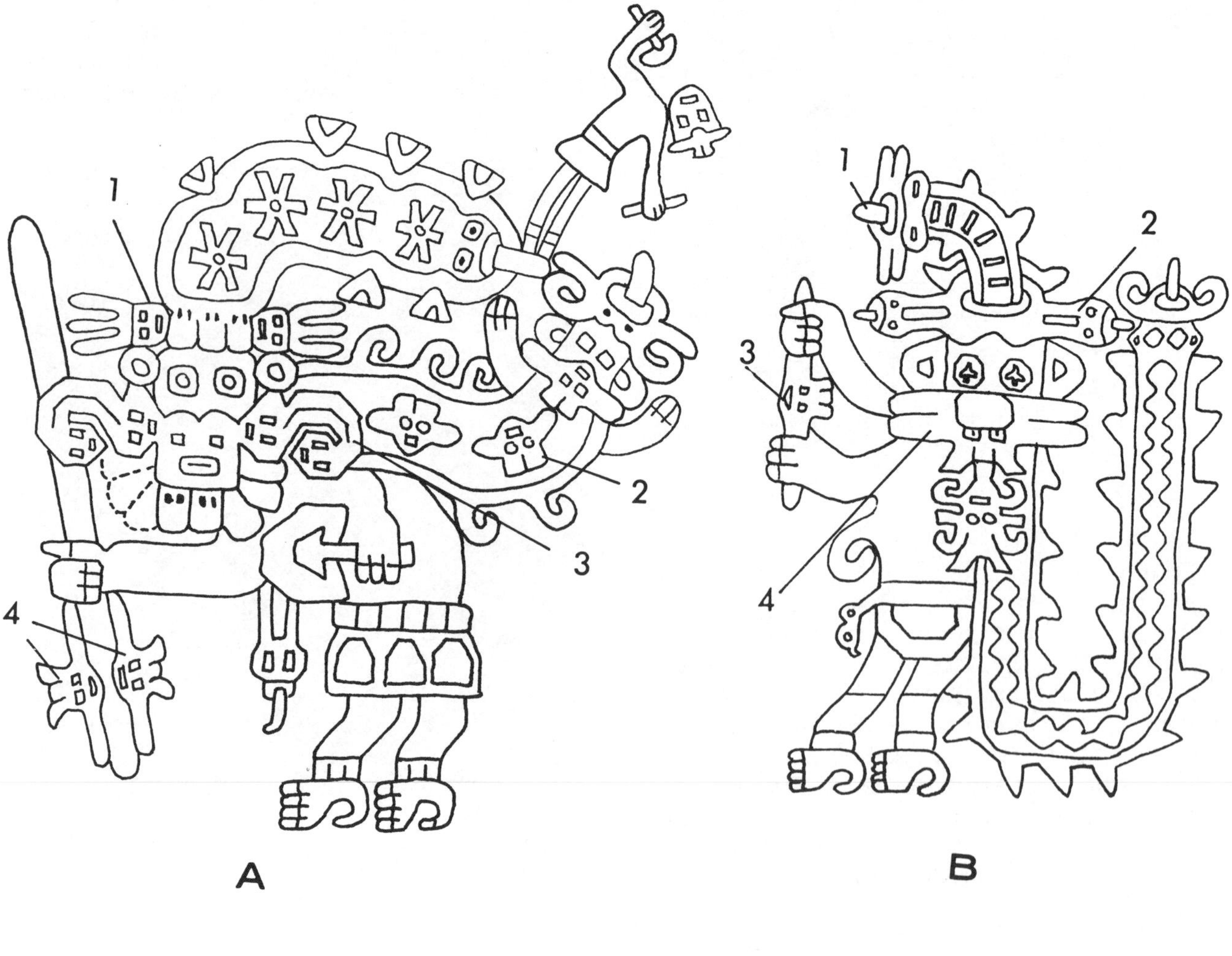

A

B

A

B

9.20. (A) Line drawing of three-dimensional needle-knit tab on Brooklyn Museum Paracas mantle with (1) centipede-kenned forehead ornament with human figure as tongue, (2) trailer with forehead-ornament "spots" ending in whisker-masked faces, (3) triple-kenned mouth mask, carrying *tumi* knife, and (4) forehead-ornament staff; (B) A needle-knit tab on the same mantle, showing a figure with (1) tongue tip-kenned with whisker mask and (2) kenned, whiskered mouth mask, (3) carrying and (4) wearing a forehead ornament. (Illustrated in D'Harcourt 1962, pl. 93, figs. 22 and 23; redrawn by the author from Tello 1959, figs. 55 and 70; courtesy UNMSM)

9.21. Photo and line drawing of a llama tab with stylized trophy heads as (1) eye border and ear, (2) rump and tail spots, (3) penis, (4) harness and bridle of forehead masks, (5) body ornaments of Chavinoid eyes, assorted plants, (6) kenned appendage figure. (D'Harcourt 1962, pl. 93, fig. 26, courtesy UWP; redrawn by the author from Tello 1959, fig. 68)

9.22. Feline Oculate Being figures in Linear substyle, Early Horizon 10 embroidery, in the Raton Collection, Paris. (D'Harcourt 1962, pl. 106; courtesy UWP)

tary wefts, gauzes, and multiple-layered weaves. EH 9 textiles are subdued in color; structure and texture carry the pattern. Individual designs have Chavinoid elements (long trailers with forked or trophy-head ends reminiscent of kennings) but are more geometric or stylized, sometimes with interlocking repeats and combined bird, serpent, feline, and anthropomorphic elements.

Early Horizon 10 marks the beginning of Necropolis at Cerro Colorado as Cavernas continued. Necropolis textiles display rectilinear EH-9 designs because, Dwyer feels, artisans were experimenting with needle knitting and were unfamiliar with its potential. The result is a Linear Substyle (Figure 9.22) with large and secondary figures of compressed concentric lines covering the entire cloth. The effect is dense and impenetrable because figures and background use the same limited range of rich colors. Figures are "visually elusive" and stand out only when a line in contrasting color traces facial features, body profiles, or interior figures shown in X-ray fashion. Needle-thin bodies, heads, eyes, and mouths float detached from fixed points of reference (Paul 1982a, 256–260) and may represent mythical, ancestral, or supernatural images or intangible concepts (Paul 1989, 72). A Broad Line Substyle using wider, bandlike outlines appears in fewer bundles and perhaps represents a family or personal style. Stylistically and iconographically related to the Linear substyle, it is probably a transitional

form that led into the subsequent Block Color substyle (Paul 1989, 74–76).

Early Intermediate 1 embroiderers, in full control of needle knitting, experimented with clarity of form and visual legibility. There was an increasing tendency to build more natural images of solid-color blocks instead of narrow parallel lines. In this Block Color Substyle, bright color units outlined in black against monochrome backgrounds define each motif. Some reflect their rectilinear narrow-line heritage; others are rounded, with overlapping legs or arms suggesting perspective.

During Early Intermediate 2, embroiderers produced block-color cloths of enormous complexity and variety. Fully curvilinear images from the natural world and supernatural beings show more realism and action. Frontal or profile torsos, heads, toed feet and fingered hands, and animal bodies show maximum information about the subjects. Complex, varied motifs are heightened by repeat positioning in vertical or horizontal rows (Stafford 1941), also an early Nasca characteristic. Three-dimensional needle-knit tabs edge these huge iconographically complex mantles.

Paul (1982a, 263–277) notes that linear and block substyles coexisted in Necropolis burials and proposes that each may have encoded a different iconography, whereas the less prevalent broad line substyle was restricted to very high-rank bundles. Within the three substyles, the Dwyers (Dwyer and Dwyer 1975, 159) feel that

9.23. Detail of Necropolis mantle with (A) supernatural figure and (B) human trophy hunter. (Reproduced by permission of Smithsonian Institution Press from Lumbreras 1974, fig. 102, p. 91; copyright © 1974 by Luis G. Lumbreras)

they can identify the embroidery of up to twenty different artisans in a single bundle.

Iconography

Early Horizon 9's main figure is the Oculate Being, a large-eyed whiskered, jaguar-spotted flying or standing figure with a U-shaped mouth carrying a trophy head or knife. His crossed canines and trophy-head-tipped streamers designate deity status (Dwyer and Dwyer 1975, 153. For Oculate Being varients, see Paul 1986). Serpent, bird, and feline forms attend him or act as small background fillers.

Early Horizon 10 elaborates these attendants and gives the Oculate Being a feline or killer-whale body holding a trophy head and knife, framed by long serrated appendages tipped with trophy heads, serpent heads, or miniature human bodies. His heart-shaped face has large, owl-like, or hexagonal eyes and a U-shaped

mouth on an arched, falling body with long flowing hair.

Early Intermediate 1 brought increasing naturalism. Iconographically distinct supernaturals include birdmen, anthropomorphized killer whales, avian–felines plus the Occulate Being with many of these attributes. Body parts are detailed: Parabola-shaped feet and hands reveal each tiny toe or finger or have long simian digits with opposable thumbs (Figure 9.23a). Eyes have black pupils, mouths individual teeth; costume tassels and fringes show individual threads (Figure 9.23b). Trophy heads alternate with beans, suggesting a connection between their spirit power and that of plant germination.

Early Intermediate 2 adds more secondary forms and complex iconographic elements. Pervasive trophy heads are kenned as beans and other vegetables. Excavated, preserved trophy heads suggest a formalized trophy-head cult. Falling or flying anthropomorphized felines and birds eat trophy heads or entire bodies, and figures carrying trophy heads, staffs, fans, vegetation, darts, and spearthrowers wear trophy heads on sashes or as pelage marks. Serpent and trophy heads ken long flowing streamers, whiskers, forehead ornament ends (Figure 9.20), costume fringes, and even the soles of feet as Chavinoid vestiges. EI 2 figures rhythmically repeated in vertical or horizontal rows regularly alternate head direction, costume details, and objects carried.

Cultural Significance

What interpretations and conclusions can we draw from these beautiful textiles?

First, they document the manner and rate of spread of Chavín motifs to the South Coast. Painted textiles indicate two strong waves of Chavín influence. Pilgrimages to Chavín and transplanted artisans at South Coast textile production centers likely maintained a continuing cross-fertilization of ideas, with textiles (large altar cloths or wall hangings?) among the agents of transmission.

Second, they point to a Chavín–local iconographic synthesis as the basis for the Nasca style. Needle knitting opened design motifs to a range of color interpretation impossible in stone carvings or painted textiles.

Third, they provide a complex visible imagery of supernatural power. Terence Grieder (1982, 150–151) identifies nine indicators of supernatural status in South Coast art: (1) frontal eyes, (2) the bloody mouth, (3) checkerboard panels, (4) darts, (5) trophy heads, (6) kenned hair, (7) bird forehead ornaments, (8) the flying pose, and (9) feline whisker masks, all present on Necropolis textiles. Gold forehead ornaments with tie strings (7) and clip-whisker masks for nasal-septum attachment (9) have been found archaeologically. On textiles, tongues (Figure 9.20b) and back ornaments (Figure 9.20a) are tip-kenned with little whisker-masked faces. Bird forehead ornaments are worn, carried (Figure 9.20b), and used as bridle and muzzle ornaments on a Brooklyn Museum mantle's elaborate three-dimensional needle-knit llama tab (Figure 9.21). Trophy heads (5) ken its sinuous eyelashes and penis (Figure 9.21) and were richly elaborated on Nasca textiles and pottery as the concepts they represented became increasingly important.

Fourth, Paracas textiles indicate organized textile production. Designs were planned and stitch-outlined before needleknitting. Most cloths probably saw ritual use during their owner's lifetime and were completed long before his death, but variations in styles and quality of unfinished wrappings suggest that others were hastily produced between death and burial as contributions by kin or other groups (Dwyer and Dwyer 1975, 159). Some bundles were perhaps renewed with "remembrance rites" wrappings because styles of outer textiles are more recent than inner ones. The labor of procuring and processing highland llama wool, coastal cotton, and montaña feathers and then designing, spinning, weaving, and embroidering the staggering quantities of textiles excavated speak eloquently of esteem for the socially prominent dead.

Finally, iconography poses interesting speculations about Paracas society and world view. The mantle figures may be ancestors or lineage leaders in a society where rank was determined by age and sex rather than wealth, buried with satellite bundles containing wives or retainers. Anthropomorphized animals may indicate affiliations with totemic clans and their patron deities (Dwyer and Dwyer 1975). Humans with trophy heads could be lineage leaders taking trophy heads to feed the Oculate Being who translates their "head essence" into vegetal growth, glossed by the plants bedecking his image. Anne Paul and Solveig Turpin (1986) consider anthropomorphic Early Intermediate 1 and 2 "falling," "flying," and "dancing" figures with their streaming hair, outstretched arms, arched backs, and nude, sometimes skeletal torsos, to be ecstatic shamans battling supernatural spirits and falling earthbound after trance experiences.

By extension, mummy mantles and cloth false-head masks representing Oculate Beings may act as "agents of transformation" by apotheosizing bundle occupants into the Occulate Being. Symbols of life taking (trophy heads, jaguars, raptorial birds) and regeneration (beans and other plant crops) offer "graphic allegory of the necessity of death to sustain the living" (Dwyer 1979, 121, 127) in a philosophy akin to Mesoamerican beliefs. Anne Paul (1986) distinguishes seven different Occulate Beings with variants and theorizes that they may instead be totemic symbols or lineage ancestors of the weavers who created the figures.

In conclusion, the iconography of Paracas textiles simultaneously reconfirms Chavín–highland influences and depicts a wide array of Paracas supernaturals and related concepts. Their iconography and the incredible amount of time required for their production also reflect hierarchical variations in the status of the bundle occupants and the importance of weavers in this culture where one bridged to the afterlife as a power-imbued, meaning-laden "stratified hill of cloth" (Paul 1989, 115).

CHAPTER 10

NASCA

Wıth the collapse of Chavinoid influences, the South Coast returned to local traditions. By A.D. 200, Nasca (Map 10: "Nazca" is an alternate spelling) had become a major cultural center, and its well-defined art style dominated contiguous valleys. At around A.D. 500, strong connections with the highland site of Huari resulted in the introduction of highland urban/religious architecture and a Tiahuanaco-influenced style sometimes called Epigonal, and Nasca's importance diminished. By A.D. 1000, when Huari contributions waned, the Ica Valley had replaced Nasca as the dominant South Coast style.

ARCHAEOLOGY

Nasca, as a primary civilization, was largely defined by Max Uhle. Excavations by William Duncan Strong (1957) and studies of settlement patterns by John Rowe (1963) have provided the archaeological context for reconstructing Nasca culture.

Chronological Divisions

Strong (1957) divided the sequence into Proto-Nazca, Early, Middle, and Late Nazca. Using Uhle's extensive pottery collections, Anna Gayton and Alfred Kroeber (1927) defined stylistic phases A, X, B, and Y, and later revised them as phases A, B, and C. Richard Roark (1965) identified important shifts in design organization by introducing the descriptive terms of Monumental, Proliferous, and Disjunctive Nazca. Further seriation of Uhle's collection tied to Strong's stratigraphy has produced a chronological framework of four major cultural phases, Nasca I, II, III, and IV, and nine ceramic periods (Menzel, Rowe, and Dawson 1964).

During Nasca I (Strong's Proto-Nasca), villages of wattle-covered cane huts dotted the Nasca, Pisco, and Ica valleys. Hunting supplemented crops of lima beans, corn, and tubers; river fish, whales, and porpoises were abundant. Textiles and pottery combine Paracas Necropolis and innovative Nasca elements.

Nasca II (Early Nasca) brought larger settlements of adobe brick, cane, and post construction. The most impressive is Cahuachi in the Nasca Valley (Map 10), probably a regional capital and administrative center coordinating water distribution for adjacent valleys. Its location and size imply a nucleated urbanized character like that of highland cities. Smaller sites may have had lesser religious and administrative roles in a short-lived "mini-empire" created by Nasca Middle-Phase-II military expansion.

By Nasca III (Middle Nasca), Cahuachi and other large sites were abandoned. Smaller centers continued in the southern valleys. Social classes included rulers, priests, wealthy individuals buried with gold ornaments and polichrome pottery, craftsworkers, warriors buried with atlatls and obsidian-tipped spears, farmers, and unskilled laborers. Some burials contain trophy heads, which were also a favorite pottery motif.

Nasca IV (Late Nasca) saw the return of large ceremonial centers with painted plaster walls and remains of animal sacrifice. Contact intensified with the Ayacucho Valley in the South Highlands, where Nasca pottery has been found at Conchopata near Huari. South Coast workmanship deteriorated as the valleys absorbed the brunt of increasing Huari expansion.

ARCHITECTURE

Early Intermediate architecture points to emerging regional kingdoms that were frequently in conflict. Cahuachi, the probable Nasca capital, covers a square kilometer (.62 mile) and contains six pyramids with walled courts set on adobe-brick-faced terraces, plus smaller huts of bound canes (quincha) daubed with mud. The 20-meter-high (65.6 foot) Great Temple is surrounded by rectangular rooms and plazas. To the north, cemeteries contain burials in log-roofed pits lined with adobe brick. Flexed bodies lie in rows facing the temple and are wrapped in cane mats in contrast to the elaborately embroidered mantles of Paracas Necropolis mummy bundles.

Other large Early Intermediate sites include Cerro Soldado in the Ica Valley and Dos Palmos in the Pisco Valley. In the Acarí Valley to the south, Tambo Viejo and Chocaventa were fortified with stone and brick walls during Phase II, perhaps to resist Nasca invasion. During Phase III, Cahuachi, Tambo Viejo, and Dos Palmos were abandoned, and a distinctive structure called La Estaquería (because of its twelve rows of twenty wooden posts) was built near Cahuachi (Map 10). Strong, its excavator, thinks that

they were roof supports of a large temple used for agricultural fertility rites together with the Phase-III "Nasca lines" on the adjacent desert floor (see later section). Plastered and painted walls are found at late Early Intermediate Huaca del Loro in the Upper Nasca Valley. More data are needed to link archaeological stages to Nasca ceramic phases and textile types.

ART

Nasca art reflects its smooth, gradual transition from Paracas antecedents in both form and decoration. Both textiles and ceramics have motifs that continued from Paracas and were modified to suit Nasca tastes and shifts in manufacturing techniques.

Pottery

Nasca painted pottery replaced Paracas postfiring resin colors with polychrome-slip painting in a palette of colors ranging from buffs and tans to oranges and browns. Figure outlines were no longer incised but were delineated with dark brown or black lines. Subject matter expanded enormously to encompass a multitude of supernatural beings, among them a so-called Anthropomorphic Mythical Being who seems to be a descendant of the Oculate Being found on late Paracas needle-knit mantles. Supernaturals, ordinary humans, birds, and even mummy-bundle images are prominently associated with trophy heads, the iconographic counterparts of well-preserved heads found in buried caches that suggest a well-organized trophy head cult.

Ceramic Phases

Nasca pottery has been described in major studies by Gayton and Kroeber (1927), Kroeber (1956), Strong (1957), Menzel, Rowe, and Dawson (1964), Roark (1965), and Proulx (1968). Their terminologies differ, but all adhere to a common chronology derived through seriation of Max Uhle's comprehensive South Coast collections, cross-tied to stratigraphy at Cahuachi and other sites. The most frequently used sequence, the work of Menzel, Rowe, and Dawson (1964), divides Nasca pottery into nine ceramic phases. Their development through the four major stages of Nasca cultural development is summarized next.

10.1. Otter–ocelot holding jícama roots (Sawyer 1975, fig. 130a; drawing by Raymond Perlman, courtesy Alan Sawyer and KAM)

10.2. Otter–ocelots with trophy head–kenned legs, signifier, tongue, and (*left*) forehead ornament in paw. From a stone vase in the Museo Nacional de Antropología e Arqueología, Lima. (Sawyer 1968, p. 56; courtesy Alan Sawyer)

During Nasca I (Strong's Proto-Nasca; Ceramic Phase 1), polichrome-slip-painted designs replaced resin-based colors but were still outline incised in the Paracas manner. Naturalistic humans, animals, birds, and agricultural plants were painted or modeled as effigies on single- or double-bridged-spout jars and flaring or conical-walled bowls.

By Nasca II (Early Nasca: Ceramic Phases 2–5), the range of naturalistic representations increased. Designs outlined in black were painted on the polished globular bodies of double-bridged-spout jars against solid-black, buff, cream, or red grounds in up to eight colors, including reds, browns, yellows, and grays. Kroeber calls this phase Nazca A; Rowe refers to it as Monumental because large images cover most of the vessel surface. Fishers, farmers, warriors, figures with monkey traits, birds (including the whippoorwill-like *vencejo*), centipedes, killer whales, peppers, and beans are easily identifiable. Other figures are supernaturals, among them ongoing Paracas anthropomorphic felines and an otterlike feline with swept-back whiskers, a protruding tongue, and ocelot spots. Because of the agricultural plants in its paws (Figure 10.1), Sawyer (1975, 94) identifies it as "a benign spiritual guardian of agriculture."

These naturalistic felines gradually developed into Whiskered Mythical Beings (Figure 10.2, left) with trophy-head kenned feet, tails, tongues, and fur, wearing swept-back whisker masks and wearing or carrying a forehead ornament in their paws (Wolfe 1981). One type, an early Anthropomorphic Mythical Being, has a small loinclothed human-body appendage to one side of the head and carries a club and/or trophy head in one hand. A long, wide, tail-like "signifier" edged with trophy heads and spikes and ending in a feline, bird, or plant "terminator" reminiscent of Chavín kennings arcs over its body (Figure 10.3). Another avian "diving" type holds trophy heads in its front paws or seems to bite into limp human bodies. Its "wings" are made of layered trophy-head (three dotted) feathers (Figure 10.4a,b). A dotted feather bustle fans out from the trophy-head "rump patch" between its splayed legs (Figure 10.4). These whiskered feline and anthropomorphic mythical beings are close kin to the Oculate Being of Ocucaje V pottery and Necropolis mantles and the earliest Nasca painted

and embroidered textiles (Proulx 1968, 17–18, 32).

During Nasca III (Late Nasca: Ceramic Phases 5–6 and Kroeber's Nazca B), key Nasca II elements become more abstract. Mythical Beings are laden with guavas, peppers, beans, and manioc. Figure 10.5 shows one with a shirt and headdress composed of vegetal forms, holding a dismembered corpse. Trophy heads with guavas and peppers sprouting from their mouths edge its long trailer "signifier," which is banded with manioc images.

Trophy heads abstracted as triangles with small slits for eyes and mouth and long hanks of black hair pervade Nasca-III imagery. Jars with sling-wrapped turbans and stitched lips closely resemble actual mummified trophy heads recovered from excavations in the Nasca area (Figure 10.6). Sawyer (1975, 78; 1979, 130–131) sees them as assurances of agricultural fertility, with the life force obtained from enemy heads redirected positively toward the captor group's crops. To Roark (1965), they reflect the expansionist warfare of the period.

Other formerly naturalistic motifs are also "mythified" and given trophy-head associations. The condor, formerly shown as a raptorial bird that feeds on human corpses (Figure 10.7), is transformed into the "Horrible Bird" (Wolfe 1981). Trophy heads form its segmented body, tip its feathers, and are carried in its beak (Figure 10.7c,e).

The same transition awaited the killer whale, formerly portrayed naturalistically as part of the Nasca biota. Its "mythicized" anthropomorphic "Bloody-Mouth" form, with a long "signifier" serrated like a whale's tail (Figure 10.8a,b,e,f,g), or a segmented body of connected heads (Figure 10.8c,d), disgorges streams of clotted blood (Figure 10.8a,c,d,h,i), trophy heads (Figure 10.8e,f), or even an entire human corpse (Figure 10.8g). To Sawyer (1977, 32), "Horrible Bird" and "Bloody Mouth" again indicate the introduction of new religious concepts.

Many late Nasca III images are embellished with complex scrolls, lancets, and volutes (Figures 10.8, 10.9) that Sawyer sees as emanations of trophy-head "life force" and thin, black clove-like or forked elements interpreted as trophy-head hair (Sawyer 1975, 104–105). Forehead ornaments, whisker masks, and the "Bloody Mouth" often become independent motifs (Fig-

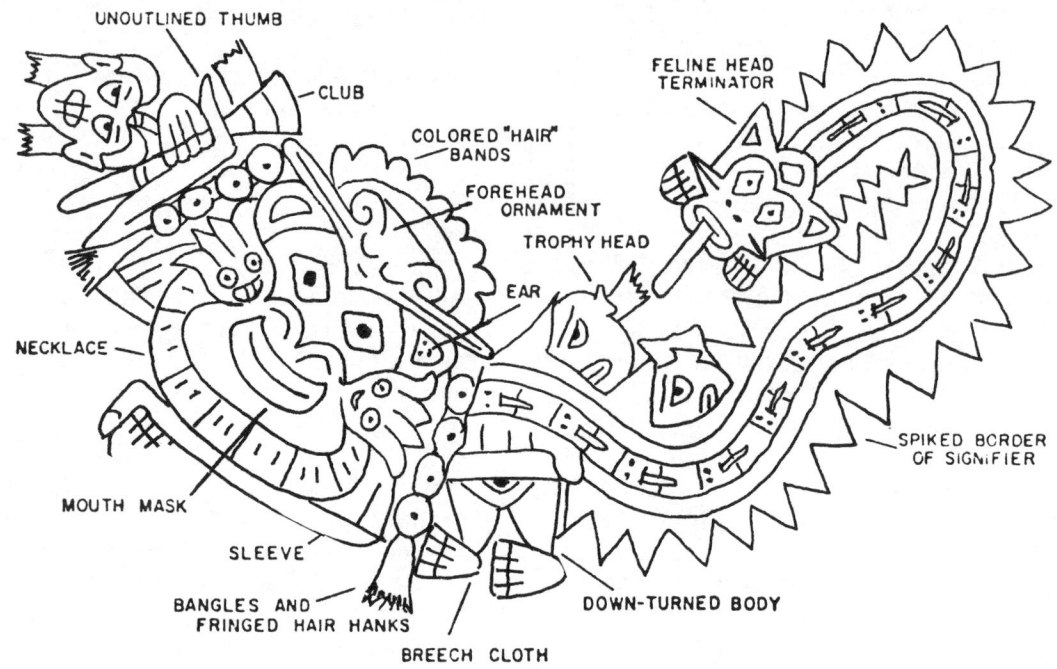

A

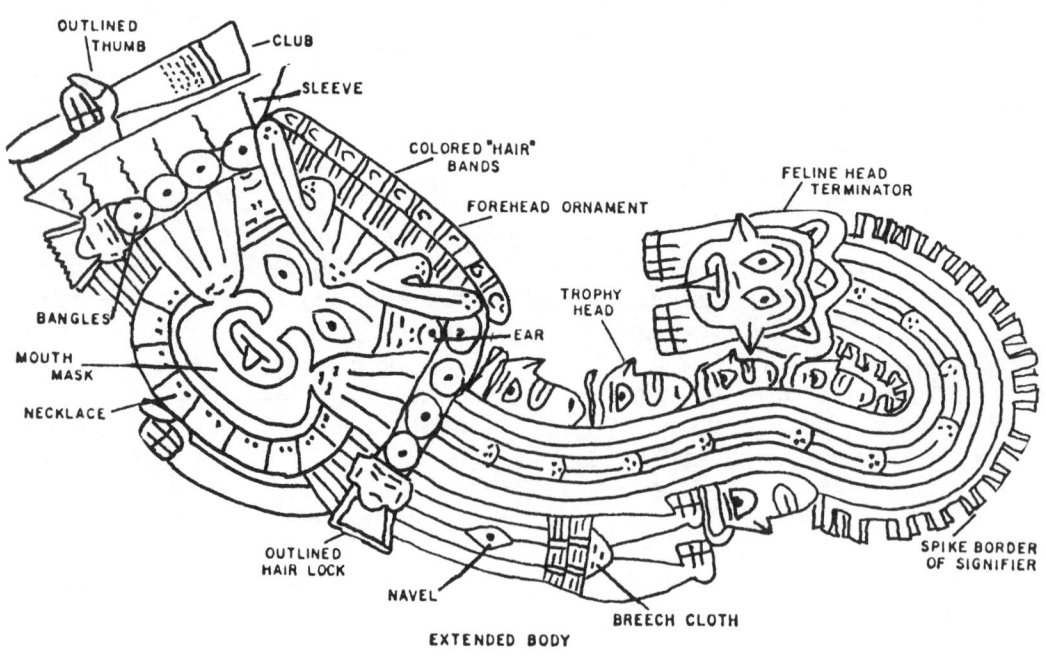

B

10.3. Whiskered Mythical Beings, with components labeled. (Proulx 1968, figs. 18 and 19; courtesy Donald A. Proulx)

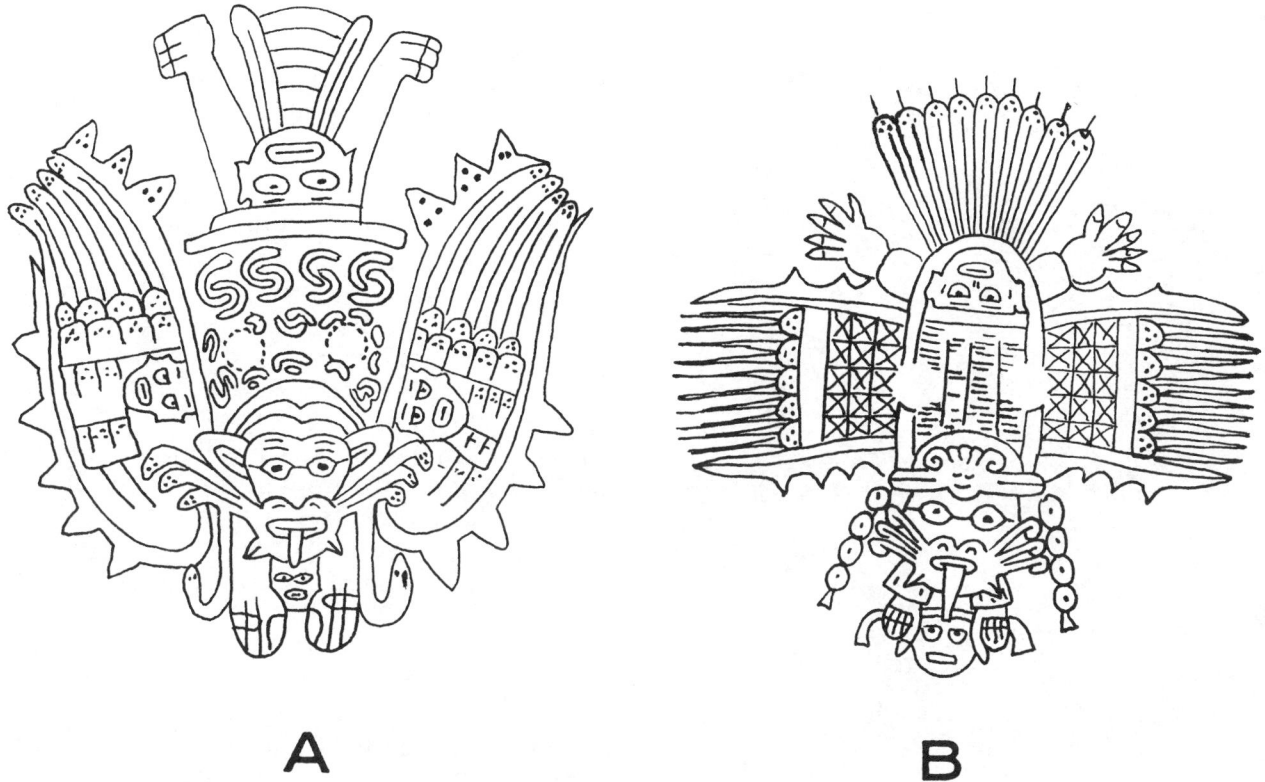

10.4. (A) "Diving" Whiskered Mythical Being; (B) Whiskered Mythical Being with splayed "tail" of trophy-head feathers. (Redrawn by the author from Seler 1923, figs. 72 and 73.)

10.5. Agricultural deity from a Middle Nasca ceramic cup. There are guavas on the tongue of the left signifier trophy head, peppers on the tongue of the right signifier trophy head, and manioc on the deity's shirt and signifier band. Art Institute of Chicago, Gaffron Collection. (Sawyer 1979, fig. 24; drawing by Sally Schaefer, courtesy Alan Sawyer)

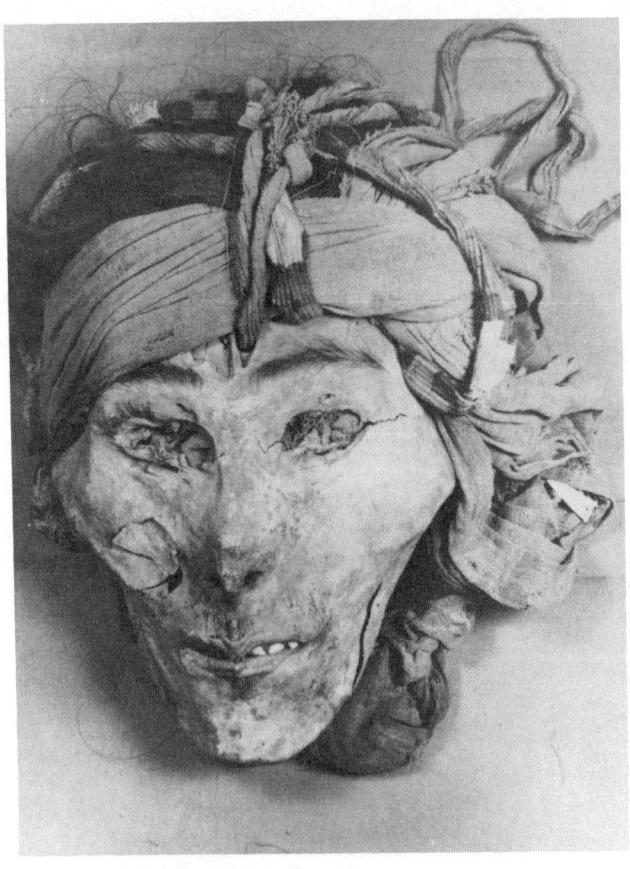

ure 10.8) or are strung together in chainlike clones reminiscent of the repeated elements in Chavín iconography (Figure 10.9). The effect is one of bursting vitality, as if the designs are procreating new forms in response to the vibrant life force they portray. Rowe aptly labels the stage "Proliferous."

Nasca IV (Nasca/Huari; Ceramic Phases 7–9, and Kroeber's Nazca C) saw motifs degenerate into simpler, poorly executed derivatives as ceramic technology declined. Designs were sloppily painted on red or cream ground, with a return to simple, modeled effigy forms with painted detail. The proliferation of "mythification" embellishments is gone: A few, such as the volute, remain abstract design elements. Bits and pieces of formerly cohesive figures float randomly through the Nasca-IV design repertoire, leading Rowe to dub this stage "Dis-

10.6. Mummified Early Intermediate period Nasca trophy head with a cactus spine pinning the lips. Collection of the Muséo Peruano de Ciencia de la Salud, Lima. (Vreeland and Cockburn, 1980, fig. 9.16, p. 162; photo by James Vreeland copyright © by CUP, reprinted with permission)

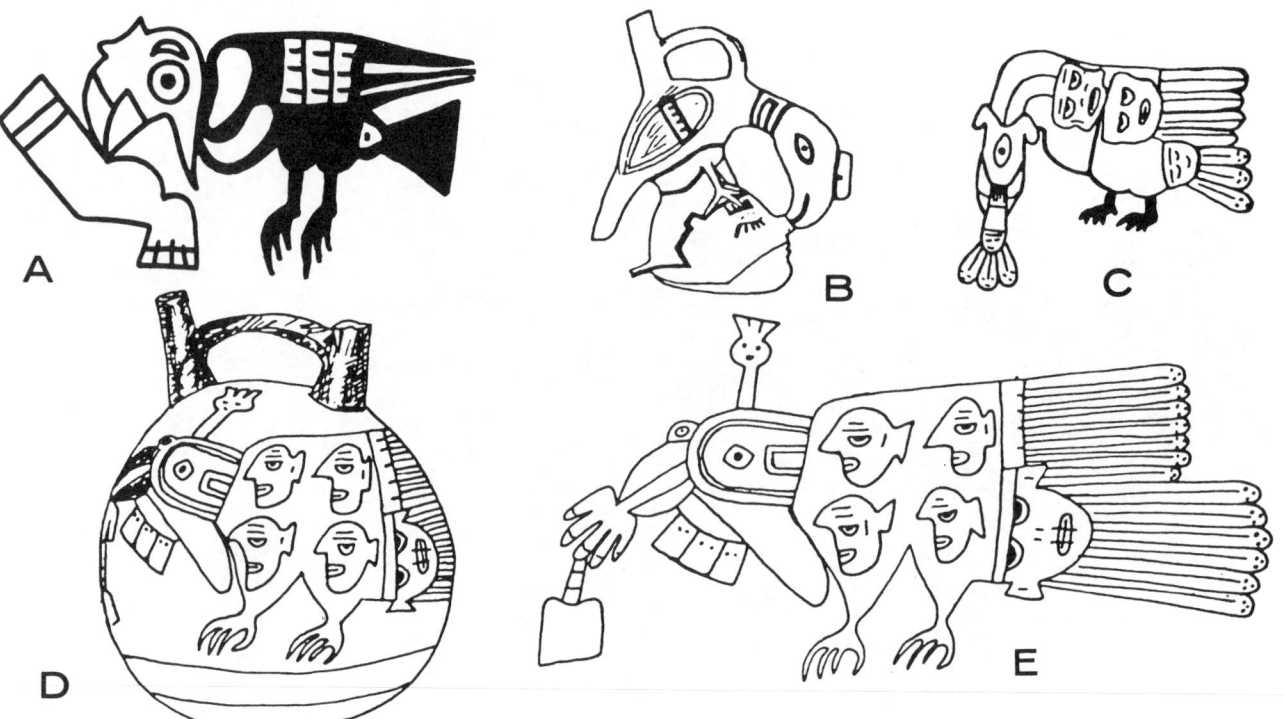

10.7. Variants and possible precursors of the "Horrible Bird" motif: (A, B) devouring human leg, head, (C) with stylized heads, (D) on vase, and (E) devouring a human arm, with trophy heads on body, wing, and tail ends. (Wolfe 1981, figs. 60–65; courtesy NP/IAS)

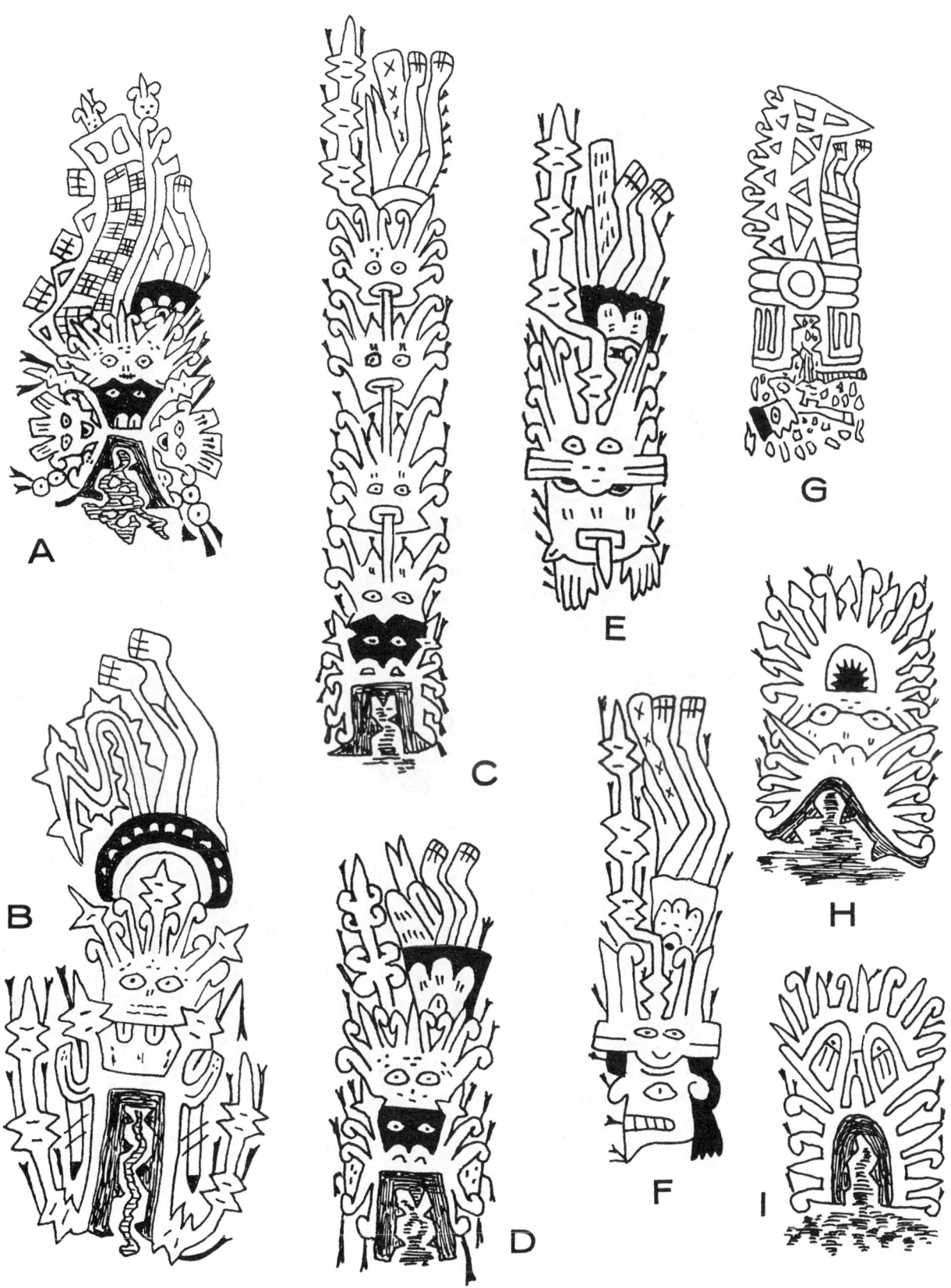

10.8. "Bloody Mouth" motifs. (Redrawn by the author from Yacovleff 1932b, fig. 11; courtesy MNCP)

junctive." To archaeologists and art historians, it represents South Coast incorporation of decorative concepts from Huarpa, the South Highland culture that preceded Huari, during the century of intense South Coast–Highland interaction just before Tiahuanacoid elements appear in South Coast pottery around A.D. 600.

Textiles

Nasca weavers shifted their emphasis from needle-knit embroidery to tapestry and, to a lesser degree, brocading. Painted plain-weave textiles continued from earlier times as well.

Painted Textiles

Alan Sawyer has used painted textiles to illustrate important aspects of Nasca design evolution (Sawyer 1979). Their images, freer than embroidered ones and less bound by the geometrical form imposed by the weaving process, are often easier to identify. Their size and grave contexts suggest use either as funerary offerings, ceremonial wall hangings, or altar cloths. Like pottery, they depict trophy heads and themes of agricultural fertility.

10.9. Abstracted version of proliferous deity with head repeats. (Drawing by Raymond Perlman in Sawyer 1975, fig. 144; courtesy Alan Sawyer and IAS)

10.10. Agricultural deity from the "Manto Calendárico." Paracas Necropolis, fardo 290-45. (Sawyer 1979, fig. 1; drawing by Sally Schaefer, courtesy Alan Sawyer)

A prime example is the (Nasca I) Manto Calendárico found by Tello (1959) on a Paracas Necropolis mummy bundle, which depicts multiple frontal humans carrying agricultural plants. Headdresses and clothing expand the theme: The vegetation deity in Figure 10.10 wears a shirt decorated with two types of beans and carries bean pods in both hands (Sawyer 1979, 30).

A second Nasca II painted textile shows Whiskered Mythical Beings as part of a ceremonial cloth border. Their winged, spotted, or feline-striped bodies have tails or streamers tipkenned with realistic trophy heads or victim bodies with streaming hair; one flicks his tongue at a head held aloft. The best preserved figure (Figure 10.11) wears a loincloth, divided shirt, necklace of slat-shaped shell pieces, turban of colored hair bands, whisker mask, and forehead ornament; his whiskers, bared canines, round, bean-decorated ears, and arched brows, however, are feline. His taloned paws hold a knife and a trophy head.

On another early painted fragment, whiskered felines with shirted human torsos face frontally with feet and arms facing left and plump (cloud-marked?) tails to the right. On the three surviving fragments of this large textile, they hold a variety of domesticated plants (in Figure 10.12, from left to right, a gourd rattle and jicama roots; a maize stalk; bean pods and a forehead ornament).

10.11. Anthropomorphic pampas cat on Early Nasca Phase A ceremonial cloth. (Photo courtesy The Cleveland Museum of Art, The Norweb Collection, 40.530)

10.12. Crop-holding ocelot–otters on Early Nasca Phase B ceremonial cloth. (Sawyer 1979, fig. 7; courtesy TM, 1966.46.1)

Another Nasca-II textile hints at the size and complexity of these hangings. Sawyer estimates that the complete web was over 8 meters (26 feet) high and 3.8 meters (12.4 feet) wide, with ten rows of forty-nine figures each and that additional pieces originally sewn on would have brought the total dimensions to 2.5 by 4 meters (8 by 13 feet), with at least 1,500 painted figures in the design (Sawyer 1979, 137). The small costumed humans carrying staffs, weapons, and crop plants may be dancing in a First Fruits ceremony. Sawyer (1979, 141) thinks that a related Middle-Nasca embroidered shirt with twenty-six plant-carrying humans, analyzed and identified by O'Neale and Whitaker (1947) was probably worn during harvest-ceremony rites. On another Middle Nasca fragment, Whiskered Mythical Beings with plant headdresses, trophy-head kilts, and tail-like "signifiers" tip-kenned with otter heads alternate in position, color, and iconographic details and are so closely packed that the background is virtually obliterated (Figure 10.13).

These huge textiles permit variations of motifs impossible on more limited ceramic surfaces. Among them are crop plants that botanists can specifically identify to further our reconstruction of Nasca culture.

The Nasca Lines

Art and imagery sometimes take strange forms. One of these is the intricate complex of lines, triangles, trapezoids, spirals, zigzags, animal, bird, reptile, insect, and marine forms deliberately created on a 30-mile (48 kilometer) plateau near the Nasca River Valley 1,300 years ago (Aveni (ed.) 1990).

The Nasca desert designs have long been known to local residents. They were published in 1939 by Toribio Mejía Xesspe (1939), Tello's assistant in the Paracas excavations. They received wider reknown through the publications of Paul Kosok (1949, 1965), a New York student surveying the South Coast in the 1940s for ancient drainage ditches, and international prominence as extraterrestrial "landing runways" in the Von Daniken publications and their spinoffs in the 1970s. Kosok mentioned them to Maria Reiche, a German math/astronomy student then in Peru, and Reiche began an intensive study of the markings, walking the desert for over four decades to discover new configurations. Over thirty distinct animal figures include a duckling, monkey (Figure 10.14), lizard, spider, sea bird, killer whale (Figure 10.15), and hummingbird (Figure 10.16). Numerous rectilinear markings also crisscross the desert floor. The effect has been compared to "the world's largest scratch pad" (Morrison and Hawkins 1978, 29).

The lines, referred to as "caminos" (roads) by the locals, occur on a plateau above the Nasca Valley named Pampa Colorada ("red plain") because its surface is littered with oxidized pebbles. A few inches below, sand retains its natural lighter color. The designs were created by removing the darker material to expose the sand. They are regular and precise and cross riverbeds and mountain ridges without losing their accuracy. They are also difficult to date: Although lines bisect and images were superimposed, stratigraphy is lacking. Pampa potsherds date between A.D. 200–600 and show animals similar to those portrayed (Figure 10.15). Carbon-14 dates stakes set at line termi-

10.13. Agricultural deities from fragments of a Middle Nasca painted ceremonial cloth. Milwaukee Public Museum, 51544b/18046. (Drawing by Milton Sonday in Sawyer 1979, fig. 25; courtesy Alan Sawyer and TM)

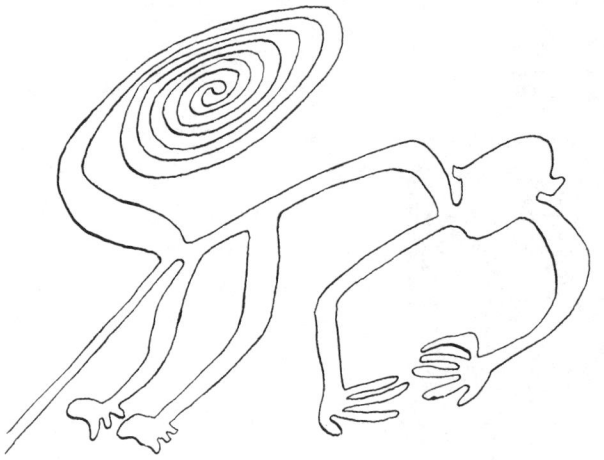

10.14. Ground figure of monkey, Nasca Plain. (Drawing by the author, after Isbell 1978, p. 194)

nations at A.D. 525. It is safe to assume that the images were made locally during the Early Intermediate Period without looking further afield.

Astronomical Interpretations

One interpretation is that the lines have astronomical associations. Maria Reiche (1974) feels that straight and fan-shaped lines may be sighting lines for astral, solar, and lunar settings, keyed to dates for planting, harvesting, return of water in the rivers, and the annual fiesta cycle. Their multiplicity, she feels, reflects the gradual shift of star positions due to precession (the change of the earth's axis of rotation) over the years.

Gerald Hawkins (1969; 1974), the noted British astronomer who interprets England's mega-

10.15. Ground figure of a killer whale (*top*); modeled Nasca effigy whale pot (*bottom*). (Drawings by the author, after Isbell 1978, p. 192)

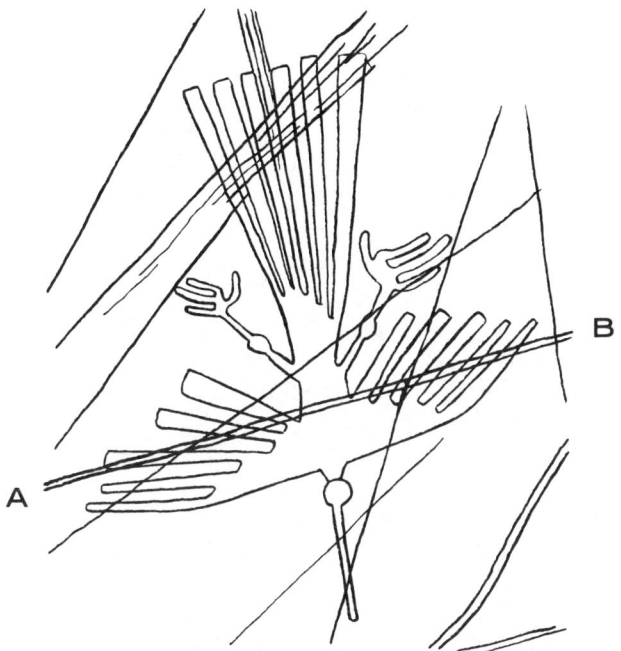

10.16. Avian ground figure with solstice alignment along wing feathers: *A* = winter solstice, *B* = summer solstice. (Drawing by the author, after Morrison 1978, p. 60)

lithic Stonehenge site as a giant eclipse predicter, however, found minimal correlation between the lines and astronomical phenomena.

Using a large map based on 1,200 air photos from which each line's azimuths could be computer-plotted to key star positions, computers programmed by Hawkins found twice the number of solar and lunar correspondences than expected by chance but no clear-cut majority for star positions. The two stone mounds of one of the largest geometric forms, the Great Rectangle, line up with the rising of the Pleiades in 610 A.D., a date close to the C-14 date of a wooden stake nearby,[1] and a line transsecting a long-beaked bird connects solar solstice positions (Figure 10.16), but most of the lines showed no clear celestial alignments. Hawkins's (1974) conclusion was that the lines do not form any cohesive celestial grid or base for a calendar system.

The lines and designs are barely perceptible at ground level but are clearly visible from nearby foothills or when viewed from above. For whose

edification were they intended? Imaginative accounts suggest UFO landing strips, but the sand underneath is soft: As Maria Reiche says, "I'm afraid the spacemen would have gotten stuck" (McIntyre 1975, 716). Like similar designs in England and the California desert, they may have been intended for celestial supernaturals, created to capture, concentrate, or disperse power, unseen by human eyes. Or they may have been conduits to supernatural power, like the "spirit paths" traced by Australian aborigines to commune with supernatural forces.

The animal figures have also generated many theories (Aveni (ed.) 1990). Perhaps they represent Nasca constellations, as we today see Pisces the Fish and Taurus the Bull. Ancestor cults are also a possibility, with memorial service for dead elders conducted at those images symbolizing their lineage totems. The close parallels on Nasca pottery may indicate ceremonies to killer whales and other animal–human combinations held at their images to gain power over them or express gratitude for plant and animal fertility. Evan Hadingham (1987, 177–178) suggests that animal images may represent "spirit helpers" contacted by shaman healers while in hallucinogen-induced spirit flights or perhaps the transformed shamans themselves.

Economic and social aspects are also implicit. William Isbell (1978, 191) feels that their dimensions (trapezoids over 2,000 feet [609.6 meters] long, great, cleared "ceremonial areas," and lines that cross rivers and mountain ridges) represent a huge energy investment, a deliberate means of diverting human labor into ceremonial activities to guarantee continuing abundance while maintaining a balance between population growth and resource availability.[2]

Interpretations Based on Ethnohistory and Ethnography

Another theory sees the markings as pathways between large, shrinelike piles of stone at line ends or the hub of radial lines. Coca leaves and Nasca shards found under the stones suggest continuing use. An offering is not even mandatory: Highland Peruvian Indians today build

---

[1] The Pleiades influenced grain preservation according to the Incas, whereas Colonial period coastal Indians felt that their brightness signaled a good or poor crop (Morrison and Hawkins 1978, 49).

[2] To others, the labor was not so great. Hawkins (Morrison and Hawkins 1978, 80) thinks that the lines in a 1 square mile area represent 3 weeks' work for a thousand people, based on reduplication of lines by Peruvian schoolboys, filmed by the BBC.

large *apacitas* (stone-pile shrines) on trails connecting mountain chapels and native shrines. As each person passes, he or she prays and adds a stone.

Anthropologist Johan Reinhard (1985a, 398) reports ongoing Central Andean beliefs associating worship of mountain peaks with rain for crops and human fertility and suggests that archaeological Chavín and Tiahuanaco were sited to be near sacred peaks that still receive native offerings today. He has documented Bolivian rain seekers walking along a straight, 2-mile-long (3.2 km) pathway to lay offerings at mountain shrines and has found offerings atop Cerro Blanco, a large dune overlooking the Nazca Valley that is regarded locally as a mountain-god creator of rain and healer of infertility (Reinhard 1985b).

Ethnohistoric sources describe complex systems of Inca shrines along pathways called *ceques* extending out from Cuzco, which subdivided the landscape into ritual areas (see Inca chapter for a fuller description). Anthony Aveni and a team of specialists representing archaeol-

ogy, anthropology, and astronomy, methodically walked and photomapped the Nasca lines between 1976 and 1984 (Aveni 1986, [ed.] 1990). They found ordered radials that may be analogous to Inca ceques. Significantly, these lines are consistently keyed to nearby water sources. The Nasca lines, too, may be walkways connecting apacita shrines, some of which (in the case of Pleiades and solstice orientations) had simultaneous astronomical functions as sighting lines, with wider trapezoidal spaces for sacred gatherings (Aveni [ed.] 1990).

Today the Nasca designs are scarred from dune buggies and jeeps of careless visitors. As Maria Reiche laments, "So many people come here now since that spaceman story" (quoted in Morrison and Hawkins 1974, 33). The Pampa Colorada had been slated for irrigation but because of public outcry is now a preserve, and an observation tower and tour flights enable visitors to see the patterns more clearly. In one instance at least, a unique example of precolumbian art has been preserved for future generations to ponder and enjoy.

CHAPTER 11

MOCHE

BY about 200 B.C., local North Coast polities began to emerge as Chavín influence weakened. In the Chicama, Virú, and Moche valleys, Salinar farmers living in villages beneath hilltop forts began producing White-on-Red stirrup-spout, strap-handle-and-spout, and bridged, false-spout jars with simple, incised, and painted geometric designs. At Cerro Arena in the Moche Valley, hundreds of stone-walled dwellings and a shared irrigation system attest to their intense cooperative farming. Subsequent Gallinazo occupations in these valleys with resist-decorated pottery that was probably introduced from the highlands are best known from excavations in the Virú Valley where the fortified 5-square-kilometer (1.9 square mile) site of Gallinazo contained a 25-meter-high (82-foot-high) adobe-brick pyramid, walled compounds, a complex irrigation system, and over 30,000 adobe rooms housing up to 10,000 people (Willey 1971, 36).

The Moche Sequence

Moche cultural development has been keyed to five stages (Moche I–V) based on changes in ceramic form and decoration. There is some disagreement among archaeologists about the exact duration of these stages, but the general outline of Moche origins and development is clear.

Some time between 250 B.C. and A.D. 100, a synthesis of Gallinazo and other local elements led to a new cultural pattern alternately referred to as Moche or Mochica. The huge site of Gallinazo was subsequently abandoned, and its forts were taken over by Moche peoples based in the Chicama and Moche valleys to the north. During Moche I–III, the Moche consolidated their presence, and between A.D. 300 and 500 (Moche III and IV), they moved southward into the Lower Virú, Santa, and Nepeña valleys, subjugating villages and enlarging them into administrative centers such as Pañamarca and Huancaco (Topic 1982, 72). By A.D. 400, the entire North Coast was a unified regional kingdom with a capital at the site of Moche (Map 10).

Around A.D. 550, during Moche V, cohesion began to falter in the face of expanding pressure from Huari in the Southern Highlands. Between A.D. 650–700, a series of harsh El Niño rains, earthquake-triggered landslides, and encroaching sands due to tectonic uplift may have altered drainage patterns and disrupted canal irrigation (Moseley 1983, 220). By A.D. 650, Moche and the southern valleys were abandoned. Populations shifted northward to the Lambayeque Valley and built Pampa Grande, an enormous, formally planned site with huge huacas and a nearby warrior–priest burial platform at Sipán, leaving the smaller upriver site of Galindo to control the now-peripheral Moche Valley. Late Moche pottery reflects the stress and tension of retrenchment with frenzied, crowded, painted figures and erratic composition. By A.D. 850, Galindo, too, was abandoned, and Pampa Grande was superseded by Chan Chan as the Middle Horizon ended around A.D. 1000 with the establishment of the Chimú culture, the last great North Coast state before the Inca.

Moche Culture

Archaeological excavation confirms that during Moche III and IV, farmers cultivated canal-irrigated plots several miles long. Corn, beans, squash, and peanuts were supplemented by fish, shrimps, and crabs that thrived on plankton stirred up by the offshore current. Other foods included beached whales, domesticated guinea pigs, and wildlife hunted by nobility from slave-borne litters.

Wealth differences were considerable and corresponded to well-defined class distinctions. Fine textiles, goldwork, and pottery were ubiquitous among the upper classes (Donnan and Mackey 1978). Burials at Moche near the Huaca de la Luna and Huaca del Sol and in mountain-slope cemeteries contain exotic items from the highlands and even distant Ecuador. Royal burials such as those at Loma Negra (in the Upper Piura Valley), Sipán (Middle Lambayeque Valley), and La Mina (Lower Jequetepeque Valley: see Lapiner 1976; Alva 1988, 1990; Donnan 1990) contain some of the most elaborate goldwork found in pre-columbian America. Such burials often contain military accoutrements. Bodies interpreted as warrior–priests are buried with battle maces and religious staffs. In life, they are depicted on pottery and murals as puma-skin-garbed, fang-masked dignitaries sitting atop pyramids or litters directing ceremonies. Running or fighting warriors with spotted-bean bodies also appear on pottery. At the lower end of the social scale, ordinary farmers and fisherfolk provided the food base and corporate labor.

Centralized cohesion was strong, and punishments were severe, including cutting off the noses of transgressors. The state organized labor forces to clear canals and controlled access to water sources that were defended by lines of forts where Andean streams entered the lowlands.

ARCHITECTURE

Although Moche architecture and grave lots were described in early archaeological reports, their distribution and settlement patterns were not well understood until the Virú Valley was intensively surveyed in the 1940s. Since then, ongoing excavations have added to the picture.

Moche, the presumed capital, is a 1-kilometer-square (.38-mile-square) site in the Lower Moche Valley. Its largest structure, the Huaca del Sol, lies west of a plain separating it from the smaller Huaca de la Luna that is set against the steep slopes of Cerro Blanco on the valley's southeastern side. Flooding from the cerro's slopes has lamentably eroded part of the plain's cemetery and adobe structures.

The Huaca del Sol, the largest adobe structure in the Americas, is built of over 143-million sun-dried adobe bricks (Hastings and Moseley 1975, 197) in at least eight stages. Its ultimate appearance is hard to reconstruct, for rains have eroded its surface; tomb looting at its upper levels has left gaping holes; and two-thirds of its western face was deliberately washed away by seventeenth-century Spaniards trying to expose additional gold from burials. Originally perhaps 50 meters (164 feet) high, its current height is 41 meters (134.5 feet) on a base measuring 228 by 136 meters (748 by 446 feet). The top is accessible by a 6-meter-wide (19.6 foot) ramp and exhibits remains of courts and rooms that covered rich (now looted) burials. The lack of hearths, domestic pottery, and wall murals points to administrative or temple functions as opposed to elite residential functions.

The Huaca de la Luna, 21 meters (69 feet) high with a 276 by 178 meter (905 by 584 foot) base, is half the size and contains an estimated 50 million bricks (Hastings and Moseley 1975, 197). It, too, has platforms and walled rooms set around courtyards on top. Now-destroyed polichrome murals showing anthropomorphized weapons and artifacts "revolting" against humans decorated the walls of what were probably pyramid-top aristocratic residences.

The Chan Chan–Moche Valley Project excavations also explored low- to moderately high-status domestic architecture at the base of Cerro Blanco and south of the central plain. Surprisingly few storage structures suggest that the Moche did not achieve the widespread redistribution of goods characteristic of the later Chimú and Inca (Topic 1982, 268–270).

One of the most interesting architectural inferences is that the Moche demanded a corporate labor tax resembling the Inca *mita*. The labor investment for monumental architecture at Moche far exceeds the estimated residential population. Huaca del Sol bricks bear over a hundred different finger-produced patterns interpreted by Moseley (1975, 192) as makers' marks (Figure 11.1), and "skins" of outer bricks

11.1. Makers' marks on bricks, Huaca del Sol, Moche Valley. (Redrawn by the author from drawing in Moseley 1975, p. 192; courtesy Michael E. Moseley)

were laid in sections as if demarcating the standardized labor responsibilities of discrete work groups. Brick markings, sizes, and composition have also helped to distinguish sequential construction phases. At Pampa Grande, Moche's successor during Phase 5, walls continued to be built with marked adobes in identifiable "task-unit" sections. The appearance of U-shaped *audiencias* may be an innovation from the north (Day 1982, 343–344; Mackey 1982, 328–329).

ART

North Coast wood sculpture and textiles are poorly preserved, although some examples of Moche weaving and a surprising number of mural fragments have survived (Schaedel 1951; Mackey and Hastings 1982; Bonavia 1985). Pottery and gold objects, however, are the most complete art sources of information about Moche life.

Metal Objects

Moche metallurgy was well developed and has been described in some detail by Jones (1979). Mosaic-inlaid ear spools, repoussé beakers, cast figurines, and ceremonial knives were the most diagnostic items. Over 700 copper, silver, and gold objects looted in 1969 from shaft tombs at Loma Negra in the Piura Valley are illustrated in color in Lapiner (1976) and have been technically analyzed by Heather Lechtman (1973). Anne-Louise Schaffer's (1985) preliminary reconstruction of their burial contexts describes personal jewelry and ornaments that adorned litters or thrones. Many illustrated warriors, trophy-head taking, and predatory animal themes. Even more important are the excavations of undisturbed warrior–priest burials at Sipán in the Lambayeque area that exposed the richest trove of pre-columbian grave objects to date, including complex gold and turquoise ear ornaments of deer, Muscovy ducks, and intricate warriors with movable parts, a 2-foot-wide (.6 meter) gold, crescent-shaped headdress, gold and copper back-flap shields with "decapitator" figures carrying knives and trophy heads, gold facial half-masks, over a thousand ceramic pieces, and cloth banners stitched with gilded copper plaques associated with the buried lords and accompanying sacrificial victims (Alva 1988, 1990; Donnan 1990).

Pottery

Moche pottery is divided into a five-phase chronology based on spout and body forms, techniques, and decoration. Early polished black and brown or cream modeled wares gave rise *ca.* A.D. 500 to more finely modeled humans and animals and complex painted themes. Between A.D. 500

A

and 700 scenes became cluttered and erratic, with "a kind of nervous tension" (Sawyer 1968, 45), reflecting growing cultural disorientation.

The two basic pottery types, painted and modeled, are distinctive. Painted wares are cream slipped with fine-line black or red–brown figures or scenes (Figure 11.2a,b). Some have small modeled figures in the upper register where the diagnostic North Coast stirrup spout is attached. Modeled vessels are three dimensional with occasional painted details. Best known are the "portrait jars" with sensitively modeled human faces.[1] Birds, animals, fruits, and vegetables are modeled so accurately that biologists can identify them by genus and species.

Together, these vessels are a comprehensive pictorial ethnography. Paleobotanists and paleozoologists have verified the archaeological presence of most of the plants and animals depicted. Architectural details, weapons, utensils, and jewelry correspond to those recovered through excavation. Some vessels portray hunting (Figure 11.2b), fishing, *chicha* making, warfare and prisoner taking, and explicit sexual activity.[2] Rulers on thrones receive visitations; grieving citizens bury their dead. Landscapes and seascapes give additional details. These realistic images may also have symbolic meanings (Donnan 1978). Other vessels show super-

[1] To appreciate portrait jar variety, consult photos 192–225 in Ubbelohde-Doering 1954 that illustrate seldom-published vessels from private European collections, the Museum fur Volkerkunde in Munich, and the Linden-Museum in Stuttgart.

[2] The Sex Institute at Indiana Univesity, Bloomington, has a modest collection of Moche erotic vessels. Others are illustrated in Benson 1972a; Gebhard 1970; and Larco Hoyle 1965.

B

11.2. Ceramic bottle (*A*) showing a sea lion hunt. Both modeling and fine lines have been used to create the design shown in the rollout (*B*). (In a private collection; reproduced in Donnan 1978, fig. 55; photo by Robert Woolard, courtesy UCLA/MCH)

natural situations and anthropomorphized animals, plants, skeletons, and weapons. Complex ceremonial and ritual activities involve interacting supernaturals and masked priests or god impersonators. Together, these vessels are an encyclopedic corpus of information on Moche life. How can we determine the emic significance of this rich pool of images?

ART HISTORY

Scholars have approached Moche ceramic images from several perspectives. Definitions of Moche style (Benson 1972a, 59–70, 119–120; Donnan 1976, 28–34) note its naturalism and realism. Relative sizes are maintained except where smaller figures may indicate lower status or, in the upper-design register, background position. Limbs and head are profile on a frontal torso. Context, arm and leg positions, and accoutrements indicate specific activities such as running, fighting, or dying. Hard-to-recognize animals or objects are shown in profile or from above. Among humans, gender is hard to tell when breasts or genitalia are absent. Bound naked prisoners stand beside their bundled weapons and clothes wearing neck nooses or are held by the hair by armed captors. Iconographic canons are consistent, yet the style permitted individuality: Vessels from different locales are occasionally similar enough to be considered the work of a single artist (Donnan 1976: Figures 61–70 and pp. 43–50).

Art historians also seek antecedents of and influences upon Moche style. Michael Kan (1972, 81–84) sees the felines on Moche headpiece and mask decorations as meek in expression, devoid of the kennings and fierce canines of their Chavín predecessors (Figure 11.3, left).

Iconographic Themes

Early iconographic studies established a typology of design themes (hunting and gathering, warfare, prisoner taking, human sacrifice, punishment, dance, sacred race, coca chewing, and mythical beings (Kutscher 1967). Elizabeth Benson (1972a) has added diverse ecological settings and social classes, deformed animals and humans, and livelihood, crafts, architectural, erotic, and burial themes. Supernaturals include a seated god associated with mountains and creation (ancestral to the Chimú Ai Apaec?), a fanged, snake-belted sun–water god who hunts, fishes, and battles monsters aided by a lizard or owl (Figure 11.3), and a "radiant god" with flame aura and hawk–warrior companions. Bound humans shown with jaguars (Figure 11.4) may be war prisoners sacrificed to a Moche feline totem, whereas humans thrown from mountain peaks into streams may provide the arid coast with water. Other scholars identify bound coca chewers carrying lime jars as highland prisoners (Sawyer 1968) and portrait vessels as images of rulers given as rewards to loyal minions.

The most extensive study using a thematic ap-

11.3. Drawing of combat between a fanged individual, wearing a serpent belt, and a *Strombus Galeatus* monster. From a vessel in the collection of the Museum fuer Voelkerkunde, Berlin; Staatliche Museen Preussischer Kulturbesitz. (Donnan 1978, fig. 219; courtesy UCLA/MCH)

11.4. Rollout from a ceramic bottle showing a fine line drawing of a prisoner with a feline captor. (Donnan 1978, fig. 245; courtesy UCLA/MCH)

proach is by Christopher Donnan (1978), known for North Coast excavations and his seriation of the Uhle pottery collection. Donnan began compiling the Archive of Moche Art in 1968 with photos of pieces in American and European collections. Examining over 70,000 photos and 7,000 specimens, he narrowed down 90 themes. Subdivisions show variation and recombination that parallels grammatical interrelationships in language: Major figures are visual "nouns," modified by "adjective" details of posture, setting, costume, and interaction and "adverb" indicators of types of actions.

In spite of individual variations and a time gap of over a thousand years, consistent theme interrelationships are revealing. Donnan observes that a trained out-of-culture observer of Santa Claus representations could, from internal evidence, identify Saint Nick by his accoutrements (stocking cap, toy sack, boots, and red fur-trimmed costume) and his major activities (toy making with elves, reindeer-sleigh rides, chimney maneuvers, and gift deliveries in fireplace stockings or under Christmas trees) in varying depictions of the old gent. Donnan and Donna McClelland (Donnan 1976, 1977; Donnan and McClelland 1979) have produced line drawings of Moche theme variants and used archaeological, biological–pathological, ethnohistorical, and ethnographic data to interpret their meaning.

The Burial Theme

The Burial Theme consists of four scenes involving burial; assembly of human/animal/supernatural beings; conch-shell transfer; and sacrifices (shown together in Figure 11.5).

The Burial Scene. The Burial Scene (Figures 11.6, 11.8, 11.9) shows a bird-headdressed iguana and a wrinkle-faced, feline-headdressed, and serpent-sashed human lowering a masked wicker bundle on ropes into a shaft chamber stacked with bowls of food, conch shells, jewelry, and textiles.

The Assembly Scene. In the Assembly Scene (Figures 11.7, 11.8, 11.9), rows of profile staff-bearing net-shirted humans gather to the left of the shaft (under Wrinkle Face) opposite rows of anthropomorphized stags or felines on the right (under Iguana). A second, large image of Iguana (lower left) and a counterpart Wrinkle Face (lower right) face the crypt, holding staffs fringed with small, round objects. To Donnan, the assembled are participants in funerary rites on behalf of the deceased.

The Conch Shell Transfer Scene. In the Conch Shell Transfer (Figures 11.10, 11.12, 11.13), a figure (Kneeler) with a crescent or double-tasseled headpiece, donut-decorated costume (resist-dyed *plangi* circles?), and tiered back ornament kneels under a gable-roofed structure atop a pyramid stair, giving or receiving a conch shell from Iguana, Wrinkle Face, and/or the Net Shirts ascending the stair. Llamas bear additional conch-shell loads on some vessels. These shells, also stacked as grave goods, were imported from coastal Ecuador as ritual or prestige items.

The Sacrifice Scene. In the Sacrifice Scene (Figures 11.11, 11.12, 11.13) depicted above the

11.5. Rollout of a bottle decorated with the Burial Theme. (Donnan and McClelland 1979, fig. 2; courtesy Donna McClelland, Christopher Donnan, and DO)

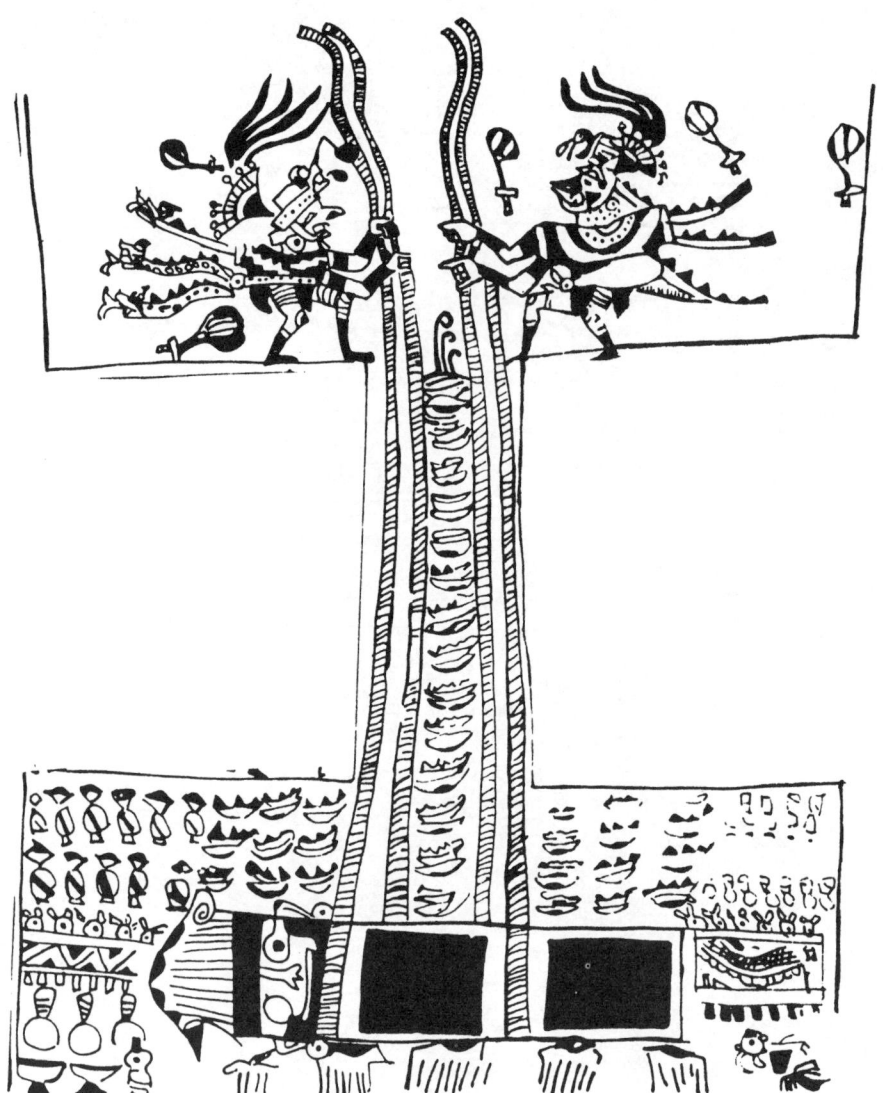

11.6. Detail of the Burial scene in fig. 11.5. (Donnan and McClelland 1979, fig. 13; courtesy Donna McClelland, Christopher Donnan, and DO)

11.7. Detail of the Assembly scene in fig. 11.5. (Donnan and McClelland 1979, fig. 14; courtesy Donna McClelland, Christopher Donnan, and DO)

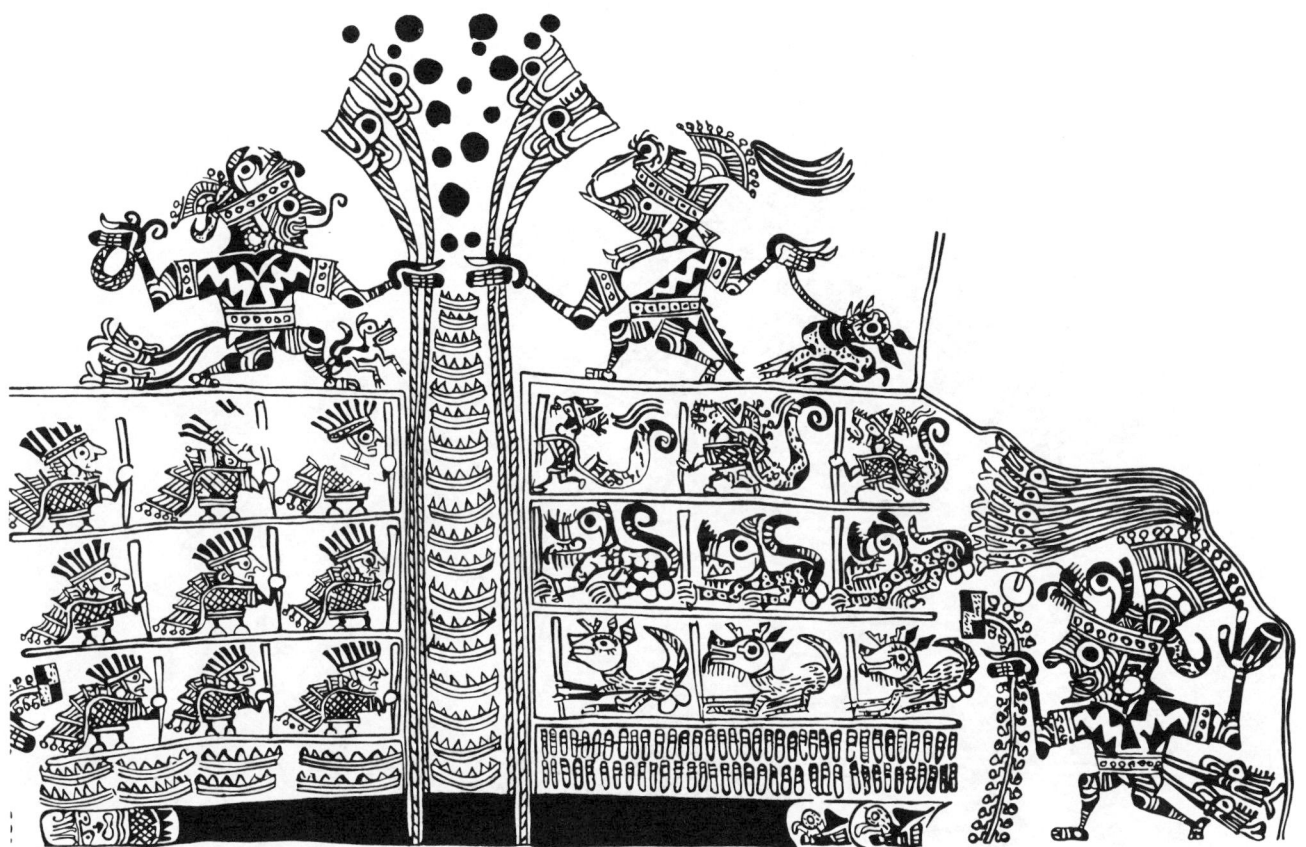

11.8. Detail of the Burial and Assembly scenes in fig. 11.5. (Donnan 1978, fig. 143; courtesy Donna McClelland, Christopher Donnan, and DO)

11.9. Detail of Burial and Assembly scenes. (Donnan 1976, fig. 2c; courtesy UCLA/CLAS)

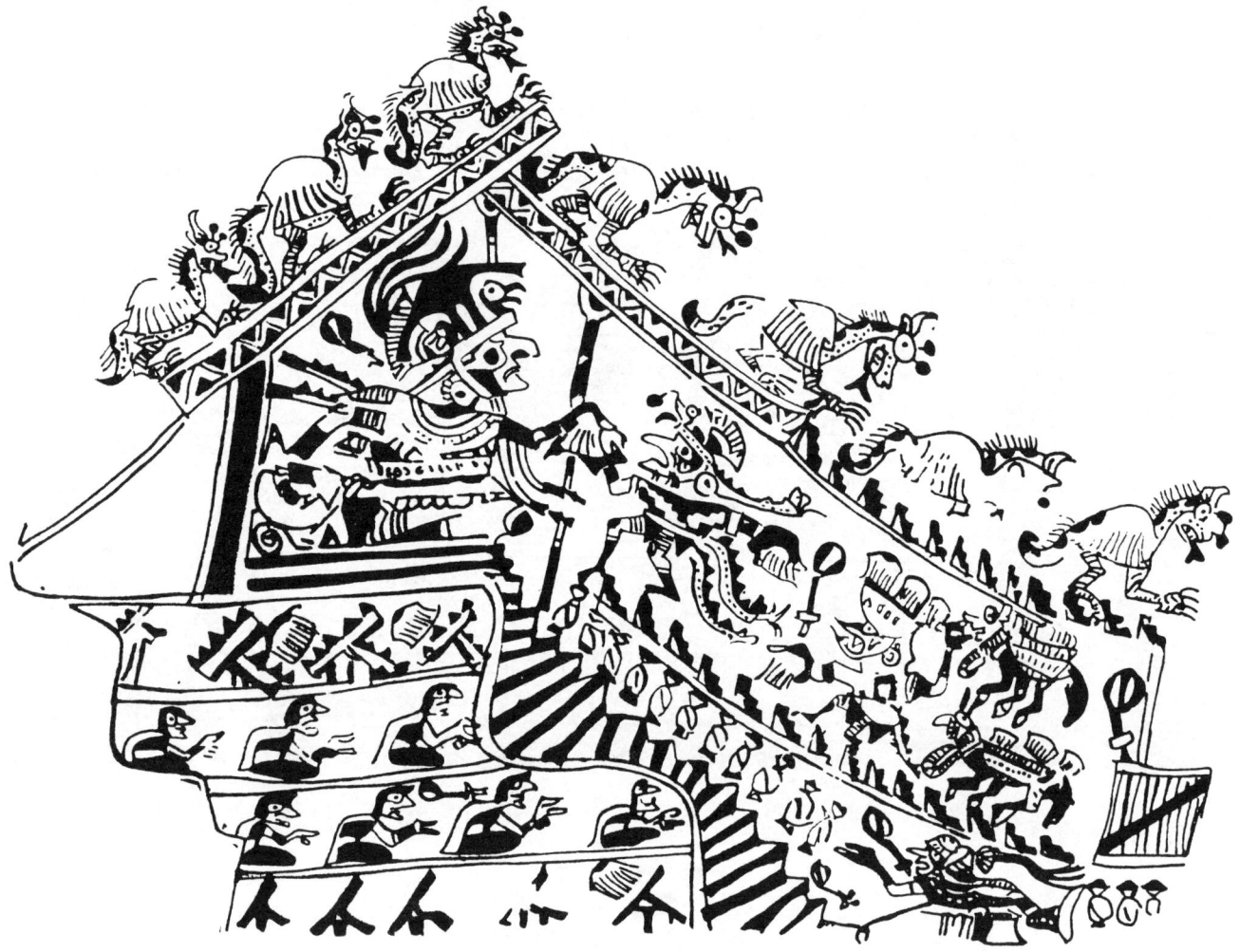

11.10. Detail of Conch Shell Transfer from fig. 11.5. (Donnan and McClelland 1979, fig. 16; courtesy Donna McClelland, Christopher Donnan, and DO)

Conch Transfer, Iguana, with a crescent tumi knife, and Wrinkle Face, carrying darts and an atlatl, face a bird splayed across a wooden rack, while Iguana or an anthropomorphized dart carries a rope with attached birds. To the left, birds devour the corpse of a naked female.

These scenes are probably sequential because Iguana and Wrinkle Face appear in all four. The Burial and Assembly scenes are the most important because they are larger and were painted first. Consistent changes in bodies, headdresses, and costume become more Chimú-like in style and make theme seriation possible. Donnan (1979, 11–12) thinks that the four scenes depict an actual event that acquired mythical overtones, perhaps the death of an important individual under the care of a shamaness, and show his burial rites and the sacrifice of the unfortunate curer in a manner very similar to a North

Coast event described by a seventeenth-century Augustinian monk.

The Presentation Theme

A second theme analyzed by Donnan (1978, 158–173, summarized here) is the Presentation Theme (Figure 11.14). In it, a crescent-head-dressed Radiant Figure (A) receives a goblet from a disc-holding Bird–Human (B), wearing a crescent-topped helmet or a headpiece with a jaguar-faced half-disc, curving lateral arcs, and a rear tuft of feathers. A small spotted dog (O) sits between them. Behind (B) are a serpent-shawled human with a tasseled cap holding a disc or goblet (C), and a wavy-neck-scarfed figure (D) with a crescent nose ornament and half-disc jaguar-face headdress like C's.

Other figures complement the scene. An elab-

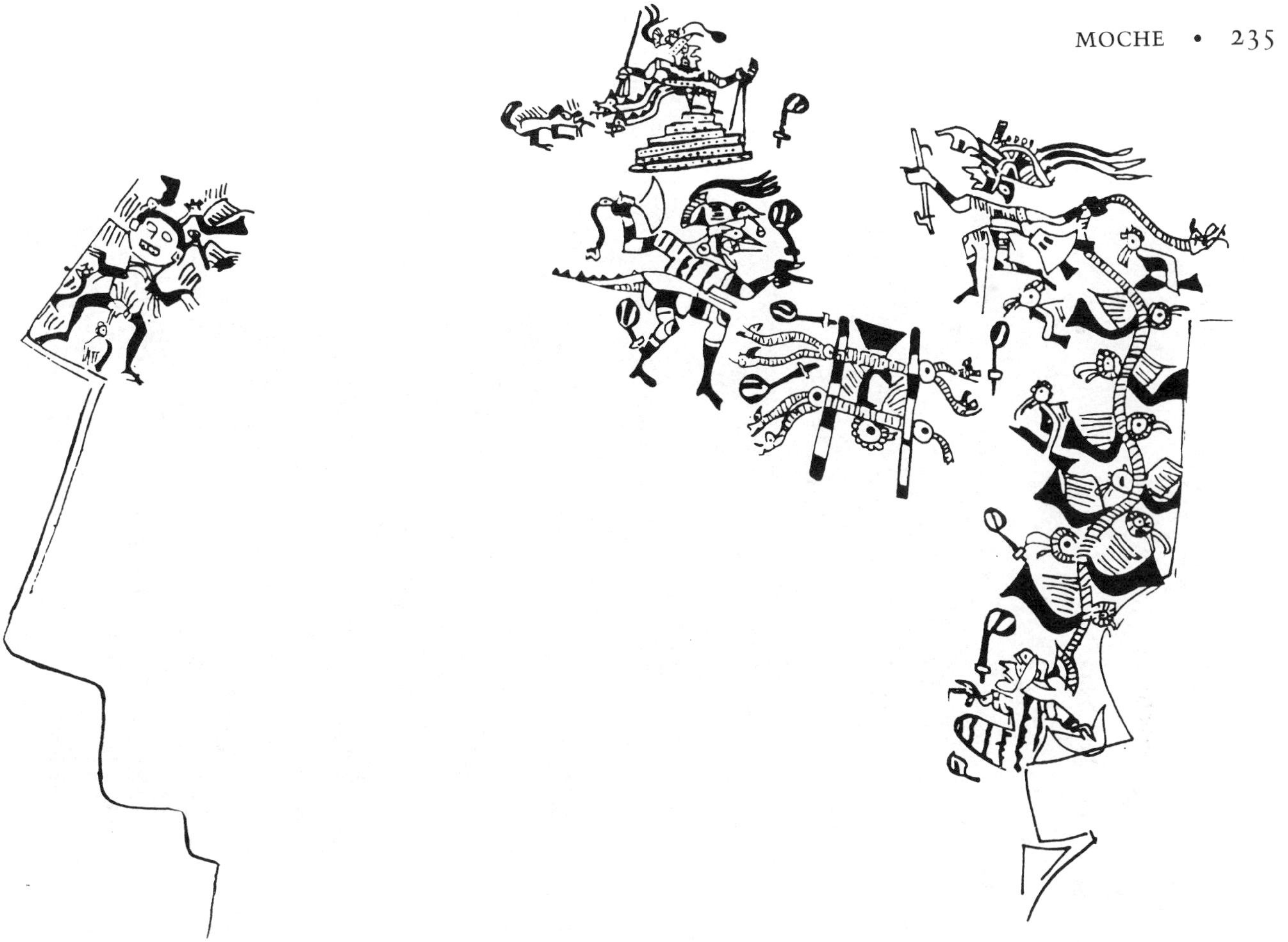

11.11. Detail of Sacrifice scene from fig. 11.5. (Donnan and McClelland 1979, fig. 15; courtesy Donna McClelland, Christopher Donnan, and DO)

11.12. Detail of Conch Shell Transfer and Sacrifice scenes (Donnan 1978, fig. 143; Courtesy Donna McClelland)

11.13. Detail of Conch Shell Transfer and Sacrifice scenes (Donnan 1976, fig. 2b; courtesy UCLA/CLAS)

orately dressed human (E) and a feline-headed human (F) draw blood from naked prisoners with bound hands (G), perhaps to fill the goblets. Also present are serpents (P), and anthropomorphized fox (Q), bird (R), and feline warriors (S), bundles of maces and darts (T) behind a round shield, a club with a human head (U), a rayed litter or throne (V), and a gourdlike *ulluchu* fruit (W). Other Presentation Theme variants add a bat-headed human captor (H), a goblet-holding anthropomorphized Muscovy duck (X), and a bowl containing three goblets (Z).

The major figures appear without the minor ones on pottery (Figures 11.15, 11.16) and in murals from the Lambayeque Valley and the Moche site of Pañamarca (Figure 11.17). The identification at Pañamarca of human (E), anthropomorphized feline (F) and anthropomorphized bat (H) warriors bringing in their captives (G) behind tassel-capped Figure C plus serpents (P), the club behind shield (T) and the bowl with goblets (Z) makes possible its hypothetical

completion (Figure 11.18) as a full-fledged Presentation Theme. Thus through familiarity with the theme's iconographic variants, twentieth-century art historians can reconstruct 1,000-year-old material with a reasonable degree of probability. From three-dimensional representations, we gain further details about the actual construction of bird-headed B's half-disc jaguar-face headdress (Figure 11.19).

Background Elements

Some researchers have traced background figures as individual motifs. Donna McClelland (1977) examines the ulluchu fruit as a possible geographic symbol, indicator of magical contexts, or identifier of specific Presentation Theme figures (Figure 11.20). More recent interpretations, noting the ulluchu's presence in war and captive scenes, propose its use as an anticoagulant in postvictory blood-drinking rituals (Alva 1990, 15). Ann Mester (1983) traces Owl,

11.14. The Presentation Theme. The letters refer to participants identified by Donnan: see the text. (Donnan 1978, fig. 239b; courtesy Donna McClelland and Christopher Donnan)

11.15. Fine line drawing of the Presentation Theme. For identification of figures, see the text. (Donnan 1976, fig. 106; courtesy UCLA/CLAS)

11.16. Fine line drawing of the Presentation Theme. For identification of figures, see the text. (Donnan 1978, fig. 242; courtesy Donna McClelland and Christopher Donnan)

11.17. Pañamarca mural with Presentation Theme figures. For identification of figures, see text. (Donnan 1978, fig. 243; courtesy Donna McClelland and Christopher Donnan)

11.18. Hypothetical reconstruction of Pañamarca mural. For identification of figures, see text. (Donnan 1978, fig. 244; courtesy Donna McClelland and Christopher Donnan)

11.19. Bird-winged, bird-headed Presentation Theme Figure B on modeled vessel (Donnan 1978, fig. 248; courtesy Christopher Donnan)

a frequent companion of Wrinkle Face, as a possible alter-ego nocturnal sun denoting femaleness, agricultural fertility, and shamanic power and proposes that vessels showing Wrinkle Face in opposition to a crab demon depict a Moche land/architectural versus maritime perception of the environment and its associated supernatural forces. Anne-Louise Schaffer (1984) notes five different contexts for vultures on Burial Theme pots including humans dressed as vultures.

Contexts can also be deduced through careful comparisons. Alana Cordy-Collins (1977b) has found Burial Theme Netshirts kneeling in totora-reed boats and others on stylized moon-like crescents (Figure 11.21) or along the break line of composite-silhouette Moche pots (Figure 11.21). Thus a crescent form and even the undecorated bottom quarter of a vessel read as a boat to viewers recalling the naturalistic alternative form. Such changes have more than mere decorative significance, for they represent "the evolution of design into symbol . . . [as] idea codification, which is the first step toward the written word" (Cordy-Collins 1977b, 433).

Related Archaeological Artifacts

One of the most exciting developments of interdisciplinary research has been the identification of archaeologically retrieved items of costume, jewelry, and ritual paraphernalia with depictions of similar objects in the Moche iconographic themes described by Donnan. Some of the items have been discovered among the over 125,000 photos of excavated artifacts at UCLA's Archive of Moche Art; others come directly from ceremonial contexts or high-status burials.

Donnan (1976, 125–128) describes a cache of copper goblets and rattles incised with motifs from the Presentation Theme and speculates that they may actually have been used in the Presentation ceremony. The headdress, back flaps, earrings, crescent nose ornament, and gold rattle associated on painted pottery with the Presentation Theme's Radiant Figure (Figure 11.14, figure A) are almost identical to similar objects that were buried with the sumptuously attired "warrior–priest" discovered in 1987 at Sipán near Pampa Grande in the Lambayeque Valley (Alva 1988), suggesting that the Sipán lord was a central participant in these ceremonies. The dog buried at his feet may correspond to the small spotted dog depicted in the Presentation Theme (Figure 11.14, figure O; Donnan 1988, 554–555). Similar artifacts accompanied a previously looted Sipán burial and an even richer, earlier burial found subsequently in the same platform (Alva 1990, 2–6). Grave goods from three additional, as-yet unexcavated burials at Sipán should further amplify these intriguing iconographic connections.

Further evidence of Moche rituals comes from Pacatnamú, about 50 kilometers (31 miles) south in the Jequetepeque Valley, where well-preserved miniature ponchos, tunics, and loincloths probably used as offerings, and slit

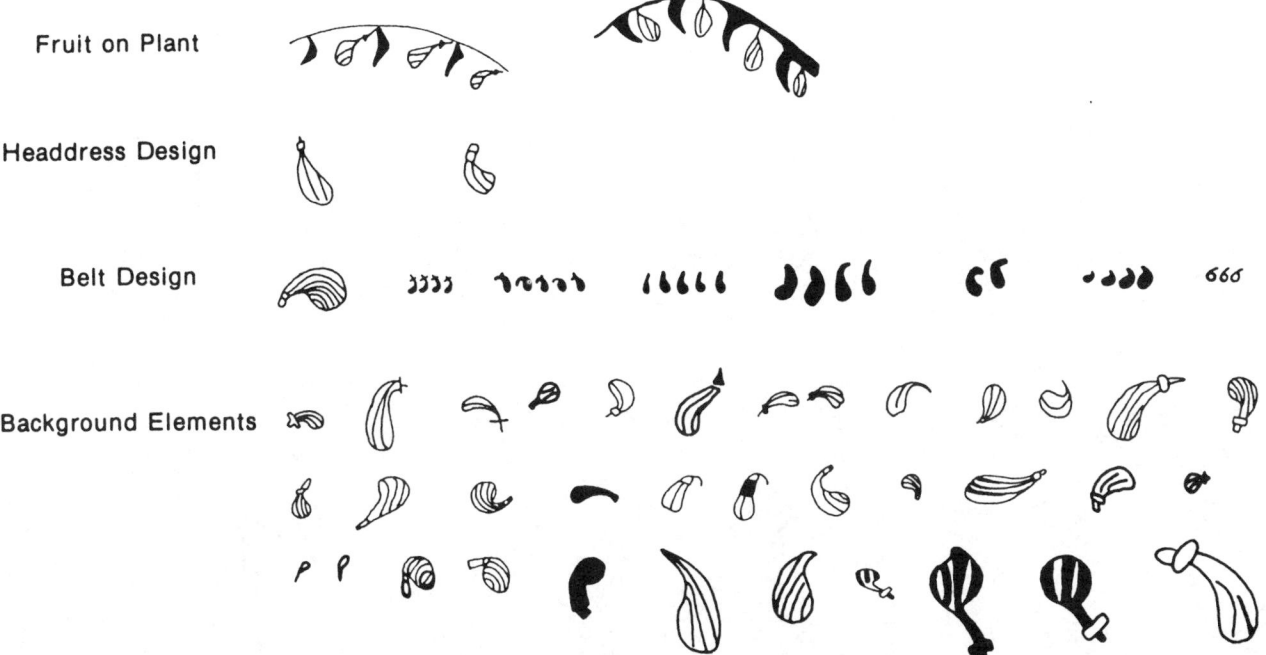

Fruit on Plant

Headdress Design

Belt Design

Background Elements

Range of Variability in the Depiction of
the Ulluchu.

11.20. Ulluchu fruit representations (McClelland 1977, fig. 2, p. 436; courtesy Donna McClelland)

A

B

11.21. (*A*) Netshirt in a totora boat symbolized by a crescent on an Phase Vb stirrup-spout bottle, Museo Amano, Lima; (*B*) Netshirt in a boat symbolized by a medial band at the break of the composite silhouette on a Phase Vd stirrup-spout bottle, Museo de Trujillo, Trujillo, Peru. (Drawings by the author)

11.22. Ceremony with cannibalism and copulation themes. (Donnan 1976, fig. 1; courtesy UCLA/CLAS)

tapestry patches with complex designs used as appliqués on full-sized tunics were uncovered. A larger piece, left from looting, shows crescent-headdressed, winged (?) figures with raised goblets, "dancers," llama sacrifice, perhaps corresponding to a sacrificed llama buried beneath a platform floor, and profile weavers at their looms, likely aspects of ceremonies held in the Quadrangle area where they were found (Donnan 1986, 113–114).

Three groups of apparently ritually mutilated young males, some with rope around their ankles, were uncovered in a trench near the main entrance to the Huaca 1 complex at Pacatnamú. They exhibit skeletal trauma that suggest repeated stab wounds while victims were prone or possibly tied to a rack or post; rib-cage fractures consistent with heart sacrifice; and decapitation or deliberate removal of key leg and arm bones after exposure prior to burial (Verano 1986). These mutilated physical remains correspond well with ceramic "Decapitator" figures of a feline supernatural holding a tumi knife and a severed head (Donnan 1990, 31) and fine-line pottery scenes of bound captives being delivered in litters to a crescent-headdressed, goblet-holding figure in a ceremonial structure. Pottery scenes of decapitated, mutilated bodies with black-costumed anthropomorphized bird onlookers also represent sacrifice and corpse exposure like those indicated by this find. Two skeletons of deliberately mutilated black vultures associated with these burials correspond to fine-line paintings where vultures appear feeding on nude, splayed female (Figures 11.11, 11.12), tethered to rack sacrifice posts (Figures 11.11, 11.12), and near the casket (Figures 11.6, 11.8) in Burial Theme scenes (Rea 1986).

Counterparts of themes identified by Donnan are being sought in Moche-influenced areas. Terence Grieder (1979, 90) thinks the Presentation Theme may be part of a larger narrative widespread enough to appear in related styles; if so, comparative iconography may clarify its meaning. When the total range of themes has been studied and integrated, we may begin to understand important beliefs underlying Moche culture.

ETHNOHISTORY

Sixteenth- and seventeenth-century Spanish accounts that postdate Moche culture by 600 to 1,000 years contain oral traditions and descriptions of Chimú customs and iconography that are probably Moche survivals (Donnan 1976, 80–91). The Burial Theme closely parallels a seventeenth-century description of how an unsuccessful curer was tied to the dead patient's body and left to be devoured by vultures. Chimú thieves were lashed to posts, likewise to be consumed by birds; a Moche modeled vessel (Donnan 1976, Plate 9) shows a victim with a patch of back skin peeled down as possible vulture enticement. Spanish writers also describe witch rites of copulation and ceremonial cannibalism that match another of Donnan's Moche themes (Figure 11.22). A seventeenth-century witch named Mollep ("the Lousy") has a centuries-earlier counterpart in three Moche modeled vases of a crouching figure sporting three fat lice. These and other similarities make Donnan feel that North Coast "customs, beliefs, and religious practices were maintained over more than 1,300 years without significant change" (1976, 85).

ETHNOGRAPHY

Ethnographic parallels for practices and artifacts on Moche vessels strengthen the case for cultural continuity. Totora-reed boats with split-cane paddles, coca-chewing equipment (lime gourds and spatulas), loaded pack llamas with ears notched for identification, panpipes, rattles, and conch-shell trumpets continue essentially

11.23. Moche vessel depicting aspects of curing, from the Viru and Chicama River valleys, Peabody Museum 30/F728. (Photo by Hillel Burger, courtesy PM/HU; copyright © 1982 by President and Fellows of Harvard College)

unchanged from Moche through Chimú, Inca, and Spanish Colonial times into the ethnographic present.

The most intriguing suggestion of continuity comes through Douglas Sharon's (1978) studies of shaman Eduardo Calderón's curing practices in the North Coast Trujillo Valley. Calderón uses a wooden owl staff like one from a high-status (shaman?) Moche burial to symbolize wisdom and death spirits on his table of power objects. He appeals to Single Woman, a legendary old spinster herbalist who may be the shawl-wearing Owl figure on a Moche vessel depicting a curing ceremony.

Working with Eduardo, Donnan has identified some of the healing ritual paraphernalia on the vessel. These include four loop-handled strands of medicinal *espingo* seeds, a rectangular bull roarer, a bowl of lime cones, a slice of hallucinogenic San Pedro cactus, and a modeled box of medicinal spheroids (?) surrounding Owl Woman above a curer (?) facing a mesa with four jars and a sacrificial (?) llama tethered to a stake (Figure 11.23). The patient, modeled and covered by a cross-bedecked blanket, rests at Owl Woman's left, near the stirrup spout.

Other possibly "curative"-related vessels show deer beside trees with hallucinogenic seed pods, sea lions mouthing or spitting out round objects (Figure 11.2), perhaps stones from their bellies used in shamanic curing of epilepsy and heart trouble, felines as protectors against evil spirits, foxes for astuteness, dogs for smelling malevolence, and serpents as mediators between good and evil. As art historians inventory additional Moche representations, we may expect further insights into the iconography behind the images.

CHAPTER 12

TIAHUANACO-HUARI

DURING the Middle Horizon (A.D. 600–1000), coastal cultures were again strongly influenced by the highlands. The source was identified in the early 1900s as Tiahuanaco (Map 10), a ceremonial center on the south end of Lake Titicaca, in Bolivia, long known for its elaborately carved stone architecture.

Tiahuanaco has been the subject of many fanciful surmises, identified as a colony for extraterrestrial in Von Daniken-type descriptions and the "lost Atlantis" in late nineteenth-century and some current sources. In the late 1800s, the indefatigable Max Uhle drew up site plans, and in 1932 Wendell Bennett undertook preliminary excavations. Since then, Bolivian archaeologists have provided new data and refined the ceramic and architectonic sequence (Ponce 1976, 1981).

Origins

The origins of Tiahuanaco's distinctive art may derive from a style called Pucara that developed between 200 B.C.–A.D. 300 around Lake Titicaca as a result of South-Coast Paracas influences. Pucara pottery shows Tiahuanacoid split-eyed, tear-banded frontal figures with digging sticks flanked by profile attendants, and Staff God figures carved in stone. At nearby Niño Korin, a medicine man's pottery, spatulas, and bone tubes dating to A.D. 300–600 also depict a Staff God and (winged?) attendants, perhaps ancestral to later Tiahuanaco forms.

Tiahuanaco-Influenced Sites

In the early 1900s, archaeologists found Tiahuanacoid designs on Central Coast Pachacamac and North Coast Moche Middle Horizon pottery and christened the derivative style "Epigonal." Subsequently, highland-influenced coastal Nasca and Lima wares were dubbed "Tiahuanacoid." Bennett (1934) excavated at Tiahuanaco and, confirming the similarities, proposed a "Tiahuanaco horizon." As more sites were put to the spade, it became clear that between A.D. 750–850 local wares throughout the Central Andean area imitated or were replaced by Tiahuanacoid products. For years, Tiahuanaco was accepted as their source, with religious missionization the probable mechanism. The Middle Horizon ended by A.D. 1000 when local cultures again took hold.

The Role of Huari

In the late 1940s and early 1950s, new data indicated that the picture was not so simple. Excavations focusing on settlement archaeology revealed that complex urban constructions accompanied intrusive Tiahuanacoid pottery and textiles at numerous coastal sites. This presented a problem, for Tiahuanaco lacked urban architecture and the large population required for such an extensive, organized expansion. Peruvian archaeologists recalled Tello's earlier suggestion that Huari, a large highland site north of Tiahuanaco (also spelled Wari; see Map 10) was strongly involved in the Tiahuanaco spread. In the late 1940s, they proposed a Huari cultural conquest of the North Coast; subsequently, archaeologists John Rowe, Donald Collier, and Gordon Willey (1950) presented the concept to a wider American audience. Bennett excavated at Huari in 1950 (1953); seriation of its pottery by Rowe (1956) and Dorothy Menzel (Menzel 1964, 1968) confirmed strong South Coast ties.

Huari's catalytic role is still unclear. The site apparently evolved from a regional Ayacucho complex called Huarpa. By A.D. 600 (late Early Intermediate), urbanization was in progress, perhaps stimulated by South Coast Nasca influence (Menzel 1964). At this time, Tiahuanaco was already an important religious center with Chavín-derived imagery—perhaps in the midst of a Chavín revival (Lanning 1967, 30). Contact was established with Huari (by Tiahuanaco missionaries or Huari pilgrims?), and Tiahuanaco Gateway of the Sun figures combined with Nasca imagery appear on large ceremonially killed pottery *keros* at the shrine site of Conchopata near Huari (Map 10).

During the early Middle Horizon, Huari strengthened its Tiahuanaco ties and expanded into the North Coast, the North Highlands, and South Coast Nasca. Following a brief crisis of an undetermined nature, the city expanded to its maximum growth. In the process, Tiahuanaco designs became abbreviated, individual motifs. Then decline and eventual disintegration set in, perhaps through competition from

rising coastal rivals (Menzel 1977, 76). By A.D. 850 Huari had collapsed, and within 200 years Huari-influenced cultures had returned to local patterns.

Huari–Tiahuanaco Connections

The nature of Tiahuanaco–Huari relationship is the subject of lively discussion. Isbell (1978, 372–376) sees Huari as a primitive state by A.D. 700, replete with unified architecture and a road system (later taken over by the Inca), tying together a network for collection and redistribution of goods. To Menzel (1977, 31), both sites were regional capitals of dual empires between A.D. 600–850, with Tiahuanaco spreading southward and Huari northward in a flush of expansion that produced the first political (and military?) unification of the Central Andean area.

The earlier notion of direct transmission of religious concepts from Tiahuanaco to Huari now seems less likely, based on architectural and iconographic differences between the two sites (Gasparini and Margolies 1980, 37–38). Iconographic interchange between the two seems to have been limited to reformulations at Huari of some Tiahuanaco designs. There was no direct exchange of material goods: No Tiahuanaco sherds are found at Huari, nor Huari sherds at Tiahuanaco (Isbell 1977, 4).

Wider Huari–Tiahuanaco Influences

North Coast

In the North Coast, Huari/Tiahuanaco influence appears initially only in a few religious centers. Contacts seem to have been peaceful and syncretistic: Murals discovered in 1972 at Huaca de la Luna, a late Moche-IV site, show "design, technique and artistic style . . . within the Moche cultural tradition" (Mackey and Hastings 1982, 304) plus the Tiahuanaco Staff God and panels of motif blocks duplicating those on Huari/Tiahuanaco ponchos (Donnan 1972, 95). Moche, with its strong military infrastructure and indigenous tradition, was never culturally subsumed. Only northern ceremonial centers have Huari material; at less important sites, Moche V grades into Chimú culture, which reformulated surviving Moche elements when Huari declined.

Central Coast

In the Central Coast, Huari influence concentrated at Pachacamac (Map 10), famous for its Inca-period oracle. During the Middle Horizon, a highland-style temple housed an earlier oracle, the remains of which may be a 6-foot-tall (1.8 meter) wooden sculpture with Tiahuanaco elements found on top of the temple ruin in the late 1930s (Lumbreras 1974, 168).

South Coast

The South Coast had a high receptivity quotient for Huari ideas through strong trade ties, with goods passing through Pacheco and Cahuachi. Chakipampa pottery retained South Coast forms but shared highland mythical figures and motifs. Ica/Nasca Middle-Horizon mummies wear tapestry tunics with Huari-influenced designs (see Figure 12.11, below). Because of these close connections, Nasca participated fully in the South Highland tradition and felt the Huari collapse with particular force.

ARCHITECTURE

Tiahuanaco

Tiahuanaco is located at 12,600 feet (3,840 meters) altitude 11 miles (17.7 kilometers) south of Lake Titicaca and covers approximately 9 square miles (23 square kilometers), making it the largest Early Intermediate and Middle Horizon site in the South Highlands. Raised, ridged fields in irrigated checkerboard plots along the western lakeshore attest to water management and farming that could have sustained up to 20,000 people (Willey 1971, 154). Lake Titicaca provided water for irrigation, lacrustine products, and warm air for an agriculturally productive microenvironment at this otherwise windswept and semibarren altitude.

At Tiahuanaco's center is a complex of presumed religious, civil, and elite residential structures. Best known is the Kalasasaya ("standing stones" in Quechua), a rectangular enclosure with a raised stone platform, a sunken courtyard lined with monoliths, and a carved stone archway popularly called "Gateway of the Sun." The monoliths include atlantid figures with hands clenched to the chest (Figure 12.1). Stones in the Kalasasaya platform walls are cut, dressed, and held in position by stone and cop-

12.1. A sculptured stone figure, Tiahuanaco, Bolivia. (Photo by Arturo Posnansky, collected 1909 by Dr. Thomas Barbour; print by Hillel Burger, 1987, courtesy PM/HU; copyright © President and Fellows of Harvard College)

per clamps or carefully fitted in the masonry style that later became the hallmark of the Incas.

South of the Kalasasaya, the Akpana ("Artificial Hill"), a 15-meter-high (49.2 foot) truncated, terraced mound, was probably a temple base. Enclosures to the west include the Putuni, possibly a palace compound, and were presumably used by the individuals buried in a cemetery still further west near the lake. To the east, a sunken 28-by-26 meter (92 by 85 foot) rectangular patio called the Semisubterranean Temple is walled with sandstone blocks set with tenoned stone heads in the Chavín manner; their wide-eyed unsmiling faces replicate those on monolithic stelae scattered throughout the site. Another large terraced platform of splendid block masonry called Puma Punku ("Puma Gate") lies approximately 700 meters (765.5 yards) southwest of the Kalasasaya. Because original construction stones and monuments were relocated during Inca and Colonial times, the original site plan and functions of structures are probably beyond recovery. Site size suggests a populace of between 20,000 to 40,000.

Excavation has also located eight satellite towns that probably provided subsistence goods and labor. By A.D. 900, excavated goods indicate Tiahuanaco trade interests further afield (Kolata 1983, 263–264). Pacific shells, cotton, and fish came from coastal centers in southern Peru and northern Chile. Bolivian selva drug use (coca, tobacco, datura) and paraphernalia are reflected in Tiahuanaco stone copies of snuff trays, mortars and pestles, and coca tubes; their wooden counterparts appear at South Coast sites. David Browman (1978a, 336) observes that "this 'drug culture' becomes one of the most frequently recognized attributes of Tiahuanaco influence." He further proposes that colonies and trading outposts for receiving raw materials extended from Ecuador to Chile and northwestern Argentina, connected by llama caravan routes that were later continued by the Inca. Tiahuanaco's craftsworkers processed raw goods into exportable finished goods probably carried by "merchant–missionaries" in ongoing peaceable interchange.

Huari

Huari, the site that was recognized Johnny-come-lately in the Middle Horizon equation, lies about 22 miles (35 kilometers) north of Ayacucho on a tributary of the Mantaro River some 450 miles (724 kilometers) northwest of Tiahuanaco (Map 10). It is a large urban site, only partially explored because of overlying cultivated fields. Excavation in the late 1970s and early 1980s by the Huari Urban Prehistory Project directed by William Isbell has exposed rectangular room clusters surrounded by high walls, zones of craft specialization, windowless storehouses, and a ceremonial precinct of temples with subterranean chambers. Corrals for llamas, aqueducts, and canals all foreshadow later Inca developments. Archaeologists think that limited food resources created population pressure, motivating expansion and conquest (Lumbreras 1974, 163), a premise awaiting reliable demographic projections.

Construction and sculpture at Huari are generally coarser than at Tiahuanaco because local stone is more porous and fieldstone was used for houses and walls. Nevertheless, Huari's subterranean structures are made of well-shaped slabs similar to Tiahuanaco's, leading to speculation that they may be tombs of Tiahuanaco missionary–priests (Gasparini and Margolies 1980, 37). Although Huari architecture influenced North Coast settlements, it had little effect in the Central and South coasts, where Huari presence appears in pottery and Tiahuanacoid iconography. In the highlands, administrative towns and storage centers (Capilla Pata near Huari, Pikillaqta near Cuzco, Viracocha Pampa near Huanuco, Pampa de las Llamas in Casma, Jincamocco) redistributed local goods. Their small warehouse-like rooms and similar formal plans seem to indicate preplanned centers constructed under state direction (Menzel 1964, 70–71).

Around A.D. 850, Huari collapsed. Tiahuanaco's religious and economic connections to the south continued until A.D. 1000. The nature of this early, pre-Incan attempt at pan-Central-Andean unification remains to be resolved.

ART

As archaeologists have shed light on the directions and intensity of Huari expansion, art historians have clarified the nature of the accompanying spread of Tiahuanacoid iconography.

Main Motifs

The most visible motifs at Tiahuanaco are carved on large, prominently displayed stone monuments. Monolithic stelae from 4 to 20 feet

(1.2 to 6 meters) tall represent square-jawed, scepter- or goblet-holding humans with enormous donut-rimmed eyes and broad, pendant tear bands, rectangular "letter-drop" mouths framing checkerboard rows of square teeth, and vacuous stares (Figure 12.1). Finely carved on their broad, wide headdress bands are low-relief human-headed feline and fish-tailed zoomorphs possibly denoting embroidery or featherwork (Lumbreras 1974, 140–141). These anthropomorphized foxes, falcons, fish, and felines have hair or belts with Chavinoid serpent- or puma-headed tabs that may ken them as powerful supernaturals.

Kenning is also a feature of other important Tiahuanaco icons. One of the most heavily kenned figures is a standing frontal "Staff God," again reminiscent of Chavín. Residents and incoming pilgrims saw these same motifs on pottery bowls and *kero* beakers, modeled or painted in geometric black outline.

The Gateway of the Sun

Tiahuanaco iconography was at its most formal and complex in the low-relief friezes on the Gateway of the Sun (Figure 12.2). The lower two-thirds of this 9-foot-high (2.7 meter), 12-foot-wide (3.6 meter) monolithic slab consists of flat, undecorated sides enclosing an open, recessed, rectangular doorway. In the upper third, a band of meanders sets off deity faces with serpent-kenned hair or radiance rays. Centered over the door, a frontal Gateway God (Figure 12.3) on a terraced base holds a vertical animal-headed staff in each outstretched hand much like the Chavín Staff God. His face, in high relief, has huge round eyes, tear bands, and an aureola of serpent-headed kennings. On either side are three identical rows of seven profile bird–men (Figure 12.3) identified as falcons (Figure 12.4a) and condors (Figure 12.4b). The feather crests on their beaked, upturned heads

12.2. Gateway of the Sun, Tiahuanaco. (Photo by Professor E. C. Pickering, 1892, courtesy PM/HU; copyright © by President and Fellows of Harvard College)

12.3. Closeup, Gateway of the Sun, Tiahuanaco, showing staff-holding Gateway God and running figures. (Photo by E. C. Pickering, 1892, courtesy PM/HU; copyright © by President and Fellows of Harvard College)

and wing tips are serpent-kenned, and they either kneel (in reverence?) or race toward the Gateway God with bent knees and taloned feet while extending a single, animal, or condor-headed staff.

Related Designs in Other Areas

The Gateway God and staff-bearing "bird attendants" (also called "falcon runners" or "winged angels") saturated the South Coast and Highlands as archetypal designs that together form what Anita Cook (1987, 60–69) refers to as the Central Deity Theme. Felines with cruller-ring noses, vertically divided black/white eyes,

serpent-head fur kennings, and N-shaped interlocking canines (Figure 12.5) and tear-banded supernaturals (Figure 12.6) were also part of the complex of diffused designs and appear widely on textiles and sheet-gold plaques.

South Highlands: Conchopata

The iconography of these forms was sometimes incompletely transmitted, partially understood, or deliberately reinterpreted and synthesized. This is particularly well illustrated at Conchopata, a "shrine site" about 10 kilometers (6.2 miles) south of Huari where Tiahuanacoid designs appear on large urnlike pots called "keros."

A

B

12.4. (A) Gateway falcon and (B) Gateway condor, and their supposed models. (Redrawn by the author from Yacovleff 1932a, fig. 15; courtesy MNCP)

12.5. Pottery vessels of the "Coastal Tiahuanaco" Atarco style. (Reproduced with permission from Luis G. Lumbreras, *The Peoples and Cultures of Ancient Peru*, trans. Betty J. Meggars, fig. 168, p. 156; copyright © 1974 by Luis G. Lumbreras and Smithsonian Institution, Washington, D.C.)

12.6. Tiahuanacoid images showing tear bands. (Redrawn by the author from Yacovleff 1932a, fig. 17; courtesy MNCP)

Relationship to Tiahuanaco and Huari. William Isbell and Anita Cook (1987) see Conchopata as an early Middle Horizon religious innovator that refined Early Intermediate, Chavín-like Pucara designs of a frontal, staff-holding deity and axe- and trophy-head-carrying attendants. Conchopata artisans combined them into what Cook (1987) calls the Central Deity Theme composed of a front-facing deity and profile attendants and then passed them to both Tiahuanaco and Huari. The accompanying, cohesive ideology, stressing hierarchy, stimulated the development of statehood at both Tiahuanaco and Huari (Isbell and Cook 1987, 26–33). At Tiahuanaco, these concepts developed true cult proportions and were memorialized on the stone facades of ceremonial structures, polychrome ceramics, and textiles from which devotees bore them further afield.

Others feel that Tiahuanaco was the religious innovator and that Conchopata was merely a minor site, perhaps the center of a local cult, that acquired Tiahuanaco iconography with associated Nasca elements during its gradual northward spread.

Iconographic Parallels. The precise logistics of South Highland interaction are unresolved, but there is no question about Conchopata/Tiahuanaco iconographic similarities.

Tiahuanacoid motifs occur on enormous, polychrome-painted Conchopata urns that may have contained chicha consumed during ancestor-cult ceremonies and were subsequently ritually broken and buried. Urns from a cache excavated in 1942 (Menzel 1964, 1968) show the Central Deity Theme; its profile attendants, alter-egos of the Tiahuanaco Gateway of the Sun's "falcon runners," are described by Menzel as winged "floating angels" with alternate bird and jaguar heads (Figure 12.7a). In a maskless variant, the torso is frontal, carrying a staff ending in a trophy head or bound human body and the rear arm bearing a wavy-handled celt (Figure 12.7b, c). Hands and feet have parallel slatlike digits and a prominent pointed thumbnail; eyes are split, with tear panels; the jaguar mouth has N-over lapping canines; and tongues, wing tips, and headband tassels are kenned with serpent, falcon, or jaguar heads with split eye, nape meander (indicating decapitation?), donut nose ring, and/or N-shaped canines. The Frontal Face Deity, holding staffs, shows the same attributes plus a kenned corona headpiece (Figure 12.8). Vertical (textile influenced) block-divider panels contain stepped frets and profile jaguar heads set in triangles like those formed by their own N-canines.

A second cache excavated at Conchopata in

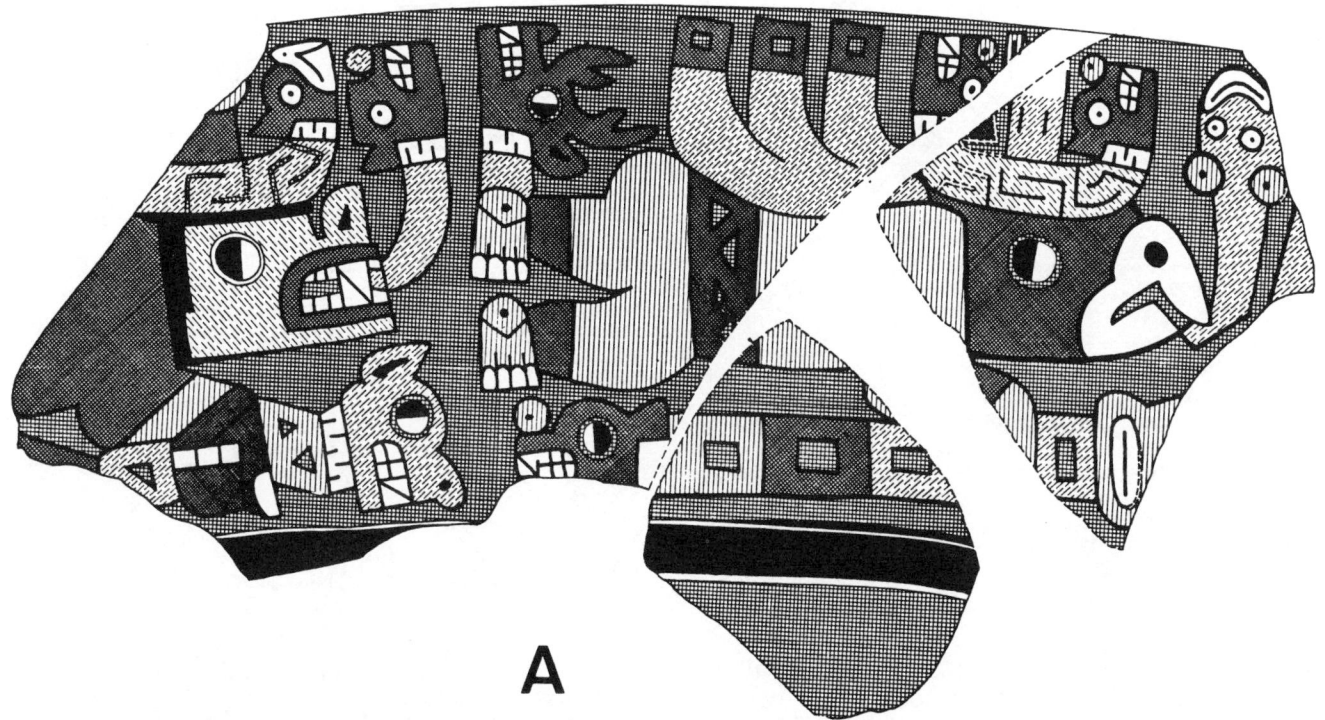

A

12.7a. Huari Floating Angels from near Conchopata, Middle Horizon 1A. (Menzel 1977, pp. 111–12; courtesy LM)

B

C

12.7b and c. Feline-headed Angels from near Conchopata, Middle Horizon 1A. (Menzel 1977, pp. 111–12; courtesy LM)

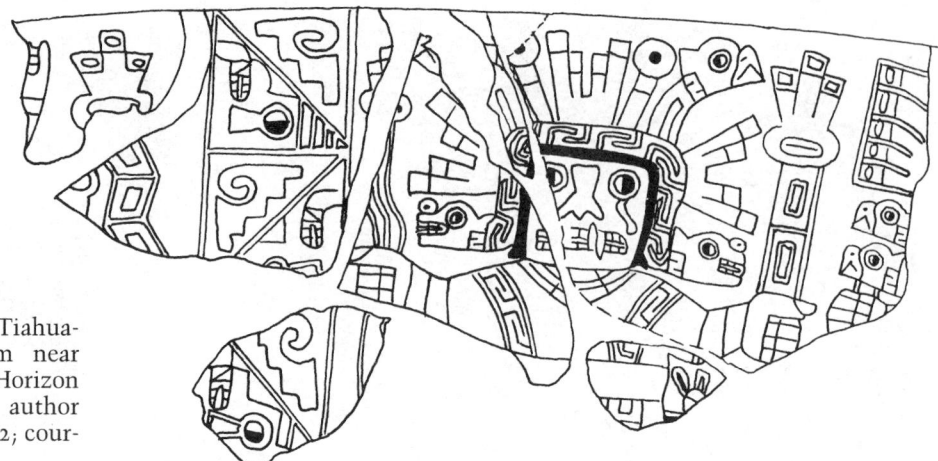

12.8. Huari deity with Tiahuanacoid attributes, from near Conchopata, Middle Horizon IA. (Redrawn by the author from Menzel 1977, fig. 62; courtesy LM)

1977 near five flexed (probably sacrificed) female burials aged 15 to 25 consisted of over 17,000 fragments of pottery, including large face–neck jars (representing mummy bundles?) with the Central Deity Theme or Nasca-related designs painted on their midsections (Cook 1987, 58–71, figures 21–30). The 1977 designs were more standardized, with fewer figures, and Profile Attendants had extended snouts and fishlike bodies, unlike the 1942 cache's bird- and jaguar-masked runners.

South Coast: Pacheco

The South Coast ceremonial/trading site of Pacheco in the Upper Nasca Valley (Map 10) produced large ritual keros of a Tiahuanacoid ware called Robles Moqo while passing Nasca-derived elements back into the highlands. Copies of highland wares show a frontal Staff God with lateral winged attendants; others add South Coast motifs: tear bands ending in human trophy heads (Figure 12.9), marine animals, and headdresses with ears of lowland corn.

Pacheco, Conchapata, and Ayapata urns also hint at Huari distribution of highland goods to the coast. Isbell (1977) describes vessels combining highland plants, llamas, and dotted checkerboard squares that resemble the presumed counting devices of the quipu-holding treasurer for the Inca empire in a late sixteenth-century drawing by Poma de Ayala: Both may represent tallying of state produce for redistribution. Other Pacheco vessels depict highland plants and steep-roofed buildings that resemble the Inca storehouses in Poma's drawing of a

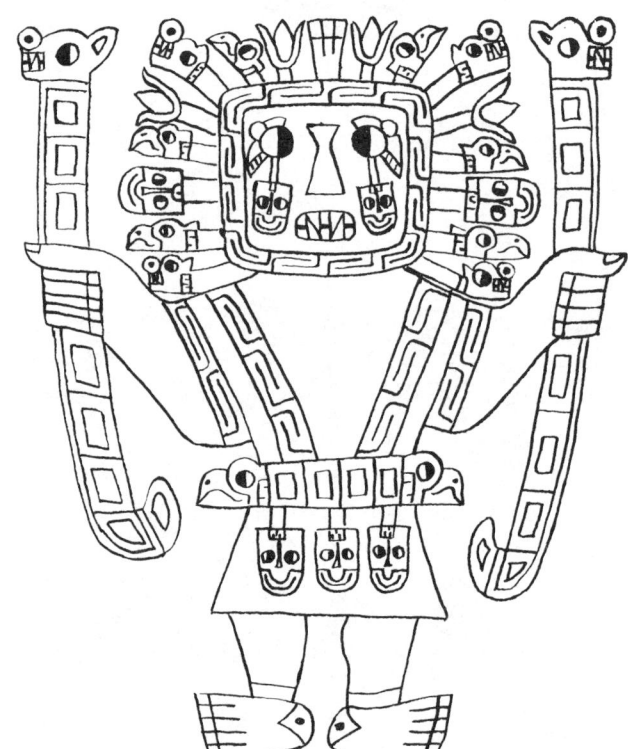

12.9. Staff God with trophy-head tear bands and trophy-head corn headdress elements, from a Pacheco urn owned by the American Museum of Natural History, New York City. (Drawing by the author)

high-ranking Inca conversing with a quipu-holding non-Inca administrator.

North Coast

In the North Coast, Tiahuanaco iconography faced strong local tradition. Tiahuanaco deities replaced naturalistic Moche forms in modeled pottery, and polychrome painting supplanted black-on-cream wares at some sites. Domestic wares remained relatively unchanged.

Textiles

No Huari textiles have survived, but in the dry South Coast their counterparts carry unmistakable Huari images. The remaining upper section of an Ica Valley Middle Horizon wall hanging (Figure 12.10, dark portion; hypothetical reconstruction of the remainder is drawn in outline) shows a frontal face with divided black/white eyes and serpent-kenned hair flanked by floating, staff-bearing bird attendants with feline heads and by three pairs of humans with ceremonial fire drills (Conklin 1970).

Other coastal textiles further document the interchange. William Conklin has stylistically seriated six Tiahuanacoid textile fragments from coastal South Peru and North Chile that were probably trade pieces. They, too, bear split-eye, staff-carrying bird runners as individual motifs. Clearly, Gateway of the Sun elements moved to new lands as a cohesive, unified theme.

Tiahuanacoid textiles also replaced Nasca weavings on Middle-Horizon mummies (Figure 12.11). The N-divided block of stepped frets and split-eye, profile jaguar head favored as a panel divider on pottery (Figure 12.8) was also suited to the rectlinear constraints of weaving, and strips of paired blocks alternating with solid color bands were frequent on tapestry funerary ponchos (Figure 12.12).

Weaving Techniques and Design Layout

Rebecca Stone (1986, 1987, 1988) has specialized in the analysis of Huari-style textiles. She believes that tapestry tunics for South Coast mummy bundles were deliberately created by multiple weavers on wide-frame or stake looms that exposed the entire design field, facilitating complex pattern and color variation and the coordination of tunic halves. These 8-foot-wide (2.4 meter) webs, with short cotton warps covered by interlocking or noninterlocked discontinuous wefts of different colors, were subsequently stitched together and worn with warps running horizontally (as "width-wise warps") and the long rows of weft-oriented design blocks

appearing vertically on the wearer (Stone 1988). Conklin (1986), in fact, proposes that Falcon "Runners" on ponchos are really flying figures because they were originally conceived and woven in horizontal lines.

Systematic, computer-analyzed patterns of color repetition vary from tunic to tunic (Stone 1987) and are sometimes strong enough to detract from the formal pattern of iconographic units of a web. Stone's (1986) analysis of complex repetitions of color in the Lima Tapestry distinguishes consistent patterns of use for whites and reds, irregular substitutions for tans and greens, and unpredictable "wild-card" appearances of blues in the thirty-eight staff-bearer-unit halves. Greater deviation from these color norms on the right half of the tunic suggests the participation of multiple weavers exercising individual creativity, perhaps in communal workshops like those shown on Moche pottery.

Motif Modifications

One of the characteristics accompanying the application of Tiahuanaco motifs to textiles was the partial transformation in their form. Falcon Runners or the Gateway God, painted in full on keros, were now reduced to a *pars pro toto* (parts symbolizing the whole motif) shorthand that abstracted their key elements. South Coast weavers squeezed, stretched, split, abstracted, or recombined block units and varied their spatial and color sequencing. The resulting transposition of elements is such that one must be familiar with the prototype motif to have any inkling of what is meant.

Alan Sawyer (1963, 27–38) has brilliantly reconstructed several of the possible recombinations from the Lima Tapestry, a Huari-style tunic found in highland Ayacucho. Designs are given rhythmic sequence by reversing colors or positions (Figure 12.13a), combining them with other elements to form a block that is color- or position-reversed (Figure 12.13b), alternating different blocks (Figure 12.13c), or rotating a block around a center axis (Figure 12.14a, b). Complete motifs may also be expanded at the center of a garment or severely narrowed at its sides to the point of making them almost unrecognizable.

The progression from realistic to abstract shows beautifully in Sawyer's figures of the

12.10. Line drawing of the Tiahuanacoid design on an Ica Middle Horizon textile (TM 1972.27), with reconstructed lower portion drawn in. (Conklin 1970, fig. 6; photo courtesy William J. Conklin)

12.12. N-divided blocks with tear-band eyes on a South Coast Middle Horizon textile. (Redrawn by the author from Yacovleff 1932b, fig. 14; courtesy MNCP)

12.11. High-status Middle Horizon mummy bundle with false head and hair, face mask, cap, headband, and divided block-patterned tunic. Probably from the Nasca area. Collection Museo Nacional de Antropología y Arqueología, Lima. (From Vreeland and Cockburn 1980, fig. 9.3, p. 142; photo by James Vreeland, copyright © by CUP, reprinted with permission)

Falcon Runner motif in various stages of compression (Figure 12.15a–d). The figure is divided into four vertical segments: (1) the hand gripping the staff; (2) the upraised head, arm, and front leg; (3) the headdress, body, and vertically oriented back foot; and (4) the wing, tailfeathers, and small serpent-foot kenning.

Figure 12.16 shows a similar winged feline holding a staff. In Figure 12.16a, the tail/wing segment is compressed and the head/front foot is expanded, whereas in Figure 12.16b, the staff, head, and wing/tail are compressed and the headdress/rear-foot section is expanded. Figure 12.17 shows how the same figure (bottom) appears when its four units (lacking some central

elements) are simplified and expanded (center) and how the design loses almost all intelligibility when the staff and head segments of A are reversed (top) and separated from the rear-foot and wing segments (B) that complete the design.

Sawyer assures us that there are other possibilities of design development far more intricate than those given here. He also shows how motif segments may be readjusted to a more normal scale to recreate the original. Combining the compressed or expanded portions (Figure 12.18, middle register) of two versions of a motif (Figure 12.18a, b, top) and readjusting the proportions produces mirror images of a backward-looking, long-tailed anthropomorphic feline (bottom). Sawyer's article was written before the era of videographics. It is interesting to speculate how a computer might explore additional variants within the vocabulary of Tiahuanaco "shorthand" design.

Interpretations of Iconography

Tiahuanaco–Inca Parallels. Some researchers have tried to project meaning into Middle-

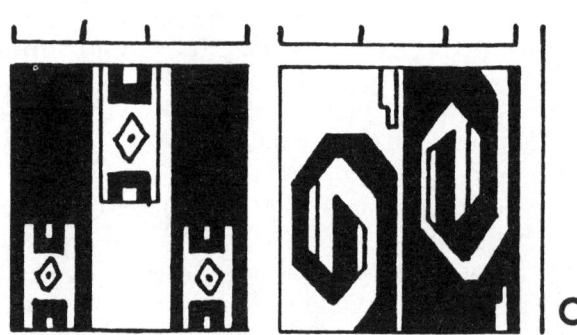

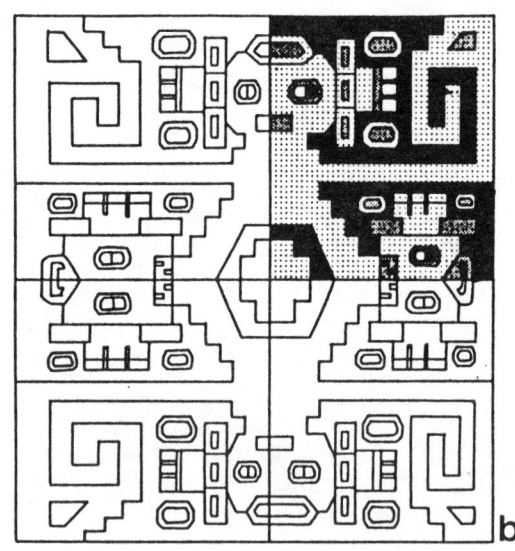

12.13. Paired elements in Tiahuanaco textile design: (*a*) stepped spirals divided by a diagonal, (*b*) stepped spiral and stylized profile heads separated by diagonal, (*c*) different paired elements alternated in checkerboard fashion (Sawyer 1963, p. 28; drawing by Milton Sonday, courtesy Alan Sawyer and TM)

12.14. Composite motifs in Tiahuanacoid textile design oriented around a central point: (*a*) profile feline (puma?) heads, (*b*) profile bird (falcon?) and sometimes human heads (Sawyer 1963, p. 28; drawing by Milton Sonday, courtesy Alan Sawyer and TM)

a. From the "Gateway of the Sun" at Tiahuanaco, Bolivia

b. T.M. 1959.5.6. Gift of Raymond
Wielgus

c. T.M. 1961.24.1 Gift of John Wise

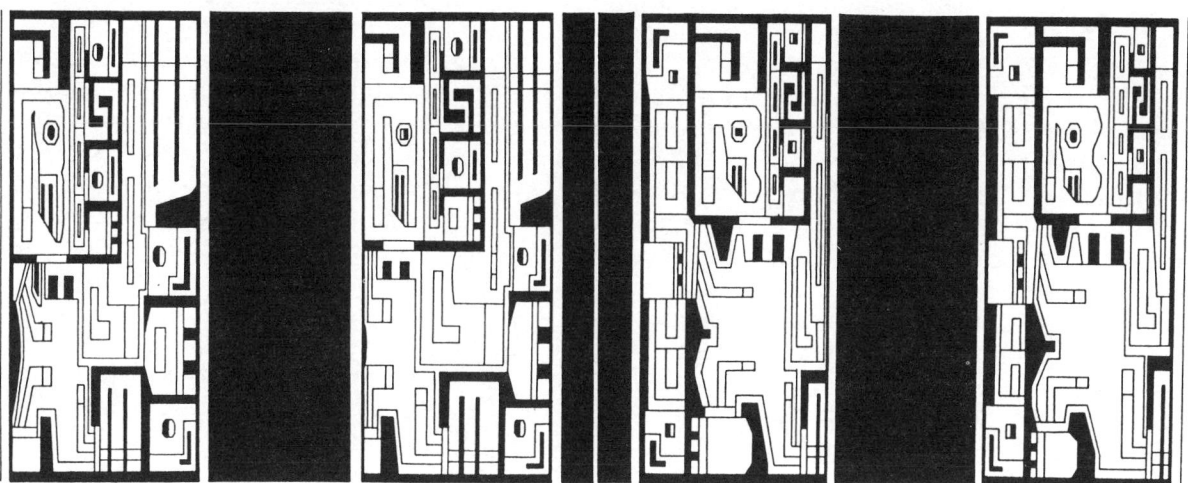

d. T.M. 1962.51.1 Gift of Junius B. Bird

12.15. Representations of falcon-headed, staff-bearing figure motifs (Type IIIA). (Sawyer 1963, fig. 1, p. 30; drawing by Milton Sonday, courtesy Alan Sawyer and TM)

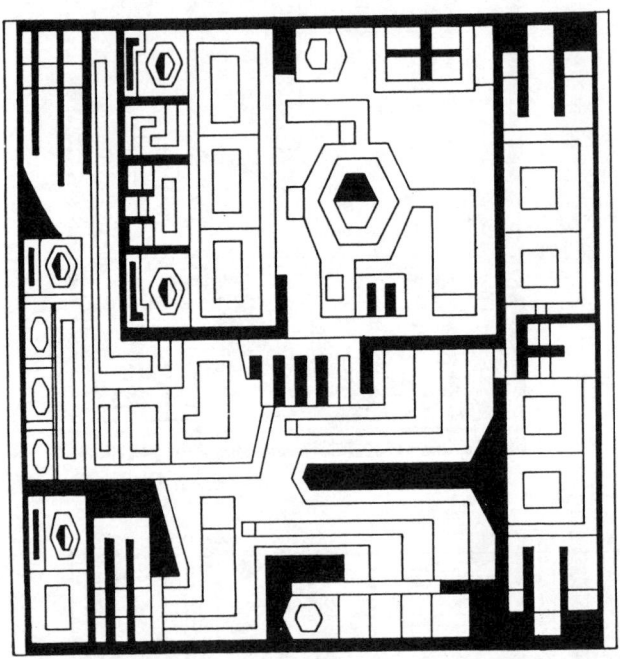 

12.16. Two puma-headed, staff-bearing figure motifs from adjoining registers in Tiahuanaco shirt, TM 1962.30.2. (Sawyer 1963, fig. 3, p. 32; drawing by Milton Sonday, courtesy Alan Sawyer and TM)

Horizon images through possible continuity into Inca times. Conklin (1970) notes that the Inca, who claimed Tiahuanaco cultural derivation, included lion and condor costumes and lighting a sacred fire in their Raimi Festival to the sun. These elements parallel the condor–feline beings and fire-drill scenes on South-Coast Huari-influenced textiles (Figure 12.10a, b).

The validity of Inca data in interpreting Huari material is further strengthened by a coastal textile analyzed by Anne Rowe (1979) on which profile musicians play animal-headed trumpets, panpipes, whistles (?), and drums like those described ethnohistorically for the Inca. Many are divinities (indicated by their vertically divided eyes and rayed headdresses) wearing the same "suspender-strap" tunic and bandlike three-pendant animal-headed belt as the Gateway God. The remaining musicians wear variants of Huari costume with decided similarities to Inca apparel.

Dorothy Menzel (1977), working with the Uhle Collection Middle-Horizon keros from Nasca, Huari, and Conchopata, sees similarities with Inca representations that suggest a direct continuation of many Huari beliefs. She feels that Huari and Moche deities merged during the Middle Horizon and continued into Chimú beliefs after the decline of Huari influence, subsequently entering the Inca inventory when the Inca absorbed the Chimú.

Menzel identifies and names several Huari figures on the basis of Inca parallels:

1. A frontal sky deity with a U-shaped halo ending in a serpent head at each shoulder, antecedent of the Divine Couple according to Inca legend. Like the Tiahuanaco Gateway God, he holds a staff in each hand (Figure 12.8).

2. Walking, running, floating, or flying feline-headed angels directly inspired from Tiahuanaco motifs (Figure 12.7a, b).

3. A divine couple consisting of a sun god with a corn-eared headdress and a moon goddess with a corn-eared costume and vegetal staffs.

4. Star animals with dot-ended wings, dorsal appendages (fur?), and tail feathers that may represent Inca constellations (Figure 12.19).

Other Interpretations. Others are less convinced. Klein (1978, 93) suggests that anthropomorphized figures may instead be identifiers of kinship groups. Reinhard, noting similarities

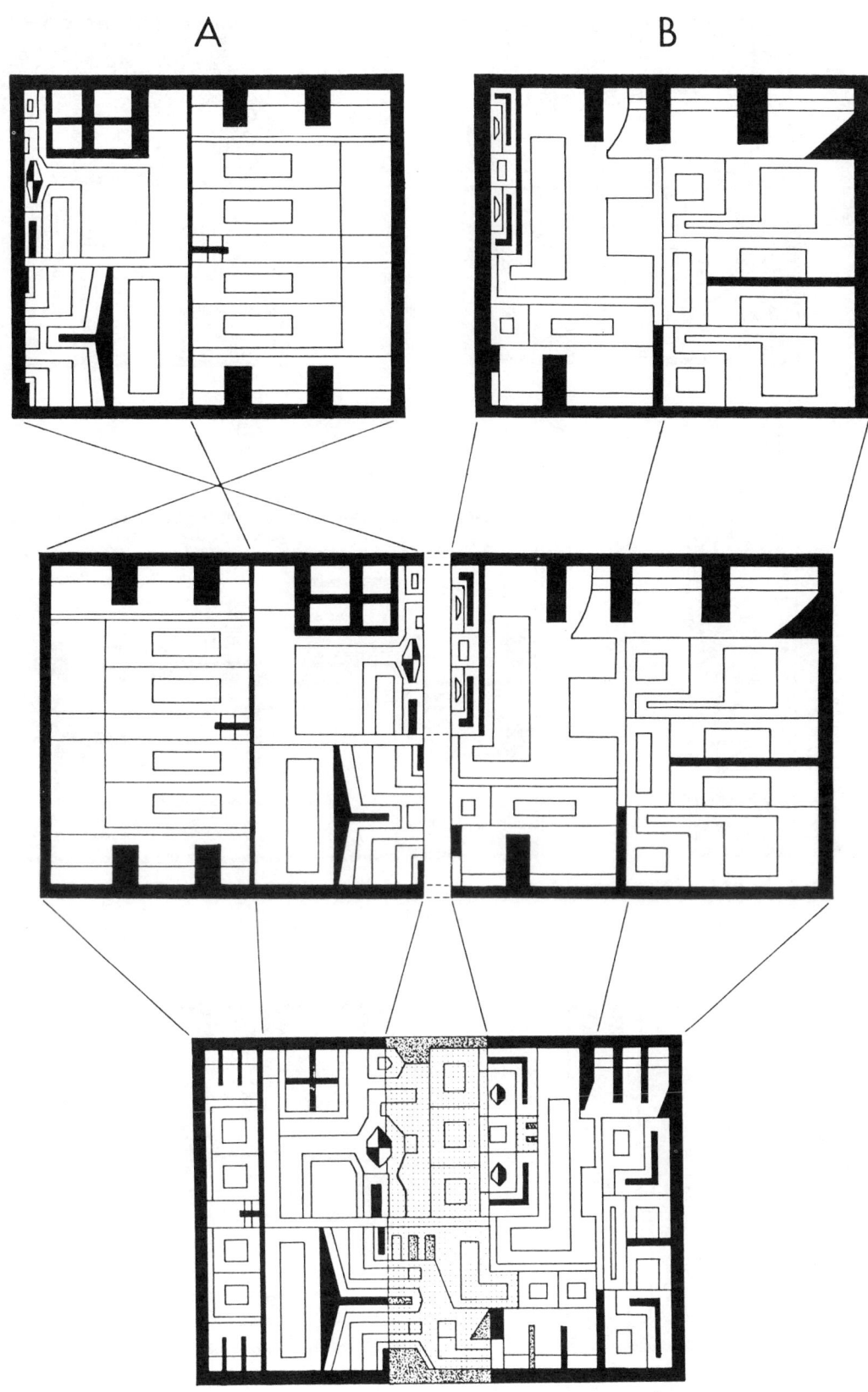

12.17. Resolution of the puma-headed, staff-bearing figure motif of the Lima tapestry. (Sawyer 1963, fig. 4, p. 33; drawing by Milton Sonday, courtesy Alan Sawyer and TM)

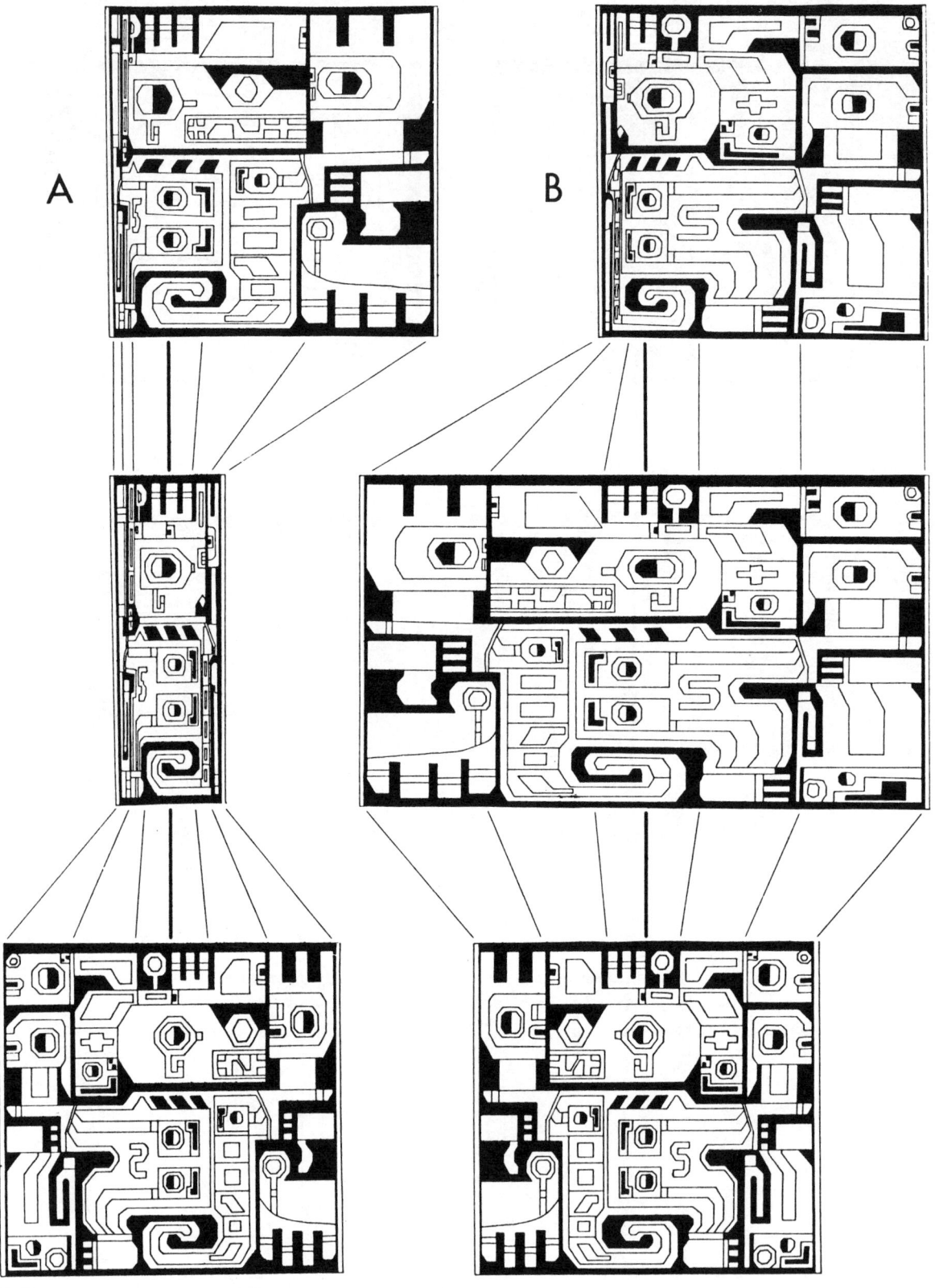

12.18. A resolution of the motif of the Museum of Primitive Art tapestry, 56.195 (*A, B, bottom*) showing expanded and compressed lateral sections (*A, B, top*) and extreme compression (*A, middle*) and expansion (*B, middle*). (Sawyer 1963, fig. 6, p. 36; drawing by Milton Sonday, courtesy Alan Sawyer and TM)

12.19. Star animals: Conchopata. (Redrawn by the author from Menzel 1977, p. 110; courtesy LM)

between the Gateway God and the Chavín Staff God, proposes that they represent an ancient weather-controlling deity because both Tiahuanaco (with adjacent Mount Illimani) and Chavín are located near sacred mountains that are still identified as the home of weather gods venerated in contemporary mountain cults (Reinhard 1985a).

Although a linear Huari-to-Chimú-to-Inca transmission is simple and attractive, it must remain only one of several hypotheses until more is known about the origins and development of Middle-Horizon iconography and the economic, social, political, and religious interactions between the polities involved in its spread. When the waning roles of late Tiahuanaco and Huari become clearer, we can better understand how the Inca, in their South Highland penetration centuries later, incorporated the remnants of this important Middle Horizon style.

CHAPTER 13

CHIMÚ

BY A.D. 1000 and the beginning of the Late Intermediate, regional polities again emerged. In the Central Highlands, the Chanka moved into the vacuum left by Huari; Wanka groups claimed the Mantaro Basin to the north. Southern Highland Lupaca and Colla established a presence in the Titicaca Basin. These small independent kingdoms are known both through excavations and Spanish descriptions. On the South and Central coasts, Chancay culture developed; It is famous for its log-roofed tombs, excavated by Julio Tello, that contained exquisite double cloth, tapestry, and gauze-weave textiles bearing both Paracas/Nasca-derived motifs and Tiahuanacoid Staff-God figures. In the Chincha/Ica valleys, graves contain gold objects, polichrome pottery, and beautiful garments decorated with macaw and toucan feathers were traded in from the Amazonian selva.

On the North Coast, remnant Moche elements formed the basis for the twelfth-to-fifteenth-century kingdom of Chimor or Chimú (A.D. 1150–1460.) Moche culture was replaced around A.D. 700 in the area of Batán Grande, a 55-square kilometer (21.1 square mile) funerary–religious complex in the La Leche Valley 300 kilometers (186 miles) north of Moche, by a new local culture called Sicán or Lambayeque that incorporated Huari, Central-Coast Pachacamac, and North-Highland Cajamarca elements in its Early Sicán (A.D. 700–850) phase. The Middle Sicán phase (A.D. 850–1000) produced a cultural florescence that has been attributed to a legendary ruler, Naymlap, who arrived by sea to establish a dynasty that ruled for three centuries. This revitalization is reflected at over fifty Batán Grande sites noted for their 40-meter-high (131 foot) pyramids and sumptuously furnished Middle Sicán tombs in what may be the largest pre-columbian cemetery in the New World (Carcedo Muro and Shimada 1985, 64). Batán Grande sites have been heavily looted and bulldozed since 1936 and have furnished an astounding array of gold artifacts in an early Chimú style.

To the south, the Chimú established their capital city of Chan Chan in the Moche Valley (Map 10) and spread rapidly to the north and south. By 1450, they dominated seventeen coastal valleys between the Tumbes River in Ecuador and the Supe River near Lima. They used conquered peoples in public-works projects, expanding the Moche irrigation and road networks, building administrative and sacred pilgrimage centers, and enlarging Chan Chan as each new ruler added a residential compound built with wealth and labor acquired through additional conquests and tribute. Ethnohistoric sources mention a dynasty of kings founded by Taycanamo, who came with an entourage from the north on seagoing balsa rafts.

The Inca adapted many features from this smoothly functioning mini-empire when they conquered the Chimú in 1460. They extended Chimor's highways and irrigation canals and built similar walled compounds in Cuzco. Like the Chimú, they used state-directed labor and relocation of populations as techniques for unification. Their political organization may also have been influenced by that of the Chimú as the Inca assimilated concepts from several conquered peoples while imposing their own.

ARCHITECTURE

The Chimú capital of Chan Chan covers 6 square miles (16 square kilometers) and had an estimated population of 25,000 to 50,000 people. It is best known for its ten rectangular *ciudadela* compounds (Map 11) enclosed in adobebrick or puddled-mud walls and named after early excavators (Uhle, Squire, Bandelier, Tello). Each compound had a single well-guarded entrance leading to a U-shaped audiencia plus courts, storerooms, servant quarters, workshop areas, a reservoir, and a burial area. Chimú compounds resemble those at late Moche Galindo, Pacatnamú, Farfán and the Huari sites of Pikillaqta, Biracochapampa, Jargampata, and Cerro Chirú, suggesting ongoing architectural and perhaps functional continuity.

Settlement-pattern studies by the 1969–1975 Chan Chan–Moche Valley Project have vastly increased our understanding of Chan Chan's building types and their probable functions. The excavators, lacking adequate organic material (for carbon-14 dating), superimposed structures, and unmixed pottery deposits, have proposed ciudadela construction sequences based on seriation of adobe-brick forms and changing audiencia architectural details possibly corresponding to the ten recorded Chimú rulers (Kolata 1982, 1983; Topic and Moseley 1985).

Construction appears to have spurted during periods of military activity. The earliest compounds were well maintained, perhaps by *panacas* of the first Chimú kings. Their rich tombs have long since been looted, but bits of fancy pottery, textiles, and spondylus shell from huaquero backfill indicate a protected elite, and the single ciudadela entrance and ramps that permitted only single-file passage also suggest highly controlled access. Ciudadelas were probably used for residence, administration, and redistribution activities by living rulers and as residence/cemeteries by their surviving royal kin. They likely reflect the same "split inheritance" followed by the Inca who appointed one son as heir and others to the panaca that would maintain his cult after death (Conrad 1982, 105–117; Kolata 1983, 362–363).

The redistribution function of compounds finds support in the multiple-row rooms within ciudadelas or adjoining annexes almost identical to known Inca storerooms. Their high walls and narrow ramp entrances regulated access and discouraged theft. Adjacent U-shaped audiencias resemble open-fronted structures depicted on Moche pottery from which seated rulers receive and dispense goods (Keatinge, Chodoff, Chodoff, Marvin, and Silverman 1975) and may have been used by rulers to receive and count tribute, fete visiting curacas with chica from jars set in floor depressions and food baked in audiencia cooking pits, and dispense goods from the adjoining storerooms (Day 1982). The plethora of Chimú storehouses and their relative paucity at Moche sites indicate that the Chimú had a far more extensive tribute and redistributive network, worthy of Inca emulation.

Outside Chan Chan's ciudadelas, smaller, lesselaborate elite compounds housed the lower nobility. Alexandra Klymyshyn (1982, 121–144) finds that they share controlled access ramps but vary in the size, number, and distribution of their wells, plazas, courts, storerooms, and audiencias. She divides them into six types, explores their construction sequence based on brick forms, and suggests their additional use by provincial curacas in temporary residence. Barrios of small, irregularly agglutinated rooms (SIARs) on Chan Chan's west side sheltered urban proletariat artisans, visiting traders, and labor crews recruited for large-scale public-works

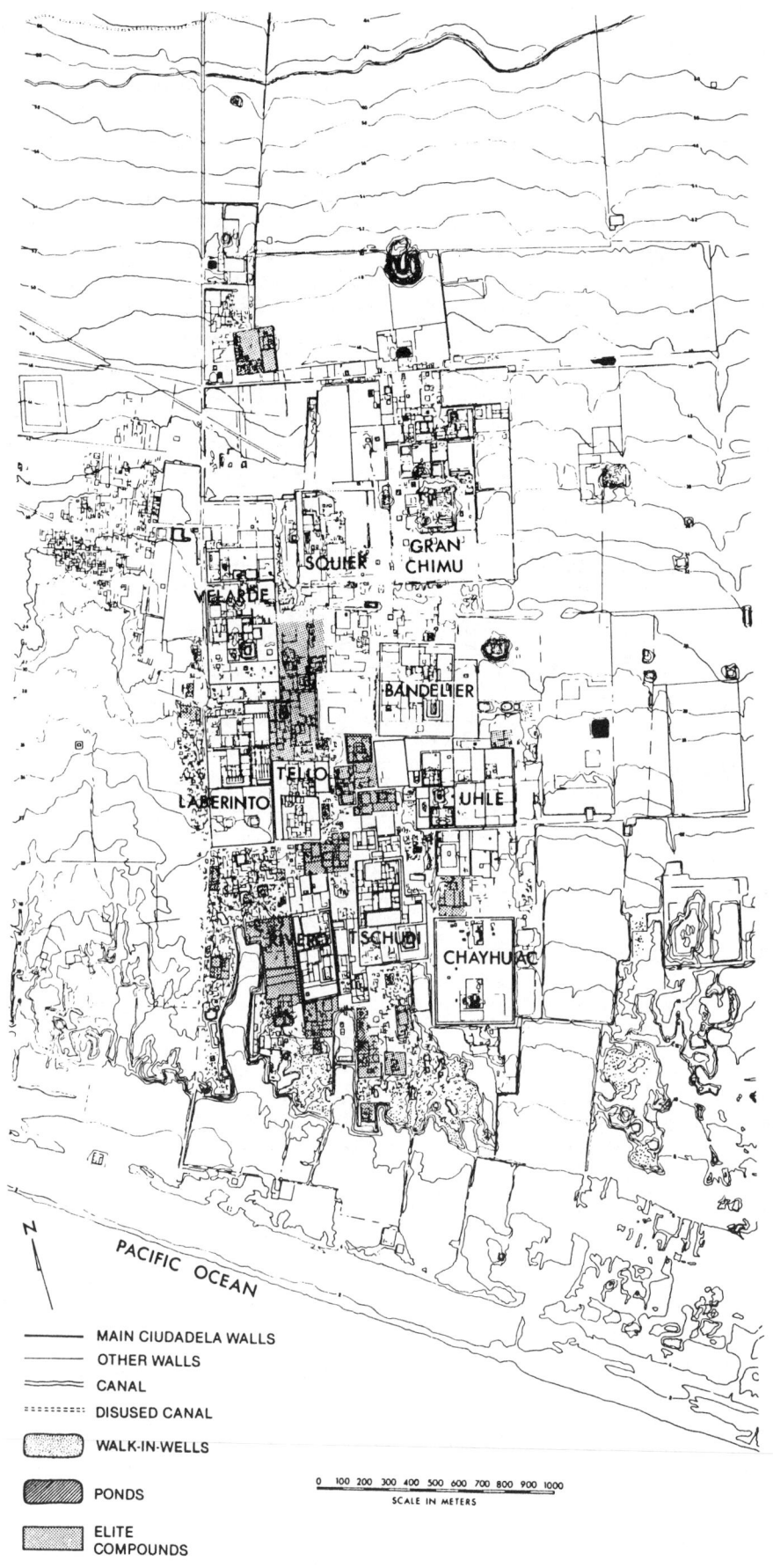

Map 11. Plan of central Chan Chan. (From Moseley and Day 1982, fig. 3.1; courtesy of Michael E. Moseley)

projects. Remains of crucibles, ash, woodworking tools, spindles and loom parts, textiles, cotton and wool fiber, and yarn indicate major crafts-working activity. Kitchen areas were identifiable by their hearths and animal refuse (Topic 1982, 145–175).

Regional centers with large populations in adjacent valleys also contain temple pyramids, walled compounds, and storehouses. Dozens of smaller towns have also been excavated. North of the Santa River, a 3-meter-high (9.8 foot), 56-kilometer (34.8 mile) wall with fifty fortification stations protected earlier Chimú boundaries (Stierlin 1984, 152). Canals, dams, and reservoirs connected the Chimú valleys and carried water 100 kilometers (62 miles) away, permitting three maize crops in a single year.

ART

Chimú artisans incorporated their Moche heritage as well as their own innovations. Much of their art is mass-produced, with a resultant loss in quality and originality of approach. Detailed, interpretive iconographic studies so far are few.

Metalwork

Chimú goldwork appears tinny, made to catch the eye rather than impress through solidness. Flat sheet-metal feathers are inserted into tubular crowns. Tiny paper-thin danglers and discs hang from headdresses and nose ornaments, burial boots, and funerary masks and are stitched to cotton and featherwork ponchos and bags, to glint as their wearer moved in the sun.[1] Casting continued, but repoussé decoration by pressing or scoring sheet metal from the backside onto a wooden or stone mould was a quicker, more economical way to produce raised designs. Sheet-metal diadems, bracelets, flat neck lunulae, elbow-length funerary "gloves," nose ornaments, beakers, ear spools, and plaques to cover walls or wooden boxes were mass produced, and sheet metal was stretch-hammered around carved wooden anvils to form three-dimensional effigy beakers, staff heads, and effigy attachments for flat pieces (Easby 1956; Emmerich 1965, 30–32). The results were paper-thin: Archaeologist Junius Bird (in the Introduction to La Farge 1981, 10) recounts with horror a huaquero's complaint that, after digging up a large cache of silver effigy beakers from Chan Chan, "when melted, they weighed practically nothing."

Gold surfaces were also produced through depletion gilding.[2] Wall plaques and huge mummy-bundle masks of tumbaga (gold/copper alloy), gold/silver, and gold/copper/silver alloys were coated with a paste of ferric-sulphate-bearing soils, salt, and/or plant acids. This etched away the nongold elements leaving a patina that, when burnished, resembled solid gold. Remains of several smelting furnaces found at Batán Grande by Izumi Shimada (Carcedo Muro and Shimada 1985, 65) attest to intensive metal production, the products of which were traded from Ancón (near present-day Lima) to Ecuador.

Chimú gold masks associated with mummies are huge, often measuring 30 inches (76.2 centimeters) wide by 16 inches (40.6 centimeters) high. They are often three dimensional, with a flat, straight top, an additive nose, and large tear-shaped "Lambayeque eyes" named after a shape frequent on masks from Batán Grande in the Lambayeque Valley, which was subdued by the Chimú around A.D. 1420 during their northward expansion. Flat "exclamation-point" ears contain ear spools, deep-set wrinkles demarcate the cheeks, and twin "staples" cover a short horizontal mouth over a wide, gently convex chin (Figure 13.1). These masks were painted in up to six colors, with red highlighting embossed areas and further ornamented with feather edging and eyes inset with gemstones. They may have covered the faces of idols in temples prior to their interment as mummy-bundle masks, associating the features of the legendary ruler Naymlap with those of the deceased (Carcedo Muro and Shimada 1985, 67–74).

Another frequent tomb object is the tumi, a ceremonial knife (Figure 13.2), often placed near the burial in packages of a dozen or more, carefully grouped by size. Its crescent blade is made of copper, gold, or halves or checkerboard squares of soldered gold and silver in elite examples. Handles are gold-leaf-covered wood

---

[1] Emmerich (1965, Figure 47) illustrates a poncho from the Miguel Mujica Collection in Lima stitched with 30,000 tiny gold placques. Another, with seven thousand plaques from Lima's Gold Museum, appears in La Farge (1981, 108–109).

[2] The term, coined by Paul Borgsoe, describes one method of mise-en-coleur or controlled coloration (see Lechtman, 1973 for her own experiments at reconstruction). The process was already used for early Moche (Vicus) pieces and continued into Inca times, duping many gold-hungry Spaniards.

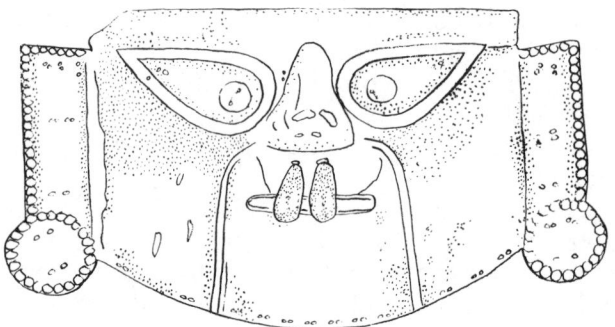

13.1. Chimú mummy mask. (Drawing by the author)

13.2. Chimú tumi. (Drawing by the author)

effigy animals or the favorite Chimú figure of the so-called Sicán Lord (equated with the mythical ruler Ñaymlap), a winged, frontal human with tear-shaped eyes wearing a huge cast-filigree crescent headdress inset with turquoise and shell. The headdress fits across the forehead in a straight line, leading to speculation that a similar headdress of perishable material was attached to the enormous mummy masks.

Gold or tumbaga vessels with two long, thin conical spouts bridged by rainbowlike filigree bands over a sharply keeled body also accompany burials. The enormous quantity of gold funerary offerings suggest that masks, tumi, and elaborate gold containers may have been ritually used during the deceased's lifetime (Carcedo Muro and Shimada 1985, 74).

Pottery

Chimú pottery provides far less information than Moche wares. The rich detailed fine-line iconography that fueled Donnan's studies is gone: Only the Moche stirrup-spout and effigy-vessel bodies came into vogue again after the Huari/Tiahuanaco interlude. Even these were modified for Chimú tastes: Spouts became wiry, with trapezoidal bends, and modeling was imitated by mass production with molding. The result was more abstract; fluid forms lacked the detail that enables biologists to identify species of Moche plant/animal effigies. Realistic "portrait" vessels are gone: Chimú potters show generalized simplifications of faces and bodies with a few incised lines for detail. Missing, too, are the wonderful Moche group-interaction scenes of warfare and erotic dalliances that pique our interest and invite interpretation.

Instead, Chimú potters added their own hallmarks. Polychromes and red ware were soon replaced (excepting some domestic wares) by smoky reduction-fired black wares burnished to a fine sheen. Water/chicha containers had mold-made effigy bodies, figures atop cube bases, and round bodies decorated with low reliefs perhaps imitating Moche antecedents (Figure 13.3a). Press molds left a sharp-rimmed indented oval containing slightly raised figures against a flecked background on vessel sides (Figure 13.3c). Increasingly thinner spouts fitted behind effigies or atop vessels, with a small monkey or human perched at the juncture of stirrup and spout (Figure 13.3b). Sometimes

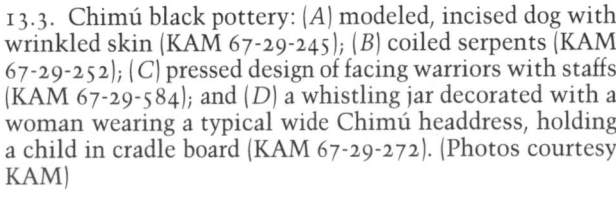

13.3. Chimú black pottery: (A) modeled, incised dog with wrinkled skin (KAM 67-29-245); (B) coiled serpents (KAM 67-29-252); (C) pressed design of facing warriors with staffs (KAM 67-29-584); and (D) a whistling jar decorated with a woman wearing a typical wide Chimú headdress, holding a child in cradle board (KAM 67-29-272). (Photos courtesy KAM)

strap handles bridged a tubular spout and a nonfunctional effigy spout. Thin, pointed "rabbit-ear-antenna" spouts were separated by a wide openwork clay arch, apparently a Huari survival by way of the Lambayeque conquest. Another favored form was the double-bridged-spout "whistling jar" (Figure 13.3d) with flat canteenlike chambers connected so that liquid poured into the first flowed into the second when the vessel was tipped and forced air through a hole in its "dummy" effigy spout with a "whoosh" like a whistling teakettle. Studies of pottery motifs on modeled forms are limited by the absence of complex iconography.

Moche and Huari influences are easier to determine. Richard Burger has demonstrated how Chimú potters revived a Moche-III scene of a god–human catching a huge fish a thousand years later as a deliberate archaism after disuse during the Tiahuanaco/Huari interlude. Chimú potters first imitated it directly, then modified it as a framed, press-molded scene adding animal "stirrup-spout sitters" and ultimately simplified the protagonists into thin, almost surrealistic, figures (Burger 1977, 95–98). More such studies are needed.

Textiles

Chimú textiles have been reknowned for years for their fine featherwork, twill weaves, and delicate gauzes. Brightly colored tropical-bird feathers were bent at the shaft and tied to two-piece cotton ponchos and mantles in scrolls, grecas, and small fish, birds, and animals like those on adobe reliefs. Northern weavers produced twills and tapestry, highland techniques probably introduced during Huari expansion. To the south, in the Chancay and Chillón valleys, fabrics were so filmy that to one Spanish conquistador's astonishment, an entire garment fit within his clenched hand.[3]

Until recently, the specifics of Chimú textile style and weaving techniques were poorly understood because most pieces were the result of huaquero activity with uncertain contextual data. In 1981, Ann Pollard Rowe, curator of New World textiles at the Textile Museum in Washington, D.C., completed analysis of textiles recovered from archaeologically controlled excavation by Thomas Pozorski of the Chan Chan–Moche Valley Project from the Las Avispas burial platform at Chan Chan. The fragments, left by looters, were associated with ninety-three female burials, probably sacrificial victims. From them, Rowe established diagnostic criteria of Chimú weaving, aiding identification of other Chimú pieces in museum and private collections and permitting educated speculations about their development, distribution, and role in Chimú culture.

Rowe found that Chimú plain weaves consistently used single cotton wefts and paired warps for a warp-face effect. Imported alpaca and other highland camelid fibers were Z-spun and S-plied. The most frequently collected pieces are tapestry panels and funerary male-tunic–loincloth–mantle sets with matching design motifs with strong Moche continuity.

SUBSTYLES

Rowe identified four Chimú textile substyles (A. Rowe 1984). Probably the earliest is the Bird Lot style (Figure 13.4a), consisting of seven matched garment sets annotated by the late Junius Bird of the American Museum of Natural History, which show considerable variety of design and technique. Turbans have checkered-brown and white-cotton plain-weave center stripes with beautifully brocaded, fringed-end panels. T-shaped loincloths were enormous, with a brocaded end panel, long checkered midsection, and narrow tie band at the other end. Wide, short tunics were made from two webs stitched at the front and sides with a V-neck opening and two smaller sleeve panels. Brocaded double cloth was a favored technique. Other sets combined plain weave, gauze, tie-dye, and/or tapestry with attached red-dyed camelid fiber tassels and medallions to give a shaggy furlike appearance.[4] Later, nonset fragments in the Toothed Crescent style (Figure 13.4b) show frontal humans with angular "fringed" headdresses holding staffs or with upraised hands and share common technical features. A third style, the Pelican style (Figure 13.4c) consists of undyed cotton-garment sets with profile pelicans brocaded on a gauze ground. Following Chimor's conquest by the Inca, matched tapestry panels bear imaginative combinations of the Plain Crescent style (Figure 13.4d) hexagon-headed figures with raised arms, outwardly bent knees and splayed feet who now wear triangular caps supporting flat headpieces with diagonal down-sloping elements that, minus their former "fringe," resemble drooping rabbit ears. These textiles show "simplified, large scale designs that obtain the maximum effect with the minimum of effort" (A. Rowe 1984, 186) per-

---

[3] The small but select Amano Museum in Lima has one of the finest collections of Chancay gauzes, stunningly illustrated in color in Tsumoyama (1979) plus a stunning leno-weave Chan Chan poncho with brocaded birds holding trophy heads in their beaks (Plate 13, p. 28).

[4] A. Rowe 1984, 44, Plates 3 and 5, and Figures 35–36. An even more spectacular example of Chimú additives is a Brooklyn Museum "short cloak" with three-dimensional cotton-stuffed, crescent-topped figures and winged bird attendants attached to a red-tasseled ground, with long pendant tassels issuing from embroidered round deity heads and a single great tassel with three-dimensional plants and flowers along its lower border. This mind-boggling piece is Photo 69 in Ubbelohde-Doering (1954).

haps because, now woven for Inca masters, their significance was lost or changed.

Featherwork variety suggests active trade with tropical areas and the keeping of captive birds. John P. O'Neill (1984, 146ff.), a specialist in Amazonian birds, identifies the most used types as Muscovy duck, various parrots, macaws, and the Paradise Tanager. Feathers were stitched onto tabards (tunic-type garment with unsewn sides) and matching crown–necklace sets with checkerboard color blocks suggestive of Inca pieces. Many of the best featherwork and woven textiles occur in Central Coast Chancay burials, perhaps due to intensified trade just before the Chimú conquest of Chancay or as grave goods of newly resident Chimú lords (O'Neill 1984, 160).

These studies open new avenues of interpretation. After the Inca conquest, Chimú tunics became longer, probably the result of Inca influence. Chimú textiles appear increasingly in South Coast sites, possibly the result of Inca population relocations or redistribution of collected mita-produced textiles as rewards to local leaders. Chimú featherwork continued as the Inca maintained tropical-feather trade. As Rowe (1984, 185–187) notes, definition of Chimú textile style furthers its recognition in other areas and the separation of Chimú influence from local styles, plus hypotheses about trade and effects of conquest that can be corroborated through ceramic, architectural, and other studies.

Adobe Sculpture

Chimú stone and wood sculpture is scarce. The preferred medium was readily available adobe low-relief decoration on architectural walls. Chan Chan's Gran Chimú, Rivero, and Tschudi compounds, the Uhle Group, and nearby Huaca Esmeralda and Huaca del Dragón have adobe friezes of textile-like designs, plants, animals, and humans with occasional Moche and Huari similarities. The Burr Frieze, uncovered in 1969 as part of a longer panel exposed between 1904–1908 and subsequently destroyed by 1925 El Niño rains, is a particularly complex example. Its background was excised through wet plaster leaving rows of plants, crescent-topped running, spear-toting birds and humans, and wavy bands of fish and crabs, all with added incised or

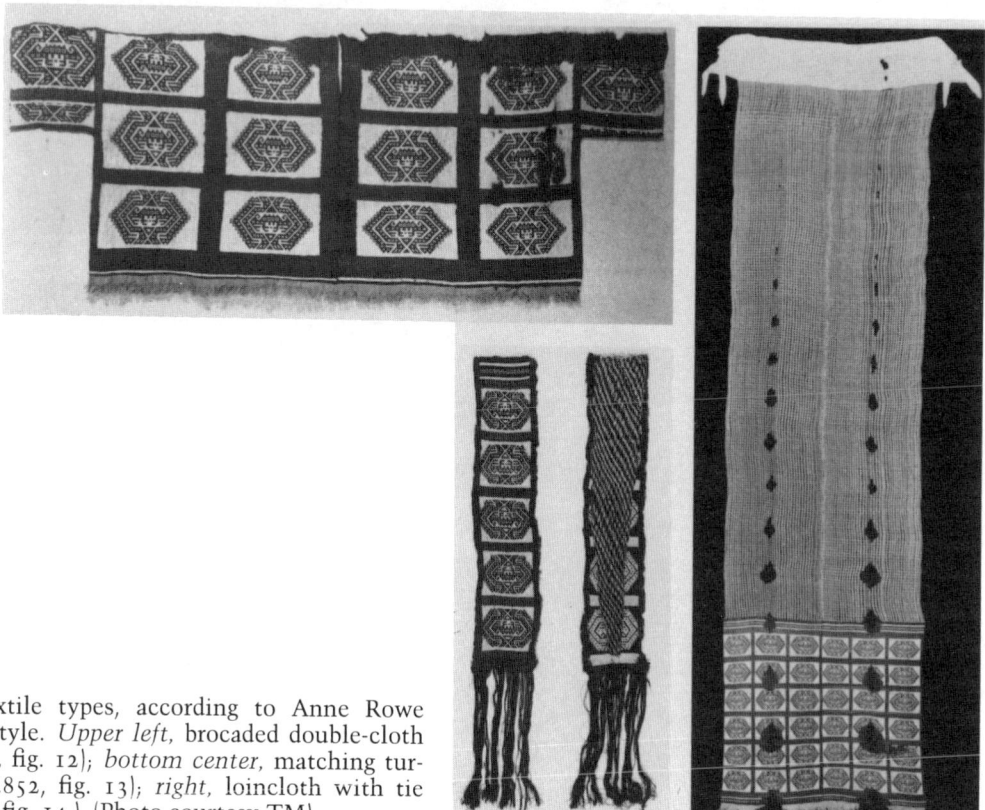

13.4a. Chimú textile types, according to Anne Rowe (1984): Bird Lot style. *Upper left,* brocaded double-cloth tunic (TM.91.851, fig. 12); *bottom center,* matching turban ends (TM.91.852, fig. 13); *right,* loincloth with tie band (TM.91.853, fig. 14.). (Photo courtesy TM)

B

C

13.4b and c. Chimú textile types, according to Anne Rowe (1984): (*b, above*) Toothed Crescent–style tunic of tapestry weave (TM.1961.3.4, pl. 12); (*c, below*) Pelican-style tunic of plain weave with brocading and complex alternate gauzes (TM.1969.39.2, pl. 13). (Photos courtesy TM)

cane-end-stamped details, representing a complex mythical scene (Hoyt and Moseley 1969, 52).

Elements of Style

Chimú design is more limited than the Moche repertoire, and Moche realism and individuality are subsumed into stylized stereotypes, harbingers of a fixed "imperial" style in which confor-

mity of concept facilitated administration by a central authority. Parallels in our own time are state-influenced sculpture and murals in mainland China and the U.S.S.R.

There is also marked similarity between designs in different media. Motifs shared by textiles and adobe reliefs are Paracas-like falling deities and frontal humans carrying stacked-triangle devices, profile humans with serrated

13.4d. Chimú textile types, according to Anne Rowe (1984): Plain Crescent style. *Upper left*, tunic (TM.91.557, fig. 112); *upper right*, loincloth (TM.91.560, fig. 114); *bottom*, mantle (TM.91.556, fig. 117). (Photo courtesy TM)

head streamers like the trailing headdresses of Paracas–Nasca textiles, profile Tiahuanacoid running, winged (tailed?) staff-bearing humans, and quadrupeds with clothespin mouths and arched multistrand tails like those on Tiahuanaco Gateway of the Sun runners and Huari polichrome pottery. On the Huaca del Dragón, two-headed dragons with a rainbowlike shared torso hold a human figure by the head. Some adobe reliefs have latticework or profile birds with stepped outlines as if imitating laid brickwork or angular textile designs. Their patterned interlocking and horizontal or diagonal-row repeating figures are purely decorative with little hint of interaction or relationships, as on Chimú textiles where similar motifs create complex positional and color alternations. On the other hand, motifs like the crescent-headdressed tumi-handle figure, sometimes identified as Ñaymlap, the Lambayeque dynasty founder (Figure 13.2), represent continuity: His splayed feet recall Tiahuanaco/Huari conventions and his staffs even earlier Chavín models. More excavations like those at Pacatnamú (Donnan 1986) are needed to document the Moche–Huari/Tiahuanaco–Chimú transition and tighten the definition of the several elements currently included under the umbrella rubric of "Chimú art."

CHAPTER 14

THE INCA

BACKGROUND

Origins

THE Inca probably began as one of several small groups, among them possible Huari descendants, that immigrated to the Cuzco Valley (Map 10). Like the Aztecs, who legitimized their rule by claiming earlier Toltec descent, the Inca said they had prior Aymara–Tiahuanaco roots (Urton 1990, 3–4).

Legends collected by Guaman Poma de Ayala, Sarmiento de Gamboa, and other Spanish chroniclers describe the creation of the sun, moon, stars, and the first humans by the deity Viracocha at Tiahuanaco, near Lake Titicaca. In one version, the first Inca ruler, Manco Capac, rose from the lake and traveled underground to Pacariqtambo ("The Inn of Origins"), located 30 kilometers (18.6 miles) south of Cuzco, and then on to Cuzco itself. In another version, Inca ancestors emerged from Tampu T'oqo ("Window Inn"), a mountain with three caves near Pacariqtambo, as a set of four brothers and four sisters who intermarried and organized the surrounding populace into ten *ayllus* (social factions: perhaps lineages) before migrating northward.

Along the way, Manco Capac and his sister–wife Mama Ocllu produced a son, Sinchi Roca, and the remaining brothers were eliminated or turned into huacas (sacred stone shrines). As a result, the legendary founding of Cuzco fell to Manco Capac, his four sisters, and Sinchi Roca, who ruled following his father. Scholars of mythohistory such as Gary Urton, who have plotted the migration route geographically, link some of the stopover places to modern towns and mountains through references from sixteenth-century documents in which claimants sought "strategic accommodations" within the Spanish Colonial administration by manipulating the old legends (Urton 1990, 124–127). Urton and others also correlate important stopovers to archaeological sites and Inca shrines located near Cuzco and Pacariqtambo. Pre-Inca pottery called Killke Ware supports a southern origin with its combination of Huari with early highland and proto-Inca elements (Lumbreras, 1974, 215).

Development and Expansion

Under their first rulers (called Inca, or "lord"), the Inca jockeyed for position in the valley. The eighth Inca, Viracocha Inca, conquered nearby Cavina, Canchi, and Cana peoples and then moved beyond Cuzco to subdue Calca in the Urubamba Valley and Muina to the south.

Recognizing the threat of Inca expansion, the Chanka confederation in the Apurimac Basin to the west decided to attack Cuzco. Viracocha Inca and his son/co-regent Urcon fled, leaving Cuzco's defense to a rival son, Pachacuti ("Earth Cacaclysm"). In a spirited battle, aided according to official Inca accounts by divine forces, Pachacuti repulsed the invaders around 1438 and had himself coronated. Rapidly consolidating his power, he expanded Cuzco and defined the geographic domains and responsibilities of regional chiefs. With a beefed-up army, he conquered the fortress city/*pucara* of Ollantaytambo (Map 10) in the Vilcañota Valley and sites in the high jungles of the eastern montaña, assigning them annual tributes of gold, silver, and the narcotic coca leaf. He then pacified the Chanka homelands and moved south, defeating the Lupaca and Colla kingdoms near Lake Titicaca. His younger brother, Capac Yupanqui, invaded Huanuco and Huamachucho in the North Highlands. In the subsequent battle for Cajamarca (Map 10), the Inca had their first contact with coastal Chimú warriors who came to aid their highland ally. Under Topa Inca, Pachacuti's youngest son, the Inca moved further north to conquer the Cañari and Palta Indians of Ecuador in 1466, establishing a regional capital at Tumibamba (Map 10). The Inca now controlled all Andean water sources to the coastal kingdoms below.

Continuing northward through Quito, the Inca finally turned to the coast and subdued Tumbes (Map 10), a northern Chimú tributary. Here they were in ideal position for a downcoast invasion of Chimor. By synchronizing pincer forays from highland Huamachucho and their Rimac Valley Cuismancu kingdom ally to the south, the Inca surrounded and starved out the Chimú, conquering Chan Chan in 1465. They then moved downcoast and subdued the Ica–Chincha kingdom. By 1474, the Inca empire of Tahuantinsuyu, Land of the Four Quarters (Chinchasuyu to the north, Collasuyu to the south, Antisuyu to the east, and Cuntisuyu to the west), had acquired its final configuration. Subsequent Incas had to cope with rebellions and internal power struggles, but until the Spaniards arrived, the empire held firm, covering over 2,700 miles (4,344 kilometers) with a population of 3-1/2 to 7 million.

Inca Culture

Numerous ethnohistoric sources describe Inca culture and the administration of Tahuantinsuyu.[1] Their lists of Inca rulers and accounts of important battles, myths, and legends come from oral traditions recalled by *quipumayocs*, professional word-rememberers whose recitations served in lieu of written history and are difficult to corroborate in the archaeological record. Other vestiges of Inca religious festivals and beliefs survive among their contemporary Quechua descendants. Excavation documents Inca terracing, irrigation, roadbuilding, relocation of populations, and warehouse redistribution of subsistence and tribute goods. From this combination of sources, we see the Inca at their height under their ruler Huayna Capac (1493–1525) as a people well adapted to their highland home, administering a vast empire from Cuzco.

Subsistence Base

Then as today, women planted dozens of potato types in holes made by men using the *taclla* footplow. Potatoes were cut up, stamped, and freeze-dried as *chuño*. Quinoa (a highland grain), the tuber oca, and corn, a more recent introduction, were cooked, and corn was fermented into mildly intoxicating chicha, which is still imbibed by Andean peasants today. Coca leaves became offerings or, chewed with lime, dulled human hunger. Guinea pigs and llama meat provided animal protein; the latter, cut into strips and dried, became *charqui*, similar to beef jerky, an easily portable nonspoiling food source when on the move. Domesticated llamas

---

[1] These include sixteenth-century Spanish conquistadores and clergymen (Cieza de León, Pedro and Hernando Pizarro, de Acosta, de Avila, and Sarmiento de Gamboa plus authors of *visitas* supplying information on geography, demography, and natural resources to the crown) and native Indian historians (Tito Cusi Yupanqui, Guaman Poma de Ayala, Santa Cruz Pachacuti, Garcilaso de la Vega).

were both pack animals and offerings, and their fur plus that of the wild alpaca and fine-haired vicuña were important textile fibers.

Inca land distribution was allocated by the ruling Inca for communal use by the residential lineages of each district. Surplus produce was collected by state officials for temple offerings and redistribution at the great public festivals. A careful annual census using the *quipu*, a mnemonic device of pendant cords bearing differently shaped, colored, and positioned knots, tallied changes in populations, herd sizes, crop production, and the like that formed the basis for land reallotment by local officials.

Social Organization

Inca society was hierarchical, with clear-cut social classes. At the top, the ruling Inca was descended directly from the sun, Inti, through Manco Capac, the first Inca. To keep the royal bloodline pure and avoid intrigues over succession, later Incas took one of their own sisters as *coya* or principal wife and designated the most capable of her sons as heir-apparent. Occasionally, rival half-brothers, offsprings of lesser wives, developed followings and claimed the throne.

The Inca population was divided into residentially localized, corporate landholding groups called *ayllus* or *panacas* that were probably related through matrilineages or other kinship ties. The ten royal ayllus consisted of the Inca's descendants with the exception of his immediate successor, who formed his own panaca consisting of his direct descendants. Royal ayllu members were privileged to wear huge gold ear spools that distended their lobes and earned them the Spanish nickname *Orejones* ("big ears").

A secondary nobility consisted of "Incas by Privilege," whose women (*iñaga*) were affiliated with the royal ayllus through intermarriage, and whose men often ruled as *curacas* (lords) in outlying or conquered lands (Urton, 1990, 28, 60). The ten nonroyal ayllus were descendants of the original ayllus created by the Inca ancestors from local ethnic populations living near Tampu T'oqo, their mythical place of emergence. Each was hierarchically ranked and associated with one of Cuzco's two major ayllu groupings or moieties, with a residential suyu or quadrant, and with a particular series of shrines (Urton 1990, 57–63, 122–123). Exceptionally beautiful girls from among them became chosen women (*Acllas*), occasionally gaining status as sacrifices, secondary wives to the Inca, or permanently chaste Virgins of the Sun (*Mamaconas*) who lived in special convents where they wove textiles and prepared chicha for festivals (Zuidema 1990, 55–59). Exceptional boys became *Yanacona*, court pages or temple attendants. Ordinary farmers and craftsworkers also belonged to ayllus affiliated with the upper (Hanan Cuzco or northern), or the lower (Hurin Cuzco or southern) moieties.

Ayllus owned land communally, cooperated in public-labor projects, and made collective, corporate decisions. Ancestors were considered active members, consulted for their input in guiding the group's fortunes. Within the royal ayllu, deceased rulers were intermediaries to the gods. Their mummies were brought out annually from the Coricancha Sun Temple in Cuzco to be reclothed, fed, given chicha, and carried in litters by their panaca descendants in public festivals while singers recited their glorious deeds.

Panacas consisted of the sisters, cousins, and other relatives of a dead Inca directed by his second son as pachaca or mayordomo of his estates. The first son usually inherited rulership and obtained wealth through conquest and tribute to sustain his own panaca and ancestral cult. Panacas ritually cared for his mummy, continued to farm his lands and lived, died, and were buried within the dead Inca's residential compound. Their financial security was guaranteed: As Burr Cartwright Brundage (1967, 43) observes: "To serve an *illapa* [royal mummy] was a sure thing." At the Spanish Conquest, the royal Capac ayllu panacas formed two moieties, with compounds of the first five Incas in Lower (Hurin) Cuzco and those from Inca Roca to Huascar in Upper (Hanan) Cuzco. Conrad and Demarest (1984) observe that panacas tied up land and tribute labor that otherwise would have reverted to the state, thus creating shortages in an "inherently unstable" system that accelerated the Inca demise.

Religion

Inca religion venerated Inti the Sun as sustainer of crops and ancestor of rulers. The walls of his temple, Coricancha, were covered with sheet gold, and a solid-gold, rayed face disc symbolized his life-nurturing sweat, heat, and light. Mummies of past Incas, his descendants, stood to either side. In a nearby room, a silver huaca of his consort Moon was attended by mummies of past coyas (royal wives). An outside garden contained life-size gold and silver replicas of the humans, plants, and animals he nurtured. The Inti Raymi Festival, celebrating his returning energy at winter solstice, is still observed today.

The reigning Inca initiated Inti Raymi with thanksgiving llama sacrifices at mountain shrines and fertilized the land with their blood after breaking the soil with a golden taclla. As Inti-incarnate, he moved down a road symbolizing the Sun's path accompanied by a beautifully adorned white llama representing the *napa* or primordial llama, took prophesies from the royal mummies, rewarded attending curacas with Inca daughters as wives, and redistributed lands, herds, and crops (Brundage 1967, 130–136).

The Ceque System. Lesser deities were worshipped in smaller Cuzco temples seen by the Spaniards and at a series of huacas or shrines that radiated out in forty-one imaginary lines (*ceques,* or "rays" in Quechua) from the Coricancha ("Golden Enclosure" of the Sun Temple) in Cuzco like rays generated by Coricancha's golden sun image, or pendant strings on a giant quipu (Zuidema 1990, 70–75). Over 400 huacas, keyed to days in the agricultural year and to mythical ancestors, places, and events, were strung out within a 12-mile (19.3 kilometer) radius on ceques that were associated with important astronomical observations and ranked in repeating sequences of three hierarchical categories according to the social class of the families and ayllus responsible for each huaca and its sacrifices.

The forty-one ceque shrine lines were grouped into *suyus* or quadrants that determined the boundaries of the four quarters of the wider Inca empire. These quadrants also functioned as a moiety system, dividing Cuzco into two distinct population groupings (moieties or *sayas,* meaning "halves"), with the southeast-to-southwest ceques in the Qollasuyu and Kuntisuyu quadrants forming Hurin Cuzco, the city's southern moiety, and the northwest–northeast Chinchasuyu and Antisuyu quadrants combining as Hanan Cuzco, the northern, upper moiety. Thus ceque shrines and attendant rituals were carefully keyed to social and residential divisions, and "in effect, the floor of the Valley of Cuzco had been mapped out in an annual ritual calendar" (Isbell 1978, 194). The southern ceques were regarded as sources of agricultural and human fertility because of their association with constellations tied to the planting season and the legendary area of Inca origins (Urton, 1990, 59).

Today these huacas are overgrown, eradicated, or at least disguised under missionary influence. Using village names, old maps, and recorded myths, Dutch-born anthropologist R. Thomas Zuidema (1964, 1977) has located many of the 328 named huacas listed by Spanish chronicler Acosta in 1590 that correspond to Cuzco's four quarters.

Economic Organization

One of the institutions that held Tahuantinsuyu together was mita, a labor tax wherein all ordinary citizens except priests and temple virgins owed the government labor hours. Craftsworkers fulfilled their mita with textiles and goldwork; subjects in distant provinces sent in tribute or maintained the roads, bridges, and mountain passes that were Tahuantinsuyu's nexus of communication. This network facilitated an empire-wide distribution system with local storage centers from which crops, herds, and textiles could flow to remote areas during famines or earthquakes and in normal times brought highland grains, potatoes, and llamas to the lowlands in exchange for maritime products, corn, cotton, or tropical montaña drugs, woods, pelts, and feathers (Murra 1956; Masuda, Shimada, and Morris, eds., 1985). The quipu documented mita work hours, types, and quantities of goods, demographic data, and the logistics of exchange.

Nature of the Inca State

Scholars differ as to whether the Inca were a benign paternalistic state or ruled with a gloved iron hand. Following military conquest, they permitted local customs and leaders (curacas) to remain but brought curaca offspring to Cuzco, ostensibly for training in Inca ways, but they were de facto hostages to encourage parental loyalty (Rowe 1961, 318). Population relocation of *mitimae* groups was another technique. Rebellious subjects were transferred to similar ecological zones for resettlement among pacified loyal groups and replaced with pro-Inca converts. Entire colonies of skilled artisans from some areas were moved to Cuzco. The spread of Quechua as a lingua franca, plus Inca military protection, architecture, techniques of llama husbandry and corn growing, and state art and religion also solidified a vast empire composed of disparate peoples and ecological zones (Collier, Rosaldo, and Wirth 1982).

ARCHITECTURE

Excavation of Inca architecture benefits from sixteenth-century eyewitness descriptions and explanations by Inca informants of its history and functions. These fill vital gaps, for many Indian structures were razed, whereas time, erosion, earthquakes, and looters have taken additional toll. Nineteenth-century explorers Squier and Bandelier photographed and measured what remained. Since then, excavations and researches by Max Uhle, John Rowe, Dorothy Menzel, Wendell Bennett, John Murra, Gordon Willey, Luís Valcarcel, Ramiros Matos Mendieta, Craig Morris, Luís Lumbreras, Richard Schaedel, and younger scholars currently in the field and combing archives have opened new interrelationships between Inca architecture and culture.[2]

Construction Techniques and Styles

The Inca are famous for their massive, beautifully fitted stonework. By A.D. 1200, the South Highland Chankas and Collas were erecting high-domed round or square funerary towers of dressed-stone blocks with corbel-arch ceilings for burial of royal families using techniques learned from the builders of Tiahuanaco. Their incorporation into Collasuyu supplied the Inca with skilled mita stoneworkers and introduced innovations such as fitting large convex-based stones on the concave upper sections of others and securing them laterally with tenons and sockets or H-shaped copper crampons. Blocks

weighing 150 tons (136 metric tons) were separated from matrix deposits with wedges and hauled on rollers using ropes attached to ledges on their surfaces that were later abraded flat. Huge polygonal stones with up to twelve facets were so closely joined in jigsaw interlock, without mortar that a razor will not fit between them (Figure 14.1a). In another style, rectangular blocks were laid in regular courses with joins mitered inward or, on sacred buildings such as Coricancha, the Golden Enclosure for the Temple of the Sun, left smooth and almost imperceptible (Figure 14.1b). The result was simple and severe, devoid of the incised decoration and tenoned heads of Chavín or the elaborately carved facades of the Maya. The size and workmanship astonished the Spaniards and was impressive even on minor structures, walls, and canal faces (Protzen 1985).

Hand-molded loaf-shaped adobes laid in mortar-on-stone foundations flat-side-up formed upper sections of both high-status and ordinary buildings (Moorehead 1979, 66–67). An example near Cuzco is the one-room hip-roofed adobe Colonial palace of Sayri Tupac, or Incahuasi, with an Inca-style entrance of double-jamb niches with wooden lintels. Another is the Temple of Viracocha in San Pedro de Cacha, south of Cuzco, a long two-halled structure divided by a center wall with ten doors. Both exhibit Inca wall niches, thickened bases, and repeat elements in adobe. For *chucllas* (peasant huts), *pirca* (fieldstone) was used. Wooden bosses protrude at the gables to tie down thatch roofs. Similar house types and construction techniques continue in rural Bolivia and Peru today.

The Cuzco, or imperial, style was developed after Pachacuti's conquest of the Chanka and continued by his successors. Its characteristics are walls of huge, perfectly joined polygonal or rectangular stones and trapezoidal inward-sloping windows and doors with shortened lintels, for stability during frequent earthquakes. The style confirms Inca presence at local administrative centers from Ecuador to Bolivia (Gasparini and Margolies 1980, 5–6).

Site Plans and Distinctive Architectural Features

Inca urban and town layouts are more uniform than those of diversified coastal cultures. Fixed

---

[2] See Gasparini and Margolies (1980) and Hemming and Ranney (1982) for well-illustrated summaries of Inca architecture and particular sites. Stierlin (1984, 197–222) has additional information and excellent color photographs.

14.1a. Inca polygonal stonework at Tambo Machay, near Cuzco. (Hemming and Ranney 1982, p. 47; photo courtesy Edward Ranney)

14.1b. Rectangular coursework in Coricancha wall, at Tambo Machay, near Cuzco. (Hemming 1982, p. 81; photo by Martín Chambi, courtesy Manuel Chambi)

elements include main palaces, plazas, a sun temple, and residences of Chosen Women (*acllahuasi*). Their particular combination varies, perhaps because Inca expansion was too rapid to develop a standard plan (Bonavia 1978, 394). Within the palaces, both in Cuzco and in provincial centers along the royal highway, vast ceremonial halls (kallankas) could hold thousands of people while sheltering and feeding travelers or during the great public festivals. Some, such as the enormous 25-by-85 foot (78 by 26 meter) kallanka at Incallacta near Cochabamba in Bolivia, probably had multiple rows of wooden columns or pillars to support their broad-beam roofs (Hemming and Ranney 1982, 35–36).

Architects deliberately adapted site plans to local topography, integrating structures with surrounding landscape (Figure 14.2), and exposing its presumed spiritually powerful features as huacas, shrines for veneration or sacrifice.[3] The Inca also built new settlements in conquered areas to store goods, control raw materials and water sources, and maintain military

[3]Of all the books about Inca architecture, John Hemming and Ranney's (1982) *Monuments of the Incas* best conveys this interrelationship between architecture and topography through Edward Ranney's sensitive, intelligently planned, magnificently developed black-and-white photos.

14.2. Machu Picchu (Hemming and Ranney 1982, p. 132; photo by Martín Chambi, courtesy Manuel Chambi)

staging areas. In smaller villages, local building styles prevailed, with few architectural traces of Inca presence.

Cuzco

The capital of Cuzco, northwest of Lake Titicaca, nestles in a valley of the Cordillera Oriental at an altitude of 3,500 meters (11,483 feet). According to Inca historians, Pachacuti rebuilt Cuzco, straightened her rivers within stone-lined canals, added reclaimed swampland, and settled the panacas into Chimú-like stone compounds a scant 60 or 70 years before the Spanish arrival. Sixteenth-century sources describe a city of 25,000, its houses set on slopes along narrow paved streets with central stone-lined water channels and room for a single horseman to either side. In spite of earthquakes, removal of stones for Colonial structures, and the fire of 1535 when the Incas tried to recapture Cuzco, much of the original layout can be reconstructed from remaining foundations (Kubler 1952, 460) and today's city streets.

Site Plan. Cuzco's plan (Map 12) is interpreted by many, but not all, scholars as a west-facing puma with the Huatanay River as its northwest/southeast axis and the Tullumayo

River as backbone. The body triangle between them contained sacred structures and the residence compounds of perhaps 9,000 Inca nobles. A third river, the Chunchumayo at the southern edge of the plebian area, converges with the Huatanay and Tullumayo at Cuzco's southeast corner of Pumac Chupan, "The Puma's Tail."

Cuzco's other axis was a road that was perpendicular to the Huatanay with exits to the Antisuyu (northeast) and Cuntisuyu (southeast) quarters of the empire. Roads to Collasuyu (the Bolivian road) and Chinchasuyu (the Ecuadorian road) branched off from the city's southeastern and northwestern sides. The main axes intersected at the puma's heart, a large public square divided by stone-slab bridges over the Huatanay into a southern Cusipata ("Joy Plaza") for celebrations and northern Huacaypata ("Holy Plaza") for rituals.

The sacred Huacaypata square contained a gold-covered conical stone for libations to the Sun. Around it stood the Kiswarkancha (to creator-god Viracocha) and Pucamarka (thunder god) temples, the Acllahuasi (Residence of the Chosen Women), and the walled compounds (*canchas*) of past and the current Inca—the "innards" or vital organs of the puma's body, so to speak. Pachacuti divided the royal panaca com-

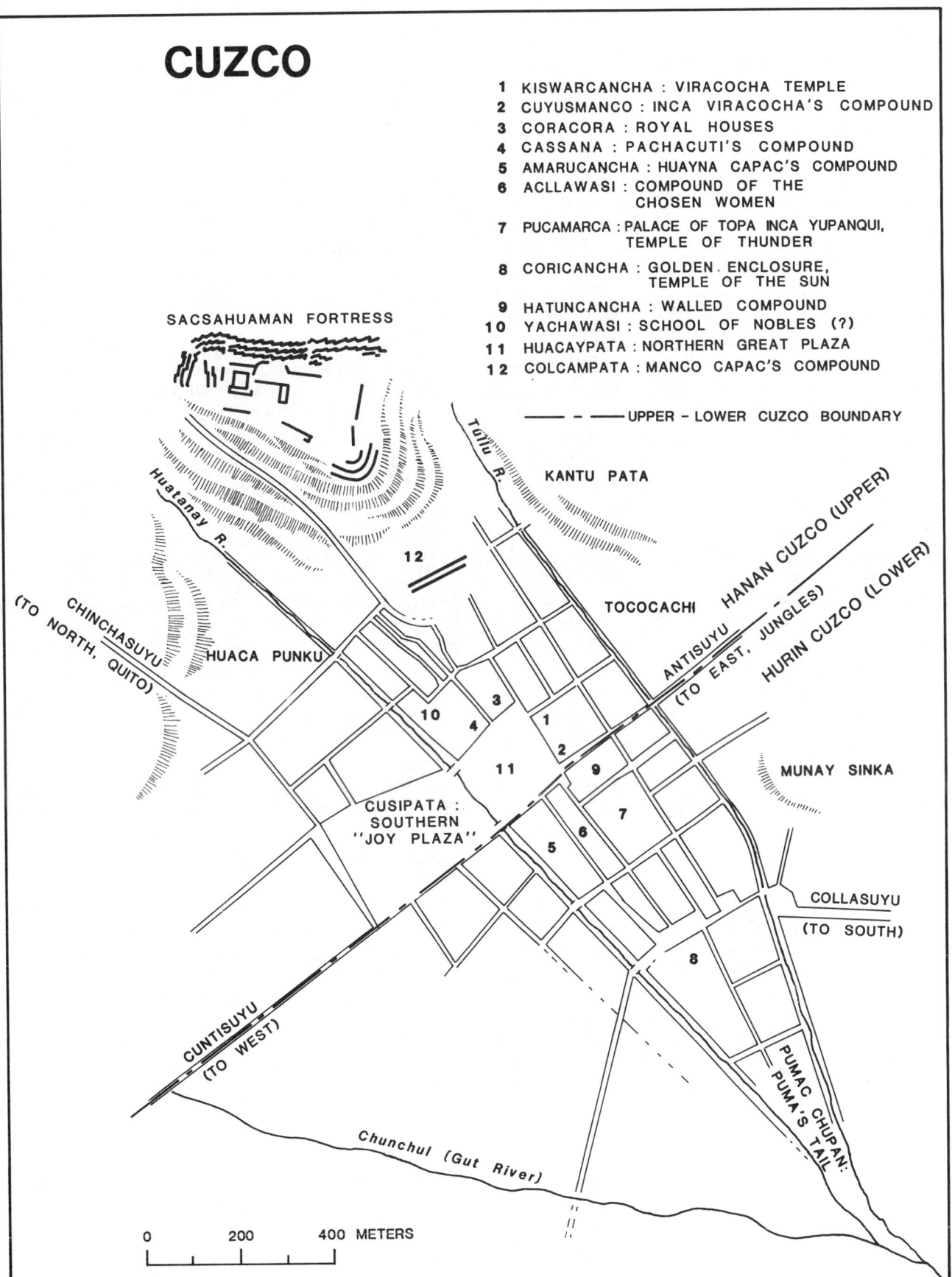

CUZCO

1 KISWARCANCHA : VIRACOCHA TEMPLE
2 CUYUSMANCO : INCA VIRACOCHA'S COMPOUND
3 CORACORA : ROYAL HOUSES
4 CASSANA : PACHACUTI'S COMPOUND
5 AMARUCANCHA : HUAYNA CAPAC'S COMPOUND
6 ACLLAWASI : COMPOUND OF THE
            CHOSEN WOMEN
7 PUCAMARCA : PALACE OF TOPA INCA YUPANQUI,
            TEMPLE OF THUNDER
8 CORICANCHA : GOLDEN ENCLOSURE,
            TEMPLE OF THE SUN
9 HATUNCANCHA : WALLED COMPOUND
10 YACHAWASI : SCHOOL OF NOBLES (?)
11 HUACAYPATA : NORTHERN GREAT PLAZA
12 COLCAMPATA : MANCO CAPAC'S COMPOUND

——— – ——— UPPER – LOWER CUZCO BOUNDARY

SACSAHUAMAN FORTRESS

KANTU PATA

Tullu R.

Huatanay R.

TOCOCACHI

ANTISUYU HANAN CUZCO (UPPER)
(TO EAST, JUNGLES)
HURIN CUZCO (LOWER)

CHINCHASUYU
(TO NORTH, QUITO)

HUACA PUNKU

12

10   4   3   1

11   2   9

MUNAY SINKA

CUSIPATA :
SOUTHERN
"JOY PLAZA"

5   6   7

COLLASUYU
(TO SOUTH)

8

CUNTISUYU
(TO WEST)

PUMAC CHUPAN:
PUMA'S TAIL

Chunchul (Gut River)

0   200   400 METERS

Map 12. Cuzco: main plazas, compounds, and Hanan and Hurin divisions

pounds into two moieties, assigning those of earlier Incas to Lower/Hurin Cuzco south of the Antisuyu–Cuntisuyu axis and those of subsequent Incas to Upper/Hanan Cuzco to the north within the triangle body. The rest of the non-noble populace lived in local barrio neighborhoods of the "legs" area across the river.

Coricancha. In the southern part of Hurin Cuzco, toward the tail and next to the Tambo Cancha palace of the first Inca, Manco Capac, Pachacuti remodeled Coricancha, the Golden Enclosure of Inti the Sun (Hemming and Ranney 1982, 78–87, including photos). This important religious center consisted of between five and seven thatch-roofed temple structures set on platforms around an open court in a walled compound, or *cancha*. Its outer walls of fitted stone were covered with over 700 gold plates, stripped off and melted down for distribution to Pizarro's soldiers in 1533. Until the earthquake of 1925, remnants of its magnificently constructed wall of precisely curved ashlars supported the Church of Santo Domingo, built directly above (Figure 14.1b).

Inside, double rooms on the east and west faced a large 35-meter square (114.8 foot) patio and contained Sun and Moon images and the mummies of past Sun-incarnate rulers and their coyas. Other rooms housed over 200 mamacona virgins, including sisters or daughters of the ruling Inca consecrated as the Sun's wives and weavers of royal rainments, plus children destined for sacrifice. Basins held water from an adjoining spring, and the Inti image was fed at an *usnu* (altar) with food and chicha thrown into a sacred fire. Outside were corrals for sacrificial llamas and the Choqquepampa or "Field of Pure Gold," with gold llamas and life-size shepherds with their slings.

Coricancha was a major focus of Inca ritual and architecture. Spanish chronicler Pedro Pizarro describes the daily feeding of the mummies of past Incas in the great square and public offerings of burned food and chicha libations to the idol of Inti the Sun when they were brought out daily from their Coricancha quarters by Villac Umu, a high priest dressed in beautiful textiles woven by the mamaconas. Facing each other across the courtyard were two temples dedicated, according to chronicler Garcilaso de la Vega, to the Moon and the planet Venus and other constellations. Niches in temple walls

facing the courtyard were inlaid with gold and precious gems as viewing seats for the Inca during important Inti rituals and suggest a cosmic interpretation for Coricancha as "Center of the Center of the Universe" (Hemming and Ranney 1982, 86). The terraced garden at the west side of the Sun Temple was the site of annual agricultural rituals during which mamaconas both planted and harvested life-sized cornstalks and ears of hammered gold. One of these stalks, plus a gold sculpture "the size of a four-year-old boy," which may have been Coricancha's sun idol, were carried by Hernando Pizarro to Spain, only to be melted down into coins by King Charles V (Hemming and Ranney 1982, 80).

Sacsahuaman. The puma's head, on the hill of Sacsahuaman northwest of the city (Map 12), was the huge fortresslike complex of Intihuasi, "House of the Sun," a second solar temple that also served as the center of government and that only Incas could enter. Its structure resembles that of other pucaras or high places of refuge overlooking cities. Pachacuti began its construction, and Huayna Capac completed it shortly before the Spanish arrival. Cieza de León, in 1550, marveled at its size and estimated that 20,000 men were needed to build it.

Sacsahuaman's base was cut into living rock above deep ravines that surround it on three sides. Its northern flank is protected by three successively terraced zigzag walls of enormous 5-meter-high (16.4 foot), up to 126-ton, polygonal blocks facilitating crossfire and extending east–west for 410 meters (448.3 yards). Their original height is unknown, for upper stones were stripped away by the Spaniards. On the hilltop are foundations of buildings described by Cieza as the palaces and storehouses from which the Inca administered Tawantinsuyu. Multiple square and rectangular rooms appear to have been storerooms for weapons, with the towers of Sallacmarka and Paucamarka as garrisons for troops.

Sacsahuaman's triple walls overlook a wide, flat parade ground. Beyond it, an undulating striated outcrop called Rodadero Hill (Sachuna) bears a double row of carved steplike platforms called *sahuacurinca* ("Throne of the Inca") that, according to Spanish sources, the Inca used as an *usnu*/altar for llama sacrifice and viewing of festivities and martial displays below. The yearly Inti Raymi Festival is still held in the same parade ground below Sacsahuaman each June. Other unusual rock forms nearby were also reshaped as sacred huacas.

Administrative Centers

To facilitate administration of their far-flung empire, the Inca built regional centers beside state roads near important conquered highland towns, with central plazas containing a tall, rectangular-stone usnu platform used as a reviewing stand or site for chicha and animal sacrifices to the Sun.

Surrounding the usnu were residences and rows of gabled, single-door hillside warehouses and granaries. Their abrupt appearance, standardized plans, absence of cemeteries, and rapid collapse at the Inca conquest indicate staffing by mitimae transients rather than by autochtonous settlements. Further confirmation comes from stockpiles of maize, quinoa, and potatoes at more than 2,000 storehouses in the Central Highlands where Inca storage-vessel sherds and standardized architecture indicate Inca planning with native Huanca production and management of crops (D'Altroy and Hastorf 1984). Inca storehouses were so well stocked that Spaniards lived for months on their contents.

One such center, Huanuco Pampa (Map 10) in the North–Central Highlands, was excavated in detail between 1963 and 1965 by the Institute of Andean Research (Morris and Thompson 1970, 1985). A 50-by-30 meter (164 by 98 foot) usnu with imperial-style masonry walls and a ramplike access stair dominates Huanuco's huge plaza as a symbol of Inca power. Over 1,000 one-story structures surround the plaza. To the east, the Inkawasi complex for administrators contains a stone-lined bath, residences, and long halls that may be counting houses with multiple doors for passage of cargo-laden llamas. The doors, of fine Inca masonry, form a direct sightline to the plaza's imposing usnu. North of the plaza, barracklike rooms may have been workshops for mita cloth production, with 497 small-windowed *qollqa* storerooms on the south side for stockpiling food. Weapons and defensive architecture are lacking. Excavators Morris and Thompson (1985, 346, 358–359) see Huanuco Pampa as a state-created artificial city of perhaps 5,000 people with Inca-style pottery (including tons of chicha jars for festivals and hospitality) and a few traces of local architecture.

The Royal Highway

Huanuco Pampa and similar centers (Cajamarca, Pumpu, Willka Waman, and Tumi Pampa) lie on the 5,200-kilometer (3,212 mile) highland trunk of the great Inca road system, the Qhapaq-Ñan, which ran from Ecuador through Cuzco to Lake Titicaca where it branched to northwestern Argentina and coastal Chile. A parallel coastal route extended for 4,000 kilometers (2,486 miles) from Ecuador to Chile, connecting coastal cities in which the Inca utilized existing adobe structures for administration: Here their pottery rather than architecture indicates their presence (Gasparini and Margolies 1980, 118–126). Link roads joined highland and coastal nodes like ladder rungs for a total distance of 12,000 kilometers (7,458 miles).

The Qhapaq-Ñan ("Beautiful Road") is one of the marvels of pre-columbian architecture and engineering (Hyslop 1984; von Hagen 1955). Built as an extension of earlier roads, its banked, paved sections were up to 8 meters (26 feet) wide and sometimes cut out of living rock. Tunnels, steep grades with stone steps, drainage gutters, and switchbacks accommodated changes in the rugged terrain, whereas rope suspension bridges spanned steep mountain gorges, rivers, and swamps. Some of these bridges continue to be used and repaired in the ancient manner today. Mital labor maintained the system and provided hundreds of *chasquis* or runners who, according to Cieza de León, could carry important messages in relays from Cuzco to Quito in Ecuador 2,000 kilometers (1,243 miles) away in 5 days (Stierlin 1984, 188).

Chasqui replacements were stationed at *tambo* roadhouses along 8- to 12-mile (12.8–19.3 kilometer) intervals. Here food and rest awaited incoming runners, and travelers moving at a slower pace, including royal processions, could spend the night. Excavation of the Tampu de Tunsukancha shows rooms and a small usnu for transients and their llama trains, homes of service personnel and a local curaca, and storehouses (Morris and Thompson 1985, 110–113).

At some locations, temple-fortresses called *pucaras* may have protected road junctures, nearby settlements, and headwaters of river valleys (Gasparini and Margolies 1980, 282–299). Paramonga, near the Central Coast Pativilca River, is a huge complex of terraced adobe walls that may have been a Chimú bastion protecting the coastal road from attack at their southern frontier. The Inca later crowned its summit with a temple. Far to the north near Tumibamba, a second capital established by Huayna Capac near Cuenca in Ecuador, the pucara of Ingapirca, consists of imperial-style stone-masonry structures surrounding a high-walled oval platform bearing twin back-to-back temples. Another possibly defensive construction is the zigzag-walled Puma Marka near Ollantaytambo, perhaps a provincial capital, in the South Highland Urubamba Valley 13 miles (20.9 kilometers) from Cuzco, still under construction when the Spaniards arrived and occupied by the Incas until 1539.

Machu Picchu

Fifty-five kilometers (34.1 miles) from Ollantaytambo, the famous "Lost City of the Incas," Machu Pichu ("Old Mountain": Map 10), spills over a 2,430-foot-high (740.6 meter) saddle of Huayna Picchu Peak, high above the Urubamba River (Figure 14.2). Begun by Pachacuti around A.D. 1450 and completed by his son Tupac Yupanqui, it was finally abandoned in 1572 after the execution of the last Inca Tupac Amaru and rediscovered and excavated in 1911 by North American archaeologist Hiram Bingham (1930).

One approaches the site along a mountain trail leading to a fortified gate and seven guardhouses. To either side, agricultural terraces capable of producing two to three annual crops and stairs leading to rainwater catchment basins carved in living rock cling to the steep slopes. Above, stone-walled houses lacking only thatch roofs are grouped within walled enclosures to either side of broad terraced plazas that may reflect a dual division of facilities for two opposing moieties or clan groups similar to the Hanan and Hurin wards of Cuzco (Gasparini and Margolies 1980, 91–92; Hemming and Ranney 1982, 118–163). One plaza has polygonal masonry temples on three sides. Northwest of this temple compound, natural-rock outcroppings are carved into broad steps. Their upright rectangular monolith was christened Intihuatana ("Hitching Post of the Sun") by Bingham but

14.3. The curved Torreón wall and Cave of the Royal Tomb grotto, Machu Picchu. (Hemming and Ranney 1982, p. 135; photo by Martín Chambi, courtesy Manuel Chambi)

was more likely a huaca or an usnu than an astronomical sighting device.

Sculptured usnus and huacas are frequent at Machu Picchu. A high curved wall (the Torreón, Figure 14.3) surrounds the top of a huge granite outcropping that has been cut into an altar. A masonry wall (right) meets the boulder's overhang to form a grotto below, which contains sculpted steplike usnus (lower right). An enclosed compound of unusual rock formations across the Great Plaza north of the Intihuatana is called the "Temple of Pachamama," the female earth deity. Everywhere, block masonry fuses organically with the rugged topography in unexpected, moving ways, as human constructions merge physically with elements they were built to revere (Figure 14.4).

Machu Picchu was interpreted by its discoverer, Hiram Bingham, as a hidden refuge and a sacred center of Chosen Women, sustained by nonresident labor working the terraces, because clefts on its west side contain female bodies spanning several generations but only five

14.4. Organic aspects of Inca architecture: walls atop rock spur of the Prison Group. (Hemming and Raney 1982, p. 157; photo courtesy Edward Ranney)

males. Actually, it is only the largest of a series of high outposts above the Urubamba linked by Inca roads and may have been an outlying royal estate. In 1982 additional terraces, buildings, and thirty untouched tombs were found 3 miles (1.8 kilometers) away, and more will likely appear as the national park that includes Machu Picchu and seven other major sites is simultaneously restored and protected from tourist abuses (Meinsch 1985, 21).

Terracing

Inca architectural skills and planning also created complex terracing and irrigation systems. Reservoirs and dams distributed drinking water to major settlements and carried water to Cuzco's fountains and Coricancha's gardens. Colonial sources record that each basin was named and had its own huaca. In the North Coast, the Inca expanded Moche–Chimú canals and constructed new dams. Stone-walled highland terraces (*andenes*) were built by mita labor on slopes with up to 60° inclines, extending from hilltops to fertile river bottomlands and connected to irrigation canals and walled roads for removal of produce. Some were built of fieldstone, others of fitted polygonal blocks laid in imaginative zigzag or trapezoidal shapes as part of larger systems conforming to the natural topography of hills and valleys (Donkin 1979,

94–130; Niles 1983, 164–167). Terraces of cut limestone with stairs may have been pleasure gardens or plots for temple crops or exotic herbs for royal use.

The most extensive array of Inca terracing occurs above the Urubamba–Vilcanota valleys where clusters of small (probably mita) settlements nestle amid the andenes worked by their inhabitants. Pisac, a hilltop city 3,300 meters (10,826 feet) high, overlooks hundreds of terraces, with walled housing compounds, two cemeteries of cliff burial niches, a temple complex (Intihuatana) containing a circular walled usnu, and possible defensive towers to guard groups of storehouses (Moorehead 1979, Hemming and Raney 1982:88–93). John Rowe thinks that Pisac may have been Pachacuti's private preserve based on its size, layout, and imperial-style masonry. If so, one can imagine the Inca looking across miles of steep cultivated terraces and full storehouses with a sense of pride at his empire's well-planned logistics and the taming of the rugged Andes through mita labor.

Future architectural data will tell us more about how exchange and redistribution, communications, and a balance between local autonomy and imperial control contributed to the efficient administration of the empire.

ART

Inca standardization in architecture finds parallels in other Inca arts. Inca style in metalwork, pottery, and textiles was conservative, with little incentive for individuality and imagination. Its strong adherence to tradition continued even after the Conquest, so that pre-columbian and early Colonial pieces are hard to tell apart except when obviously Spanish motifs are present. Much Inca art was state art, produced during mita labor-hours and sent to Cuzco for temple use, edification of the nobility, gift giving by the Inca, or redistribution through local administrative centers. Recognizable through the uniformity, however, is the debt that particular arts owe to earlier regional states incorporated into the empire.

Metalwork

When the Inca conquered Chimor, they relocated entire guilds of Chimú metallurgists to Cuzco where they could impart their skills to Inca artisans working the enormous quantities of gold and silver panned and mined by mita labor. The amounts were staggering and far surpass the take from Mesoamerica: Lothrop, using tallies by Spanish chroniclers, estimates that the loot from Aztec Tenochtitlán and Moctezuma's possessions totaled 759 pounds of silver and 8,055 pounds of gold compared to 134,000 pounds of silver and 17,500 pounds of gold from the sack of Cuzco and the ransom of the captive Inca Atahualpa (quoted in Emmerich 1965, 52).

Status Indicators

Gold and silver were owned by the state and limited to religious objects and personal ornaments of the nobility: Commoners used objects of copper, bronze, clay, and wood. Inca rulers ate with golden utensils and drank from gold, silver, or tumbaga beakers. Their golden throne stools (tianas) were encrusted with gems and rested on a gold dias with holes for wooden, gold-sheathed litter poles so the Inca might lead processions or travel carried by fourteen to twenty strong men. The royal staff and crown, topped with a red double fringe, were also of gold. Palace walls in the royal compound bore golden plaques of embossed llamas, birds, and human figures, and sheet-gold sculpture filled wall-niche shrines. Outside, gardens contained gold and silver basins with running water for resident animals. The Inca and his "Orejon" nobles alone wore heavy gold, turquoise-inlaid ear spools. Even small ear cleaners and coca-powder dippers, topped by delicate birds and animals, were cast in gold. Coyas wore gold and silver jewelry and fastened their robes with long slender topu pins.

When an Inca died, some of his gold was used for a throne on which his sumptuously adorned mummy (malqui) could join others in the Coricancha beside the great Sun disc. Life-size gold portrait images (pucarinas) and effigies of his sacred animal or symbol (huauhqui) were cast for ancestor veneration by his panaca within his royal compound. Pucarinas were feted and fed as if they were still alive and carried to visit pucarinas in other compounds for great sentimental drinking sessions in which the exploits of the Incas they represented were extolled in recitation and song. A deceased Inca's remaining wealth sustained his panaca; his successor had to slowly amass new reserves to build and furnish his own palace. Spanish sources note that Huayna Capac (reigning 1493–1525) had still not completed his palace after 7 years' effort when the conquistadores arrived (Emmerich 1965, 47).

Religious Uses

Precious metals were also made into stereotyped votive figurines buried in the fields for fertility or placed with human offerings (Figure 14.5). They include little gold and silver llamas and doll-like standing figures holding corn and musical instruments or with hands to their chests. The latter were clothed with miniature wool skirts and capes complete with topu pins, tiny coca bags, and brilliant feather headpieces. One such brightly costumed figure was found in 1953 resting reverently against the huddled, frozen body of a child drugged and left as an offering on the 20,000-foot (6,096 meter) slopes of Cerro el Plomo near Santiago, Chile (McIntyre 1973, 731–738).

Techniques of Manufacture

Inca metallurgists also experimented with new techniques and alloys. They were masters of

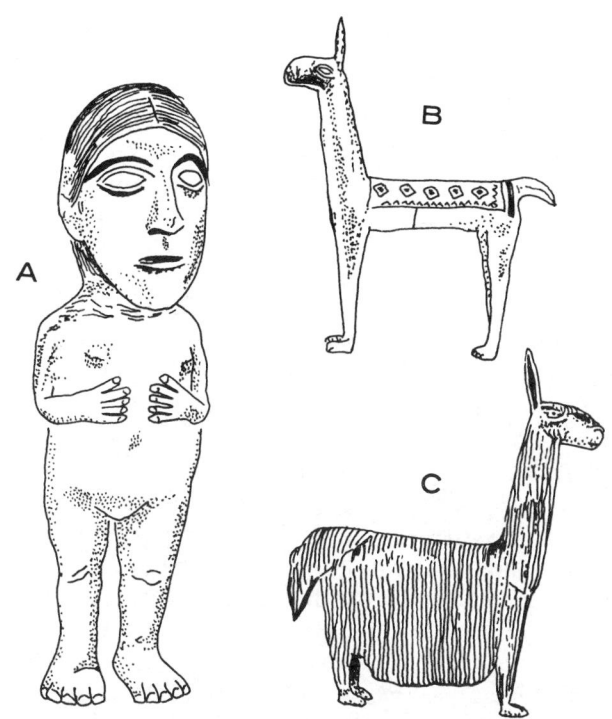

14.5. Inca silver and gold votive figures; collection of the American Museum of Natural History, New York: (*A*) human, (*B*), (*C*) llamas. (Drawings by the author)

casting, hammering, annealing, embossing, soldering, and gilding, and shortly before the Conquest they learned to inlay one metal with strips of another. They panned for platinum in the Chinchasuyu streams of Ecuador and combined Collasuyu tin with local copper for bronze tools, tumi knives, and star-headed battle maces. Smelting was done in a tall, cylindrical wind furnace (*huaira*) with openings to catch hillside breezes.

Today we possess only a small fraction of the original Inca output, for the Spaniards melted down thousands of objects from plundered tombs and cities as individual booty and the crown's "Royal Fifth." Additional loot came in 1553 from the 17-by-22-foot (5.1 by 6.7 meter) palace room filled to a man's height once with gold and twice with silver as Pizarro's required ransom for the release of Atahuallpa. With the Inca as captive, Pizarro sent collection envoys who stripped plaques from Cuzco's Coricancha, palaces, and royal compounds with crowbars and plundered gold huacas in other cities. The 24 tons (21.7 metric tons) of loot took months to melt into bullion, with each cavalryman allotted 90 pounds (40.8 kilos) of gold and 180

pounds (81.6 kilos) of silver and footsoldiers receiving less. The Royal Fifth went to the king as choice artifacts and was promptly converted into coinage (McIntyre 1973, 786). Loot was still trickling in from provincial storehouses and temples when more recent Spanish arrivals, eager to reach Cuzco, had Atahuallpa garroted in the Cajamarca plaza. Legend has it that unreceived treasure is scattered in caches throughout the Andes. The finest pieces, melted into ingots, are lost forever.

Pottery

Oxidation-fired Inca pottery was hand modeled and then slipped in white, red, black, or brown and polished or painted in polychrome-geometric, small-animal, or insect designs showing Nasca influence. Effigy pots retained the Chimú single spout and stirrup spout. Low shallow plates had a short modeled handle and two nublike buttons or lug handles at opposite sides of the rim. The most diagnostic form was the *aryballos* for carrying or storing liquids (Figure 14.6). Its ample globular body, pointed at the

14.6. Aryballos for storing liquids; Krannert Art Museum 67-29-399. (Photo courtesy KAM)

bottom, has lateral strap handles so that a rope could pass through them and around a small animal-effigy nubbin at the back for easy carrying. The long neck had an everted lip with small loops for lashing on a flat lid to prevent evaporation and spillage. Heights ranged from miniatures to 80 cms (31.5 inches), with the tan-or maroon-slipped body painted with checkerboard designs, crosshatching, and other restrained motifs. Clay keros, probably derived from Tiahuanaco antecedents adopted by the Chimú, were made in pairs for chicha toasting among commoners as a simpler version of the gold and silver ones used by the nobility. Another pottery form was the *paccha*, a drinking device up to 2 feet (61 centimeters) long with an effigy bowl connected to a long extension ending in a mouthpiece (Lothrop 1955, 237–242). The context of its use remains speculative.

The finest Inca imperial ware was given as gifts to loyal minions by the Inca; utilitarian storage jars confirm Inca presence at administrative centers. Provincial areas, however, retained their own artistic traditions. On the North Coast, burnished black keros and pacchas bear sculpturesque effigy animals. Whistling jars continue, as do single-spout and stirrup-spout jars, often minus the little monkey at the spout base. Their effigy animals carry keros on their backs or drink from them and sit atop small cubelike or rectangular vessel bodies. Some bear crescent-headdressed "Nyamlap" figures holding keros. Gold and silver "face keros" with double-rimmed eyes, deep cheek lines, a thin mouth, and hawklike noses remained a local specialty. Copper tumis now had wider blades and shorter handles that were topped by little animals or multiple-action figures. In the South Coast, ceramic emphasis on polychrome painting over modeling continued.

Wood and Stone Objects

Vessel forms produced in metal and clay carried over into wood and stone. Low stone bowls with double lugs opposite an animal head mimic pottery ones. Llama mortars and bowls with a cuplike depression in their backs are smooth, sleek, and stylized. They lack the inlay and detail of their gold and silver counterparts and were evidently used in agricultural rites or buried in fields in lieu of, or in addition to, live sacrifices. The great genius of Inca stoneworking lay in their Cyclopean masonry, not in small figures.

The best known wooden objects are keros and, in lesser numbers, pacchas. Keros ranging from 1-to-2-quart (.95 to 1.9 liter) capacities were incised with textile and geometric designs (sometimes pigment filled), lacquered, or painted in mineral reds, yellows, greens, blues, and blacks.

Keros continued into Colonial times. Because Inca style is so conservative, it is hard to distinguish between immediately pre- and early post-Conquest examples. Rowe has dated Colonial keros by their procession scenes and details of Spanish costume. By the end of the sixteenth century, they were decorated with fine lacquer inlay and round lead or tin inserts. Eventually formal figure placement gave way to a freer style with more elaborate polichrome inlay as the kero tradition flourished. Some keros were carved as snarling jaguar heads or human faces. Rowe sees late keros showing historical events such as fights with tropical groups as part of the strong cultural survival that led to the Inca Rebellion of 1780 (Rowe 1961, 340–341; for illustrations, see La Farge 1981, 158–160). He notes that lacquer-inlay decoration continued until 1821 and Peru's independence from Spain.

Textiles

Techniques and Fibers

Inca textiles also utilized the weaving and design heritage of incorporated groups. Elements of the Paracas/Nasca weaving tradition passed to the South Highland Collas and subsequently to the Inca after their subjugation of the Colla. The Inca conquered the South Coast Ica Valley in 1476, thereby initiating additional mita obligations and exchange of textile expertise. They also adopted the checkerboard design field of small, square motif units found on Tiahuanaco/Huari ponchos and cloths.

Tapestry and warp-faced weaves predominated among Inca techniques. Their longevity confirms their importance: Tapestry survived in the highlands until the early nineteenth century, whereas most Quechua/Aymara weaving is warp-faced today.[4] Fibers included the warm, readily available wool of New World cameloids

[4] A. Rowe (1977, 114). Rowe's book illustrates highland archaeological and ethnographic warp-faced textiles. Bolivian examples and instructions for replicating them appear in Cason and Cahlander (1976), whereas Nass (1980), in a delightful hand-illustrated book gives loom setups for simplified versions of pieces in Rowe's book. Also see d'Harcourt (1962) for clear diagrams and detail photos of most Late Horizon techniques.

plus lowland cotton. Vicuña was the finest, used infrequently, however, because of its shortness. Alpaca, nearly as fine but longer and more easily spun, was the favored fiber. To assure a constant supply, herd size and ownership were government controlled and tallied by quipu. Coarser llama and bast fibers became 'awasqa, the rough cloth reserved for commoners.

Types and Roles of Clothing

Inca untailored clothing was made from rectangular or shaped webs direct from the loom. Highland Indian garb today is similar, though male costume shows more change because Indian men interacted more closely with the Spaniards. Women carry produce and children in handwoven utility cloths and wear shawls (*llicllas*, still fastened with a silver tupi pin) over a dress or blouse, several skirts gathered with a handwoven belt (*chumpi*), and in some areas a handwoven headband as in pre-columbian times. Men's heavy blanketlike *yacolla* mantles, slit-necked tunics (*uncas*), belts, coca bags (*runcus* or *chuspas*), and slings also have pre-columbian antecedents, though the knit ear-flap caps and wool trousers that replaced the *huara* loincloth are Spanish innovations.[5]

Clothing indicated status within Inca society: Coarse 'awasqa cloths were restricted to the lower classes, whereas the nobility used kumbi (*qompi*), fine tapestry of alpaca or vicuña fiber with square *t'oqapu* designs, possibly woven on an upright frame loom (Figure 14.7). The Inca alone wore the red-wool *maskapaicha* fringe enclosed in golden tubes, the *llautu* forehead band, and the finest kumbi textiles of vicuña and bat fur with restricted designs. His clothing was so sacred that it was burned once a year, and the ashes thrown to the wind lest anyone collect them, for textiles captured part of the essence of their wearer through sympathetic magic and could be used to do him harm. Particular colors and designs also identified regional groups and were encouraged by the Inca government both to sustain ethnic pride and facilitate identification of subject peoples (Murra 1962; Rowe 1979).

Several groups produced kumbi. Fine webs

14.7. Fragments from an Inca tunic with all-over t'oqapu designs (TM.91.535). (Photo courtesy TM)

from the looms of cloistered mamaconas clothed the Inca and shrine statues. Curaca wives wove kumbi for their husbands to wear and give to the Inca while attending Inti Raymi or during their obligatory tribute presentation every fourth month in Cuzco. Male specialists wove fine mita kumbi, using vicuña, alpaca, cotton, and tropical-bird feathers inventoried in state storehouses to be used by the Inca as gifts to "hostage" children of absent curacas or to visiting dignitaries as indicators of royal favor. Cloth gifts to newly incorporated peoples helped established the pattern of reciprocal obligations and mita labor. Kumbi also covered the stone huaca on Lake Titicaca's Island of the Sun, whereas its concave face was covered with gold

[5] Inca costume is described in Colonial sources and illustrated in drawings accompanying Felipe Huaman Poma de Ayala's *Nueva Crónica y Buen Gobierno* (Guaman Pomade Ayala, 1978). Also see Gosta Montell (1929).

(Father Cobo, quoted in Hemming and Ranney, 1982, 56).

Locally, fine textiles mollified offended parties in disputes, sealing the settlement, or were gifts at weddings, rites of passage, or burial garb of the dead. They were cast into rivers as offerings with llamas, flowers, and ashes of animals sacrificed at the major annual festivals. Ware-

house stocks of utilitarian mita textiles were available for local use and to itinerant marching armies.

Inca South Coast and Highland ponchos confirm standardized Inca layout and design. John Rowe (1979, 245–257) found four common de-

14.8a. Inca poncho design layouts, according to John Rowe (1979): black and white checkerboard. (TM.1966.7.172, fig. 3 photo courtesy TM)

14.8b. Inca poncho design layouts, according to John Rowe (1979): key checkerboard (TM.91.147, fig. 4). (Photo courtesy TM)

14.8c. Inca poncho design layouts, according to John Rowe (1979): t'oqapu waistband (TM. 91.120, fig. 7). (Photo courtesy TM)

14.8d. Inca poncho design layouts, according to John Rowe (1979): diamond waistband (TM.1964.12.2, fig. 9). (Photo courtesy TM)

14.9a. All-t'oqapu tunic, Robert Woods Bliss Collection, Dumbarton Oaks, B-518.PT. (From Rowe, J., 1979, fig. 14; courtesy TM and DO)

sign placements: a waistband of one or several square/rectangular *t'oqapu* (individual motif) design rows (Figure 14.8c); checkerboard patterning in black/white squares beneath a solid-red, stepped-triangle yoke area (Figure 14.8a); a wide waistband of stepped diamonds (Figure 14.8d); and checkerboard layouts with the upper two-thirds filled by seven or eight rows of a stylized percentage-sign-like design in alternate color squares and the lower third with five broad bands of alternating colors (Figure 14.8b; see also A. Rowe 1978). A few ponchos are unique, perhaps royal tunics, with all-over checkerboard t'oqapu units in varying colors and orientations (including a miniature black-and-white checkerboard poncho unit; see Figure 14.9a). Their orderly field of repeated designs recalls the rich play of rectilinear units on certain earlier, Middle Horizon Huari-style tunics (Figure 14.9b). German scholar Thomas Barthel (1971) has identified several hundred different Inca tocapu variants with possible logographic meanings; others suggest that they may have heraldic, ethnic, or calendric significance.

14.9b. Huari-style tunic, probably Middle Horizon 2B, with feline, avian, and anthropomorphic block elements (TM.91.351). (Photo courtesy TM)

Rock Sculpture and Huacas

In contrast to the Aztecs, with their monolithic stone Coatlicue and Xochipilli figures and clay Xipe images and the resplendent Maya stelae and altars, the Inca produced few large-scale naturalistic sculptures. Instead, they worshipped hundreds of features of the natural landscape that, according to their legends, were the transformed bodies of early leaders and natural forces. They reshaped many of these rocks and outcroppings, called huacas (sacred objects or shrines), by carving in steps and depressions so they could be used as altars, sacrificial stones, and for divination.

Masonry-lined caves at Cochequilla, 32 miles (51.4 kilometers) northwest of Cuzco and the reshaped grotto under the Torreón at Machu Picchu (Figure 14.3) attest to their reverence toward the earth. A series of carved stones at Sahuite, 120 miles (193 kilometers) southwest of Cuzco, is more elaborately carved. One has a complex scenario of warriors, llamas, pumas, and other animals over a network of miniature platforms, usnus, steps, and deep grooves (perhaps used for flowing liquids during divination) carved on its curved base (Hemming and Ranney 1982, 164–167). Others have miniature staircases or formed ceremonial seats or benches. At Kenko, northeast of Cuzco, a huge rock outcrop carved with steps and platforms is laced with deeply cut zigzag channels leading to a natural cave cleft perhaps associated with underworld forces and death. To Hemming, the reshaping of these rock huacas represents "a unique visual language" and "an accomplishment as important as the architecture, and in fact provides the key to understanding both the architecture and the culture as a whole" (Hemming and Ranney 1982, 9).

The Nature of Inca Art

Interpretive studies of Inca art are relatively few, perhaps because the Inca directed their energies toward maintaining a recently consolidated empire rather than a formalized artistic expression (Kubler 1984, 469). They left no written language, no illustrated codices or carved narrative stelae, no sculpted portraits of rulers. Pottery and textiles bear geometric designs of stylized animal and human figures rather than iconographically complex scenes. Stone and metal images depict stereotypic forms devoid of the elaborate kennings or anthropomorphized bird/animal hybrids produced by Chavín, Paracas, Nasca, Moche, and by other earlier artisans.

Because their complex worship of sacred places involved reshaping natural forms as huacas, there was less need to create religious images; of those produced in gold and silver, most disappeared in Spanish meltdowns. Stone walls were seldom painted: Duccio Bonavia (1985, 188) cites a chronicler's mention of walls along the royal roads painted with animals and fish but concludes that highland murals were few, with most destroyed by the Spaniards as works of the devil. Although the Inca maintained an extensive verbal lore, they have bequeathed a sparse pictorial record to art historians. Scholars are learning as much about Inca culture from architecture, artifact contexts, settlement patterns, site distributions, and ethnohistoric accounts as they are from Inca art.

EPILOGUE

In 1525, the Inca Huayna Capac died during an epidemic in Ecuador, possibly the victim of advancing smallpox introduced by the Spaniards who, moving southward from Colombia, reached Tumbes in northern Peru in 1532. His son Huascar (Hummingbird), supported by the Hanan Cuzco moiety, had himself crowned Inca in Cuzco, whereas an illegitimate half-brother, Atahuallpa ("Heroic Turkey"), backed by the Hurin Cuzcos, controlled the northern Quito provinces where he had recently distinguished himself as a general. Upon his father's death, Atahuallpa moved southward with his general Quisquis to oust Huascar. Quisquis crossed the Apurimac, met, and defeated Huascar's forces, whereas Atahuallpa moved more slowly toward Cuzco awaiting the outcome.

While resting at the royal baths in Cajamarca (Map 10), Atahuallpa heard of the arrival of bearded strangers and, secure amid his retinue, arranged to meet them there. The Spaniards, under Francisco Pizarro, fired a cannon from Cajamarca's central usnu platform at the unarmed crowds in the plaza and in the ensuing slaughter took Atahuallpa prisoner in a lightning strike. After exacting a hefty ransom, they eventually tried him for crimes of incest and fratricide and killed him. By 1532, Pizarro and his 102 foot soldiers and 62 horsemen controlled the nerve center of an empire encompassing 350,000 miles.

One of the first Spanish moves was the crowning of one of Huayna Capac's other sons, Topa Hulallpa. He was almost immediately poisoned, and his brother Manco Capac replaced him as puppet ruler. Reviled by both the Spaniards and his own people, Manco escaped in 1536 to the Yucay Valley where he mounted an army to retake Cuzco. The siege was a long one, and eventually his unseasoned peasant troops deserted and returned to their fields. Manco retreated to Ollantaytambo and then to Vitcos, harrassing the Spaniards with continuing raids. He was assassinated there by Spaniards inimical to Pizarro and succeeded by his 10-year-old son Sayri Tupac who capitulated to the Spaniards and returned to Cuzco to be Christianized.

In 1560, another of Manco's sons, Titu Cusi, fled to the Urubamba highlands to escape Spanish control. His successor, Tupac Amaru, was brought to Cuzco after the Spanish capture of Vitcos and beheaded in 1572. During this desperate resistance, the Spaniards had effectively dismantled the mita system, the communications network of chasqui runners, coastal/highland and montaña trade, and governmental redistribution of goods. Food production collapsed as Indians, already decimated by diseases for which they had no immunity, were resettled away from the mountain terraces into *reducciones* between 1560 and 1570. Its rulers gone and its institutions dismantled, the once-powerful Inca empire joined the other great precolumbian civilizations that modern scholarship attempts to retrieve from the past.

CONCLUSION

THE preceding examples have shown interpretations of pre-columbian art that combine meticulous scholarship and intuition within a framework of interdisciplinary, international cooperation. The results have been far-ranging. Scholars have defined the major pre-columbian art styles. We know how the pre-columbian peoples presented their subject matter, how they generated designs, how they influenced one another, and something of their underlying world views. We are beginning to understand how art functioned as an important element in particular political, social, and economic contexts, both reinforcing tradition and creating change. We have identified previously unknown secular personae including, perhaps, individual artists, and confirmed the deliberate use of art to achieve secular goals. Pre-columbian art research as a discipline has gained legitimacy through processual studies and an increasingly accurate materialist–historical orientation.

The results of these studies have fueled the excitement of researchers (and, I hope, the readers of this book) because they represent only a small part of what we may eventually know 50 or a 100 years from now as research strategies improve and new art finds come to light. Yet important as they are to the reconstruction of pre-columbian culture, they also provide insights germane to our twentieth-century condition. It seems fitting to conclude this survey of recent research by putting it into a wider perspective.

The studies cited in this book show that pre-columbian peoples grappled with basic concerns that are still with us today. Diseases then, too, were cured through medicines, surgery, and the invocation of divine forces. Unemployment was minimized by annual labor responsibilities in a sort of proto-WPA. Equilibrium between population growth and resources then, as now, was crucial: An imbalance probably hastened the central-lowland Maya collapse. Delicate negotiations and political posturing accompanied economic ventures. When eroding trade networks sapped prosperity and internal dysfunction left the late Classic Maya vulnerable, archaeology confirms that their quality of life also declined. And surely the Fifth Sun's destruction by cataclysm preoccupied the Aztecs as the specter of potential nuclear destruction does us. Echoes of pre-columbian concerns resonate in our lives today. What, then, beyond increasingly refined scholarly insights into pre-columbian cultural dynamics can the art of these peoples contribute to us?

First, immense aesthetic satisfaction. Pre-columbian art has fired the imaginations of casual viewers and professional artists alike, proving that timeless human creativity can communicate directly across language, time, place, and culture.

Second, perspectives on contemporary functions of art. Pre-columbian art centered around still-viable concerns, though we express them differently today. We preserve history and legend through films and books instead of stelae and codices. We celebrate historic mega-events with serious (and commercial) art as Mesoamerican cultures commemorated 52-year cycles with architecture and stelae. We, too, idealize important dead in public sculpture, and living rulers publicize their accomplishments on billboards, murals, and television to consolidate political power. Pacal's repeated image recalls the media saturation of political campaigns, and the Palenque accession tablets parallel contemporary inaugural pomp and pageantry. Religious icons are still intermediaries or repositories of supernatural power. In death, material wealth is bequeathed and not stockpiled in tombs, but we, too, dispatch the deceased with solace-inspiring ceremony, symbolism, and artwork. Decoration of utilitarian objects for beauty, enjoyment, or just plain fun continues as a timeless human tendency.

Contrasts, too, abound. Art denotes culture to contemporary opera, gallery, and theater patrons. We create, underwrite, and collect art for financial investment. Art sells products, tapping carefully researched subliminal associations. We still portray the natural world, but our images no longer influence it, for we control environments with technology instead of art.

Technology, indeed, has generated new art forms (holography, moog music, computer graphics) and materials (acrylic paints, Plexiglas, sophisticated alloys). Traditional media are modified with new tools (sculptors' electric jackhammers, theremins in music). We can access the art of prior ages and distant areas as never before. Responding to these influences, twentieth-century art changes rapidly; fads come and go, and individual artists, unlike their usually anonymous pre-columbian counterparts, are this week's hot items and next year's has-beens. Knowledge about, and possession of, art is no longer elitist as television, videodisks, bookstores, and museums make available a cosmopolitan array of art forms inconceivable in the past.

Third, pre-columbian studies reconfirm art's contribution to cultural vitality in this era of intense visual communication. Art is still the tickler and stretcher of our imaginations, the complement of a full life.

Besides providing aesthetic satisfaction, giving perspective to twentieth-century art and reconfirming art's role as a cultural universal, the study of pre-columbian art offers further important insights:

It documents millennia of human inventiveness and resilience. Native Americans met complex problems head on and survived. Art often accompanies pre-columbian responses to warfare, external relations, social tensions, and religious syncretism, and is part of a coherent if incomplete legacy of cultural successes, failures, and alternatives. Some artistic expressions were short circuits; others are inappropriate to our times. Nonetheless, pre-columbian perceptions of the interrelationships between humans, humans and environment, and humans and the supernatural are relevant to any age.

Anyone who enters the mindset (as we perceive it) behind the Teotihuacán Tlalocs, Chavín kennings of mythical power, or Maya funerary vases can never again be fully ethnocentric. Pre-columbian art leads us beyond Judaeo–Christian morality and Western rationalistic materialism into radically different cultures and responses that require an open-minded appreciation of alternative solutions. In exploring pre-columbian art, we replace divisive, tunnel-vision ethnocentrism with a healthy curiosity about and appreciation of the wider human endeavor. Just as a family tree documents an individual's "roots," the pre-columbian past offers vistas of broader human roots, reminding us of human adaptability and change, and offers perspective in facing our own unknown future.

Much of pre-columbian art also reflects a holistic world in which humans interact with, rather than dominate, their environment. Human good depended on the viability of a seamless interrelated system with components meshed like stitches in a piece of knitting; catastrophes reflected imbalance or disharmony, to be corrected by ritual and appeals to supernaturals. World-renewal rites kept the delicately meshed system on course. Our contemporary emphases on mechanization and increased productivity have replaced holistic perspectives: incredibly, we are ravaging the very resources on which our lives depend. If there is a wider lesson to be learned from precolumbian art, it is that humans are part of an interdependent life network of forces in symbiotic interplay. Today's technology can preserve the balance that pre-columbian shamans sought through ritual, or can alter and even destroy all life, including our own.

Implicit in this preservation is encouragement of art as an aspect of cultural well-being, by both encouraging artistic creativity and the appreciation of art. This means making public access to the art and culture of other ages and peoples as easily available as information on how to fix a faucet or learn Italian. To an inner-city mugger or a crack addict, such concerns are light years away; to a starving Third World villager, an unobtainable, irrelevant luxury. Nevertheless, whether we are aware of it or not, we are all inheritors of our collective human past.

Pre-columbian art is a significant part of that heritage. As Terence Grieder has stated, "It is ironic to find many of our compatriots preoccupied with a search for messages from deep space while neglecting communications from deep time, which are practically extraterrestrial in their strangeness to modern Americans." (Grieder 1979, 90).

It is frustrating that, just when mass media have made widespread dissemination of precolumbian art research possible, pre-columbian archaeological sites are under siege by population expansion, vandals, and pothunters as never before. Urban expansion, dams, highways, oil refineries, and even pig farms have destroyed parts of several important sites described in this book. It is imperative that legislation and enforceable protective measures be developed to suppress the construction and looting that destroy the archaeological contexts

so essential to our understanding of these ancient cultures.

In conclusion, I cite the compelling description by Edmund Carpenter et al., (1959, 31) of the Eskimo carver who liberates the image in a block of raw material: "As the carver holds the unworked ivory lightly in his hand, turning it this way and that, he whispers, 'Who are you? Who hides there?' And then, 'Ah, seal!'" He finds the hidden form and releases it rather than creating it. So, too, researchers attempt to release the meaning and purpose behind pre-columbian art without forcing interpretations. The process is tricky, frustrating, and immeasurably exciting; the results never entirely verifiable.

Today knowledge of the pre-columbian world is snowballing. Scholars have recovered historical data from Tikal's architecture, stelae, and altars; seen the political implications of art in Palenque's ritual transfers of the divine mandate of rulership; documented Huari's impressive spread, Inca imperial organization, the economic aspects of Olmec trade, Bonampak's raids and victory/heir recognition rituals, and Aztec rituals of world renewal. Research goals have broadened as information from other disciplines allows us to extract increasingly specific data from particular styles, leading to regional models and the beginnings of multidisciplinary syntheses. New techniques of archaeological retrieval and computer processing of statistical and visual data make future prospects even more exciting as we stand to recover and humanize even more of a past that would otherwise have been lost.

Perhaps somewhere the shades of great pre-columbian shamans and savants watch our programs, grimacing with a "No, no, dummy, you're all wrong" or nodding eagerly, "That's *it!* How could you have found that out when we left so few clues?" We are forever denied the satisfaction of direct communication with them, but we *can* share something of their world through their art. The studies go on, and with each, more of the past becomes clearer. We can only hope that the best is yet to come.

GLOSSARY

Ahau. Title, "Lord," used by rulers; important day, ending the 20-day Mayan month, named after the sun god, Kinich Ahau: Its glyph is a stylized version of his face.

Amaranth. A spinachlike vegetable with edible leaves and seeds.

Apotropaic. Evil-deflecting or protective.

Art. Product of creative skill and imagination that communicates meaning and emotionally affects its users.

Atadura moldings. "Tied" columns (Spanish: *moldes de atadura*) in Yucatec Middle and Late Classic architecture imitating the cord-lashed houseposts of Mayan huts.

Atl-tlachinolli. Water–fire glyph denoting Aztec Flowery War.

Attribute analysis. Study of how elements of sound, color, proportion, and motion are combined in a work of art.

Audiencia. U-shaped adobe rooms in Central Andean architecture.

Aural arts. Art forms primarily perceived through sound.

Axis mundi. Sacred world axis connecting earth to upper and lower worlds, often in the form of a Tree of Life.

Ayllu. Inca lineage or wider kinship group.

Bacab. Maya deities who hold up the four corners of the sky.

Bajo. Lakelike lowland Maya reservoir.

Barrio. Residential area within Mesoamerican cities.

Batab. Maya village chief, often a noble.

Binder molding. See *Atadura moldings.*

Caban. Seventeenth Maya day: the spiral from its glyph denotes Earth.

Cabeza colosal (Spanish: "giant head"). Large Olmec carved stone portrait sculptures, presumably of rulers.

Calendar Round. Combination of the interdititating Mesoamerican 260-day (ritual) and 365-day (solar) calendars, which coincide every 52 years.

Callejón (Spanish: "big avenue"). Long, narrow intermontaine basins in the Central Andes.

Calmecac. Aztec school of higher learning for training priests and sons of nobles.

Calpulli. Clanlike Aztec residential grouping with social and political functions.

Candelero. Perforated Teotihuacán clay "candlestick holder" with one or two holes, presumably for holding incense or blood offerings.

Cauac. Nineteenth Maya day sign, a profile face with "grape-cluster" bubbles under lowered eyelid. Cauac grape clusters, beadlike chains, and dotted lines identify stone objects and the Cauac Monster, a zoomorphic earth/water deity.

Celt. An ungrooved axe head.

Cenote. Yucatán sinkhole or natural well of collapsed limestone.

Ceques. Lines connecting *huacas* that radiate from the Inca capital, Cuzco.

Chacmool (Yucatec: "red jaguar"). Recumbent, bent-kneed human figure with head raised, holding offering bowl on its stomach.

Chicha. Mildly intoxicating Central Andean drink of fermented corn.

Chinampa. Islandlike "floating garden" of soil on built up reed bed, anchored to shallow lake bottoms in Central Mexico.

Chultún. Bottle-shaped, clay-lined underground Mayan storage chamber.

Chuño. Freeze-dried potatoes, an Inca staple.

Codex (plural: *codices*). Mesoamerican "folding-screen" genealogies, historical and religious manuscripts, painted on deerskin or homemade paper.

Comal. Round Mesoamerican clay griddle for roasting tortillas.

Contextual analysis. Study of the cultural context of a work of art including its origins, manufacture, and artist creator.

Copal. Mesoamerican resin from coniferous trees, burned as incense during rituals.

Cuauhxicalli. Aztec "eagle bowl" for receiving sacrificial hearts and blood.

Culture area. Geographic area within which inhabitants share a high percentage of cultural traits.

Danzantes. Life-size Mesoamerican "dancing" figures in stone relief at Monte Albán, Oaxaca.

Emic. Perceptions of themselves by those within a culture.

Escuintle. (Nahuatl) small, plump, hairless domesticated dog, an Aztec food source.

Ethnoarchaeology. Interpretation of archaeological data using insights from ethnography.

Ethnography. The graphic, recorded description of cultures.

Ethnology. Search for broad cultural values through cross-cultural comparisons.

Etic. Perception of a culture by nonmembers.

Florero. Small globular clay vessel form from Teotihuacán.

Formal analysis. Study of how parts of artworks are organized and interrelated.

Geomancy. Animistic topography; belief that surface features reflect spiritual energies affecting human endeavors.

Halach Uinic. Royal title of Maya ruler.

Huaca. (Inca) sacred place.

Huaquero. South American term for pot-hunter or tomb looter.

Iconics. How art elements may be recombined to create new forms.

Iconography. Study of symbols with visually, audially, or kinetically implied meaning.

Iconology. The historical or interpretive study of symbols.

Illapa. An Incan royal mummy.

Incensario. Clay Mesoamerican incense burner.

Inti. The Inca sun deity.

Kan cross. Equal-armed cross: Mayan symbol for water.

Kennings. Visual metaphors used extensively in Chavín art.

Kero. Chimú and Inca wooden or metal beaker for drinking *chicha.*

Kinetic arts. Artworks based on movement.

Kinich Ahau. The Maya sun god, recognizable by his scrolled eye, twisted "cruller" ornament above a Roman nose, and tau-shaped upper incisors.

Long Count. Mayan dating system totaling the days within five different time units, starting from a base date of 13.0.0.0.4 Ahau 8 Cumku (3113 B.C.)

Macana. Aztec obsidian-edged battle club.

Maguey. Fleshy-leafed Mesoamerican xerophyte: fibers used for cordage and rough cloth; fermented sap, for intoxicant beverage *pulque.*

Malacate. Spindle whorl, added to drop spindle shaft to increase and sustain rotation.

Manikin scepter. Serpent-footed deity image: Emblem of Mayan rulership.

Mano (Spanish: "hand"). Bun-shaped grinding stone used with *metate.*

Metate. Mesoamerican quern; tripod, slab-shaped grinding stone for preparing cornmeal for tortillas.

Midden. Archaeological refuse area or garbage pit.

Milpa. Mesoamerican hand-cultivated corn plot.

Mita. Labor tax owed Inca rulers.

Mitimae. Inca practice of resettling conquered peoples or shifting indigenous populations where needed.

Montaña (Spanish: "mountain"). Eastern slopes of the Central Andes leading to the Amazon Basin.

Necropolis. Tomb cluster with architecture suggesting "city of the dead."

Obsidian. Amber, banded gray, green translucent, or black opaque natural volcanic glass.

Oca. Edible Central Andean highland tuber.

Panaca. Dead Inca's kin who administered his estates and maintained his memorial cult.

Pars pro toto. Artistic representation wherein part of a thing denotes the whole.

Plangi. Resist technique by which bound cloth, dyed, produced uncolored ring or donut-shaped designs.

Pochteca. Aztec itinerant merchants, perhaps also spies.

Punctation. Indention on clay using pointed object.

Qualitative analysis. Evaluation of the aesthetic qualities of artworks.

Quinoa. Milletlike high-altitude Central Andean grain.

Quipu. Central Andean mnemonic device with pendant strings bearing knots of different types, sizes, spacing, and colors.

Ramón. Breadnut (from *Brosimum utile* tree): important supplement of lowland Maya diet.

Reducción. Spanish resettlements of Indian populations to facilitate administration and production of exports.

Sacbé. Raised causeway connecting ceremonial areas in Mayan sites or adjacent sites.

Sascab. Crushed, eroded limestone, used by the Maya as mortar.

Stela. Upright stone monument, usually with commemorative inscriptions.

Style. Systematic arrangement of formal elements characterizing distinctive groups of artwork.

Strata. Horizontal layers by which a site is excavated.

Tablero. Recessed panel set above *talud* in Teotihuacán architecture.

Taclla. Inca footplow, basically a digging stick with footrest.

Tahuantinsuyu. The Inca "Empire of the Four Quarters."

Talud. Slope at base of Teotihuacán pyramid bodies.

Tecomate. Globular, neckless Mesoamerican jars imitating gourds.

Temazcal. Mesoamerican sweat lodge.

Texiptla. Aztec human deity impersonator.

Tezontle. Porous, lightweight Mesoamerican lava used in construction.

Tlachtli. Sacred Mesoamerican ball game, or I-shaped court in which it was played.

Tortilla. Thin, round, roasted Mesoamerican corn patty.

Tzompantli. Aztec rack for public display of sacrificial skulls.

Usnu. Altarlike structure in patios within Inca settlements.

Vecindad (Spanish: "neighborhood"). Sector of urban settlement with cohesive sense of identity.

Vision serpent (concept of Linda Schele, 1986, 46–47). Serpent intermediary disgorging ancestor image, summoned through autosacrificial bloodletting.

Visual arts. Art forms perceived by sight, such as sculpture, painting, ceramics, metalwork.

Volador. Mesoamerican Gulf Coast ritual "flying pole" dance with solar and calendric connotations featuring "bird men" suspended on ropes from a high revolving platform.

Adams, Richard E. (ed.)
1977   *The Origins of Maya Civilization.* Albu-
        querque: University of New Mexico Press.
Adams, Richard E. W., and Robert C. Aldrich
1980   (eds.) "A Re-Evaluation of the Bonampak
        Murals, A Preliminary Statement on the
        Paintings and Texts." In Robertson (ed.)
        1980, pp. 45–59.
Altroy, Terrence N. d', and Christine Hastor
1984   "The Distribution and Contents of Inca
        State Storehouses in the Xauxa region of
        Peru." *American Antiquity* 49, no. 2:
        334–349.
Alva, Walter
1988   "Discovering the New World's Richest Un-
        looted Tomb." *National Geographic* 174,
        no. 4 (October): 510–549.
1990   "The Moche of Ancient Peru: New Tomb of
        Royal Splendor." *National Geographic* 177,
        no. 6 (June): 2–15.
Anawalt, Patricia Rieff
1981   "Costume and Analysis and the Prove-
        nience of the Borgia Group Codices."
        American Antiquity 46, no. 4: 837–852.
1982   "Analysis of the Aztec Quechquemitl: An
        Exercise in Inference." In Boone (ed.) 1982b,
        pp. 37–72.
1984   "Memory Clothing: Costumes Associated
        with Aztec Human Sacrifice." In Boone (ed.)
        1984, pp. 165–193.
1990   "The Emperor's Cloak: Aztec Pomp, Toltec
        Circumstance." *American Antiquity* 55,
        no. 2 (April): 291–307.
Anderson, Richard L.
1989   *Art in Small Scale Societies.* Englewood
        Cliffs, N.J.: Prentice-Hall.
Anton, Ferdinand
1972   *The Art of Ancient Peru.* New York: G. P.
        Putnam's Sons.
Aveni, Anthony F.
1977   (ed.) *Native American Astronony.* Austin:
        University of Texas Press.
1980   *Sky Watchers of Ancient Mexico.* Austin:
        University of Texas Press.
1986   "The Nasca Lines: Patterns in the Desert."
        Archaeology 39, no. 4 (July/August): 32–39.
1990   (ed.) *The Lines of Nazca.* Memoirs of
        the American Philosophical Society, vol.
        183. Philadelphia: American Philosophical
        Society.
Badner, Mino
1972   *A Possible Focus of Andean Artistic Influ-
        ence in Mesoamerica.* Studies in Pre-
        Columbian Art and Archaeology, no. 9.
        Washington, D.C.: Dumbarton Oaks.

Bankes, George
1977   *Peru before Pizarro.* Oxford: Phaidon Press, Ltd.

Barbour, Warren T. D.
1976   *The Figurines and Figure Chronology of Ancient Teotihuacán, Mexico.* Ph.D. diss. Department of Anthropology, University of Rochester. Ann Arbor, Mich.: University Microfilms (BWH 76-23976).

Barnet, Sylvan
1981   *A Short Guide to Writing about Art.* Boston: Little, Brown & Co.

Barthel, Thomas S.
1971   "Viracochas Prunkgewand" (Tocapu-Studien) 1. *Tribus,* no. 20:63–124. Stuttgart: Linden-Museum für Voelkerkunde.
1991   *From the Mouth of the Dark Cave: Commemorative Sculpture of the Late Classic Maya.* Norman: University of Oklahoma Press.

Baudez, Claude F., and Peter Mathews
1979   "Capture and Sacrifice at Palenque." In Robertson (ed.) 1979a, pp. 31–40.

Bennett, Wendell C.
1934   *Excavations at Tiahuanaco.* Anthropological Papers of the American Museum of Natural History, vol. 34, no. 3. New York: American Museum of Natural History.
1953   *Excavations at Wari, Ayacucho, Peru.* Yale University Publications in Anthropology, no. 49. New Haven: Yale University.

Benson, Elizabeth P.
1968   (ed.) *Dumbarton Oaks Conference on the Olmec.* Washington, D.C.: Dumbarton Oaks.
1971   (ed.) *Dumbarton Oaks Conference on Chavín.* Washington, D.C.: Dumbarton Oaks.
1972a   *The Mochica: A Culture of Peru.* New York: Praeger.
1972b   (ed.) *The Cult of the Feline: A Conference on Precolumbian Iconography.* Washington, D.C.: Dumbarton Oaks.
1974   *A Man and a Feline in Mochica Art.* Studies in Pre-Columbian Art and Archaeology, no. 14. Washington, D.C.: Dumbarton Oaks.
1975   (ed.) *Death and the Afterlife in Pre-Columbian America: A Conference at Dumbarton Oaks, October 27th, 1973.* Washington, D.C.: Dumbarton Oaks.
1976   "Ritual Cloth and Palenque Kings." In Robertson (ed.) 1976, pp. 445–58.
1979   (ed.) *Pre-columbian Metallurgy of South America.* Washington, D.C.: Dumbarton Oaks.
1981a   (ed.) *The Olmec and their Neighbors: Essays in Memory of Matthew W. Stirling.* Washington, D.C.: Dumbarton Oaks.
1981b   (ed.) *Mesoamerican Sites and World-Views: A Conference at Dumbarton Oaks.* Washington, D.C.: Dumbarton Oaks.
1986   (ed.) *City-States of the Maya: Art and Architecture.* Denver: Rocky Mountain Institute for Pre-Columbian Studies.

Benson, Elizabeth P., and Gillett Griffin
1988   (eds.) *Maya Iconography.* Princeton, N.J.: Princeton University Press.

Berdan, Frances F.
1987   "The Economics of Aztec Luxury Trade and Tribute." In Boone (ed.) 1987, pp. 161–183.

Berlin, Heinrich
1958   "El glifo émblema en las inscripciones Mayas." *Journal de la Société des Américanistes de Paris* 47:111–119.

Berlo, Janet C.
1982   "Artistic Specialization at Teotihuacán: The Ceramic Incense Burner." In Cordy-Collins (ed.) 1982, pp. 83–100.
1983   (ed.) *Text and Image in Pre-Columbian Art: Essays on the Interrelationship of the Verbal and Visual Arts.* Oxford: Oxford University Press.
1985   *The Art of Pre-Hispanic Mesoamerica: An Annotated Bibliography.* Boston: G. K. Hall.
1989   "Early Writing in Central Mexico, in Tlilli, in Tlapalli before A.D. 1000." In Diehl and Berlo (eds.) 1989, pp. 19–47.

Bernal, Ignacio
1969   *The Olmec World.* Trans. by Doris Heyden and Fernando Horcasitas. Berkeley: University of California Press.

Berrin, Kathleen
1988   (ed.) *Feathered Serpents and Flowering Trees: Reconstructing the Murals of Teotihuacán.* San Francisco: The Fine Arts Museums of San Francisco.

Bingham, Hiram
1930   *Machu Picchu, A Citadel of the Incas: Report of the Explorations and Excavations made in 1911, 1912, and 1915 under the Auspices of Yale University and the National Geographic Society.* Memoirs of the National Geographic Society. New Haven: Yale University Press.

Bird, Junius, and Louisa Bellinger
1954   *Paracas Fabrics and Nazca Needlework, 3rd Century B.C.–3rd Century A.D.: The Textile Museum, Catalogue Raisonné.* Washington, D.C.: The Textile Museum.

Blasco, María Concepción, and Luis J. Ramos
1974   "Cabezas Cortadas en la Cerámica Nazca." *Cuadernos Prehispánicos* (Año 2) no. 2. Valladolíd, Spain: Seminario Americanista de la Universidad, Casa de Colón.

Bonavía, Duccio
1978   "Ecological Factors Affecting the Urban Transformation in the Pre-Columbian Era." Browman (ed.) 1978b, pp. 393–410.
1985   *Mural Painting in Ancient Peru.* Bloomington: Indiana University Press.

Bonifaz Nuño, Rubén
1981   *The Art in the Great Temple; Mexico–Tenochtitlan.* (With photographs by Fernando Robles.) Mexico: Instituto Nacional de Antropología e Historia/Secretaría de Educación Pública.

Boone, Elizabeth Hill
1982a   "Towards a More Precise Definition of the Aztec Painting Style." In Cordy-Collins (ed.) 1982, pp. 153–168.
1982b   (ed.) *The Art and Iconography of Late Post-Classic Central Mexico.* Washington, D.C.: Dumbarton Oaks.
1982c   (ed.) *Falsifications and Misreconstructions of Pre-columbian Art.* Washington, D.C.: Dumbarton Oaks.
1984   (ed.) *Ritual Human Sacrifice in Mesoamerica.* Washington, D.C.: Dumbarton Oaks.
1987   (ed.) *The Aztec Templo Mayor (1983 Conference).* Washington, D.C.: Dumbarton Oaks.

Bowie, Theodore, and Cornelia V. Christenson
1970   (eds.) *Studies in Erotic Art.* New York and London: Basic Books.

Bricker, Victoria Reifler
1981   *The Indian Christ, The Indian King: The Historical Substrate of Maya Myth and Ritual.* Austin: University of Texas Press.

Broda, Johanna
1970   "Tlacaxipehualiztli: A Reconstruction of an Aztec Calendar Festival from 16th Century Sources." *Revista Español de Antropología Americana* 5:197–273.
1987   "The Provenience of the Offerings: Tribute and Cosmovision." In Boone (ed.) 1987, pp. 211–256.

Browman, David L.
1978a   "Toward the Development of the Tiahuanaco (Tiwanaku) State." In Browman (ed.) 1978b, pp. 327–349.
1978b   (ed.) *Advances in Andean Archaeology.* The Hague/Paris: Mouton.
1978c   *Cultural Continuity in Mesoamerica.* The Hague/Paris: Mouton.

Brown, Betty Ann
1984   "Ochpaniztli in Historical Perspective." In Boone (ed.) 1984, pp. 195–210.

Brown, Kenneth
1977   "Toward a Schematic Explanation of Cultural Change within the Middle Classic Period of the Valley of Guatemala." In Sanders and Michels (eds.) 1977, pp. 411, 440.

Brundage, Burr Cartwright
1967   *Lords of Cuzco: A History and Description of the Inca People in their Final Days.* Norman: University of Oklahoma Press.
1969   *Empire of the Inca.* Norman: University of Oklahoma Press.
1979   *The Fifth Sun; Aztec Gods, Aztec World.* Austin: University of Texas Press.
1982   *The Phoenix of the Western World: Quetzalcoatl and the Sky Religion.* Norman: University of Oklahoma Press.
1985   *The Jade Steps, A Ritual Life of the Aztecs.* Salt Lake City: University of Utah Press.

Burger, Richard L.
1977   "The Moche Sources of Archaism in Chimu Ceramics." *Ñawpa Paccha* 14 (1976): 95–106.
1981   "The Radiocarbon Evidence for the Temporal Priority of Chavín de Huantar." *American Antiquity* 46, no. 3:593–602. Berkeley: Institute of Andean Studies.
1982   "Pójoc and Waman Wain: Two Early Horizon Villages in the Chavín Heartland." *Ñawpa Paccha* 20:3–40.
1984   *The Prehistoric Occupation of Chavín de Huantar, Peru.* University of California Publications in Anthropology, vol. 14. Berkeley: University of California Press.
1989   "An Overview of Peruvian Archaeology (1976–1986)." In *Annual Review of Anthropology* 18:37–69.

Burger, Richard L., and Lucy Salazar Burger
1980   "Ritual and Religion in Huaricoto." *Archaeology* 33, no. 6:26–32.
1985   "The Early Ceremonial Center of Huaricoto." In Donnan (ed.) 1985, pp. 111–138.

Burland, Cottie A.
1967   *The Gods of Mexico.* New York: G. P. Putnam's Sons.

Calnek, Edward E.
1972   "Settlement Patterns and Chinampa Agriculture at Tenochtitlan." *American Antiquity* 17, no. 1:104–115.
1976   "The Internal Structure of Tenochtitlan." In Wolf (ed.) 1976, pp. 287–302.

Carcedo Muro, Paloma, and Izumi Shimada
1985   "Behind the Golden Mask: Sicán Gold Artifacts from Batán Grande, Peru." In Benson (ed.) 1985, pp. 60–75.

Carlson, John
1981   "A Geomantic Model for the Interpretation of Mesoamerican Sites: An Essay in Cross-Cultural Comparison." In Benson (ed.) 1981b, pp. 143–216.

Carpenter, Edmund; Frederick Varley; and Robert Flaherty

1959   *Eskimo.* Toronto: University of Toronto Press.

Carr, Robert F., and James E. Hazard
1961   Map of the Ruins of Tikal, El Peten, Guatemala. Tikal Report 11. Philadelphia: University of Pennsylvania Press.

Carrión Cachot, Rebeca
1948   "La Cultura Chavín, Dos Nuevas Colonias: Kuntur Wasi y Ancór," Revista del Museo Nacional 2, 1:99–172.

Caso, Alfonso
1946   "Calendario y Escritura de las Antiguas Culturas de Monte Albán." In *Obras Completas (Miguel Othón Mendizábel)* 1:113–143. México.
1958   *The People of the Sun.* Norman: University of Oklahoma Press.
1966   "Dioses y Signos Teotihuacanos." In *Teotihuacán: Onceava Mesa Redonda* 1:249–279. Mexico: Sociedad Mexicana de Antropología.

Cason, Marjorie, and Adele Cahlander
1976   *The Art of Bolivian Highland Weaving.* New York: Watson-Guptill.

Chase, Arlen F., and Diane Z. Chase
1987   *Investigations at the Classic Maya City of Caracol. Belize: 1985–1987.* Pre-Columbian Art Research Monograph 3. San Francisco: Precolumbian Art Research Institute.
1989   "The Investigation of Classic Period Maya Warfare at Carcacol, Belize." *Mayab,* no. 5:4–18.

Chase, Arlen F., and Prudence M. Rice
1985   (eds.) *The Lowland Maya Postclassic.* Austin: University of Texas Press.

Cheek, Charles D.
1977   "Teotihuacán Influence at Kaminaljuyú. In Sanders and Michels (eds.) 1977, pp. 441–452.

Clewlow, C. William, Jr., Richard A. Cowan, James F. O'Connell, and Carlos Benemann
1967   *Colossal Heads of the Olmec Culture.* Contributions of the University of California Archaeological Research Facility, no. 4. Berkeley: University of California Press.

Coe, Michael D.
1962   "An Olmec Design on an Early Peruvian Vessel." *American Antiquity* 27, no. 1: 579–580.
1963   "Olmec and Chavín: Rejoinder to Lanning." *American Antiquity* 29, no. 1:101–104.
1965a   *The Jaguar's Children: Preclassic Central Mexico.* New York: Museum of Primitive Art.
1965b   "The Olmec Style and Its Distributions." In *Handbook of Middle American Indians* 3:739–775. Austin: University of Texas Press.
1972   "Olmec Jaguars and Olmec Kings." In Benson (ed.) 1972b, pp. 1–12.
1973   *The Maya Scribe and His World.* New York: The Grolier Club.
1975   *Classic Maya Pottery at Dumbarton Oaks.* Washington, D.C.: Dumbarton Oaks.
1977   "Olmec and Maya: A Study in Relationships." In Adams (ed.) 1977, pp. 183–195.
1978   *Lords of the Underworld: Masterpieces of Classic Maya Ceramics.* Princeton, N.J.: Princeton University Press.
1981   "San Lorenzo Tenochtitlan." In *Supplement to the Handbook of Middle American Indians* 1:117–146. Austin: University of Texas Press.
1987   *The Maya.* 4th ed. New York: Thames and Hudson.
1989a   "The Olmec Heartland: Evolution of Ideology." In Sharer and Grove (eds.) 1989, pp. 68–82.
1989b   "The Hero Twins: Myth and Image." In Kerr (ed.) 1989, pp. 161–184.

Coe, Michael D., and Richard A. Diehl
1980   *In the Land of the Olmec.* 2 vols. Austin: University of Texas Press.

Coggins, Clemency
1975   "Painting and Drawing Styles at Tikal: An Historical and Iconographic Reconstruction." Ph.D. diss., Harvard University.
1979   "A New Order and the Role of the Calendar: Some Characteristics of the Middle Classic Period at Tikal." In Hammond and Willey (eds.) 1979, pp. 38–50.
1980   "The Shape of Time: Political Implications of a Four-Part Figure." *American Antiquity* 45, no. 4:727–739.
1983   "An Instrument of Expansion: Monte Albán, Teotihuacán, and Tikal." In Miller (ed.) 1983, pp. 49–68.

Coggins, Clemency, and Orrin Shane III
1984   *Cenote of Sacrifice: Maya Treasures from the Sacred Well at Chichén Itzá.* Austin: University of Texas Press.

Cohodas, Marvin
1974   "The Iconography of the Panels of the Sun, Cross, and Foliated Cross at Palenque: Part II." In Robertson (ed.) 1974a, pp. 95–107.
1976   "The Iconography of the Panels of the Sun, Cross and Foliated Cross at Palenque: Part III." In Robertson (ed.) 1976, pp. 155–176.
1978   "Diverse Architectural Styles and the Ball Game Cult: The Late Middle Classic Period in Yucatan." In Pasztory (ed.) 1978.
1980   "Radial Pyramids and Radial-Associated Assemblages of the Central Maya Area." *Jour-*

nal of the Society of Architectural Historians 39, no. 3. (October 1980): 208–223.

1989a "Transformations in the Painting of Ceramic Texts by the Metropolitan Master." In Hanks and Rice (eds.) 1989.

1989b "The Epiclassic Problem: A Review and Alternative Model." In Diehl and Berlo (eds.) 1989, pp. 219–240.

Cole, John R.
1980 "Cult Archaeology and Unscientific Method and Theory." In Schiffer (ed.) 1980, 3:1–33.

Collier, Donald
1955 *Cultural Chronology and Change as Reflected in the Ceramics of the Virú Valley, Peru.* Fieldiana: Anthropology 42. Chicago: Chicago Natural History Museum.

Collier, George, Renato Rosaldo, and John Wirth
1982 (eds.) *The Inca and Aztec States, 1400–1800.* New York: Academic Press.

Conklin, William J.
1970 "Peruvian Textile Fragments from the Beginning of the Middle Horizon." *The Textile Museum Journal* 3, no. 1 (December): 15–24.

1971 "Chavín Textiles and the Origins of Peruvian Weaving." *The Textile Museum Journal* 3, no. 2:13–19.

1985a "Pucara and Tiahuanaco Tapestry: Time and Style in a Sierra Weaving Tradition." *Ñawpa Paccha* 21 (1983): 1–44.

1985b "The Architecture of Huaca de los Reyes." In Donnan (ed.) 1985, pp. 139–164.

1986 "The Mythic Geometry of the Ancient Southern Sierra." In Rowe, A. P. (ed.) 1986, pp. 123–136.

Conrad, Geoffrey N.
1982 "The Burial Platforms of Chan Chan." In Moseley and Day (eds.) 1982, pp. 119–144.

Conrad, Geoffrey W., and Arthur Demarest
1984 *Religion and Empire: The Dynamics of Aztec and Inca Expansion.* Cambridge: Cambridge University Press.

Cook, Anita G.
1983 "Aspects of State Ideology in Huari and Tiwanaku Iconography: The Central Deity and the Sacrificer." In Sandweiss (ed.) 1983, pp. 161–185.

1987 "The Middle Horizon Ceramic Offering from Conchopata." *Ñawpa Pacha* 22–23: 47–90.

Cordy-Collins, Alana
1976 "An Iconographic Study of Chavín Textiles from the South Coast of Peru: The Discovery of a Pre-Columbian Catechism." Ph.D. diss., University of California Institute of Archaeology, Los Angeles.

1977a "Chavín Art: Its Shamanistic/Hallucinogenic Origins." In Cordy-Collins and Stern (eds.) 1977, pp. 353–362.

1977b "The Moon Is a Boat! A Study in Iconographic Methodology." In Cordy-Collins and Stern (eds.) 1977, pp. 421–434.

1979 "Cotton and the Staff God: Analysis of an Ancient Chavín Textile." In Rowe, A. P., Benson, E. P., and Schaffer, A.-M. (eds.) 1979, pp. 51–60.

1982 "Psychoactive Painted Peruvian Plants, The Shamanism Textile." *Journal of Ethnobiology* 2, no. 2:144–153.

1982 (ed.) *Pre-Columbian Art History: Selected Readings,* 2nd ed. Palo Alto, Calif.: Peek Publications.

Cordy-Collins, Alana, and Jean Stern
1977 (eds.) *Pre-Columbian Art History: Selected Readings.* Palo Alto, Calif.: Peek Publications.

Covarrubias, Miguel
1946 "El Arte 'Olmeca' o de La Venta," *Cuadernos Americanos* 28, no. 4 [English version] "Olmec Art, or the Art of La Venta," translated by Robert T. Pirazzini. In Cordy-Collins and Stern (eds.) 1977, pp. 1–34.

Culbert, T. Patrick
1973 (ed.) *The Classic Maya Collapse.* Albuquerque: University of New Mexico Press.

1988 "The Collapse of Classic Maya Civilization." In Yoffee and Cowgill (eds.) 1988, pp. 69–101.

Czwarno, R. M., F. M. Meddens, and A. Morgan
1989 *The Middle Horizon Period in Peru.* BAR International Series, no. 525. Oxford: BAR.

Davies, Nigel
1974 *The Aztecs: A History.* New York: G. P. Putnam's Sons.

Davis, Whitney
1978 "So-called Jaguar Human Copulation Scenes in Olmec Art." *American Antiquity* 43, no. 3:453–457.

Dawson, Lawrence E.
1979 "Painted Cloth Mummy Masks of Ica, Peru." In Rowe, A. P., Benson, E. P., and Schaffer, A.-M. (eds.).

Day, Kent C.
1982 "Ciudadelas: Their Form and Function." In Moseley and Day (eds.) 1982, pp. 55–67.

DeBoer, Warren, and James A. Moore
1983 "The Measurement and Meaning of Stylistic Diversity." *Ñawpa Paccha,* no. 20 (1982): 147–162.

de la Fuente, Beatriz
1973 *Escultura Monumental Olmeca.* Mexico: Instituto de Investigaciones Estéticas, Universidad Nacional Autónoma de México.

1977   *Los Hombres de Piedra, Escultura Olmeca.* Mexico: Instituto de Investigaciones Estéticas, Universidad Nacional Autónoma de Mexico.

Demarest, Arthur, and Geoffrey Conrad
1983   "Ideological Adaptation and the Rise of the Aztec and Inca Empires." In Leventhal and Kolata (eds.) 1983, pp. 373–400.

Diehl, Richard, and Janet Berlo
1989   (eds.) *Mesoamerica after the Decline of Teotihuacán,* A.D. 700–900. Washington D.C.: Dumbarton Oaks.

Donkin, R. A.
1979   *Agricultural Terracing in the Aboriginal World.* Viking Publications in Anthropology, no. 6. Tucson: University of Arizona Press.

Donnan, Christopher B.
1972   "Moche-Huari Murals from Northern Peru." *Archaeology* 25, no. 2:85–95.
1976   *Moche Art and Iconography.* UCLA Latin American Studies, vol. 33.
1977   "The Thematic Approach to Moche Iconography." In Cordy-Collins and Stern (eds.) 1977, pp. 407–420. (Reprinted from *Journal of Latin American Lore* 1, no. 2, 1975.)
1978   *Moche Art of Peru: Pre-Columbian Symbolic Communication.* Los Angeles: University of California Press.
1985   (ed.) *Early Ceremonial Architecture in the Andes.* Washington, D.C.: Dumbarton Oaks.
1986   "An Elaborate Textile Fragment from the Major Quadrangle." In Donnan and Cook (eds.) 1986, pp. 109–116.
1988   "Iconography of the Moche: Unravelling the Mystery of the Warrior-Priest." *National Geographic* 174, no. 4 (October): 550–555.
1990   "Masterworks of Art Reveal a Remarkable Pre-Inca World." *National Geographic* 177, no. 6 (June): 16–33.

Donnan, Christopher, and Guillermo A. Cook
1986   (eds.) *The Pacatnamu Papers,* 1. Los Angeles: Museum of Cultural History, University of California.

Donnan, Christopher, and Carol J. Mackey
1978   *Ancient Burial Patterns of the Moche Valley, Peru.* Austin: University of Texas Press.

Donnan, Christopher, and Donna McClelland
1979   *The Burial Theme in Moche Iconography.* Studies in Pre-Columbian Art and Archaeology, no. 21. Washington, D.C.: Dumbarton Oaks.

Dow, James W.
1967   "Astronomical Orientations at Teotihuacán: A Case in Astroarchaeology." *American Antiquity* 32, no. 3:326–334.

Durán, Fray Diego
1971   *Book of the Gods and Rites and the Ancient Calendar.* (Translated and edited by Fernando Horcasitas and Doris Heyden.) Norman: University of Oklahoma Press.

Dwyer, Edward, and Jane Powell Dwyer
1975   "The Paracas Cemeteries: Mortuary Patterns in a Peruvian South Coastal Tradition." In Benson (ed.) 1975, 145–161.

Dwyer, Jane Powell
1971   *Chronology and Iconography of Late Paracas and Early Nasca Textile Designs.* Ph.D. diss., Department of Anthropology, University of California.
1979   "The Chronology and Iconography of Paracas-Style Textiles." In Rowe, Benson, and Schaffer (eds.) 1979, pp. 105–128.

Eastby, Dudley T., Jr.
1956   "Ancient American Goldsmiths." *Natural History* 65, no. 8:401–409.

Edmondson, Monro S.
1971   *The Book of Counsel: The Popol Vuh of the Quiché Maya.* Middle American Research Institute, Publication no. 35. New Orleans: Tulane University.

Edwards, Emily
1966   *Painted Walls of Mexico.* Austin: University of Texas Press.

Emmerich, Andre
1965   *Sweat of the Sun and Tears of the Moon: Gold and Silver in Pre-Columbian Art.* Seattle: University of Washington Press.

Engel, Frederic André
1976   *An Ancient World Preserved: Relics and Records of Prehistory in the Andes.* New York: Crown Publishers.

Fash, William L., and Barbara W. Fash
1990   "Scribes, Warriors, and Kings, the Lives of the Copan Maya." *Archaeology* 43 (May-June): 26–35.

Feldman, Robert A.
1983   "From Maritime Chiefdom to Agricultural State in Formative Coastal Peru." In Leventhal and Kolata (eds.) 1983, pp. 289–310.

Ferguson, William M., and John Q. Royce
1977   *Maya Ruins of Mexico in Color.* Norman: University of Oklahoma Press.

Fitzer, P. M.
1981   "Symbolic One-Leggedness: Pacal as Tezcatlipoca." *American Antiquity* 46, no. 1:163–166.

Foncerrada de Molina, Marta
1980   "Mural Painting in Cacaxtla and Teotihuacán Cosmopolitism." In Robertson (ed.) 1980, pp. 183–198.

Freidel, David A., and Linda Schele
1988a   "Kingship in the Late Preclassic Maya

Lowlands." *American Anthropologist* 90, no. 3 (September): 547–567.

1988b "Symbol and Power: A History of the Lowland Maya Cosmogram." In Benson and Griffin (eds.) 1988, pp. 44–93.

Furst, Peter

1968 "The Olmec Were-Jaguar Motif in the Light of Ethnographic Reality." In Benson (ed.) 1968, pp. 143–174.

1974 "Morning Glory and Mother Goddess at Tepantitla, Teotihuacán: Iconography and Analogy in Pre-Columbian Art." In Hammond (ed.) 1974, pp. 187–215.

1976 "Fertility, Vision Quest and Auto-Sacrifice: Some Thoughts on Ritual Blood-Letting among the Maya." In Robertson (ed.) 1976, pp. 181–193.

1981 "Jaguar Baby or Toad Mother: A New Look at an Old Problem in Olmec Iconography." In Benson (ed.) 1981a, pp. 149–162.

Gallenkamp, Charles, and R. E. Johnson

1985 *Maya: Treasures of an Ancient Civilization.* New York: Harry N. Abrams.

Gasparini, Graziano and Luise Margolies

1980 *Inca Architecture.* Bloomington: Indiana University Press.

Gay, Carlo

1972 *Xochipala: The Beginnings of Olmec Art.* Princeton, N.J.: Princeton University Press.

Gayton, Anna, and Alfred L. Kroeber

1927 *The Uhle Pottery Collections from Nazca.* University of California Publications in American Archaeology and Ethnology, vol. 24, no. 1. Berkeley: University of California Press.

Gebhard, Paul

1970 "Sexual Motifs in Prehistoric Peruvian Ceramics." In Bowie and Christenson (eds.), pp. 109–169.

Gendorp, Paul

1980 "Dragon-Mouth Entrances: Zoomorph Portals in the Architecture of Central Yucatan." In Robertson (ed.) 1980, pp. 138–150.

Gordon, G. B., and J. Alden Mason

1925–1928 *Examples of Maya Pottery in the Museum and Other Collections.* Philadelphia: University Museum.

Gorenstein, Shirley

1975 *Not Forever on Earth: Prehistory of Mexico.* New York: Scribner's Sons.

Gossen, Gary H.

1974 *Chamulas in the World of the Sun: Time and Space in a Maya Oral Tradition.* Cambridge, Mass.: Harvard University Press.

Graham, John A.

1976 "Maya, Olmecs and Izapans at Abaj Takalik." *Actes du XLII Congrès International des Americanistes* 8:179–188.

1977 "Discoveries at Abaj Takalik, Guatemala." *Archaeology* 30, no. 3:196–197.

1981a "Abaj Takalik: The Olmec Style and Its Antecedents in Pacific Guatemala." In Graham (ed.) 1981b, pp. 163–176.

1981b (ed.) *Ancient Mesoamerica: Selected Readings.* Palo Alto, Calif.: Peek Publications.

Graham, John A., Robert Heizer, and Edwin M. Shook

1978 *Abaj Takalik 1976: Exploratory Excavations.* University of California Archaeological Research Facility, no. 36:383–423.

Graham, Mark

1986 "Review of 'The Blood of Kings' [Linda Schele and Mary Ellen Miller]." In *African Arts* 20, no. 1 (November): 95–97.

Grieder, Terence

1979 "Review of *Moche Art of Peru* [Donnan]." In *African Arts* 11, no. 3 (May): 90.

1982 *Origins of Pre-Columbian Art.* Austin: University of Texas Press.

Grieder, Terence, and Alberto Bueno Mendoza

1981 "Peru Before Pottery." *Archaeology* 32, no. 2:44–51.

1985 "Ceremonial Architecture at La Galgada." In Donnan (ed.) 1985, pp. 93–109.

Grove, David

1973 "Olmec Altars and Myths." *Archaeology* 26, no. 2:128–135.

1981 "Olmec Monuments: Mutilation as a Clue to Meaning." In Benson (ed.) 1981a, pp. 49–68.

1984 *Chalcatzingo, Excavations on the Olmec Frontier.* New York/London: Thames and Hudson.

1987 "Torches, 'Knuckle Dusters', and the Legitimization of Formative Period Rulership." *Mexicon* 10, no. 3:60–65.

1989 "Olmec: What's in a Name?" In Sharer and Grove (eds.) 1989.

In Press "Formative Period Horizons in Mesoamerica: Shared Cosmology and Evolving Symbols of Power." Paper presented at the symposium "Latin American Horizons," Dumbarton Oaks, October 1986.

Grove, David, and Susan D. Gillespie

In Press "Ideology and Evolution at the Pre-State Level: Formative Period Mesoamerica." Revised version of paper presented May 1987 at the School of American Research advanced seminar "Ideology and the Cultural Evolution of Pre-Columbian Civilizations."

Guaman Poma de Ayala, Felipe

1978 *Letter to a King: A Peruvian Chief's Account of Life under the Incas and under Spanish Rule, by Huaman Poma (Don Felipe Huaman Poma de Ayala).* Arranged, edited, and translated from Nueva Cronica y Buen Gobierno, with an introduction by Christopher Dilke. New York: E. P. Dutton.

Hadingham, Evan
1987   *Lines to the Mountain Gods: Nasca and the Mysteries of Peru.* New York: Random House.

Hall, Grant D., Stanley M. Tarka, Jr., W. Jeffrey Hurst, David Stuart, and Richard E. W. Adams
1990   "Cacao Residues in Ancient Maya Vessels from Río Azul, Guatemala." *American Antiquity* 55, no. 1 (January): 141–142.

Hammond, Norman
1974   (ed.) *Mesoamerican Archaeology: New Approaches.* Austin: University of Texas Press.

Hammond, Norman, and Gordon R. Willey
1979   (eds.) *Maya Archaeology and Ethnohistory.* Austin: University of Texas Press.

Hanks, William F., and Don Rice
1989   (eds.) *Word and Image in Maya Culture: Explorations in Language, Writing, and Representation.* Salt Lake City: University of Utah Press.

Harcourt, Raoul d'
1962   *Textiles of Ancient Peru and Their Techniques.* Grace G. Denny and Carolyn M. Osborne (eds.); translated by Sadie Brown. Seattle: University of Washington Press.

Haselberger, Herta
1961   "Methods of Studying Ethnological Art." *Current Anthropology* 2, no. 4 (October): 341–384.

Hastings, Charles M., and Michael E. Moseley
1975   "The Adobes of Huaca del Sol and Huaca de la Luna." *American Antiquity* 40, no. 2: 196–203.

Hawkins, Gerald S.
1969   *Ancient Lines in the Peruvian Desert.* Cambridge, Mass.: Smithsonian Institution Astrophysical Observatory.
1974   "Prehistoric Desert Markings in Peru." *National Geographic Society Research Reports,* 1967 Projects, pp. 117–144. Washington, D.C.: National Geographic Society.

Heine-Geldern, Robert von
1959   "Representations of the Asiatic Tiger in the Art of the Chavín Culture: A Proof of Early Contacts between China and Peru." In *Actas, 33rd International Congress of Americanists,* pp. 321–326. San José, Costa Rica.

Heizer, Robert F.
1968   "New Observations on La Venta." In Benson (ed.) 1968, pp. 9–27.

Heizer, Robert F., John A. Graham, and Lewis K. Napton
1968   *The 1968 Investigation at La Venta.* University of California Archaeological Research Facility, Contribution 5. Department of Anthropology, Berkeley.

Hellmuth, Nicholas
1978   "Teotihuacán Art in the Escuintla, Guatemala Region." In Pasztory (ed.) 1978, pp. 71–85.
1987   *Monster und Menschen in der Mayakunst/ Monsters and Men in Maya Art.* Graz: Akademische Druk-u. Verlagsanstalt.

Hemming, John, and Edward Ranney
1982   *Monuments of the Incas.* A New York Graphic Society Book. Boston: Little, Brown and Company.

Henderson, John S.
1988   "Current Research: Mesoamerica." *American Antiquity* 53, no. 4: 864–866.

Heyden, Doris
1975   "An Interpretation of the Cave Underneath the Pyramid of the Sun in Teotihuacán, Mexico." *American Antiquity* 40, no. 2: 131–147.
1981   "Caves, Gods and Myths: World-View and Planning in Teotihuacán." In Benson (ed.) 1981b, pp. 1–35.
1987   "Symbolism of Ceramics from the Templo Mayor." In Boone (ed.) 1987, pp. 109–130.

Heyden, Doris, and Paul Gendrop
1975   *Pre-columbian Architecture of Mesoamerica.* New York: H. N. Abrams.

Heyden, Doris, and Luis Francisco Villaseñor
1984   *The Great Temple and the Aztec Gods.* Mexico City: Editorial Minutiae Mexicana.

Hicks, Frederick
1979   "'Flowery War' in Aztec History." *American Ethnologist* 6: 87–92.

Holland, William R.
1964   "Contemporary Tzotzil Cosmological Concepts as a Basis for Interpreting Prehistoric Maya Civilization." *American Antiquity* 29, no. 3 (January): 301–306.

Houston, Stephen, and David Stuart
1989   *The Way Glyph: Evidence for "Co-Essences" among the Classic Maya.* Research Reports on Ancient Maya Writing. Washington, D.C.: Center for Maya Research.

Hoyt, Margaret A., and Michael E. Moseley
1969–1970   "The Burr Frieze: A Rediscovery at Chan Chan." *Ñawpa Paccha* 7–8, pp. 41–58.

Hyslop, John
1984   *The Inka Road System.* New York: Academic Press.

Isbell, William H.
1977   *The Rural Foundation for Urbanism: Economic and Stylistic Interaction between Rural and Urban Communities in Eighth-Century Peru.* Illinois Studies in Anthropol-

ogy, no. 10. Urbana: University of Illinois Press.

1978   "The Prehistoric Ground Drawings of Peru." *Scientific American* (October). (Reprinted in *Pre-Columbian Archaeology: Readings from Scientific American*, Gordon R. Willey and Jeremy A. Sabloff (eds.) 1980. San Francisco: W. H. Freeman and Company.)

1983   "Shared Ideology and Parallel Political Development: Huari and Tiwanaku." In Sandweiss (ed.) 1983, pp. 186–208.

1987   "Conchopata, Ideological Innovator in Middle Horizon 1A." *Ñawpa Pacha* 22–23:91–114.

Isbell, William H. and Anita G. Cook
1987   "Ideological Origins of an Andean Conquest State." *Archaeology* 40, no. 4 (July/August): 26–33.

Isbell, William H., and Katharina J. Schreiber
1978   "Was Huari a State?" *American Antiquity* 43, no. 3:372–389.

Izumi, Seiichi
1971   "The Development of the Formative Culture in the Ceja de la Montaña: A Viewpoint Based on the Materials from the Kotosh Site." In Benson (ed.) 1971, pp. 49–72.

Izumi, Seiichi, and Toshihko Sono
1963   *Andes 2, Excavations at Kotosh, Peru, 1960.* Tokyo: Kadokawa Publishing Company.

Jennings, Gary
1980   *Aztec.* New York: Atheneum.

Jennings, Jesse
1983   (ed.) *Ancient South Americans.* New York: W. H. Freeman.

Jones, Christopher
1969   *The Twin Pyramid Group Pattern, A Classic Maya Architectural Assemblage at Tikal, Guatemala.* Ph.D. diss., Department of Anthropology, University of Pennsylvania.

Jones, Christopher, and Linton Satterthwaite
1982   *The Monuments and Inscriptions of Tikal.* Tikal Report, no. 33, pt. a. Philadelphia: University of Pennsylvania Press.

Jones, Julie
1979   "Mochica Works of Art in Metal: A Review." In Benson (ed.) 1979, pp. 53–104.

1985   *The Art of Precolumbian Gold: The Jan Mitchell Collection.* Boston: Little, Brown and Company.

Joralemon, P. David
1971   *A Study of Olmec Iconography.* Studies in Pre-Columbian Art and Archaeology, no. 7. Washington, D. C.: Dumbarton Oaks.

1974   "Ritual Blood-Sacrifice among the Ancient Maya: Part I." In Robertson (ed.) 1974b, pp. 59–75.

1976   "The Olmec Dragon: A Study in Pre-Columbian Iconography." In Nicholson (ed.) 1976, pp. 27–71.

Josserand, Kathryn, and Karen Dakin
1988   (eds.) *Smoke and Mist: Mesoamerican Studies in Memory of Thelma D. Sullivan.* BAR International Series, vol. 402.

Joyce, Rosemary A., Richard Edging, Karl Lorenz, and Susan D. Gillespie
1990   "Olmec Bloodletting: An Iconic Study." In Robertson (ed.) 1990. Norman: University of Oklahoma Press.

Joyce, T. A.
1922   "The 'Paccha' of Ancient Peru." *Journal of the Royal Anthropological Institute of Great Britain and Ireland* 54:141–149.

Justeson, John S. and Lyle Campbell
1984   (eds.) *Phoneticism in Mayan Hieroglyphic Writing.* Institute for Mesoamerican Studies Publication 9. Albany: State University of New York at Albany.

Kan, Michael
1972   "The Feline Motif in Northern Peru." In Benson (ed.) 1972b.

Kano, Chiaki
1979   *The Origins of the Chavín Culture.* Studies in Pre-Columbian Art and Archaeology, no. 22. Washington, D.C.: Dumbarton Oaks.

Katz, Friedrich
1972   *The Ancient American Civilizations.* History of Civilization series. New York and Washington: Praeger.

Keatinge, Richard W.
1978   "The Pacatnamu Textiles." *Archaeology* 31, no. 2:30–41.

Keatinge, Richard W., David Chodoff, Deborah P. Chodoff, Murray Marvin, and Helaine Silverman
1975   "From the Sacred to the Secular. First Report on a Prehistoric Architectural Tradition on the Peruvian North Coast." *Archaeology* 128, no. 2:128–129.

Keen, Benjamin
1971   *The Aztec Image in Western Thought.* New Brunswick, N.J.: Rutgers University Press.

Kelley, David H.
1965   "Glyphic Evidence for a Dynastic Sequence at Quiriguá, Guatemala." *American Antiquity* 27, no. 3:323–335.

1976   *Deciphering the Maya Script.* Austin: University of Texas Press.

Kendall, Aubin
1977   *The Art and Architecture of Pre-Columbian Middle America: An Annotated Bibliography of Works in English.* Boston: G. K. Hall.

Kennedy, Alison Bailey
1982   "Ecce Bufo, The Toad in Nature and in Olmec Iconography." *Current Anthropology* 25, no. 3:273–290.

Kerr, Barbara, and Justin Kerr
1988 "Some Observations on Maya Painters." In Benson and Griffin (eds.) 1988, pp. 236–259.

Kerr, Justin
1989 (ed.) *The Maya Vase Book, Volume 1: A Corpus of Rollout Photographs of Maya Vases.* New York: Kerr Associates.

King, Mary Elizabeth
1965a *Textiles and Basketry of the Paracas Period, Ica Valley, Peru.* Ph.D. diss., University of Arizona.
1965b *Ancient Peruvian Textiles from the Collection of the Textile Museum, Washington, D.C.* New York: The Museum of Primitive Art.

Kinzhalov, Rostislav V.
1978 "Toward the Reconstruction of the Olmec Mythological System." In Browman (ed.) 1978c, pp. 279–288.

Kirchhoff, Paul
1952 "Mesoamerica: Its Geographic Limits, Ethnic Composition, and Cultural Characteristics." In Tax et al. (1952), pp. 17–30.

Klein, Cecelia
1975 "Post-Classic Mexican Death Imagery as a Sign of Cyclic Completion." In Benson (ed.) 1975, 69–85.
1976 *The Face of the Earth: Frontality in Two-Dimensional Mesoamerican Art.* Outstanding Dissertations in the Fine Arts series (Ph.D. diss., Columbia University, 1972). New York and London: Garland Publishing, Inc.
1977 "The Identity of the Central Deity on the Aztec Calendar Stone." In Cordy-Collins and Stern (eds.) 1977, pp. 167–189.
1978 Review of *The Archaeology of Ancient Peru and the Work of Max Uhle*, by Dorothy Menzel. In *African Arts* 11, no. 3 (April): 91–94.
1986 "Masking Empire: The Material Effects of Masks in Aztec History." *Art History* 9, no. 2 (June): 135–167.
1987 "The Ideology of Autosacrifice at the Templo Mayor." In Boone (ed.) 1987, pp. 293–370.
1988a "Mayamania: 'The Blood of Kings' in Retrospect," *Art Journal* 47, no. 1 (Spring, 1988): 42–46.
1988b "Rethinking Cihuacóatl: Aztec Political Imagery of the Conquered Woman." In Josserand and Dakin (eds.) 1988, pp. 237–277.
1990 Review of *Feathered Serpents and Flowering Trees*, ed. Kathleen Berrin (1988). In *African Arts* 23 (July): 93–96.

Klymyshyn, Alexandra A.
1982 "Elite Compounds in Chan Chan." In Moseley and Day (eds.) 1982, pp. 119–145.

Kolata, Alan Louis
1982 "Chronology and Settlement Growth at Chan Chan." In Moseley and Day (eds.) 1982, pp. 67–86.
1983 "Chan Chan and Cuzco: On the Nature of the Ancient Andean City." In Leventhal and Kolata (eds.) 1983, pp. 345–371.

Kosok, Paul
1965 *Life, Land and Water in Ancient Peru.* Brooklyn, N.Y.: Long Island University Press.

Kosok, Paul, and Maria Reiche
1949 "Ancient Drawings on the Desert of Peru." *Archaeology* 2, no. 4: 206–215.

Kowalski, Jeff Karl
1987 *The House of the Governor: A Maya Palace at Uxmal, Yucatan, Mexico.* Norman and London: University of Oklahoma Press.

Kvietok, D. P., and D. H. Sandweiss
1985 (eds.) *Recent Studies in Andean Prehistory and Protohistory.* Cornell Latin American Studies Program. Ithaca: Cornell University Press.

Krochok, Ruth
1988 "Epigraphic Evidence for Political Change at Chichén Itzá." Paper presented at the 53rd Annual Meeting of the Society for American Archaeology, Phoenix, Arizona, April 28, 1988.

Kroeber, Alfred L.
1925 *The Uhle Pottery Collections from Moche.* Publications in American Archaeology and Ethnology, vol. 21: 191–234. Berkeley: University of California Press.
1953 *Paracas Cavernas and Chavín.* Publications in American Archaeology and Ethnology, vol. 40, no. 88. Berkeley: University of California Press.
1954 "Proto-Lima, A Middle Period Culture of Peru." *Fieldiana: Anthropology* 44, no. 1. Chicago: Chicago Natural History Museum.
1956 *Toward Definition of the Nazca Style.* Publications in American Archaeology and Ethnology, vol. 43, no. 4. Berkeley: University of California Press.

Kroeber, Alfred L., and William Duncan Strong
1924 *The Uhle Pottery Collections from Ica, with Three Appendices by Max Uhle.* Publications in American Archaeology and Ethnology, vol. 21, no. 3. Berkeley: University of California Press.

Kubler, George
1952 *Cuzco: Reconstruction of the Town and Restoration of its Monuments.* UNESCO.
1962 *The Shape of Time: Remarks on the History of Things.* New Haven: Yale University Press.

1967a *The Iconography of the Art of Teotihuacán.* Studies in Pre-Columbian Art and Archaeology, no. 4. Washington, D.C.: Dumbarton Oaks.

1967b "Style and the Representation of Historical Time." *Annals of the New York Academy of Sciences* 138.

1972 "The Paired Attendants of the Temple Tablets at Palenque." In *Religion in Mesoamerica: XII Mesa Redonda*, pp. 317–328. Mexico: Sociedad Mexicana de Antropología.

1973 "Iconographic Aspects of Architectural Profiles at Teotihuacán and in Mesoamerica." In *The Iconography of Middle American Sculpture.* New York: Metropolitan Museum of Art.

1980 "Eclecticism at Cacaxtla." In Robertson (ed.) 1980, pp. 163–172.

1984 *The Art and Architecture of Ancient America: The Mexican, Maya and Andean Peoples.* Pelican History of Art series. Harmondsworth, England, and Baltimore: Penguin Books.

Kutscher, Gerdt
1967 "Iconographic Studies as an Aid in the Reconstruction of Early Chimú Civilization." In Rowe and Menzel (eds.) 1967, pp. 115–124.

La Farge, Henry A.
1981 (ed.) *Museums of the Andes.* Great Museums of the World series. Tokyo: Newsweek, Inc., and Kodansha, Ltd.

Langley, James C.
1986 *Symbolic Notation of Teotihuacán Art: Elements of Writing in a Mesoamerican Culture of the Classic Period.* BAR International Series, vol. 313. Oxford: BAR.

Lanning, Edward P.
1967 *Peru before the Incas.* Englewood Cliffs, N.J.: Prentice-Hall.

Lapiner, Alan C.
1976 *Pre-Columbian Art of South America.* New York: Harry N. Abrams.

Larco Hoyle, Rafael
1965 *Checcan: Essay on Erotic Elements in Peruvian Art.* Geneva: Nagel.

Lathrap, Donald W.
1971 "The Tropical Forest and the Cultural Context of Chavín." In Benson (ed.) 1971, pp. 73–100.

1973 "Gifts of the Cayman: Some Thoughts on the Subsistence Basis of Chavín." In *Variation in Anthropology: Essays in Honor of John C. McGregor*, Donald W. Lathrap and Jody Douglas (eds.), pp. 91–105. Urbana: Illinois Archaeological Survey. (Reprinted in

Cordy-Collins and Stern [eds.] 1977, pp. 333–351.

1974 "The Moist Tropics, the Arid Lands, and the Appearance of Great Art Styles in the New World." In *Art and Environment in Native America.* Mary Elizabeth King and Idris R. Traylor, Jr. (eds.), Special Publications, no. 7. Lubbock: Texas Tech University Museum.

1985 "Jaws: the Control of Power in the Early Nuclear American Ceremonial Center." In Donnan (ed.) 1985, pp. 241–267.

Lechtman, Heather
1968 "Ancient Methods of Gilding Silver: Examples from the Old and the New Worlds." In *Science and Archaeology*, Robert H. Brill (ed.), pp. 2–30. Cambridge, Mass: MIT Press.

1973 "The Gilding of Metals in Pre-Columbian Peru." In *Application of Science in Examination of Works of Art*, William J. Young (ed.), pp. 38–52. Boston: Museum of Fine Arts.

León Portilla, Miguel
1987 "The Ethnohistorical Record for the Huey Teocalli of Tenochtitlan." In Boone (ed.) 1987, pp. 71–96.

Leventhal, Richard M., and Alan L. Kolata
1983 (eds.) *Civilization in the Ancient Americas: Essays in Honor of Gordon R. Willey.* Albuquerque: University of New Mexico Press and Peabody Museum of Archaeology and Ethnology, Harvard University.

Lincoln, Charles E.
1986 "The Chronology of Chichén Itzá: A Review of the Literature." In Sabloff and Andrews (eds.) 1986, pp. 141–196.

1988 "Dual Kingship at Chichén Itzá." Paper presented at the 53rd Annual Meeting of the Society for American Archaeology, Phoenix, Arizona, April 28, 1988.

Littmann, Edwin R.
1973 "The Physical Aspects of Some Teotihuacán Murals." Appendix 2 in Miller, A. G. (1973), pp. 175–189.

Loten, H. Stanley, and David M. Pendergast
1984 *A Lexicon for Maya Architecture.* Archaeology Monograph 8. Toronto: Royal Ontario Museum.

Lothrop, Samuel K.
1955 "Peruvian Pacchas and Keros." *American Antiquity* 21, no. 3:233–243.

Lothrop, Samuel, et al.
1961 (eds.) *Essays in Pre-Columbian Art and Archaeology.* Cambridge: Harvard University Press.

Lounsbury, Floyd G.
1985 "The Identities of the Mythological Figures

in the Cross Group Inscriptions at Palenque." In Robertson and Benson (eds.) 1985, pp. 45–58.

Love, Bruce
1987 *Glyph T93 and Maya 'Hand-Scattering' Events.* Research Reports on Ancient Maya Writing, nos. 4 and 5. Washington, D.C.: Center for Maya Research.

Lowe, Gareth, Thomas A. Lee,
and Eduardo Martínez Espinosa
1982 *Izapa: An Introduction to the Ruins and Monuments.* New World Archaeological Foundation Papers, no. 31. Provo, Utah.

Lowe, John W. G.
1985 *The Dynamics of Apocalypse: A Systems Simulation of the Classic Maya Collapse.* Albuquerque: University of New Mexico Press.

Lumbreras, Luís Guillermo
1971 "Towards a Re-Evaluation of Chavín." In Benson (ed.) 1971, pp. 1–28.
1974 *The Peoples and Cultures of Ancient Peru.* Translated by Betty J. Meggers. Washington, D.C.: Smithsonian Institution.
1977 "Excavaciones en el Templo Antiguo de Chavín (sector R): informe de la Sexta Campana." *Nawpa Pacha* 15:1–38.

Lyon, Patricia Jean
1978 "Female Supernaturals in Ancient Peru." *Ñawpa Pacha* 16:95–140.

Mackey, Carol J.
1982 "The Middle Horizon as Viewed from the Moche Valley." In Moseley and Day (eds.) 1982, pp. 321–332.

Mackey, Carol J., and Charles M. Hastings
1982 "Moche Murals from the Huaca de la Luna." In Cordy-Collins (ed.) 1982.

MacLeod, Barbara
1990 "Deciphering the Primary Standard Sequence." Ph.D. diss., Department of Anthropology, University of Texas at Austin, 1990.

Maquet, Jacques
1986 *The Aesthetic Experience: An Anthropologist Looks at the Visual Arts.* New Haven: Yale University Press.

Marcus, Joyce
1973 "Territorial Organization of the Lowland Classic Maya." *Science* 180 (4089): 911–916.
1976 *Emblem and State in the Classic Maya Lowlands: An Epigraphic Approach to Territorial Organization.* Washington, D.C.: Dumbarton Oaks.
1989 "Zapotec Chiefdoms and the Nature of Formative Religions." In Sharer and Grove (eds.) 1989, pp. 148–197.

Margain, Carlos R.
1971 "Pre-Columbian Architecture of Central Mexico." In *Handbook of Middle American Indians* 10, Gordon Ekholm and Ignacio Bernal (eds.), pp. 45–91. Austin: University of Texas Press.

Marquina, Ignacio
1951 *Arquitectura Prehispánica.* Mexico: Instituto Nacional de Antropología e Historia and Secretaría de Educación Pública.

Mastache, Alba Guadalupe, and Robert H. Cobean
1989 "The Coyotlatelco Culture and the Origins of the Toltec State." In Diehl and Berlo (eds.) 1989, pp. 46–67.

Masuda, Shozo, Izumi Shimada, and Craig Morris
1985 (eds.) *Andean Ecology and Civilization: An Inter-Disciplinary Perspective on Andean Ecological Complementarity.* Tokyo: University of Tokyo Press.

Matheny, Ray T.
1986 "Early States in the Maya Lowlands during the Late Preclassic Period: Edzná and El Mirador." In Benson (ed.) 1986, pp. 1–44.

Mathews, Peter
1980 "Notes on the Dynastic Sequence of Bonampak, Part 1." In Robertson (ed.) 1980, pp. 60–73.
1983 *Corpus of Maya Hieroglyphic Inscriptions* 6, pt. 1. Cambridge: Peabody Museum, Harvard University.

Mathews, Peter, and Linda Schele
1974 "Lords of Palenque—The Glyphic Evidence." In Robertson (ed.) 1974a, pp. 63–75.

Mathews, Zena Pearlstone
1982 "The Art of Art History: A Reply to Trubowitz and Rosenthal." *American Antiquity* 47, no. 1:198–200.

Matos Moctezuma, Eduardo
1984 "The Templo Mayor of Tenochtitlan: Economics and Ideology." In Boone (ed.) 1984, pp. 133–164.
1987 "Symbolism of the Templo Mayor." In Boone (ed.) 1987, pp. 185–209.
1988 *The Great Temple of the Aztecs: Treasures of Tenochtitlan.* London: Thames and Hudson.

McClelland, Donna D.
1977 "The Ulluchu: A Moche Symbolic Fruit." In Cordy-Collins and Stern (eds.) 1977, pp. 435–452.

McIntyre, Loren
1973 "Lost Empire of the Incas." *National Geographic* 144, no. 6 (December): 729–787.
1975 "Mystery of the Ancient Nazca Lines." *National Geographic Magazine* 147, no. 5: 716–728.

McVicker, Donald E.
1975   "Approaches to the Mural Art of Teotihuacán." In "The Art of Pre-Columbian
America" (unpublished seminar papers),
pt. 2, pp. 204–246. New Orleans: Tulane
University.
1985   "The 'Mayanized' Mexicans." *American
Antiquity* 50, no. 1:82–101.
Means, Phillip Ainsworth
1932   *A Study of Peruvian Textiles*. Boston: Museum of Fine Arts.
Meinsch, Lynn A.
1985   "Machu Picchu, Conserving an Inca Treasure." *Archaeology* 36, no. 6 (November-
December): 18–25.
Mejía Xesspe, Toribio
1939   "Acueductos y Caminos Antiguos de la
Hoya del Río Grande de Nasca." In *International Congress of Americanists* 1:
559–569. Lima.
Menzel, Dorothy
1964   "Style and Time in the Middle Horizon."
Ñawpa Pacha 2:1–105.
1968   "New data on the Huari Empire in Middle
Horizon Epoch 2a." *Ñawpa Pacha* 6:
47–114.
1977   *The Archaeology of Ancient Peru and the
Work of Max Uhle*. Berkeley: R. H. Lowie
Museum of Anthropology, University of
California.
Menzel, Dorothy, John H. Rowe,
and Lawrence E. Dawson
1964   *The Paracas Pottery of Ica: A Study in Style
and Time*. Publications in American Archaeology and Ethnology, vol. 50. Berkeley
and Los Angeles: University of California
Press.
Master, Ann
1983   "The Owl in Moche Iconography: Implications for Ethnic Dualism on the North
Coast of Peru." Paper presented at the 11th
Annual Midwest Conference on Andean and
Amazonian Archaeology and Ethnohistory,
Bloomington, Indiana, February 26–27,
1983.
Metraux, Alfred
1949   "Warfare, Cannibalism, and Human Tro-
phies." In *Handbook of South American In-
dians* 5, pp. 383–409. Washington, D.C.:
Smithsonian Institution.
Milbrath, Susan
1979   *A Study of Olmec Sculptural Chronology*.
Studies in Pre-Columbian Art and Archaeol-
ogy, no. 23. Washington, D.C.: Dumbarton
Oaks.
Miles, Susan W.
1965   "Sculpture of the Guatemala-Chiapas High-

lands and the Pacific Slopes and Associated
Hieroglyphs." In *Handbook of Middle
American Indians* 2:237–275. Austin: University of Texas Press.
Miller, Arthur G.
1973   *The Mural Painting of Teotihuacán*. Washington, D.C.: Dumbarton Oaks.
1974   "West and East in Maya Thought: Death and
Rebirth at Palenque and Tulum." In Robertson (ed.) 1974, pp. 45–49.
1983   (ed.) *Highland-Lowland Interaction in Mesoamerica: Interdisciplinary Approaches*.
Washington, D.C.: Dumbarton Oaks.
1986   *Maya Rulers of Time/Los Soberanos Maya
del Tiempo: A Study of Architectural
Sculpture at Tikal*. Philadelphia: University
Museum, Publication Division of University of Pennsylvania Press.
Miller, Mary Ellen
1985   "A Re-Examination of the Mesoamerican
Chacmool." *The Art Bulletin* 67, no. 1
(March): 7–17.
1986a   *The Art of Mesoamerica from Olmec to
Aztec*. World of Art series. London: Thames
and Hudson.
1986b   *The Murals of Bonampak*. Princeton, N.J.:
Princeton University Press.
1986c   "Copan, Honduras: Conference with a Per-
ished City." In Benson (ed.) 1986, pp.
72–108.
Millon, Clara
1972   "The History of Mural Art in Teotihuacan."
In *Teotihuacán: XI Mesa Redonda* 2. Mexico: Sociedad Mexicana de Antropología.
1973   "Painting, Writing and Polity in Teotihuacán." *American Antiquity* 38,
no. 3:294–314.
Millon, René
1967   "Teotihuacán." *Scientific American* 216,
no. 6:38–48.
1973   (ed.) *Urbanization at Teotihuacán, Mexico*
1, pts. 1 and 2. Austin: University of Texas
Press.
1981   "Teotihuacán: City, State and Civilization."
In *Supplement to the Handbook of Middle
American Indians* 1, pp. 198–243. Austin:
University of Texas Press.
Millon, Rene, Bruce Drewitt, and George Cowgill
1973   *Urbanization at Teotihuacán, Vol. 1: The
Teotihuacán Map* (Pt. 1, text; Pt. 2, maps).
Austin: University of Texas.
Millon, Rene, Bruce Drewitt,
and James A. Bennyhoff
1965   *The Pyramid of the Sun at Teotihuacán:
1959 Investigations*. Transactions of the
American Philosophical Society, n.s., vol.
55, no. 6. Philadelphia: American Philo-
sophical Society.

Molina Montes, Augusto F.
1987   "Templo Mayor Architecture: So What's New?" In Boone (ed.) 1987, pp. 97–107.

Montell, Gosta
1929   *Dress and Ornaments in Ancient Peru.* Göteborg: Elanders Boktryckeri Aktiebolag.

Moorehead, Elisabeth L.
1979   "Highland Inca Architecture in Adoba." *Ñawpa Pacha* 16 (1978): 65–94.

Morris, Craig, and Donald E. Thompson
1970   "Huanuco Viejo: An Inca Administrative Center." *American Antiquity* 35, no. 3: 344–362.
1985   *Huanuco Pampa: An Inca City and Its Hinterland.* London: Thames and Hudson.

Morrison, Tony, and Gerald S. Hawkins
1978   *Pathways to the Gods: The Mystery of the Andes Lines.* New York: Harper & Row.

Moseley, Michael E.
1975   "Prehistoric Principles of Labor Organization in the Moche Valley, Peru." *American Antiquity* 40, no. 2, 191–196.
1983   "Central Andean Civilizations." In Jennings (ed.) 1983, pp. 179–239.
1985   "The Exploration and Explanation of Early Monumental Architecture in the Andes." In Donnan 1975, pp. 29–58.

Moseley, Michael E., and Kent C. Day
1982   (eds.) *Chan Chan, Andean Desert City.* Albuquerque: University of New Mexico Press.

Moseley, Michael E., and Eric E. Deeds
1982   "The Land in Front of Chan Chan: Agrarian Expansion, Reform and Collapse in the Moche Valley." In Moseley and Day (eds.) 1982, pp. 25–54.

Murra, John V.
1956   *The Economic Organization of the Inca State.* Ph.D. diss., University of Chicago.
1962   "Cloth and Its Functions in the Inca State." *American Anthropologist* 64, no. 4: 710–728.

Muse, Mike, and Terry Stocker
1974   "The Cult of the Cross: Interpretations in Olmec Iconography." *Journal of the Steward Anthropological Society* 5: 67–68.

Nass, Ulla
1980   *Weaves of the Incas.* Flourtown, Pa.: Sylvan and Ulla Nass.

Nicholson, H. B.
1960   "The Mixteca-Puebla Concept in Mesoamerican Archaeology: A Re-examination." In *International Congress of Anthropological and Ethnological Sciences: Men and Cultures,* Fifth International Congress, pp. 612–618. (Reprinted in Graham [ed.] 1981b, pp. 253–258.)
1971a   "Major Sculpture in Pre-Hispanic Central Mexico." In *Handbook of Middle American Indians* 10, Gordon F. Ekholm and Ignacio Bernal (eds.), pp. 92–134. Austin: University of Texas Press.
1971b   "Religion in Pre-Hispanic Central Mexico." *Handbook of Middle American Indians* 10: 395–446.
1972   "The Cult of Xipe Totec in Mesoamerica." In *Religion in Mesoamerica: XII Mesa Redonda,* pp. 213–218. Mexico: Sociedad Mexicana de Antropología.
1973   "The Late Pre-Hispanic Central Mexican (Aztec) Iconographic System." In *The Iconography of Middle American Sculpture.* New York: Metropolitan Museum of Art.
1976a   (ed.) *Origins of Religious Art and Iconography in Preclassic Mesoamerica.* Los Angeles: UCLA Latin American Center and Ethnic Arts Council of Los Angeles.
1976b   "Preclassic Mesoamerican Iconography from the Perspective of the Postclassic: Problems in Interpretational Analysis." In H. B. Nicholson (ed.) 1976a.
1977   "An Aztec Stone Image of a Fertility Goddess." In Cordy-Collins and Stern (eds.) 1977, pp. 145–165.
1982   "Revelation of the Great Temple." *Natural History* 91, no. 7 (July) 48–58.
1987   "Symposium on the Aztec Templo Mayor: Discussion." In Boone (ed.) 1987, pp. 463–484.

Nicholson, Irene
1967   *Mexican and Central American Mythology.* London: Hamlyn.

Niles, Susan A.
1983   "Style and Function in Inca Agricultural Works Near Cuzco." *Ñawpa Pacha* 20 (1982): 163–182.

Norman, V. Garth
1973   *Izapa Sculpture.* New World Archaeological Foundation Papers, no. 30, pts. 1 and 2. Provo, Utah: New World Archaeological Foundation.

Nuño, Rubén, and Fernando Robles
1981   *The Art in the Great Temple.* Mexico: Instituto Nacional de Antropología e Historia. (U.S. distribution by William Kaufman, Inc., Los Angeles.)

Nuttall, Zelia
1975   (ed.) *The Codex Nuttall, A Picture Manuscript from Ancient Mexico; The Peabody Museum Facsimile Edited By Zelia Nuttall,* with Introduction by Arthur G. Miller. New York: Dover.

O'Neale, Lila M.
1937   *Archaeological Explorations in Peru; pt. 3, Textiles of the Early Nazca Period.* Field Museum of Natural History, Anthropol-

ogy Memoirs, vol. 2, no. 3, pp. 110–218. Chicago.

1942 "Textile Periods in Ancient Peru: II, Paracas Cavernas and the Grand Necropolis." *Publications in American Archaeology and Ethnology* 39, no. 2:143–202. Berkeley: University of California Press.

O'Neale, Lila M., and Thomas W. Whitaker

1947 "Embroideries of the Early Nazca Period and the Crop Plants Depicted on Them." *Southwestern Journal of Anthropology* 3, no. 4: 294–321.

O'Neill, John P.

1984 "Featherwork." In Rowe, A. P., 1984, pp. 144–184.

Padden, R. C.

1967 *The Hummingbird and the Hawk: Conquest and Sovereignty in the Valley of Mexico, 1503–1541.* New York: Harper & Row.

Parsons, Lee A.

1981 "Post-Olmec Stone Sculpture: The Olmec-Izapan Transition on the Southern Pacific Coast and Highlands." In Benson (ed.) 1981a, pp. 257–288.

1986 *The Origins of Maya Art: Monumental Sculpture of Kaminaljuyu, Guatemala, and the Southern Pacific Coast.* Studies in Pre-Columbian Art and Archaeology, no. 28. Washington, D.C.: Dumbarton Oaks.

Pasztory, Esther

1973 "The Gods of Teotihuacan: A Synthetic Approach in Teotihuacan Iconography." In *Atti del XL Congresso Internazionale digli Americanisti (Rome and Genoa),* 1 (1972): pp. 147–159.

1974 *The Iconography of the Teotihuacán Tlaloc.* Studies in Pre-Columbian Art and Archaeology, no. 15. Washington, D.C.: Dumbarton Oaks.

1976 *The Murals of Tepantitla, Teotihuacán.* New York: Garland.

1978 (ed.) *Middle Class Mesoamerica: A. D. 400–700.* New York: Columbia University Press.

1978 "Artistic Traditions of the Middle Classic Period." In Pasztory (ed.), pp. 108–142.

1983 *Aztec Art.* New York: Harry N. Abrams.

1988a "The Aztec Tlaloc: God of Antiquity." In Josserand and Dakin (eds.) 1988, pp. 289–327.

1988b "A Reinterpretation of Teotihuacán and Its Mural and Painting Tradition." In Berrin (ed.) 1988, pp. 45–77.

(n.d.) "The Nature of the Teotihuacán Image System." Paper presented at the symposium "Art, Polity, and the City of Teotihuacán," October 8–9, 1988, at Dumbarton Oaks, Washington, D.C.

Patterson, Thomas C.

1971 "Chavín: An Interpretation of its Spread and Influence." In Benson (ed.) 1971, pp. 29–48.

1985 "The Huaca Florida, Rimac Valley, Peru." In Donnan (ed.) 1985, pp. 59–69.

Paul, Anne C.

1980 "Paracas Ritual Attire: Symbols of Authority in Ancient Peru." Ph.D. diss., Department of Art, University of Texas at Austin.

1981 "Re-Establishing Provenience of Two Paracas Mantles." *The Textile Museum Journal* 19 and 20.

1982 "The Chronological Relationship of the Linear, Block Color, and Broad Line Styles of Paracas Embroidered Images." In Cordy-Collins (ed.) 1982, pp. 255–277.

1982b "The Symbolism of Paracas Turbans: A Consideration of Style, Serpents and Hair." *Ñawpa Pacha* 20:41–60.

1986 "Continuity in Paracas Textile Iconography and Its Implications for the Meaning of Linear Style Images." In Rowe, A. P. (ed.) 1986, pp. 81–100.

1989 *Paracas Ritual Attire: Symbols of Authority in Ancient Peru.* Norman and London: University of Oklahoma Press.

Paul, Anne C., and Susan A. Niles

1985 "Identifying Hands at Work on a Paracas Mantle." *The Textile Museum Journal* 23.

Paul, Anne C., and Solveig A. Turpin

1986 "The Ecstatic Shaman Theme of Paracas Textiles." *Archaeology* 39, no. 5 (September/October): 20–27.

Peters, Daniel

1983 *Tikal: A Novel about the Maya.* New York: Random House.

Pollock, H. E. D.

1980 *The Puuc: An Architectural Survey of the Hill Country of Yucatan and Northern Campeche, Mexico.* Memoirs of the Peabody Museum, vol. 19. Cambridge: Harvard University Press.

Ponce Sanginés, Carlos

1976 *La Cerámica de la Época I de Tiwanaku.* Instituto Nacional de Arqueología, Publicación 18. La Paz.

1981 *El Templo Semisubterraneo de Tiwanaku.* La Paz: Editorial Juveníl.

Posnansky, Arthur

1945 *Tiahuanaco: The Cradle of American Man.* 2 vols. New York: J. J. Augustin.

Pozorski, Thomas

1982 "Early Social Stratification and Subsistence Systems: The Caballo Muerto Complex." In Moseley and Day (eds.) 1982, pp. 225–254.

Pozorski, Thomas, and Sheila Pozorski

1987 "Chavín, the Early Horizon and the Initial

Period." In *The Origins and Development of the Andean State*, Jonathan Haas (ed.): pp. 36–46. Cambridge, England: Cambridge University Press.

Proskouriakoff, Tatiana
1960 "Historical Implications of a Pattern of Dates at Piedras Negras, Guatemala." *American Antiquity* 25, no. 4:454–475.
1961 "Portraits of Women in Maya Art." In *Essays in Pre-Columbian Art and Archaeology*, Samuel K. Lothrop et al. (eds.), pp. 81–99. Cambridge, Mass.: Harvard University Press.
1963 *An Album of Maya Architecture.* Norman: University of Oklahoma Press.
1968 "The Jog and the Jaguar Signs in Maya Writing." *American Antiquity* 33, no. 2: 247–251.

Protzen, Jean-Pierre
1985 "Inca Quarrying and Stone Cutting." *Ñawpa Pacha* 21 (1983): 183–214.

Proulx, Donald A.
1968 *Local Differences and Time Differences in Nasca Pottery.* University of California Publications in Anthropology, vol. 5. Berkeley.

Puleston, Dennis
1979 "An Epistemological Pathology and the Collapse, or Why the Maya Kept the Short Count." In Hammond and Willey 1979, pp. 63–74.

Quirarte, Jacinto
1973 *Izapa-Style Art, A Study of Form and Meaning.* Studies in Pre-Columbian Art and Archaeology, no. 10. Washington, D.C.: Dumbarton Oaks.
1974 "Terrestrial/Celestial Polymorphs as Narrative Frames." In Robertson (ed.) 1974a, pp. 129–136.
1976 "The Relationship of Izapan-Style Art to Olmec and Maya Art: A Review." In Nicholson, H. B. (ed.) 1976, pp. 73–86.
1977 "Early Art Styles of Mesoamerica and Early Classic Maya Art." In Adams, R. E. W. (ed.) 1977, pp. 249–283.
1981 "Tricephalic Units in Olmec, Izapan-Style, and Maya Art." In Benson (ed.) 1981a, pp. 289–308.
1983 "Outside Influence at Cacaxtla." In Miller (ed.) 1983, pp. 201–221.

Rands, Robert
1955 "Some Manifestations of Water in Mesoamerican Art." In *Anthropological Papers*, Bureau of American Ethnology Bulletin 157, pp. 265–393. Washington, D. C.: Smithsonian Institution.
1957 "Comparative Notes on the Hand-Eye and Related motifs." *American Antiquity* 22: 247–257.

Ravines, Rogger
1970 (ed.) *100 Años de Arqueología en el Perú.* Fuentes e Investigaciones para la Historia del Peru, 3. Lima: Instituto de Estudios Peruanos.
1985 "Early Monumental Architecture of the Jequetepeque Valley, Peru." In Donnan (ed.) 1985, pp. 209–226.

Rea, Amadeo M.
1986 Black Vultures and Human Victims: Archaeological evidence from Pacatnamu." In Donnan and Cook (eds.) 1986, pp. 139–144.

Recinos, Adrian
1950 *Popol Vuh: The Sacred Book of the Quiché Maya.* Norman: University of Oklahoma Press.

Reents, Doris Jane
1985 "The Late Classic Maya Holmul Style Polychrome Pottery." Ph.D. diss. University of Texas at Austin.

Reents-Budet, Dorie
1987 "The Discovery of a Ceramic Artist and Royal Patron among the Classic Maya." *Mexicon* 9:123–126.

Reese, Thomas F.
1985 (ed.) *Studies in Ancient American and European Art: The Collected Essays of George Kubler.* New Haven: Yale University Press.

Reiche, Maria
1974 *Peruvian Ground Drawings.* Munich: Kunstraum.

Reinhard, Johan
1985a "Chavín and Tiahuanaco: A New Look at Two Andean Ceremonial Centers." *National Geographic Research Reports* 1, no. 3 (Summer 1985): 395–422. Washington, D.C.: National Geographic Society
1985b *The Nasca Lines: A New Perspective on Origins and Meaning.* Lima: Editorial Los Pinos.

Roark, Richard Paul
1965 "From Monumental to Proliferous in Nasca Pottery." *Ñawpa Pacha*, no. 3, pp. 1–92.

Robertson, Donald
1974 "Some Remarks on Stone Relief Sculpture at Palenque." In Robertson (ed.) 1974b, pp. 103–124.

Robertson, Merle Greene
1974a (ed.) *Primera Mesa Redonda de Palenque*, pt. 1. Pebble Beach, Calif.: Robert Louis Stevenson School.
1974b (ed.) *Primera Mesa Redonda de Palenque.* pt. 2. Pebble Beach, Calif.: Robert Louis Stevenson School.
1974c "The Quadripartite Badge—A Badge of Rulership." In Robertson (ed.) 1974, pp. 77–93.
1976 (ed.) *Segunda Mesa Redonda de Palenque:*

The Art, Iconography, and Dynastic History of Palenque, pt. 3. Pebble Beach, Calif.: Robert Louis Stevenson School.

1977 "Painting Practices and Their Change through Time of the Palenque Stucco Sculptors." In *Social Process in Maya Prehistory: Studies in Honor of Sir Eric Thompson*, Norman Hammond (ed.), 1977, pp. 297–326. New York: Academic Press.

1979a (ed.) *Tercera Mesa Redonda de Palenque, 1978*, vol. 4. Monterey, Calif.: Herald Printers.

1979b "An Iconographic Approach to the Identity of the Figures on the Piers of the Temple of the Inscriptions, Palenque." In Robertson (ed.), 1979a, vol. 4.

1980 (ed.) *Third Palenque Round Table, 1978*, vol. 5, pt. 2. Austin: University of Texas Press.

1983 *The Sculpture of Palenque*. Vol. 1, *The Temple of the Inscriptions*. Princeton, N.J.: Princeton University Press.

1985a *The Sculpture of Palenque*. Vol. 2, *The Early Buildings of the Palace and the Wall Paintings*. Princeton, N.J.: Princeton University Press.

1985b *The Sculpture of Palenque*, Vol. 3, *The Late Buildings of the Palace*. Princeton, N.J.: Princeton University Press.

1990 (ed.) *Sixth Palenque Round Table, 1986*, vol. 8. Virginia M. Fields, volume ed. Norman: University of Oklahoma Press.

Robertson, Merle Greene, and Elizabeth P. Benson
1985 (eds.) *Fourth Palenque Round Table, 1980*, Vol. 6. San Francisco: Pre-Columbian Art Research Institute.

Robertson, Merle Greene, and Virginia M. Fields
1985 (eds.) *Fifth Palenque Round Table, 1983*, vol. 7. San Francisco: Pre-Columbian Art Research Institute.

Robertson, Merle Greene, Marjorie S. Rosenblum Scandizzo, and John R. Scandizzo
1976 "Physical Deformities in the Ruling Lineage of Palenque, and the Dynastic Implications." In Robertson (ed.) 1976, pp. 59–86.

Robicsek, Francis
1978 *The Smoking Gods: Tobacco in Maya Art, History and Religion*. Norman: University of Oklahoma Press.

Robicsek, Francis, and Donald M. Hales
1981 *The Maya Book of the Dead: The Ceramic Codex*. Charlottesville: University of Virginia Art Museum.

1984 "Maya Heart Sacrifice: Cultural Perspective and Surgical Technique." In Boone (ed.) 1984, pp. 49–90.

1988 "A Ceramic Codex Fragment: The Sacrifice of Xbalanque." In Benson and Griffin (eds.) 1988, pp. 260–276.

Roe, Peter G.
1974 *Further Exploration of the Rowe Chavín Seriation and Its Implications for North Central Coast Chronology*. Studies in Pre-Columbian Art and Archaeology, no. 13. Washington, D.C.: Dumbarton Oaks.

1978 "Recent Discoveries in Chavín Art: Some Speculations on Methodology and Significance in the Analysis of a Figural Style." *El Dorado* 3, no. 1:1–41.

1982a "Cupisnique Pottery: A Cache from Tembladera." In Cordy-Collins (ed.) 1982, pp. 231–253.

1982b *The Cosmic Zygote, Cosmology in the Amazon Basin*. New Brunswick, N.J.: Rutgers University Press.

Román Berrelleza, Juan Alberto
1987 "Offering 48 of the Templo Mayor: A Case of Child Sacrifice." In Boone (ed.) 1987, pp. 131–143.

Rowe, Ann Pollard
1977 *Warp Patterned Weaving of the Andes*. Washington, D.C.: The Textile Museum.

1978 "Technical Features of Inca Tapestry Tunics." *The Textile Museum Journal* 17: 5–28.

1979 "Textile Evidence for Huari Music." *The Textile Museum Journal* 18:5–16.

1981 "Textiles from the Burial Platform of Las Avispas at Chan Chan." *Ñawpa Pacha* 18 (1980): 81–148.

1984 *Costumes and Featherwork of the Lords of Chimor: Textiles from Peru's North Coast*, with feather identification by John P. O'Neill. Washington, D.C.: The Textile Museum.

1986 (ed.) *The Junius B. Bird Conference on Andean Textiles, April 7th and 8th, 1984*. Washington, D.C.: The Textile Museum.

Rowe, Ann Pollard, Elizabeth P. Benson, and Anne-Louise Schaffer
1979 (eds.) *The Junius B. Bird Pre-Columbian Textile Conference*. Washington, D.C.: The Textile Museum and Dumbarton Oaks.

Rowe, John H.
1956 "Archaeological Explorations in Southern Peru, 1954–1955." *American Antiquity* 22, pt. 1:135–151.

1961 "The Chronology of Inca Wooden Cups." In Lothrop et al. (eds.) 1961, pp. 317–341.

1962 *Chavín Art: An Inquiry into Its Form and Meaning*. New York: Museum of Primitive Art.

1963 "Urban Settlements in Ancient Peru." *Ñawpa Pacha* 1:1–28.

1967   "Form and Meaning in Chavín Art." In Rowe and Menzel (eds.) 1967, pp. 72–103.

1971   "The Influence of Chavín Art on Later Styles." In Benson (ed.) 1971, pp. 101–124.

1979   "Standardization in Inca Tapestry Tunics." In Rowe, A. P., Benson, and Schaffer (eds.), 1976, pp. 239–264.

Rowe, John H., Donald Collier, and Gordon Willey

1950   "Reconnaissance Notes on the Site of Huari, near Ayacucho, Peru." *American Antiquity* 16, no. 2:120–137.

Rowe, John H., and Dorothy Menzel

1967   (eds.) *Peruvian Archaeology: Selected Readings.* Palo Alto, Calif.: Peek Publications.

Ruppert, Karl, J. Eric S. Thompson, and Tatiana Proskouriakoff

1955   *Bonampak, Chiapas, Mexico.* Carnegie Institution of Washington Publication 602. Washington, D.C.

Sabloff, Jeremy A.

1982   "Introduction." In *Archaeology: Myth and Reality: Readings from* Scientific American, pp. 1–11. San Francisco: W. H. Freeman.

Sabloff, Jeremy, and E. Wyllys Andrews V.

1986   (eds.) *Late Lowland Maya Civilization: Classic to Postclassic.* Albuquerque: University of New Mexico Press.

Sahagún, Bernardino de

1950–   *General History of the Things of New Spain*
1976   *(Florentine Codex).* Translated by Arthur Anderson and Charles Dibble (12 vols.) Santa Fe: School of American Research.

Samaniego, Lorenzo, Enrique Vergara, and Henning Bischoff

1985   "New Evidence on Cerro Sechín, Casma Valley, Peru." In Donnan (ed.) 1985, pp. 165–190.

Sanders, William T.

1974   "Chiefdom to State: Political Evolution at Kaminaljuyu, Guatemala." In *Reconstructing Complex Societies: An Archaeological Colloquium,* Charlotte B. Moore (ed.). Supplement, *Bulletin of the American Schools of Oriental Research* 20:97–121. Cambridge, Mass.

Sanders, William T., Jeffrey R. Parsons, and Robert S. Santley

1979   *The Basin of Mexico: Ecological Processes in the Evolution of a Civilization.* New York: Academic Press.

Sanders, William T., and Barbara J. Price

1968   *Mesoamerica, The Evolution of a Civilization.* New York: Random Hosue.

Sanders, William T., and Joseph W. Michels

1977   (eds.) *Teotihuacán and Kaminaljuyú: A Study in Prehistoric Contact.* University Park: Pennsylvania State University Press.

Sandweiss, Daniel H.

1983   (ed.) *Investigations of the Andean Past: Papers from the First Annual Northeast Conference on Andean Archaeology and Ethnohistory.* Ithaca, N.Y.: Cornell University Latin American Studies Program.

Santley, Robert S.

1983   "Obsidian Trade and Teotihuacán Influence in Mesoamerica." In Miller, A. (ed.) 1983, pp. 69–124.

1989   "Obsidian Working, Long-Distance Exchange, and the Teotihuacán Presence on the South Gulf Coast." In Diehl and Berlo (eds.) 1989, pp. 131–151.

Sawyer, Alan R.

1961   "Paracas and Nazca Iconography." In Samuel K. Lothrop et al. (eds.) 1961, pp. 269–298. (Reprinted in Cordy-Collins and Stern [eds.] 1977, pp. 363–392.)

1963   "Tiahuanaco Tapestry Design." *The Textile Museum Journal* 1, no. 2:27–38. (Reprinted in Rowe and Menzel [eds.] 1967, pp. 165–176.)

1968   *Mastercraftsmen of Ancient Peru.* New York: The Solomon R. Guggenheim Foundation.

1972   "The Feline in Paracas Art." In Benson (ed.) 1972b, pp. 91–112.

1975   *Ancient Andean Arts in the Collections of the Krannert Art Museum.* Champaign-Urbana: University of Illinois Press.

1979   "Painted Nasca Textiles." In Rowe, A. P., Benson, and Schaffer (eds.) 1979, pp. 129–150.

Scarborough, Vernon, and David Wilcox

1989   (eds.) *International Symposium on the Mesoamerican Ball Game.* Tucson: University of Arizona Press.

Schaedel, Richard

1951   "Mochica Murals at Pañamarca." *Archaeology* 4, no. 3:145–154.

Schaffer, Anne-Louise

1984   "Cathartidae in Moche Art and Culture." In *Proceedings of the 44th International Congress of Americanists, Manchester, 1982,* Norman Hammond (ed.), pp. 29–68. Oxford: BAR.

1985   "Impressions in metal: reconstructing burial context at Loma Negra, Peru." In Kvietok and Sandweiss (eds.), 1985.

Schele, Linda

1974   "Observations on the Cross Motif at Palenque." In Robertson (ed.), 1974a, pp. 41–61.

1976   "Accession Iconography of Chan Bahlum in the Group of the Cross at Palenque." In Robertson (ed.) 1976, pp. 9–34.

1977   "Palenque: The Hosue of the Dying Sun." In Aveni (ed.) 1977, pp. 42–56.

1981 "Sacred Site and World View at Palenque." In Benson (ed.) 1981, pp. 87–114.

1984 "Human Sacrifice among the Classic Maya." In Boone (ed.) 1984, pp. 7–48.

1986 "Architectural Development and Political History at Palenque." In Benson (ed.) 1986, pp. 110–137.

Schele, Linda, and David Freidel
1990 *A Forest of Kings, the Untold Story of the Ancient Maya.* New York: Morrow.

Schele, Linda, and Mary E. Miller
1986 *The Blood of Kings: Dynasty and Ritual in Maya Art.* Fort Worth: Kimball Art Museum.

Schiffer, Michael B.
1980 (ed.) *Advances in Archaeological Method and Theory,* vol. 3. New York: Academic Press.

Scott, John F.
1978 *The Danzantes of Monte Alban, Part 1: Text, Part 2: Catalogue.* Studies in Pre-Columbian Art and Archaeology, no. 19. Washington, D.C.: Dumbarton Oaks.

Séjourné, Laurette
1956 *Burning Water: Thought and Religion in Ancient Mexico.* (Drawings by Abel Mendoza.) New York: Vanguard Press.

1966 *Arqueología de Teotihuacán: La Cerámica.* (Illustrations by Abel Mendoza and Manuel Romero.) Mexico: Fondo de Cultura Económica.

Seler, Eduard
1923 "Die buntbemalten Gefaesse vor Nazca im suedlichen Peru und Hauptelemente ihrer Versierung." In *Gesammelte Abhandlungen zur Amerikanischen Sprach und Altertumskunde* 4. Berlin.

Sharer, Robert J.
1974 "The Prehistory of the Southeastern Maya Periphery." *Current Anthropology* 15, no. 2:165–187.

1985 "Terminal Events in the Southeastern Lowlands: A View from Quiriguá." In Chase and Rice (eds.) 1985, pp. 245–253.

Sharer, Robert J., and David Grove
1989 (eds.) *Regional Perspectives on the Olmec.* Cambridge and New York: Cambridge University Press.

Sharon, Douglas
1972 "The San Pedro Cactus in Peruvian Folk Healing." In *Flesh of the Gods: The Ritual Use of Hallucinogens.* Peter Furst (ed.), 1972, pp. 114–135. New York: Praeger.

1974 *The Symbol System of a North Peruvian Shaman.* Ph.D. diss., Department of Anthropology, University of California at Los Angeles.

1979 *Wizard of the Four Winds: A Shaman's Story.* New York: The Free Press.

Sharon, Douglas, and Christopher B. Donnan
1974 "Shamanism in Moche Iconography." In *Ethnoarchaeology,* Christopher B. Donnan and C. William Clewlow, Jr. (eds.). Institute of Archaeology Monograph 4. Los Angeles: University of California.

Sheets, Payson D.
1980 (ed.) *Archaeology and Volcanism in Central America: The Zapotitlan Valley of El Salvador.* Austin: University of Texas Press.

Shimada, Izumii
1978 "Commodity and Labor Flow at Moche V Pampa Grande." *American Antiquity* 43, no. 4:569–593.

Smith, Virginia G.
1984 *Izapa Relief Carving: Form, Content, Rules for Design, and Role in Mesoamerican Art History and Archaeology.* Studies in Pre-Columbian Art and Archaeology, no. 27. Washington D. C.: Dumbarton Oaks.

Sodi Morales, Demetrio
1976 *The Maya World.* Mexico: Editorial Minutiae Mexicana.

Solís Olguín, Felipe R.
1982 "The Formal Pattern of Anthropomorphic Sculpture and the Ideology of the Aztec State." In Boone (ed.) 1982b, pp. 73–110.

Spickard, Lynda E.
1983 "The Development of Huari Administrative Architecture." In Sandweiss (ed.) 1983, pp. 136–160.

Stafford, Cora E.
1941 *Paracas Embroideries: A Study of Repeated Patterns.* New York: J. J. Augustin.

Stierlin, Henri
1964 *Living Architecture: Mayan.* New York: Grosset and Dunlap.

1984 *Art of the Incas and Its Origins.* New York: Rizzoli.

Stocker, Terrance, Sarah Meltzoff, and Steve Armsey
1980 "Crocodilians and Olmecs: Further Interpretations in Formative Period Iconography." *American Antiquity* 45, no. 4 (October): 740–758.

Stocker, Terrance L., and Michael W. Spence
1973 "Trilobal Eccentrics at Teotihuacán and Tula." *American Antiquity* 38, no. 2 (April): 195–199.

Stone, Andrea
1989 "Disconnection, Foreign Insignia, and Political Expansion: Teotihuacán and the Warrior Stelae of Piedras Negras." In Diehl and Berlo (eds.) 1989, pp. 153–172.

Stone, Doris
1982 *Aspects of the Mixteca-Puebla Style and*

Central Mexican Culture in Southern Meso-America. (Papers from a symposium organized by Doris Stone, with contributions by John Paddock, Donald L. Brockington, Donald Robertson, Robert Chadwick, James R. Ramsey, Jacinto Quirarte, and Doris Stone.) Middle American Research Institute Occasional Papers, no. 4. New Orleans: Tulane University.

Stone, Rebecca

1983 "Possible Uses, Roles and Meanings of Chavín-Related Painted Textiles of South Coast Peru." In Sandweiss (ed.) 1983, pp. 51–74.

1986 "Color Patterning and the Huari Artist: The 'Lima Tapestry' Revisited." In A. Rowe (ed.) 1986, pp. 137–149.

1987 "Technique and Form in Huari-Style Tapestry Tunics: The Andean Artist, A.D. 500–800." Ph.D. diss., Yale University.

1988 "The Width-Wise Warp in the Creation of the Huari-Style Tunic: Implications of Innovation in Textile Technology for Design and Culture." Paper presented at the 46th International Congress of Americanists, July 4–8, 1988, Amsterdam.

Strong, William Duncan

1957 *Paracas, Nazca and Tiahuanacoid Cultural Relationships in South Coastal Peru.* Memoirs of the Society for American Archaeology, no. 13. Salt Lake City: SAA.

Stuart, David

1984 "A Note on the 'Hand-Scattering' Glyph. In Juteson and Campbell (eds.) 1984, pp. 307–310.

1988 "Blood Symbolism in Maya Iconography." In Benson and Griffin (eds.) 1988, pp. 175–221.

1989 "Hieroglyphs on Maya Vessels." In Kerr (ed.) 1989, pp. 149–160.

Sugiyama, Saburo

1989 "Burials Dedicated to the Old Temple of Quetzalcóatl at Teotihuacán, Mexico." *American Antiquity* 54, no. 1:85–106.

Sullivan, Thelma D.

1982 "Tlazoltéotl-Ixcuina: The Great Spinner and Weaver." In Boone (ed.) 1982b, pp. 7–35.

Tate, Carolyn

1982 "The Maya Cauac Monster's Formal Development and Dynastic Contexts." In Cordy-Collins (ed.) 1982, pp. 33–54.

Taube, Karl

1985 "The Classic Maya Maize God: A Reappraisal." In Robertson, M. G., and Fields (eds.) 1985, pp. 171–182.

1988 "Classic Maya Scaffold Sacrifice." In Benson and Griffin (eds.) 1988, pp. 331–351.

Tax, Sol, and members of the Viking Fund Seminar on Middle American Ethnology

1952 *Heritage of Conquest: The Ethnology of Middle America.* Glencoe, Ill.: Free Press.

Taylor, Dicey

1982 "Problems in the Study of Narrative Scenes on Classic Maya Vases." In Boone (ed.) 1982c, pp. 107–124.

Tello, Julio C.

1942 *Origen y Desarollo de las Civilizaciones Prehistóricas Andinas.* 37 Congreso Internacional de Americanistas, Actas y Memorias, 1:589–720. Lima.

1959 *Paracas, Part 1.* Lima: Impresa Gráfica Scheuch.

1960 *Chavín, Cultura Matríz de la Civilización Andina, Primera Parte,* Publicación Antropólogica del Archivo "Julio C. Tello," vol. 2. Lima: Universidad de San Marcos.

1970 "Las Ruinas de Huari." In Ravines (ed.) 1970.

1980 *Paracas, Part 2: Cavernas y Necropolis.* Lima: Universidad Mayor de San Marcos.

Terada, Kazuo

1985 "Early Ceremonial Architecture in the Cajamarca Valley." In Donnan (ed.) 1985, pp. 191–208.

Terada, Kazuo, and Yoshio Onuki

1985 *The Formative Period in the Cajamarca Basin, Peru: Excavations at Huacaloma and Layzon, 1982.* Tokyo: University of Tokyo Press.

Thompson, J. Eric S.

1960 *Maya Hieroglyphic Writing.* Norman: University of Oklahoma Press.

1961 "A Blood-Drawing Ceremony Painted on a Maya Vase." *Estudios de la Cultura Maya* 1:13–20.

Tolstoy, Paul

1989 "Coapexco and Tlatilco." In Sharer and Grove (eds.) 1989, pp. 85–121.

Topic, John R.

1982 "Lower-Class Social and Economic Organization at Chan Chan." In Moseley and Day (eds.) 1982, pp. 145–176.

Topic, John R., and Michael E. Moseley

1985 "Chan Chan: A Case Study of Urban Change in Peru." *Ñawpa Pacha* 21 (1983): 153–182.

Topic, Theresa Lange

1982 "The Early Intermediate Period as Viewed from the Moche Valley." In Moseley and Day (eds.) 1982, pp. 255–284.

Townsend, Richard Fraser

1979 *State and Cosmos in the Art of Tenochtitlan.* Studies in Pre-Columbian Art and Archaeology, no. 20. Washington, D.C.: Dumbarton Oaks.

1987 "Coronation at Tenochtitlan." In Boone (ed.) 1987, pp. 371–409.

Troike, Nancy P.
1981 "Fundamental Changes in the Interpretation of the Mixtec Codices." In Graham (ed.) 1981b, pp. 277–295.

Tsunoyama, Yukihiro
1979 (ed.) *Textiles of the Andes: Catalog of Amano Collection.* San Francisco: Heian/ Dohosha. (Printed in Japan.)

Tushingham, A. Douglas, Ursula M. Franklin, and Christopher Toogood
1979 *Studies in Ancient Peruvian Metalworking: An Investigation of Objects from the Museo Oro del Peru Exhibited in Canada in 1976–1977 under the Title 'Gold for the Gods.'* Ontario: Royal Ontario Museum.

Ubbelohde-Doering, Heinrich
1954 *The Art of Ancient Peru.* New York: Praeger.

Uhle, Max
1914 *The Nazca Pottery of Ancient Peru.* Proceedings of the Davenport Academy of Sciences, vol. 13:1–16. Davenport, Iowa.

Umberger, Emily
1982 *Aztec Mexico: Discovery of Templo Mayor.* Brochure accompanying the exhibition "Aztec Mexico: Discovery of Templo Mayor," at the American Museum of Natural History, July 27–October 6, 1982. New York: AMNH.
1987 "Events Commemorated by Date Plaques at the Templo Mayor: Further Thoughts on the Solar Metaphor." In Boone (ed.) 1987, pp. 411–449.

Urton, Gary
1990 *History of a Myth: Pacariqtambo and the Origins of the Incas.* Austin: University of Texas Press.

Verano, John W.
1986 "A Mass Burial of Mutilated Individuals at Pacatnamú." In Donnan and Cook (eds.) 1986, pp. 117–138.

Villagra Caleti, Agustin
1971 "Mural Painting in Central Mexico." In Wauchope, Robert, Gordon F. Ekholm, and Ignacio Bernal (eds.), pp. 135–156.

Vogt, Evon Z.
1983 "Some New Themes in Settlement Pattern Research." In Vogt and Leventhal (eds.) 1983, pp. 3–20.

Vogt, Evon Z., and Richard M. Leventhal
1983 (eds.) *Prehistoric Settlement Patterns: Essays in Honor of Gordon R. Willey.* Albuquerque: University of New Mexico Press and Peabody Museum of Archaeology and Ethnography, Harvard University.

Von Daniken, Erich
1974 *In Search of Ancient Gods: My Pictorial Evidence for the Impossible.* New York: G. P. Putnam's Sons.

Von Hagen, Victor
1955 *Highway of the Sun.* New York: Duell, Sloan and Pearce.

Von Winning, Hasso
1947 "A Symbol for Dripping Water in the Teotihuacán Culture." *El Mexico Antiguo* 6:333–341.
1948 "The Teotihuacán Owl-and-Weapon Symbol and Its Association with 'Serpent Head X' at Kaminaljuyú." *American Antiquity* 14, no. 2:129–132.
1958 "Figurines with Movable Limbs from Ancient Mexico." *Ethnos* 23, no. 1:1–60.
1961 "Teotihuacán Symbols: The Reptile's Eye Glyph." *Ethnos* 26, no. 3:121–166.
1968 "Der Netzjaguar in Teotihuacán, Mexico: eine ikonographische Untersuchung." *Baessler-Archiv*, Neue Folge 16:31–46. Berlin: Museum fuer Völkerkunde.
1976 "Late and Terminal Preclassic: The Emergence of Teotihuacán." In Nicholson (ed.) 1976, pp. 141–156.
1977 "The Old Fire God and His Symbolism at Teotihuacan." *Contributions to Ethnology and Linguistics, Archaeology and Physical Anthropology of Indian America.* Berlin: Ibero-Amerikanisches Institut Preussischer Kulturbesitz.
1979 "The 'Binding of the Years' and the 'New Fire' in Teotihuacan." *Contributions to Ethnology and Linguistics, Archaeology and Physical Anthropology of Indian America.* Berlin: Ibero-Amerikanisches Institut Preussischer Kulturbesitz.
1987 *La Iconografía de Teotihuacán: Los Dioses y Los Signos.* 2 vols. Mexico: Universidad Nacional Autónoma de Mexico.

Vreeland Jr., James M.
1978 "Paracas." *Americas* 30, no. 10 (October): 36–44.

Vreeland, Jr., James M., and Aidan Cockburn
1980 "Mummies of Peru." In *Mummies, Disease and Ancient Cultures*, Aidan and Eve Cockburn (eds.), pp. 135–174. Cambridge and New York: Cambridge University Press.

Wauchope, Robert
1962 *Lost Tribes and Sunken Continents.* Chicago: University of Chicago Press.

Wauchope, Robert, Gordon F. Ekholm, and Ignacio Bernal
1971 (eds.) *Archaeology of Northern Mesoamerica, Part One.* Vol. 10, *Handbook of Middle American Indiana.* Austin: University of Texas Press.

Weaver, Muriel Porter
1981 *The Aztecs, Maya, and Their Predecessors* (2nd ed.). New York: Academic Press.

Webster, David
1989 (ed.) *The House of the Bacabs, Copán, Honduras*. Studies in Pre-Columbian Art and Archaeology, no. 29. Washington D.C.: Dumbarton Oaks.

Wicke, Charles R.
1971 *Olmec: An Early Art Style of Precolumbian Mexico*. Tucson: University of Arizona Press.

Wilkerson, S. Jeffrey K.
1984 "In Search of the Mountains of Foam." In Boone (ed.) 1984, pp. 101–132.

Willey, Gordon R.
1951 "The Chavín Problem: A Review and Critique." *Southwestern Journal of Anthropology* 7, no. 2:103–144.
1962 "The Early Great Styles and the Rise of Pre-Columbian Civilization." *American Anthropologist* 64, no. 1:1–14.
1971 *South America*. Vol. 2, *An Introduction to American Archaeology*. Englewood Cliffs, N.J.: Prentice-Hall.
1976 "The Rise of Maya Civilization, A Summary View." In Adams (ed.) 1976, pp. 383–423.

Williams, Carlos
1985 "A Scheme for the Early Monumental Architecture of the Central Coast of Peru." In Donnan 1985, pp. 227–240.

Winfield Capitaine, Fernando
1988 *La Estela 1 de La Mojarra, Veracruz, Mexico*. Research Reports on Ancient Maya Writing, no. 16. Washington, D.C.: Center for Maya Research.

Wolf, Eric R.
1976 (ed.) *The Valley of Mexico: Studies in Pre-Hispanic Ecology and Society*. Albuquerque: University of New Mexico Press.

Wolfe, Elizabeth Farkass
1981 "The Spotted Cat and the Horrible Bird: Stylistic Change in Nasca 1-5 Ceramic Decoration." *Ñawpa Pacha* 19:1–62.

Wray, Christine Brewster
1983 "Spatial Patterning and the Function of a Huari Architectural Compound." In Sandweiss (ed.) 1983, pp. 122–135.

Wren, Linnea H.
1984 "Chichén Itzá: The Site and its People." In Coggins and Shane (eds.) 1984, pp. 13–21.

Yacovleff, Eugenio
1932a "Las falconidas en el arte y en las creencias de los antiguos Peruanos." *Revista del Museo Nacional* 1, no. 1:33–111.
1932b "Arte antiguo Peruano, la deidad primitiva de los Nasca." *Revista del Museo Nacional* 1, no. 2.

Yoffe, Norman, and George Cowgill
1988 (eds.) *The Collapse of Ancient States and Civilizations*. Tucson: University of Arizona Press.

Zeitlin, Robert N.
1978 "Long-Distance Exchange and the Growth of a Regional Center on the Southern Isthmus of Tehuantepec, Mexico." In *Prehistoric Coastal Adaptations: The Economy and Ecology of Maritime Middle America*, Barbara L. Stark and Barbara Voorhees (eds.), pp. 183–210.

Zuidema, R. Thomas
1964 *The Ceque System of Cuzco*. Leiden: E. J. Brill.
1977 "The Inca Calendar." In *Native American Astronomy*, Anthony F. Aveni (ed.), pp. 219–259. Austin: University of Texas Press.
1982 "Catachillay: The Role of the Pleiades and of the Southern Cross and Alpha and Beta Centauri in the Calendar of the Incas." In *Ethnoastronomy and Archaeoastronomy in the American Tropics*, Annals of the New York Academy of Sciences, vol. 385; Anthony F. Aveni and Gary Urton (eds.), pp. 203–229 (New York: New York Academy of Sciences).
1990 *Inca Civilization in Cuzco*. Austin: University of Texas Press.

INDEX